# A Guide to the
# PROJECT MANAGEMENT
# BODY OF KNOWLEDGE

*(PMBOK® GUIDE)*

**Sixth Edition**

Library of Congress Cataloging-in-Publication Data

Names: Project Management Institute, publisher.
Title: A guide to the project management body of knowledge (PMBOK guide) / Project Management Institute.
Other titles: PMBOK guide
Description: Sixth edition. | Newtown Square, PA: Project Management Institute, 2017. | Series: PMBOK guide | Includes bibliographical references and index.
Identifiers: LCCN 2017032505 (print) | LCCN 2017035597 (ebook) | ISBN 9781628253900 (ePUP) | ISBN 9781628253917 (kindle) | ISBN 9781628253924 ( Web PDF) | ISBN 9781628251845 (paperback)
Subjects: LCSH: Project management. | BISAC: BUSINESS & ECONOMICS / Project Management.
Classification: LCC HD69.P75 (ebook) | LCC HD69.P75 G845 2017 (print) | DDC 658.4/04--dc23
LC record available at https://lccn.loc.gov/2017032505

ISBN: 978-1-62825-184-5

Published by:
    Project Management Institute, Inc.
    14 Campus Boulevard
    Newtown Square, Pennsylvania 19073-3299 USA
    Phone: +1 610-356-4600
    Fax: +1 610-356-4647
    Email: customercare@pmi.org
    Website: www.PMI.org

To place a Trade Order or for pricing information, please contact Independent Publishers Group:
    Independent Publishers Group
    Order Department
    814 North Franklin Street
    Chicago, IL 60610 USA
    Phone: +1 800-888-4741
    Fax: +1 312- 337-5985
    Email: orders@ipgbook.com (For orders only)

For all other inquiries, please contact the PMI Book Service Center.
    PMI Book Service Center
    P.O. Box 932683, Atlanta, GA 31193-2683 USA
    Phone: 1-866-276-4764 (within the U.S. or Canada) or +1-770-280-4129 (globally)
    Fax: +1-770-280-4113
    Email: info@bookorders.pmi.org

10  9  8  7

# NOTICE

The Project Management Institute, Inc. (PMI) standards and guideline publications, of which the document contained herein is one, are developed through a voluntary consensus standards development process. This process brings together volunteers and/or seeks out the views of persons who have an interest in the topic covered by this publication. While PMI administers the process and establishes rules to promote fairness in the development of consensus, it does not write the document and it does not independently test, evaluate, or verify the accuracy or completeness of any information or the soundness of any judgments contained in its standards and guideline publications.

PMI disclaims liability for any personal injury, property or other damages of any nature whatsoever, whether special, indirect, consequential or compensatory, directly or indirectly resulting from the publication, use of application, or reliance on this document. PMI disclaims and makes no guaranty or warranty, expressed or implied, as to the accuracy or completeness of any information published herein, and disclaims and makes no warranty that the information in this document will fulfill any of your particular purposes or needs. PMI does not undertake to guarantee the performance of any individual manufacturer or seller's products or services by virtue of this standard or guide.

In publishing and making this document available, PMI is not undertaking to render professional or other services for or on behalf of any person or entity, nor is PMI undertaking to perform any duty owed by any person or entity to someone else. Anyone using this document should rely on his or her own independent judgment or, as appropriate, seek the advice of a competent professional in determining the exercise of reasonable care in any given circumstances. Information and other standards on the topic covered by this publication may be available from other sources, which the user may wish to consult for additional views or information not covered by this publication.

PMI has no power, nor does it undertake to police or enforce compliance with the contents of this document. PMI does not certify, test, or inspect products, designs, or installations for safety or health purposes. Any certification or other statement of compliance with any health or safety-related information in this document shall not be attributable to PMI and is solely the responsibility of the certifier or maker of the statement.

# TABLE OF CONTENTS

**PART 1.**
**A GUIDE TO THE PROJECT MANAGEMENT BODY OF KNOWLEDGE** *(PMBOK® Guide)*

## PART 2.
## THE STANDARD FOR PROJECT MANAGEMENT

# PART 3.
# APPENDICES, GLOSSARY, AND INDEX

# LIST OF TABLES AND FIGURES

**PART 2.**
**The Standard For Project Management**

**PART 3.**
**APPENDICES, GLOSSARY, AND INDEX**

# Part 1

# A Guide to the Project Management Body of Knowledge

## (*PMBOK® GUIDE*)

# 1

## INTRODUCTION

### 1.1 OVERVIEW AND PURPOSE OF THIS GUIDE

Project management is not new. It has been in use for hundreds of years. Examples of project outcomes include:

◆ Pyramids of Giza,

◆ Olympic games,

◆ Great Wall of China,

◆ Taj Mahal,

◆ Publication of a children's book,

◆ Panama Canal,

◆ Development of commercial jet airplanes,

◆ Polio vaccine,

◆ Human beings landing on the moon,

◆ Commercial software applications,

◆ Portable devices to use the global positioning system (GPS), and

◆ Placement of the International Space Station into Earth's orbit.

The outcomes of these projects were the result of leaders and managers applying project management practices, principles, processes, tools, and techniques to their work. The managers of these projects used a set of key skills and applied knowledge to satisfy their customers and other people involved in and affected by the project. By the mid-20th century, project managers began the work of seeking recognition for project management as a profession. One aspect of this work involved obtaining agreement on the content of the body of knowledge (BOK) called project management. This BOK became known as the Project Management Body of Knowledge (PMBOK). The Project Management Institute (PMI) produced a baseline of charts and glossaries for the PMBOK. Project managers soon realized that no single book could contain the entire PMBOK. Therefore, PMI developed and published *A Guide to the Project Management Body of Knowledge (PMBOK® Guide)*.

PMI defines the project management body of knowledge (PMBOK) as a term that describes the knowledge within the profession of project management. The project management body of knowledge includes proven traditional practices that are widely applied as well as innovative practices that are emerging in the profession.

The body of knowledge (BOK) includes both published and unpublished materials. This body of knowledge is constantly evolving. This *PMBOK® Guide* identifies a subset of the project management body of knowledge that is generally recognized as good practice.

◆ *Generally recognized* means the knowledge and practices described are applicable to most projects most of the time, and there is consensus about their value and usefulness.

◆ *Good practice* means there is general agreement that the application of the knowledge, skills, tools, and techniques to project management processes can enhance the chance of success over many projects in delivering the expected business values and results.

The project manager works with the project team and other stakeholders to determine and use the appropriate generally recognized good practices for each project. Determining the appropriate combination of processes, inputs, tools, techniques, outputs and life cycle phases to manage a project is referred to as "tailoring" the application of the knowledge described in this guide.

This *PMBOK® Guide* is different from a methodology. A methodology is a system of practices, techniques, procedures, and rules used by those who work in a discipline. This *PMBOK® Guide* is a foundation upon which organizations can build methodologies, policies, procedures, rules, tools and techniques, and life cycle phases needed to practice project management.

## 1.1.1 THE STANDARD FOR PROJECT MANAGEMENT

This guide is based on *The Standard for Project Management* [1]. A standard is a document established by an authority, custom, or general consent as a model or example. As an American National Standards Institute (ANSI) standard, *The Standard for Project Management* was developed using a process based on the concepts of consensus, openness, due process, and balance. *The Standard for Project Management* is a foundational reference for PMI's project management professional development programs and the practice of project management. Because project management needs to be tailored to fit the needs of the project, the standard and the guide are both based on *descriptive* practices, rather than *prescriptive* practices. Therefore, the standard identifies the processes that are considered good practices on most projects, most of the time. The standard also identifies the inputs and outputs that are usually associated with those processes. The standard does not require that any particular process or practice be performed. *The Standard for Project Management* is included as Part 2 of *A Guide to the Project Management Body of Knowledge (PMBOK® Guide).*

The *PMBOK® Guide* provides more detail about key concepts, emerging trends, considerations for tailoring the project management processes, and information on how tools and techniques are applied to projects. Project managers may use one or more methodologies to implement the project management processes outlined in the standard.

The scope of this guide is limited to the discipline of project management, rather than the full spectrum of portfolios, programs, and projects. Portfolios and programs will be addressed only to the degree they interact with projects. PMI publishes two other standards that address the management of portfolios and programs:

◆ *The Standard for Portfolio Management* [2], and

◆ *The Standard for Program Management* [3].

## 1.1.2 COMMON VOCABULARY

A common vocabulary is an essential element of a professional discipline. *The PMI Lexicon of Project Management Terms* [4] provides the foundational professional vocabulary that can be consistently used by organizations, portfolio, program, and project managers and other project stakeholders. The *Lexicon* will continue to evolve over time. The glossary to this guide includes the vocabulary in the *Lexicon* along with additional definitions. There may be other industry-specific terms used in projects that are defined by that industry's literature.

## 1.1.3 CODE OF ETHICS AND PROFESSIONAL CONDUCT

PMI publishes the *Code of Ethics and Professional Conduct* [5] to instill confidence in the project management profession and to help an individual in making wise decisions, particularly when faced with difficult situations where the individual may be asked to compromise his or her integrity or values. The values that the global project management community defined as most important were responsibility, respect, fairness, and honesty. The *Code of Ethics and Professional Conduct* affirms these four values as its foundation.

The *Code of Ethics and Professional Conduct* includes both aspirational standards and mandatory standards. The aspirational standards describe the conduct that practitioners, who are also PMI members, certification holders, or volunteers, strive to uphold. Although adherence to the aspirational standards is not easily measured, conduct in accordance with these is an expectation for those who consider themselves to be professionals—it is not optional. The mandatory standards establish firm requirements and, in some cases, limit or prohibit practitioner behavior. Practitioners who are also PMI members, certification holders, or volunteers and who do not conduct themselves in accordance with these standards will be subject to disciplinary procedures before PMI's Ethics Review Committee.

## 1.2 FOUNDATIONAL ELEMENTS

This section describes foundational elements necessary for working in and understanding the discipline of project management.

### 1.2.1 PROJECTS

A project is a temporary endeavor undertaken to create a unique product, service, or result.

◆ **Unique product, service, or result.** Projects are undertaken to fulfill objectives by <u>producing deliverables</u>. An objective is defined as an outcome toward which work is to be directed, a strategic position to be attained, a purpose to be achieved, a result to be obtained, a product to be produced, or a service to be performed. A deliverable is defined as any unique and verifiable product, result, or capability to perform a service that is required to be produced to complete a process, phase, or project. Deliverables may be tangible or intangible.

Fulfillment of project objectives may produce one or more of the following deliverables:

■ A unique product that can be either a component of another item, an enhancement or correction to an item, or a new end item in itself (e.g., the correction of a defect in an end item);

■ A unique service or a capability to perform a service (e.g., a business function that supports production or distribution);

■ A unique result, such as an outcome or document (e.g., a research project that develops knowledge that can be used to determine whether a trend exists or a new process will benefit society); and

■ A unique combination of one or more products, services, or results (e.g., a software application, its associated documentation, and help desk services).

Repetitive elements may be present in some project deliverables and activities. This repetition does not change the fundamental and unique characteristics of the project work. For example, office buildings can be constructed with the same or similar materials and by the same or different teams. However, each building project remains unique in key characteristics (e.g., location, design, environment, situation, people involved).

Projects are undertaken at all organizational levels. A project can involve a single individual or a group. A project can involve a single organizational unit or multiple organizational units from multiple organizations.

Examples of projects include but are not limited to:

- Developing a new pharmaceutical compound for market,
- Expanding a tour guide service,
- Merging two organizations,
- Improving a business process within an organization,
- Acquiring and installing a new computer hardware system for use in an organization,
- Exploring for oil in a region,
- Modifying a computer software program used in an organization,
- Conducting research to develop a new manufacturing process, and
- Constructing a building.

◆ **Temporary endeavor.** The temporary nature of projects indicates that a project has a definite beginning and end. Temporary does not necessarily mean a project has a short duration. The end of the project is reached when one or more of the following is true:

- The project's objectives have been achieved;
- The objectives will not or cannot be met;
- Funding is exhausted or no longer available for allocation to the project;
- The need for the project no longer exists (e.g., the customer no longer wants the project completed, a change in strategy or priority ends the project, the organizational management provides direction to end the project);
- The human or physical resources are no longer available; or
- The project is terminated for legal cause or convenience.

Projects are temporary, but their deliverables may exist beyond the end of the project. Projects may produce deliverables of a social, economic, material, or environmental nature. For example, a project to build a national monument will create a deliverable expected to last for centuries.

◆ **Projects drive change.** Projects drive change in organizations. From a business perspective, a project is aimed at moving an organization from one state to another state in order to achieve a specific objective (see Figure 1-1). Before the project begins, the organization is commonly referred to as being in the current state. The desired result of the change driven by the project is described as the future state.

For some projects, this may involve creating a transition state where multiple steps are made along a continuum to achieve the future state. The successful completion of a project results in the organization moving to the future state and achieving the specific objective. For more information on project management and change, see *Managing Change in Organizations: A Practice Guide* [6].

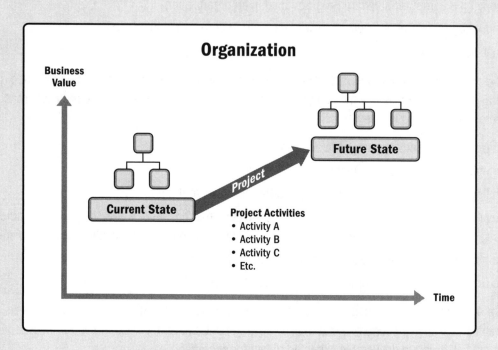

Figure 1-1. Organizational State Transition via a Project

---

◆ **Projects enable business value creation.** PMI defines business value as the net quantifiable benefit derived from a business endeavor. The benefit may be tangible, intangible, or both. In business analysis, business value is considered the return, in the form of elements such as time, money, goods, or intangibles in return for something exchanged (see *Business Analysis for Practitioners: A Practice Guide*, p. 185 [7]).

Business value in projects refers to the benefit that the results of a specific project provide to its stakeholders. The benefit from projects may be tangible, intangible, or both.

Examples of tangible elements include:

- Monetary assets,
- Stockholder equity,
- Utility,
- Fixtures,
- Tools, and
- Market share.

Examples of intangible elements include:

- Goodwill,
- Brand recognition,
- Public benefit,
- Trademarks,
- Strategic alignment, and
- Reputation.

◆ **Project Initiation Context.** Organizational leaders initiate projects in response to factors acting upon their organizations. There are four fundamental categories for these factors, which illustrate the context of a project (see Figure 1-2):

- Meet regulatory, legal, or social requirements;
- Satisfy stakeholder requests or needs;
- Implement or change business or technological strategies; and
- Create, improve, or fix products, processes, or services.

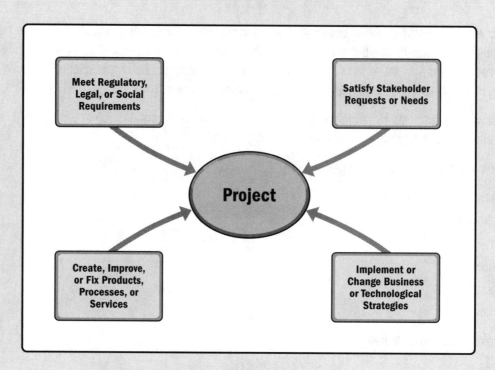

**Figure 1-2. Project Initiation Context**

These factors influence an organization's ongoing operations and business strategies. Leaders respond to these factors in order to keep the organization viable. Projects provide the means for organizations to successfully make the changes necessary to deal with these factors. These factors ultimately should link to the strategic objectives of the organization and the business value of each project.

Table 1-1 illustrates how example factors could align with one or more of the fundamental factor categories.

**Table 1-1. Examples of Factors that Lead to the Creation of a Project**

| Specific Factor | Examples of Specific Factors | Meet Regulatory, Legal, or Social Requirements | Satisfy Stakeholder Requests or Needs | Create, Improve, or Fix Products, Processes, or Services | Implement or Change Business or Technological Strategies |
|---|---|---|---|---|---|
| New technology | An electronics firm authorizes a new project to develop a faster, cheaper, and smaller laptop based on advances in computer memory and electronics technology | | | X | X |
| Competitive forces | Lower pricing on products by a competitor results in the need to lower production costs to remain competitive | | | | X |
| Material issues | A municipal bridge developed cracks in some support members resulting in a project to fix the problems | X | | X | |
| Political changes | A newly elected official instigating project funding changes to a current project | | | | X |
| Market demand | A car company authorizes a project to build more fuel-efficient cars in response to gasoline shortages | | X | X | X |
| Economic changes | An economic downturn results in a change in the priorities for a current project | | | | X |
| Customer request | An electric utility authorizes a project to build a substation to serve a new industrial park | | X | X | |
| Stakeholder demands | A stakeholder requires that a new output be produced by the organization | | X | | |
| Legal requirement | A chemical manufacturer authorizes a project to establish guidelines for the proper handling of a new toxic material | X | | | |
| Business process improvements | An organization implements a project resulting from a Lean Six Sigma value stream mapping exercise | | | X | |
| Strategic opportunity or business need | A training company authorizes a project to create a new course to increase its revenues | | | X | X |
| Social need | A nongovernmental organization in a developing country authorizes a project to provide potable water systems, latrines, and sanitation education to communities suffering from high rates of infectious diseases | | X | | |
| Environmental considerations | A public company authorizes a project to create a new service for electric car sharing to reduce pollution | | | X | X |

## 1.2.2 THE IMPORTANCE OF PROJECT MANAGEMENT

Project management is the application of knowledge, skills, tools, and techniques to project activities to meet the project requirements. Project management is accomplished through the appropriate application and integration of the project management processes identified for the project. Project management enables organizations to execute projects effectively and efficiently.

Effective project management helps individuals, groups, and public and private organizations to:

◆ Meet business objectives;

◆ Satisfy stakeholder expectations;

◆ Be more predictable;

◆ Increase chances of success;

◆ Deliver the right products at the right time;

◆ Resolve problems and issues;

◆ Respond to risks in a timely manner;

◆ Optimize the use of organizational resources;

◆ Identify, recover, or terminate failing projects;

◆ Manage constraints (e.g., scope, quality, schedule, costs, resources);

◆ Balance the influence of constraints on the project (e.g., increased scope may increase cost or schedule); and

◆ Manage change in a better manner.

Poorly managed projects or the absence of project management may result in:

◆ Missed deadlines,

◆ Cost overruns,

◆ Poor quality,

◆ Rework,

◆ Uncontrolled expansion of the project,

◆ Loss of reputation for the organization,

◆ Unsatisfied stakeholders, and

◆ Failure in achieving the objectives for which the project was undertaken.

Projects are a key way to create value and benefits in organizations. In today's business environment, organizational leaders need to be able to manage with tighter budgets, shorter timelines, scarcity of resources, and rapidly changing technology. The business environment is dynamic with an accelerating rate of change. To remain competitive in the world economy, companies are embracing project management to consistently deliver business value.

Effective and efficient project management should be considered a strategic competency within organizations. It enables organizations to:

◆ Tie project results to business goals,

◆ Compete more effectively in their markets,

◆ Sustain the organization, and

◆ Respond to the impact of business environment changes on projects by appropriately adjusting project management plans (see Section 4.2).

## 1.2.3 RELATIONSHIP OF PROJECT, PROGRAM, PORTFOLIO, AND OPERATIONS MANAGEMENT

### 1.2.3.1 OVERVIEW

Using project management processes, tools, and techniques puts in place a sound foundation for organizations to achieve their goals and objectives. A project may be managed in three separate scenarios: as a stand-alone project (outside of a portfolio or program), within a program, or within a portfolio. Project managers interact with portfolio and program managers when a project is within a program or portfolio. For example, multiple projects may be needed to accomplish a set of goals and objectives for an organization. In those situations, projects may be grouped together into a program. A program is defined as a group of related projects, subsidiary programs, and program activities managed in a coordinated manner to obtain benefits not available from managing them individually. Programs are not large projects. A very large project may be referred to as a megaproject. As a guideline, megaprojects cost US$1 billion or more, affect 1 million or more people, and run for years.

Some organizations may employ the use of a project portfolio to effectively manage multiple programs and projects that are underway at any given time. A portfolio is defined as projects, programs, subsidiary portfolios, and operations managed as a group to achieve strategic objectives. Figure 1-3 illustrates an example of how portfolios, programs, projects, and operations are related in a specific situation.

Program management and portfolio management differ from project management in their life cycles, activities, objectives, focus, and benefits. However, portfolios, programs, projects, and operations often engage with the same stakeholders and may need to use the same resources (see Figure 1-3), which may result in a conflict in the organization. This type of a situation increases the need for coordination within the organization through the use of portfolio, program, and project management to achieve a workable balance in the organization.

Figure 1-3 illustrates a sample portfolio structure indicating relationships between the programs, projects, shared resources, and stakeholders. The portfolio components are grouped together in order to facilitate the effective governance and management of the work that helps to achieve organizational strategies and priorities. Organizational and portfolio planning impact the components by means of prioritization based on risk, funding, and other considerations. The portfolio view allows organizations to see how the strategic goals are reflected in the portfolio. This portfolio view also enables the implementation and coordination of appropriate portfolio, program, and project governance. This coordinated governance allows authorized allocation of human, financial, and physical resources based on expected performance and benefits.

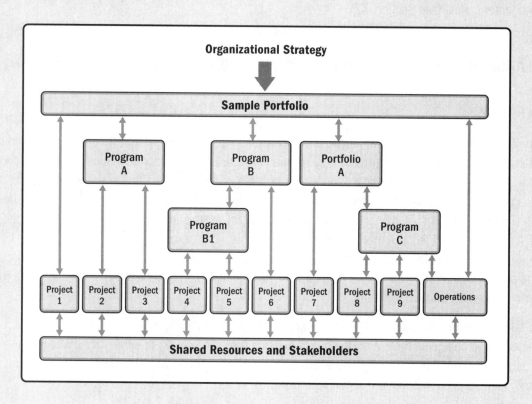

Figure 1-3. Portfolio, Programs, Projects, and Operations

Looking at project, program, and portfolio management from an organizational perspective:

◆ Program and project management focus on doing programs and projects the "right" way; and

◆ Portfolio management focuses on doing the "right" programs and projects.

Table 1-2 gives a comparative overview of portfolios, programs, and projects.

**Table 1-2. Comparative Overview of Portfolios, Programs, and Projects**

| Organizational Project Management | | | |
|---|---|---|---|
| | **Projects** | **Programs** | **Portfolios** |
| **Definition** | A project is a temporary endeavor undertaken to create a unique product, service, or result. | A program is a group of related projects, subsidiary programs, and program activities that are managed in a coordinated manner to obtain benefits not available from managing them individually. | A portfolio is a collection of projects, programs, subsidiary portfolios, and operations managed as a group to achieve strategic objectives. |
| **Scope** | Projects have defined objectives. Scope is progressively elaborated throughout the project life cycle. | Programs have a scope that encompasses the scopes of its program components. Programs produce benefits to an organization by ensuring that the outputs and outcomes of program components are delivered in a coordinated and complementary manner. | Portfolios have an organizational scope that changes with the strategic objectives of the organization. |
| **Change** | Project managers expect change and implement processes to keep change managed and controlled. | Programs are managed in a manner that accepts and adapts to change as necessary to optimize the delivery of benefits as the program's components deliver outcomes and/or outputs. | Portfolio managers continuously monitor changes in the broader internal and external environments. |
| **Planning** | Project managers progressively elaborate high-level information into detailed plans throughout the project life cycle. | Programs are managed using high-level plans that track the interdependencies and progress of program components. Program plans are also used to guide planning at the component level. | Portfolio managers create and maintain necessary processes and communication relative to the aggregate portfolio. |
| **Management** | Project managers manage the project team to meet the project objectives. | Programs are managed by program managers who ensure that program benefits are delivered as expected, by coordinating the activities of a program's components. | Portfolio managers may manage or coordinate portfolio management staff, or program and project staff that may have reporting responsibilities into the aggregate portfolio. |
| **Monitoring** | Project managers monitor and control the work of producing the products, services, or results that the project was undertaken to produce. | Program managers monitor the progress of program components to ensure the overall goals, schedules, budget, and benefits of the program will be met. | Portfolio managers monitor strategic changes and aggregate resource allocation, performance results, and risk of the portfolio. |
| **Success** | Success is measured by product and project quality, timeliness, budget compliance, and degree of customer satisfaction. | A program's success is measured by the program's ability to deliver its intended benefits to an organization, and by the program's efficiency and effectiveness in delivering those benefits. | Success is measured in terms of the aggregate investment performance and benefit realization of the portfolio. |

## 1.2.3.2 PROGRAM MANAGEMENT

Program management is defined as the application of knowledge, skills, and principles to a program to achieve the program objectives and to obtain benefits and control not available by managing program components individually. A program component refers to projects and other programs within a program. Project management focuses on interdependencies within a project to determine the optimal approach for managing the project. Program management focuses on the interdependencies between projects and between projects and the program level to determine the optimal approach for managing them. Actions related to these program and project-level interdependencies may include:

◆ Aligning with the organizational or strategic direction that affects program and project goals and objectives;

◆ Allocating the program scope into program components;

◆ Managing interdependencies among the components of the program to best serve the program;

◆ Managing program risks that may impact multiple projects in the program;

◆ Resolving constraints and conflicts that affect multiple projects within the program;

◆ Resolving issues between component projects and the program level;

◆ Managing change requests within a shared governance framework;

◆ Allocating budgets across multiple projects within the program; and

◆ Assuring benefits realization from the program and component projects.

An example of a program is a new communications satellite system with projects for the design and construction of the satellite and the ground stations, the launch of the satellite, and the integration of the system.

For more information on program management, see *The Standard for Program Management* [3].

## 1.2.3.3 PORTFOLIO MANAGEMENT

A portfolio is defined as projects, programs, subsidiary portfolios, and operations managed as a group to achieve strategic objectives.

Portfolio management is defined as the centralized management of one or more portfolios to achieve strategic objectives. The programs or projects of the portfolio may not necessarily be interdependent or directly related.

The aim of portfolio management is to:

◆ Guide organizational investment decisions.

◆ Select the optimal mix of programs and projects to meet strategic objectives.

◆ Provide decision-making transparency.

◆ Prioritize team and physical resource allocation.

◆ Increase the likelihood of realizing the desired return on investment.

◆ Centralize the management of the aggregate risk profile of all components.

Portfolio management also confirms that the portfolio is consistent with and aligned with organizational strategies.

Maximizing the value of the portfolio requires careful examination of the components that comprise the portfolio. Components are prioritized so that those contributing the most to the organization's strategic objectives have the required financial, team, and physical resources.

For example, an infrastructure organization that has the strategic objective of maximizing the return on its investments may put together a portfolio that includes a mix of projects in oil and gas, power, water, roads, rail, and airports. From this mix, the organization may choose to manage related projects as one portfolio. All of the power projects may be grouped together as a power portfolio. Similarly, all of the water projects may be grouped together as a water portfolio. However, when the organization has projects in designing and constructing a power plant and then operates the power plant to generate energy, those related projects can be grouped in one program. Thus, the power program and similar water program become integral components of the portfolio of the infrastructure organization.

For more information on portfolio management, see *The Standard for Portfolio Management* [2].

### 1.2.3.4 OPERATIONS MANAGEMENT

Operations management is an area that is outside the scope of formal project management as described in this guide.

Operations management is concerned with the ongoing production of goods and/or services. It ensures that business operations continue efficiently by using the optimal resources needed to meet customer demands. It is concerned with managing processes that transform inputs (e.g., materials, components, energy, and labor) into outputs (e.g., products, goods, and/or services).

### 1.2.3.5 OPERATIONS AND PROJECT MANAGEMENT

Changes in business or organizational operations may be the focus of a project—especially when there are substantial changes to business operations as a result of a new product or service delivery. Ongoing operations are outside of the scope of a project; however, there are intersecting points where the two areas cross.

Projects can intersect with operations at various points during the product life cycle, such as;

◆ When developing a new product, upgrading a product, or expanding outputs;

◆ While improving operations or the product development process;

◆ At the end of the product life cycle; and

◆ At each closeout phase.

At each point, deliverables and knowledge are transferred between the project and operations for implementation of the delivered work. This implementation occurs through a transfer of project resources or knowledge to operations or through a transfer of operational resources to the project.

### 1.2.3.6 ORGANIZATIONAL PROJECT MANAGEMENT (OPM) AND STRATEGIES

Portfolios, programs, and projects are aligned with or driven by organizational strategies and differ in the way each contributes to the achievement of strategic goals:

◆ Portfolio management aligns portfolios with organizational strategies by selecting the right programs or projects, prioritizing the work, and providing the needed resources.

◆ Program management harmonizes its program components and controls interdependencies in order to realize specified benefits.

◆ Project management enables the achievement of organizational goals and objectives.

Within portfolios or programs, projects are a means of achieving organizational goals and objectives. This is often accomplished in the context of a strategic plan that is the primary factor guiding investments in projects. Alignment with the organization's strategic business goals can be achieved through the systematic management of portfolios, programs, and projects through the application of organizational project management (OPM). OPM is defined as a framework in which portfolio, program, and project management are integrated with organizational enablers in order to achieve strategic objectives.

The purpose of OPM is to ensure that the organization undertakes the right projects and allocates critical resources appropriately. OPM also helps to ensure that all levels in the organization understand the strategic vision, the initiatives that support the vision, the objectives, and the deliverables. Figure 1-4 shows the organizational environment where strategy, portfolio, programs, projects, and operations interact.

For more information on OPM, refer to *Implementing Organizational Project Management: A Practice Guide* [8].

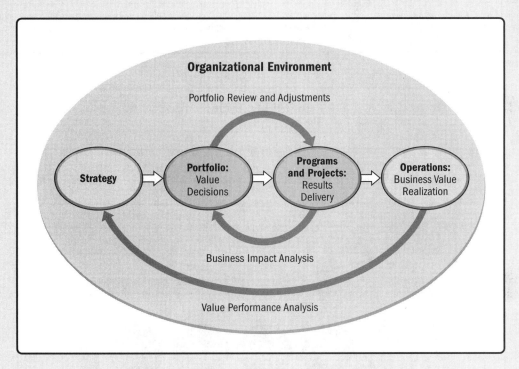

**Figure 1-4. Organizational Project Management**

## 1.2.4 COMPONENTS OF THE GUIDE

Projects comprise several key components that, when effectively managed, result in their successful completion. This guide identifies and explains these components. The various components interrelate to one another during the management of a project.

The key components are described briefly in Table 1-3. These components are more fully explained in the sections that follow the table.

**Table 1-3. Description of *PMBOK® Guide* Key Components**

| *PMBOK® Guide* Key Component | Brief Description |
|---|---|
| Project life cycle (Section 1.2.4.1) | The series of phases that a project passes through from its start to its completion. |
| Project phase (Section 1.2.4.2) | A collection of logically related project activities that culminates in the completion of one or more deliverables. |
| Phase gate (Section 1.2.4.3) | A review at the end of a phase in which a decision is made to continue to the next phase, to continue with modification, or to end a program or project. |
| Project management processes (Section 1.2.4.4) | A systematic series of activities directed toward causing an end result where one or more inputs will be acted upon to create one or more outputs. |
| Project Management Process Group (Section 1.2.4.5) | A logical grouping of project management inputs, tools and techniques, and outputs. The Project Management Process Groups include Initiating, Planning, Executing, Monitoring and Controlling, and Closing. Project Management Process Groups are not project phases. |
| Project Management Knowledge Area (Section 1.2.4.6) | An identified area of project management defined by its knowledge requirements and described in terms of its component processes, practices, inputs, outputs, tools, and techniques. |

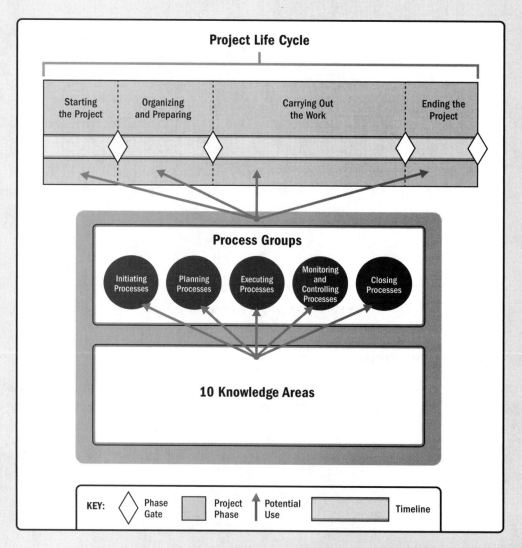

Figure 1-5. Interrelationship of *PMBOK® Guide* Key Components in Projects

## 1.2.4.1 PROJECT AND DEVELOPMENT LIFE CYCLES

A project life cycle is the series of phases that a project passes through from its start to its completion. It provides the basic framework for managing the project. This basic framework applies regardless of the specific project work involved. The phases may be sequential, iterative, or overlapping. All projects can be mapped to the generic life cycle shown in Figure 1-5.

Project life cycles can be predictive or adaptive. Within a project life cycle, there are generally one or more phases that are associated with the development of the product, service, or result. These are called a development life cycle. Development life cycles can be predictive, iterative, incremental, adaptive, or a hybrid model:

◆ In a predictive life cycle, the project scope, time, and cost are determined in the early phases of the life cycle. Any changes to the scope are carefully managed. Predictive life cycles may also be referred to as waterfall life cycles.

◆ In an iterative life cycle, the project scope is generally determined early in the project life cycle, but time and cost estimates are routinely modified as the project team's understanding of the product increases. Iterations develop the product through a series of repeated cycles, while increments successively add to the functionality of the product.

◆ In an incremental life cycle, the deliverable is produced through a series of iterations that successively add functionality within a predetermined time frame. The deliverable contains the necessary and sufficient capability to be considered complete only after the final iteration.

◆ Adaptive life cycles are agile, iterative, or incremental. The detailed scope is defined and approved before the start of an iteration. Adaptive life cycles are also referred to as agile or change-driven life cycles. See Appendix X3.

◆ A hybrid life cycle is a combination of a predictive and an adaptive life cycle. Those elements of the project that are well known or have fixed requirements follow a predictive development life cycle, and those elements that are still evolving follow an adaptive development life cycle.

It is up to the project management team to determine the best life cycle for each project. The project life cycle needs to be flexible enough to deal with the variety of factors included in the project. Life cycle flexibility may be accomplished by:

◆ Identifying the process or processes needed to be performed in each phase,

◆ Performing the process or processes identified in the appropriate phase,

◆ Adjusting the various attributes of a phase (e.g., name, duration, exit criteria, and entrance criteria).

Project life cycles are independent of product life cycles, which may be produced by a project. A product life cycle is the series of phases that represent the evolution of a product, from concept through delivery, growth, maturity, and to retirement.

## 1.2.4.2 PROJECT PHASE

A project phase is a collection of logically related project activities that culminates in the completion of one or more deliverables. The phases in a life cycle can be described by a variety of attributes. Attributes may be measurable and unique to a specific phase. Attributes may include but are not limited to:

◆ Name (e.g., Phase A, Phase B, Phase 1, Phase 2, proposal phase),

◆ Number (e.g., three phases in the project, five phases in the project),

◆ Duration (e.g., 1 week, 1 month, 1 quarter),

◆ Resource requirements (e.g., people, buildings, equipment),

◆ Entrance criteria for a project to move into that phase (e.g., specified approvals documented, specified documents completed), and

◆ Exit criteria for a project to complete a phase (e.g., documented approvals, completed documents, completed deliverables).

Projects may be separated into distinct phases or subcomponents. These phases or subcomponents are generally given names that indicate the type of work done in that phase. Examples of phase names include but are not limited to:

◆ Concept development,

◆ Feasibility study,

◆ Customer requirements,

◆ Solution development,

◆ Design,

◆ Prototype,

◆ Build,

◆ Test,

◆ Transition,

◆ Commissioning,

◆ Milestone review, and

◆ Lessons learned.

The project phases may be established based on various factors including, but not limited to:

◆ Management needs;

◆ Nature of the project;

◆ Unique characteristics of the organization, industry, or technology;

◆ Project elements including, but not limited to, technology, engineering, business, process, or legal; and

◆ Decision points (e.g., funding, project go/no-go, and milestone review).

Using multiple phases may provide better insight to managing the project. It also provides an opportunity to assess the project performance and take necessary corrective or preventive actions in subsequent phases. A key component used with project phases is the phase review (see Section 1.2.4.3).

### 1.2.4.3 PHASE GATE

A phase gate is held at the end of a phase. The project's performance and progress are compared to project and business documents including but not limited to:

◆ Project business case (see Section 1.2.6.1),

◆ Project charter (see Section 4.1),

◆ Project management plan (see Section 4.2), and

◆ Benefits management plan (see Section 1.2.6.2).

A decision (e.g., go/no-go decision) is made as a result of this comparison to:

◆ Continue to the next phase,

◆ Continue to the next phase with modification,

◆ End the project,

◆ Remain in the phase, or

◆ Repeat the phase or elements of it.

Depending on the organization, industry, or type of work, phase gates may be referred to by other terms such as, phase review, stage gate, kill point, and phase entrance or phase exit. Organizations may use these reviews to examine other pertinent items which are beyond the scope of this guide, such as product-related documents or models.

## 1.2.4.4 PROJECT MANAGEMENT PROCESSES

The project life cycle is managed by executing a series of project management activities known as project management processes. Every project management process produces one or more outputs from one or more inputs by using appropriate project management tools and techniques. The output can be a deliverable or an outcome. Outcomes are an end result of a process. Project management processes apply globally across industries.

Project management processes are logically linked by the outputs they produce. Processes may contain overlapping activities that occur throughout the project. The output of one process generally results in either:

◆ An input to another process, or

◆ A deliverable of the project or project phase.

Figure 1-6 shows an example of how inputs, tools and techniques, and outputs relate to each other within a process, and with other processes.

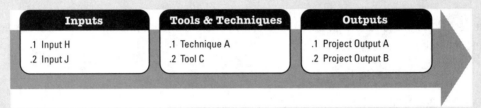

**Figure 1-6. Example Process: Inputs, Tools & Techniques, and Outputs**

The number of process iterations and interactions between processes varies based on the needs of the project. Processes generally fall into one of three categories:

◆ **Processes used once or at predefined points in the project.** The processes *Develop Project Charter and Close Project or Phase* are examples.

◆ **Processes that are performed periodically as needed.** The process *Acquire Resources* is performed as resources are needed. The process *Conduct Procurements* is performed prior to needing the procured item.

◆ **Processes that are performed continuously throughout the project.** The process *Define Activities* may occur throughout the project life cycle, especially if the project uses rolling wave planning or an adaptive development approach. Many of the monitoring and control processes are ongoing from the start of the project, until it is closed out.

Project management is accomplished through the appropriate application and integration of logically grouped project management processes. While there are different ways of grouping processes, the *PMBOK® Guide* groups processes into five categories called Process Groups.

# 1.2.4.5 PROJECT MANAGEMENT PROCESS GROUPS

A Project Management Process Group is a logical grouping of project management processes to achieve specific project objectives. Process Groups are independent of project phases. Project management processes are grouped into the following five Project Management Process Groups:

◆ **Initiating Process Group.** Those processes performed to define a new project or a new phase of an existing project by obtaining authorization to start the project or phase.

◆ **Planning Process Group.** Those processes required to establish the scope of the project, refine the objectives, and define the course of action required to attain the objectives that the project was undertaken to achieve.

◆ **Executing Process Group.** Those processes performed to complete the work defined in the project management plan to satisfy the project requirements.

◆ **Monitoring and Controlling Process Group.** Those processes required to track, review, and regulate the progress and performance of the project; identify any areas in which changes to the plan are required; and initiate the corresponding changes.

◆ **Closing Process Group.** Those processes performed to formally complete or close the project, phase, or contract.

Process flow diagrams are used throughout this guide. The project management processes are linked by specific inputs and outputs where the result or outcome of one process may become the input to another process that is not necessarily in the same Process Group. Note that Process Groups are not the same as project phases (see Section 1.2.4.2).

# 1.2.4.6 PROJECT MANAGEMENT KNOWLEDGE AREAS

In addition to Process Groups, processes are also categorized by Knowledge Areas. A Knowledge Area is an identified area of project management defined by its knowledge requirements and described in terms of its component processes, practices, inputs, outputs, tools, and techniques.

Although the Knowledge Areas are interrelated, they are defined separately from the project management perspective. The ten Knowledge Areas identified in this guide are used in most projects most of the time. The ten Knowledge Areas described in this guide are:

◆ **Project Integration Management.** Includes the processes and activities to identify, define, combine, unify, and coordinate the various processes and project management activities within the Project Management Process Groups.

◆ **Project Scope Management.** Includes the processes required to ensure the project includes all the work required, and only the work required, to complete the project successfully.

◆ **Project Schedule Management.** Includes the processes required to manage the timely completion of the project.

◆ **Project Cost Management.** Includes the processes involved in planning, estimating, budgeting, financing, funding, managing, and controlling costs so the project can be completed within the approved budget.

◆ **Project Quality Management.** Includes the processes for incorporating the organization's quality policy regarding planning, managing, and controlling project and product quality requirements, in order to meet stakeholders' expectations.

◆ **Project Resource Management.** Includes the processes to identify, acquire, and manage the resources needed for the successful completion of the project.

◆ **Project Communications Management.** Includes the processes required to ensure timely and appropriate planning, collection, creation, distribution, storage, retrieval, management, control, monitoring, and ultimate disposition of project information.

◆ **Project Risk Management.** Includes the processes of conducting risk management planning, identification, analysis, response planning, response implementation, and monitoring risk on a project.

◆ **Project Procurement Management.** Includes the processes necessary to purchase or acquire products, services, or results needed from outside the project team.

◆ **Project Stakeholder Management.** Includes the processes required to identify the people, groups, or organizations that could impact or be impacted by the project, to analyze stakeholder expectations and their impact on the project, and to develop appropriate management strategies for effectively engaging stakeholders in project decisions and execution.

The needs of a specific project may require one or more additional Knowledge Areas, for example, construction may require financial management or safety and health management. Table 1-4 maps the Project Management Process Groups and Knowledge Areas. Sections 4 through 13 provide more detail about each Knowledge Area. This table is an overview of the basic processes described in Sections 4 through 13.

**Table 1-4. Project Management Process Group and Knowledge Area Mapping**

| Knowledge Areas | Project Management Process Groups | | | | |
|---|---|---|---|---|---|
| | **Initiating Process Group** | **Planning Process Group** | **Executing Process Group** | **Monitoring and Controlling Process Group** | **Closing Process Group** |
| **4. Project Integration Management** | 4.1 Develop Project Charter | 4.2 Develop Project Management Plan | 4.3 Direct and Manage Project Work<br>4.4 Manage Project Knowledge | 4.5 Monitor and Control Project Work<br>4.6 Perform Integrated Change Control | 4.7 Close Project or Phase |
| **5. Project Scope Management** | | 5.1 Plan Scope Management<br>5.2 Collect Requirements<br>5.3 Define Scope<br>5.4 Create WBS | | 5.5 Validate Scope<br>5.6 Control Scope | |
| **6. Project Schedule Management** | | 6.1 Plan Schedule Management<br>6.2 Define Activities<br>6.3 Sequence Activities<br>6.4 Estimate Activity Durations<br>6.5 Develop Schedule | | 6.6 Control Schedule | |
| **7. Project Cost Management** | | 7.1 Plan Cost Management<br>7.2 Estimate Costs<br>7.3 Determine Budget | | 7.4 Control Costs | |
| **8. Project Quality Management** | | 8.1 Plan Quality Management | 8.2 Manage Quality | 8.3 Control Quality | |
| **9. Project Resource Management** | | 9.1 Plan Resource Management<br>9.2 Estimate Activity Resources | 9.3 Acquire Resources<br>9.4 Develop Team<br>9.5 Manage Team | 9.6 Control Resources | |
| **10. Project Communications Management** | | 10.1 Plan Communications Management | 10.2 Manage Communications | 10.3 Monitor Communications | |
| **11. Project Risk Management** | | 11.1 Plan Risk Management<br>11.2 Identify Risks<br>11.3 Perform Qualitative Risk Analysis<br>11.4 Perform Quantitative Risk Analysis<br>11.5 Plan Risk Responses | 11.6 Implement Risk Responses | 11.7 Monitor Risks | |
| **12. Project Procurement Management** | | 12.1 Plan Procurement Management | 12.2 Conduct Procurements | 12.3 Control Procurements | |
| **13. Project Stakeholder Management** | 13.1 Identify Stakeholders | 13.2 Plan Stakeholder Engagement | 13.3 Manage Stakeholder Engagement | 13.4 Monitor Stakeholder Engagement | |

## 1.2.4.7 PROJECT MANAGEMENT DATA AND INFORMATION

Throughout the life cycle of a project, a significant amount of data is collected, analyzed, and transformed. Project data are collected as a result of various processes and are shared within the project team. The collected data are analyzed in context, aggregated, and transformed to become project information during various processes. Information is communicated verbally or stored and distributed in various formats as reports. See Section 4.3 for more detail on this topic.

Project data are regularly collected and analyzed throughout the project life cycle. The following definitions identify key terminology regarding project data and information:

◆ **Work performance data.** The raw observations and measurements identified during activities performed to carry out the project work. Examples include reported percent of work physically completed, quality and technical performance measures, start and finish dates of schedule activities, number of change requests, number of defects, actual costs, actual durations, etc. Project data are usually recorded in a Project Management Information System (PMIS) (see Section 4.3.2.2) and in project documents.

◆ **Work performance information.** The performance data collected from various controlling processes, analyzed in context and integrated based on relationships across areas. Examples of performance information are status of deliverables, implementation status for change requests, and forecast estimates to complete.

◆ **Work performance reports.** The physical or electronic representation of work performance information compiled in project documents, which is intended to generate decisions or raise issues, actions, or awareness. Examples include status reports, memos, justifications, information notes, electronic dashboards, recommendations, and updates.

Figure 1-7 shows the flow of project information across the various processes used in managing the project.

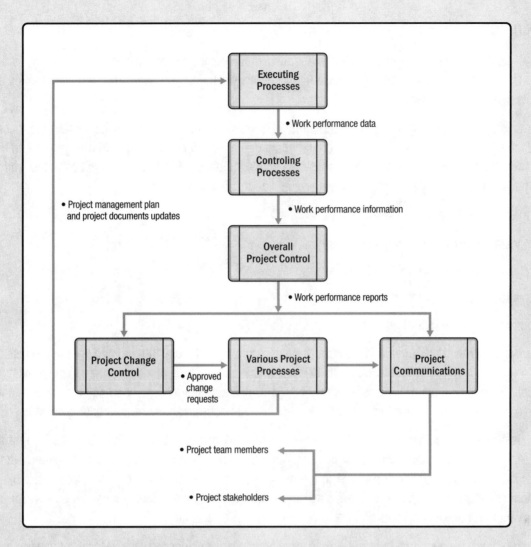

**Figure 1-7. Project Data, Information, and Report Flow**

## 1.2.5 TAILORING

Usually, project managers apply a project management methodology to their work. A methodology is a system of practices, techniques, procedures, and rules used by those who work in a discipline. This definition makes it clear that this guide itself is not a methodology.

This guide and *The Standard for Project Management* [1] are recommended references for tailoring, because these standard documents identify the subset of the project management body of knowledge that is generally recognized as good practice. "Good practice" does not mean that the knowledge described should always be applied uniformly to all projects. Specific methodology recommendations are outside the scope of this guide.

Project management methodologies may be:

◆ Developed by experts within the organization,

◆ Purchased from vendors,

◆ Obtained from professional associations, or

◆ Acquired from government agencies.

The appropriate project management processes, inputs, tools, techniques, outputs, and life cycle phases should be selected to manage a project. This selection activity is known as tailoring project management to the project. The project manager collaborates with the project team, sponsor, organizational management, or some combination thereof, in the tailoring. In some cases, the organization may require specific project management methodologies be used.

Tailoring is necessary because each project is unique; not every process, tool, technique, input, or output identified in the *PMBOK® Guide* is required on every project. Tailoring should address the competing constraints of scope, schedule, cost, resources, quality, and risk. The importance of each constraint is different for each project, and the project manager tailors the approach for managing these constraints based on the project environment, organizational culture, stakeholder needs, and other variables.

In tailoring project management, the project manager should also consider the varying levels of governance that may be required and within which the project will operate, as well as considering the culture of the organization. In addition, consideration of whether the customer of the project is internal or external to the organization may affect project management tailoring decisions.

Sound project management methodologies take into account the unique nature of projects and allow tailoring, to some extent, by the project manager. However, the tailoring that is included in the methodology may still require additional tailoring for a given project.

# 1.2.6 PROJECT MANAGEMENT BUSINESS DOCUMENTS

The project manager needs to ensure that the project management approach captures the intent of business documents. These documents are defined in Table 1-5. These two documents are interdependent and iteratively developed and maintained throughout the life cycle of the project.

**Table 1-5. Project Business Documents**

| Project Business Documents | Definition |
|---|---|
| Project business case | A documented economic feasibility study used to establish the validity of the benefits of a selected component lacking sufficient definition and that is used as a basis for the authorization of further project management activities. |
| Project benefits management plan | The documented explanation defining the processes for creating, maximizing, and sustaining the benefits provided by a project. |

The project sponsor is generally accountable for the development and maintenance of the project business case document. The project manager is responsible for providing recommendations and oversight to keep the project business case, project management plan, project charter, and project benefits management plan success measures in alignment with one another and with the goals and objectives of the organization.

Project managers should appropriately tailor the noted project management documents for their projects. In some organizations, the business case and benefits management plan are maintained at the program level. Project managers should work with the appropriate program managers to ensure the project management documents are aligned with the program documents. Figure 1-8 illustrates the interrelationship of these critical project management business documents and the needs assessment. Figure 1-8 shows an approximation of the life cycle of these various documents against the project life cycle.

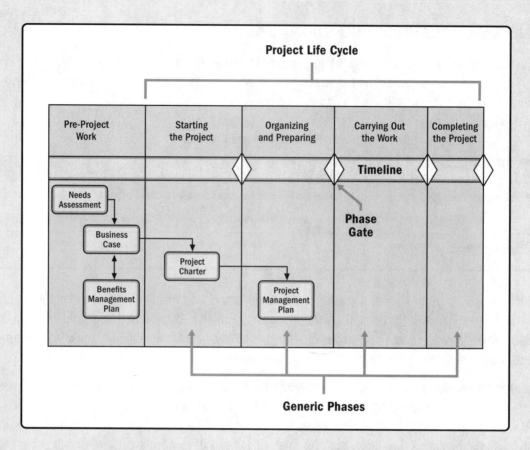

**Figure 1-8. Interrelationship of Needs Assessment and Critical Business/Project Documents**

### 1.2.6.1 PROJECT BUSINESS CASE

The project business case is a documented economic feasibility study used to establish the validity of the benefits of a selected component lacking sufficient definition and that is used as a basis for the authorization of further project management activities. The business case lists the objectives and reasons for project initiation. It helps measure the project success at the end of the project against the project objectives. The business case is a project business document that is used throughout the project life cycle. The business case may be used before the project initiation and may result in a go/no-go decision for the project.

A needs assessment often precedes the business case. The needs assessment involves understanding business goals and objectives, issues, and opportunities and recommending proposals to address them. The results of the needs assessment may be summarized in the business case document.

The process of defining the business need, analyzing the situation, making recommendations, and defining evaluation criteria is applicable to any organization's projects. A business case may include but is not limited to documenting the following:

◆ Business needs:

- Determination of what is prompting the need for action;

- Situational statement documenting the business problem or opportunity to be addressed including the value to be delivered to the organization;

- Identification of stakeholders affected; and

- Identification of the scope.

◆ Analysis of the situation:

- Identification of organizational strategies, goals, and objectives;

- Identification of root cause(s) of the problem or main contributors of an opportunity;

- Gap analysis of capabilities needed for the project versus existing capabilities of the organization;

- Identification of known risks;

- Identification of critical success factors;

- Identification of decision criteria by which the various courses of action may be assessed;

Examples of criteria categories used for analysis of a situation are:

- ○ *Required.* This is a criterion that is "required" to be fulfilled to address the problem or opportunity.

- ○ *Desired.* This is a criterion that is "desired" to be fulfilled to address the problem or opportunity.

- ○ *Optional.* This is a criterion that is not essential. Fulfillment of this criterion may become a differentiator between alternative courses of action.

- Identification of a set of options to be considered for addressing the business problem or opportunity. Options are alternative courses of action that may be taken by the organization. Options may also be described as business scenarios. For example, a business case could present the following three options:

- ○ *Do nothing.* This is also referred to as the "business as usual" option. Selection of this option results in the project not being authorized.

- ○ *Do the minimum work possible to address the problem or opportunity.* The minimum may be established by identifying the set of documented criteria that are key in addressing the problem or opportunity.

- ○ *Do more than the minimum work possible to address the problem or opportunity.* This option meets the minimum set of criteria and some or all of the other documented criteria. There may be more than one of these options documented in the business case.

◆ Recommendation:

  ■ A statement of the recommended option to pursue in the project;

  ■ Items to include in the statement may include but are not limited to:

    ○ Analysis results for the potential option;

    ○ Constraints, assumptions, risks, and dependencies for the potential options; and

    ○ Success measures (see Section 1.2.6.4).

  ■ An implementation approach that may include but is not limited to:

    ○ Milestones,

    ○ Dependencies, and

    ○ Roles and responsibilities.

◆ Evaluation:

  ■ Statement describing the plan for measuring benefits the project will deliver. This should include any ongoing operational aspects of the recommended option beyond initial implementation.

The business case document provides the basis to measure success and progress throughout the project life cycle by comparing the results with the objectives and the identified success criteria. See *Business Analysis for Practitioners: A Practice Guide* [7].

## 1.2.6.2 PROJECT BENEFITS MANAGEMENT PLAN

The project benefits management plan is the document that describes how and when the benefits of the project will be delivered, and describes the mechanisms that should be in place to measure those benefits. A project benefit is defined as an outcome of actions, behaviors, products, services, or results that provide value to the sponsoring organization as well as to the project's intended beneficiaries. Development of the benefits management plan begins early in the project life cycle with the definition of the target benefits to be realized. The benefits management plan describes key elements of the benefits and may include but is not limited to documenting the following:

◆ **Target benefits** (e.g., the expected tangible and intangible value to be gained by the implementation of the project; financial value is expressed as net present value);

◆ **Strategic alignment** (e.g., how well the project benefits align to the business strategies of the organization);

◆ **Timeframe for realizing benefits** (e.g., benefits by phase, short-term, long-term, and ongoing);

◆ **Benefits owner** (e.g., the accountable person to monitor, record, and report realized benefits throughout the timeframe established in the plan);

◆ **Metrics** (e.g., the measures to be used to show benefits realized, direct measures, and indirect measures);

◆ **Assumptions** (e.g., factors expected to be in place or to be in evidence); and

◆ **Risks** (e.g., risks for realization of benefits).

Developing the benefits management plan makes use of the data and information documented in the business case and needs assessment. For example, the cost-benefit analyses recorded in the documents illustrate the estimate of costs compared to the value of the benefits realized by the project. The benefits management plan and the project management plan include a description of how the business value resulting from the project becomes part of the organization's ongoing operations, including the metrics to be used. The metrics provide verification of the business value and validation of the project's success.

Development and maintenance of the project benefits management plan is an iterative activity. This document complements the business case, project charter, and project management plan. The project manager works with the sponsor to ensure that the project charter, project management plan, and the benefits management plan remain in alignment throughout the life cycle of the project. See *Business Analysis for Practitioners: A Practice Guide* [7], *The Standard for Program Management* [3], and *The Standard for Portfolio Management* [2].

## 1.2.6.3 PROJECT CHARTER AND PROJECT MANAGEMENT PLAN

The project charter is defined as a document issued by the project sponsor that formally authorizes the existence of a project and provides the project manager with the authority to apply organizational resources to project activities.

The project management plan is defined as the document that describes how the project will be executed, monitored, and controlled.

See Section 4 on Project Integration Management for more information on the project charter and the project management plan.

## 1.2.6.4 PROJECT SUCCESS MEASURES

One of the most common challenges in project management is determining whether or not a project is successful.

Traditionally, the project management metrics of time, cost, scope, and quality have been the most important factors in defining the success of a project. More recently, practitioners and scholars have determined that project success should also be measured with consideration toward achievement of the project objectives.

Project stakeholders may have different ideas as to what the successful completion of a project will look like and which factors are the most important. It is critical to clearly document the project objectives and to select objectives that are measurable. Three questions that the key stakeholders and the project manager should answer are:

◆ What does success look like for this project?

◆ How will success be measured?

◆ What factors may impact success?

The answer to these questions should be documented and agreed upon by the key stakeholders and the project manager.

Project success may include additional criteria linked to the organizational strategy and to the delivery of business results. These project objectives may include but are not limited to:

◆ Completing the project benefits management plan;

◆ Meeting the agreed-upon financial measures documented in the business case. These financial measures may include but are not limited to:

- Net present value (NPV),
- Return on investment (ROI),
- Internal rate of return (IRR),
- Payback period (PBP), and
- Benefit-cost ratio (BCR).

- ◆ Meeting business case nonfinancial objectives;

- ◆ Completing movement of an organization from its current state to the desired future state;

- ◆ Fulfilling contract terms and conditions;

- ◆ Meeting organizational strategy, goals, and objectives;

- ◆ Achieving stakeholder satisfaction;

- ◆ Acceptable customer/end-user adoption;

- ◆ Integration of deliverables into the organization's operating environment;

- ◆ Achieving agreed-upon quality of delivery;

- ◆ Meeting governance criteria; and

- ◆ Achieving other agreed-upon success measures or criteria (e.g., process throughput).

The project team needs to be able to assess the project situation, balance the demands, and maintain proactive communication with stakeholders in order to deliver a successful project.

When the business alignment for a project is constant, the chance for project success greatly increases because the project remains aligned with the strategic direction of the organization.

It is possible for a project to be successful from a scope/schedule/budget viewpoint, and to be unsuccessful from a business viewpoint. This can occur when there is a change in the business needs or the market environment before the project is completed.

# 2

## THE ENVIRONMENT IN WHICH PROJECTS OPERATE

### 2.1 OVERVIEW

Projects exist and operate in environments that may have an influence on them. These influences can have a favorable or unfavorable impact on the project. Two major categories of influences are enterprise environmental factors (EEFs) and organizational process assets (OPAs).

EEFs originate from the environment outside of the project and often outside of the enterprise. EEFs may have an impact at the organizational, portfolio, program, or project level. See Section 2.2 for additional information on EEFs.

OPAs are internal to the organization. These may arise from the organization itself, a portfolio, a program, another project, or a combination of these. Figure 2-1 shows the breakdown of project influences into EEFs and OPAs. See Section 2.3 for additional information on OPAs.

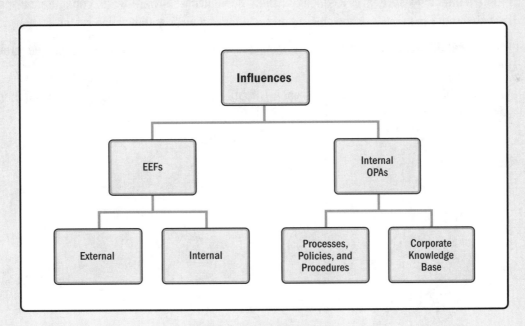

Figure 2-1. Project Influences

In addition to EEFs and OPAs, organizational systems play a significant role in the life cycle of the project. System factors that impact the power, influence, interests, competencies, and political capabilities of the people to act within the organizational system are discussed further in the section on organizational systems (see Section 2.4).

## 2.2 ENTERPRISE ENVIRONMENTAL FACTORS

Enterprise environmental factors (EEFs) refer to conditions, not under the control of the project team, that influence, constrain, or direct the project. These conditions can be internal and/or external to the organization. EEFs are considered as inputs to many project management processes, specifically for most planning processes. These factors may enhance or constrain project management options. In addition, these factors may have a positive or negative influence on the outcome.

EEFs vary widely in type or nature. These factors need to be considered if the project is to be effective. EEFs include but are not limited to the factors described in Sections 2.2.1 and 2.2.2.

### 2.2.1 EEFS INTERNAL TO THE ORGANIZATION

The following EEFs are internal to the organization:

◆ **Organizational culture, structure, and governance.** Examples include vision, mission, values, beliefs, cultural norms, leadership style, hierarchy and authority relationships, organizational style, ethics, and code of conduct.

◆ **Geographic distribution of facilities and resources.** Examples include factory locations, virtual teams, shared systems, and cloud computing.

◆ **Infrastructure.** Examples include existing facilities, equipment, organizational telecommunications channels, information technology hardware, availability, and capacity.

◆ **Information technology software.** Examples include scheduling software tools, configuration management systems, web interfaces to other online automated systems, and work authorization systems.

◆ **Resource availability.** Examples include contracting and purchasing constraints, approved providers and subcontractors, and collaboration agreements.

◆ **Employee capability.** Examples include existing human resources expertise, skills, competencies, and specialized knowledge.

## 2.2.2 EEFS EXTERNAL TO THE ORGANIZATION

The following EEFs are external to the organization.

◆ **Marketplace conditions.** Examples include competitors, market share brand recognition, and trademarks.

◆ **Social and cultural influences and issues.** Examples include political climate, codes of conduct, ethics, and perceptions.

◆ **Legal restrictions.** Examples include country or local laws and regulations related to security, data protection, business conduct, employment, and procurement.

◆ **Commercial databases.** Examples include benchmarking results, standardized cost estimating data, industry risk study information, and risk databases.

◆ **Academic research.** Examples include industry studies, publications, and benchmarking results.

◆ **Government or industry standards.** Examples include regulatory agency regulations and standards related to products, production, environment, quality, and workmanship.

◆ **Financial considerations.** Examples include currency exchange rates, interest rates, inflation rates, tariffs, and geographic location.

◆ **Physical environmental elements.** Examples include working conditions, weather, and constraints.

## 2.3 ORGANIZATIONAL PROCESS ASSETS

Organizational process assets (OPAs) are the plans, processes, policies, procedures, and knowledge bases specific to and used by the performing organization. These assets influence the management of the project.

OPAs include any artifact, practice, or knowledge from any or all of the performing organizations involved in the project that can be used to execute or govern the project. The OPAs also include the organization's lessons learned from previous projects and historical information. OPAs may include completed schedules, risk data, and earned value data. OPAs are inputs to many project management processes. Since OPAs are internal to the organization, the project team members may be able to update and add to the organizational process assets as necessary throughout the project. They may be grouped into two categories:

◆ Processes, policies, and procedures; and

◆ Organizational knowledge bases.

Generally, the assets in the first category are not updated as part of the project work. Processes, policies, and procedures are usually established by the project management office (PMO) or another function outside of the project. These can be updated only by following the appropriate organizational policies associated with updating processes, policies, or procedures. Some organizations encourage the team to tailor templates, life cycles, and checklists for the project. In these instances, the project management team should tailor those assets to meet the needs of the project.

The assets in the second category are updated throughout the project with project information. For example, information on financial performance, lessons learned, performance metrics and issues, and defects are continually updated throughout the project.

## 2.3.1 PROCESSES, POLICIES, AND PROCEDURES

The organization's processes and procedures for conducting project work include but are not limited to:

◆ **Initiating and Planning:**

- Guidelines and criteria for tailoring the organization's set of standard processes and procedures to satisfy the specific needs of the project;

- Specific organizational standards such as policies (e.g., human resources policies, health and safety policies, security and confidentiality policies, quality policies, procurement policies, and environmental policies);

- Product and project life cycles, and methods and procedures (e.g., project management methods, estimation metrics, process audits, improvement targets, checklists, and standardized process definitions for use in the organization);

- Templates (e.g., project management plans, project documents, project registers, report formats, contract templates, risk categories, risk statement templates, probability and impact definitions, probability and impact matrices, and stakeholder register templates); and

- Preapproved supplier lists and various types of contractual agreements (e.g., fixed-price, cost-reimbursable, and time and material contracts).

◆ **Executing, Monitoring, and Controlling:**

- Change control procedures, including the steps by which performing organization standards, policies, plans, and procedures or any project documents will be modified, and how any changes will be approved and validated;

- Traceability matrices;

- Financial controls procedures (e.g., time reporting, required expenditure and disbursement reviews, accounting codes, and standard contract provisions);

- Issue and defect management procedures (e.g., defining issue and defect controls, identifying and resolving issues and defects, and tracking action items);

- Resource availability control and assignment management;

- Organizational communication requirements (e.g., specific communication technology available, authorized communication media, record retention policies, videoconferencing, collaborative tools, and security requirements);

- Procedures for prioritizing, approving, and issuing work authorizations;

- Templates (e.g., risk register, issue log, and change log);

- Standardized guidelines, work instructions, proposal evaluation criteria, and performance measurement criteria; and

- Product, service, or result verification and validation procedures.

- **Closing.** Project closure guidelines or requirements (e.g., final project audits, project evaluations, deliverable acceptance, contract closure, resource reassignment, and knowledge transfer to production and/or operations).

## 2.3.2 ORGANIZATIONAL KNOWLEDGE REPOSITORIES

The organizational knowledge repositories for storing and retrieving information include but are not limited to:

- Configuration management knowledge repositories containing the versions of software and hardware components and baselines of all performing organization standards, policies, procedures, and any project documents;

- Financial data repositories containing information such as labor hours, incurred costs, budgets, and any project cost overruns;

- Historical information and lessons learned knowledge repositories (e.g., project records and documents, all project closure information and documentation, information regarding both the results of previous project selection decisions and previous project performance information, and information from risk management activities);

- Issue and defect management data repositories containing issue and defect status, control information, issue and defect resolution, and action item results;

- Data repositories for metrics used to collect and make available measurement data on processes and products; and

- Project files from previous projects (e.g., scope, cost, schedule, and performance measurement baselines, project calendars, project schedule network diagrams, risk registers, risk reports, and stakeholder registers).

# 2.4 ORGANIZATIONAL SYSTEMS

## 2.4.1 OVERVIEW

Projects operate within the constraints imposed by the organization through their structure and governance framework. To operate effectively and efficiently, the project manager needs to understand where responsibility, accountability, and authority reside within the organization. This understanding will help the project manager effectively use his or her power, influence, competence, leadership, and political capabilities to successfully complete the project.

The interaction of multiple factors within an individual organization creates a unique system that impacts the project operating in that system. The resulting organizational system determines the power, influence, interests, competence, and political capabilities of the people who are able to act within the system. The system factors include but are not limited to:

◆ Management elements,

◆ Governance frameworks, and

◆ Organizational structure types.

The complete information and explanation of the organizational system factors and how the combination of these factors impacts a project are beyond the scope of this guide. There are disciplines with associated literature, methodologies, and practices that address these factors in more depth than is possible within this guide. This section provides an overview of these factors and their interrelationship.

This overview begins by discussing systems in general. A system is a collection of various components that together can produce results not obtainable by the individual components alone. A component is an identifiable element within the project or organization that provides a particular function or group of related functions. The interaction of the various system components creates the organizational culture and capabilities. There are several principles regarding systems:

◆ Systems are dynamic,

◆ Systems can be optimized,

◆ System components can be optimized,

◆ Systems and their components cannot be optimized at the same time, and

◆ Systems are nonlinear in responsiveness (a change in the input does not produce a predictable change in the output).

Multiple changes may occur within the system and between the system and its environment. When these changes take place, adaptive behavior occurs within the components that in turn add to the system's dynamics. The system's dynamics are defined by the interaction between the components based on the relationships and dependencies that exist between the components.

Systems are typically the responsibility of an organization's management. The organization's management examines the optimization trade-offs between the components and the system in order to take the appropriate action to achieve the best outcomes for the organization. The results of this examination will impact the project under consideration. Therefore, it is important that the project manager take these results into account when determining how to fulfill the project's objectives. In addition, the project manager should take into account the organization's governance framework.

## 2.4.2 ORGANIZATIONAL GOVERNANCE FRAMEWORKS

Recent PMI research reveals that governance refers to organizational or structural arrangements at all levels of an organization designed to determine and influence the behavior of the organization's members [9]. This research suggests that the concept of governance is multidimensional and:

◆ Includes consideration of people, roles, structures, and policies; and

◆ Requires providing direction and oversight through data and feedback.

### 2.4.2.1 GOVERNANCE FRAMEWORK

Governance is the framework within which authority is exercised in organizations. This framework includes but is not limited to:

◆ Rules,

◆ Policies,

◆ Procedures,

◆ Norms,

◆ Relationships,

◆ Systems, and

◆ Processes.

This framework influences how:

◆ Objectives of the organization are set and achieved,

◆ Risk is monitored and assessed, and

◆ Performance is optimized.

### 2.4.2.2 GOVERNANCE OF PORTFOLIOS, PROGRAMS, AND PROJECTS

The *Governance of Portfolios, Programs, and Projects: A Practice Guide* [10] describes a common governance framework aligning organizational project management (OPM) and portfolio, program, and project management. The practice guide describes four governance domains of alignment, risk, performance, and communications. Each domain has the following functions: oversight, control, integration, and decision making. Each function has governance supporting processes and activities for stand-alone projects, or projects operating within the portfolio or program environments.

Project governance refers to the framework, functions, and processes that guide project management activities in order to create a unique product, service, or result to meet organizational, strategic, and operational goals. There is no one governance framework that is effective in all organizations. A governance framework should be tailored to the organizational culture, types of projects, and the needs of the organization in order to be effective.

For more information regarding project governance, including its implementation, see *Governance of Portfolios, Programs, and Projects: A Practice Guide* [10].

### 2.4.3 MANAGEMENT ELEMENTS

Management elements are the components that comprise the key functions or principles of general management in the organization. The general management elements are allocated within the organization according to its governance framework and the organizational structure type selected.

The key functions or principles of management include but are not limited to:

◆ Division of work using specialized skills and availability to perform work;

◆ Authority given to perform work;

◆ Responsibility to perform work appropriately assigned based on such attributes as skill and experience;

◆ Discipline of action (e.g., respect for authority, people, and rules);

◆ Unity of command (e.g., only one person gives orders for any action or activity to an individual);

◆ Unity of direction (e.g., one plan and one head for a group of activities with the same objective);

◆ General goals of the organization take precedence over individual goals;

◆ Paid fairly for work performed;

- ◆ Optimal use of resources;

- ◆ Clear communication channels;

- ◆ Right materials to the right person for the right job at the right time;

- ◆ Fair and equal treatment of people in the workplace;

- ◆ Clear security of work positions;

- ◆ Safety of people in the workplace;

- ◆ Open contribution to planning and execution by each person; and

- ◆ Optimal morale.

Performance of these management elements are assigned to selected individuals within the organization. These individuals may perform the noted functions within various organizational structures. For example, in a hierarchical structure, there are horizontal and vertical levels within the organization. These hierarchical levels range from the line management level through to the executive management level. The responsibility, accountability, and authority assigned to the hierarchical level indicate how the individual may perform the noted function within that organizational structure.

## 2.4.4 ORGANIZATIONAL STRUCTURE TYPES

Determination of the appropriate organizational structure type is a result of the study of tradeoffs between two key variables. The variables are the organizational structure types available for use and how to optimize them for a given organization. There is not a one-size-fits-all structure for any given organization. The final structure for a given organization is unique due to the numerous variables to be considered. Sections 2.4.4.1 and 2.4.4.2 give examples of some of the factors to be included when considering the two variables given. Section 2.4.4.3 discusses one organizational structure that is prevalent in project management.

### 2.4.4.1 ORGANIZATIONAL STRUCTURE TYPES

Organizational structures take many forms or types. Table 2-1 compares several types of organizational structures and their influence on projects.

## 2.4.4.2 FACTORS IN ORGANIZATION STRUCTURE SELECTION

Each organization considers numerous factors for inclusion in its organizational structure. Each factor may carry a different level of importance in the final analysis. The combination of the factor, its value, and relative importance provides the organization's decision makers with the right information for inclusion in the analysis.

Factors to consider in selecting an organizational structure include but are not limited to:

◆ Degree of alignment with organizational objectives,

◆ Specialization capabilities,

◆ Span of control, efficiency, and effectiveness,

◆ Clear path for escalation of decisions,

◆ Clear line and scope of authority,

◆ Delegation capabilities,

◆ Accountability assignment,

◆ Responsibility assignment,

◆ Adaptability of design,

◆ Simplicity of design,

◆ Efficiency of performance,

◆ Cost considerations,

◆ Physical locations (e.g., colocated, regional, and virtual), and

◆ Clear communication (e.g., policies, status of work, and organization's vision).

## Table 2-1. Influences of Organizational Structures on Projects

| Organizational Structure Type | Project Characteristics | | | | | |
|---|---|---|---|---|---|---|
| | Work Groups Arranged by: | Project Manager's Authority | Project Manager's Role | Resource Availability | Who Manages the Project Budget? | Project Management Administrative Staff |
| **Organic or Simple** | Flexible; people working side-by-side | Little or none | Part-time; may or may not be a designated job role like coordinator | Little or none | Owner or operator | Little or none |
| **Functional (centralized)** | Job being done (e.g., engineering, manufacturing) | Little or none | Part-time; may or may not be a designated job role like coordinator | Little or none | Functional manager | Part-time |
| **Multi-divisional (may replicate functions for each division with little centralization)** | One of: product; production processes; portfolio; program; geographic region; customer type | Little or none | Part-time; may or may not be a designated job role like coordinator | Little or none | Functional manager | Part-time |
| **Matrix – strong** | By job function, with project manager as a function | Moderate to high | Full-time designated job role | Moderate to high | Project manager | Full-time |
| **Matrix – weak** | Job function | Low | Part-time; done as part of another job and not a designated job role like coordinator | Low | Functional manager | Part-time |
| **Matrix – balanced** | Job function | Low to moderate | Part-time; embedded in the functions as a skill and may not be a designated job role like coordinator | Low to moderate | Mixed | Part-time |
| **Project-oriented (composite, hybrid)** | Project | High to almost total | Full-time designated job role | High to almost total | Project manager | Full-time |
| **Virtual** | Network structure with nodes at points of contact with other people | Low to moderate | Full-time or part-time | Low to moderate | Mixed | Could be full-time or part-time |
| **Hybrid** | Mix of other types | Mixed | Mixed | Mixed | Mixed | Mixed |
| **PMO*** | Mix of other types | High to almost total | Full-time designated job role | High to almost total | Project manager | Full-time |

*PMO refers to a portfolio, program, or project management office or organization.

## 2.4.4.3 PROJECT MANAGEMENT OFFICE

A project management office (PMO) is an organizational structure that standardizes the project-related governance processes and facilitates the sharing of resources, methodologies, tools, and techniques. The responsibilities of a PMO can range from providing project management support functions to the direct management of one or more projects.

There are several types of PMOs in organizations. Each type varies in the degree of control and influence it has on projects within the organization, such as:

◆ **Supportive.** Supportive PMOs provide a consultative role to projects by supplying templates, best practices, training, access to information, and lessons learned from other projects. This type of PMO serves as a project repository. The degree of control provided by the PMO is low.

◆ **Controlling.** Controlling PMOs provide support and require compliance through various means. The degree of control provided by the PMO is moderate. Compliance may involve:

- Adoption of project management frameworks or methodologies;
- Use of specific templates, forms, and tools; and
- Conformance to governance frameworks.

◆ **Directive.** Directive PMOs take control of the projects by directly managing the projects. Project managers are assigned by and report to the PMO. The degree of control provided by the PMO is high.

The project management office may have organization-wide responsibility. It may play a role in supporting strategic alignment and delivering organizational value. The PMO integrates data and information from organizational strategic projects and evaluates how higher-level strategic objectives are being fulfilled. The PMO is the natural liaison between the organization's portfolios, programs, projects, and the organizational measurement systems (e.g., balanced scorecard).

The projects supported or administered by the PMO may not be related other than by being managed together. The specific form, function, and structure of a PMO are dependent upon the needs of the organization that it supports.

A PMO may have the authority to act as an integral stakeholder and a key decision maker throughout the life of each project in order to keep it aligned with the business objectives. The PMO may:

◆ Make recommendations,

◆ Lead knowledge transfer,

◆ Terminate projects, and

◆ Take other actions, as required.

A primary function of a PMO is to support project managers in a variety of ways, which may include but are not limited to:

◆ Managing shared resources across all projects administered by the PMO;

◆ Identifying and developing project management methodology, best practices, and standards;

◆ Coaching, mentoring, training, and oversight;

◆ Monitoring compliance with project management standards, policies, procedures, and templates by means of project audits;

◆ Developing and managing project policies, procedures, templates, and other shared documentation (organizational process assets); and

◆ Coordinating communication across projects.

# 3

# THE ROLE OF THE PROJECT MANAGER

## 3.1 OVERVIEW

The project manager plays a critical role in the leadership of a project team in order to achieve the project's objectives. This role is clearly visible throughout the project. Many project managers become involved in a project from its initiation through closing. However, in some organizations, a project manager may be involved in evaluation and analysis activities prior to project initiation. These activities may include consulting with executive and business unit leaders on ideas for advancing strategic objectives, improving organizational performance, or meeting customer needs. In some organizational settings, the project manager may also be called upon to manage or assist in business analysis, business case development, and aspects of portfolio management for a project. A project manager may also be involved in follow-on activities related to realizing business benefits from the project. The role of a project manager may vary from organization to organization. Ultimately, the project management role is tailored to fit the organization in the same way that the project management processes are tailored to fit the project.

A simple analogy may help in understanding the roles of a project manager for a large project by comparing them to the roles of a conductor for a large orchestra:

◆ **Membership and roles.** A large project and an orchestra each comprise many members, each playing a different role. A large orchestra may have more than 100 musicians who are led by a conductor. These musicians may play 25 different kinds of instruments placed into major sections, such as strings, woodwinds, brass, and percussion. Similarly, a large project may have more than 100 project members led by a project manager. Team members may fulfill many different roles, such as design, manufacturing, and facilities management. Like the major sections of the orchestra, they represent multiple business units or groups within an organization. The musicians and the project members make up each leader's team.

◆ **Responsibility for team.** The project manager and conductor are both responsible for what their teams produce—the project outcome or the orchestra concert, respectively. The two leaders need to take a holistic view of their team's products in order to plan, coordinate, and complete them. The two leaders begin by reviewing the vision, mission, and objectives of their respective organizations to ensure alignment with their products. The two leaders establish their interpretation of the vision, mission, and objectives involved in successfully completing their products. The leaders use their interpretation to communicate and motivate their teams toward the successful completion of their objectives.

◆ **Knowledge and skills:**

■ The conductor is not expected to be able to play every instrument in the orchestra, but should possess musical knowledge, understanding, and experience. The conductor provides the orchestra with leadership, planning, and coordination through communications. The conductor provides written communication in the form of musical scores and practice schedules. The conductor also communicates in real time with the team by using a baton and other body movements.

■ The project manager is not expected to perform every role on the project, but should possess project management knowledge, technical knowledge, understanding, and experience. The project manager provides the project team with leadership, planning, and coordination through communications. The project manager provides written communications (e.g., documented plans and schedules) and communicates in real time with the team using meetings and verbal or nonverbal cues.

The remainder of this section covers the key aspects of the role of the project manager. While there are thousands of books and articles available on the subject, this section is not intended to cover the entire spectrum of information available. Rather, it is designed to present an overview that will provide the practitioner with a basic understanding of the subject in preparation for a more concentrated study on the various aspects discussed.

## 3.2 DEFINITION OF A PROJECT MANAGER

The role of a project manager is distinct from that of a functional manager or operations manager. Typically, the functional manager focuses on providing management oversight for a functional or business unit. Operations managers are responsible for ensuring that business operations are efficient. The project manager is the person assigned by the performing organization to lead the team that is responsible for achieving the project objectives.

## 3.3 THE PROJECT MANAGER'S SPHERE OF INFLUENCE

### 3.3.1 OVERVIEW

Project managers fulfill numerous roles within their sphere of influence. These roles reflect the project manager's capabilities and are representative of the value and contributions of the project management profession. This section highlights the roles of the project manager in the various spheres of influence shown in Figure 3-1.

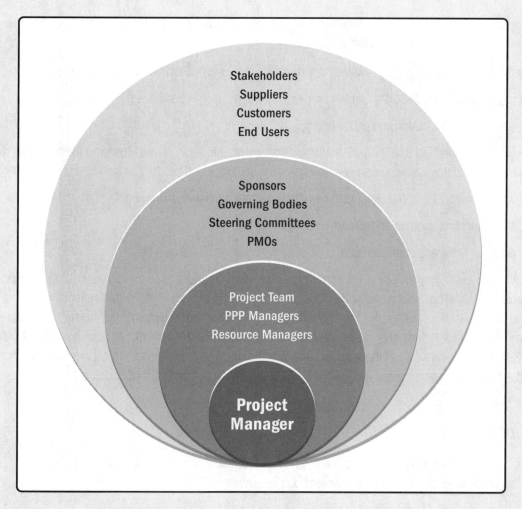

**Figure 3-1. Example of Project Manager's Sphere of Influence**

## 3.3.2 THE PROJECT

The project manager leads the project team to meet the project's objectives and stakeholders' expectations. The project manager works to balance the competing constraints on the project with the resources available.

The project manager also performs communication roles between the project sponsor, team members, and other stakeholders. This includes providing direction and presenting the vision of success for the project. The project manager uses soft skills (e.g., interpersonal skills and the ability to manage people) to balance the conflicting and competing goals of the project stakeholders in order to achieve consensus. In this context, consensus means that the relevant stakeholders support the project decisions and actions even when there is not 100% agreement.

Research shows that successful project managers consistently and effectively use certain essential skills. Research reveals that the top 2% of project managers as designated by their bosses and team members distinguish themselves by demonstrating superior relationship and communication skills while displaying a positive attitude [12].

The ability to communicate with stakeholders, including the team and sponsors applies across multiple aspects of the project including, but not limited to, the following:

◆ Developing finely tuned skills using multiple methods (e.g., verbal, written, and nonverbal);

◆ Creating, maintaining, and adhering to communications plans and schedules;

◆ Communicating predictably and consistently;

◆ Seeking to understand the project stakeholders' communication needs (communication may be the only deliverable that some stakeholders received until the project's end product or service is completed);

◆ Making communications concise, clear, complete, simple, relevant, and tailored;

◆ Including important positive and negative news;

◆ Incorporating feedback channels; and

◆ Relationship skills involving the development of extensive networks of people throughout the project manager's spheres of influence. These networks include formal networks such as organizational reporting structures. However, the informal networks that project managers develop, maintain, and nurture are more important. Informal networks include the use of established relationships with individuals such as subject matter experts and influential leaders. Use of these formal and informal networks allows the project manager to engage multiple people in solving problems and navigating the bureaucracies encountered in a project.

### 3.3.3 THE ORGANIZATION

The project manager proactively interacts with other project managers. Other independent projects or projects that are part of the same program may impact a project due to but not limited to the following:

◆ Demands on the same resources,

◆ Priorities of funding,

◆ Receipt or distribution of deliverables, and

◆ Alignment of project goals and objectives with those of the organization.

Interacting with other project managers helps to create a positive influence for fulfilling the various needs of the project. These needs may be in the form of human, technical, or financial resources and deliverables required by the team for project completion. The project manager seeks ways to develop relationships that assist the team in achieving the goals and objectives of the project.

In addition, the project manager maintains a strong advocacy role within the organization. The project manager proactively interacts with managers within the organization during the course of the project. The project manager also works with the project sponsor to address internal political and strategic issues that may impact the team or the viability or quality of the project.

The project manager may work toward increasing the project management competency and capability within the organization as a whole and is involved in both tacit and explicit knowledge transfer or integration initiatives (see Section 4.4 on Manage Project Knowledge). The project manager also works to:

◆ Demonstrate the value of project management,

◆ Increase acceptance of project management in the organization, and

◆ Advance the efficacy of the PMO when one exists in the organization.

Depending on the organizational structure, a project manager may report to a functional manager. In other cases, a project manager may be one of several project managers who report to a PMO or a portfolio or program manager who is ultimately responsible for one or more organization-wide projects. The project manager works closely with all relevant managers to achieve the project objectives and to ensure the project management plan aligns with the portfolio or program plan. The project manager also works closely and in collaboration with other roles, such as organizational managers, subject matter experts, and those involved with business analysis. In some situations, the project manager may be an external consultant placed in a temporary management role.

## 3.3.4 THE INDUSTRY

The project manager stays informed about current industry trends. The project manager takes this information and sees how it may impact or apply to the current projects. These trends include but are not limited to:

◆ Product and technology development;

◆ New and changing market niches;

◆ Standards (e.g., project management, quality management, information security management);

◆ Technical support tools;

◆ Economic forces that impact the immediate project;

◆ Influences affecting the project management discipline; and

◆ Process improvement and sustainability strategies.

### 3.3.5 PROFESSIONAL DISCIPLINE

Continuing knowledge transfer and integration is very important for the project manager. This professional development is ongoing in the project management profession and in other areas where the project manager maintains subject matter expertise. This knowledge transfer and integration includes but is not limited to:

◆ Contribution of knowledge and expertise to others within the profession at the local, national, and global levels (e.g., communities of practice, international organizations); and

◆ Participation in training, continuing education, and development:

■ In the project management profession (e.g., universities, PMI);

■ In a related profession (e.g., systems engineering, configuration management); and

■ In other professions (e.g., information technology, aerospace).

### 3.3.6 ACROSS DISCIPLINES

A professional project manager may choose to orient and educate other professionals regarding the value of a project management approach to the organization. The project manager may serve as an informal ambassador by educating the organization as to the advantages of project management with regard to timeliness, quality, innovation, and resource management.

## 3.4 PROJECT MANAGER COMPETENCES

### 3.4.1 OVERVIEW

Recent PMI studies applied the *Project Manager Competency Development (PMCD) Framework* to the skills needed by project managers through the use of The PMI Talent Triangle® shown in Figure 3-2. The talent triangle focuses on three key skill sets:

◆ **Technical project management.** The knowledge, skills, and behaviors related to specific domains of project, program, and portfolio management. The technical aspects of performing one's role.

◆ **Leadership.** The knowledge, skills, and behaviors needed to guide, motivate, and direct a team, to help an organization achieve its business goals.

◆ **Strategic and business management.** The knowledge of and expertise in the industry and organization that enhances performance and better delivers business outcomes.

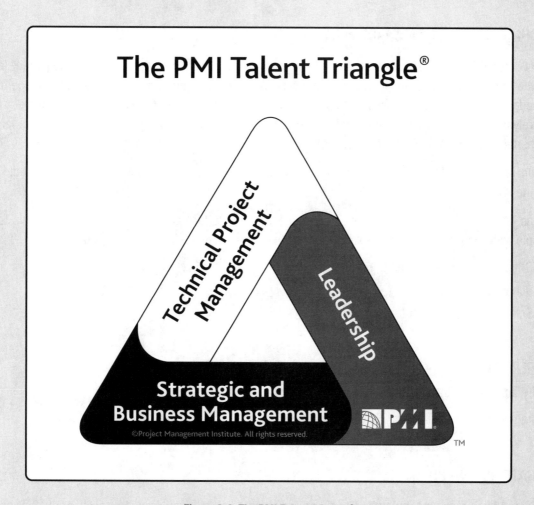

**Figure 3-2. The PMI Talent Triangle®**

While technical project management skills are core to program and project management, PMI research indicates that they are not enough in today's increasingly complicated and competitive global marketplace. Organizations are seeking added skills in leadership and business intelligence. Members of various organizations state their belief that these competencies can support longer-range strategic objectives that contribute to the bottom line. To be the most effective, project managers need to have a balance of these three skill sets.

## 3.4.2 TECHNICAL PROJECT MANAGEMENT SKILLS

Technical project management skills are defined as the skills to effectively apply project management knowledge to deliver the desired outcomes for programs or projects. There are numerous technical project management skills. The Knowledge Areas in this guide describe many of these necessary project management skills. Project managers frequently rely on expert judgment to perform well. Being aware of personal expertise and where to find others with the needed expertise are important for success as a project manager.

According to research. the top project managers consistently demonstrated several key skills including, but not limited to, the ability to:

◆ Focus on the critical technical project management elements for each project they manage. This focus is as simple as having the right artifacts readily available. At the top of the list were the following:

  ■ Critical success factors for the project,
  ■ Schedule,
  ■ Selected financial reports, and
  ■ Issue log.

◆ Tailor both traditional and agile tools, techniques, and methods for each project.

◆ Make time to plan thoroughly and prioritize diligently.

◆ Manage project elements, including, but not limited to, schedule, cost, resources, and risks.

## 3.4.3 STRATEGIC AND BUSINESS MANAGEMENT SKILLS

Strategic and business management skills involve the ability to see the high-level overview of the organization and effectively negotiate and implement decisions and actions that support strategic alignment and innovation. This ability may include a working knowledge of other functions such as finance, marketing, and operations. Strategic and business management skills may also include developing and applying pertinent product and industry expertise. This business knowledge is also known as domain knowledge. Project managers should be knowledgeable enough about the business to be able to:

◆ Explain to others the essential business aspects of a project;

◆ Work with the project sponsor, team, and subject matter experts to develop an appropriate project delivery strategy; and

◆ Implement that strategy in a way that maximizes the business value of the project.

In order to make the best decisions regarding the successful delivery of their projects, project managers should seek out and consider the expertise of the operational managers who run the business in their organization. These managers should know the work performed in their organization and how project plans will affect that work. The more the project manager is able to know about the project's subject matter, the better. At a minimum, the project manager should be knowledgeable enough to explain to others the following aspects of the organization:

◆ Strategy;

◆ Mission;

◆ Goals and objectives;

◆ Products and services;

◆ Operations (e.g., location, type, technology);

◆ The market and the market condition, such as customers, state of the market (i.e., growing or shrinking), and time-to-market factors, etc.; and

◆ Competition (e.g., what, who, position in the market place).

The project manager should apply the following knowledge and information about the organization to the project to ensure alignment:

◆ Strategy,

◆ Mission,

◆ Goals and objectives,

◆ Priority,

◆ Tactics, and

◆ Products or services (e.g., deliverables).

Strategic and business skills help the project manager to determine which business factors should be considered for their project. The project manager determines how these business and strategic factors could affect the project while understanding the interrelationship between the project and the organization. These factors include but are not limited to:

◆ Risks and issues,

◆ Financial implications,

◆ Cost versus benefits analysis (e.g., net present value, return on investment), including the various options considered,

◆ Business value,

◆ Benefits realization expectations and strategies, and

◆ Scope, budget, schedule, and quality.

Through the application of this business knowledge, a project manager has the ability to make the appropriate decisions and recommendations for a project. As conditions change, the project manager should be continuously working with the project sponsor to keep the business and the project strategies aligned.

## 3.4.4 LEADERSHIP SKILLS

Leadership skills involve the ability to guide, motivate, and direct a team. These skills may include demonstrating essential capabilities such as negotiation, resilience, communication, problem solving, critical thinking, and interpersonal skills. Projects are becoming increasingly more complicated with more and more businesses executing their strategy through projects. Project management is more than just working with numbers, templates, charts, graphs, and computing systems. A common denominator in all projects is people. People can be counted, but they are not numbers.

### 3.4.4.1 DEALING WITH PEOPLE

A large part of the project manager's role involves dealing with people. The project manager should study people's behaviors and motivations. The project manager should strive to be a good leader, because leadership is crucial to the success of projects in organizations. A project manager applies leadership skills and qualities when working with all project stakeholders, including the project team, the steering team, and project sponsors.

### 3.4.4.2 QUALITIES AND SKILLS OF A LEADER

Research shows that the qualities and skills of a leader include but are not limited to:

◆ Being a visionary (e.g., help to describe the products, goals, and objectives of the project; able to dream and translate those dreams for others);

◆ Being optimistic and positive;

◆ Being collaborative;

◆ Managing relationships and conflict by:

   ■ Building trust;

   ■ Satisfying concerns;

   ■ Seeking consensus;

   ■ Balancing competing and opposing goals;

   ■ Applying persuasion, negotiation, compromise, and conflict resolution skills;

   ■ Developing and nurturing personal and professional networks;

   ■ Taking a long-term view that relationships are just as important as the project; and

   ■ Continuously developing and applying political acumen.

◆ Communicating by:

   ■ Spending sufficient time communicating (research shows that top project managers spend about 90% of their time on a project in communicating);

   ■ Managing expectations;

   ■ Accepting feedback graciously;

   ■ Giving feedback constructively; and

   ■ Asking and listening.

◆ Being respectful (helping others retain their autonomy), courteous, friendly, kind, honest, trustworthy, loyal, and ethical;

◆ Exhibiting integrity and being culturally sensitive, courageous, a problem solver, and decisive;

◆ Giving credit to others where due;

◆ Being a life-long learner who is results- and action-oriented;

◆ Focusing on the important things, including:

  ■ Continuously prioritizing work by reviewing and adjusting as necessary;

  ■ Finding and using a prioritization method that works for them and the project;

  ■ Differentiating high-level strategic priorities, especially those related to critical success factors for the project;

  ■ Maintaining vigilance on primary project constraints;

  ■ Remaining flexible on tactical priorities; and

  ■ Being able to sift through massive amounts of information to obtain the most important information.

◆ Having a holistic and systemic view of the project, taking into account internal and external factors equally;

◆ Being able to apply critical thinking (e.g., application of analytical methods to reach decisions) and identify him or herself as a change agent.

◆ Being able to build effective teams, be service-oriented, and have fun and share humor effectively with team members.

### 3.4.4.3 POLITICS, POWER, AND GETTING THINGS DONE

Leadership and management are ultimately about being able to get things done. The skills and qualities noted help the project manager to achieve the project goals and objectives. At the root of many of these skills and qualities is the ability to deal with politics. Politics involves influence, negotiation, autonomy, and power.

Politics and its associated elements are not "good" or "bad," "positive" or "negative" alone. The better the project manager understands how the organization works, the more likely he or she will be successful. The project manager observes and collects data about the project and organizational landscapes. The data then needs to be reviewed in the context of the project, the people involved, the organization, and the environment as a whole. This review yields the information and knowledge necessary for the project manager to plan and implement the most appropriate action. The project manager's action is a result of selecting the right kind of power to influence and negotiate with others. Exercise of power also carries with it the responsibility of being sensitive to and respectful of other people. The effective action of the project manager maintains the autonomy of those involved. The project manager's action results in the right people performing the activities necessary to fulfill the project's objectives.

Power can originate with traits exhibited by the individual or the organization. Power is often supported by other people's perception of the leader. It is essential for project managers to be aware of their relationships with other people. Relationships enable project managers to get things done on the project. There are numerous forms of power at the disposal of project managers. Power and its use can be complex given its nature and the various factors at play in a project. Various forms of power include but are not limited to:

◆ Positional (sometimes called formal, authoritative, legitimate) (e.g., formal position granted in the organization or team);

◆ Informational (e.g., control of gathering or distribution);

◆ Referent (e.g., respect or admiration others hold for the individual, credibility gained);

◆ Situational (e.g., gained due to unique situation such as a specific crisis);

◆ Personal or charismatic (e.g., charm, attraction);

◆ Relational (e.g., participates in networking, connections, and alliances);

◆ Expert (e.g., skill, information possessed; experience, training, education, certification);

◆ Reward-oriented (e.g., ability to give praise, monetary or other desired items);

◆ Punitive or coercive (e.g., ability to invoke discipline or negative consequences);

◆ Ingratiating (e.g., application of flattery or other common ground to win favor or cooperation);

◆ Pressure-based (e.g., limit freedom of choice or movement for the purpose of gaining compliance to desired action);

◆ Guilt-based (e.g., imposition of obligation or sense of duty);

◆ Persuasive (e.g., ability to provide arguments that move people to a desired course of action); and

◆ Avoiding (e.g., refusing to participate).

Top project managers are proactive and intentional when it comes to power. These project managers will work to acquire the power and authority they need within the boundaries of organizational policies, protocols, and procedures rather than wait for it to be granted.

## 3.4.5 COMPARISON OF LEADERSHIP AND MANAGEMENT

The words *leadership* and *management* are often used interchangeably. However, they are not synonymous. The word *management* is more closely associated with directing another person to get from one point to another using a known set of expected behaviors. In contrast, leadership involves working with others through discussion or debate in order to guide them from one point to another.

The method that a project manager chooses to employ reveals a distinct difference in behavior, self-perception, and project role. Table 3-1 compares management and leadership on several important levels.

Project managers need to employ both leadership and management in order to be successful. The skill is in finding the right balance for each situation. The way in which management and leadership are employed often shows up in the project manager's leadership style.

Table 3-1. Team Management and Team Leadership Compared

| Management | Leadership |
| --- | --- |
| Direct using positional power | Guide, influence, and collaborate using relational power |
| Maintain | Develop |
| Administrate | Innovate |
| Focus on systems and structure | Focus on relationships with people |
| Rely on control | Inspire trust |
| Focus on near-term goals | Focus on long-range vision |
| Ask how and when | Ask what and why |
| Focus on bottom line | Focus on the horizon |
| Accept status quo | Challenge status quo |
| Do things right | Do the right things |
| Focus on operational issues and problem solving | Focus on vision, alignment, motivation, and inspiration |

### 3.4.5.1 LEADERSHIP STYLES

Project managers may lead their teams in many ways. The style a project manager selects may be a personal preference, or the result of the combination of multiple factors associated with the project. The style a project manager uses may change over time based on the factors in play. Major factors to consider include but are not limited to:

◆ Leader characteristics (e.g., attitudes, moods, needs, values, ethics);

◆ Team member characteristics (e.g., attitudes, moods, needs, values, ethics);

◆ Organizational characteristics (e.g., its purpose, structure, and type of work performed); and

◆ Environmental characteristics (e.g., social situation, economic state, and political elements).

Research describes numerous leadership styles that a project manager can adopt. Some of the most common examples of these styles include but are not limited to:

◆ Laissez-faire (e.g., allowing the team to make their own decisions and establish their own goals, also referred to as taking a hands-off style);

◆ Transactional (e.g., focus on goals, feedback, and accomplishment to determine rewards; management by exception);

◆ Servant leader (e.g., demonstrates commitment to serve and put other people first; focuses on other people's growth, learning, development, autonomy, and well-being; concentrates on relationships, community and collaboration; leadership is secondary and emerges after service);

◆ Transformational (e.g., empowering followers through idealized attributes and behaviors, inspirational motivation, encouragement for innovation and creativity, and individual consideration);

◆ Charismatic (e.g., able to inspire; is high-energy, enthusiastic, self-confident; holds strong convictions); and

◆ Interactional (e.g., a combination of transactional, transformational, and charismatic).

### 3.4.5.2 PERSONALITY

Personality refers to the individual differences in characteristic patterns of thinking, feeling, and behaving. Personality characteristics or traits include but are not limited to:

◆ Authentic (e.g., accepts others for what and who they are, show open concern);

◆ Courteous (e.g., ability to apply appropriate behavior and etiquette);

◆ Creative (e.g., ability to think abstractly, to see things differently, to innovate);

◆ Cultural (e.g., measure of sensitivity to other cultures including values, norms, and beliefs);

◆ Emotional (e.g., ability to perceive emotions and the information they present and to manage them; measure of interpersonal skills);

◆ Intellectual (e.g., measure of human intelligence over multiple aptitudes);

◆ Managerial (e.g., measure of management practice and potential);

◆ Political (e.g., measure of political intelligence and making things happen);

◆ Service-oriented (e.g., evidence of willingness to serve other people);

◆ Social (e.g., ability to understand and manage people); and

◆ Systemic (e.g., drive to understand and build systems).

An effective project manager will have some level of ability with each of these characteristics in order to be successful. Each project, organization, and situation requires that the project manager emphasize different aspects of personality.

## 3.5 PERFORMING INTEGRATION

The role of the project manager is twofold when performing integration on the project:

◆ Project managers play a key role in working with the project sponsor to understand the strategic objectives and ensure the alignment of the project objectives and results with those of the portfolio, program, and business areas. In this way, project managers contribute to the integration and execution of the strategy.

◆ Project managers are responsible for guiding the team to work together to focus on what is really essential at the project level. This is achieved through the integration of processes, knowledge, and people.

Integration is a critical skill for project managers. Integration is covered more in depth in the Project Integration Management Knowledge Area of this guide. Sections 3.5.1 through 3.5.4 focus on integration that takes place at three different levels: the process, cognitive, and context levels. Section 3.5.4 concludes by addressing complexity and integration.

### 3.5.1 PERFORMING INTEGRATION AT THE PROCESS LEVEL

Project management may be seen as a set of processes and activities that are undertaken to achieve the project objectives. Some of these processes may take place once (e.g., the initial creation of the project charter), but many others overlap and occur several times throughout the project. One example of this process overlap and multiple occurrences is a change in a requirement that impacts scope, schedule, or budget and requires a change request. Several project management processes such as the Control Scope process and the Perform Integrated Change Control process may involve a change request. The Perform Integrated Change Control process occurs throughout the project for integrating change requests.

Although there is no stated definition on how to integrate the project processes, it is clear that a project has a small chance of meeting its objective when the project manager fails to integrate the project processes where they interact.

### 3.5.2 INTEGRATION AT THE COGNITIVE LEVEL

There are many different ways to manage a project, and the method selected typically depends on the specific characteristics of the project including its size, how complicated the project or organization may be, and the culture of the performing organization. It is clear that the personal skills and abilities of the project manager are closely related to the way in which the project is managed.

The project manager should strive to become proficient in all of the Project Management Knowledge Areas. In concert with proficiency in these Knowledge Areas, the project manager applies experience, insight, leadership, and technical and business management skills to the project. Finally, it is through the project manager's ability to integrate the processes in these Knowledge Areas that makes it possible to achieve the desired project results.

### 3.5.3 INTEGRATION AT THE CONTEXT LEVEL

There have been many changes in the context in which business and projects take place today compared to a few decades ago. New technologies have been introduced. Social networks, multicultural aspects, virtual teams, and new values are part of the new reality of projects. An example is knowledge and people integration in the context of a large cross-functional project implementation involving multiple organizations. The project manager considers the implications of this context in communications planning and knowledge management for guiding the project team.

Project managers need to be cognizant of the project context and these new aspects when managing the integration. Then project managers can decide how to best use these new elements of the environment in their projects to achieve success.

## 3.5.4 INTEGRATION AND COMPLEXITY

Some projects may be referred to as complex and considered difficult to manage. In simple terms, complex and complicated are concepts often used to describe what is considered to be intricate or complicated.

Complexity within projects is a result of the organization's system behavior, human behavior, and the uncertainty at work in the organization or its environment. In *Navigating Complexity: A Practice Guide* [13], these three dimensions of complexity are defined as:

◆ **System behavior.** The interdependencies of components and systems.

◆ **Human behavior.** The interplay between diverse individuals and groups.

◆ **Ambiguity.** Uncertainty of emerging issues and lack of understanding or confusion.

Complexity itself is a perception of an individual based on personal experience, observation, and skill. Rather than being complex, a project is more accurately described as containing complexity. Portfolios, programs, and projects may contain elements of complexity.

When approaching the integration of a project, the project manager should consider elements that are both inside and outside of the project. The project manager should examine the characteristics or properties of the project. Complexity as a characteristic or property of a project is typically defined as:

◆ Containing multiple parts,

◆ Possessing a number of connections between the parts,

◆ Exhibiting dynamic interactions between the parts, and

◆ Exhibiting behavior produced as a result of those interactions that cannot be explained as the simple sum of the parts (e.g., emergent behavior).

Examining these various items that appear to make the project complex should help the project manager identify key areas when planning, managing, and controlling the project to ensure integration.

# 4

## PROJECT INTEGRATION MANAGEMENT

Project Integration Management includes the processes and activities to identify, define, combine, unify, and coordinate the various processes and project management activities within the Project Management Process Groups. In the project management context, integration includes characteristics of unification, consolidation, communication, and interrelationship. These actions should be applied from the start of the project through completion. Project Integration Management includes making choices about:

◆ Resource allocation,

◆ Balancing competing demands,

◆ Examining any alternative approaches,

◆ Tailoring the processes to meet the project objectives, and

◆ Managing the interdependencies among the Project Management Knowledge Areas.

The Project Integration Management processes are:

**4.1 Develop Project Charter**—The process of developing a document that formally authorizes the existence of a project and provides the project manager with the authority to apply organizational resources to project activities.

**4.2 Develop Project Management Plan**—The process of defining, preparing, and coordinating all plan components and consolidating them into an integrated project management plan.

**4.3 Direct and Manage Project Work**—The process of leading and performing the work defined in the project management plan and implementing approved changes to achieve the project's objectives.

**4.4 Manage Project Knowledge**—The process of using existing knowledge and creating new knowledge to achieve the project's objectives and contribute to organizational learning.

**4.5 Monitor and Control Project Work**—The process of tracking, reviewing, and reporting overall progress to meet the performance objectives defined in the project management plan.

**4.6 Perform Integrated Change Control**—The process of reviewing all change requests; approving changes and managing changes to deliverables, organizational process assets, project documents, and the project management plan; and communicating the decisions.

**4.7 Close Project or Phase**—The process of finalizing all activities for the project, phase, or contract.

Figure 4-1 provides an overview of the Project Integration Management processes. The Project Integration Management processes are presented as discrete processes with defined interfaces while, in practice, they overlap and interact in ways that cannot be completely detailed in the *PMBOK® Guide*.

## Project Integration Management Overview

### 4.1 Develop Project Charter

.1 Inputs
  .1 Business documents
  .2 Agreements
  .3 Enterprise environmental factors
  .4 Organizational process assets

.2 Tools & Techniques
  .1 Expert judgment
  .2 Data gathering
  .3 Interpersonal and team skills
  .4 Meetings

.3 Outputs
  .1 Project charter
  .2 Assumption log

### 4.2 Develop Project Management Plan

.1 Inputs
  .1 Project charter
  .2 Outputs from other processes
  .3 Enterprise environmental factors
  .4 Organizational process assets

.2 Tools & Techniques
  .1 Expert judgment
  .2 Data gathering
  .3 Interpersonal and team skills
  .4 Meetings

.3 Outputs
  .1 Project management plan

### 4.3 Direct and Manage Project Work

.1 Inputs
  .1 Project management plan
  .2 Project documents
  .3 Approved change requests
  .4 Enterprise environmental factors
  .5 Organizational process assets

.2 Tools & Techniques
  .1 Expert judgment
  .2 Project management information system
  .3 Meetings

.3 Outputs
  .1 Deliverables
  .2 Work performance data
  .3 Issue log
  .4 Change requests
  .5 Project management plan updates
  .6 Project documents updates
  .7 Organizational process assets updates

### 4.4 Manage Project Knowledge

.1 Inputs
  .1 Project management plan
  .2 Project documents
  .3 Deliverables
  .4 Enterprise environmental factors
  .5 Organizational process assets

.2 Tools & Techniques
  .1 Expert judgment
  .2 Knowledge management
  .3 Information management
  .4 Interpersonal and team skills

.3 Outputs
  .1 Lessons learned register
  .2 Project management plan updates
  .3 Organizational process assets updates

### 4.5 Monitor and Control Project Work

.1 Inputs
  .1 Project management plan
  .2 Project documents
  .3 Work performance information
  .4 Agreements
  .5 Enterprise environmental factors
  .6 Organizational process assets

.2 Tools & Techniques
  .1 Expert judgment
  .2 Data analysis
  .3 Decision making
  .4 Meetings

.3 Outputs
  .1 Work performance reports
  .2 Change requests
  .3 Project management plan updates
  .4 Project documents updates

### 4.6 Perform Integrated Change Control

.1 Inputs
  .1 Project management plan
  .2 Project documents
  .3 Work performance reports
  .4 Change requests
  .5 Enterprise environmental factors
  .6 Organizational process assets

.2 Tools & Techniques
  .1 Expert judgment
  .2 Change control tools
  .3 Data analysis
  .4 Decision making
  .5 Meetings

.3 Outputs
  .1 Approved change requests
  .2 Project management plan updates
  .3 Project documents updates

### 4.7 Close Project or Phase

.1 Inputs
  .1 Project charter
  .2 Project management plan
  .3 Project documents
  .4 Accepted deliverables
  .5 Business documents
  .6 Agreements
  .7 Procurement documentation
  .8 Organizational process assets

.2 Tools & Techniques
  .1 Expert judgment
  .2 Data analysis
  .3 Meetings

.3 Outputs
  .1 Project documents updates
  .2 Final product, service, or result transition
  .3 Final report
  .4 Organizational process assets updates

**Figure 4-1. Project Integration Management Overview**

## KEY CONCEPTS FOR PROJECT INTEGRATION MANAGEMENT

Project Integration Management is specific to project managers. Whereas other Knowledge Areas may be managed by specialists (e.g., cost analysis, scheduling specialists, risk management experts), the accountability of Project Integration Management cannot be delegated or transferred. The project manager is the one who combines the results in all the other Knowledge Areas and has the overall view of the project. The project manager is ultimately responsible for the project as a whole.

Projects and project management are integrative by nature. For example, a cost estimate needed for a contingency plan involves integrating the processes in the Project Cost Management, Project Schedule Management, and Project Risk Management Knowledge Areas. When additional risks associated with various staffing alternatives are identified, then one or more of those processes may be revisited.

The links among the processes in the Project Management Process Groups are often iterative. For example, the Planning Process Group provides the Executing Process Group with a documented project management plan early in the project and then updates the project management plan if changes occur as the project progresses.

Project Integration Management is about:

◆ Ensuring that the deliverable due dates of the product, service, or result; project life cycle; and the benefits management plan are aligned;

◆ Providing a project management plan to achieve the project objectives;

◆ Ensuring the creation and the use of the appropriate knowledge to and from the project as necessary;

◆ Managing the performance and changes of the activities in the project management plan;

◆ Making integrated decisions regarding key changes impacting the project;

◆ Measuring and monitoring the project's progress and taking appropriate action to meet project objectives;

◆ Collecting data on the results achieved, analyzing the data to obtain information, and communicating this information to relevant stakeholders;

◆ Completing all the work of the project and formally closing each phase, contract, and the project as a whole; and

◆ Managing phase transitions when necessary.

The more complex the project and the more varied the expectations of the stakeholders, the more a sophisticated approach to integration is needed.

## TRENDS AND EMERGING PRACTICES IN PROJECT INTEGRATION MANAGEMENT

The Project Integration Management Knowledge Area requires combining the results from all the other Knowledge Areas. Evolving trends in integration processes include but are not limited to:

◆ **Use of automated tools.** The volume of data and information that project managers need to integrate makes it necessary to use a project management information system (PMIS) and automated tools to collect, analyze, and use information to meet project objectives and realize project benefits.

◆ **Use of visual management tools.** Some project teams use visual management tools, rather than written plans and other documents, to capture and oversee critical project elements. Making key project elements visible to the entire team provides a real-time overview of the project status, facilitates knowledge transfer, and empowers team members and other stakeholders to help identify and solve issues.

◆ **Project knowledge management.** The increasingly mobile and transitory work force requires a more rigorous process of identifying knowledge throughout the project life cycle and transferring it to the target audience so that the knowledge is not lost.

◆ **Expanding the project manager's responsibilities.** Project managers are being called on to initiate and finalize the project, such as project business case development and benefits management. Historically, these activities have been the responsibility of management and the project management office, but project managers are more frequently collaborating with them to better meet project objectives and deliver benefits. Project managers are also engaging in more comprehensive identification and engagement of stakeholders. This includes managing the interfaces with various functional and operational departments and senior management personnel.

◆ **Hybrid methodologies.** Some project management methodologies are evolving to incorporate successfully applied new practices. Examples include the use of agile and other iterative practices; business analysis techniques for requirements management; tools for identifying complex elements in projects; and organizational change management methods to prepare for transitioning the project outputs into the organization.

## TAILORING CONSIDERATIONS

Because each project is unique, the project manager may need to tailor the way that Project Integration Management processes are applied. Considerations for tailoring include but are not limited to:

◆ **Project life cycle.** What is an appropriate project life cycle? What phases should comprise the project life cycle?

◆ **Development life cycle.** What development life cycle and approach are appropriate for the product, service, or result? Is a predictive or adaptive approach appropriate? If adaptive, should the product be developed incrementally or iteratively? Is a hybrid approach best?

◆ **Management approaches.** What management processes are most effective based on the organizational culture and the complexity of the project?

◆ **Knowledge management.** How will knowledge be managed in the project to foster a collaborative working environment?

◆ **Change.** How will change be managed in the project?

◆ **Governance.** What control boards, committees, and other stakeholders are part of the project? What are the project status reporting requirements?

◆ **Lessons learned.** What information should be collected throughout and at the end of the project? How will historical information and lessons learned be made available to future projects?

◆ **Benefits.** When and how should benefits be reported: at the end of the project or at the end of each iteration or phase?

## CONSIDERATIONS FOR AGILE/ADAPTIVE ENVIRONMENTS

Iterative and agile approaches promote the engagement of team members as local domain experts in integration management. The team members determine how plans and components should integrate.

The expectations of the project manager as noted in the *Key Concepts for Integration Management* do not change in an adaptive environment, but control of the detailed product planning and delivery is delegated to the team. The project manager's focus is on building a collaborative decision-making environment and ensuring the team has the ability to respond to changes. This collaborative approach can be further enhanced when team members possess a broad skill base rather than a narrow specialization.

# 4.1 DEVELOP PROJECT CHARTER

Develop Project Charter is the process of developing a document that formally authorizes the existence of a project and provides the project manager with the authority to apply organizational resources to project activities. The key benefits of this process are that it provides a direct link between the project and the strategic objectives of the organization, creates a formal record of the project, and shows the organizational commitment to the project. This process is performed once or at predefined points in the project. The inputs, tools and techniques, and outputs of the process are depicted in Figure 4-2. Figure 4-3 depicts the data flow diagram for the process.

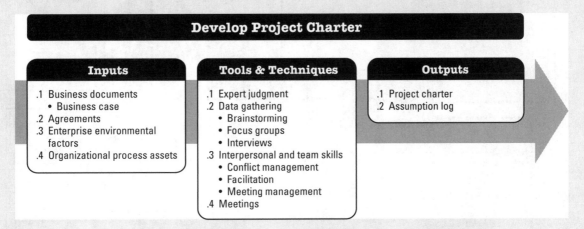

**Figure 4-2. Develop Project Charter: Inputs, Tools & Techniques, and Outputs**

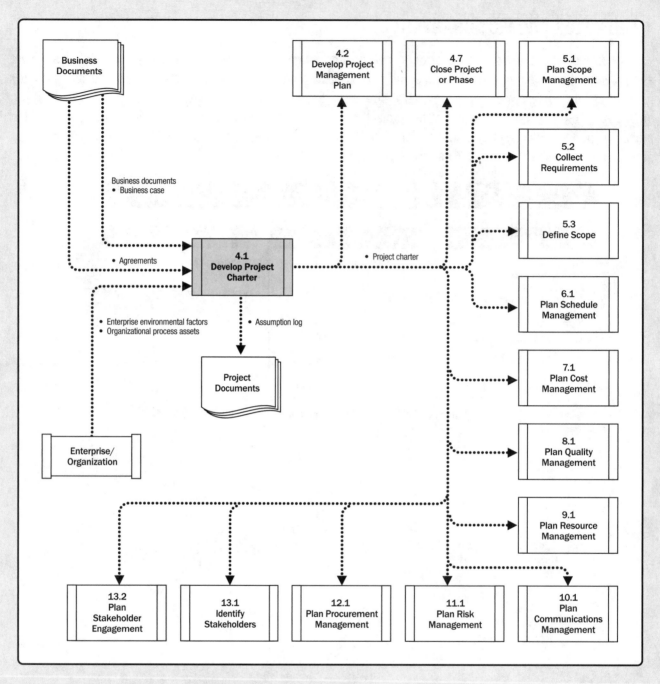

Figure 4-3. Develop Project Charter: Data Flow Diagram

The project charter establishes a partnership between the performing and requesting organizations. In the case of external projects, a formal contract is typically the preferred way to establish an agreement. A project charter may still be used to establish internal agreements within an organization to ensure proper delivery under the contract. The approved project charter formally initiates the project. A project manager is identified and assigned as early in the project as is feasible, preferably while the project charter is being developed and always prior to the start of planning. The project charter can be developed by the sponsor or the project manager in collaboration with the initiating entity. This collaboration allows the project manager to have a better understanding of the project purpose, objectives, and expected benefits. This understanding will better allow for efficient resource allocation to project activities. The project charter provides the project manager with the authority to plan, execute, and control the project.

Projects are initiated by an entity external to the project such as a sponsor, program, or project management office (PMO), or a portfolio governing body chairperson or authorized representative. The project initiator or sponsor should be at a level that is appropriate to procure funding and commit resources to the project. Projects are initiated due to internal business needs or external influences. These needs or influences often trigger the creation of a needs analysis, feasibility study, business case, or description of the situation that the project will address. Chartering a project validates alignment of the project to the strategy and ongoing work of the organization. A project charter is not considered to be a contract because there is no consideration or money promised or exchanged in its creation.

## 4.1.1 DEVELOP PROJECT CHARTER: INPUTS

### 4.1.1.1 BUSINESS DOCUMENTS

The business case (described in Section 1.2.6.1) and the benefits management plan (described in Section 1.2.6.2) are sources of information about the project's objectives and how the project will contribute to the business goals. Although the business documents are developed prior to the project, they are reviewed periodically.

◆ **Business case.** The approved business case, or similar, is the business document most commonly used to create the project charter. The business case describes the necessary information from a business standpoint to determine whether the expected outcomes of the project justify the required investment. It is commonly used for decision making by managers or executives above the project level. Typically, the business need and the cost-benefit analysis are contained in the business case to justify and establish boundaries for the project. For more information on the business case, see Section 1.2.6.1. The business case is created as a result of one or more of the following:

- *Market demand* (e.g., an automobile manufacturer authorizing a project to build more fuel-efficient cars in response to gasoline shortages),

- *Organizational need* (e.g., due to high overhead costs, a company may combine staff functions and streamline processes to reduce costs),

- *Customer request* (e.g., an electric utility authorizing a project to build a new substation to serve a new industrial park),

- *Technological advance* (e.g., an airline authorizing a new project to develop electronic tickets instead of paper tickets based on technological advances),

- *Legal requirement* (e.g., a paint manufacturer authorizing a project to establish guidelines for handling toxic materials),

- *Ecological impacts* (e.g., a company authorizing a project to lessen its environmental impact), or

- *Social need* (e.g., a nongovernmental organization in a developing country authorizing a project to provide potable water systems, latrines, and sanitation education to communities suffering from high rates of cholera).

The project charter incorporates the appropriate information for the project from the business documents. The project manager does not update or modify the business documents since they are not project documents; however, the project manager may make recommendations.

### 4.1.1.2 AGREEMENTS

Described in Section 12.2.3.2. Agreements are used to define initial intentions for a project. Agreements may take the form of contracts, memorandums of understanding (MOUs), service level agreements (SLA), letters of agreement, letters of intent, verbal agreements, email, or other written agreements. Typically, a contract is used when a project is being performed for an external customer.

### 4.1.1.3 ENTERPRISE ENVIRONMENTAL FACTORS

The enterprise environmental factors that can influence the Develop Project Charter process include but are not limited to:

- Government or industry standards (e.g., product standards, quality standards, safety standards, and workmanship standards),

- Legal and regulatory requirements and/or constraints,

- Marketplace conditions,

- Organizational culture and political climate,

- Organizational governance framework (a structured way to provide control, direction, and coordination through people, policies, and processes to meet organizational strategic and operational goals), and

- Stakeholders' expectations and risk thresholds.

### 4.1.1.4 ORGANIZATIONAL PROCESS ASSETS

The organizational process assets that can influence the Develop Project Charter process include but are not limited to:

◆ Organizational standard policies, processes, and procedures;

◆ Portfolio, program, and project governance framework (governance functions and processes to provide guidance and decision making);

◆ Monitoring and reporting methods;

◆ Templates (e.g., project charter template); and

◆ Historical information and lessons learned repository (e.g., project records and documents, information about the results of previous project selection decisions, and information about previous project performance).

### 4.1.2 DEVELOP PROJECT CHARTER: TOOLS AND TECHNIQUES

### 4.1.2.1 EXPERT JUDGMENT

Expert judgment is defined as judgment provided based upon expertise in an application area, Knowledge Area, discipline, industry, etc., as appropriate for the activity being performed. Such expertise may be provided by any group or person with specialized education, knowledge, skill, experience, or training.

For this process, expertise should be considered from individuals or groups with specialized knowledge of or training in the following topics:

◆ Organizational strategy,

◆ Benefits management,

◆ Technical knowledge of the industry and focus area of the project,

◆ Duration and budget estimation, and

◆ Risk identification.

## 4.1.2.2 DATA GATHERING

Data-gathering techniques that can be used for this process include but are not limited to:

◆ **Brainstorming.** This technique is used to identify a list of ideas in a short period of time. It is conducted in a group environment and is led by a facilitator. Brainstorming comprises two parts: idea generation and analysis. Brainstorming can be used to gather data and solutions or ideas from stakeholders, subject matter experts, and team members when developing the project charter.

◆ **Focus groups.** Described in Section 5.2.2.2. Focus groups bring together stakeholders and subject matter experts to learn about the perceived project risk, success criteria, and other topics in a more conversational way than a one-on-one interview.

◆ **Interviews.** Described in Section 5.2.2.2. Interviews are used to obtain information on high-level requirements, assumptions or constraints, approval criteria, and other information from stakeholders by talking directly to them.

## 4.1.2.3 INTERPERSONAL AND TEAM SKILLS

Interpersonal and team skills that can be used for this process include but are not limited to:

◆ **Conflict management.** Described in Section 9.5.2.1. Conflict management can be used to help bring stakeholders into alignment on the objectives, success criteria, high-level requirements, project description, summary milestones, and other elements of the charter.

◆ **Facilitation.** Facilitation is the ability to effectively guide a group event to a successful decision, solution, or conclusion. A facilitator ensures that there is effective participation, that participants achieve a mutual understanding, that all contributions are considered, that conclusions or results have full buy-in according to the decision process established for the project, and that the actions and agreements achieved are appropriately dealt with afterward.

◆ **Meeting management.** Described in Section 10.2.2.6. Meeting management includes preparing the agenda, ensuring that a representative for each key stakeholder group is invited, and preparing and sending the follow-up minutes and actions.

## 4.1.2.4 MEETINGS

For this process, meetings are held with key stakeholders to identify the project objectives, success criteria, key deliverables, high-level requirements, summary milestones, and other summary information.

## 4.1.3 DEVELOP PROJECT CHARTER: OUTPUTS

### 4.1.3.1 PROJECT CHARTER

The project charter is the document issued by the project initiator or sponsor that formally authorizes the existence of a project and provides the project manager with the authority to apply organizational resources to project activities. It documents the high-level information on the project and on the product, service, or result the project is intended to satisfy, such as:

◆ Project purpose;

◆ Measurable project objectives and related success criteria;

◆ High-level requirements;

◆ High-level project description, boundaries, and key deliverables;

◆ Overall project risk;

◆ Summary milestone schedule;

◆ Preapproved financial resources;

◆ Key stakeholder list;

◆ Project approval requirements (i.e., what constitutes project success, who decides the project is successful, and who signs off on the project);

◆ Project exit criteria (i.e., what are the conditions to be met in order to close or to cancel the project or phase);

◆ Assigned project manager, responsibility, and authority level; and

◆ Name and authority of the sponsor or other person(s) authorizing the project charter.

At a high level, the project charter ensures a common understanding by the stakeholders of the key deliverables, milestones, and the roles and responsibilities of everyone involved in the project.

### 4.1.3.2 ASSUMPTION LOG

High-level strategic and operational assumptions and constraints are normally identified in the business case before the project is initiated and will flow into the project charter. Lower-level activity and task assumptions are generated throughout the project such as defining technical specifications, estimates, the schedule, risks, etc. The assumption log is used to record all assumptions and constraints throughout the project life cycle.

## 4.2 DEVELOP PROJECT MANAGEMENT PLAN

Develop Project Management Plan is the process of defining, preparing, and coordinating all plan components and consolidating them into an integrated project management plan. The key benefit of this process is the production of a comprehensive document that defines the basis of all project work and how the work will be performed. This process is performed once or at predefined points in the project. The inputs, tools and techniques, and outputs of the process are depicted in Figure 4-4. Figure 4-5 depicts the data flow diagram for the process.

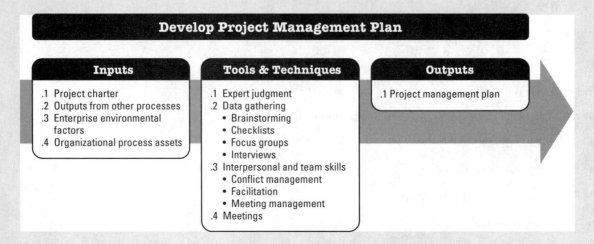

Figure 4-4. Develop Project Management Plan: Inputs, Tools & Techniques, and Outputs

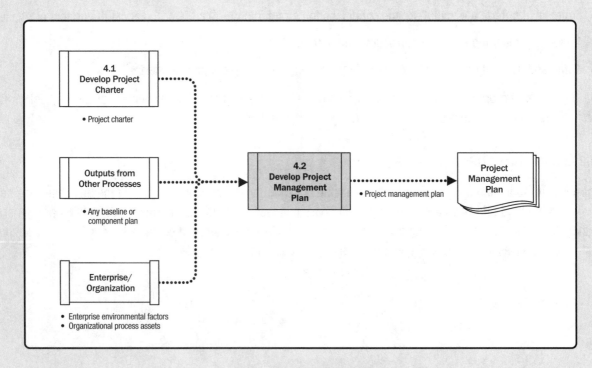

Figure 4-5. Develop Project Management Plan: Data Flow Diagram

The project management plan defines how the project is executed, monitored and controlled, and closed. The project management plan's content varies depending on the application area and complexity of the project.

The project management plan may be either summary level or detailed. Each component plan is described to the extent required by the specific project. The project management plan should be robust enough to respond to an ever-changing project environment. This agility may result in more accurate information as the project progresses.

The project management plan should be baselined; that is, it is necessary to define at least the project references for scope, time, and cost, so that the project execution can be measured and compared to those references and performance can be managed. Before the baselines are defined, the project management plan may be updated as many times as necessary. No formal process is required at that time. But, once it is baselined, it may only be changed through the Perform Integrated Change Control process. Consequently, change requests will be generated and decided upon whenever a change is requested. This results in a project management plan that is progressively elaborated by controlled and approved updates extending through project closure.

Projects that exist in the context of a program or portfolio should develop a project management plan that is consistent with the program or portfolio management plan. For example, if the program management plan indicates all changes exceeding a specified cost need to be reviewed by the change control board (CCB), then this process and cost threshold need to be defined in the project management plan.

## 4.2.1 DEVELOP PROJECT MANAGEMENT PLAN: INPUTS

### 4.2.1.1 PROJECT CHARTER

Described in Section 4.1.3.1. The project team uses the project charter as a starting point for initial project planning. The type and amount of information in the project charter varies depending on the complexity of the project and the information known at the time of its creation. At a minimum, the project charter should define the high-level information about the project that will be elaborated in the various components of the project management plan.

### 4.2.1.2 OUTPUTS FROM OTHER PROCESSES

Outputs from many of the other processes described in Sections 5 through 13 are integrated to create the project management plan. Subsidiary plans and baselines that are an output from other planning processes are inputs to this process. In addition, changes to these documents may necessitate updates to the project management plan.

### 4.2.1.3 ENTERPRISE ENVIRONMENTAL FACTORS

The enterprise environmental factors that can influence the Develop Project Management Plan process include but are not limited to:

◆ Government or industry standards (e.g., product standards, quality standards, safety standards, and workmanship standards);

◆ Legal and regulatory requirements and/or constraints;

◆ Project management body of knowledge for vertical market (e.g., construction) and/or focus area (e.g., environmental, safety, risk, or agile software development);

◆ Organizational structure, culture, management practices, and sustainability;

◆ Organizational governance framework (a structured way to provide control, direction, and coordination through people, policies, and processes to meet organizational strategic and operational goals); and

◆ Infrastructure (e.g., existing facilities and capital equipment).

### 4.2.1.4 ORGANIZATIONAL PROCESS ASSETS

The organizational process assets that can influence the Develop Project Management Plan process include but are not limited to:

◆ Organizational standard policies, processes, and procedures;

◆ Project management plan template, including:

  ■ Guidelines and criteria for tailoring the organization's set of standard processes to satisfy the specific needs of the project, and

  ■ Project closure guidelines or requirements such as the product validation and acceptance criteria.

◆ Change control procedures, including the steps by which official organizational standards, policies, plans, procedures, or any project documents will be modified and how any changes will be approved and validated;

◆ Monitoring and reporting methods, risk control procedures, and communication requirements;

◆ Project information from previous similar projects (e.g., scope, cost, schedule and performance measurement baselines, project calendars, project schedule network diagrams, and risk registers); and

◆ Historical information and lessons learned repository.

## 4.2.2 DEVELOP PROJECT MANAGEMENT PLAN: TOOLS AND TECHNIQUES

### 4.2.2.1 EXPERT JUDGMENT

Described in Section 4.1.2.1. Expertise should be considered from individuals or groups with specialized knowledge of or training in the following topics:

◆ Tailoring the project management process to meet the project needs, including the dependencies and interactions among those processes and the essential inputs and outputs;

◆ Developing additional components of the project management plan if needed;

◆ Determining the tools and techniques to be used for accomplishing those processes;

◆ Developing technical and management details to be included in the project management plan;

◆ Determining resources and skill levels needed to perform project work;

◆ Defining the level of configuration management to apply on the project;

◆ Determining which project documents will be subject to the formal change control process; and

◆ Prioritizing the work on the project to ensure the project resources are allocated to the appropriate work at the appropriate time.

### 4.2.2.2 DATA GATHERING

Data-gathering techniques that can be used for this process include but are not limited to:

◆ **Brainstorming.** Described in Section 4.1.2.2. Brainstorming is frequently used when developing the project management plan to gather ideas and solutions about the project approach. Attendees include the project team members although other subject matter experts (SMEs) or stakeholders may also participate.

◆ **Checklists.** Described in Section 11.2.2.2. Many organizations have standardized checklists available based in their own experience or use checklists from the industry. A checklist may guide the project manager to develop the plan or may help to verify that all the required information is included in the project management plan.

◆ **Focus groups.** Described in Section 5.2.2.2. Focus groups bring together stakeholders to discuss the project management approach and the integration of the different components of the project management plan.

◆ **Interviews.** Described in Section 5.2.2.2. Interviews are used to obtain specific information from stakeholders to develop the project management plan or any component plan or project document.

### 4.2.2.3 INTERPERSONAL AND TEAM SKILLS

The interpersonal and team skills used when developing the project management plan include:

◆ **Conflict management.** Described in Section 9.5.2.1. Conflict management may be necessary to bring diverse stakeholders into alignment on all aspects of the project management plan.

◆ **Facilitation.** Described in Section 4.1.2.3. Facilitation ensures that there is effective participation, that participants achieve a mutual understanding, that all contributions are considered, and that conclusions or results have full buy-in according to the decision process established for the project.

◆ **Meeting management.** Described in Section 10.2.2.6. Meeting management is necessary to ensure that the numerous meetings that are necessary to develop, unify, and agree on the project management plan are well run.

### 4.2.2.4 MEETINGS

For this process, meetings are used to discuss the project approach, determine how work will be executed to accomplish the project objectives, and establish the way the project will be monitored and controlled.

The project kick-off meeting is usually associated with the end of planning and the start of executing. Its purpose is to communicate the objectives of the project, gain the commitment of the team for the project, and explain the roles and responsibilities of each stakeholder. The kick-off may occur at different points in time depending on the characteristics of the project:

◆ For small projects, there is usually only one team that performs the planning and the execution. In this case, the kick-off occurs shortly after initiation, in the Planning Process Group, because the team is involved in planning.

◆ In large projects, a project management team normally does the majority of the planning, and the remainder of the project team is brought on when the initial planning is complete, at the start of the development/implementation. In this instance, the kick-off meeting takes place with processes in the Executing Process Group.

Multiphase projects will typically include a kick-off meeting at the beginning of each phase.

### 4.2.3 DEVELOP PROJECT MANAGEMENT PLAN: OUTPUTS

### 4.2.3.1 PROJECT MANAGEMENT PLAN

The project management plan is the document that describes how the project will be executed, monitored and controlled, and closed. It integrates and consolidates all of the subsidiary management plans and baselines, and other information necessary to manage the project. The needs of the project determine which components of the project management plan are needed.

Project management plan components include but are not limited to:

◆ **Subsidiary management plans:**

■ *Scope management plan.* Described in Section 5.1.3.1. Establishes how the scope will be defined, developed, monitored, controlled, and validated.

■ *Requirements management plan.* Described in Section 5.1.3.2. Establishes how the requirements will be analyzed, documented, and managed.

■ *Schedule management plan.* Described in Section 6.1.3.1. Establishes the criteria and the activities for developing, monitoring, and controlling the schedule.

■ *Cost management plan.* Described in Section 7.1.3.1. Establishes how the costs will be planned, structured, and controlled.

■ *Quality management plan.* Described in Section 8.1.3.1. Establishes how an organization´s quality policies, methodologies, and standards will be implemented in the project.

■ *Resource management plan.* Described in Section 9.1.3.1 Provides guidance on how project resources should be categorized, allocated, managed, and released.

■ *Communications management plan.* Described in Section 10.1.3.1. Establishes how, when, and by whom information about the project will be administered and disseminated.

■ *Risk management plan.* Described in Section 11.1.3.1. Establishes how the risk management activities will be structured and performed.

■ *Procurement management plan.* Described in Section 12.1.3.1. Establishes how the project team will acquire goods and services from outside of the performing organization.

■ *Stakeholder engagement plan.* Described in Section 13.2.3.1. Establishes how stakeholders will be engaged in project decisions and execution, according to their needs, interests, and impact.

◆ **Baselines:**

■ *Scope baseline.* Described in Section 5.4.3.1. The approved version of a scope statement, work breakdown structure (WBS), and its associated WBS dictionary, which is used as a basis for comparison.

■ *Schedule baseline.* Described in Section 6.5.3.1. The approved version of the schedule model that is used as a basis for comparison to the actual results.

■ *Cost baseline.* Described in Section 7.3.3.1. The approved version of the time-phased project budget that is used as a basis for comparison to the actual results.

◆ **Additional components.** Most components of the project management plan are produced as outputs from other processes, though some are produced during this process. Those components developed as part of this process will be dependent on the project; however, they often include but are not limited to:

- *Change management plan.* Describes how the change requests throughout the project will be formally authorized and incorporated.

- *Configuration management plan.* Describes how the information about the items of the project (and which items) will be recorded and updated so that the product, service, or result of the project remains consistent and/or operative.

- *Performance measurement baseline.* An integrated scope-schedule-cost plan for the project work against which project execution is compared to measure and manage performance.

- *Project life cycle.* Describes the series of phases that a project passes through from its initiation to its closure.

- *Development approach.* Describes the product, service, or result development approach, such as predictive, iterative, agile, or a hybrid model.

- *Management reviews.* Identifies the points in the project when the project manager and relevant stakeholders will review the project progress to determine if performance is as expected, or if preventive or corrective actions are necessary.

While the project management plan is one of the primary documents used to manage the project, other project documents are also used. These other documents are not part of the project management plan; however, they are necessary to manage the project effectively. Table 4-1 is a representative list of the project management plan components and project documents.

**Table 4-1. Project Management Plan and Project Documents**

| Project Management Plan | Project Documents | |
|---|---|---|
| 1. Scope management plan | 1. Activity attributes | 20. Quality metrics |
| 2. Requirements management plan | 2. Activity list | 21. Quality report |
| 3. Schedule management plan | 3. Assumption log | 22. Requirements documentation |
| 4. Cost management plan | 4. Basis of estimates | 23. Requirements traceability matrix |
| 5. Quality management plan | 5. Change log | 24. Resource breakdown structure |
| 6. Resource management plan | 6. Cost estimates | 25. Resource calendars |
| 7. Communications management plan | 7. Cost forecasts | 26. Resource requirements |
| 8. Risk management plan | 8. Duration estimates | 27. Risk register |
| 9. Procurement management plan | 9. Issue log | 28. Risk report |
| 10. Stakeholder engagement plan | 10. Lessons learned register | 29. Schedule data |
| 11. Change management plan | 11. Milestone list | 30. Schedule forecasts |
| 12. Configuration management plan | 12. Physical resource assignments | 31. Stakeholder register |
| 13. Scope baseline | 13. Project calendars | 32. Team charter |
| 14. Schedule baseline | 14. Project communications | 33. Test and evaluation documents |
| 15. Cost baseline | 15. Project schedule | |
| 16. Performance measurement baseline | 16. Project schedule network diagram | |
| 17. Project life cycle description | 17. Project scope statement | |
| 18. Development approach | 18. Project team assignments | |
| 19. Management reviews | 19. Quality control measurements | |

## 4.3 DIRECT AND MANAGE PROJECT WORK

Direct and Manage Project Work is the process of leading and performing the work defined in the project management plan and implementing approved changes to achieve the project's objectives. The key benefit of this process is that it provides overall management of the project work and deliverables, thus improving the probability of project success. This process is performed throughout the project. The inputs, tools and techniques, and outputs of the process are depicted in Figure 4-6. Figure 4-7 depicts the data flow diagram for the process.

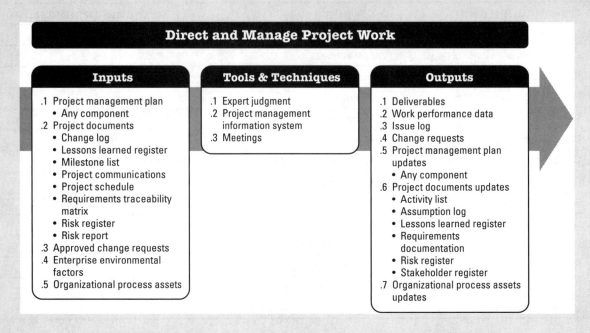

Figure 4-6. Direct and Manage Project Work: Inputs, Tools & Techniques, and Outputs

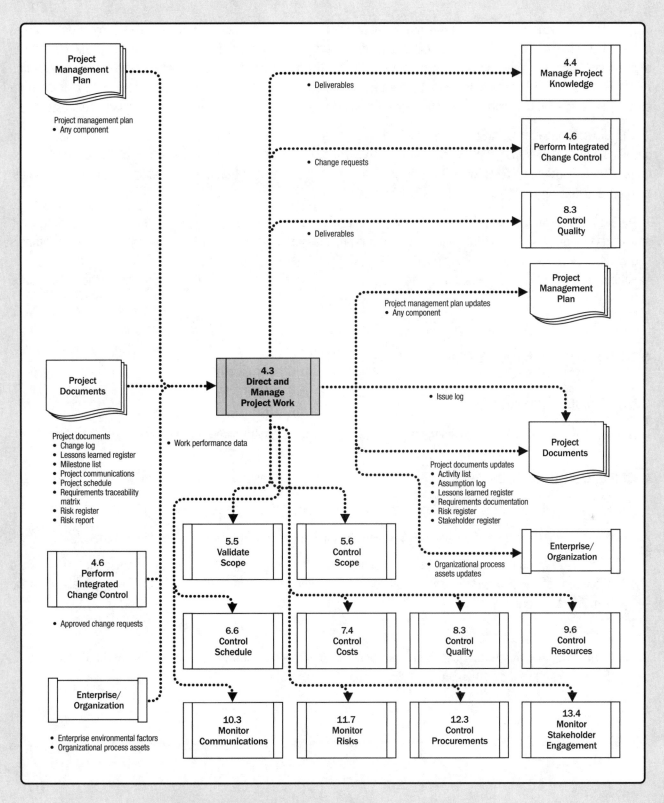

**Figure 4-7. Direct and Manage Project Work: Data Flow Diagram**

Direct and Manage Project Work involves executing the planned project activities to complete project deliverables and accomplish established objectives. Available resources are allocated, their efficient use is managed, and changes in project plans stemming from analyzing work performance data and information are carried out. The Direct and Manage Project Work process is directly affected by the project application area. Deliverables are produced as outputs from processes performed to accomplish the project work as planned and scheduled in the project management plan.

The project manager, along with the project management team, directs the performance of the planned project activities and manages the various technical and organizational interfaces that exist in the project. Direct and Manage Project Work also requires review of the impact of all project changes and the implementation of approved changes: corrective action, preventive action, and/or defect repair.

During project execution, the work performance data is collected and communicated to the applicable controlling processes for analysis. Work performance data analysis provides information about the completion status of deliverables and other relevant details about project performance. The work performance data will also be used as an input to the Monitoring and Controlling Process Group, and can be used as feedback into lessons learned to improve the performance of future work packages.

## 4.3.1 DIRECT AND MANAGE PROJECT WORK: INPUTS

### 4.3.1.1 PROJECT MANAGEMENT PLAN

Described in Section 4.2.3.1. Any component of the project management plan may be an input to this process.

### 4.3.1.2 PROJECT DOCUMENTS

Project documents that can be considered as inputs for this process include but are not limited to:

◆ **Change log.** Described in Section 4.6.3.3. The change log contains the status of all change requests.

◆ **Lessons learned register.** Described in Section 4.4.3.1. Lessons learned are used to improve the performance of the project and to avoid repeating mistakes. The register helps identify where to set rules or guidelines so the team's actions are aligned.

◆ **Milestone list.** Described in Section 6.2.3.3. The milestone list shows the scheduled dates for specific milestones.

◆ **Project communications.** Described in Section 10.2.3.1. Project communications include performance reports, deliverable status, and other information generated by the project.

- **Project schedule.** Described in Section 6.5.3.2. The schedule includes at least the list of work activities, their durations, resources, and planned start and finish dates.

- **Requirements traceability matrix.** Described in Section 5.2.3.2. The requirements traceability matrix links product requirements to the deliverables that satisfy them and helps to focus on the final outcomes.

- **Risk register.** Described in Section 11.2.3.1. The risk register provides information on threats and opportunities that may impact project execution.

- **Risk report.** Described in Section 11.2.3.2. The risk report provides information on sources of overall project risk along with summary information on identified individual project risks.

### 4.3.1.3 APPROVED CHANGE REQUESTS

Described in Section 4.6.3.1. Approved change requests are an output of the Perform Integrated Change Control process, and include those requests reviewed and approved for implementation by the project manager or by the change control board (CCB) when applicable. The approved change request may be a corrective action, a preventive action, or a defect repair. Approved change requests are scheduled and implemented by the project team and can impact any area of the project or project management plan. The approved change requests can also modify the formally controlled project management plan components or project documents.

### 4.3.1.4 ENTERPRISE ENVIRONMENTAL FACTORS

The enterprise environmental factors that can influence the Direct and Manage Project Work process include but are not limited to:

- Organizational structure, culture, management practices, and sustainability;

- Infrastructure (e.g., existing facilities and capital equipment); and

- Stakeholder risk thresholds (e.g., allowable cost overrun percentage).

### 4.3.1.5 ORGANIZATIONAL PROCESS ASSETS

The organizational process assets that can influence the Direct and Manage Project Work process include but are not limited to:

◆ Organizational standard policies, processes, and procedures;

◆ Issue and defect management procedures defining issue and defect controls, issue and defect identification and resolution, and action item tracking;

◆ Issue and defect management database(s) containing historical issue and defect status, issue and defect resolution, and action item results;

◆ Performance measurement database used to collect and make available measurement data on processes and products;

◆ Change control and risk control procedures; and

◆ Project information from previous projects (e.g., scope, cost, schedule, performance measurement baselines, project calendars, project schedule network diagrams, risk registers, risk reports, and lessons learned repository).

## 4.3.2 DIRECT AND MANAGE PROJECT WORK: TOOLS AND TECHNIQUES

### 4.3.2.1 EXPERT JUDGMENT

Described in Section 4.1.2.1. Expertise should be considered from individuals or groups with specialized knowledge or training in the following topics:

◆ Technical knowledge on the industry and focus area of the project,

◆ Cost and budget management,

◆ Legal and procurement,

◆ Legislation and regulations, and

◆ Organizational governance.

### 4.3.2.2 PROJECT MANAGEMENT INFORMATION SYSTEM (PMIS)

The PMIS provides access to information technology (IT) software tools, such as scheduling software tools, work authorization systems, configuration management systems, information collection and distribution systems, as well as interfaces to other online automated systems such as corporate knowledge base repositories. Automated gathering and reporting on key performance indicators (KPI) can be part of this system.

### 4.3.2.3 MEETINGS

Meetings are used to discuss and address pertinent topics of the project when directing and managing project work. Attendees may include the project manager, the project team, and appropriate stakeholders involved or affected by the topics addressed. Each attendee should have a defined role to ensure appropriate participation. Types of meetings include but are not limited to: kick-off, technical, sprint or iteration planning, Scrum daily standups, steering group, problem solving, progress update, and retrospective meetings.

## 4.3.3 DIRECT AND MANAGE PROJECT WORK: OUTPUTS

### 4.3.3.1 DELIVERABLES

A deliverable is any unique and verifiable product, result, or capability to perform a service that is required to be produced to complete a process, phase, or project. Deliverables are typically the outcomes of the project and can include components of the project management plan.

Change control should be applied once the first version of a deliverable has been completed. The control of the multiple versions or editions of a deliverable (e.g., documents, software, and building blocks) is supported by configuration management tools and procedures.

### 4.3.3.2 WORK PERFORMANCE DATA

Work performance data are the raw observations and measurements identified during activities being performed to carry out the project work. Data are often viewed as the lowest level of detail from which information is derived by other processes. Data is gathered through work execution and passed to the controlling processes for further analysis.

Examples of work performance data include work completed, key performance indicators (KPIs), technical performance measures, actual start and finish dates of schedule activities, story points completed, deliverables status, schedule progress, number of change requests, number of defects, actual costs incurred, actual durations, etc.

### 4.3.3.3 ISSUE LOG

Throughout the life cycle of a project, the project manager will normally face problems, gaps, inconsistencies, or conflicts that occur unexpectedly and that require some action so they do not impact the project performance. The issue log is a project document where all the issues are recorded and tracked. Data on issues may include:

◆ Issue type,

◆ Who raised the issue and when,

◆ Description,

◆ Priority,

◆ Who is assigned to the issue,

◆ Target resolution date,

◆ Status, and

◆ Final solution.

The issue log will help the project manager effectively track and manage issues, ensuring that they are investigated and resolved. The issue log is created for the first time as an output of this process, although issues may happen at any time during the project. The issue log is updated as a result of the monitoring and control activities throughout the project's life cycle.

### 4.3.3.4 CHANGE REQUESTS

A change request is a formal proposal to modify any document, deliverable, or baseline. When issues are found while project work is being performed, change requests can be submitted, which may modify project policies or procedures, project or product scope, project cost or budget, project schedule, or quality of the project or product results. Other change requests cover the needed preventive or corrective actions to forestall negative impact later in the project. Any project stakeholder may request a change. Change requests are processed for review and disposition through the Perform Integrated Change Control process (Section 4.6). Change requests can be initiated from inside or outside the project and they can be optional or legally/contractually mandated. Change requests may include:

◆ **Corrective action.** An intentional activity that realigns the performance of the project work with the project management plan.

◆ **Preventive action.** An intentional activity that ensures the future performance of the project work is aligned with the project management plan.

◆ **Defect repair.** An intentional activity to modify a nonconforming product or product component.

◆ **Updates.** Changes to formally controlled project documents, plans, etc., to reflect modified or additional ideas or content.

### 4.3.3.5 PROJECT MANAGEMENT PLAN UPDATES

Any change to the project management plan goes through the organization's change control process via a change request. Any component of the project management plan may require a change request as a result of this process.

### 4.3.3.6 PROJECT DOCUMENTS UPDATES

Project documents that may be updated as a result of carrying out this process include but are not limited to:

- ◆ **Activity list.** Described in Section 6.2.3.1. The activity list may be updated with additional or modified activities to be performed to complete project work.

- ◆ **Assumption log.** Described in Section 4.1.3.2. New assumptions and constraints may be added, and the status of existing assumptions and constraints may be updated or closed out.

- ◆ **Lessons learned register.** Described in Section 4.4.3.1. Any lessons learned that will improve performance for current or future projects is recorded as it is learned.

- ◆ **Requirements documentation.** Described in Section 5.2.3.1. New requirements may be identified during this process. Progress on meeting requirements can also be updated.

- ◆ **Risk register.** Described in Section 11.2.3.1. New risks may be identified and existing risks may be updated during this process. Risks are recorded in the risk register via risk management processes.

- ◆ **Stakeholder register.** Described in Section 13.1.3.1. Where additional information on existing or new stakeholders is gathered as a result of this process, it is recorded in the stakeholder register.

### 4.3.3.7 ORGANIZATIONAL PROCESS ASSETS UPDATES

Any organizational process asset can be updated as a result of this process.

## 4.4 MANAGE PROJECT KNOWLEDGE

Manage Project Knowledge is the process of using existing knowledge and creating new knowledge to achieve the project's objectives and contribute to organizational learning. The key benefits of this process are that prior organizational knowledge is leveraged to produce or improve the project outcomes, and knowledge created by the project is available to support organizational operations and future projects or phases. This process is performed throughout the project. The inputs, tools and techniques, and outputs of the process are depicted in Figure 4-8. Figure 4-9 depicts the data flow diagram for the process.

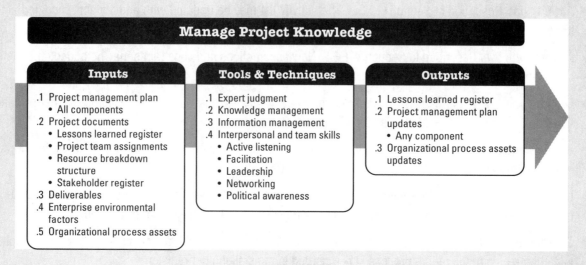

**Figure 4-8. Manage Project Knowledge: Inputs, Tools & Techniques, and Outputs**

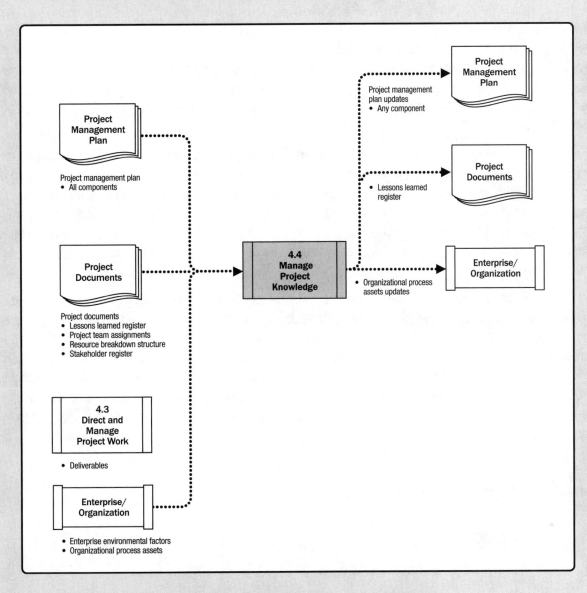

**Figure 4-9. Manage Project Knowledge: Data Flow Diagram**

Knowledge is commonly split into "explicit" (knowledge that can be readily codified using words, pictures, and numbers) and "tacit" (knowledge that is personal and difficult to express, such as beliefs, insights, experience, and "know-how"). Knowledge management is concerned with managing both tacit and explicit knowledge for two purposes: reusing existing knowledge and creating new knowledge. The key activities that underpin both purposes are knowledge sharing and knowledge integration (of knowledge from different domains, contextual knowledge, and project management knowledge).

It is a common misconception that managing knowledge involves just documenting it so it can be shared. Another common misconception is that managing knowledge involves just obtaining lessons learned at the end of the project, in order to use it in the future projects. Only codified explicit knowledge can be shared in this way. But codified explicit knowledge lacks context and is open to different interpretations, so even though it can easily be shared, it isn't always understood or applied in the right way. Tacit knowledge has context built in but is very difficult to codify. It resides in the minds of individual experts or in social groups and situations, and is normally shared through conversations and interactions between people.

From an organizational perspective, knowledge management is about making sure the skills, experience, and expertise of the project team and other stakeholders are used before, during, and after the project. Because knowledge resides in the minds of people and people cannot be forced to share what they know (or to pay attention to others' knowledge), the most important part of knowledge management is creating an atmosphere of trust so that people are motivated to share their knowledge. Even the best knowledge management tools and techniques will not work if people are not motivated to share what they know or to pay attention to what others know. In practice, knowledge is shared using a mixture of knowledge management tools and techniques (interactions between people) and information management tools and techniques (in which people codify part of their explicit knowledge by documenting it so it can be shared).

## 4.4.1 MANAGE PROJECT KNOWLEDGE: INPUTS

### 4.4.1.1 PROJECT MANAGEMENT PLAN

Described in Section 4.2.3.1. All components of the project management plan are inputs.

### 4.4.1.2 PROJECT DOCUMENTS

Project documents that can be considered as inputs for this process include but are not limited to:

◆ **Lessons learned register.** Described in Section 4.4.3.1. The lessons learned register provides information on effective practices in knowledge management.

◆ **Project team assignments.** Described in Section 9.3.3.2. Project team assignments provide information on the type of competencies and experience available in the project and the knowledge that may be missing.

◆ **Resource breakdown structure.** Described in Section 9.2.3.3. The resource breakdown structure includes information on the composition of the team and may help to understand what knowledge is available as a group and what knowledge is missing.

◆ **Stakeholder register.** Described in Section 13.1.3.1. The stakeholder register contains details about the identified stakeholders to help understand the knowledge they may have.

### 4.4.1.3 DELIVERABLES

A deliverable is any unique and verifiable product, result, or capability to perform a service that is required to be produced to complete a process, phase, or project. Deliverables are typically tangible components completed to meet the project objectives and can include components of the project management plan.

### 4.4.1.4 ENTERPRISE ENVIRONMENTAL FACTORS

The enterprise environmental factors that can influence the Manage Project Knowledge process include but are not limited to:

◆ **Organizational, stakeholder, and customer culture.** The existence of trusting working relationships and a no-blame culture is particularly important in managing knowledge. Other factors include the value placed on learning and social behavioral norms.

◆ **Geographic distribution of facilities and resources.** The location of team members helps determine methods for gaining and sharing knowledge.

◆ **Organizational knowledge experts.** Some organizations have a team or individual that specializes in knowledge management.

◆ **Legal and regulatory requirements and/or constraints.** These include confidentiality of project information.

### 4.4.1.5 ORGANIZATIONAL PROCESS ASSETS

Knowledge about project management is often embedded in processes and routines. The organizational process assets that can influence the Manage Project Knowledge process include but are not limited to:

◆ **Organizational standard policies, processes, and procedures.** These may include: confidentiality and access to information; security and data protection; record retention policies; use of copyrighted information; destruction of classified information; format and maximum size of files; registry data and metadata; authorized technology and social media; etc.

◆ **Personnel administration.** These include, for example, employee development and training records, and competency frameworks that refer to knowledge-sharing behaviors.

◆ **Organizational communication requirements.** Formal, rigid communication requirements are good for sharing information. Informal communication is more effective for creating new knowledge and integrating knowledge across diverse stakeholder groups.

◆ **Formal knowledge-sharing and information-sharing procedures.** These include learning reviews before, during, and after projects and project phases; for example, identifying, capturing, and sharing lessons learned from the current project and other projects.

## 4.4.2 MANAGE PROJECT KNOWLEDGE: TOOLS AND TECHNIQUES

### 4.4.2.1 EXPERT JUDGMENT

Described in Section 4.1.2.1. Expertise should be considered from individuals or groups with specialized knowledge or training in the following topics:

◆ Knowledge management,

◆ Information management,

◆ Organizational learning,

◆ Knowledge and information management tools, and

◆ Relevant information from other projects.

### 4.4.2.2 KNOWLEDGE MANAGEMENT

Knowledge management tools and techniques connect people so they can work together to create new knowledge, share tacit knowledge, and integrate the knowledge of diverse team members. The tools and techniques appropriate in a project depend on the nature of the project, especially the degree of innovation involved, the project complexity, and the level of diversity (including diversity of disciplines) among team members.

Tools and techniques include but are not limited to:

◆ Networking, including informal social interaction and online social networking. Online forums where people can ask open questions ("What does anyone know about...?") are useful for starting knowledge-sharing conversations with specialists;

◆ Communities of practice (sometimes called communities of interest or just communities) and special interest groups;

◆ Meetings, including virtual meetings where participants can interact using communications technology;

◆ Work shadowing and reverse shadowing;

◆ Discussion forums such as focus groups;

◆ Knowledge-sharing events such as seminars and conferences;

◆ Workshops, including problem-solving sessions and learning reviews designed to identify lessons learned;

◆ Storytelling;

◆ Creativity and ideas management techniques;

◆ Knowledge fairs and cafés; and

◆ Training that involves interaction between learners.

All of these tools and techniques can be applied face-to-face or virtually, or both. Face-to-face interaction is usually the most effective way to build the trusting relationships that are needed to manage knowledge. Once relationships are established, virtual interaction can be used to maintain the relationship.

## 4.4.2.3 INFORMATION MANAGEMENT

Information management tools and techniques are used to create and connect people to information. They are effective for sharing simple, unambiguous, codified explicit knowledge. They include but are not limited to:

◆ Methods for codifying explicit knowledge; for example, for producing lessons to be learned entries for the lessons learned register;

◆ Lessons learned register;

◆ Library services;

◆ Information gathering, for example, web searches and reading published articles; and

◆ Project management information system (PMIS). Described in Section 4.3.2.2. Project management information systems often include document management systems.

Tools and techniques that connect people to information can be enhanced by adding an element of interaction, for example, include a "contact me" function so users can get in touch with the originators of the lessons and ask for advice specific to their project and context.

Interaction and support also helps people find relevant information. Asking for help is generally quicker and easier than trying to identify search terms. Search terms are often difficult to select because people may not know which keywords or key phrases to use to access the information they need.

Knowledge and information management tools and techniques should be connected to project processes and process owners. Communities of practice and subject matter experts (SMEs), for example, may generate insights that lead to improved control processes; having an internal sponsor can ensure improvements are implemented. Lessons learned register entries may be analyzed to identify common issues that can be addressed by changes to project procedures.

### 4.4.2.4 INTERPERSONAL AND TEAM SKILLS

The interpersonal and team skills used include but are not limited to:

◆ **Active listening.** Described in Section 10.2.2.6. Active listening helps reduce misunderstandings and improves communication and knowledge sharing.

◆ **Facilitation.** Described in Section 4.1.2.3. Facilitation helps effectively guide a group to a successful decision, solution, or conclusion.

◆ **Leadership.** Described in Section 3.4.4. Leadership is used to communicate the vision and inspire the project team to focus on the appropriate knowledge and knowledge objectives.

◆ **Networking.** Described in Section 10.2.2.6. Networking allows informal connections and relations among project stakeholders to be established and creates the conditions to share tacit and explicit knowledge.

◆ **Political awareness.** Described in Section 10.1.2.6. Political awareness helps the project manager to plan communications based on the project environment as well as the organization's political environment.

### 4.4.3 MANAGE PROJECT KNOWLEDGE: OUTPUTS

### 4.4.3.1 LESSONS LEARNED REGISTER

The lessons learned register can include the category and description of the situation. The lessons learned register may also include the impact, recommendations, and proposed actions associated with the situation. The lessons learned register may record challenges, problems, realized risks and opportunities, or other content as appropriate.

The lessons learned register is created as an output of this process early in the project. Thereafter it is used as an input and updated as an output in many processes throughout the project. The persons or teams involved in the work are also involved in capturing the lessons learned. Knowledge can be documented using videos, pictures, audios, or other suitable means that ensure the efficiency of the lessons captured.

At the end of a project or phase, the information is transferred to an organizational process asset called a lessons learned repository.

#### 4.4.3.2 PROJECT MANAGEMENT PLAN UPDATES

Any change to the project management plan goes through the organization's change control process via a change request. Any component of the project management plan may be updated as a result of this process.

#### 4.4.3.3 ORGANIZATIONAL PROCESS ASSETS UPDATES

All projects create new knowledge. Some of this knowledge is codified, embedded in deliverables, or embedded in improvements to processes and procedures as a result of the Manage Project Knowledge process. Existing knowledge can also be codified or embedded for the first time as a result of this process; for example, if an existing idea for a new procedure is piloted in the project and found to be successful.

Any organizational process asset can be updated as a result of this process.

## 4.5 MONITOR AND CONTROL PROJECT WORK

Monitor and Control Project Work is the process of tracking, reviewing, and reporting the overall progress to meet the performance objectives defined in the project management plan. The key benefits of this process are that it allows stakeholders to understand the current state of the project, to recognize the actions taken to address any performance issues, and to have visibility into the future project status with cost and schedule forecasts. This process is performed throughout the project. The inputs, tools and techniques, and outputs of the process are depicted in Figure 4-10. Figure 4-11 depicts the data flow diagram for the process.

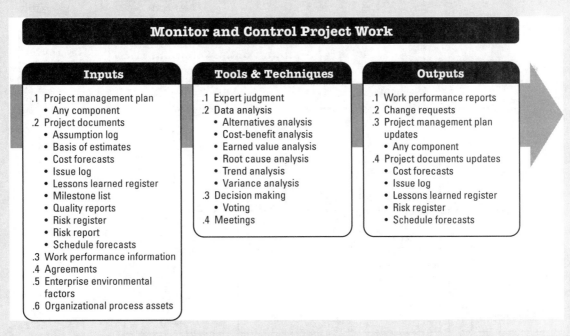

Figure 4-10. Monitor and Control Project Work: Inputs, Tools & Techniques, and Outputs

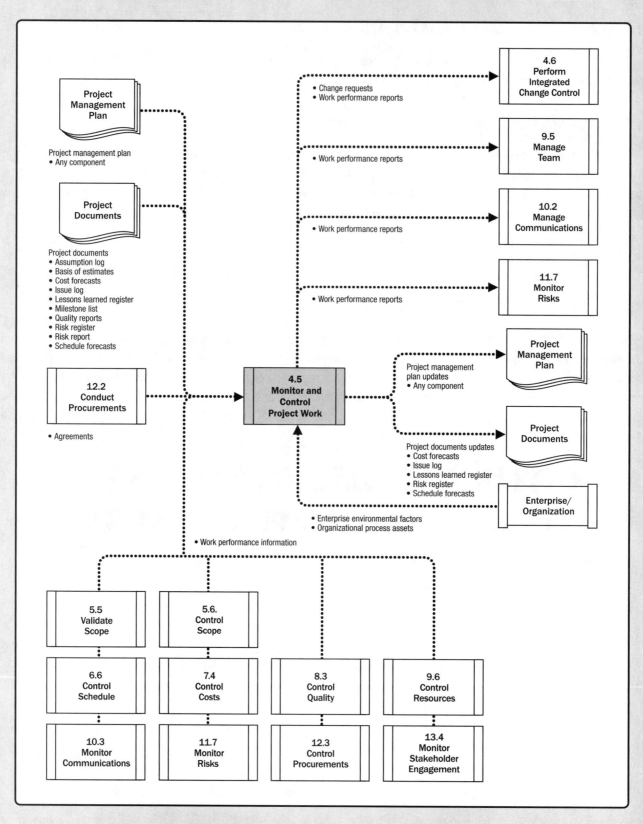

**Figure 4-11. Monitor and Control Project Work: Data Flow Diagram**

Monitoring is an aspect of project management performed throughout the project. Monitoring includes collecting, measuring, and assessing measurements and trends to effect process improvements. Continuous monitoring gives the project management team insight into the health of the project and identifies any areas that may require special attention. Control includes determining corrective or preventive actions or replanning and following up on action plans to determine whether the actions taken resolved the performance issue. The Monitor and Control Project Work process is concerned with:

◆ Comparing actual project performance against the project management plan;

◆ Assessing performance periodically to determine whether any corrective or preventive actions are indicated, and then recommending those actions as necessary;

◆ Checking the status of individual project risks;

◆ Maintaining an accurate, timely information base concerning the project's product(s) and their associated documentation through project completion;

◆ Providing information to support status reporting, progress measurement, and forecasting;

◆ Providing forecasts to update current cost and current schedule information;

◆ Monitoring implementation of approved changes as they occur;

◆ Providing appropriate reporting on project progress and status to program management when the project is part of an overall program; and

◆ Ensuring that the project stays aligned with the business needs.

## 4.5.1 MONITOR AND CONTROL PROJECT WORK: INPUTS

### 4.5.1.1 PROJECT MANAGEMENT PLAN

Described in Section 4.2.3.1. Monitoring and controlling project work involves looking at all aspects of the project. Any component of the project management plan may be an input for this process.

### 4.5.1.2 PROJECT DOCUMENTS

Project documents that can be considered as inputs for this process include but are not limited to:

◆ **Assumption log.** Described in Section 4.1.3.2. The assumption log contains information about assumptions and constraints identified as affecting the project.

◆ **Basis of estimates.** Described in Sections 6.4.3.2 and 7.2.3.2. Basis of estimates indicates how the various estimates were derived and can be used to make a decision on how to respond to variances.

◆ **Cost forecasts.** Described in Section 7.4.3.2. Based on the project's past performance, the cost forecasts are used to determine if the project is within defined tolerance ranges for budget and to identify any necessary change requests.

◆ **Issue log.** Described in Section 4.3.3.3. The issue log is used to document and monitor who is responsible for resolving specific issues by a target date.

◆ **Lessons learned register.** Described in Section 4.4.3.1. The lessons learned register may have information on effective responses for variances, and corrective and preventive actions.

◆ **Milestone list.** Described in Section 6.2.3.3. The milestone list shows the scheduled dates for specific milestones and is used to check if the planned milestones have been met.

◆ **Quality reports.** Described in Section 8.2.3.1. The quality report includes quality management issues; recommendations for process, project, and product improvements; corrective actions recommendations (includes rework, defect/bugs repair, 100% inspection, and more); and the summary of findings from the Control Quality process.

◆ **Risk register.** Described in Section 11.2.3.1. The risk register provides information on threats and opportunities that have occurred during project execution.

◆ **Risk report.** Described in Section 11.2.3.2. The risk report provides information on the overall project risks as well as information on specified individual risks.

◆ **Schedule forecasts.** Described in Section 6.6.3.2. Based on the project's past performance, the schedule forecasts are used to determine if the project is within defined tolerance ranges for schedule and to identify any necessary change requests.

### 4.5.1.3 WORK PERFORMANCE INFORMATION

Work performance data is gathered through work execution and passed to the controlling processes. To become work performance information, the work performance data are compared with the project management plan components, project documents, and other project variables. This comparison indicates how the project is performing.

Specific work performance metrics for scope, schedule, budget, and quality are defined at the start of the project as part of the project management plan. Performance data are collected during the project through the controlling processes and compared to the plan and other variables to provide a context for work performance.

For example, work performance data on cost may include funds that have been expended. However, to be useful, that data has to be compared to the budget, the work that was performed, the resources used to accomplish the work, and the funding schedule. This additional information provides the context to determine if the project is on budget or if there is a variance. It also indicates the degree of variance from the plan, and by comparing it to the variance thresholds in the project management plan it can indicate if preventive or corrective action is required. Interpreting work performance data and the additional information as a whole provides a context that provides a sound foundation for project decisions.

### 4.5.1.4 AGREEMENTS

Described in Section 12.2.3.2. A procurement agreement includes terms and conditions, and may incorporate other items that the buyer specifies regarding what the seller is to perform or provide. If the project is outsourcing part of the work, the project manager needs to oversee the contractor's work to make certain that all the agreements meet the specific needs of the project while adhering to organizational procurement policies.

### 4.5.1.5 ENTERPRISE ENVIRONMENTAL FACTORS

The enterprise environmental factors that can influence the Monitor and Control Project Work process include but are not limited to:

◆ Project management information systems such as scheduling, cost, resourcing tools, performance indicators, databases, project records, and financials;

◆ Infrastructure (e.g., existing facilities and equipment, organization's telecommunications channels);

◆ Stakeholders' expectations and risk thresholds; and

◆ Government or industry standards (e.g., regulatory agency regulations, product standards, quality standards, and workmanship standards).

### 4.5.1.6 ORGANIZATIONAL PROCESS ASSETS

The organizational process assets that can influence the Monitor and Control Project Work process include but are not limited to:

◆ Organizational standard policies, processes, and procedures;

◆ Financial controls procedures (e.g., required expenditure and disbursement reviews, accounting codes, and standard contract provisions);

◆ Monitoring and reporting methods;

◆ Issue management procedures defining issue controls, issue identification, and resolution and action item tracking;

◆ Defect management procedures defining defect controls, defect identification, and resolution and action item tracking; and

◆ Organizational knowledge base, in particular process measurement and the lessons learned repository.

### 4.5.2 MONITOR AND CONTROL PROJECT WORK: TOOLS AND TECHNIQUES

### 4.5.2.1 EXPERT JUDGMENT

Described in Section 4.1.2.1. Expertise should be considered from individuals or groups with specialized knowledge or training in the following topics:

◆ Earned value analysis,

◆ Interpretation and contextualization of data,

◆ Techniques to estimate duration and costs,

◆ Trend analysis,

◆ Technical knowledge on the industry and focus area of the project,

◆ Risk management, and

◆ Contract management.

### 4.5.2.2 DATA ANALYSIS

Data analysis techniques that can be used include but are not limited to:

◆ **Alternatives analysis.** Alternatives analysis is used to select the corrective actions or a combination of corrective and preventive actions to implement when a deviation occurs.

◆ **Cost-benefit analysis.** Described in Section 8.1.2.3. Cost-benefit analysis helps to determine the best corrective action in terms of cost in case of project deviations.

◆ **Earned value analysis.** Described in Section 7.4.2.2. Earned value provides an integrated perspective on scope, schedule, and cost performance.

◆ **Root cause analysis.** Described in Section 8.2.2.2. Root cause analysis focuses on identifying the main reasons of a problem. It can be used to identify the reasons for a deviation and the areas the project manager should focus on in order to achieve the objectives of the project.

◆ **Trend analysis.** Trend analysis is used to forecast future performance based on past results. It looks ahead in the project for expected slippages and warns the project manager ahead of time that there may be problems later in the schedule if established trends persist. This information is made available early enough in the project timeline to give the project team time to analyze and correct any anomalies. The results of trend analysis can be used to recommend preventive actions if necessary.

◆ **Variance analysis**. Variance analysis reviews the differences (or variance) between planned and actual performance. This can include duration estimates, cost estimates, resources utilization, resources rates, technical performance, and other metrics.

Variance analysis may be conducted in each Knowledge Area based on its particular variables. In Monitor and Control Project Work, the variance analysis reviews the variances from an integrated perspective considering cost, time, technical, and resource variances in relation to each other to get an overall view of variance on the project. This allows for the appropriate preventive or corrective actions to be initiated.

### 4.5.2.3 DECISION MAKING

A decision-making technique that can be used includes but is not limited to voting. Described in Section 5.2.2.4. Voting can include making decisions based on unanimity, majority, or plurality.

### 4.5.2.4 MEETINGS

Meetings may be face-to-face, virtual, formal, or informal. They may include project team members and other project stakeholders when appropriate. Types of meetings include but are not limited to user groups and review meetings.

## 4.5.3 MONITOR AND CONTROL PROJECT WORK: OUTPUTS

### 4.5.3.1 WORK PERFORMANCE REPORTS

Work performance information is combined, recorded, and distributed in a physical or electronic form in order to create awareness and generate decisions or actions. Work performance reports are the physical or electronic representation of work performance information intended to generate decisions, actions, or awareness. They are circulated to the project stakeholders through the communication processes as defined in the project communications management plan.

Examples of work performance reports include status reports and progress reports. Work performance reports can contain earned value graphs and information, trend lines and forecasts, reserve burndown charts, defect histograms, contract performance information, and risk summaries. They can be presented as dashboards, heat reports, stop light charts, or other representations useful for creating awareness and generating decisions and actions.

### 4.5.3.2 CHANGE REQUESTS

Described in Section 4.3.3.4. As a result of comparing planned results to actual results, change requests may be issued to expand, adjust, or reduce project scope, product scope, or quality requirements and schedule or cost baselines. Change requests may necessitate the collection and documentation of new requirements. Changes can impact the project management plan, project documents, or product deliverables. Change requests are processed for review and disposition through the Perform Integrated Change Control process (Section 4.6). Changes may include but are not limited to:

- ◆ **Corrective action.** An intentional activity that realigns the performance of the project work with the project management plan.

- ◆ **Preventive action.** An intentional activity that ensures the future performance of the project work is aligned with the project management plan.

- ◆ **Defect repair.** An intentional activity that modifies a nonconforming product or product component.

### 4.5.3.3 PROJECT MANAGEMENT PLAN UPDATES

Any change to the project management plan goes through the organization's change control process via a change request. Changes identified during the Monitor and Control Project Work process may affect the overall project management plan.

### 4.5.3.4 PROJECT DOCUMENTS UPDATES

Project documents that may be updated as a result of carrying out this process include but are not limited to:

◆ **Cost forecasts.** Described in Section 7.4.3.2. Changes in cost forecasts resulting from this process are recorded using cost management processes.

◆ **Issue log.** Described in Section 4.3.3.3. New issues raised as a result of this process are recorded in the issue log.

◆ **Lessons learned register.** Described in Section 4.4.3.1. The lessons learned register is updated with effective responses for variances and corrective and preventive actions.

◆ **Risk register.** Described in Section 11.2.3.1. New risks identified during this process are recorded in the risk register and managed using the risk management processes.

◆ **Schedule forecasts.** Described in Section 6.6.3.2. Changes in schedule forecasts resulting from this process are recorded using schedule management processes.

## 4.6 PERFORM INTEGRATED CHANGE CONTROL

Perform Integrated Change Control is the process of reviewing all change requests; approving changes and managing changes to deliverables, project documents, and the project management plan; and communicating the decisions. This process reviews all requests for changes to project documents, deliverables, or the project management plan and determines the resolution of the change requests. The key benefit of this process is that it allows for documented changes within the project to be considered in an integrated manner while addressing overall project risk, which often arises from changes made without consideration of the overall project objectives or plans. This process is performed throughout the project. The inputs, tools and techniques, and outputs of the process are depicted in Figure 4-12. Figure 4-13 depicts the data flow diagram for the process.

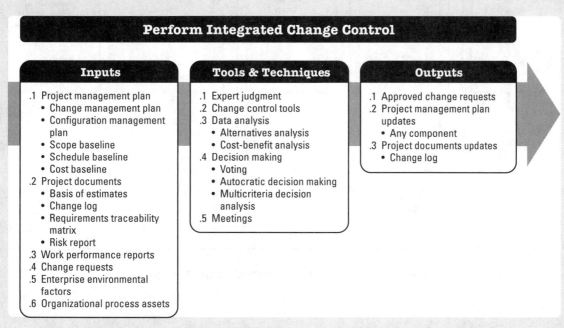

**Perform Integrated Change Control**

| Inputs | Tools & Techniques | Outputs |
|---|---|---|
| .1 Project management plan<br>  • Change management plan<br>  • Configuration management plan<br>  • Scope baseline<br>  • Schedule baseline<br>  • Cost baseline<br>.2 Project documents<br>  • Basis of estimates<br>  • Change log<br>  • Requirements traceability matrix<br>  • Risk report<br>.3 Work performance reports<br>.4 Change requests<br>.5 Enterprise environmental factors<br>.6 Organizational process assets | .1 Expert judgment<br>.2 Change control tools<br>.3 Data analysis<br>  • Alternatives analysis<br>  • Cost-benefit analysis<br>.4 Decision making<br>  • Voting<br>  • Autocratic decision making<br>  • Multicriteria decision analysis<br>.5 Meetings | .1 Approved change requests<br>.2 Project management plan updates<br>  • Any component<br>.3 Project documents updates<br>  • Change log |

Figure 4-12. Perform Integrated Change Control: Inputs, Tools & Techniques, and Outputs

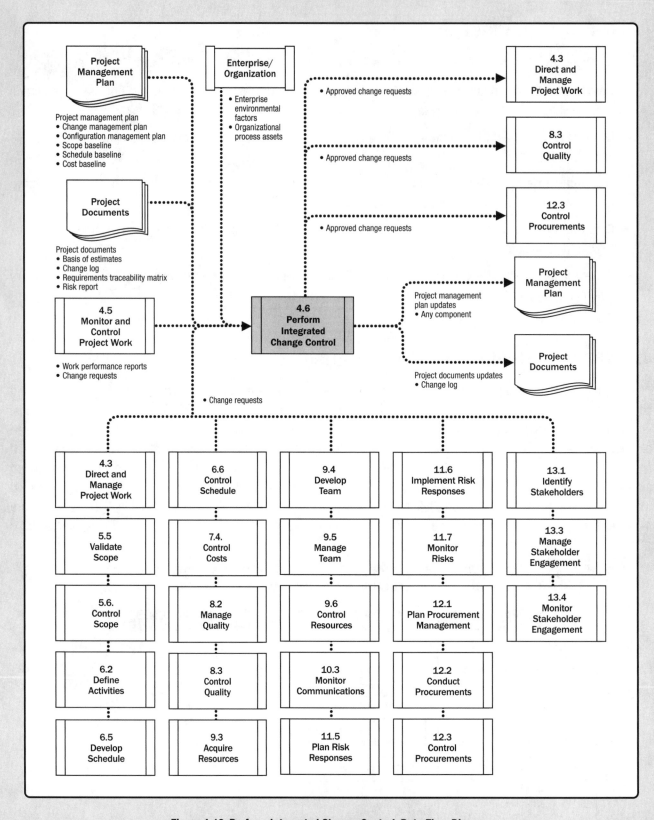

**Figure 4-13. Perform Integrated Change Control: Data Flow Diagram**

The Perform Integrated Change Control process is conducted from project start through completion and is the ultimate responsibility of the project manager. Change requests can impact the project scope and the product scope, as well as any project management plan component or any project document. Changes may be requested by any stakeholder involved with the project and may occur at any time throughout the project life cycle. The applied level of change control is dependent upon the application area, complexity of the specific project, contract requirements, and the context and environment in which the project is performed.

Before the baselines are established, changes are not required to be formally controlled by the Perform Integrated Change Control process. Once the project is baselined, change requests go through this process. As a general rule, each project's configuration management plan should define which project artifacts need to be placed under configuration control. Any change in a configuration element should be formally controlled and will require a change request.

Although changes may be initiated verbally, they should be recorded in written form and entered into the change management and/or configuration management system. Change requests may require information on estimated schedule impacts and estimated cost impacts prior to approval. Whenever a change request may impact any of the project baselines, a formal integrated change control process is always required. Every documented change request needs to be either approved, deferred, or rejected by a responsible individual, usually the project sponsor or project manager. The responsible individual will be identified in the project management plan or by organizational procedures. When required, the Perform Integrated Change Control process includes a change control board (CCB), which is a formally chartered group responsible for reviewing, evaluating, approving, deferring, or rejecting changes to the project and for recording and communicating such decisions.

Approved change requests can require new or revised cost estimates, activity sequences, schedule dates, resource requirements, and/or analysis of risk response alternatives. These changes can require adjustments to the project management plan and other project documents. Customer or sponsor approval may be required for certain change requests after CCB approval, unless they are part of the CCB.

# 4.6.1 PERFORM INTEGRATED CHANGE CONTROL: INPUTS

## 4.6.1.1 PROJECT MANAGEMENT PLAN

Described in Section 4.2.3.1. Project management plan components include but are not limited to:

◆ **Change management plan.** Described in Section 4.2.3.1. The change management plan provides the direction for managing the change control process and documents the roles and responsibilities of the change control board (CCB).

◆ **Configuration management plan.** Described in Section 4.2.3.1. The configuration management plan describes the configurable items of the project and identifies the items that will be recorded and updated so that the product of the project remains consistent and operable.

◆ **Scope baseline.** Described in Section 5.4.3.1. The scope baseline provides the project and product definition.

◆ **Schedule baseline.** Described in Section 6.5.3.1. The schedule baseline is used to assess the impact of the changes in the project schedule.

◆ **Cost baseline.** Described in Section 7.3.3.1. The cost baseline is used to assess the impact of the changes to the project cost.

## 4.6.1.2 PROJECT DOCUMENTS

Project documents that can be considered as inputs for this process include but are not limited to:

◆ **Basis of estimates.** Described in Section 6.4.3.2. Basis of estimates indicate how the duration, cost, and resources estimates were derived and can be used to calculate the impact of the change in time, budget, and resources.

◆ **Change log.** Described in Section 6.4.3.3. The change log is used to record all submitted change requests.

◆ **Requirements traceability matrix.** Described in Section 5.2.3.2. The requirements traceability matrix helps assess the impact of the change on the project scope.

◆ **Risk report.** Described in Section 11.2.3.2. The risk report presents information on sources of overall and individual project risks involved by the change requested.

## 4.6.1.3 WORK PERFORMANCE REPORTS

Described in Section 4.5.3.1. Work performance reports of particular interest to the Perform Integrated Change Control process include resource availability, schedule and cost data, earned value reports, and burnup or burndown charts.

## 4.6.1.4 CHANGE REQUESTS

Many processes produce change requests as an output. Change requests (described in Section 4.3.3.4) may include corrective action, preventive action, defect repairs, as well as updates to formally controlled documents or deliverables to reflect modified or additional ideas or content. Changes may or may not impact the project baselines—sometimes only the performance against the baseline is affected. Decisions on those changes are usually made by the project manager.

Change requests that have an impact on the project baselines should normally include information about the cost of implementing the change, modifications in the scheduled dates, resource requirements, and risks. These changes should be approved by the CCB (if it exists) and by the customer or sponsor, unless they are part of the CCB. Only approved changes should be incorporated into a revised baseline.

## 4.6.1.5 ENTERPRISE ENVIRONMENTAL FACTORS

The enterprise environmental factors that can influence the Perform Integrated Change Control process include but are not limited to:

◆ Legal restrictions, such as country or local regulations;

◆ Government or industry standards (e.g., product standards, quality standards, safety standards, and workmanship standards);

◆ Legal and regulatory requirements and/or constraints;

◆ Organizational governance framework (a structured way to provide control, direction, and coordination through people, policies, and processes to meet organizational strategic and operational goals); and

◆ Contracting and purchasing constraints.

## 4.6.1.6 ORGANIZATIONAL PROCESS ASSETS

The organizational process assets that can influence the Perform Integrated Change Control process include but are not limited to:

◆ Change control procedures, including the steps by which organizational standards, policies, plans, procedures, or any project documents will be modified, and how any changes will be approved and validated;

◆ Procedures for approving and issuing change authorizations; and

◆ Configuration management knowledge base containing the versions and baselines of all official organizational standards, policies, procedures, and any project documents.

## 4.6.2 PERFORM INTEGRATED CHANGE CONTROL: TOOLS AND TECHNIQUES

### 4.6.2.1 EXPERT JUDGMENT

Described in Section 4.1.2.1. Expertise should be considered from individuals or groups with specialized knowledge of or training in the following topics:

◆ Technical knowledge of the industry and focus area of the project,

◆ Legislation and regulations,

◆ Legal and procurement,

◆ Configuration management, and

◆ Risk management.

### 4.6.2.2 CHANGE CONTROL TOOLS

In order to facilitate configuration and change management, manual or automated tools may be used. Configuration control is focused on the specification of both the deliverables and the processes, while change control is focused on identifying, documenting, and approving or rejecting changes to the project documents, deliverables, or baselines.

Tool selection should be based on the needs of the project stakeholders including organizational and environmental considerations and/or constraints. Tools should support the following configuration management activities:

◆ **Identify configuration item.** Identification and selection of a configuration item to provide the basis for which the product configuration is defined and verified, products and documents are labeled, changes are managed, and accountability is maintained.

◆ **Record and report configuration item status.** Information recording and reporting about each configuration item.

◆ **Perform configuration item verification and audit.** Configuration verification and configuration audits ensure that the composition of a project's configuration items is correct and that corresponding changes are registered, assessed, approved, tracked, and correctly implemented. This ensures that the functional requirements defined in the configuration documentation are met.

Tools should support the following change management activities as well:

◆ **Identify changes.** Identifying and selecting a change item for processes or project documents.

◆ **Document changes.** Documenting the change into a proper change request.

◆ **Decide on changes.** Reviewing the changes; approving, rejecting, deferring, or making any other decision about changes to the project documents, deliverables, or baselines.

◆ **Track changes.** Verifying that the changes are registered, assessed, approved, and tracked and communicating final results to stakeholders.

Tools are also used to manage the change requests and the resulting decisions. Additional considerations should be made for communications to assist the change control board (CCB) members in their duties, as well as to distribute the decisions to the appropriate stakeholders.

### 4.6.2.3 DATA ANALYSIS

Data analysis techniques that can be used for this process include but are not limited to:

◆ **Alternatives analysis.** Described in Section 9.2.2.5. This technique is used to assess the requested changes and decide which are accepted, rejected, or need to be modified to be finally accepted.

◆ **Cost-benefit analysis.** Described in Section 8.1.2.3. This analysis helps to determine if the requested change is worth its associated cost.

### 4.6.2.4 DECISION MAKING

Decision-making techniques that can be used for this process include but are not limited to:

◆ **Voting.** Described in Section 5.2.2.4. Voting can take the form of unanimity, majority, or plurality to decide on whether to accept, defer, or reject change requests.

◆ **Autocratic decision making.** In this decision-making technique, one individual takes the responsibility for making the decision for the entire group.

◆ **Multicriteria decision analysis.** Described in Section 8.1.2.4. This technique uses a decision matrix to provide a systematic analytical approach to evaluate the requested changes according to a set of predefined criteria.

### 4.6.2.5 MEETINGS

Change control meetings are held with a change control board (CCB) that is responsible for meeting and reviewing the change requests and approving, rejecting, or deferring change requests. Most changes will have some sort of impact on time, cost, resources, or risks. Assessing the impact of the changes is an essential part of the meeting. Alternatives to the requested changes may also be discussed and proposed. Finally, the decision is communicated to the request owner or group.

The CCB may also review configuration management activities. The roles and responsibilities of these boards are clearly defined and agreed upon by the appropriate stakeholders and are documented in the change management plan. CCB decisions are documented and communicated to the stakeholders for information and follow-up actions.

## 4.6.3 PERFORM INTEGRATED CHANGE CONTROL: OUTPUTS

### 4.6.3.1 APPROVED CHANGE REQUESTS

Change requests (described in Section 4.3.3.4) are processed according to the change management plan by the project manager, CCB, or an assigned team member. As a result, changes may be approved, deferred, or rejected. Approved change requests will be implemented through the Direct and Manage Project Work process. Deferred or rejected change requests are communicated to the person or group requesting the change.

The disposition of all change requests are recorded in the change log as a project document update.

### 4.6.3.2 PROJECT MANAGEMENT PLAN UPDATES

Any formally controlled component of the project management plan may be changed as a result of this process. Changes to baselines are only made from the last baseline forward. Past performance is not changed. This protects the integrity of the baselines and the historical data of past performance.

### 4.6.3.3 PROJECT DOCUMENTS UPDATES

Any formally controlled project document may be changed as a result of this process. A project document that is normally updated as a result of this process is the change log. The change log is used to document changes that occur during a project.

# 4.7 CLOSE PROJECT OR PHASE

Close Project or Phase is the process of finalizing all activities for the project, phase, or contract. The key benefits of this process are the project or phase information is archived, the planned work is completed, and organizational team resources are released to pursue new endeavors. This process is performed once or at predefined points in the project. The inputs, tools and techniques, and outputs of the process are depicted in Figure 4-14. Figure 4-15 depicts the data flow diagram for the process.

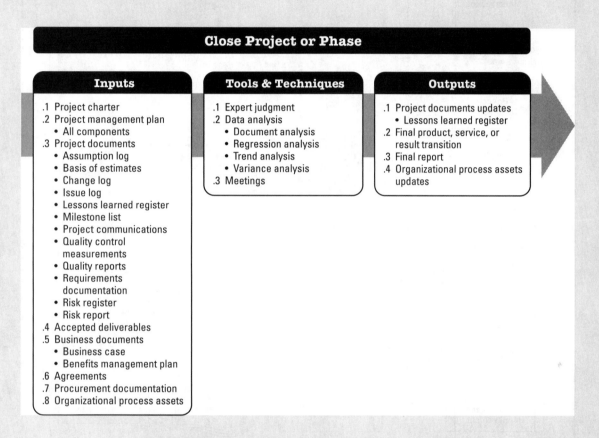

**Figure 4-14. Close Project or Phase: Inputs, Tools & Techniques, and Outputs**

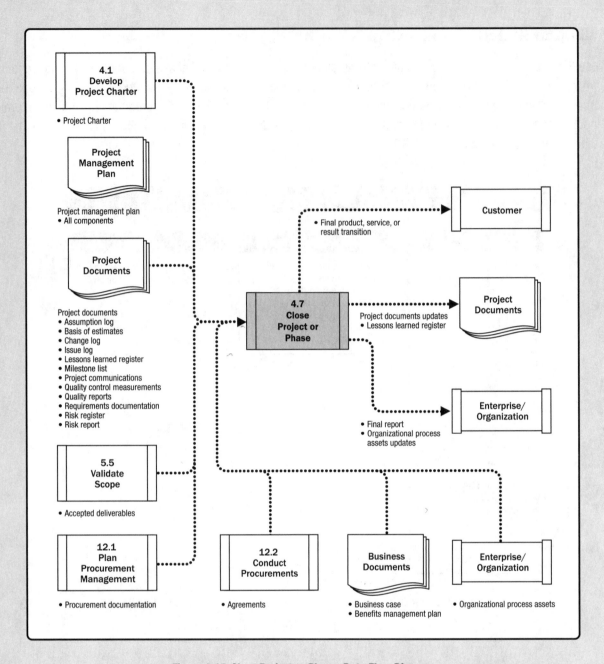

**Figure 4-15. Close Project or Phase: Data Flow Diagram**

When closing the project, the project manager reviews the project management plan to ensure that all project work is completed and that the project has met its objectives. The activities necessary for the administrative closure of the project or phase include but are not limited to:

◆ Actions and activities necessary to satisfy completion or exit criteria for the phase or project such as:

■ Making certain that all documents and deliverables are up-to-date and that all issues are resolved;

■ Confirming the delivery and formal acceptance of deliverables by the customer;

■ Ensuring that all costs are charged to the project;

■ Closing project accounts;

■ Reassigning personnel;

■ Dealing with excess project material;

■ Reallocating project facilities, equipment, and other resources; and

■ Elaborating the final project reports as required by organizational policies.

◆ Activities related to the completion of the contractual agreements applicable to the project or project phase such as:

■ Confirming the formal acceptance of the seller's work,

■ Finalizing open claims,

■ Updating records to reflect final results, and

■ Archiving such information for future use.

◆ Activities needed to:

■ Collect project or phase records,

■ Audit project success or failure,

■ Manage knowledge sharing and transfer,

■ Identify lessons learned, and

■ Archive project information for future use by the organization.

◆ Actions and activities necessary to transfer the project's products, services, or results to the next phase or to production and/or operations.

◆ Collecting any suggestions for improving or updating the policies and procedures of the organization, and sending them to the appropriate organizational unit.

◆ Measuring stakeholder satisfaction.

The Close Project or Phase process also establishes the procedures to investigate and document the reasons for actions taken if a project is terminated before completion. In order to successfully achieve this, the project manager needs to engage all the proper stakeholders in the process.

### 4.7.1 CLOSE PROJECT OR PHASE: INPUTS

#### 4.7.1.1 PROJECT CHARTER

Described in Section 4.1.3.1. The project charter documents the project success criteria, the approval requirements, and who will sign off on the project.

#### 4.7.1.2 PROJECT MANAGEMENT PLAN

Described in Section 4.2.3.1. All components of the project management plan are an input to this process.

#### 4.7.1.3 PROJECT DOCUMENTS

Project documents that may be inputs for this process include but are not limited to:

◆ **Assumption log.** Described in Section 4.1.3.2. The assumption log has a record of all the assumptions and constraints that guided the technical specifications, estimates, schedule, risks, etc.

◆ **Basis of estimates.** Described in Sections 6.4.3.2 and 7.2.3.2. The basis of estimates is used to evaluate how the estimation of durations, cost, resources, and cost control compared to the actual results.

◆ **Change log.** Described in Section 4.6.3.3. The change log contains the status of all change requests throughout the project or phase.

◆ **Issue log.** Described in Section 4.3.3.3. The issue log is used to check that there is no open issue.

◆ **Lessons learned register.** Described in Section 4.4.3.1. The lessons learned in the phase or project will be finalized before being entered into the lessons learned repository.

◆ **Milestone list.** Described in Section 6.2.3.3. The milestone list shows the final dates on which the project milestones have been accomplished.

◆ **Project communications.** Described in Section 10.2.3.1. Project communications include any and all communications that have been created throughout the project.

◆ **Quality control measurements.** Described in Section 8.3.3.1. The quality control measurements document the results of Control Quality activities and demonstrate compliance with the quality requirements.

◆ **Quality reports.** Described in Section 8.2.3.1. The information presented in the quality report may include all quality assurance issues managed or escalated by the team, recommendations for improvement, and the summary of findings from the Control Quality process.

◆ **Requirements documentation.** Described in Section 5.2.3.1. Requirements documentation is used to demonstrate compliance with the project scope.

- ◆ **Risk register.** Described in Section 11.2.3.1. The risk register provides information on risks that have occurred throughout the project.

- ◆ **Risk report.** Described in Section 11.2.3.2. The risk report provides information on the risk status and is used to check that there are no open risks at the end of the project.

### 4.7.1.4 ACCEPTED DELIVERABLES

Described in Section 5.5.3.1. Accepted deliverables may include approved product specifications, delivery receipts, and work performance documents. Partial or interim deliverables may also be included for phased or cancelled projects.

### 4.7.1.5 BUSINESS DOCUMENTS

Described in Section 1.2.6. Business documents include but are not limited to:

- ◆ **Business case.** The business case documents the business need and the cost benefit analysis that justify the project.

- ◆ **Benefits management plan.** The benefits management plan outlines the target benefits of the project.

The business case is used to determine if the expected outcomes from the economic feasibility study used to justify the project occurred. The benefits management plan is used to measure whether the benefits of the project were achieved as planned.

### 4.7.1.6 AGREEMENTS

Described in Section 12.2.3.2. The requirements for formal procurement closure are usually defined in the terms and conditions of the contract and are included in the procurement management plan. A complex project may involve managing multiple contracts simultaneously or in sequence.

### 4.7.1.7 PROCUREMENT DOCUMENTATION

Described in Section 12.3.1.4. To close the contract, all procurement documentation is collected, indexed, and filed. Information on contract schedule, scope, quality, and cost performance along with all contract change documentation, payment records, and inspection results are cataloged. "As-built" plans/drawing or "as-developed" documents, manuals, troubleshooting, and other technical documentation should also be considered as part of the procurement documentation when closing a project. This information can be used for lessons learned information and as a basis for evaluating contractors for future contracts.

### 4.7.1.8 ORGANIZATIONAL PROCESS ASSETS

The organizational process assets that can influence the Close Project or Phase process include but are not limited to:

◆ Project or phase closure guidelines or requirements (e.g., lessons learned, final project audits, project evaluations, product validations, acceptance criteria, contract closure, resource reassignment, team performance appraisals, and knowledge transfer).

◆ Configuration management knowledge base containing the versions and baselines of all official organizational standards, policies, procedures, and any project documents.

## 4.7.2 CLOSE PROJECT OR PHASE: TOOLS AND TECHNIQUES

### 4.7.2.1 EXPERT JUDGMENT

Described in Section 4.1.2.1. Expertise should be considered from individuals or groups with specialized knowledge or training in the following topics:

◆ Management control,

◆ Audit,

◆ Legal and procurement, and

◆ Legislation and regulations.

### 4.7.2.2 DATA ANALYSIS

Data analysis techniques that can be used in project closeout include but are not limited to:

◆ **Document analysis.** Described in Section 5.2.2.3. Assessing available documentation will allow identifying lessons learned and knowledge sharing for future projects and organizational assets improvement.

◆ **Regression analysis.** This technique analyzes the interrelationships between different project variables that contributed to the project outcomes to improve performance on future projects.

◆ **Trend analysis.** Described in Section 4.5.2.2. Trend analysis can be used to validate the models used in the organization and to implement adjustments for future projects.

◆ **Variance analysis.** Described in Section 4.5.2.2. Variance analysis can be used to improve the metrics of the organization by comparing what was initially planned and the end result.

### 4.7.2.3 MEETINGS

Meetings are used to confirm that the deliverables have been accepted, to validate that the exit criteria have been met, to formalize the completion of the contracts, to evaluate the satisfaction of the stakeholders, to gather lessons learned, to transfer knowledge and information from the project, and to celebrate success. Attendees may include project team members and other stakeholders involved in or affected by the project. Meetings may be face-to-face, virtual, formal, or informal. Types of meetings include but are not limited to close-out reporting meetings, customer wrap-up meetings, lessons learned meetings, and celebration meetings.

## 4.7.3 CLOSE PROJECT OR PHASE: OUTPUTS

### 4.7.3.1 PROJECT DOCUMENTS UPDATES

All project documents may be updated and marked as final versions as a result of project closure. Of particular interest is the lessons learned register, which is finalized to include final information on phase or project closure. The final lessons learned register may include information on benefits management, accuracy of the business case, project and development life cycles, risk and issue management, stakeholder engagement, and other project management processes.

### 4.7.3.2 FINAL PRODUCT, SERVICE, OR RESULT TRANSITION

A product, service, or result, once delivered by the project, may be handed over to a different group or organization that will operate, maintain, and support it throughout its life cycle.

This output refers to this transition of the final product, service, or result that the project was authorized to produce (or in the case of phase closure, the intermediate product, service, or result of that phase) from one team to another.

### 4.7.3.3 FINAL REPORT

The final report provides a summary of the project performance. It can include information such as:

◆ Summary level description of the project or phase.

◆ Scope objectives, the criteria used to evaluate the scope, and evidence that the completion criteria were met.

◆ Quality objectives, the criteria used to evaluate the project and product quality, the verification and actual milestone delivery dates, and reasons for variances.

◆ Cost objectives, including the acceptable cost range, actual costs, and reasons for any variances.

◆ Summary of the validation information for the final product, service, or result.

◆ Schedule objectives including whether results achieved the benefits that the project was undertaken to address. If the benefits are not met at the close of the project, indicate the degree to which they were achieved and estimate for future benefits realization.

◆ Summary of how the final product, service, or result achieved the business needs identified in the business plan. If the business needs are not met at the close of the project, indicate the degree to which they were achieved and estimate for when the business needs will be met in the future.

◆ Summary of any risks or issues encountered on the project and how they were addressed.

### 4.7.3.4 ORGANIZATIONAL PROCESS ASSET UPDATES

Organizational process assets that are updated include but are not limited to:

◆ **Project documents.** Documentation resulting from the project's activities; for example, project management plan; scope, cost, schedule, and project calendars; and change management documentation.

◆ **Operational and support documents.** Documents required for an organization to maintain, operate, and support the product or service delivered by the project. These may be new documents or updates to existing documents.

◆ **Project or phase closure documents.** Project or phase closure documents, consisting of formal documentation that indicates completion of the project or phase and the transfer of the completed project or phase deliverables to others, such as an operations group or to the next phase. During project closure, the project manager reviews prior phase documentation, customer acceptance documentation from the Validate Scope process (Section 5.5), and the agreement (if applicable) to ensure that all project requirements are completed prior to finalizing the closure of the project. If the project was terminated prior to completion, the formal documentation indicates why the project was terminated and formalizes the procedures for the transfer of the finished and unfinished deliverables of the cancelled project to others.

◆ **Lessons learned repository.** Lessons learned and knowledge gained throughout the project are transferred to the lessons learned repository for use by future projects.

# 5

## PROJECT SCOPE MANAGEMENT

Project Scope Management includes the processes required to ensure that the project includes all the work required, and only the work required, to complete the project successfully. Managing the project scope is primarily concerned with defining and controlling what is and is not included in the project.

The Project Scope Management processes are:

**5.1 Plan Scope Management**—The process of creating a scope management plan that documents how the project and product scope will be defined, validated, and controlled.

**5.2 Collect Requirements**—The process of determining, documenting, and managing stakeholder needs and requirements to meet project objectives.

**5.3 Define Scope**—The process of developing a detailed description of the project and product.

**5.4 Create WBS**—The process of subdividing project deliverables and project work into smaller, more manageable components.

**5.5 Validate Scope**—The process of formalizing acceptance of the completed project deliverables.

**5.6 Control Scope**—The process of monitoring the status of the project and product scope and managing changes to the scope baseline.

Figure 5-1 provides an overview of the Project Scope Management processes. The Project Scope Management processes are presented as discrete processes with defined interfaces while, in practice, they overlap and interact in ways that cannot be completely detailed in the *PMBOK® Guide*.

**Project Scope Management Overview**

## 5.1 Plan Scope Management

.1 Inputs
  .1 Project charter
  .2 Project management plan
  .3 Enterprise environmental factors
  .4 Organizational process assets

.2 Tools & Techniques
  .1 Expert judgment
  .2 Data analysis
  .3 Meetings

.3 Outputs
  .1 Scope management plan
  .2 Requirements management plan

## 5.2 Collect Requirements

.1 Inputs
  .1 Project charter
  .2 Project management plan
  .3 Project documents
  .4 Business documents
  .5 Agreements
  .6 Enterprise environmental factors
  .7 Organizational process assets

.2 Tools & Techniques
  .1 Expert judgment
  .2 Data gathering
  .3 Data analysis
  .4 Decision making
  .5 Data representation
  .6 Interpersonal and team skills
  .7 Context diagram
  .8 Prototypes

.3 Outputs
  .1 Requirements documentation
  .2 Requirements traceability matrix

## 5.3 Define Scope

.1 Inputs
  .1 Project charter
  .2 Project management plan
  .3 Project documents
  .4 Enterprise environmental factors
  .5 Organizational process assets

.2 Tools & Techniques
  .1 Expert judgment
  .2 Data analysis
  .3 Decision making
  .4 Interpersonal and team skills
  .5 Product analysis

.3 Outputs
  .1 Project scope statement
  .2 Project documents updates

## 5.4 Create WBS

.1 Inputs
  .1 Project management plan
  .2 Project documents
  .3 Enterprise environmental factors
  .4 Organizational process assets

.2 Tools & Techniques
  .1 Expert judgment
  .2 Decomposition

.3 Outputs
  .1 Scope baseline
  .2 Project documents updates

## 5.5 Validate Scope

.1 Inputs
  .1 Project management plan
  .2 Project documents
  .3 Verified deliverables
  .4 Work performance data

.2 Tools & Techniques
  .1 Inspection
  .2 Decision making

.3 Outputs
  .1 Accepted deliverables
  .2 Work performance information
  .3 Change requests
  .4 Project documents updates

## 5.6 Control Scope

.1 Inputs
  .1 Project management plan
  .2 Project documents
  .3 Work performance data
  .4 Organizational process assets

.2 Tools & Techniques
  .1 Data analysis

.3 Outputs
  .1 Work performance information
  .2 Change requests
  .3 Project management plan updates
  .4 Project documents updates

**Figure 5-1. Project Scope Management Overview**

# KEY CONCEPTS FOR PROJECT SCOPE MANAGEMENT

In the project context, the term "scope" can refer to:

◆ **Product scope.** The features and functions that characterize a product, service, or result.

◆ **Project scope.** The work performed to deliver a product, service, or result with the specified features and functions. The term "project scope" is sometimes viewed as including product scope.

Project life cycles can range along a continuum from predictive approaches at one end to adaptive or agile approaches at the other. In a predictive life cycle, the project deliverables are defined at the beginning of the project and any changes to the scope are progressively managed. In an adaptive or agile life cycle, the deliverables are developed over multiple iterations where a detailed scope is defined and approved for each iteration when it begins.

Projects with adaptive life cycles are intended to respond to high levels of change and require ongoing stakeholder engagement. The overall scope of an adaptive project will be decomposed into a set of requirements and work to be performed, sometimes referred to as a product backlog. At the beginning of an iteration, the team will work to determine how many of the highest-priority items on the backlog list can be delivered within the next iteration. Three processes (Collect Requirements, Define Scope, and Create WBS) are repeated for each iteration. On the contrary, in a predictive project, these processes are performed toward the beginning of the project and updated as necessary, using the integrated change control process.

In an adaptive or agile life cycle, the sponsor and customer representatives should be continuously engaged with the project to provide feedback on deliverables as they are created and to ensure that the product backlog reflects their current needs. Two processes (Validate Scope and Control Scope) are repeated for each iteration. On the contrary, in a predictive project, Validate Scope occurs with each deliverable or phase review and Control Scope is an ongoing process.

In predictive projects, the scope baseline for the project is the approved version of the project scope statement, work breakdown structure (WBS), and its associated WBS dictionary. A baseline can be changed only through formal change control procedures and is used as a basis for comparison while performing Validate Scope and Control Scope processes as well as other controlling processes. Projects with adaptive life cycles use backlogs (including product requirements and user stories) to reflect their current needs.

Completion of the project scope is measured against the project management plan, while completion of the product scope is measured against the product requirements. The term "requirement" is defined as a condition or capability that is required to be present in a product, service, or result to satisfy an agreement or other formally imposed specification.

Validate Scope is the process of formalizing acceptance of the completed project deliverables. The verified deliverables obtained from the Control Quality process are an input to the Validate Scope process. One of the outputs of Validate Scope is accepted deliverables that are formally signed off and approved by the authorized stakeholder. Therefore, the stakeholder needs to get involved early on during planning (sometimes initiating as well) and to provide inputs about quality of deliverables so that Control Quality can assess the performance and recommend necessary changes.

## TRENDS AND EMERGING PRACTICES IN PROJECT SCOPE MANAGEMENT

Requirements have always been a concern in project management and have continued to gain more attention in the profession. As the global environment becomes more complex, organizations are starting to recognize how to use business analysis to their competitive advantage by defining, managing, and controlling requirements activities. Activities of business analysis may start before a project is initiated and a project manager is assigned. According to *Requirements Management: A Practice Guide* [14], the requirements management process starts with a needs assessment, which may begin in portfolio planning, in program planning, or within a discrete project.

Eliciting, documenting, and managing stakeholder requirements takes place within the Project Scope Management processes. Trends and emerging practices for Project Scope Management include but are not limited to a focus on collaborating with business analysis professionals to:

◆ Determine problems and identify business needs;

◆ Identify and recommend viable solutions for meeting those needs;

◆ Elicit, document, and manage stakeholder requirements in order to meet business and project objectives; and

◆ Facilitate the successful implementation of the product, service, or end result of the program or project [7].

The process ends with the requirements closure, which transitions the product, service, or result to the recipient in order to measure, monitor, realize, and sustain benefits over time.

The role with responsibility to conduct business analysis should be assigned to resources with sufficient business analysis skills and expertise. If a business analyst is assigned to a project, requirement-related activities are the responsibility of that role. The project manager is responsible for ensuring that requirements-related work is accounted for in the project management plan and that requirements-related activities are performed on time and within budget and deliver value.

The relationship between a project manager and a business analyst should be a collaborative partnership. A project will have a higher likelihood of being successful if project managers and business analysts fully understand each other's roles and responsibilities to successfully achieve project objectives.

## TAILORING CONSIDERATIONS

Because each project is unique, the project manager will need to tailor the way Project Scope Management processes are applied. Considerations for tailoring include but are not limited to:

◆ **Knowledge and requirements management.** Does the organization have formal or informal knowledge and requirements management systems? What guidelines should the project manager establish for requirements to be reused in the future?

◆ **Validation and control.** Does the organization have existing formal or informal validation and control-related policies, procedures, and guidelines?

◆ **Development approach.** Does the organization use agile approaches in managing projects? Is the development approach iterative or incremental? Is a predictive approach used? Will a hybrid approach be productive?

◆ **Stability of requirements.** Are there areas of the project with unstable requirements? Do unstable requirements necessitate the use of lean, agile, or other adaptive techniques until they are stable and well defined?

◆ **Governance.** Does the organization have formal or informal audit and governance policies, procedures, and guidelines?

## CONSIDERATIONS FOR AGILE/ADAPTIVE ENVIRONMENTS

In projects with evolving requirements, high risk, or significant uncertainty, the scope is often not understood at the beginning of the project or it evolves during the project. Agile methods deliberately spend less time trying to define and agree on scope in the early stage of the project and spend more time establishing the process for its ongoing discovery and refinement. Many environments with emerging requirements find that there is often a gap between the real business requirements and the business requirements that were originally stated. Therefore, agile methods purposefully build and review prototypes and release versions in order to refine the requirements. As a result, scope is defined and redefined throughout the project. In agile approaches, the requirements constitute the backlog.

# 5.1 PLAN SCOPE MANAGEMENT

Plan Scope Management is the process of creating a scope management plan that documents how the project and product scope will be defined, validated, and controlled. The key benefit of this process is that it provides guidance and direction on how scope will be managed throughout the project. This process is performed once or at predefined points in the project. The inputs, tools and techniques, and outputs of this process are depicted in Figure 5-2. Figure 5-3 depicts the data flow diagram of the process.

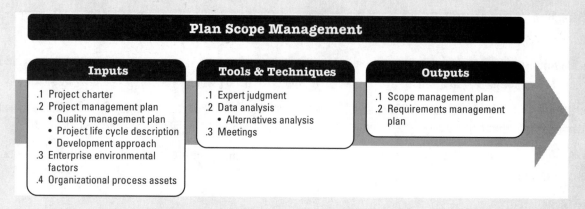

Figure 5-2. Plan Scope Management: Inputs, Tools & Techniques, and Outputs

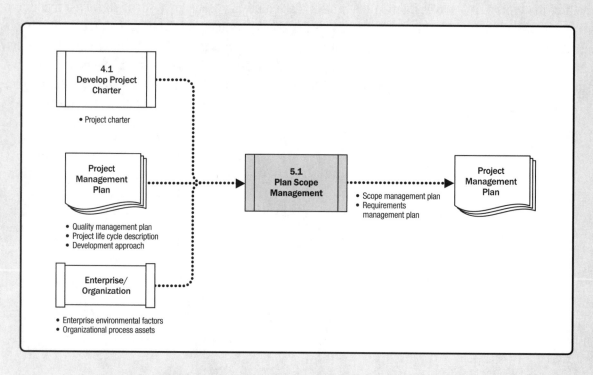

Figure 5-3. Plan Scope Management: Data Flow Diagram

The scope management plan is a component of the project or program management plan that describes how the scope will be defined, developed, monitored, controlled, and validated. The development of the scope management plan and the detailing of the project scope begin with the analysis of information contained in the project charter (Section 4.1.3.1), the latest approved subsidiary plans of the project management plan (Section 4.2.3.1), historical information contained in the organizational process assets (Section 2.3), and any other relevant enterprise environmental factors (Section 2.2).

## 5.1.1 PLAN SCOPE MANAGEMENT: INPUTS

### 5.1.1.1 PROJECT CHARTER

Described in Section 4.1.3.1. The project charter documents the project purpose, high-level project description, assumptions, constraints, and high-level requirements that the project is intended to satisfy.

### 5.1.1.2 PROJECT MANAGEMENT PLAN

Described in Section 4.2.3.1. Project management plan components include but are not limited to:

◆ **Quality management plan.** Described in Section 8.1.3.1. The way the project and product scope will be managed can be influenced by how the organization's quality policy, methodologies, and standards are implemented on the project.

◆ **Project life cycle description.** The project life cycle determines the series of phases that a project passes through from its inception to the end of the project.

◆ **Development approach.** The development approach defines whether waterfall, iterative, adaptive, agile, or a hybrid development approach will be used.

### 5.1.1.3 ENTERPRISE ENVIRONMENTAL FACTORS

The enterprise environmental factors that can influence the Plan Scope Management process include but are not limited to:

◆ Organization's culture,

◆ Infrastructure,

◆ Personnel administration, and

◆ Marketplace conditions.

### 5.1.1.4 ORGANIZATIONAL PROCESS ASSETS

The organizational process assets that can influence the Plan Scope Management process include but are not limited to:

◆ Policies and procedures, and

◆ Historical information and lessons learned repositories.

## 5.1.2 PLAN SCOPE MANAGEMENT: TOOLS AND TECHNIQUES

### 5.1.2.1 EXPERT JUDGMENT

Described in Section 4.1.2.1 Expertise should be considered from individuals or groups with specialized knowledge or training in the following topics:

◆ Previous similar projects, and

◆ Information in the industry, discipline, and application area.

### 5.1.2.2 DATA ANALYSIS

A data analysis technique that can be used for this process includes but is not limited to alternatives analysis. Various ways of collecting requirements, elaborating the project and product scope, creating the product, validating the scope, and controlling the scope are evaluated.

### 5.1.2.3 MEETINGS

Project teams may attend project meetings to develop the scope management plan. Attendees may include the project manager, the project sponsor, selected project team members, selected stakeholders, anyone with responsibility for any of the scope management processes, and others as needed.

## 5.1.3 PLAN SCOPE MANAGEMENT: OUTPUTS

### 5.1.3.1 SCOPE MANAGEMENT PLAN

The scope management plan is a component of the project management plan that describes how the scope will be defined, developed, monitored, controlled, and validated. The components of a scope management plan include:

◆ Process for preparing a project scope statement;

◆ Process that enables the creation of the WBS from the detailed project scope statement;

◆ Process that establishes how the scope baseline will be approved and maintained; and

◆ Process that specifies how formal acceptance of the completed project deliverables will be obtained.

The scope management plan can be formal or informal, broadly framed or highly detailed, based on the needs of the project.

### 5.1.3.2 REQUIREMENTS MANAGEMENT PLAN

The requirements management plan is a component of the project management plan that describes how project and product requirements will be analyzed, documented, and managed. According to *Business Analysis for Practitioners: A Practice Guide* [7], some organizations refer to it as a business analysis plan. Components of the requirements management plan can include but are not limited to:

◆ How requirements activities will be planned, tracked, and reported;

◆ Configuration management activities such as: how changes will be initiated; how impacts will be analyzed; how they will be traced, tracked, and reported; as well as the authorization levels required to approve these changes;

◆ Requirements prioritization process;

◆ Metrics that will be used and the rationale for using them; and

◆ Traceability structure that reflects the requirement attributes captured on the traceability matrix.

## 5.2 COLLECT REQUIREMENTS

Collect Requirements is the process of determining, documenting, and managing stakeholder needs and requirements to meet objectives. The key benefit of this process is that it provides the basis for defining the product scope and project scope. This process is performed once or at predefined points in the project. The inputs, tools and techniques, and outputs of this process are depicted in Figure 5-4. Figure 5-5 depicts the data flow diagram of the process.

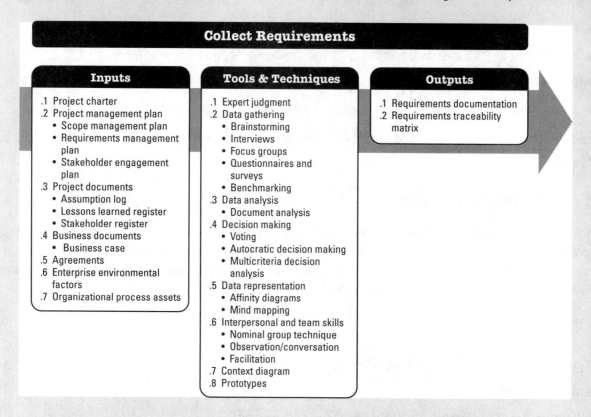

**Figure 5-4. Collect Requirements: Inputs, Tools & Techniques, and Outputs**

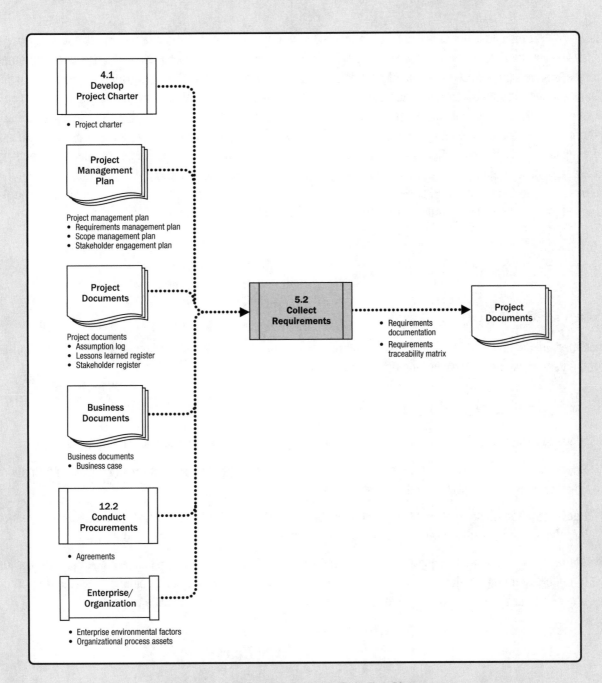

**Figure 5-5. Collect Requirements: Data Flow Diagram**

The *PMBOK® Guide* does not specifically address product requirements since those are industry specific. Note that *Business Analysis for Practitioners: A Practice Guide* [7] provides more in-depth information about product requirements. The project's success is directly influenced by active stakeholder involvement in the discovery and decomposition of needs into project and product requirements and by the care taken in determining, documenting, and managing the requirements of the product, service, or result of the project. Requirements include conditions or capabilities that are required to be present in a product, service, or result to satisfy an agreement or other formally imposed specification. Requirements include the quantified and documented needs and expectations of the sponsor, customer, and other stakeholders. These requirements need to be elicited, analyzed, and recorded in enough detail to be included in the scope baseline and to be measured once project execution begins. Requirements become the foundation of the WBS. Cost, schedule, quality planning, and procurement are all based on these requirements.

## 5.2.1 COLLECT REQUIREMENTS: INPUTS

### 5.2.1.1 PROJECT CHARTER

Described in Section 4.1.3.1. The project charter documents the high-level project description and high-level requirements that will be used to develop detailed requirements.

### 5.2.1.2 PROJECT MANAGEMENT PLAN

Described in Section 4.2.3.1. Project management plan components include but are not limited to:

◆ **Scope management plan.** Described in Section 5.1.3.1. The scope management plan contains information on how the project scope will be defined and developed.

◆ **Requirements management plan.** Described in Section 5.1.3.2. The requirements management plan has information on how project requirements will be collected, analyzed, and documented.

◆ **Stakeholder engagement plan.** Described in Section 13.2.3.1. The stakeholder engagement plan is used to understand stakeholder communication requirements and the level of stakeholder engagement in order to assess and adapt to the level of stakeholder participation in requirements activities.

### 5.2.1.3 PROJECT DOCUMENTS

Examples of project documents that can be considered as inputs for this process include but are not limited to:

◆ **Assumption Log.** Described in Section 4.1.3.2. The assumption log identified assumptions about the product, project, environment, stakeholders, and other factors that can influence requirements.

◆ **Lessons learned register.** Described in Section 4.4.3.1. The lessons learned register is used to provide information on effective requirements collection techniques, especially for projects that are using an iterative or adaptive product development methodology.

◆ **Stakeholder Register.** Described in Section 13.1.3.1. The stakeholder register is used to identify stakeholders who can provide information on the requirements. It also captures requirements and expectations that stakeholders have for the project.

### 5.2.1.4 BUSINESS DOCUMENTS

Described in Section 1.2.6. A business document that can influence the Collect Requirements process is the business case, which can describe required, desired, and optional criteria for meeting the business needs.

### 5.2.1.5 AGREEMENTS

Described in Section 12.2.3.2. Agreements can contain project and product requirements.

### 5.2.1.6 ENTERPRISE ENVIRONMENTAL FACTORS

The enterprise environmental factors that can influence the Collect Requirements process include but are not limited to:

◆ Organization's culture,

◆ Infrastructure,

◆ Personnel administration, and

◆ Marketplace conditions.

### 5.2.1.7 ORGANIZATIONAL PROCESS ASSETS

The organizational process assets that can influence the Collect Requirements process include but are not limited to:

◆ Policies and procedures, and

◆ Historical information and lessons learned repository with information from previous projects.

## 5.2.2 COLLECT REQUIREMENTS: TOOLS AND TECHNIQUES

### 5.2.2.1 EXPERT JUDGMENT

Described in Section 4.1.2.1. Expertise should be considered from individuals or groups with specialized knowledge or training in the following topics:

- ◆ Business analysis,
- ◆ Requirements elicitation,
- ◆ Requirements analysis,
- ◆ Requirements documentation,
- ◆ Project requirements in previous similar projects,
- ◆ Diagramming techniques,
- ◆ Facilitation, and
- ◆ Conflict management.

### 5.2.2.2 DATA GATHERING

Data-gathering techniques that can be used for this process include but are not limited to:

- ◆ **Brainstorming.** Described in Section 4.1.2.2. Brainstorming is a technique used to generate and collect multiple ideas related to project and product requirements.

- ◆ **Interviews.** An interview is a formal or informal approach to elicit information from stakeholders by talking to them directly. It is typically performed by asking prepared and spontaneous questions and recording the responses. Interviews are often conducted on an individual basis between an interviewer and an interviewee, but may involve multiple interviewers and/or multiple interviewees. Interviewing experienced project participants, sponsors, other executives, and subject matter experts can aid in identifying and defining the features and functions of the desired product deliverables. Interviews are also useful for obtaining confidential information.

- ◆ **Focus groups.** Focus groups bring together prequalified stakeholders and subject matter experts to learn about their expectations and attitudes about a proposed product, service, or result. A trained moderator guides the group through an interactive discussion designed to be more conversational than a one-on-one interview.

- ◆ **Questionnaires and surveys.** Questionnaires and surveys are written sets of questions designed to quickly accumulate information from a large number of respondents. Questionnaires and/or surveys are most appropriate with varied audiences, when a quick turnaround is needed, when respondents are geographically dispersed, and where statistical analysis could be appropriate.

- ◆ **Benchmarking.** Described in Section 8.1.2.2. Benchmarking involves comparing actual or planned products, processes, and practices to those of comparable organizations to identify best practices, generate ideas for improvement, and provide a basis for measuring performance. The organizations compared during benchmarking can be internal or external.

## 5.2.2.3 DATA ANALYSIS

Described in Section 4.5.2.2. Data analysis techniques that can be used for this process include but are not limited to document analysis. Document analysis consists of reviewing and assessing any relevant documented information. In this process, document analysis is used to elicit requirements by analyzing existing documentation and identifying information relevant to the requirements. There is a wide range of documents that may be analyzed to help elicit relevant requirements. Examples of documents that may be analyzed include but are not limited to:

- ◆ Agreements;

- ◆ Business plans;

- ◆ Business process or interface documentation;

- ◆ Business rules repositories;

- ◆ Current process flows;

- ◆ Marketing literature;

- ◆ Problem/issue logs;

- ◆ Policies and procedures;

- ◆ Regulatory documentation such as laws, codes, or ordinances, etc.;

- ◆ Requests for proposal; and

- ◆ Use cases.

## 5.2.2.4 DECISION MAKING

Decision-making techniques that can be used in the Collect Requirements process include but are not limited to:

◆ **Voting.** Voting is a collective decision-making technique and an assessment process having multiple alternatives with an expected outcome in the form of future actions. These techniques can be used to generate, classify, and prioritize product requirements. Examples of voting techniques include:

- *Unanimity.* A decision that is reached whereby everyone agrees on a single course of action.

- *Majority.* A decision that is reached with support obtained from more than 50% of the members of the group. Having a group size with an uneven number of participants can ensure that a decision will be reached, rather than resulting in a tie.

- *Plurality.* A decision that is reached whereby the largest block in a group decides, even if a majority is not achieved. This method is generally used when the number of options nominated is more than two.

◆ **Autocratic decision making.** In this method, one individual takes responsibility for making the decision for the group.

◆ **Multicriteria decision analysis.** A technique that uses a decision matrix to provide a systematic analytical approach for establishing criteria, such as risk levels, uncertainty, and valuation, to evaluate and rank many ideas.

## 5.2.2.5 DATA REPRESENTATION

Data representation techniques that can be used for this process include but are not limited to:

◆ **Affinity diagrams.** Affinity diagrams allow large numbers of ideas to be classified into groups for review and analysis.

◆ **Mind mapping.** Mind mapping consolidates ideas created through individual brainstorming sessions into a single map to reflect commonality and differences in understanding and to generate new ideas.

## 5.2.2.6 INTERPERSONAL AND TEAM SKILLS

Described in Section 4.1.2.3. The interpersonal and team skills that can be used in this process include but are not limited to:

◆ **Nominal group technique.** The nominal group technique enhances brainstorming with a voting process used to rank the most useful ideas for further brainstorming or for prioritization. The nominal group technique is a structured form of brainstorming consisting of four steps:

- A question or problem is posed to the group. Each person silently generates and writes down their ideas.

- The moderator writes down the ideas on a flip chart until all ideas are recorded.

- Each recorded idea is discussed until all group members have a clear understanding.

- Individuals vote privately to prioritize the ideas, usually using a scale of 1 – 5, with 1 being the lowest and 5 being the highest. Voting may take place in many rounds to reduce and focus in on ideas. After each round, the votes are tallied and the highest scoring ideas are selected.

◆ **Observation/conversation.** Observation and conversation provide a direct way of viewing individuals in their environment and how they perform their jobs or tasks and carry out processes. It is particularly helpful for detailed processes when the people who use the product have difficulty or are reluctant to articulate their requirements. Observation is also known as "job shadowing." It is usually done externally by an observer viewing a business expert performing a job. It can also be done by a "participant observer" who actually performs a process or procedure to experience how it is done to uncover hidden requirements.

◆ **Facilitation.** Described in Section 4.1.2.3. Facilitation is used with focused sessions that bring key stakeholders together to define product requirements. Workshops can be used to quickly define cross-functional requirements and reconcile stakeholder differences. Because of their interactive group nature, well-facilitated sessions can build trust, foster relationships, and improve communication among the participants, which can lead to increased stakeholder consensus. In addition, issues can be discovered earlier and resolved more quickly than in individual sessions.

Facilitation skills are used in the following situations, but are not limited to:

- *Joint application design/development (JAD).* JAD sessions are used in the software development industry. These facilitated sessions focus on bringing business subject matter experts and the development team together to gather requirements and improve the software development process.

- *Quality function deployment (QFD).* In the manufacturing industry, QFD is another facilitation technique that helps determine critical characteristics for new product development. QFD starts by collecting customer needs, also known as voice of the customer (VOC). These needs are then objectively sorted and prioritized, and goals are set for achieving them.

- *User stories.* User stories, which are short, textual descriptions of required functionality, are often developed during a requirements workshop. User stories describe the stakeholder role, who benefits from the feature (role), what the stakeholder needs to accomplish (goal), and the benefit to the stakeholder (motivation).

## 5.2.2.7 CONTEXT DIAGRAM

The context diagram is an example of a scope model. Context diagrams visually depict the product scope by showing a business system (process, equipment, computer system, etc.), and how people and other systems (actors) interact with it (see Figure 5-6). Context diagrams show inputs to the business system, the actor(s) providing the input, the outputs from the business system, and the actor(s) receiving the output.

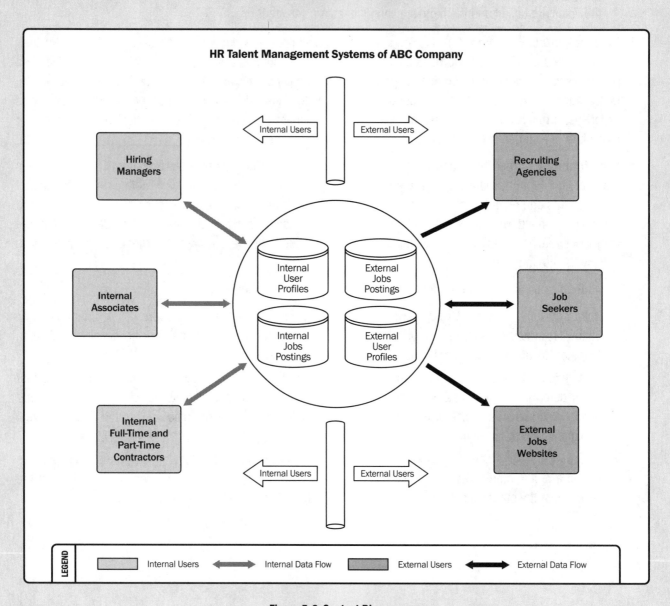

**Figure 5-6. Context Diagram**

## 5.2.2.8 PROTOTYPES

Prototyping is a method of obtaining early feedback on requirements by providing a model of the expected product before actually building it. Examples of prototypes are small-scale products, computer generated 2D and 3D models, mock-ups, or simulations. Prototypes allow stakeholders to experiment with a model of the final product rather than being limited to discussing abstract representations of their requirements. Prototypes support the concept of progressive elaboration in iterative cycles of mock-up creation, user experimentation, feedback generation, and prototype revision. When enough feedback cycles have been performed, the requirements obtained from the prototype are sufficiently complete to move to a design or build phase.

Storyboarding is a prototyping technique showing sequence or navigation through a series of images or illustrations. Storyboards are used on a variety of projects in a variety of industries, such as film, advertising, instructional design, and on agile and other software development projects. In software development, storyboards use mock-ups to show navigation paths through web pages, screens, or other user interfaces.

## 5.2.3 COLLECT REQUIREMENTS: OUTPUTS

### 5.2.3.1 REQUIREMENTS DOCUMENTATION

Requirements documentation describes how individual requirements meet the business need for the project. Requirements may start out at a high level and become progressively more detailed as more information about the requirements is known. Before being baselined, requirements need to be unambiguous (measurable and testable), traceable, complete, consistent, and acceptable to key stakeholders. The format of the requirements document may range from a simple document listing all the requirements categorized by stakeholder and priority, to more elaborate forms containing an executive summary, detailed descriptions, and attachments.

Many organizations categorize requirements into different types, such as business and technical solutions, the former referring to stakeholder needs and the latter as to how those needs will be implemented. Requirements can be grouped into classifications allowing for further refinement and detail as the requirements are elaborated. These classifications include:

◆ **Business requirements.** These describe the higher-level needs of the organization as a whole, such as the business issues or opportunities, and reasons why a project has been undertaken.

◆ **Stakeholder requirements.** These describe needs of a stakeholder or stakeholder group.

◆ **Solution requirements.** These describe features, functions, and characteristics of the product, service, or result that will meet the business and stakeholder requirements. Solution requirements are further grouped into functional and nonfunctional requirements:

  ■ *Functional requirements.* Functional requirements describe the behaviors of the product. Examples include actions, processes, data, and interactions that the product should execute.

  ■ *Nonfunctional requirements.* Nonfunctional requirements supplement functional requirements and describe the environmental conditions or qualities required for the product to be effective. Examples include: reliability, security, performance, safety, level of service, supportability, retention/purge, etc.

◆ **Transition and readiness requirements.** These describe temporary capabilities, such as data conversion and training requirements, needed to transition from the current as-is state to the desired future state.

◆ **Project requirements.** These describe the actions, processes, or other conditions the project needs to meet. Examples include milestone dates, contractual obligations, constraints, etc.

◆ **Quality requirements.** These capture any condition or criteria needed to validate the successful completion of a project deliverable or fulfillment of other project requirements. Examples include tests, certifications, validations, etc.

## 5.2.3.2 REQUIREMENTS TRACEABILITY MATRIX

The requirements traceability matrix is a grid that links product requirements from their origin to the deliverables that satisfy them. The implementation of a requirements traceability matrix helps ensure that each requirement adds business value by linking it to the business and project objectives. It provides a means to track requirements throughout the project life cycle, helping to ensure that requirements approved in the requirements documentation are delivered at the end of the project. Finally, it provides a structure for managing changes to the product scope.

Tracing requirements includes but is not limited to:

◆ Business needs, opportunities, goals, and objectives;

◆ Project objectives;

◆ Project scope and WBS deliverables;

◆ Product design;

◆ Product development;

◆ Test strategy and test scenarios; and

◆ High-level requirements to more detailed requirements.

Attributes associated with each requirement can be recorded in the requirements traceability matrix. These attributes help to define key information about the requirement. Typical attributes used in the requirements traceability matrix may include: a unique identifier, a textual description of the requirement, the rationale for inclusion, owner, source, priority, version, current status (such as active, cancelled, deferred, added, approved, assigned, completed), and status date. Additional attributes to ensure that the requirement has met stakeholders' satisfaction may include stability, complexity, and acceptance criteria. Figure 5-7 provides an example of a requirements traceability matrix with its associated attributes.

| Requirements Traceability Matrix | | | | | | | | |
|---|---|---|---|---|---|---|---|---|
| Project Name: | | | | | | | | |
| Cost Center: | | | | | | | | |
| Project Description: | | | | | | | | |
| ID | Associate ID | Requirements Description | Business Needs, Opportunities, Goals, Objectives | Project Objectives | WBS Deliverables | Product Design | Product Development | Test Cases |
| 001 | 1.0 | | | | | | | |
| | 1.1 | | | | | | | |
| | 1.2 | | | | | | | |
| | 1.2.1 | | | | | | | |
| 002 | 2.0 | | | | | | | |
| | 2.1 | | | | | | | |
| | 2.1.1 | | | | | | | |
| 003 | 3.0 | | | | | | | |
| | 3.1 | | | | | | | |
| | 3.2 | | | | | | | |
| 004 | 4.0 | | | | | | | |
| 005 | 5.0 | | | | | | | |

Figure 5-7. Example of a Requirements Traceability Matrix

## 5.3 DEFINE SCOPE

Define Scope is the process of developing a detailed description of the project and product. The key benefit of this process is that it describes the product, service, or result boundaries and acceptance criteria. This process is performed once or at predefined points in the project. The inputs, tools and techniques, and outputs of this process are depicted in Figure 5-8. Figure 5-9 depicts the data flow diagram of the process.

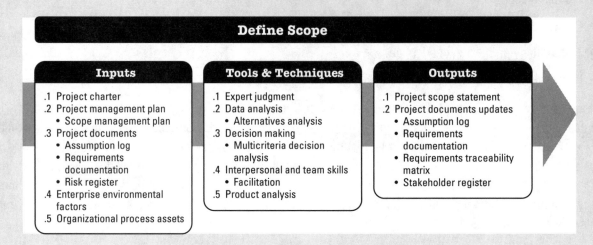

### Define Scope

| Inputs | Tools & Techniques | Outputs |
|---|---|---|
| .1 Project charter<br>.2 Project management plan<br>  • Scope management plan<br>.3 Project documents<br>  • Assumption log<br>  • Requirements<br>    documentation<br>  • Risk register<br>.4 Enterprise environmental<br>   factors<br>.5 Organizational process assets | .1 Expert judgment<br>.2 Data analysis<br>  • Alternatives analysis<br>.3 Decision making<br>  • Multicriteria decision<br>   analysis<br>.4 Interpersonal and team skills<br>  • Facilitation<br>.5 Product analysis | .1 Project scope statement<br>.2 Project documents updates<br>  • Assumption log<br>  • Requirements<br>   documentation<br>  • Requirements traceability<br>   matrix<br>  • Stakeholder register |

**Figure 5-8. Define Scope: Inputs, Tools & Techniques, and Outputs**

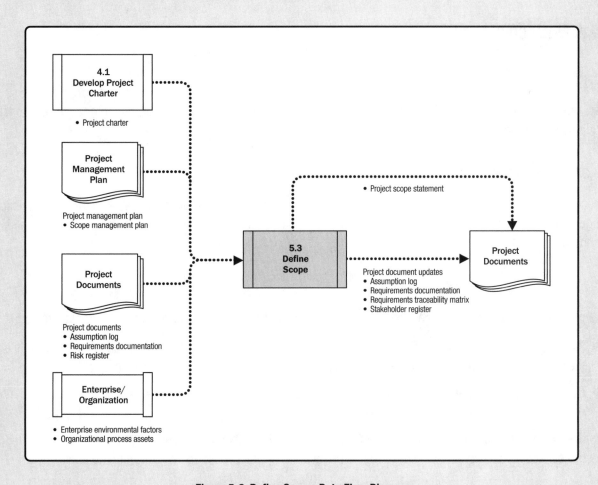

**Figure 5-9. Define Scope: Data Flow Diagram**

Since all the requirements identified in Collect Requirements may not be included in the project, the Define Scope process selects the final project requirements from the requirements documentation developed during the Collect Requirements process. It then develops a detailed description of the project and product, service, or result.

The preparation of a detailed project scope statement builds upon the high-level project description that is documented during project initiation. During project planning, the project scope is defined and described with greater specificity as more information about the project is known. Existing risks, assumptions, and constraints are analyzed for completeness and added or updated as necessary. The Define Scope process can be highly iterative. In iterative life cycle projects, a high-level vision will be developed for the overall project, but the detailed scope is determined one iteration at a time, and the detailed planning for the next iteration is carried out as work progresses on the current project scope and deliverables.

## 5.3.1 DEFINE SCOPE: INPUTS

### 5.3.1.1 PROJECT CHARTER

Described in Section 4.1.3.1. The project charter provides the high-level project description, product characteristics, and approval requirements.

### 5.3.1.2 PROJECT MANAGEMENT PLAN

Described in Section 4.2.3.1. A project management plan component includes but is not limited to the scope management plan as described in Section 5.1.3.1, which documents how the project scope will be defined, validated, and controlled.

### 5.3.1.3 PROJECT DOCUMENTS

Examples of project documents that can be considered as inputs for this process include but are not limited to:

◆ **Assumption log.** Described in Section 4.1.3.2. The assumption log identifies assumptions and constraints about the product, project, environment, stakeholders, and other factors that can influence the project and product scope.

◆ **Requirements documentation.** Described in Section 5.2.3.1. Requirements documentation identifies requirements that will be incorporated into the scope.

◆ **Risk register.** Described in Section 11.2.3.1. The risk register contains response strategies that may affect the project scope, such as reducing or changing project and product scope to avoid or mitigate a risk.

### 5.3.1.4 ENTERPRISE ENVIRONMENTAL FACTORS

The enterprise environmental factors that can influence the Define Scope process include but are not limited to:

◆ Organization's culture,

◆ Infrastructure,

◆ Personnel administration, and

◆ Marketplace conditions.

### 5.3.1.5 ORGANIZATIONAL PROCESS ASSETS

The organizational process assets that can influence the Define Scope process include but are not limited to:

◆ Policies, procedures, and templates for a project scope statement;

◆ Project files from previous projects; and

◆ Lessons learned from previous phases or projects.

## 5.3.2 DEFINE SCOPE: TOOLS AND TECHNIQUES

### 5.3.2.1 EXPERT JUDGMENT

Described in Section 4.1.2.1. Expertise should be considered from individuals or groups with knowledge of or experience with similar projects.

### 5.3.2.2 DATA ANALYSIS

An example of a data analysis technique that can be used in this process includes but is not limited to alternatives analysis. Alternatives analysis can be used to evaluate ways to meet the requirements and the objectives identified in the charter.

### 5.3.2.3 DECISION MAKING

Described in Section 5.2.2.4. A decision-making technique that can be used in this process includes but is not limited to multicriteria decision analysis. Described in Section 8.1.2.4, multicriteria decision analysis is a technique that uses a decision matrix to provide a systematic analytical approach for establishing criteria, such as requirements, schedule, budget, and resources, in order to refine the project and product scope for the project.

### 5.3.2.4 INTERPERSONAL AND TEAM SKILLS

Described in Section 4.1.2.3. An example of an interpersonal and team skills technique is facilitation. Facilitation is used in workshops and working sessions with key stakeholders who have a variety of expectations or fields of expertise. The goal is to reach a cross-functional and common understanding of the project deliverables and project and product boundaries.

### 5.3.2.5 PRODUCT ANALYSIS

Product analysis can be used to define products and services. It includes asking questions about a product or service and forming answers to describe the use, characteristics, and other relevant aspects of what is going to be delivered.

Each application area has one or more generally accepted methods for translating high-level product or service descriptions into meaningful deliverables. Requirements are captured at a high level and decomposed to the level of detail needed to design the final product. Examples of product analysis techniques include but are not limited to:

◆ Product breakdown,

◆ Requirements analysis,

◆ Systems analysis,

◆ Systems engineering,

◆ Value analysis, and

◆ Value engineering.

## 5.3.3 DEFINE SCOPE: OUTPUTS

### 5.3.3.1 PROJECT SCOPE STATEMENT

The project scope statement is the description of the project scope, major deliverables, and exclusions. The project scope statement documents the entire scope, including project and product scope. It describes the project's deliverables in detail. It also provides a common understanding of the project scope among project stakeholders. It may contain explicit scope exclusions that can assist in managing stakeholder expectations. It enables the project team to perform more detailed planning, guides the project team's work during execution, and provides the baseline for evaluating whether requests for changes or additional work are contained within or outside the project's boundaries.

The degree and level of detail to which the project scope statement defines the work that will be performed and the work that is excluded can help determine how well the project management team can control the overall project scope. The detailed project scope statement, either directly or by reference to other documents, includes the following:

◆ **Product scope description.** Progressively elaborates the characteristics of the product, service, or result described in the project charter and requirements documentation.

◆ **Deliverables.** Any unique and verifiable product, result, or capability to perform a service that is required to be produced to complete a process, phase, or project. Deliverables also include ancillary results, such as project management reports and documentation. These deliverables may be described at a summary level or in great detail.

◆ **Acceptance criteria.** A set of conditions that is required to be met before deliverables are accepted.

◆ **Project exclusions.** Identifies what is excluded from the project. Explicitly stating what is out of scope for the project helps manage stakeholders' expectations and can reduce scope creep.

Although the project charter and the project scope statement are sometimes perceived as containing a certain degree of redundancy, they are different in the level of detail contained in each. The project charter contains high-level information, while the project scope statement contains a detailed description of the scope components. These components are progressively elaborated throughout the project. Table 5-1 describes some of the key elements for each document.

**Table 5-1. Elements of the Project Charter and Project Scope Statement**

| Project Charter | Project Scope Statement |
|---|---|
| Project purpose | Project scope description (progressively elaborated) |
| Measurable project objectives and related success criteria | Project deliverables |
| High-level requirements | Acceptance criteria |
| High-level project description, boundaries, and key deliverables | Project exclusions |
| Overall project risk | |
| Summary milestone schedule | |
| Preapproved financial resources | |
| Key stakeholder list | |
| Project approval requirements (i.e., what constitutes success, who decides the project is successful, who signs off on the project) | |
| Project exit criteria (i.e., what are the conditions to be met in order to close or to cancel the project or phase | |
| Assigned project manager, responsibility, and authority level | |
| Name and authority of the sponsor or other person(s) authorizing the project charter | |

## 5.3.3.2 PROJECT DOCUMENTS UPDATES

Project documents that may be updated as a result of carrying out this process include but are not limited to:

◆ **Assumption log.** Described in Section 4.1.3.2. The assumption log is updated with additional assumptions or constraints that were identified during this process.

◆ **Requirements documentation.** Described in Section 5.2.3.1. Requirements documentation may be updated with additional or changed requirements.

◆ **Requirements traceability matrix.** Described in Section 5.2.3.2. The requirements traceability matrix may be updated to reflect updates in requirement documentation.

◆ **Stakeholder register.** Described in Section 13.1.3.1. Where additional information on existing or new stakeholders is gathered as a result of this process, it is recorded in the stakeholder register.

## 5.4 CREATE WBS

Create WBS is the process of subdividing project deliverables and project work into smaller, more manageable components. The key benefit of this process is that it provides a framework of what has to be delivered. This process is performed once or at predefined points in the project. The inputs, tools and techniques, and outputs of this process are depicted in Figure 5-10. Figure 5-11 depicts the data flow diagram of the process.

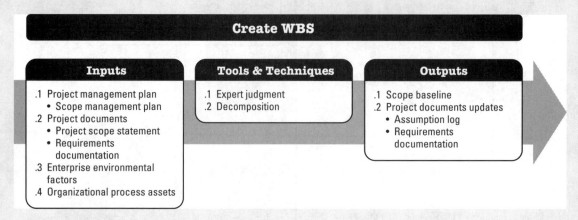

**Figure 5-10. Create WBS: Inputs, Tools & Techniques, and Outputs**

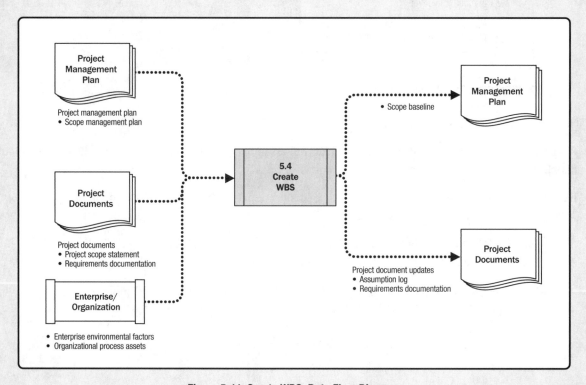

**Figure 5-11. Create WBS: Data Flow Diagram**

The WBS is a hierarchical decomposition of the total scope of work to be carried out by the project team to accomplish the project objectives and create the required deliverables. The WBS organizes and defines the total scope of the project and represents the work specified in the current approved project scope statement.

The planned work is contained within the lowest level of WBS components, which are called work packages. A work package can be used to group the activities where work is scheduled and estimated, monitored, and controlled. In the context of the WBS, work refers to work products or deliverables that are the result of activity and not to the activity itself.

## 5.4.1 CREATE WBS: INPUTS

### 5.4.1.1 PROJECT MANAGEMENT PLAN

A project management plan component includes but is not limited to the scope management plan. Described in Section 5.1.3.1, the scope management plan documents how the WBS will be created from the project scope statement.

### 5.4.1.2 PROJECT DOCUMENTS

Examples of project documents that can be considered as inputs for this process include but are not limited to:

◆ **Project scope statement.** Described in Section 5.3.3.1. The project scope statement describes the work that will be performed and the work that is excluded.

◆ **Requirements documentation.** Described in Section 5.2.3.1. Detailed requirements describe how individual requirements meet the business need for the project.

### 5.4.1.3 ENTERPRISE ENVIRONMENTAL FACTORS

The enterprise environmental factors that can influence the Create WBS process include but are not limited to industry-specific WBS standards that are relevant to the nature of the project. These industry-specific standards may serve as external reference sources for creating the WBS.

### 5.4.1.4 ORGANIZATIONAL PROCESS ASSETS

The organizational process assets that can influence the Create WBS process include but are not limited to:

◆ Policies, procedures, and templates for the WBS;

◆ Project files from previous projects; and

◆ Lessons learned from previous projects.

## 5.4.2 CREATE WBS: TOOLS AND TECHNIQUES

### 5.4.2.1 EXPERT JUDGMENT

Described in Section 4.1.2.1. Expertise should be considered from individuals or groups with knowledge of or experience with similar projects.

### 5.4.2.2 DECOMPOSITION

Decomposition is a technique used for dividing and subdividing the project scope and project deliverables into smaller, more manageable parts. The work package is the work defined at the lowest level of the WBS for which cost and duration can be estimated and managed. The level of decomposition is often guided by the degree of control needed to effectively manage the project. The level of detail for work packages will vary with the size and complexity of the project. Decomposition of the total project work into work packages generally involves the following activities:

◆ Identifying and analyzing the deliverables and related work,

◆ Structuring and organizing the WBS,

◆ Decomposing the upper WBS levels into lower-level detailed components,

◆ Developing and assigning identification codes to the WBS components, and

◆ Verifying that the degree of decomposition of the deliverables is appropriate.

A portion of a WBS with some branches of the WBS decomposed down through the work package level is shown in Figure 5-12.

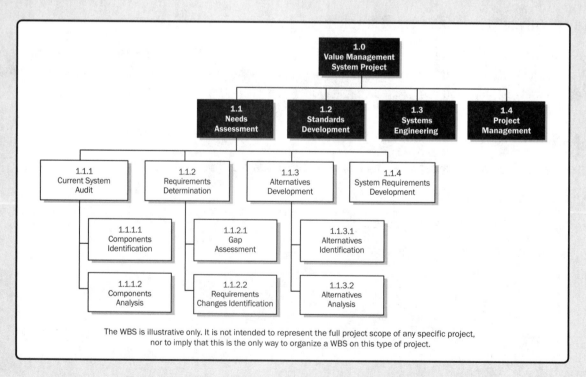

**Figure 5-12. Sample WBS Decomposed Down Through Work Packages**

A WBS structure may be created through various approaches. Some of the popular methods include the top-down approach, the use of organization-specific guidelines, and the use of WBS templates. A bottom-up approach can be used to group subcomponents. The WBS structure can be represented in a number of forms, such as:

◆ Using phases of the project life cycle as the second level of decomposition, with the product and project deliverables inserted at the third level, as shown in Figure 5-13;

◆ Using major deliverables as the second level of decomposition, as shown in Figure 5-14; and

◆ Incorporating subcomponents that may be developed by organizations outside the project team, such as contracted work. The seller then develops the supporting contract WBS as part of the contracted work.

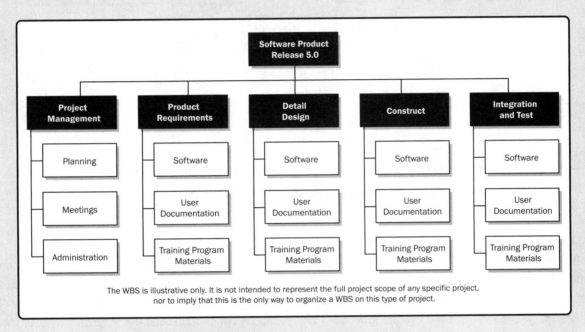

Figure 5-13. Sample WBS Organized by Phase

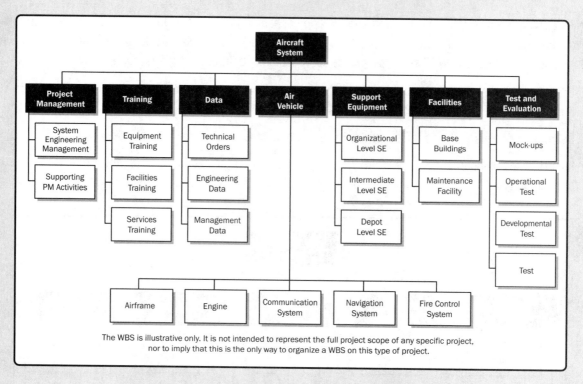

The WBS is illustrative only. It is not intended to represent the full project scope of any specific project, nor to imply that this is the only way to organize a WBS on this type of project.

**Figure 5-14. Sample WBS with Major Deliverables**

Decomposition of the upper-level WBS components requires subdividing the work for each of the deliverables or subcomponents into its most fundamental components, where the WBS components represent verifiable products, services, or results. If an agile approach is used, epics can be decomposed into user stories. The WBS may be structured as an outline, an organizational chart, or other method that identifies a hierarchical breakdown. Verifying the correctness of the decomposition requires determining that the lower-level WBS components are those that are necessary and sufficient for completion of the corresponding higher-level deliverables. Different deliverables can have different levels of decomposition. To arrive at a work package, the work for some deliverables needs to be decomposed only to the next level, while others need additional levels of decomposition. As the work is decomposed to greater levels of detail, the ability to plan, manage, and control the work is enhanced. However, excessive decomposition can lead to nonproductive management effort, inefficient use of resources, decreased efficiency in performing the work, and difficulty aggregating data over different levels of the WBS.

Decomposition may not be possible for a deliverable or subcomponent that will be accomplished far into the future. The project management team usually waits until the deliverable or subcomponent is agreed on, so the details of the WBS can be developed. This technique is sometimes referred to as rolling wave planning.

The WBS represents all product and project work, including the project management work. The total of the work at the lowest levels should roll up to the higher levels so that nothing is left out and no extra work is performed. This is sometimes called the 100 percent rule.

For specific information regarding the WBS, refer to the *Practice Standard for Work Breakdown Structures – Second Edition* [15]. This standard contains industry-specific examples of WBS templates that can be tailored to specific projects in a particular application area.

## 5.4.3 CREATE WBS: OUTPUTS

### 5.4.3.1 SCOPE BASELINE

The scope baseline is the approved version of a scope statement, WBS, and its associated WBS dictionary, which can be changed only through formal change control procedures and is used as a basis for comparison. It is a component of the project management plan. Components of the scope baseline include:

◆ **Project scope statement.** The project scope statement includes the description of the project scope, major deliverables, and exclusions (Section 5.3.3.1).

◆ **WBS.** The WBS is a hierarchical decomposition of the total scope of work to be carried out by the project team to accomplish the project objectives and create the required deliverables. Each descending level of the WBS represents an increasingly detailed definition of the project work.

   ■ *Work package.* The lowest level of the WBS is a work package with a unique identifier. These identifiers provide a structure for hierarchical summation of costs, schedule, and resource information and form a code of accounts. Each work package is part of a control account. A control account is a management control point where scope, budget, and schedule are integrated and compared to the earned value for performance measurement. A control account has two or more work packages, though each work package is associated with a single control account.

   ■ *Planning package.* A control account may include one or more planning packages. A planning package is a work breakdown structure component below the control account and above the work package with known work content but without detailed schedule activities.

◆ **WBS dictionary.** The WBS dictionary is a document that provides detailed deliverable, activity, and scheduling information about each component in the WBS. The WBS dictionary is a document that supports the WBS. Most of the information included in the WBS dictionary is created by other processes and added to this document at a later stage. Information in the WBS dictionary may include but is not limited to:

- Code of account identifier,
- Description of work,
- Assumptions and constraints,
- Responsible organization,
- Schedule milestones,
- Associated schedule activities,
- Resources required,
- Cost estimates,
- Quality requirements,
- Acceptance criteria,
- Technical references, and
- Agreement information.

### 5.4.3.2 PROJECT DOCUMENTS UPDATES

Project documents that may be updated as a result of carrying out this process include but are not limited to:

- **Assumption log.** Described in Section 4.1.3.2. The assumption log is updated with additional assumptions or constraints that were identified during the Create WBS process.
- **Requirements documentation.** Described in Section 5.2.3.1. Requirements documentation may be updated to include approved changes resulting from the Create WBS process.

## 5.5 VALIDATE SCOPE

Validate Scope is the process of formalizing acceptance of the completed project deliverables. The key benefit of this process is that it brings objectivity to the acceptance process and increases the probability of final product, service, or result acceptance by validating each deliverable. This process is performed periodically throughout the project as needed. The inputs, tools and techniques, and outputs of this process are depicted in Figure 5-15. Figure 5-16 depicts the data flow diagram of the process.

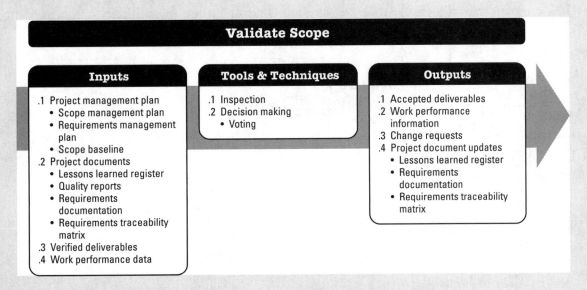

**Figure 5-15. Validate Scope: Inputs, Tools & Techniques, and Outputs**

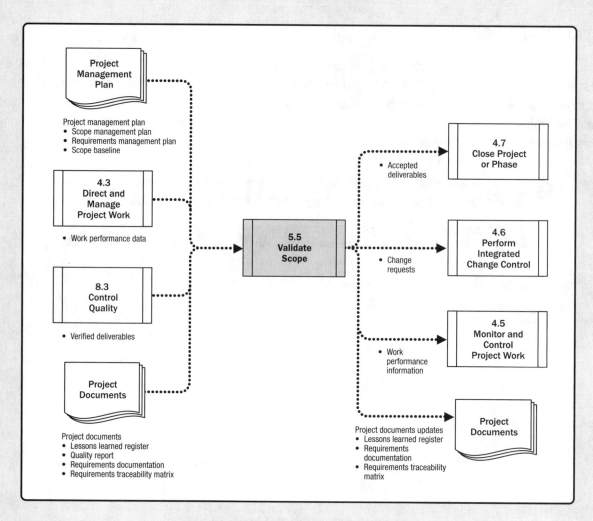

**Figure 5-16. Validate Scope: Data Flow Diagram**

The verified deliverables obtained from the Control Quality process are reviewed with the customer or sponsor to ensure they are completed satisfactorily and have received formal acceptance of the deliverables by the customer or sponsor. In this process, the outputs obtained as a result of the Planning processes in the Project Scope Management Knowledge Area, such as the requirements documentation or the scope baseline, as well as the work performance data obtained from the Execution processes in other Knowledge Areas, are the basis for performing the validation and for final acceptance.

The Validate Scope process differs from the Control Quality process in that the former is primarily concerned with acceptance of the deliverables, while the latter is primarily concerned with correctness of the deliverables and meeting the quality requirements specified for the deliverables. Control Quality is generally performed before Validate Scope, although the two processes may be performed in parallel.

## 5.5.1 VALIDATE SCOPE: INPUTS

### 5.5.1.1 PROJECT MANAGEMENT PLAN

Described in Section 4.2.3.1. Project management plan components include but are not limited to:

- **Scope management plan.** Described in Section 5.1.3.1. The project management plan specifies how formal acceptance of the completed project deliverables will be obtained.

- **Requirements management plan.** Described in Section 5.1.3.2. The requirements management plan describes how the project requirements are validated.

- **Scope baseline.** Described in Section 5.4.3.1. The scope baseline is compared to actual results to determine if a change, corrective action, or preventive action is necessary.

### 5.5.1.2 PROJECT DOCUMENTS

Project documents that can be considered as inputs for this process include but are not limited to:

- **Lessons learned register:** Described in Section 4.4.3.1. Lessons learned earlier in the project can be applied to later phases in the project to improve the efficiency and effectiveness of validating deliverables.

- **Quality reports.** Described in Section 8.2.3.1. The information presented in the quality report may include all quality assurance issues managed or escalated by the team, recommendations for improvement, and the summary of findings from the Control Quality process. This information is reviewed prior to product acceptance.

- **Requirements documentation.** Described in Section 5.2.3.1. Requirements are compared to the actual results to determine if a change, corrective action, or preventive action is necessary.

- **Requirements traceability matrix.** Described in Section 5.2.3.2. The requirements traceability matrix contains information about requirements, including how they will be validated.

### 5.5.1.3 VERIFIED DELIVERABLES

Verified deliverables are project deliverables that are completed and checked for correctness through the Control Quality process.

### 5.5.1.4 WORK PERFORMANCE DATA

Described in Section 4.3.3.2. Work performance data can include the degree of compliance with requirements, number of nonconformities, severity of the nonconformities, or the number of validation cycles performed in a period of time.

## 5.5.2 VALIDATE SCOPE: TOOLS AND TECHNIQUES

### 5.5.2.1 INSPECTION

Described in Section 8.3.2.3. Inspection includes activities such as measuring, examining, and validating to determine whether work and deliverables meet requirements and product acceptance criteria. Inspections are sometimes called reviews, product reviews, and walkthroughs. In some application areas, these different terms have unique and specific meanings.

### 5.5.2.2 DECISION MAKING

Described in Section 5.2.2.4. An example of decision making that may be used in this process includes but is not limited to voting. Voting is used to reach a conclusion when the validation is performed by the project team and other stakeholders.

## 5.5.3 VALIDATE SCOPE: OUTPUTS

### 5.5.3.1 ACCEPTED DELIVERABLES

Deliverables that meet the acceptance criteria are formally signed off and approved by the customer or sponsor. Formal documentation received from the customer or sponsor acknowledging formal stakeholder acceptance of the project's deliverables is forwarded to the Close Project or Phase process (Section 4.7).

### 5.5.3.2 WORK PERFORMANCE INFORMATION

Work performance information includes information about project progress, such as which deliverables have been accepted and which have not been accepted and the reasons why. This information is documented as described in Section 10.3.3.1 and communicated to stakeholders.

### 5.5.3.3 CHANGE REQUESTS

The completed deliverables that have not been formally accepted are documented, along with the reasons for non-acceptance of those deliverables. Those deliverables may require a change request for defect repair. The change requests (described in Section 4.3.3.4) are processed for review and disposition through the Perform Integrated Change Control process (Section 4.6).

#### 5.5.3.4 PROJECT DOCUMENTS UPDATES

Project documents that may be updated as a result of carrying out this process include but are not limited to:

◆ **Lessons learned register.** Described in Section 4.4.3.1. The lessons learned register is updated with information on challenges encountered and how they could have been avoided as well as approaches that worked well for validating deliverables.

◆ **Requirements documentation.** Described in Section 5.2.3.1. The requirements documentation may be updated with the actual results of validation activity. Of particular interest is when the actual results are better than the requirement or where a requirement was waived.

◆ **Requirements traceability matrix.** Described in Section 5.2.3.2. The requirements traceability matrix is updated with the results of the validation, including the method used and the outcome.

## 5.6 CONTROL SCOPE

Control Scope is the process of monitoring the status of the project and product scope and managing changes to the scope baseline. The key benefit of this process is that the scope baseline is maintained throughout the project. This process is performed throughout the project. The inputs, tools and techniques, and outputs of this process are depicted in Figure 5-17. Figure 5-18 depicts the data flow diagram of the process.

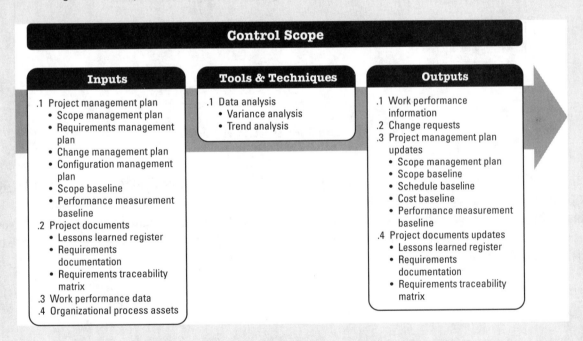

Figure 5-17. Control Scope: Inputs, Tools & Techniques, and Outputs

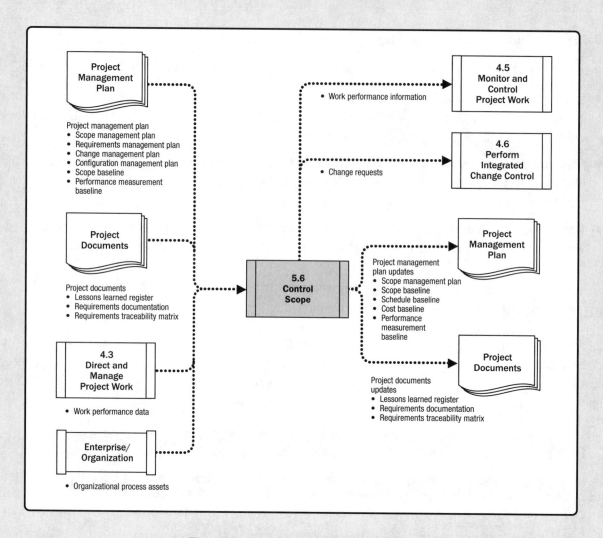

**Figure 5-18. Control Scope: Data Flow Diagram**

Controlling the project scope ensures all requested changes and recommended corrective or preventive actions are processed through the Perform Integrated Change Control process (see Section 4.6). Control Scope is also used to manage the actual changes when they occur and is integrated with the other control processes. The uncontrolled expansion to product or project scope without adjustments to time, cost, and resources is referred to as scope creep. Change is inevitable; therefore, some type of change control process is mandatory for every project.

## 5.6.1 CONTROL SCOPE: INPUTS

### 5.6.1.1 PROJECT MANAGEMENT PLAN

Described in Section 4.2.3.1. Project management plan components include but are not limited to:

- ◆ **Scope management plan.** Described in Section 5.1.3.1. The scope management plan documents how the project and product scope will be controlled.

- ◆ **Requirements management plan.** Described in Section 5.1.3.2. The requirements management plan describes how the project requirements will be managed.

- ◆ **Change management plan.** Described in Section 4.2.3.1. The change management plan defines the process for managing change on the project.

- ◆ **Configuration management plan.** Described in Section 4.2.3.1. The configuration management plan defines those items that are configurable, those items that require formal change control, and the process for controlling changes to such items.

- ◆ **Scope baseline.** Described in Section 5.4.3.1. The scope baseline is compared to actual results to determine if a change, corrective action, or preventive action is necessary.

- ◆ **Performance measurement baseline.** Described in Section 4.2.3.1. When using earned value analysis, the performance measurement baseline is compared to actual results to determine if a change, corrective action, or preventive action is necessary.

### 5.6.1.2 PROJECT DOCUMENTS

Project documents that can be considered as inputs for this process include but are not limited to:

- ◆ **Lessons learned register.** Described in Section 4.4.3.1. Lessons learned earlier in the project can be applied to later phases in the project to improve scope control.

- ◆ **Requirements documentation.** Described in Section 5.2.3.1. Requirements documentation is used to detect any deviation in the agreed-upon scope for the project or product.

- ◆ **Requirements traceability matrix.** Described in Section 5.2.3.2. The requirements traceability matrix helps to detect the impact of any change or deviation from the scope baseline on the project objectives. It may also provide status of requirements being controlled.

### 5.6.1.3 WORK PERFORMANCE DATA

Work performance data can include the number of change requests received, the number of requests accepted, and the number of deliverables verified, validated, and completed.

### 5.6.1.4 ORGANIZATIONAL PROCESS ASSETS

The organizational process assets that can influence the Control Scope process include but are not limited to:

◆ Existing formal and informal scope, control-related policies, procedures, guidelines; and

◆ Monitoring and reporting methods and templates to be used.


## 5.6.2 CONTROL SCOPE: TOOLS AND TECHNIQUES

### 5.6.2.1 DATA ANALYSIS

Data analysis techniques that can be used in the Control Scope process include but are not limited to:

◆ **Variance analysis.** Described in Section 4.5.2.2. Variance analysis is used to compare the baseline to the actual results and determine if the variance is within the threshold amount or if corrective or preventive action is appropriate.

◆ **Trend analysis.** Described in Section 4.5.2.2. Trend analysis examines project performance over time to determine if performance is improving or deteriorating.

Important aspects of project scope control include determining the cause and degree of variance relative to the scope baseline (Section 5.4.3.1) and deciding whether corrective or preventive action is required.


## 5.6.3 CONTROL SCOPE: OUTPUTS

### 5.6.3.1 WORK PERFORMANCE INFORMATION

Work performance information produced includes correlated and contextualized information on how the project and product scope are performing compared to the scope baseline. It can include the categories of the changes received, the identified scope variances and their causes, how they impact schedule or cost, and the forecast of the future scope performance.

### 5.6.3.2 CHANGE REQUESTS

Described in Section 4.3.3.4. Analysis of project performance may result in a change request to the scope and schedule baselines or other components of the project management plan. Change requests are processed for review and disposition through the Perform Integrated Change Control process (Section 4.6).

### 5.6.3.3 PROJECT MANAGEMENT PLAN UPDATES

Any change to the project management plan goes through the organization's change control process via a change request. Components that may require a change request for the project management plan include but are not limited to:

◆ **Scope management plan.** Described in Section 5.1.3.1. The scope management plan may be updated to reflect a change in how the scope is managed.

◆ **Scope baseline.** Described in Section 5.4.3.1. Changes to the scope baseline are incorporated in response to approved changes in scope, scope statement, the WBS, or the WBS dictionary. In some cases, scope variances can be so severe that a revised scope baseline is needed to provide a realistic basis for performance measurement.

◆ **Schedule baseline.** Described in Section 6.5.3.1. Changes to the schedule baseline are incorporated in response to approved changes in scope, resources, or schedule estimates. In some cases, schedule variances can be so severe that a revised schedule baseline is needed to provide a realistic basis for performance measurement.

◆ **Cost baseline.** Described in Section 7.3.3.1. Changes to the cost baseline are incorporated in response to approved changes in scope, resources, or cost estimates. In some cases, cost variances can be so severe that a revised cost baseline is needed to provide a realistic basis for performance measurement.

◆ **Performance measurement baseline.** Described in Section 4.2.3.1. Changes to the performance measurement baseline are incorporated in response to approved changes in scope, schedule performance, or cost estimates. In some cases, the performance variances can be so severe that a change request is put forth to revise the performance measurement baseline to provide a realistic basis for performance measurement.

### 5.6.3.4 PROJECT DOCUMENTS UPDATES

Project documents that may be updated as a result of carrying out this process include but are not limited to:

◆ **Lessons learned register.** Described in Section 4.4.3.1. The lessons learned register can be updated with techniques that are efficient and effective in controlling scope, including causes of variances and corrective actions chosen.

◆ **Requirements documentation.** Described in Section 5.2.3.1. Requirements documentation may be updated with additional or changed requirements.

◆ **Requirements traceability matrix.** Described in Section 5.2.3.2. The requirements traceability matrix may be updated to reflect updates in requirement documentation.

# 6

## PROJECT SCHEDULE MANAGEMENT

Project Schedule Management includes the processes required to manage the timely completion of the project. The Project Schedule Management processes are:

**6.1 Plan Schedule Management**—The process of establishing the policies, procedures, and documentation for planning, developing, managing, executing, and controlling the project schedule.

**6.2 Define Activities**—The process of identifying and documenting the specific actions to be performed to produce the project deliverables.

**6.3 Sequence Activities**—The process of identifying and documenting relationships among the project activities.

**6.4 Estimate Activity Durations**—The process of estimating the number of work periods needed to complete individual activities with the estimated resources.

**6.5 Develop Schedule**—The process of analyzing activity sequences, durations, resource requirements, and schedule constraints to create the project schedule model for project execution and monitoring and controlling.

**6.6 Control Schedule**—The process of monitoring the status of the project to update the project schedule and manage changes to the schedule baseline.

Figure 6-1 provides an overview of the Project Schedule Management processes. The Project Schedule Management processes are presented as discrete processes with defined interfaces while, in practice, they overlap and interact in ways that cannot be completely detailed in the *PMBOK® Guide*.

**Project Schedule Management Overview**

**6.1 Plan Schedule Management**

.1 Inputs
   .1 Project charter
   .2 Project management plan
   .3 Enterprise environmental factors
   .4 Organizational process assets

.2 Tools & Techniques
   .1 Expert judgment
   .2 Data analysis
   .3 Meetings

.3 Outputs
   .1 Schedule management plan

**6.4 Estimate Activity Durations**

.1 Inputs
   .1 Project management plan
   .2 Project documents
   .3 Enterprise environmental factors
   .4 Organizational process assets

.2 Tools & Techniques
   .1 Expert judgment
   .2 Analogous estimating
   .3 Parametric estimating
   .4 Three-point estimating
   .5 Bottom-up estimating
   .6 Data analysis
   .7 Decision making
   .8 Meetings

.3 Outputs
   .1 Duration estimates
   .2 Basis of estimates
   .3 Project documents updates

**6.2 Define Activities**

.1 Inputs
   .1 Project management plan
   .2 Enterprise environmental factors
   .3 Organizational process assets

.2 Tools & Techniques
   .1 Expert judgment
   .2 Decomposition
   .3 Rolling wave planning
   .4 Meetings

.3 Outputs
   .1 Activity list
   .2 Activity attributes
   .3 Milestone list
   .4 Change requests
   .5 Project management plan updates

**6.5 Develop Schedule**

.1 Inputs
   .1 Project management plan
   .2 Project documents
   .3 Agreements
   .4 Enterprise environmental factors
   .5 Organizational process assets

.2 Tools & Techniques
   .1 Schedule network analysis
   .2 Critical path method
   .3 Resource optimization
   .4 Data analysis
   .5 Leads and lags
   .6 Schedule compression
   .7 Project management information system
   .8 Agile release planning

.3 Outputs
   .1 Schedule baseline
   .2 Project schedule
   .3 Schedule data
   .4 Project calendars
   .5 Change requests
   .6 Project management plan updates
   .7 Project documents updates

**6.3 Sequence Activities**

.1 Inputs
   .1 Project management plan
   .2 Project documents
   .3 Enterprise environmental factors
   .4 Organizational process assets

.2 Tools & Techniques
   .1 Precedence diagramming method
   .2 Dependency determination and integration
   .3 Leads and lags
   .4 Project management information system

.3 Outputs
   .1 Project schedule network diagrams
   .2 Project documents updates

**6.6 Control Schedule**

.1 Inputs
   .1 Project management plan
   .2 Project documents
   .3 Work performance data
   .4 Organizational process assets

.2 Tools & Techniques
   .1 Data analysis
   .2 Critical path method
   .3 Project management information system
   .4 Resource optimization
   .5 Leads and lags
   .6 Schedule compression

.3 Outputs
   .1 Work performance information
   .2 Schedule forecasts
   .3 Change requests
   .4 Project management plan updates
   .5 Project documents updates

**Figure 6-1. Project Schedule Management Overview**

## KEY CONCEPTS FOR PROJECT SCHEDULE MANAGEMENT

Project scheduling provides a detailed plan that represents how and when the project will deliver the products, services, and results defined in the project scope and serves as a tool for communication, managing stakeholders' expectations, and as a basis for performance reporting.

The project management team selects a scheduling method, such as critical path or an agile approach. Then, the project-specific data, such as the activities, planned dates, durations, resources, dependencies, and constraints, are entered into a scheduling tool to create a schedule model for the project. The result is a project schedule. Figure 6-2 provides a scheduling overview that shows how the scheduling method, scheduling tool, and outputs from the Project Schedule Management processes interact to create a schedule model.

For smaller projects, defining activities, sequencing activities, estimating activity durations, and developing the schedule model are so tightly linked that they are viewed as a single process that can be performed by a person over a relatively short period of time. These processes are presented here as distinct elements because the tools and techniques for each process are different. Some of these processes are presented more fully in the *Practice Standard for Scheduling* [16].

When possible, the detailed project schedule should remain flexible throughout the project to adjust for knowledge gained, increased understanding of the risk, and value-added activities.

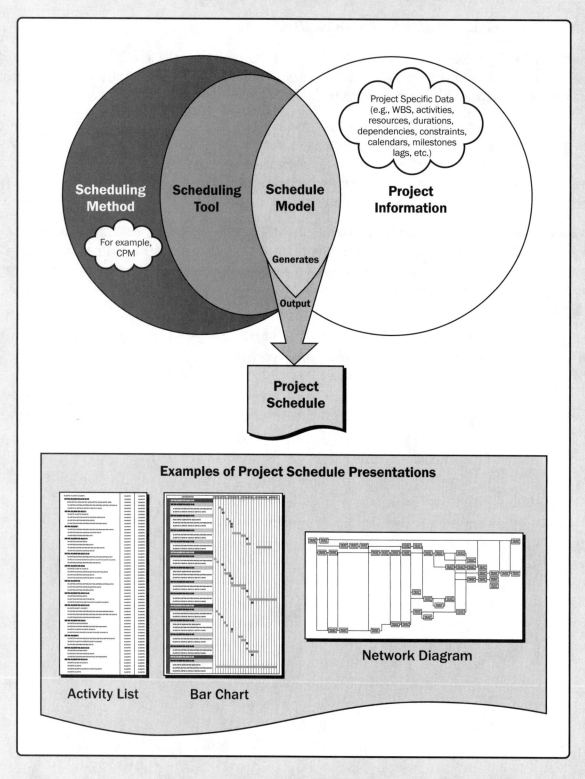

Figure 6-2. Scheduling Overview

## TRENDS AND EMERGING PRACTICES IN PROJECT SCHEDULE MANAGEMENT

With high levels of uncertainty and unpredictability in a fast-paced, highly competitive global marketplace where long term scope is difficult to define, it is becoming even more important to have a contextual framework for effective adoption and tailoring of development practices to respond to the changing needs of the environment. Adaptive planning defines a plan but acknowledges that once work starts, the priorities may change and the plan needs to reflect this new knowledge.

Some of the emerging practices for project scheduling methods include but are not limited to:

◆ **Iterative scheduling with a backlog.** This is a form of rolling wave planning based on adaptive life cycles, such as the agile approach for product development. The requirements are documented in user stories that are then prioritized and refined just prior to construction, and the product features are developed using time-boxed periods of work. This approach is often used to deliver incremental value to the customer or when multiple teams can concurrently develop a large number of features that have few interconnected dependencies. This scheduling method is appropriate for many projects as indicated by the widespread and growing use of adaptive life cycles for product development. The benefit of this approach is that it welcomes changes throughout the development life cycle.

◆ **On-demand scheduling.** This approach, typically used in a Kanban system, is based on the theory-of-constraints and pull-based scheduling concepts from lean manufacturing to limit a team's work in progress in order to balance demand against the team's delivery throughput. On-demand scheduling does not rely on a schedule that was developed previously for the development of the product or product increments, but rather pulls work from a backlog or intermediate queue of work to be done immediately as resources become available. On-demand scheduling is often used for projects that evolve the product incrementally in operational or sustainment environments, and where tasks may be made relatively similar in size and scope or can be bundled by size and scope.

## TAILORING CONSIDERATIONS

Because each project is unique, the project manager may need to tailor the way Project Schedule Management processes are applied. Considerations for tailoring include but are not limited to:

◆ **Life cycle approach.** What is the most appropriate life cycle approach that allows for a more detailed schedule?

◆ **Resource availability.** What are the factors influencing durations (such as the correlation between available resources and their productivity)?

◆ **Project dimensions.** How will the presence of project complexity, technological uncertainty, product novelty, pace, or progress tracking (such as earned value, percentage complete, red-yellow-green (stop light) indicators) impact the desired level of control?

◆ **Technology support.** Is technology used to develop, record, transmit, receive, and store project schedule model information and is it readily accessible?

For more specific information regarding scheduling, refer to the *Practice Standard for Scheduling* [16].

## CONSIDERATIONS FOR AGILE/ADAPTIVE ENVIRONMENTS

Adaptive approaches use short cycles to undertake work, review the results, and adapt as necessary. These cycles provide rapid feedback on the approaches and suitability of deliverables, and generally manifest as iterative scheduling and on-demand, pull-based scheduling, as discussed in the section on Key Trends and Emerging Practices in Project Schedule Management.

In large organizations, there may be a mixture of small projects and large initiatives requiring long-term roadmaps to manage the development of these programs using scaling factors (e.g., team size, geographical distribution, regulatory compliance, organizational complexity, and technical complexity). To address the full delivery life cycle for larger, enterprise-wide systems, a range of techniques utilizing a predictive approach, adaptive approach, or a hybrid of both, may need to be adopted. The organization may need to combine practices from several core methods, or adopt a method that has already done so, and adopt a few principles and practices of more traditional techniques.

The role of the project manager does not change based on managing projects using a predictive development life cycle or managing projects in adaptive environments. However, to be successful in using adaptive approaches, the project manager will need to be familiar with the tools and techniques to understand how to apply them effectively.

# 6.1 PLAN SCHEDULE MANAGEMENT

Plan Schedule Management is the process of establishing the policies, procedures, and documentation for planning, developing, managing, executing, and controlling the project schedule. The key benefit of this process is that it provides guidance and direction on how the project schedule will be managed throughout the project. This process is performed once or at predefined points in the project. The inputs, tools and techniques, and outputs of the process are depicted in Figure 6-3. Figure 6-4 depicts the data flow diagram for the process.

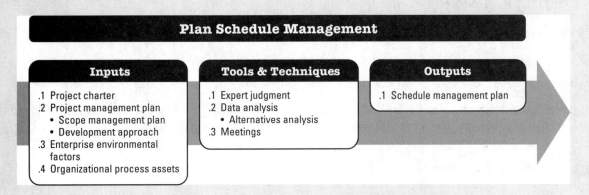

**Figure 6-3. Plan Schedule Management: Inputs, Tools & Techniques, and Outputs**

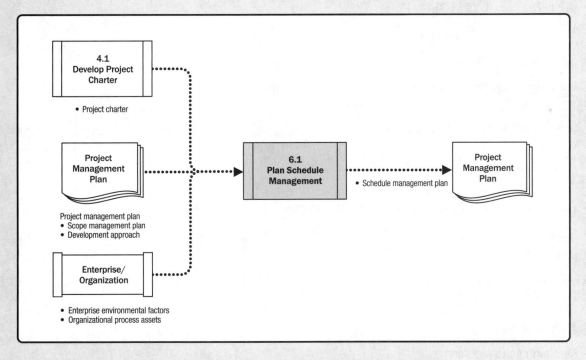

**Figure 6-4. Plan Schedule Management: Data Flow Diagram**

## 6.1.1 PLAN SCHEDULE MANAGEMENT: INPUTS

### 6.1.1.1 PROJECT CHARTER

Described in Section 4.1.3.1. The project charter defines the summary milestone schedule that will influence the management of the project schedule.

### 6.1.1.2 PROJECT MANAGEMENT PLAN

Described in Section 4.3.2.1. Project management plan components include but are not limited to:

◆ **Scope management plan.** Described in Section 5.1.3.1. The scope management plan describes how the scope will be defined and developed, which will provide information on how the schedule will be developed.

◆ **Development approach.** Described in Section 4.2.3.1. The product development approach will help define the scheduling approach, estimating techniques, scheduling tools, and techniques for controlling the schedule.

### 6.1.1.3 ENTERPRISE ENVIRONMENTAL FACTORS

The enterprise environmental factors that can influence the Plan Schedule Management process include but are not limited to:

◆ Organizational culture and structure,

◆ Team resource availability and skills and physical resource availability,

◆ Scheduling software, and

◆ Commercial databases, such as standardized estimating data.

### 6.1.1.4 ORGANIZATIONAL PROCESS ASSETS

The organizational process assets that can influence the Plan Schedule Management process include but are not limited to:

◆ Historical information and lessons learned repositories;

◆ Existing formal and informal schedule development, management- and control-related policies, procedures, and guidelines;

◆ Guidelines and criteria for tailoring the organization's set of standard processes and procedures to satisfy the specific needs of the project,

◆ Templates and forms; and

◆ Monitoring and reporting tools.

## 6.1.2 PLAN SCHEDULE MANAGEMENT: TOOLS AND TECHNIQUES

### 6.1.2.1 EXPERT JUDGMENT

Described in Section 4.1.2.1 Expertise should be considered from individuals or groups with specialized knowledge or training in previous, similar projects:

◆ Schedule development, management, and control;

◆ Scheduling methodologies (e.g., predictive or adaptive life cycle);

◆ Scheduling software; and

◆ The specific industry for which the project is developed.

### 6.1.2.2 DATA ANALYSIS

A data analysis technique that can be used for this process includes but is not limited to alternatives analysis. Alternatives analysis can include determining which schedule methodology to use, or how to combine various methods on the project. It can also include determining how detailed the schedule needs to be, the duration of waves for rolling wave planning, and how often it should be reviewed and updated. An appropriate balance between the level of detail needed to manage the schedule and the amount of time it takes to keep it up to date needs to be reached for each project.

### 6.1.2.3 MEETINGS

Project teams may hold planning meetings to develop the schedule management plan. Participants at these meetings may include the project manager, the project sponsor, selected project team members, selected stakeholders, anyone with responsibility for schedule planning or execution, and others as needed.

## 6.1.3 PLAN SCHEDULE MANAGEMENT: OUTPUTS

### 6.1.3.1 SCHEDULE MANAGEMENT PLAN

The schedule management plan is a component of the project management plan that establishes the criteria and the activities for developing, monitoring, and controlling the schedule. The schedule management plan may be formal or informal, highly detailed, or broadly framed based on the needs of the project, and includes appropriate control thresholds.

The schedule management plan can establish the following:

◆ **Project schedule model development.** The scheduling methodology and the scheduling tool to be used in the development of the project schedule model are specified.

◆ **Release and iteration length.** When using an adaptive life cycle, the time-boxed periods for releases, waves, and iterations are specified. Time-boxed periods are durations during which the team works steadily toward completion of a goal. Time-boxing helps to minimize scope creep as it forces the teams to process essential features first, then other features when time permits.

◆ **Level of accuracy.** The level of accuracy specifies the acceptable range used in determining realistic activity duration estimates and may include an amount for contingencies.

◆ **Units of measure.** Each unit of measurement (such as staff hours, staff days, or weeks for time measures, or meters, liters, tons, kilometers, or cubic yards for quantity measures) is defined for each of the resources.

◆ **Organizational procedures links.** The work breakdown structure (WBS) (Section 5.4) provides the framework for the schedule management plan, allowing for consistency with the estimates and resulting schedules.

◆ **Project schedule model maintenance.** The process used to update the status and record progress of the project in the schedule model during the execution of the project is defined.

◆ **Control thresholds.** Variance thresholds for monitoring schedule performance may be specified to indicate an agreed-upon amount of variation to be allowed before some action needs to be taken. Thresholds are typically expressed as percentage deviations from the parameters established in the baseline plan.

◆ **Rules of performance measurement.** Earned value management (EVM) rules or other physical measurement rules of performance measurement are set. For example, the schedule management plan may specify:

  ▪ Rules for establishing percent complete,
  ▪ EVM techniques (e.g., baselines, fixed-formula, percent complete, etc.) to be employed (for more specific information, refer to the *Practice Standard for Earned Value Management* [17]), and
  ▪ Schedule performance measurements such as schedule variance (SV) and schedule performance index (SPI) used to assess the magnitude of variation to the original schedule baseline.

◆ **Reporting formats.** The formats and frequency for the various schedule reports are defined.

# 6.2 DEFINE ACTIVITIES

Define Activities is the process of identifying and documenting the specific actions to be performed to produce the project deliverables. The key benefit of this process is that it decomposes work packages into schedule activities that provide a basis for estimating, scheduling, executing, monitoring, and controlling the project work. This process is performed throughout the project. The inputs, tools and techniques, and outputs of this process are depicted in Figure 6-5. Figure 6-6 depicts the data flow diagram of the process.

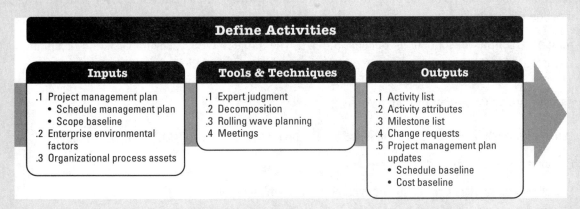

**Figure 6-5. Define Activities: Inputs, Tools & Techniques, and Outputs**

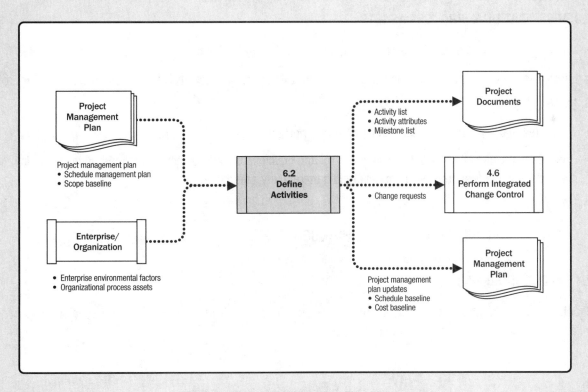

**Figure 6-6. Define Activities: Data Flow Diagram**

## 6.2.1 DEFINE ACTIVITIES: INPUTS

### 6.2.1.1 PROJECT MANAGEMENT PLAN

Described in Section 4.2.3.1. Project management plan components include but are not limited to:

◆ **Schedule management plan.** Described in Section 6.1.3.1. The schedule management plan defines the schedule methodology, the duration of waves for rolling wave planning, and the level of detail necessary to manage the work.

◆ **Scope baseline.** Described in Section 5.4.3.1. The project WBS, deliverables, and aceptance criteria documented in the scope baseline are considered explicitly while defining activities.

### 6.2.1.2 ENTERPRISE ENVIRONMENTAL FACTORS

Enterprise environmental factors that influence the Define Activities process include but are not limited to:

◆ Organizational cultures and structure,

◆ Published commercial information from commercial databases, and

◆ Project management information system (PMIS).

### 6.2.1.3 ORGANIZATIONAL PROCESS ASSETS

The organizational process assets that can influence the Define Activities process include but are not limited to:

◆ Lessons learned repository containing historical information regarding activity lists used by previous similar projects,

◆ Standardized processes,

◆ Templates that contain a standard activity list or a portion of an activity list from a previous project, and

◆ Existing formal and informal activity planning-related policies, procedures, and guidelines, such as the scheduling methodology, that are considered in developing the activity definitions.

## 6.2.2 DEFINE ACTIVITIES: TOOLS AND TECHNIQUES

### 6.2.2.1 EXPERT JUDGMENT

Described in Section 4.1.2.1. Expertise should be considered from individuals or groups with specialized knowledge of similar past projects and the work being performed.

### 6.2.2.2 DECOMPOSITION

Described in Section 5.4.2.2. Decomposition is a technique used for dividing and subdividing the project scope and project deliverables into smaller, more manageable parts. Activities represent the effort needed to complete a work package. The Define Activities process defines the final outputs as activities rather than deliverables, as done in the Create WBS process (Section 5.4).

The activity list, WBS, and WBS dictionary can be developed either sequentially or concurrently, with the WBS and WBS dictionary used as the basis for development of the final activity list. Each work package within the WBS is decomposed into the activities required to produce the work package deliverables. Involving team members in the decomposition can lead to better and more accurate results.

### 6.2.2.3 ROLLING WAVE PLANNING

Rolling wave planning is an iterative planning technique in which the work to be accomplished in the near term is planned in detail, while work further in the future is planned at a higher level. It is a form of progressive elaboration applicable to work packages, planning packages, and release planning when using an agile or waterfall approach. Therefore, work can exist at various levels of detail depending on where it is in the project life cycle. During early strategic planning when information is less defined, work packages may be decomposed to the known level of detail. As more is known about the upcoming events in the near term, work packages can be decomposed into activities.

### 6.2.2.4 MEETINGS

Meetings may be face-to-face, virtual, formal, or informal. Meetings may be held with team members or subject matter experts to define the activities needed to complete the work.

## 6.2.3 DEFINE ACTIVITIES: OUTPUTS

### 6.2.3.1 ACTIVITY LIST

The activity list includes the schedule activities required on the project. For projects that use rolling wave planning or agile techniques, the activity list will be updated periodically as the project progresses. The activity list includes an activity identifier and a scope of work description for each activity in sufficient detail to ensure that project team members understand what work is required to be completed.

### 6.2.3.2 ACTIVITY ATTRIBUTES

Activity attributes extend the description of the activity by identifying multiple components associated with each activity. The components for each activity evolve over time. During the initial stages of the project, they include the unique activity identifier (ID), WBS ID, and activity label or name. When completed, they may include activity descriptions, predecessor activities, successor activities, logical relationships, leads and lags (Section 6.3.2.3), resource requirements, imposed dates, constraints, and assumptions. Activity attributes can be used to identify the place where the work has to be performed, the project calendar the activity is assigned to, and the type of effort involved. Activity attributes are used for schedule development and for selecting, ordering, and sorting the planned schedule activities in various ways within reports

### 6.2.3.3 MILESTONE LIST

A milestone is a significant point or event in a project. A milestone list identifies all project milestones and indicates whether the milestone is mandatory, such as those required by contract, or optional, such as those based on historical information. Milestones have zero duration because they represent a significant point or event.

### 6.2.3.4 CHANGE REQUESTS

Described in Section 4.3.3.4. Once the project has been baselined, the progressive elaboration of deliverables into activities may reveal work that was not initially part of the project baselines. This may result in a change request. Change requests are processed for review and disposition through the Perform Integrated Change Control process (Section 4.6).

### 6.2.3.5 PROJECT MANAGEMENT PLAN UPDATES

Any change to the project management plan goes through the organization's change control process via a change request. Components that may require a change request for the project management plan include but are not limited to:

◆ **Schedule baseline.** Described in Section 6.5.3.1. Throughout the project, work packages are progressively elaborated into activities. This process may reveal work that was not part of the initial schedule baseline, necessitating a change to delivery dates or other significant schedule milestones that are part of the schedule baseline.

◆ **Cost baseline.** Described in Section 7.3.3.1. Changes to the cost baseline are incorporated in response to approved changes in schedule activities.

# 6.3 SEQUENCE ACTIVITIES

Sequence Activities is the process of identifying and documenting relationships among the project activities. The key benefit of this process is that it defines the logical sequence of work to obtain the greatest efficiency given all project constraints. This process is performed throughout the project. The inputs, tools and techniques, and outputs of this process are depicted in Figure 6-7. Figure 6-8 depicts the data flow diagram of the process.

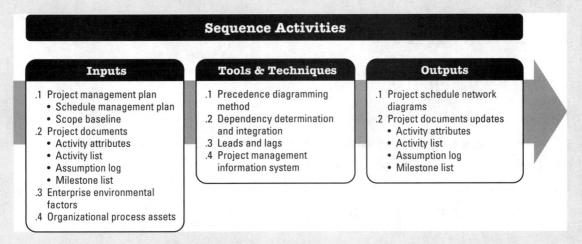

**Figure 6-7. Sequence Activities: Inputs, Tools & Techniques, and Outputs**

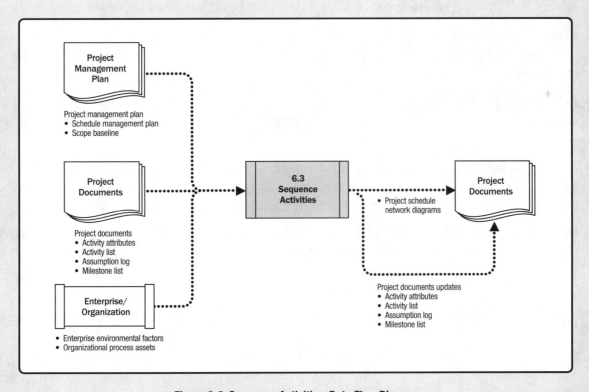

**Figure 6-8. Sequence Activities: Data Flow Diagram**

Every activity except the first and last should be connected to at least one predecessor and at least one successor activity with an appropriate logical relationship. Logical relationships should be designed to create a realistic project schedule. It may be necessary to use lead or lag time between activities to support a realistic and achievable project schedule. Sequencing can be performed by using project management software or by using manual or automated techniques. The Sequence Activities process concentrates on converting the project activities from a list to a diagram to act as a first step to publish the schedule baseline.

## 6.3.1 SEQUENCE ACTIVITIES: INPUTS

### 6.3.1.1 PROJECT MANAGEMENT PLAN

Described in Section 4.2.3.1. Project management plan components include but are not limited to:

◆ **Schedule management plan.** Described in Section 6.1.3.1. The schedule management plan defines the method used and the level of accuracy along with other criteria required to sequence activities.

◆ **Scope baseline.** Described in Section 5.4.3.1. The project WBS, deliverables, and acceptance criteria documented in the scope baseline are considered explicitly while sequencing activities.

### 6.3.1.2 PROJECT DOCUMENTS

Project documents that can be considered as inputs for this process include but are not limited to:

◆ **Activity attributes.** Described in Section 6.2.3.2. Activity attributes may describe a necessary sequence of events or defined predecessor or successor relationships, as well as defined lead and lag and logical relationships between the activities.

◆ **Activity list.** Described in Section 6.2.3.1. The activity list contains all schedule activities required on the project that are to be sequenced. Dependencies and other constraints for these activities can influence the sequencing of the activities.

◆ **Assumption log.** Described in Section 4.1.3.2. Assumptions and constraints recorded in the assumption log may influence the way activities are sequenced, the relationship between activities, and the need for leads and lags, and may give rise to individual project risks that may impact the project schedule.

◆ **Milestone list.** Described in Section 6.2.3.3. The milestone list may have scheduled dates for specific milestones, which may influence the way activities are sequenced.

### 6.3.1.3 ENTERPRISE ENVIRONMENTAL FACTORS

The enterprise environmental factors that can influence the Sequence Activities process include but are not limited to:

◆ Government or industry standards,

◆ Project management information system (PMIS),

◆ Scheduling tools, and

◆ Organization work authorization systems.

### 6.3.1.4 ORGANIZATIONAL PROCESS ASSETS

The organizational process assets that can influence the Sequence Activities process include but are not limited to:

◆ Portfolio and program plans and project dependencies and relationships;

◆ Existing formal and informal activity planning-related policies, procedures, and guidelines, such as the scheduling methodology that is considered in developing logical relationships;

◆ Templates that can be used to expedite the preparation of networks for project activities. Related activity attributes information in templates can also contain additional descriptive information useful in sequencing activities; and

◆ Lessons learned repository containing historical information that can help optimize the sequencing process.

## 6.3.2 SEQUENCE ACTIVITIES: TOOLS AND TECHNIQUES

### 6.3.2.1 PRECEDENCE DIAGRAMMING METHOD

The precedence diagramming method (PDM) is a technique used for constructing a schedule model in which activities are represented by nodes and are graphically linked by one or more logical relationships to show the sequence in which the activities are to be performed.

PDM includes four types of dependencies or logical relationships. A predecessor activity is an activity that logically comes before a dependent activity in a schedule. A successor activity is a dependent activity that logically comes after another activity in a schedule. These relationships are defined below and are illustrated in Figure 6-9:

◆ **Finish-to-start (FS).** A logical relationship in which a successor activity cannot start until a predecessor activity has finished. For example, installing the operating system on a PC (successor) cannot start until the PC hardware is assembled (predecessor).

◆ **Finish-to-finish (FF).** A logical relationship in which a successor activity cannot finish until a predecessor activity has finished. For example, writing a document (predecessor) is required to finish before editing the document (successor) can finish.

◆ **Start-to-start (SS).** A logical relationship in which a successor activity cannot start until a predecessor activity has started. For example, level concrete (successor) cannot begin until pour foundation (predecessor) begins.

◆ **Start-to-finish (SF).** A logical relationship in which a predecessor activity cannot finish until a successor activity has started. For example, a new accounts payable system (successor) has to start before the old accounts payable system can be shut down (predecessor).

In PDM, FS is the most commonly used type of precedence relationship. The SF relationship is very rarely used, but is included to present a complete list of the PDM relationship types.

Two activities can have two logical relationships at the same time (for example, SS and FF). Multiple relationships between the same activities are not recommended, so a decision has to be made to select the relationship with the highest impact. Closed loops are also not recommended in logical relationships.

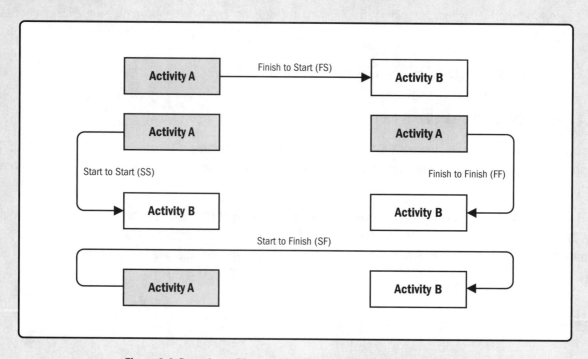

Figure 6-9. Precedence Diagramming Method (PDM) Relationship Types

## 6.3.2.2 DEPENDENCY DETERMINATION AND INTEGRATION

Dependencies may be characterized by the following attributes: mandatory or discretionary, internal or external (as described below). Dependency has four attributes, but two can be applicable at the same time in the following ways: mandatory external dependencies, mandatory internal dependencies, discretionary external dependencies, or discretionary internal dependencies.

◆ **Mandatory dependencies.** Mandatory dependencies are those that are legally or contractually required or inherent in the nature of the work. Mandatory dependencies often involve physical limitations, such as on a construction project, where it is impossible to erect the superstructure until after the foundation has been built, or on an electronics project, where a prototype has to be built before it can be tested. Mandatory dependencies are sometimes referred to as hard logic or hard dependencies. Technical dependencies may not be mandatory. The project team determines which dependencies are mandatory during the process of sequencing the activities. Mandatory dependencies should not be confused with assigning schedule constraints in the scheduling tool.

◆ **Discretionary dependencies.** Discretionary dependencies are sometimes referred to as preferred logic, preferential logic, or soft logic. Discretionary dependencies are established based on knowledge of best practices within a particular application area or some unusual aspect of the project where a specific sequence is desired, even though there may be other acceptable sequences. For example, generally accepted best practices recommend that during construction, the electrical work should start after finishing the plumbing work. This order is not mandatory and both activities may occur at the same time (in parallel), but performing the activities in sequential order reduces the overall project risk. Discretionary dependencies should be fully documented since they can create arbitrary total float values and can limit later scheduling options. When fast tracking techniques are employed, these discretionary dependencies should be reviewed and considered for modification or removal. The project team determines which dependencies are discretionary during the process of sequencing the activities.

◆ **External dependencies.** External dependencies involve a relationship between project activities and non-project activities. These dependencies are usually outside of the project team's control. For example, the testing activity in a software project may be dependent on the delivery of hardware from an external source, or governmental environmental hearings may need to be held before site preparation can begin on a construction project. The project management team determines which dependencies are external during the process of sequencing the activities.

◆ **Internal dependencies.** Internal dependencies involve a precedence relationship between project activities and are generally inside the project team's control. For example, if the team cannot test a machine until they assemble it, there is an internal mandatory dependency. The project management team determines which dependencies are internal during the process of sequencing the activities.

### 6.3.2.3 LEADS AND LAGS

A lead is the amount of time a successor activity can be advanced with respect to a predecessor activity. For example, on a project to construct a new office building, the landscaping could be scheduled to start 2 weeks prior to the scheduled punch list completion. This would be shown as a finish-to-start with a 2-week lead as shown in Figure 6-10. Lead is often represented as a negative value for lag in scheduling software.

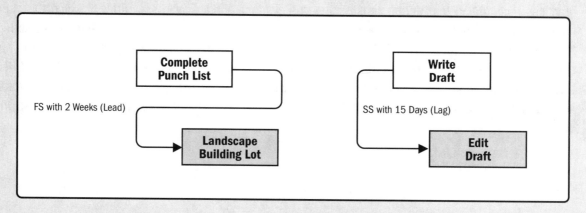

**Figure 6-10. Examples of Lead and Lag**

A lag is the amount of time a successor activity will be delayed with respect to a predecessor activity. For example, a technical writing team may begin editing the draft of a large document 15 days after they begin writing it. This can be shown as a start-to-start relationship with a 15-day lag as shown in Figure 6-10. Lag can also be represented in project schedule network diagrams as shown in Figure 6-11 in the relationship between activities *H* and *I* (as indicated by the nomenclature SS+10 (start-to-start plus 10 days lag) even though the offset is not shown relative to a timescale).

The project management team determines the dependencies that may require a lead or a lag to accurately define the logical relationship. The use of leads and lags should not replace schedule logic. Also, duration estimates do not include any leads or lags. Activities and their related assumptions should be documented.

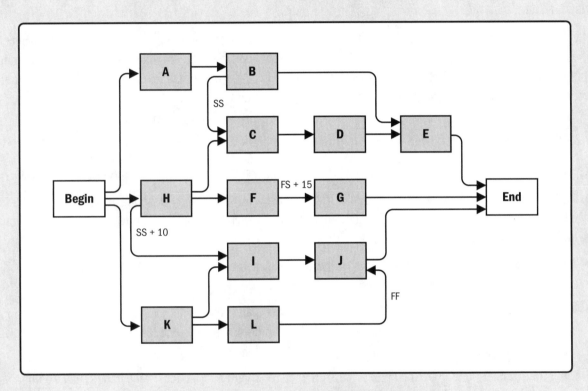

**Figure 6-11. Project Schedule Network Diagram**

### 6.3.2.4 PROJECT MANAGEMENT INFORMATION SYSTEM (PMIS)

Described in Section 4.3.2.2. Project management information systems includes scheduling software that has the capability to help plan, organize, and adjust the sequence of the activities; insert the logical relationships, lead and lag values; and differentiate the different types of dependencies.

## 6.3.3 SEQUENCE ACTIVITIES: OUTPUTS

### 6.3.3.1 PROJECT SCHEDULE NETWORK DIAGRAMS

A project schedule network diagram is a graphical representation of the logical relationships, also referred to as dependencies, among the project schedule activities. Figure 6-11 illustrates a project schedule network diagram. A project schedule network diagram is produced manually or by using project management software. It can include full project details, or have one or more summary activities. A summary narrative can accompany the diagram and describe the basic approach used to sequence the activities. Any unusual activity sequences within the network should be fully described within the narrative.

Activities that have multiple predecessor activities indicate a path convergence. Activities that have multiple successor activities indicate a path divergence. Activities with divergence and convergence are at greater risk as they are affected by multiple activities or can affect multiple activities. Activity I is called a path convergence, as it has more than one predecessor, while activity K is called a path divergence, as it has more than one successor.

### 6.3.3.2 PROJECT DOCUMENTS UPDATES

Project documents that may be updated as a result of carrying out this process include but are not limited to:

◆ **Activity attributes.** Described in Section 6.2.3.2. Activity attributes may describe a necessary sequence of events or defined predecessor or successor relationships, as well as defined lead and lag and logical relationships between the activities.

◆ **Activity list.** Described in Section 6.2.3.1. The activity list may be impacted by the change in relationships among the project activities during the sequencing activities.

◆ **Assumption log.** Described in Section 4.1.3.2. Assumptions and constraints recorded in the assumption log may need to be updated based on the sequencing, relationship determination, and leads and lags, and may give rise to individual project risks that may impact the project schedule.

◆ **Milestone list.** Described in Section 6.2.3.3. The scheduled dates for specific milestones may be impacted by changes in relationships among the project activities during the sequencing activities.

## 6.4 ESTIMATE ACTIVITY DURATIONS

Estimate Activity Durations is the process of estimating the number of work periods needed to complete individual activities with estimated resources. The key benefit of this process is that it provides the amount of time each activity will take to complete. This process is performed throughout the project. The inputs, tools and techniques, and outputs of this process are depicted in Figure 6-12. Figure 6-13 depicts the data flow diagram of the process.

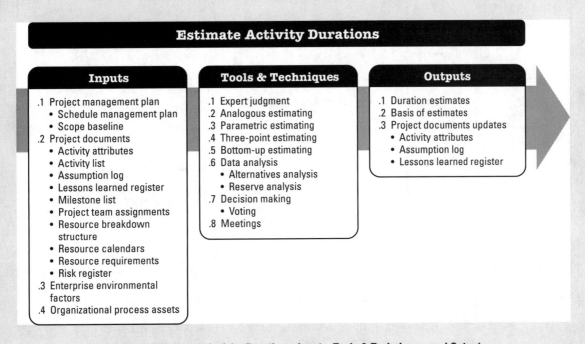

**Estimate Activity Durations**

| Inputs | Tools & Techniques | Outputs |
|---|---|---|
| .1 Project management plan<br>  • Schedule management plan<br>  • Scope baseline<br>.2 Project documents<br>  • Activity attributes<br>  • Activity list<br>  • Assumption log<br>  • Lessons learned register<br>  • Milestone list<br>  • Project team assignments<br>  • Resource breakdown structure<br>  • Resource calendars<br>  • Resource requirements<br>  • Risk register<br>.3 Enterprise environmental factors<br>.4 Organizational process assets | .1 Expert judgment<br>.2 Analogous estimating<br>.3 Parametric estimating<br>.4 Three-point estimating<br>.5 Bottom-up estimating<br>.6 Data analysis<br>  • Alternatives analysis<br>  • Reserve analysis<br>.7 Decision making<br>  • Voting<br>.8 Meetings | .1 Duration estimates<br>.2 Basis of estimates<br>.3 Project documents updates<br>  • Activity attributes<br>  • Assumption log<br>  • Lessons learned register |

**Figure 6-12. Estimate Activity Durations: Inputs, Tools & Techniques, and Outputs**

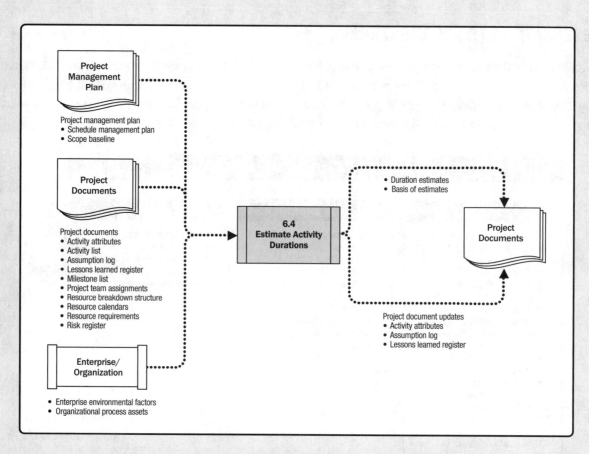

**Figure 6-13. Estimate Activity Durations: Data Flow Diagram**

Estimating activity durations uses information from the scope of work, required resource types or skill levels, estimated resource quantities, and resource calendars. Other factors that may influence the duration estimates include constraints imposed on the duration, effort involved, or type of resources (e.g., fixed duration, fixed effort or work, fixed number of resources), as well as the schedule network analysis technique used. The inputs for the estimates of duration originate from the person or group on the project team who is most familiar with the nature of the work in the specific activity. The duration estimate is progressively elaborated, and the process considers the quality and availability of the input data. For example, as more detailed and precise data are available about the project engineering and design work, the accuracy and quality of the duration estimates improve.

The Estimate Activity Durations process requires an estimation of the amount of work effort required to complete the activity and the amount of available resources estimated to complete the activity. These estimates are used to approximate the number of work periods (activity duration) needed to complete the activity using the appropriate project and resource calendars. In many cases, the number of resources that are expected to be available to accomplish an activity, along with the skill proficiency of those resources, may determine the activity's duration. A change to a driving resource allocated to the activity will usually have an effect on the duration, but this is not a simple "straight-line" or linear relationship. Sometimes, the intrinsic nature of the work (i.e., constraints imposed on the duration, effort involved, or number of resources) will take a predetermined amount of time to complete regardless of the resource allocation (e.g., a 24-hour stress test). Other factors for consideration when estimating duration include:

◆ **Law of diminishing returns.** When one factor (e.g., resource) used to determine the effort required to produce a unit of work is increased while all other factors remain fixed, a point will eventually be reached at which additions of that one factor start to yield progressively smaller or diminishing increases in output.

◆ **Number of resources.** Increasing the number of resources to twice the original number of the resources does not always reduce the time by half, as it may increase extra duration due to risk, and at some point adding too many resources to the activity may increase duration due to knowledge transfer, learning curve, additional coordination, and other factors involved.

◆ **Advances in technology.** This may also play an important role in determining duration estimates. For example, an increase in the output of a manufacturing plant may be achieved by procuring the latest advances in technology, which may impact duration and resource needs.

◆ **Motivation of staff.** The project manager also needs to be aware of Student Syndrome—or procrastination—when people start to apply themselves only at the last possible moment before the deadline, and Parkinson's Law where work expands to fill the time available for its completion.

All data and assumptions that support duration estimating are documented for each activity duration estimate.

## 6.4.1 ESTIMATE ACTIVITY DURATIONS: INPUTS

### 6.4.1.1 PROJECT MANAGEMENT PLAN

Described in Section 4.2.3.1. Project management plan components include but are not limited to:

◆ **Schedule management plan.** Described in Section 6.1.3.1. The schedule management plan defines the method used, as well as the level of accuracy and other criteria required to estimate activity durations.

◆ **Scope baseline.** Described in Section 5.4.3.1. The scope baseline includes the WBS dictionary, which contains technical details that can influence the effort and duration estimates.

### 6.4.1.2 PROJECT DOCUMENTS

Project documents that can be considered as inputs for this process include but are not limited to:

◆ **Activity attributes.** Described in Section 6.2.3.2. Activity attributes may describe defined predecessor or successor relationships, as well as defined lead and lag and logical relationships between the activities that may impact duration estimates.

◆ **Activity list.** Described in Section 6.2.3.1. The activity list contains all schedule activities required on the project, which are to be estimated. Dependencies and other constraints for these activities can influence the duration estimates.

◆ **Assumption log.** Described in Section 4.1.3.2. Assumptions and constraints recorded in the assumption log may give rise to individual project risks that may impact the project schedule.

◆ **Lessons learned register.** Described in Section 4.4.3.1. Lessons learned earlier in the project with regard to effort and duration estimating can be applied to later phases in the project to improve the accuracy and precision of effort and duration estimates.

◆ **Milestone list.** Described in Section 6.2.3.3. The milestone list may have scheduled dates for specific milestones that may impact the duration estimates.

◆ **Project team assignments.** Described in Section 9.3.3.2. The project is staffed when the appropriate people have been assigned to the team.

◆ **Resource breakdown structure.** Described in Section 9.2.3.3. The resource breakdown structure provides a hierarchical structure of the identified resources by resource category and resource type.

◆ **Resource calendars.** Described in Section 9.2.1.2. The resource calendars influence the duration of schedule activities due to the availability of specific resources, type of resources, and resources with specific attributes. Resource calendars specify when and how long identified project resources will be available during the project.

◆ **Resource requirements.** Described in Section 9.2.3.1. The estimated activity resource requirements will have an effect on the duration of the activity, since the level to which the resources assigned to the activity meet the requirements will significantly influence the duration of most activities. For example, if additional or lower-skilled resources are assigned to an activity, there may be reduced efficiency or productivity due to increased communication, training, and coordination needs leading to a longer duration estimate.

◆ **Risk register.** Described in Section 11.2.3.1. Individual project risks may impact resource selection and availability. Updates to the risk register are included with project documents updates, described in Section 11.5.3.2, from Plan Risk Responses.

### 6.4.1.3 ENTERPRISE ENVIRONMENTAL FACTORS

The enterprise environmental factors that can influence the Estimate Activity Durations process include but are not limited to:

◆ Duration estimating databases and other reference data,

◆ Productivity metrics,

◆ Published commercial information, and

◆ Location of team members.

### 6.4.1.4 ORGANIZATIONAL PROCESS ASSETS

The organizational process assets that can influence the Estimate Activity Durations process include but are not limited to:

◆ Historical duration information,

◆ Project calendars,

◆ Estimating policies,

◆ Scheduling methodology, and

◆ Lessons learned repository.

## 6.4.2 ESTIMATE ACTIVITY DURATIONS: TOOLS AND TECHNIQUES

### 6.4.2.1 EXPERT JUDGMENT

Described in Section 4.1.2.1. Expertise should be considered from individuals or groups with specialized knowledge or training in the following topics:

◆ Schedule development, management, and control;

◆ Expertise in estimating; and

◆ Discipline or application knowledge.

### 6.4.2.2 ANALOGOUS ESTIMATING

Analogous estimating is a technique for estimating the duration or cost of an activity or a project using historical data from a similar activity or project. Analogous estimating uses parameters from a previous, similar project, such as duration, budget, size, weight, and complexity, as the basis for estimating the same parameter or measure for a future project. When estimating durations, this technique relies on the actual duration of previous, similar projects as the basis for estimating the duration of the current project. It is a gross value estimating approach, sometimes adjusted for known differences in project complexity. Analogous duration estimating is frequently used to estimate project duration when there is a limited amount of detailed information about the project.

Analogous estimating is generally less costly and less time-consuming than other techniques, but it is also less accurate. Analogous duration estimates can be applied to a total project or to segments of a project and may be used in conjunction with other estimating methods. Analogous estimating is most reliable when the previous activities are similar in fact and not just in appearance, and the project team members preparing the estimates have the needed expertise.

### 6.4.2.3 PARAMETRIC ESTIMATING

Parametric estimating is an estimating technique in which an algorithm is used to calculate cost or duration based on historical data and project parameters. Parametric estimating uses a statistical relationship between historical data and other variables (e.g., square footage in construction) to calculate an estimate for activity parameters, such as cost, budget, and duration.

Durations can be quantitatively determined by multiplying the quantity of work to be performed by the number of labor hours per unit of work. For example, duration on a design project is estimated by the number of drawings multiplied by the number of labor hours per drawing, or on a cable installation, the meters of cable multiplied by the number of labor hours per meter. If the assigned resource is capable of installing 25 meters of cable per hour, the duration required to install 1,000 meters is 40 hours (1,000 meters divided by 25 meters per hour).

This technique can produce higher levels of accuracy depending on the sophistication and underlying data built into the model. Parametric schedule estimates can be applied to a total project or to segments of a project, in conjunction with other estimating methods.

### 6.4.2.4 THREE-POINT ESTIMATING

The accuracy of single-point duration estimates may be improved by considering estimation uncertainty and risk. Using three-point estimates helps define an approximate range for an activity's duration:

◆ **Most likely ($tM$).** This estimate is based on the duration of the activity, given the resources likely to be assigned, their productivity, realistic expectations of availability for the activity, dependencies on other participants, and interruptions.

◆ **Optimistic ($tO$).** The activity duration based on analysis of the best-case scenario for the activity.

◆ **Pessimistic ($tP$).** The duration based on analysis of the worst-case scenario for the activity.

Depending on the assumed distribution of values within the range of the three estimates, the expected duration, $tE$, can be calculated. One commonly used formula is triangular distribution:

$$tE = (tO + tM + tP) / 3.$$

Triangular distribution is used when there is insufficient historical data or when using judgmental data. Duration estimates based on three points with an assumed distribution provide an expected duration and clarify the range of uncertainty around the expected duration.

### 6.4.2.5 BOTTOM-UP ESTIMATING

Bottom-up estimating is a method of estimating project duration or cost by aggregating the estimates of the lower-level components of the WBS. When an activity's duration cannot be estimated with a reasonable degree of confidence, the work within the activity is decomposed into more detail. The detail durations are estimated. These estimates are then aggregated into a total quantity for each of the activity's durations. Activities may or may not have dependencies between them that can affect the application and use of resources. If there are dependencies, this pattern of resource usage is reflected and documented in the estimated requirements of the activity.

### 6.4.2.6 DATA ANALYSIS

Data analysis techniques that can be used for this process include but are not limited to:

◆ **Alternatives analysis.** Alternatives analysis is used to compare various levels of resource capability or skills; scheduling compression techniques (described in Section 6.5.2.6); different tools (manual versus automated); and make, rent, or buy decisions regarding the resources. This allows the team to weigh resource, cost, and duration variables to determine an optimal approach for accomplishing project work.

◆ **Reserve analysis.** Reserve analysis is used to determine the amount of contingency and management reserve needed for the project. Duration estimates may include contingency reserves, sometimes referred to as schedule reserves, to account for schedule uncertainty. Contingency reserves are the estimated duration within the schedule baseline, which is allocated for identified risks that are accepted. Contingency reserves are associated with the known-unknowns, which may be estimated to account for this unknown amount of rework. The contingency reserve may be a percentage of the estimated activity duration or a fixed number of work periods. Contingency reserves may be separated from the individual activities and aggregated. As more precise information about the project becomes available, the contingency reserve may be used, reduced, or eliminated. Contingency should be clearly identified in the schedule documentation.

Estimates may also be produced for the amount of management reserve of schedule for the project. Management reserves are a specified amount of the project budget withheld for management control purposes and are reserved for unforeseen work that is within scope of the project. Management reserves are intended to address the unknown-unknowns that can affect a project. Management reserve is not included in the schedule baseline, but it is part of the overall project duration requirements. Depending on contract terms, use of management reserves may require a change to the schedule baseline.

### 6.4.2.7 DECISION MAKING

Described in Section 5.2.2.4. Decision-making techniques that can be used in this process include but are not limited to voting. One variation of the voting method that is often used in agile-based projects is called the fist of five (also called fist to five). In this technique, the project manager asks the team to show their level of support for a decision by holding up a closed fist (indicating no support) up to five fingers (indicating full support). If a team member holds up fewer than three fingers, the team member is given the opportunity to discuss any objections with the team. The project manager continues the fist-of-five process until the team achieves consensus (everyone holds up three or more fingers) or agrees to move on to the next decision.

### 6.4.2.8 MEETINGS

The project team may hold meetings to estimate activity durations. When using an agile approach, it is necessary to conduct sprint or iteration planning meetings to discuss prioritized product backlog items (user stories) and decide which of these items the team will commit to work on in the upcoming iteration. The team breaks down user stories to low-level tasks, with estimates in hours, and then validates that the estimates are achievable based on team capacity over the duration (iteration). This meeting is usually held on the first day of the iteration and is attended by the product owner, the Scrum team, and the project manager. The outcome of the meeting includes an iteration backlog, as well as assumptions, concerns, risks, dependencies, decisions, and actions.

## 6.4.3 ESTIMATE ACTIVITY DURATIONS: OUTPUTS

### 6.4.3.1 DURATION ESTIMATES

Duration estimates are quantitative assessments of the likely number of time periods that are required to complete an activity, a phase, or a project. Duration estimates do not include any lags as described in Section 6.3.2.3. Duration estimates may include some indication of the range of possible results. For example:

◆ A range of 2 weeks ± 2 days, which indicates that the activity will take at least 8 days and not more than 12 (assuming a 5-day work week); or

◆ A 15% probability of exceeding 3 weeks, which indicates a high probability—85%—that the activity will take 3 weeks or less.

## 6.4.3.2 BASIS OF ESTIMATES

The amount and type of additional details supporting the duration estimate vary by application area. Regardless of the level of detail, the supporting documentation should provide a clear and complete understanding of how the duration estimate was derived.

Supporting detail for duration estimates may include:

◆ Documentation of the basis of the estimate (i.e., how it was developed),

◆ Documentation of all assumptions made,

◆ Documentation of any known constraints,

◆ Indication of the range of possible estimates (e.g., ±10%) to indicate that the duration is estimated between a range of values),

◆ Indication of the confidence level of the final estimate, and

◆ Documentation of individual project risks influencing this estimate.

## 6.4.3.3 PROJECT DOCUMENTS UPDATES

Project documents that may be updated as a result of carrying out this process include but are not limited to:

◆ **Activity attributes.** Described in Section 6.2.3.2. Activity duration estimates produced during this process are documented as part of the activity attributes.

◆ **Assumption log.** Described in Section 4.1.3.2. This includes assumptions made in developing the duration estimate, such as resource skill levels and availability, as well as a basis of estimates for durations. Additionally, constraints arising out of the scheduling methodology and scheduling tool are also documented.

◆ **Lessons learned register.** Described in Section 4.4.3.1. The lessons learned register can be updated with techniques that were efficient and effective in developing effort and duration estimates.

## 6.5 DEVELOP SCHEDULE

Develop Schedule is the process of analyzing activity sequences, durations, resource requirements, and schedule constraints to create a schedule model for project execution and monitoring and controlling. The key benefit of this process is that it generates a schedule model with planned dates for completing project activities. This process is performed throughout the project. The inputs, tools and techniques, and outputs of this process are depicted in Figure 6-14. Figure 6-15 depicts the data flow diagram of the process.

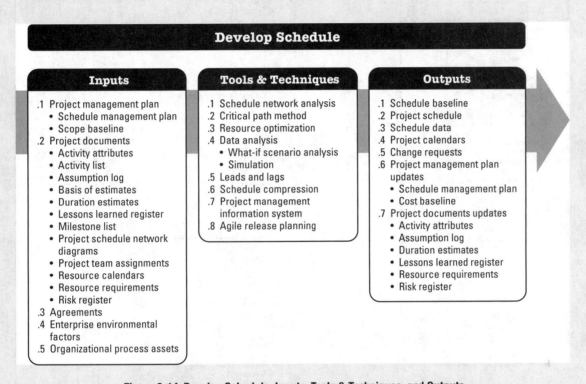

**Figure 6-14. Develop Schedule: Inputs, Tools & Techniques, and Outputs**

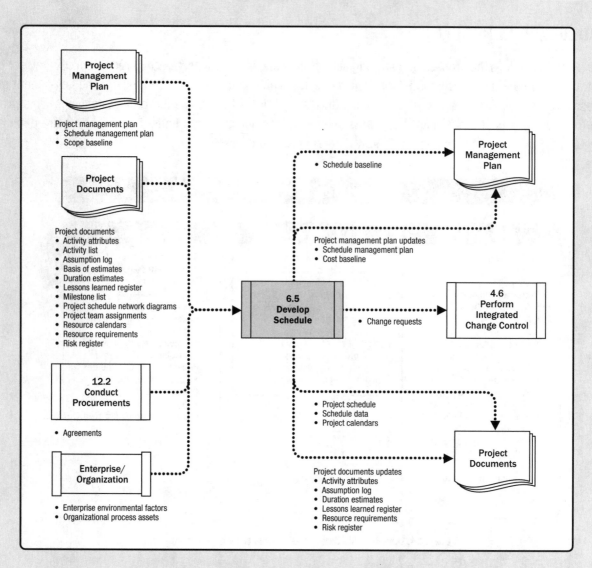

**Figure 6-15. Develop Schedule: Data Flow Diagram**

Developing an acceptable project schedule is an iterative process. The schedule model is used to determine the planned start and finish dates for project activities and milestones based on the best available information. Schedule development can require the review and revision of duration estimates, resource estimates, and schedule reserves to establish an approved project schedule that can serve as a baseline to track progress. Key steps include defining the project milestones, identifying and sequencing activities, and estimating durations. Once the activity start and finish dates have been determined, it is common to have the project staff assigned to the activities review their assigned activities. The staff confirms that the start and finish dates present no conflict with resource calendars or assigned activities on other projects or tasks and thus are still valid. The schedule is then analyzed to determine conflicts with logical relationships and if resource leveling is required before the schedule is approved and baselined. Revising and maintaining the project schedule model to sustain a realistic schedule continues throughout the duration of the project.

For more specific information regarding scheduling, refer to the *Practice Standard for Scheduling*.

## 6.5.1 DEVELOP SCHEDULE: INPUTS

### 6.5.1.1 PROJECT MANAGEMENT PLAN

Described in Section 4.2.3.1. Project management plan components include but are not limited to:

◆ **Schedule management plan.** Described in Section 6.1.3.1. The schedule management plan identifies the scheduling method and tool used to create the schedule and how the schedule is to be calculated.

◆ **Scope baseline.** Described in Section 5.4.3.1. The scope statement, WBS, and WBS dictionary have details about the project deliverables that are considered when building the schedule model.

### 6.5.1.2 PROJECT DOCUMENTS

Project documents that can be considered as inputs for this process include but are not limited to:

◆ **Activity attributes.** Described in Section 6.2.3.2. The activity attributes provide the details used to build the schedule model.

◆ **Activity list.** Described in Section 6.2.3.1. The activity list identifies the activities that will be included in the schedule model.

◆ **Assumption log.** Described in Section 4.1.3.2. Assumptions and constraints recorded in the assumption log may give rise to individual project risks that may impact the project schedule.

◆ **Basis of estimates.** Described in Section 6.4.3.2. The amount and type of additional details supporting the duration estimate vary by application area. Regardless of the level of detail, the supporting documentation should provide a clear and complete understanding of how the duration estimate was derived.

◆ **Duration estimates.** Described in Section 6.4.3.1. The duration estimates contain the quantitative assessments of the likely number of work periods that will be required to complete an activity. This will be used to calculate the schedule.

◆ **Lessons learned register.** Described in Section 4.4.3.1. Lessons learned earlier in the project with regard to developing the schedule model can be applied to later phases in the project to improve the validity of the schedule model.

◆ **Milestone list.** Described in Section 6.2.3.3. The milestone list has scheduled dates for specific milestones.

◆ **Project schedule network diagrams.** Described in Section 6.3.3.1. The project schedule network diagrams contain the logical relationships of predecessors and successors that will be used to calculate the schedule.

◆ **Project team assignments.** Described in Section 9.3.3.2. The project team assignments specify which resources are assigned to each activity.

◆ **Resource calendars.** Described in Sections 9.2.1.2. The resource calendars contain information on the availability of resources during the project.

◆ **Resource requirements.** Described in Section 9.2.3.1. The activity resource requirements identify the types and quantities of resources required for each activity used to create the schedule model.

◆ **Risk register.** Described in Section 11.2.3.1. The risk register provides the details of all identified risks, and their characteristics, that affect the schedule model. Risk information relevant to the schedule is reflected in schedule reserves using the expected or mean risk impact.

## 6.5.1.3 AGREEMENTS

Described in Section 12.2.3.2. Vendors may have an input to the project schedule as they develop the details of how they will perform the project work to meet contractual commitments.

### 6.5.1.4 ENTERPRISE ENVIRONMENTAL FACTORS

The enterprise environmental factors that can influence the Develop Schedule process include but are not limited to:

◆ Government or industry standards, and

◆ Communication channels.

### 6.5.1.5 ORGANIZATIONAL PROCESS ASSETS

The organizational process assets that can influence the Develop Schedule process include but are not limited to:

◆ Scheduling methodology containing the policies governing schedule model development and maintenance, and

◆ Project calendar(s).

## 6.5.2 DEVELOP SCHEDULE: TOOLS AND TECHNIQUES

### 6.5.2.1 SCHEDULE NETWORK ANALYSIS

Schedule network analysis is the overarching technique used to generate the project schedule model. It employs several other techniques such as critical path method (described in Section 6.5.2.2), resource optimization techniques (described in Section 6.5.2.3), and modeling techniques (described in Section 6.5.2.4). Additional analysis includes but is not limited to:

◆ Assessing the need to aggregate schedule reserves to reduce the probability of a schedule slip when multiple paths converge at a single point in time or when multiple paths diverge from a single point in time, to reduce the probability of a schedule slip.

◆ Reviewing the network to see if the critical path has high-risk activities or long lead items that would necessitate use of schedule reserves or the implementation of risk responses to reduce the risk on the critical path.

Schedule network analysis is an iterative process that is employed until a viable schedule model is developed.

## 6.5.2.2 CRITICAL PATH METHOD

The critical path method is used to estimate the minimum project duration and determine the amount of schedule flexibility on the logical network paths within the schedule model. This schedule network analysis technique calculates the early start, early finish, late start, and late finish dates for all activities without regard for any resource limitations by performing a forward and backward pass analysis through the schedule network, as shown in Figure 6-16. In this example, the longest path includes activities A, C, and D, and therefore the sequence of A-C-D is the critical path. The critical path is the sequence of activities that represents the longest path through a project, which determines the shortest possible project duration. The longest path has the least total float—usually zero. The resulting early and late start and finish dates are not necessarily the project schedule; rather they indicate the time periods within which the activity could be executed, using the parameters entered in the schedule model for activity durations, logical relationships, leads, lags, and other known constraints. The critical path method is used to calculate the critical path(s) and the amount of total and free float or schedule flexibility on the logical network paths within the schedule model.

On any network path, the total float or schedule flexibility is measured by the amount of time that a schedule activity can be delayed or extended from its early start date without delaying the project finish date or violating a schedule constraint. A critical path is normally characterized by zero total float on the critical path. As implemented with the precedence diagramming method sequencing, critical paths may have positive, zero, or negative total float depending on the constraints applied. Positive total float is caused when the backward pass is calculated from a schedule constraint that is later than the early finish date that has been calculated during forward pass calculation. Negative total float is caused when a constraint on the late dates is violated by duration and logic. Negative float analysis is a technique that helps to find possible accelerated ways of bringing a delayed schedule back on track. Schedule networks may have multiple near-critical paths. Many software packages allow the user to define the parameters used to determine the critical path(s). Adjustments to activity durations (when more resources or less scope can be arranged), logical relationships (when the relationships were discretionary to begin with), leads and lags, or other schedule constraints may be necessary to produce network paths with a zero or positive total float. Once the total float and the free float have been calculated, the free float is the amount of time that a schedule activity can be delayed without delaying the early start date of any successor or violating a schedule constraint. For example the free float for Activity B, in Figure 6-16, is 5 days.

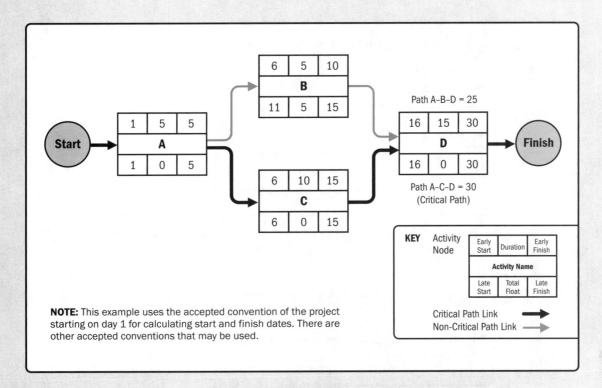

**Figure 6-16. Example of Critical Path Method**

### 6.5.2.3 RESOURCE OPTIMIZATION

Resource optimization is used to adjust the start and finish dates of activities to adjust planned resource use to be equal to or less than resource availability. Examples of resource optimization techniques that can be used to adjust the schedule model due to demand and supply of resources include but are not limited to:

◆ **Resource leveling.** A technique in which start and finish dates are adjusted based on resource constraints with the goal of balancing the demand for resources with the available supply. Resource leveling can be used when shared or critically required resources are available only at certain times or in limited quantities, or are over-allocated, such as when a resource has been assigned to two or more activities during the same time period (as shown in Figure 6-17), or there is a need to keep resource usage at a constant level. Resource leveling can often cause the original critical path to change. Available float is used for leveling resources. Consequently, the critical path through the project schedule may change.

◆ **Resource smoothing.** A technique that adjusts the activities of a schedule model such that the requirements for resources on the project do not exceed certain predefined resource limits. In resource smoothing, as opposed to resource leveling, the project's critical path is not changed and the completion date may not be delayed. In other words, activities may only be delayed within their free and total float. Resource smoothing may not be able to optimize all resources.

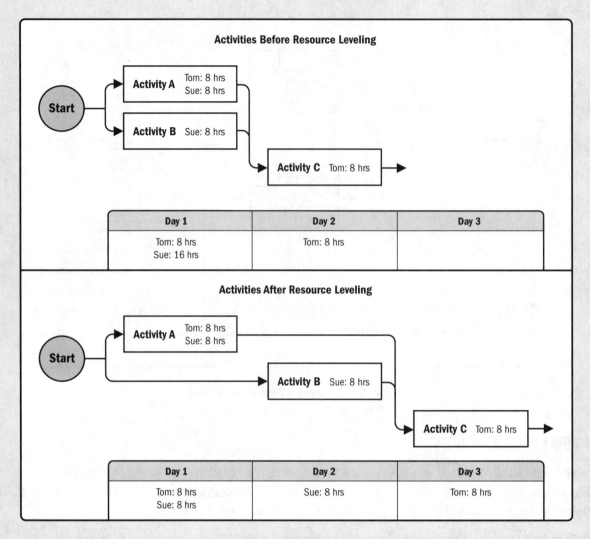

**Figure 6-17. Resource Leveling**

### 6.5.2.4 DATA ANALYSIS

Data analysis techniques that can be used for this process include but are not limited to:

◆ **What-if scenario analysis.** What-if scenario analysis is the process of evaluating scenarios in order to predict their effect, positive or negative, on project objectives. This is an analysis of the question, "What if the situation represented by scenario X happens?" A schedule network analysis is performed using the schedule to compute the different scenarios, such as delaying a major component delivery, extending specific engineering durations, or introducing external factors, such as a strike or a change in the permit process. The outcome of the what-if scenario analysis can be used to assess the feasibility of the project schedule under different conditions, and in preparing schedule reserves and response plans to address the impact of unexpected situations.

◆ **Simulation.** Simulation models the combined effects of individual project risks and other sources of uncertainty to evaluate their potential impact on achieving project objectives. The most common simulation technique is Monte Carlo analysis (see Section 11.4.2.5), in which risks and other sources of uncertainty are used to calculate possible schedule outcomes for the total project. Simulation involves calculating multiple work package durations with different sets of activity assumptions, constraints, risks, issues, or scenarios using probability distributions and other representations of uncertainty (see Section 11.4.2.4). Figure 6-18 shows a probability distribution for a project with the probability of achieving a certain target date (i.e., project finish date). In this example, there is a 10% probability that the project will finish on or before the target date of May 13, while there is a 90% probability of completing the project by May 28.

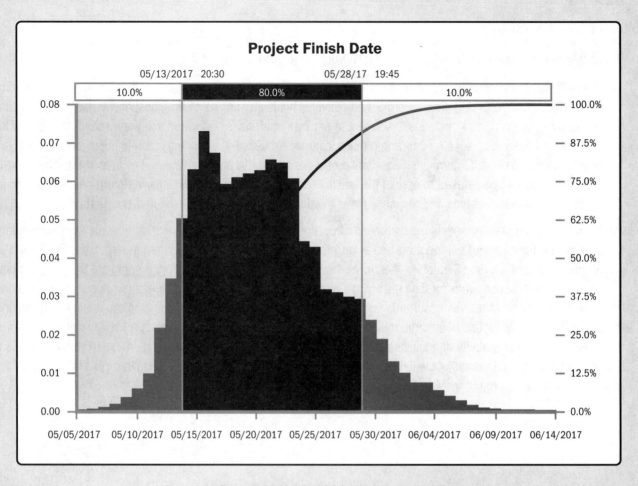

**Figure 6-18. Example Probability Distribution of a Target Milestone**

For more information on how Monte Carlo simulation is used for schedule models, see the *Practice Standard for Scheduling.*

### 6.5.2.5 LEADS AND LAGS

Described in Section 6.3.2.3. Leads and lags are refinements applied during network analysis to develop a viable schedule by adjusting the start time of the successor activities. Leads are used in limited circumstances to advance a successor activity with respect to the predecessor activity, and lags are used in limited circumstances where processes require a set period of time to elapse between the predecessors and successors without work or resource impact.

### 6.5.2.6 SCHEDULE COMPRESSION

Schedule compression techniques are used to shorten or accelerate the schedule duration without reducing the project scope in order to meet schedule constraints, imposed dates, or other schedule objectives. A helpful technique is the negative float analysis. The critical path is the one with the least float. Due to violating a constraint or imposed date, the total float can become negative. Schedule compression techniques are compared in Figure 6-19 and include:

◆ **Crashing.** A technique used to shorten the schedule duration for the least incremental cost by adding resources. Examples of crashing include approving overtime, bringing in additional resources, or paying to expedite delivery to activities on the critical path. Crashing works only for activities on the critical path where additional resources will shorten the activity's duration. Crashing does not always produce a viable alternative and may result in increased risk and/or cost.

◆ **Fast tracking.** A schedule compression technique in which activities or phases normally done in sequence are performed in parallel for at least a portion of their duration. An example is constructing the foundation for a building before completing all of the architectural drawings. Fast tracking may result in rework and increased risk. Fast tracking only works when activities can be overlapped to shorten the project duration on the critical path. Using leads in case of schedule acceleration usually increases coordination efforts between the activities concerned and increases quality risk. Fast tracking may also increase project costs.

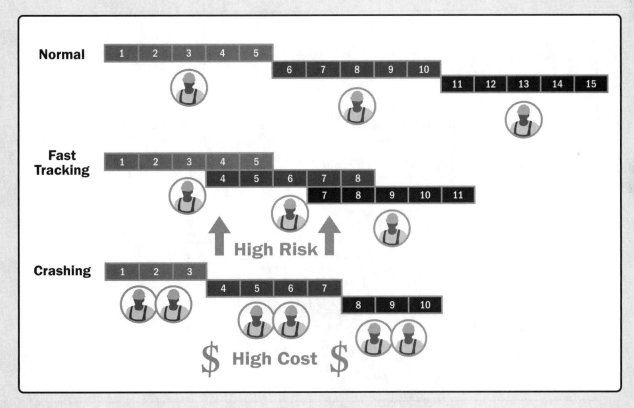

**Figure 6-19. Schedule Compression Comparison**

### 6.5.2.7 PROJECT MANAGEMENT INFORMATION SYSTEM (PMIS)

Described in Section 4.3.2.2. Project management information systems include scheduling software that expedites the process of building a schedule model by generating start and finish dates based on the inputs of activities, network diagrams, resources, and activity durations.

### 6.5.2.8 AGILE RELEASE PLANNING

Agile release planning provides a high-level summary timeline of the release schedule (typically 3 to 6 months) based on the product roadmap and the product vision for the product's evolution. Agile release planning also determines the number of iterations or sprints in the release, and allows the product owner and team to decide how much needs to be developed and how long it will take to have a releasable product based on business goals, dependencies, and impediments.

Since features represent value to the customer, the timeline provides a more easily understood project schedule as it defines which feature will be available at the end of each iteration, which is exactly the depth of information the customer is looking for.

Figure 6-20 shows the relationship among product vision, product roadmap, release planning, and iteration planning.

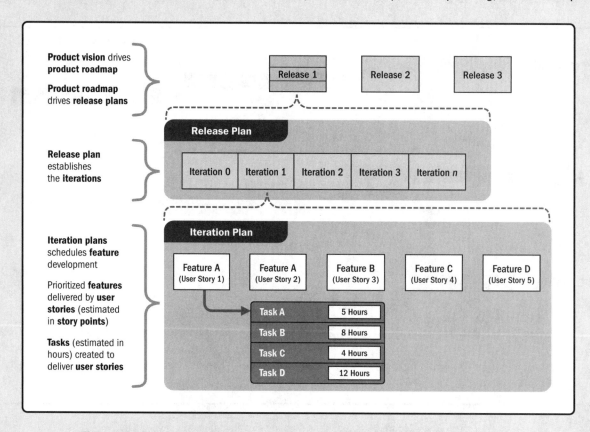

**Figure 6-20. Relationship Between Product Vision, Release Planning, and Iteration Planning**

### 6.5.3 DEVELOP SCHEDULE: OUTPUTS

#### 6.5.3.1 SCHEDULE BASELINE

A schedule baseline is the approved version of a schedule model that can be changed only through formal change control procedures and is used as a basis for comparison to actual results. It is accepted and approved by the appropriate stakeholders as the schedule baseline with baseline start dates and baseline finish dates. During monitoring and controlling, the approved baseline dates are compared to the actual start and finish dates to determine if variances have occurred. The schedule baseline is a component of the project management plan.

#### 6.5.3.2 PROJECT SCHEDULE

The project schedule is an output of a schedule model that presents linked activities with planned dates, durations, milestones, and resources. At a minimum, the project schedule includes a planned start date and planned finish date for each activity. If resource planning is done at an early stage, the project schedule remains preliminary until resource assignments have been confirmed and scheduled start and finish dates are established. This process usually occurs no later than the completion of the project management plan (Section 4.2.3.1). A target project schedule model may also be developed with a defined target start and target finish for each activity. The project schedule may be presented in summary form, sometimes referred to as the master schedule or milestone schedule, or presented in detail. Although a project schedule model can be presented in tabular form, it is more often presented graphically, using one or more of the following formats:

◆ **Bar charts.** Also known as Gantt charts, bar charts represent schedule information where activities are listed on the vertical axis, dates are shown on the horizontal axis, and activity durations are shown as horizontal bars placed according to start and finish dates. Bar charts are relatively easy to read and are commonly used. Depending on the audience, float can be depicted or not. For control and management communications, the broader, more comprehensive summary activity is used between milestones or across multiple interdependent work packages and is displayed in bar chart reports. An example is the summary schedule portion of Figure 6-21 that is presented in a WBS-structured format.

◆ **Milestone charts.** These charts are similar to bar charts, but only identify the scheduled start or completion of major deliverables and key external interfaces. An example is the milestone schedule portion of Figure 6-21.

◆ **Project schedule network diagrams.** These diagrams are commonly presented in the activity-on-node diagram format showing activities and relationships without a time scale, sometimes referred to as a pure logic diagram, as shown in Figure 6-11, or presented in a time-scaled schedule network diagram format that is sometimes called a logic bar chart, as shown for the detailed schedule in Figure 6-21. These diagrams, with activity date information, usually show both the project network logic and the project's critical path schedule activities. This example also shows how each work package is planned as a series of related activities. Another presentation of the project schedule network diagram is a time-scaled logic diagram. These diagrams include a time scale and bars that represent the duration of activities with the logical relationships. They are optimized to show the relationships between activities where any number of activities may appear on the same line of the diagram in sequence.

Figure 6-21 shows schedule presentations for a sample project being executed, with the work in progress reported through as-of date or status date. For a simple project schedule model, Figure 6-21 reflects schedule presentations in the forms of (1) a milestone schedule as a milestone chart, (2) a summary schedule as a bar chart, and (3) a detailed schedule as a project schedule linked bar chart diagram. Figure 6-21 also visually shows the relationships among the different levels of detail of the project schedule.

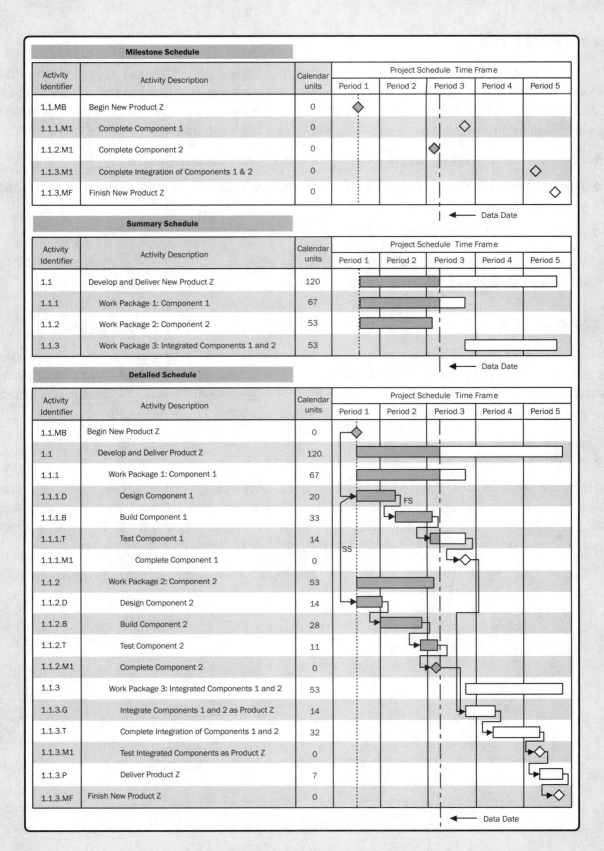

**Figure 6-21. Project Schedule Presentations—Examples**

### 6.5.3.3 SCHEDULE DATA

The schedule data for the project schedule model is the collection of information for describing and controlling the schedule. The schedule data includes, at a minimum, the schedule milestones, schedule activities, activity attributes, and documentation of all identified assumptions and constraints. The amount of additional data varies by application area. Information frequently supplied as supporting detail includes but is not limited to:

◆ Resource requirements by time period, often in the form of a resource histogram;

◆ Alternative schedules, such as best-case or worst-case, not resource-leveled or resource-leveled, or with or without imposed dates; and

◆ Applied schedule reserves.

Schedule data could also include such items as resource histograms, cash-flow projections, order and delivery schedules, or other relevant information.

### 6.5.3.4 PROJECT CALENDARS

A project calendar identifies working days and shifts that are available for scheduled activities. It distinguishes time periods in days or parts of days that are available to complete scheduled activities from time periods that are not available for work. A schedule model may require more than one project calendar to allow for different work periods for some activities to calculate the project schedule. The project calendars may be updated.

### 6.5.3.5 CHANGE REQUESTS

Described in Section 4.3.3.4. Modifications to the project scope or project schedule may result in change requests to the scope baseline, and/or other components of the project management plan. Change requests are processed for review and disposition through the Perform Integrated Change Control process (Section 4.6). Preventive actions may include recommended changes to eliminate or reduce the probability of negative schedule variances.

## 6.5.3.6 PROJECT MANAGEMENT PLAN UPDATES

Any change to the project management plan goes through the organization's change control process via a change request. Components that may require a change request for the project management plan include but are not limited to:

◆ **Schedule management plan.** Described in Section 6.1.3.1. The schedule management plan may be updated to reflect a change in the way the schedule was developed and will be managed.

◆ **Cost baseline.** Described in Section 7.3.3.1. Changes to the cost baseline are incorporated in response to approved changes in scope, resources, or cost estimates. In some cases, cost variances can be so severe that a revised cost baseline is needed to provide a realistic basis for performance measurement.

## 6.5.3.7 PROJECT DOCUMENTS UPDATES

Project documents that may be updated as a result of carrying out this process include but are not limited to:

◆ **Activity attributes.** Described in Section 6.2.3.2. Activity attributes are updated to include any revised resource requirements and any other revisions generated by the Develop Schedule process.

◆ **Assumption log.** Described in Section 4.1.3.2. The assumption log may be updated with changes to assumptions in duration, resource utilization, sequencing, or other information that is revealed as a result of developing the schedule model.

◆ **Duration estimates.** Described in Section 6.4.3.1. The number and availability of resources, along with the activity dependencies can result in a change to the duration estimates. If the resource-leveling analysis changes the resource requirements, then the duration estimates will likely need to be updated as well.

◆ **Lessons learned register.** Described in Section 4.4.3.1. The lessons learned register can be updated with techniques that were efficient and effective in developing the schedule model.

◆ **Resource requirements.** Described in Section 9.2.3.1. Resource leveling can have a significant effect on preliminary estimates for the types and quantities of resources required. If the resource-leveling analysis changes the resource requirements, then the resource requirements are updated.

◆ **Risk register.** Described in Section 11.2.3.1. The risk register may need to be updated to reflect opportunities or threats perceived through scheduling assumptions.

# 6.6 CONTROL SCHEDULE

Control Schedule is the process of monitoring the status of the project to update the project schedule and managing changes to the schedule baseline. The key benefit of this process is that the schedule baseline is maintained throughout the project. This process is performed throughout the project. The inputs, tools and techniques, and outputs of this process are depicted in Figure 6-22. Figure 6-23 depicts the data flow diagram of the process.

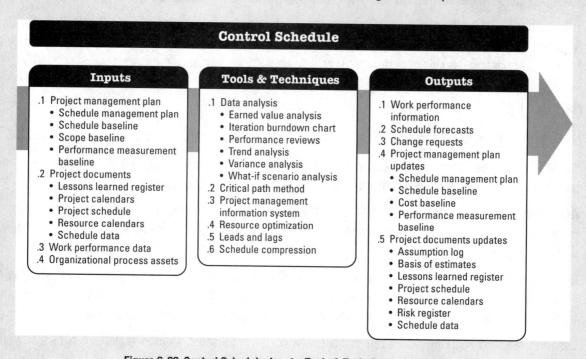

**Figure 6-22. Control Schedule: Inputs, Tools & Techniques, and Outputs**

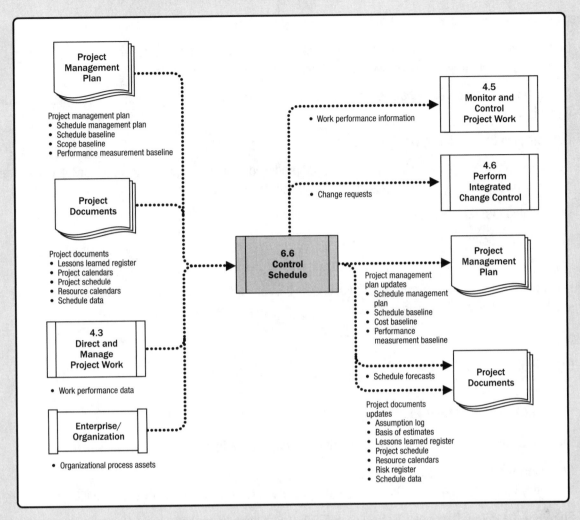

**Figure 6-23. Control Schedule: Data Flow Diagram**

Updating the schedule model requires knowing the actual performance to date. Any change to the schedule baseline can only be approved through the Perform Integrated Change Control process (Section 4.6). Control Schedule, as a component of the Perform Integrated Change Control process, is concerned with:

◆ Determining the current status of the project schedule,

◆ Influencing the factors that create schedule changes,

◆ Reconsidering necessary schedule reserves,

◆ Determining if the project schedule has changed, and

◆ Managing the actual changes as they occur.

When an agile approach is used, Control Schedule is concerned with:

◆ Determining the current status of the project schedule by comparing the total amount of work delivered and accepted against the estimates of work completed for the elapsed time cycle;

◆ Conducting retrospectives (scheduled reviews to record lessons learned) for correcting processes and improving, if required;

◆ Reprioritizing the remaining work plan (backlog);

◆ Determining the rate at which the deliverables are produced, validated, and accepted (velocity) in the given time per iteration (agreed-upon work cycle duration, typically 2 weeks or 1 month);

◆ Determining that the project schedule has changed; and

◆ Managing the actual changes as they occur.

When work is being contracted, regular and milestone status updates from contractors and suppliers are a means of ensuring the work is progressing as agreed upon to ensure the schedule is under control. Scheduled status reviews and walkthroughs should be done to ensure the contractor reports are accurate and complete.

## 6.6.1 CONTROL SCHEDULE: INPUTS

### 6.6.1.1 PROJECT MANAGEMENT PLAN

Described in Section 4.2.3.1. Project management plan components include but are not limited to:

◆ **Schedule management plan.** Described in Section 6.1.3.1. The schedule management plan describes the frequency that the schedule will be updated, how reserve will be used, and how the schedule will be controlled.

◆ **Schedule baseline.** Described in Section 6.5.3.1. The schedule baseline is compared with actual results to determine if a change, corrective action, or preventive action is necessary.

◆ **Scope baseline.** Described in Section 5.4.3.1. The project WBS, deliverables, and acceptance criteria documented in the scope baseline are considered explicitly when monitoring and controlling the schedule baseline.

◆ **Performance measurement baseline.** Described in Section 4.2.3.1. When using earned value analysis the performance measurement baseline is compared to actual results to determine if a change, corrective action, or preventive action is necessary.

## 6.6.1.2 PROJECT DOCUMENTS

Project documents that can be considered as inputs for this process include but are not limited to:

◆ **Lessons learned register.** Described in Section 4.4.3.1. Lessons learned earlier in the project can be applied to later phases in the project to improve schedule control.

◆ **Project calendars.** Described in Section 6.5.3.4. A schedule model may require more than one project calendar to allow for different work periods for some activities to calculate the schedule forecasts.

◆ **Project schedule.** Described in Section 6.5.3.2. Project schedule refers to the most recent version with notations to indicate updates, completed activities, and started activities as of the indicated date.

◆ **Resource calendars.** Described in Section 9.2.1.2. Resource calendars show the availability of team and physical resources.

◆ **Schedule data.** Described in Section 6.5.3.3. Schedule data will be reviewed and updated in the Control Schedule process.

## 6.6.1.3 WORK PERFORMANCE DATA

Described in Section 4.3.3.2. Work performance data contains data on project status such as which activities have started, their progress (e.g., actual duration, remaining duration, and physical percent complete), and which activities have finished.

## 6.6.1.4 ORGANIZATIONAL PROCESS ASSETS

The organizational process assets that can influence the Control Schedule process include but are not limited to:

◆ Existing formal and informal schedule control-related policies, procedures, and guidelines;

◆ Schedule control tools; and

◆ Monitoring and reporting methods to be used.

## 6.6.2 CONTROL SCHEDULE: TOOLS AND TECHNIQUES

### 6.6.2.1 DATA ANALYSIS

Data analysis techniques that can be used for this process include but are not limited to:

◆ **Earned value analysis.** Described in Section 7.4.2.2. Schedule performance measurements such as schedule variance (SV) and schedule performance index (SPI) are used to assess the magnitude of variation to the original schedule baseline.

◆ **Iteration burndown chart.** This chart tracks the work that remains to be completed in the iteration backlog. It is used to analyze the variance with respect to an ideal burndown based on the work committed from iteration planning (see Section 6.4.2.8). A forecast trend line can be used to predict the likely variance at iteration completion and take appropriate actions during the course of the iteration. A diagonal line representing the ideal burndown and daily actual remaining work is then plotted. A trend line is then calculated to forecast completion based on remaining work. Figure 6-24 is an example of an iteration burndown chart.

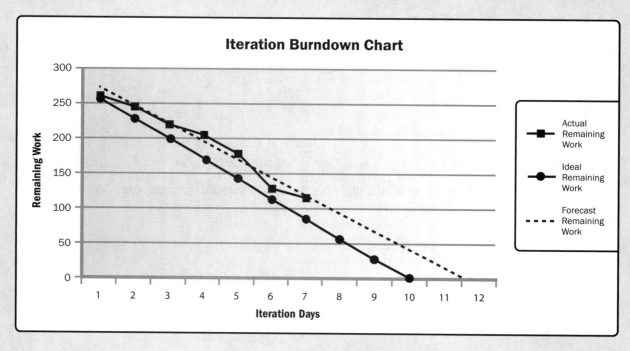

Figure 6-24. Iteration Burndown Chart

◆ **Performance reviews.** Performance reviews measure, compare, and analyze schedule performance against the schedule baseline such as actual start and finish dates, percent complete, and remaining duration for work in progress.

◆ **Trend analysis.** Described in Section 4.5.2.2. Trend analysis examines project performance over time to determine whether performance is improving or deteriorating. Graphical analysis techniques are valuable for understanding performance to date and for comparing to future performance goals in the form of completion dates.

◆ **Variance analysis.** Variance analysis looks at variances in planned versus actual start and finish dates, planned versus actual durations, and variances in float. Part of variance analysis is determining the cause and degree of variance relative to the schedule baseline (see Section 6.5.3.1), estimating the implications of those variances for future work to completion, and deciding whether corrective or preventive action is required. For example, a major delay on any activity not on the critical path may have little effect on the overall project schedule, while a much shorter delay on a critical or near-critical activity may require immediate action.

◆ **What-if scenario analysis.** Described in Section 6.5.2.4. What-if scenario analysis is used to assess the various scenarios guided by the output from the Project Risk Management processes to bring the schedule model into alignment with the project management plan and approved baseline.

## 6.6.2.2 CRITICAL PATH METHOD

Described in Section 6.5.2.2. Comparing the progress along the critical path can help determine schedule status. The variance on the critical path will have a direct impact on the project end date. Evaluating the progress of activities on near critical paths can identify schedule risk.

## 6.6.2.3 PROJECT MANAGEMENT INFORMATION SYSTEM (PMIS)

Described in Section 4.3.2.2. Project management information systems include scheduling software that provides the ability to track planned dates versus actual dates, to report variances to and progress made against the schedule baseline, and to forecast the effects of changes to the project schedule model.

## 6.6.2.4 RESOURCE OPTIMIZATION

Described in Section 6.5.2.3. Resource optimization techniques involve the scheduling of activities and the resources required by those activities while taking into consideration both the resource availability and the project time.

### 6.6.2.5 LEADS AND LAGS

Adjusting leads and lags is applied during network analysis to find ways to bring project activities that are behind into alignment with the plan. For example, on a project to construct a new office building, the landscaping can be adjusted to start before the exterior work of the building is completed by increasing the lead time in the relationship, or a technical writing team can adjust the start of editing the draft of a large document immediately after the document is written by eliminating or decreasing lag time.

### 6.6.2.6 SCHEDULE COMPRESSION

Schedule compression techniques (see Section 6.5.2.6) are used to find ways to bring project activities that are behind into alignment with the plan by fast tracking or crashing the schedule for the remaining work.

## 6.6.3 CONTROL SCHEDULE: OUTPUTS

### 6.6.3.1 WORK PERFORMANCE INFORMATION

Described in Section 4.5.1.3. Work performance information includes information on how the project work is performing compared to the schedule baseline. Variances in the start and finish dates and the durations can be calculated at the work package level and control account level. For projects using earned value analysis, the (SV) and (SPI) are documented for inclusion in work performance reports (see Section 4.5.3.1).

### 6.6.3.2 SCHEDULE FORECASTS

Schedule updates are forecasts of estimates or predictions of conditions and events in the project's future based on information and knowledge available at the time of the forecast. Forecasts are updated and reissued based on work performance information provided as the project is executed. The information is based on the project's past performance and expected future performance based on corrective or preventive actions. This can include earned value performance indicators, as well as schedule reserve information that could impact the project in the future.

### 6.6.3.3 CHANGE REQUESTS

Described in Section 4.3.3.4. Schedule variance analysis, as well as reviews of progress reports, results of performance measures, and modifications to the project scope or project schedule, may result in change requests to the schedule baseline, scope baseline, and/or other components of the project management plan. Change requests are processed for review and disposition through the Perform Integrated Change Control process (Section 4.6). Preventive actions may include recommended changes to eliminate or reduce the probability of negative schedule variances.

### 6.6.3.4 PROJECT MANAGEMENT PLAN UPDATES

Any change to the project management plan goes through the organization's change control process via a change request. Components that may require a change request for the project management plan include but are not limited to:

◆ **Schedule management plan.** Described in Section 6.1.3.1. The schedule management plan may be updated to reflect a change in the way the schedule is managed.

◆ **Schedule baseline.** Described in Section 6.5.3.1. Changes to the schedule baseline are incorporated in response to approved change requests related to change in project scope, resources, or activity duration estimates. The schedule baseline may be updated to reflect changes caused by schedule compression techniques or performance issues.

◆ **Cost baseline.** Described in Section 7.3.3.1. Changes to the cost baseline are incorporated in response to approved changes in scope, resources, or cost estimates.

◆ **Performance measurement baseline.** Described in Section 4.2.3.1. Changes to the performance measurement baseline are incorporated in response to approved changes in scope, schedule performance, or cost estimates. In some cases, the performance variances can be so severe that a change request is put forth to revise the performance measurement baseline to provide a realistic basis for performance measurement.

### 6.6.3.5 PROJECT DOCUMENTS UPDATES

Project documents that may be updated as a result of carrying out this process include but are not limited to:

◆ **Assumption log.** Described in Section 4.1.3.2. Schedule performance may indicate the need to revise assumptions on activity sequencing, durations, and productivity.

◆ **Basis of estimates.** Described in Section 6.4.3.2. Schedule performance may indicate the need to revise the way duration estimates were developed.

◆ **Lessons learned register.** Described in Section 4.4.3.1. The lessons learned register can be updated with techniques that were effective in maintaining the schedule, causes of variances, and corrective actions that were used to respond to schedule variances.

◆ **Project schedule.** An updated project schedule (see Section 6.5.3.2) will be generated from the schedule model populated with updated schedule data to reflect the schedule changes and manage the project.

◆ **Resource calendars.** Described in Section 9.2.1.2. Resource calendars are updated to reflect changes to the utilization of resource calendars that were the result of optimizing resources, schedule compression, and corrective or preventive actions.

◆ **Risk register.** Described in Section 11.2.3.1. The risk register and risk response plans within it, may be updated based on the risks that may arise due to schedule compression techniques.

◆ **Schedule data.** Described in Section 6.5.3.3. New project schedule network diagrams may be developed to display approved remaining durations and approved modifications to the schedule. In some cases, project schedule delays can be so severe that a new target schedule with forecasted start and finish dates is needed to provide realistic data for directing the work, measuring performance, and measuring progress.

# 7

## PROJECT COST MANAGEMENT

Project Cost Management includes the processes involved in planning, estimating, budgeting, financing, funding, managing, and controlling costs so that the project can be completed within the approved budget. The Project Cost Management processes are:

**7.1 Plan Cost Management**—The process of defining how the project costs will be estimated, budgeted, managed, monitored, and controlled.

**7.2 Estimate Costs**—The process of developing an approximation of the monetary resources needed to complete project work.

**7.3 Determine Budget**—The process of aggregating the estimated costs of individual activities or work packages to establish an authorized cost baseline.

**7.4 Control Costs**—The process of monitoring the status of the project to update the project costs and manage changes to the cost baseline.

Figure 7-1 provides an overview of the Project Cost Management processes. The Project Cost Management processes are presented as discrete processes with defined interfaces, while in practice they overlap and interact in ways that cannot be completely detailed in the *PMBOK® Guide*. These processes interact with each other and with processes in other Knowledge Areas.

On some projects, especially those of smaller scope, cost estimating and cost budgeting are tightly linked and can be viewed as a single process that can be performed by a single person over a relatively short period of time. They are presented here as distinct processes because the tools and techniques for each are different. The ability to influence cost is greatest at the early stages of the project, making early scope definition critical (see Section 5.3).

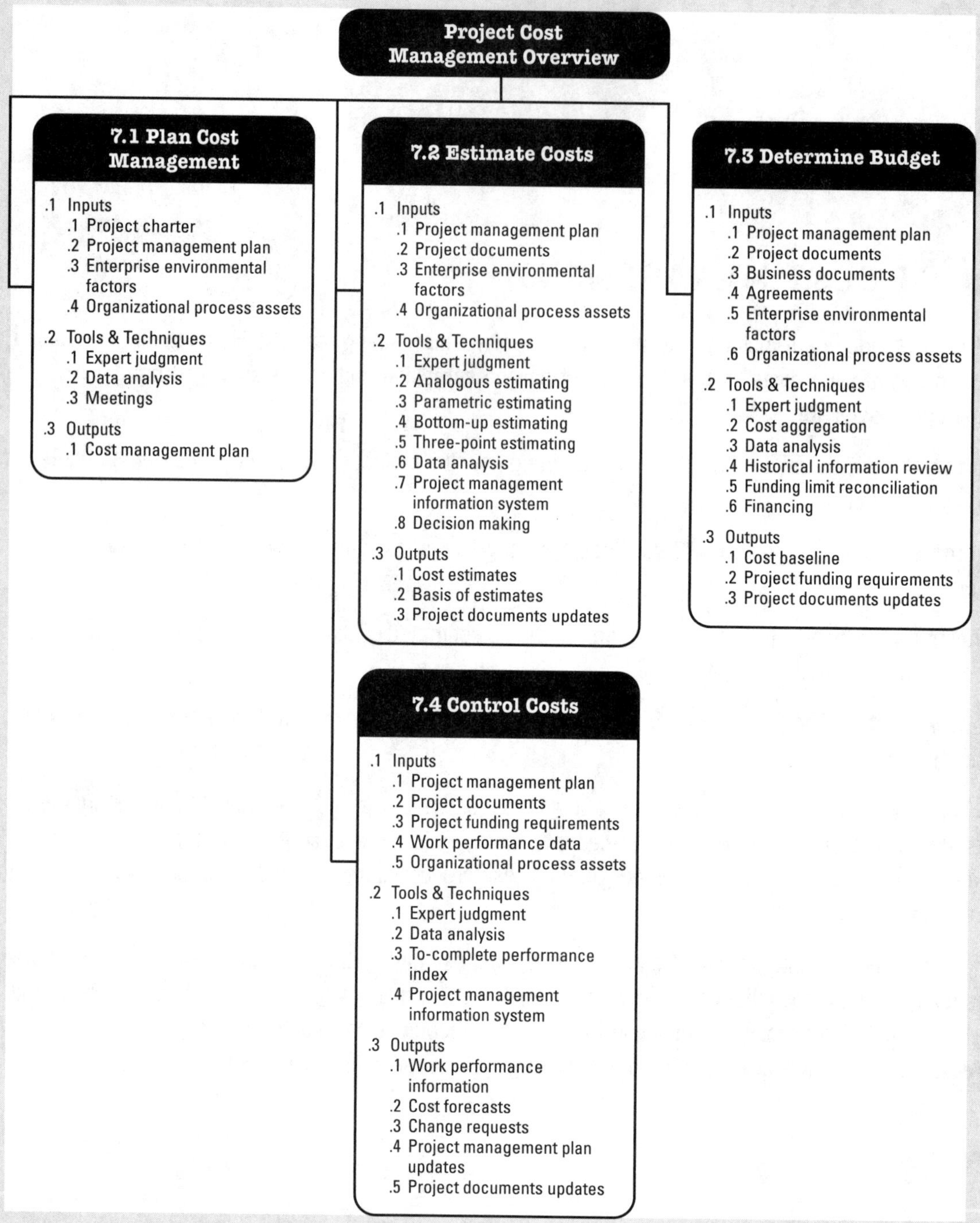

```
                        ┌─────────────────────────┐
                        │   Project Cost          │
                        │ Management Overview     │
                        └─────────────────────────┘
```

**7.1 Plan Cost Management**

.1 Inputs
    .1 Project charter
    .2 Project management plan
    .3 Enterprise environmental
       factors
    .4 Organizational process assets

.2 Tools & Techniques
    .1 Expert judgment
    .2 Data analysis
    .3 Meetings

.3 Outputs
    .1 Cost management plan

**7.2 Estimate Costs**

.1 Inputs
    .1 Project management plan
    .2 Project documents
    .3 Enterprise environmental
       factors
    .4 Organizational process assets

.2 Tools & Techniques
    .1 Expert judgment
    .2 Analogous estimating
    .3 Parametric estimating
    .4 Bottom-up estimating
    .5 Three-point estimating
    .6 Data analysis
    .7 Project management
       information system
    .8 Decision making

.3 Outputs
    .1 Cost estimates
    .2 Basis of estimates
    .3 Project documents updates

**7.3 Determine Budget**

.1 Inputs
    .1 Project management plan
    .2 Project documents
    .3 Business documents
    .4 Agreements
    .5 Enterprise environmental
       factors
    .6 Organizational process assets

.2 Tools & Techniques
    .1 Expert judgment
    .2 Cost aggregation
    .3 Data analysis
    .4 Historical information review
    .5 Funding limit reconciliation
    .6 Financing

.3 Outputs
    .1 Cost baseline
    .2 Project funding requirements
    .3 Project documents updates

**7.4 Control Costs**

.1 Inputs
    .1 Project management plan
    .2 Project documents
    .3 Project funding requirements
    .4 Work performance data
    .5 Organizational process assets

.2 Tools & Techniques
    .1 Expert judgment
    .2 Data analysis
    .3 To-complete performance
       index
    .4 Project management
       information system

.3 Outputs
    .1 Work performance
       information
    .2 Cost forecasts
    .3 Change requests
    .4 Project management plan
       updates
    .5 Project documents updates

**Figure 7-1. Project Cost Management Overview**

## KEY CONCEPTS FOR PROJECT COST MANAGEMENT

Project Cost Management is primarily concerned with the cost of the resources needed to complete project activities. Project Cost Management should consider the effect of project decisions on the subsequent recurring cost of using, maintaining, and supporting the product, service, or result of the project. For example, limiting the number of design reviews can reduce the cost of the project but could increase the resulting product's operating costs.

Another aspect of cost management is recognizing that different stakeholders measure project costs in different ways and at different times. For example, the cost of an acquired item may be measured when the acquisition decision is made or committed, the order is placed, the item is delivered, or the actual cost is incurred or recorded for project accounting purposes. In many organizations, predicting and analyzing the prospective financial performance of the project's product is performed outside of the project. In others, such as a capital facilities project, Project Cost Management can include this work. When such predictions and analyses are included, Project Cost Management may address additional processes and numerous general financial management techniques such as return on investment, discounted cash flow, and investment payback analysis.

## TRENDS AND EMERGING PRACTICES IN PROJECT COST MANAGEMENT

Within the practice of Project Cost Management, trends include the expansion of earned value management (EVM) to include the concept of earned schedule (ES).

ES is an extension to the theory and practice of EVM. Earned schedule theory replaces the schedule variance measures used in traditional EVM (earned value – planned value) with ES and actual time (AT). Using the alternate equation for calculating schedule variance ES – AT, if the amount of earned schedule is greater than 0, then the project is considered ahead of schedule. In other words, the project earned more than planned at a given point in time. The schedule performance index (SPI) using earned schedule metrics is ES/AT. This indicates the efficiency with which work is being accomplished. Earned schedule theory also provides formulas for forecasting the project completion date, using earned schedule, actual time, and estimated duration.

## TAILORING CONSIDERATIONS

Because each project is unique, the project manager may need to tailor the way Project Cost Management processes are applied. Considerations for tailoring include but are not limited to:

◆ **Knowledge management.** Does the organization have a formal knowledge management and financial database repository that a project manager is required to use and that is readily accessible?

◆ **Estimating and budgeting.** Does the organization have existing formal or informal cost estimating and budgeting-related policies, procedures, and guidelines?

◆ **Earned value management.** Does the organization use earned value management in managing projects?

◆ **Use of agile approach.** Does the organization use agile methodologies in managing projects? How does this impact cost estimating?

◆ **Governance.** Does the organization have formal or informal audit and governance policies, procedures, and guidelines?

## CONSIDERATIONS FOR AGILE/ADAPTIVE ENVIRONMENTS

Projects with high degrees of uncertainty or those where the scope is not yet fully defined may not benefit from detailed cost calculations due to frequent changes. Instead, lightweight estimation methods can be used to generate a fast, high-level forecast of project labor costs, which can then be easily adjusted as changes arise. Detailed estimates are reserved for short-term planning horizons in a just-in-time fashion.

In cases where high-variability projects are also subject to strict budgets, the scope and schedule are more often adjusted to stay within cost constraints.

# 7.1 PLAN COST MANAGEMENT

Plan Cost Management is the process of defining how the project costs will be estimated, budgeted, managed, monitored, and controlled. The key benefit of this process is that it provides guidance and direction on how the project costs will be managed throughout the project. This process is performed once or at predefined points in the project. The inputs, tools and techniques, and outputs of this process are depicted in Figure 7-2. Figure 7-3 depicts the data flow diagram of the process.

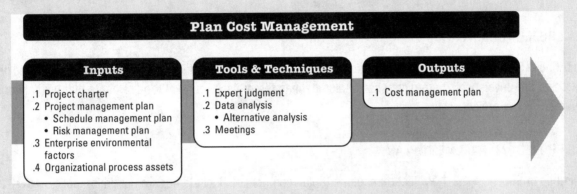

**Figure 7-2. Plan Cost Management: Inputs, Tools & Techniques, and Outputs**

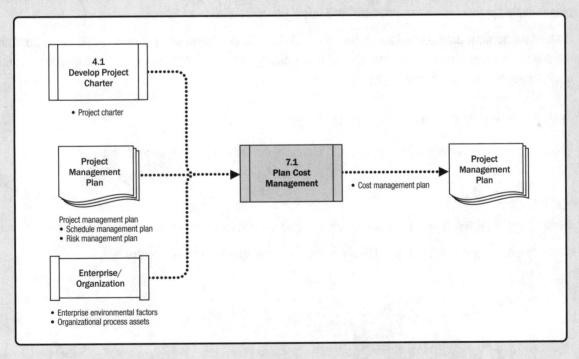

**Figure 7-3. Plan Cost Management: Data Flow Diagram**

The cost management planning effort occurs early in project planning and sets the framework for each of the cost management processes so that performance of the processes will be efficient and coordinated. The cost management processes and their associated tools and techniques are documented in the cost management plan. The cost management plan is a component of the project management plan.

## 7.1.1 PLAN COST MANAGEMENT: INPUTS

### 7.1.1.1 PROJECT CHARTER

Described in Section 4.2.3.1. The project charter provides the preapproved financial resources from which the detailed project costs are developed. The project charter also defines the project approval requirements that will influence the management of the project costs.

### 7.1.1.2 PROJECT MANAGEMENT PLAN

Described in Section 4.2.3.1. Project management plan components include but are not limited to:

◆ **Schedule management plan.** Described in Section 6.1.3.1. The schedule management plan establishes the criteria and the activities for developing, monitoring, and controlling the schedule. The schedule management plan provides processes and controls that will impact cost estimation and management.

◆ **Risk management plan.** Described in Section 11.1.3.1. The risk management plan provides the approach for identifying, analyzing, and monitoring risks. The risk management plan provides processes and controls that will impact cost estimation and management.

### 7.1.1.3 ENTERPRISE ENVIRONMENTAL FACTORS

The enterprise environmental factors that can influence the Plan Cost Management process include but are not limited to:

◆ Organizational culture and structure can influence cost management.

◆ Market conditions describe what products, services, and results are available in the regional and global markets.

◆ Currency exchange rates for project costs are sourced from more than one country.

◆ Published commercial information such as resource cost rate information is often available from commercial databases that track skills and human resource costs, and provide standard costs for material and equipment. Published seller price lists are another source of information.

◆ Project management information system provides alternative possibilities for managing cost.

◆ Productivity differences in different parts of the world can have a large influence on the cost of projects.

### 7.1.1.4 ORGANIZATIONAL PROCESS ASSETS

The organizational process assets that can influence the Plan Cost Management process include but are not limited to:

◆ Financial controls procedures (e.g., time reporting, required expenditure and disbursement reviews, accounting codes, and standard contract provisions);

◆ Historical information and lessons learned repository;

◆ Financial databases; and

◆ Existing formal and informal cost estimating and budgeting-related policies, procedures, and guidelines.

## 7.1.2 PLAN COST MANAGEMENT: TOOLS AND TECHNIQUES

### 7.1.2.1 EXPERT JUDGMENT

Described in Section 4.1.2.1 Expertise should be considered from individuals or groups with specialized knowledge or training in the following topics:

◆ Previous similar projects;

◆ Information in the industry, discipline, and application area;

◆ Cost estimating and budgeting; and

◆ Earned value management.

## 7.1.2.2 DATA ANALYSIS

A data analysis technique that can be used for this process includes but is not limited to alternatives analysis. Alternatives analysis can include reviewing strategic funding options such as: self-funding, funding with equity, or funding with debt. It can also include consideration of ways to acquire project resources such as making, purchasing, renting, or leasing.

## 7.1.2.3 MEETINGS

Project teams may hold planning meetings to develop the cost management plan. Attendees may include the project manager, the project sponsor, selected project team members, selected stakeholders, anyone with responsibility for project costs, and others as needed.

## 7.1.3 PLAN COST MANAGEMENT: OUTPUTS

### 7.1.3.1 COST MANAGEMENT PLAN

The cost management plan is a component of the project management plan and describes how the project costs will be planned, structured, and controlled. The cost management processes and their associated tools and techniques are documented in the cost management plan.

For example, the cost management plan can establish the following:

◆ **Units of measure.** Each unit used in measurements (such as staff hours, staff days, or weeks for time measures; meters, liters, tons, kilometers, or cubic yards for quantity measures; or lump sum in currency form) is defined for each of the resources.

◆ **Level of precision.** This is the degree to which cost estimates will be rounded up or down (e.g., US$995.59 to US$1,000), based on the scope of the activities and magnitude of the project.

◆ **Level of accuracy.** The acceptable range (e.g., ±10%) used in determining realistic cost estimates is specified, and may include an amount for contingencies.

◆ **Organizational procedures links.** The work breakdown structure (WBS) (Section 5.4) provides the framework for the cost management plan, allowing for consistency with the estimates, budgets, and control of costs. The WBS component used for the project cost accounting is called the control account. Each control account is assigned a unique code or account number(s) that links directly to the performing organization's accounting system.

◆ **Control thresholds.** Variance thresholds for monitoring cost performance may be specified to indicate an agreed-upon amount of variation to be allowed before some action needs to be taken. Thresholds are typically expressed as percentage deviations from the baseline plan.

◆ **Rules of performance measurement.** Earned value management (EVM) rules of performance measurement are set. For example, the cost management plan may:

  ■ Define the points in the WBS at which measurement of control accounts will be performed;

  ■ Establish the EVM techniques (e.g., weighted milestones, fixed-formula, percent complete, etc.) to be employed; and

  ■ Specify tracking methodologies and the EVM computation equations for calculating projected estimate at completion (EAC) forecasts to provide a validity check on the bottom-up EAC.

◆ **Reporting formats.** The formats and frequency for the various cost reports are defined.

◆ **Additional details.** Additional details about cost management activities include but are not limited to:

  ■ Description of strategic funding choices,

  ■ Procedure to account for fluctuations in currency exchange rates, and

  ■ Procedure for project cost recording.

For more specific information regarding earned value management, refer to the *Practice Standard for Earned Value Management – Second Edition* [17].

# 7.2 ESTIMATE COSTS

Estimate Costs is the process of developing an approximation of the cost of resources needed to complete project work. The key benefit of this process is that it determines the monetary resources required for the project. This process is performed periodically throughout the project as needed. The inputs, tools and techniques, and outputs of this process are depicted in Figure 7-4. Figure 7-5 depicts the data flow diagram of the process.

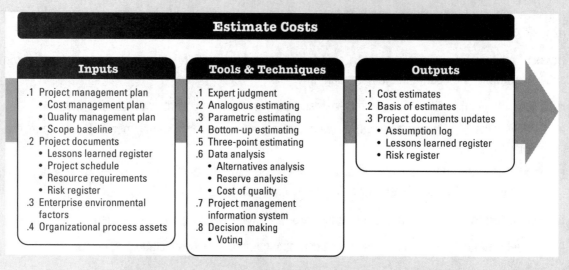

**Figure 7-4. Estimate Costs: Inputs, Tools & Techniques, and Outputs**

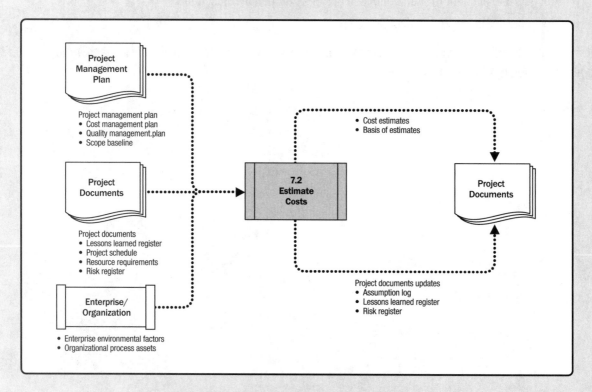

**Figure 7-5. Estimate Costs: Data Flow Diagram**

A cost estimate is a quantitative assessment of the likely costs for resources required to complete the activity. It is a prediction that is based on the information known at a given point in time. Cost estimates include the identification and consideration of costing alternatives to initiate and complete the project. Cost trade-offs and risks should be considered, such as make versus buy, buy versus lease, and the sharing of resources in order to achieve optimal costs for the project.

Cost estimates are generally expressed in units of some currency (i.e., dollars, euros, yen, etc.), although in some instances other units of measure, such as staff hours or staff days, are used to facilitate comparisons by eliminating the effects of currency fluctuations.

Cost estimates should be reviewed and refined during the course of the project to reflect additional detail as it becomes available and assumptions are tested. The accuracy of a project estimate will increase as the project progresses through the project life cycle. For example, a project in the start up phase may have a rough order of magnitude (ROM) estimate in the range of −25% to +75%. Later in the project, as more information is known, definitive estimates could narrow the range of accuracy to −5% to +10%. In some organizations, there are guidelines for when such refinements can be made and the degree of confidence or accuracy that is expected.

Costs are estimated for all resources that will be charged to the project. This includes but is not limited to labor, materials, equipment, services, and facilities, as well as special categories such as an inflation allowance, cost of financing, or contingency costs. Cost estimates may be presented at the activity level or in summary form.

## 7.2.1 ESTIMATE COSTS: INPUTS

### 7.2.1.1 PROJECT MANAGEMENT PLAN

Described in Section 4.2.3.1. Project management plan components include but are not limited to:

◆ **Cost management plan.** Described in Section 7.1.3.1. The cost management plan describes estimating methods that can be used and the level of precision and accuracy required for the cost estimate.

◆ **Quality management plan.** Described in Section 8.1.3.1. The quality management plan describes the activities and resources necessary for the project management team to achieve the quality objectives set for the project.

◆ **Scope baseline.** Described in Section 5.4.3.1. The scope baseline includes the project scope statement, WBS, and WBS dictionary:

■ *Project scope statement.* The scope statement (Section 5.3.3.1) includes the deliverables and acceptance criteria.

■ *Work breakdown structure.* The WBS (Section 5.4.3.1) provides the relationships among all the project deliverables and their various components.

■ *WBS dictionary.* The WBS dictionary (Section 5.4.3) and related detailed statements of work provide an identification of the deliverables and a description of the work in each WBS component required to produce each deliverable.

### 7.2.1.2 PROJECT DOCUMENTS

Project documents that can be considered as inputs for this process include but are not limited to:

◆ **Lessons learned register.** Described in Section 4.4.3.1. Lessons learned earlier in the project with regard to developing cost estimates can be applied to later phases in the project to improve the accuracy and precision of the cost estimates.

◆ **Project schedule.** Described in Section 6.5.3.2. The schedule includes the type, quantity, and amount of time that team and physical resources will be active on the project. The duration estimates (Section 6.4.3.1) will affect cost estimates when resources are charged per unit of time and when there are seasonal fluctuations in costs. The schedule also provides useful information for projects that incorporate the cost of financing (including interest charges).

◆ **Resource requirements.** Described in Section 9.2.3.1. Resource requirements identify the types and quantities of resources required for each work package or activity.

◆ **Risk register.** Described in Section 11.2.3.1. The risk register contains details of individual project risks that have been identified and prioritized, and for which risk responses are required. The risk register provides detailed information that can be used to estimate costs.

### 7.2.1.3 ENTERPRISE ENVIRONMENTAL FACTORS

The enterprise environmental factors that can influence the Estimate Costs process include but are not limited to:

◆ **Market conditions.** These conditions describe what products, services, and results are available in the market, from whom, and under what terms and conditions. Regional and/or global supply and demand conditions greatly influence resource costs.

◆ **Published commercial information.** Resource cost rate information is often available from commercial databases that track skills and human resource costs, and provide standard costs for material and equipment. Published seller price lists are another source of information.

◆ **Exchange rates and inflation.** For large-scale projects that extend multiple years with multiple currencies, the fluctuations of currencies and inflation need to be understood and built into the Estimate Cost process.

### 7.2.1.4 ORGANIZATIONAL PROCESS ASSETS

The organizational process assets that can influence the Estimate Costs process include but are not limited to:

◆ Cost estimating policies,

◆ Cost estimating templates,

◆ Historical information and lessons learned repository.

## 7.2.2 ESTIMATE COSTS: TOOLS AND TECHNIQUES

### 7.2.2.1 EXPERT JUDGMENT

Described in Section 4.1.2.1. Expertise should be considered from individuals or groups with specialized knowledge or training in the following topics:

◆ Previous similar projects;

◆ Information in the industry, discipline, and application area; and

◆ Cost estimating methods.

## 7.2.2.2 ANALOGOUS ESTIMATING

Described in Section 6.4.2.2. Analogous cost estimating uses values, or attributes, of a previous project that are similar to the current project. Values and attributes of the projects may include but are not limited to: scope, cost, budget, duration, and measures of scale (e.g., size, weight). Comparison of these project values, or attributes, becomes the basis for estimating the same parameter or measurement for the current project.

## 7.2.2.3 PARAMETRIC ESTIMATING

Described in Section 6.4.2.3. Parametric estimating uses a statistical relationship between relevant historical data and other variables (e.g., square footage in construction) to calculate a cost estimate for project work. This technique can produce higher levels of accuracy depending on the sophistication and underlying data built into the model. Parametric cost estimates can be applied to a total project or to segments of a project, in conjunction with other estimating methods.

## 7.2.2.4 BOTTOM-UP ESTIMATING

Described in Section 6.4.2.5. Bottom-up estimating is a method of estimating a component of work. The cost of individual work packages or activities is estimated to the greatest level of specified detail. The detailed cost is then summarized or "rolled up" to higher levels for subsequent reporting and tracking purposes. The cost and accuracy of bottom-up cost estimating are typically influenced by the size or other attributes of the individual activity or work package.

## 7.2.2.5 THREE-POINT ESTIMATING

Described in Section 6.4.2.4. The accuracy of single-point cost estimates may be improved by considering estimation uncertainty and risk and using three estimates to define an approximate range for an activity's cost:

◆ **Most likely ($cM$).** The cost of the activity, based on realistic effort assessment for the required work and any predicted expenses.

◆ **Optimistic ($cO$).** The cost based on analysis of the best-case scenario for the activity.

◆ **Pessimistic ($cP$).** The cost based on analysis of the worst-case scenario for the activity.

Depending on the assumed distribution of values within the range of the three estimates, the expected cost, $cE$, can be calculated using a formula. Two commonly used formulas are triangular and beta distributions. The formulas are:

- **Triangular distribution.** $cE = (cO + cM + cP) / 3$
- **Beta distribution.** $cE = (cO + 4cM + cP) / 6$

Cost estimates based on three points with an assumed distribution provide an expected cost and clarify the range of uncertainty around the expected cost.

### 7.2.2.6 DATA ANALYSIS

Data analysis techniques that can be used in the Estimate Costs process include but are not limited to:

- **Alternatives analysis.** Alternatives analysis is a technique used to evaluate identified options in order to select which options or approaches to use to execute and perform the work of the project. An example would be evaluating the cost, schedule, resource, and quality impacts of buying versus making a deliverable.

- **Reserve analysis.** Cost estimates may include contingency reserves (sometimes called contingency allowances) to account for cost uncertainty. Contingency reserves are the budget within the cost baseline that is allocated for identified risks. Contingency reserves are often viewed as the part of the budget intended to address the known-unknowns that can affect a project. For example, rework for some project deliverables could be anticipated, while the amount of this rework is unknown. Contingency reserves may be estimated to account for this unknown amount of rework. Contingency reserves can be provided at any level from the specific activity to the entire project. The contingency reserve may be a percentage of the estimated cost, a fixed number, or may be developed by using quantitative analysis methods.

  As more precise information about the project becomes available, the contingency reserve may be used, reduced, or eliminated. Contingency should be clearly identified in cost documentation. Contingency reserves are part of the cost baseline and the overall funding requirements for the project.

- **Cost of quality.** Assumptions about costs of quality (Section 8.1.2.3) may be used to prepare the estimates. This includes evaluating the cost impact of additional investment in conformance versus the cost of nonconformance. It can also include looking at short-term cost reductions versus the implication of more frequent problems later on in the product life cycle.

### 7.2.2.7 PROJECT MANAGEMENT INFORMATION SYSTEM (PMIS)

Described in Section 4.3.2.2. The project management information system can include spreadsheets, simulation software, and statistical analysis tools to assist with cost estimating. Such tools simplify the use of some cost-estimating techniques and thereby facilitate rapid consideration of cost estimate alternatives.

### 7.2.2.8 DECISION MAKING

The decision-making techniques that can be used in the Estimate Costs process include but are not limited to voting. Described in Section 5.2.2.4, voting is an assessment process having multiple alternatives with an expected outcome in the form of future actions. These techniques are useful for engaging team members to improve estimate accuracy and commitment to the emerging estimates.

## 7.2.3 ESTIMATE COSTS: OUTPUTS

### 7.2.3.1 COST ESTIMATES

Cost estimates include quantitative assessments of the probable costs required to complete project work, as well as contingency amounts to account for identified risks, and management reserve to cover unplanned work. Cost estimates can be presented in summary form or in detail. Costs are estimated for all resources that are applied to the cost estimate. This includes but is not limited to direct labor, materials, equipment, services, facilities, information technology, and special categories such as cost of financing (including interest charges), an inflation allowance, exchange rates, or a cost contingency reserve. Indirect costs, if they are included in the project estimate, can be included at the activity level or at higher levels.

### 7.2.3.2 BASIS OF ESTIMATES

The amount and type of additional details supporting the cost estimate vary by application area. Regardless of the level of detail, the supporting documentation should provide a clear and complete understanding of how the cost estimate was derived.

Supporting detail for cost estimates may include:

◆ Documentation of the basis of the estimate (i.e., how it was developed),

◆ Documentation of all assumptions made,

◆ Documentation of any known constraints,

◆ Documentation of identified risks included when estimating costs,

◆ Indication of the range of possible estimates (e.g., US$10,000 (±10%) to indicate that the item is expected to cost between a range of values), and

◆ Indication of the confidence level of the final estimate.

### 7.2.3.3 PROJECT DOCUMENTS UPDATES

Project documents that may be updated as a result of carrying out this process include but are not limited to:

◆ **Assumption log.** Described in Section 4.1.3.2. During the Cost Estimates process, new assumptions may be made, new constraints may be identified, and existing assumptions or constraints may be revisited and changed. The assumption log should be updated with this new information.

◆ **Lessons learned register.** Described in Section 4.4.3.1. The lessons learned register can be updated with techniques that were efficient and effective in developing cost estimates.

◆ **Risk register.** Described in Section 11.2.3.1. The risk register may be updated when appropriate risk responses are chosen and agreed upon during the Estimate Cost process.

## 7.3 DETERMINE BUDGET

Determine Budget is the process of aggregating the estimated costs of individual activities or work packages to establish an authorized cost baseline. The key benefit of this process is that it determines the cost baseline against which project performance can be monitored and controlled. This process is performed once or at predefined points in the project. The inputs, tools and techniques, and outputs of this process are depicted in Figure 7-6. Figure 7-7 depicts the data flow diagram of the process.

A project budget includes all the funds authorized to execute the project. The cost baseline is the approved version of the time-phased project budget that includes contingency reserves, but excludes management reserves.

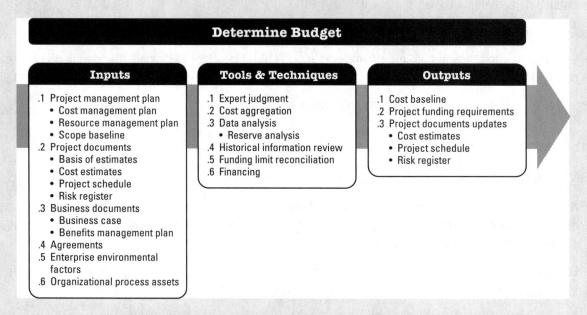

**Determine Budget**

| Inputs | Tools & Techniques | Outputs |
|---|---|---|
| .1 Project management plan<br>• Cost management plan<br>• Resource management plan<br>• Scope baseline<br>.2 Project documents<br>• Basis of estimates<br>• Cost estimates<br>• Project schedule<br>• Risk register<br>.3 Business documents<br>• Business case<br>• Benefits management plan<br>.4 Agreements<br>.5 Enterprise environmental factors<br>.6 Organizational process assets | .1 Expert judgment<br>.2 Cost aggregation<br>.3 Data analysis<br>• Reserve analysis<br>.4 Historical information review<br>.5 Funding limit reconciliation<br>.6 Financing | .1 Cost baseline<br>.2 Project funding requirements<br>.3 Project documents updates<br>• Cost estimates<br>• Project schedule<br>• Risk register |

**Figure 7-6. Determine Budget: Inputs, Tools & Techniques, and Outputs**

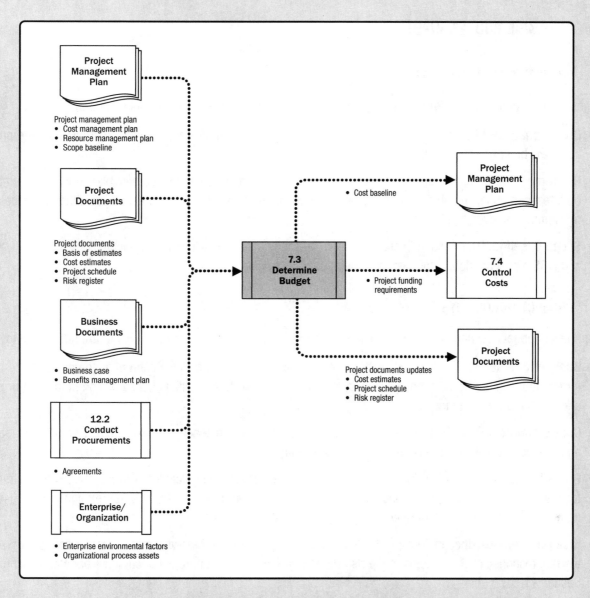

Figure 7-7. Determine Budget: Data Flow Diagram

## 7.3.1 DETERMINE BUDGET: INPUTS

### 7.3.1.1 PROJECT MANAGEMENT PLAN

Described in Section 4.2.3.1. Project management plan components include but are not limited to:

◆ **Cost management plan.** Described in Section 7.1.3.1. The cost management plan describes how the project costs will be structured into the project budget.

◆ **Resource management plan.** Described in Section 9.1.3.1. The resource management plan provides information on rates (personnel and other resources), estimation of travel costs, and other foreseen costs that are necessary to estimate the overall project budget.

◆ **Scope baseline.** Described in Section 5.4.3.1. The scope baseline includes the project scope statement, WBS, and WBS dictionary details for cost estimation and management.

### 7.3.1.2 PROJECT DOCUMENTS

Examples of project documents that can be considered as inputs for this process include but are not limited to:

◆ **Basis of estimates.** Described in Section 7.2.3.2. Supporting detail for cost estimates contained in the basis for estimates should specify any basic assumptions dealing with the inclusion or exclusion of indirect or other costs in the project budget.

◆ **Cost estimates.** Described in Section 7.2.3.1. Cost estimates for each activity within a work package are aggregated to obtain a cost estimate for each work package.

◆ **Project schedule.** Described in Section 6.5.3.2. The project schedule includes planned start and finish dates for the project's activities, milestones, work packages, and control accounts. This information can be used to aggregate costs to the calendar periods in which the costs are planned to be incurred.

◆ **Risk register.** Described in Section 11.2.3.1. The risk register should be reviewed to consider how to aggregate the risk response costs. Updates to the risk register are included with project documents updates described in Section 11.5.3.3.

### 7.3.1.3 BUSINESS DOCUMENTS

Described in Section 1.2.6. The business documents that can be considered as inputs for this process include but are not limited to:

◆ **Business case.** The business case identifies the critical success factors for the project, including financial success factors.

◆ **Benefits management plan.** The benefits management plan includes the target benefits, such as net present value calculations, timeframe for realizing benefits, and the metrics associated with the benefits.

### 7.3.1.4 AGREEMENTS

Described in Section 12.2.3.2. Applicable agreement information and costs relating to products, services, or results that have been or will be purchased are included when determining the budget.

### 7.3.1.5 ENTERPRISE ENVIRONMENTAL FACTORS

The enterprise environmental factors that can influence the Determine Budget process include but are not limited to exchange rates. For large-scale projects that extend multiple years with multiple currencies, the fluctuations of currencies need to be understood and built into the Determine Budget process.

### 7.3.1.6 ORGANIZATIONAL PROCESS ASSETS

The organizational process assets that can influence the Determine Budget process include but are not limited to:

◆ Existing formal and informal cost budgeting-related policies, procedures, and guidelines;

◆ Historical information and lessons learned repository.

◆ Cost budgeting tools; and

◆ Reporting methods.

## 7.3.2 DETERMINE BUDGET: TOOLS AND TECHNIQUES

### 7.3.2.1 EXPERT JUDGMENT

Described in Section 4.1.2.1. Expertise should be considered from individuals or groups with specialized knowledge or training in the following topics:

◆ Previous similar projects;

◆ Information in the industry, discipline, and application area;

◆ Financial principles; and

◆ Funding requirement and sources.

### 7.3.2.2 COST AGGREGATION

Cost estimates are aggregated by work packages in accordance with the WBS. The work package cost estimates are then aggregated for the higher component levels of the WBS (such as control accounts) and, ultimately, for the entire project.

### 7.3.2.3 DATA ANALYSIS

A data analysis technique that can be used in the Determine Budget process includes but is not limited to reserve analysis, which can establish the management reserves for the project. Management reserves are an amount of the project budget withheld for management control purposes and are reserved for unforeseen work that is within scope of the project. Management reserves are intended to address the unknown unknowns that can affect a project. The management reserve is not included in the cost baseline but is part of the overall project budget and funding requirements. When an amount of management reserves is used to fund unforeseen work, the amount of management reserve used is added to the cost baseline, thus requiring an approved change to the cost baseline.

### 7.3.2.4 HISTORICAL INFORMATION REVIEW

Reviewing historical information can assist in developing parametric estimates or analogous estimates. Historical information may include project characteristics (parameters) to develop mathematical models to predict total project costs. Such models may be simple (e.g., residential home construction is based on a certain cost per square foot of space) or complex (e.g., one model of software development costing uses multiple separate adjustment factors, each of which has numerous points within it).

Both the cost and accuracy of analogous and parametric models can vary widely. They are most likely to be reliable when:

◆ Historical information used to develop the model is accurate,

◆ Parameters used in the model are readily quantifiable, and

◆ Models are scalable, such that they work for large projects, small projects, and phases of a project.

### 7.3.2.5 FUNDING LIMIT RECONCILIATION

The expenditure of funds should be reconciled with any funding limits on the commitment of funds for the project. A variance between the funding limits and the planned expenditures will sometimes necessitate the rescheduling of work to level out the rate of expenditures. This is accomplished by placing imposed date constraints for work into the project schedule.

### 7.3.2.6 FINANCING

Financing entails acquiring funding for projects. It is common for long-term infrastructure, industrial, and public services projects to seek external sources of funds. If a project is funded externally, the funding entity may have certain requirements that are required to be met.

### 7.3.3 DETERMINE BUDGET: OUTPUTS

#### 7.3.3.1 COST BASELINE

The cost baseline is the approved version of the time-phased project budget, excluding any management reserves, which can only be changed through formal change control procedures. It is used as a basis for comparison to actual results. The cost baseline is developed as a summation of the approved budgets for the different schedule activities.

Figure 7-8 illustrates the various components of the project budget and cost baseline. Cost estimates for the various project activities, along with any contingency reserves (see Section 7.2.2.6) for these activities, are aggregated into their associated work package costs. The work package cost estimates, along with any contingency reserves estimated for the work packages, are aggregated into control accounts. The summation of the control accounts make up the cost baseline. Since the cost estimates that make up the cost baseline are directly tied to the schedule activities, this enables a time-phased view of the cost baseline, which is typically displayed in the form of an S-curve, as is illustrated in Figure 7-9. For projects that use earned value management, the cost baseline is referred to as the performance measurement baseline.

Management reserves (Section 7.3.2.3) are added to the cost baseline to produce the project budget. As changes warranting the use of management reserves arise, the change control process is used to obtain approval to move the applicable management reserve funds into the cost baseline.

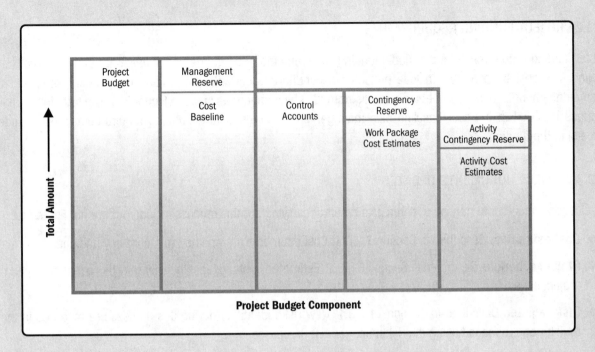

**Figure 7-8. Project Budget Components**

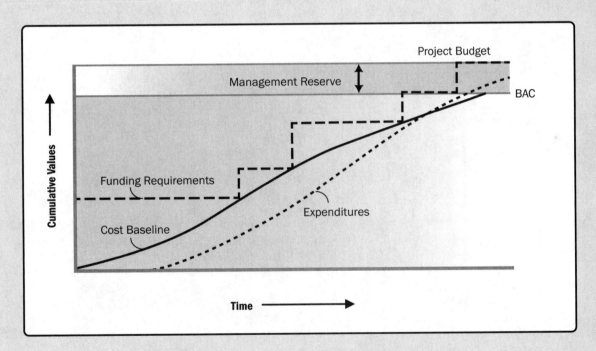

**Figure 7-9. Cost Baseline, Expenditures, and Funding Requirements**

## 7.3.3.2 PROJECT FUNDING REQUIREMENTS

Total funding requirements and periodic funding requirements (e.g., quarterly, annually) are derived from the cost baseline. The cost baseline will include projected expenditures plus anticipated liabilities. Funding often occurs in incremental amounts, and may not be evenly distributed, which appear as steps in Figure 7-9. The total funds required are those included in the cost baseline plus management reserves, if any. Funding requirements may include the source(s) of the funding.

## 7.3.3.3 PROJECT DOCUMENTS UPDATES

Project documents that may be updated as a result of carrying out this process include but are not limited to:

◆ **Cost estimates.** Described in Section 7.2.3.1. Cost estimates are updated to record any additional information.

◆ **Project schedule.** Described in Section 6.5.3.2. Estimated costs for each activity may be recorded as part of the project schedule.

◆ **Risk register.** Described in Section 11.2.3.1. New risks identified during this process are recorded in the risk register and managed using the risk management processes.

# 7.4 CONTROL COSTS

Control Costs is the process of monitoring the status of the project to update the project costs and managing changes to the cost baseline. The key benefit of this process is that the cost baseline is maintained throughout the project. This process is performed throughout the project. The inputs, tools and techniques, and outputs of this process are depicted in Figure 7-10. Figure 7-11 depicts the data flow diagram of the process.

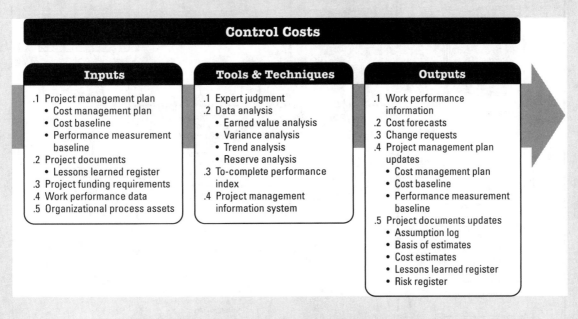

**Figure 7-10. Control Costs: Inputs, Tools & Techniques, and Outputs**

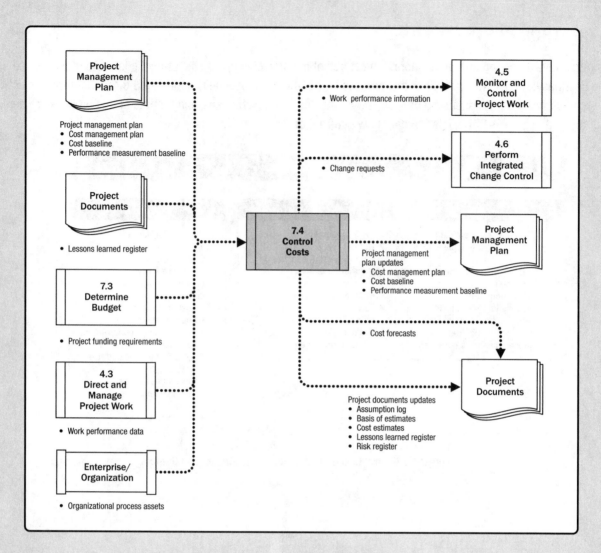

**Figure 7-11. Control Costs: Data Flow Diagram**

Updating the budget requires knowledge of the actual costs spent to date. Any increase to the authorized budget can only be approved through the Perform Integrated Change Control process (Section 4.6). Monitoring the expenditure of funds without regard to the value of work being accomplished for such expenditures has little value to the project, other than to track the outflow of funds. Much of the effort of cost control involves analyzing the relationship between the consumption of project funds and the work being accomplished for such expenditures. The key to effective cost control is the management of the approved cost baseline.

Project cost control includes:

◆ Influencing the factors that create changes to the authorized cost baseline;

◆ Ensuring that all change requests are acted on in a timely manner;

◆ Managing the actual changes when and as they occur;

◆ Ensuring that cost expenditures do not exceed the authorized funding by period, by WBS component, by activity, and in total for the project;

◆ Monitoring cost performance to isolate and understand variances from the approved cost baseline;

◆ Monitoring work performance against funds expended;

◆ Preventing unapproved changes from being included in the reported cost or resource usage;

◆ Informing appropriate stakeholders of all approved changes and associated cost; and

◆ Bringing expected cost overruns within acceptable limits.


## 7.4.1 CONTROL COSTS: INPUTS

### 7.4.1.1 PROJECT MANAGEMENT PLAN

Described in Section 4.2.3.1. Project management plan components include but are not limited to:

◆ **Cost management plan.** Described in Section 7.1.3.1. The cost management plan describes how the project costs will be managed and controlled.

◆ **Cost baseline.** Described in Section 7.3.3.1. The cost baseline is compared with actual results to determine if a change, corrective action, or preventive action is necessary.

◆ **Performance measurement baseline.** Described in Section 4.2.3.1. When using earned value analysis, the performance measurement baseline is compared to actual results to determine if a change, corrective action, or preventive action is necessary.

### 7.4.1.2. PROJECT DOCUMENTS

Examples of project documents that can be considered as inputs for this process include but are not limited to the lessons learned register. Described in Section 4.4.3.1. Lessons learned earlier in the project can be applied to later phases in the project to improve cost control.

### 7.4.1.3 PROJECT FUNDING REQUIREMENTS

Described in Section 7.3.3.2. The project funding requirements include projected expenditures plus anticipated liabilities.

### 7.4.1.4 WORK PERFORMANCE DATA

Described in Section 4.3.3.2. Work performance data contains data on project status such as which costs have been authorized, incurred, invoiced, and paid.

### 7.4.1.5 ORGANIZATIONAL PROCESS ASSETS

The organizational process assets that can influence the Control Costs process include but are not limited to:

◆ Existing formal and informal cost control-related policies, procedures, and guidelines;

◆ Cost control tools; and

◆ Monitoring and reporting methods to be used.

## 7.4.2 CONTROL COSTS: TOOLS AND TECHNIQUES

### 7.4.2.1 EXPERT JUDGMENT

Described in Section 4.1.2.1. Examples of expert judgment during the Control Costs process include but are not limited to:

◆ Variance analysis,

◆ Earned value analysis,

◆ Forecasting, and

◆ Financial analysis.

## 7.4.2.2 DATA ANALYSIS

Data analysis techniques that can be used to control costs include but are not limited to:

◆ **Earned value analysis (EVA).** Earned value analysis compares the performance measurement baseline to the actual schedule and cost performance. EVM integrates the scope baseline with the cost baseline and schedule baseline to form the performance measurement baseline. EVM develops and monitors three key dimensions for each work package and control account:

■ *Planned value.* Planned value (PV) is the authorized budget assigned to scheduled work. It is the authorized budget planned for the work to be accomplished for an activity or work breakdown structure (WBS) component, not including management reserve. This budget is allocated by phase over the life of the project, but at a given point in time, planned value defines the physical work that should have been accomplished. The total of the PV is sometimes referred to as the performance measurement baseline (PMB). The total planned value for the project is also known as budget at completion (BAC).

■ *Earned value.* Earned value (EV) is a measure of work performed expressed in terms of the budget authorized for that work. It is the budget associated with the authorized work that has been completed. The EV being measured needs to be related to the PMB, and the EV measured cannot be greater than the authorized PV budget for a component. The EV is often used to calculate the percent complete of a project. Progress measurement criteria should be established for each WBS component to measure work in progress. Project managers monitor EV, both incrementally to determine current status and cumulatively to determine the long-term performance trends.

■ *Actual cost.* Actual cost (AC) is the realized cost incurred for the work performed on an activity during a specific time period. It is the total cost incurred in accomplishing the work that the EV measured. The AC needs to correspond in definition to what was budgeted in the PV and measured in the EV (e.g., direct hours only, direct costs only, or all costs including indirect costs). The AC will have no upper limit; whatever is spent to achieve the EV will be measured.

◆ **Variance analysis.** Described in Section 4.5.2.2. Variance analysis, as used in EVM, is the explanation (cause, impact, and corrective actions) for cost (CV = EV − AC), schedule (SV = EV − PV), and variance at completion (VAC = BAC − EAC) variances. Cost and schedule variances are the most frequently analyzed measurements. For projects not using formal earned value analysis, similar variance analyses can be performed by comparing planned cost against actual cost to identify variances between the cost baseline and actual project performance. Further analysis can be performed to determine the cause and degree of variance relative to the schedule baseline and any corrective or preventive actions needed. Cost performance measurements are used to assess the magnitude of variation to the original cost baseline. An important aspect of project cost control includes determining the cause and degree of variance relative to the cost baseline (see Section 7.3.3.1) and deciding whether corrective or preventive action is required. The percentage range of acceptable variances will tend to decrease as more work is accomplished. Examples of variance analysis include but are not limited to:

■ *Schedule variance.* Schedule variance (SV) is a measure of schedule performance expressed as the difference between the earned value and the planned value. It is the amount by which the project is ahead or behind the planned delivery date, at a given point in time. It is a measure of schedule performance on a project. It is equal to the earned value (EV) minus the planned value (PV). The EVA schedule variance is a useful metric in that it can indicate when a project is falling behind or is ahead of its baseline schedule. The EVA schedule variance will ultimately equal zero when the project is completed because all of the planned values will have been earned. Schedule variance is best used in conjunction with critical path method (CPM) scheduling and risk management. Equation: SV = EV − PV.

■ *Cost variance.* Cost variance (CV) is the amount of budget deficit or surplus at a given point in time, expressed as the difference between earned value and the actual cost. It is a measure of cost performance on a project. It is equal to the earned value (EV) minus the actual cost (AC). The cost variance at the end of the project will be the difference between the budget at completion (BAC) and the actual amount spent. The CV is particularly critical because it indicates the relationship of physical performance to the costs spent. Negative CV is often difficult for the project to recover. Equation: CV = EV − AC.

- *Schedule performance index.* The schedule performance index (SPI) is a measure of schedule efficiency expressed as the ratio of earned value to planned value. It measures how efficiently the project team is accomplishing the work. It is sometimes used in conjunction with the cost performance index (CPI) to forecast the final project completion estimates. An SPI value less than 1.0 indicates less work was completed than was planned. An SPI greater than 1.0 indicates that more work was completed than was planned. Since the SPI measures all project work, the performance on the critical path also needs to be analyzed to determine whether the project will finish ahead of or behind its planned finish date. The SPI is equal to the ratio of the EV to the PV. Equation: SPI = EV/PV.

- *Cost performance index.* The cost performance index (CPI) is a measure of the cost efficiency of budgeted resources, expressed as a ratio of earned value to actual cost. It is considered the most critical EVA metric and measures the cost efficiency for the work completed. A CPI value of less than 1.0 indicates a cost overrun for work completed. A CPI value greater than 1.0 indicates a cost underrun of performance to date. The CPI is equal to the ratio of the EV to the AC. Equation: CPI = EV/AC.

◆ **Trend analysis.** Described in Section 4.5.2.2. Trend analysis examines project performance over time to determine if performance is improving or deteriorating. Graphical analysis techniques are valuable for understanding performance to date and for comparison to future performance goals in the form of BAC versus estimate at completion (EAC) and completion dates. Examples of the trend analysis techniques include but are not limited to:

- *Charts.* In earned value analysis, three parameters of planned value, earned value, and actual cost can be monitored and reported on both a period-by-period basis (typically weekly or monthly) and on a cumulative basis. Figure 7-12 uses S-curves to display EV data for a project that is performing over budget and behind the schedule.

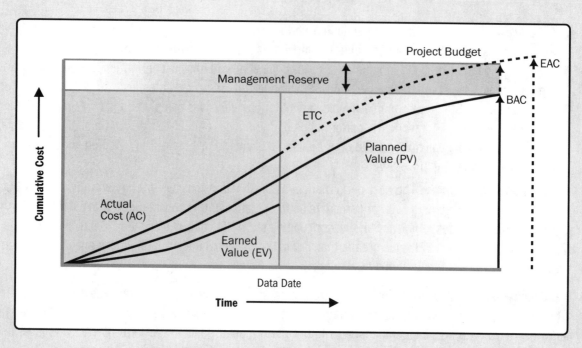

**Figure 7-12. Earned Value, Planned Value, and Actual Costs**

- *Forecasting.* As the project progresses, the project team may develop a forecast for the estimate at completion (EAC) that may differ from the budget at completion (BAC) based on the project performance. If it becomes obvious that the BAC is no longer viable, the project manager should consider the forecasted EAC. Forecasting the EAC involves making projections of conditions and events in the project's future based on current performance information and other knowledge available at the time of the forecast. Forecasts are generated, updated, and reissued based on work performance data (Section 4.3.3.2) that is provided as the project is executed. The work performance information covers the project's past performance and any information that could impact the project in the future.

EACs are typically based on the actual costs incurred for work completed, plus an estimate to complete (ETC) the remaining work. It is incumbent on the project team to predict what it may encounter to perform the ETC, based on its experience to date. Earned value analysis works well in conjunction with manual forecasts of the required EAC costs. The most common EAC forecasting approach is a manual, bottom-up summation by the project manager and project team.

The project manager's bottom-up EAC method builds upon the actual costs and experience incurred for the work completed, and requires a new estimate to complete the remaining project work. Equation: EAC = AC + Bottom-up ETC.

The project manager's manual EAC is quickly compared with a range of calculated EACs representing various risk scenarios. When calculating EAC values, the cumulative CPI and SPI values are typically used. While EVM data quickly provide many statistical EACs, only three of the more common methods are described as follows:

- ○ *EAC forecast for ETC work performed at the budgeted rate.* This EAC method accepts the actual project performance to date (whether favorable or unfavorable) as represented by the actual costs, and predicts that all future ETC work will be accomplished at the budgeted rate. When actual performance is unfavorable, the assumption that future performance will improve should be accepted only when supported by project risk analysis. Equation: $EAC = AC + (BAC - EV)$.

- ○ *EAC forecast for ETC work performed at the present CPI.* This method assumes that what the project has experienced to date can be expected to continue in the future. The ETC work is assumed to be performed at the same cumulative cost performance index (CPI) as that incurred by the project to date. Equation: $EAC = BAC / CPI$.

- ○ *EAC forecast for ETC work considering both SPI and CPI factors.* In this forecast, the ETC work will be performed at an efficiency rate that considers both the cost and schedule performance indices. This method is most useful when the project schedule is a factor impacting the ETC effort. Variations of this method weight the CPI and SPI at different values (e.g., 80/20, 50/50, or some other ratio) according to the project manager's judgment. Equation: $EAC = AC + [(BAC - EV) / (CPI \times SPI)]$.

◆ **Reserve analysis.** Described in Section 7.2.2.6. During cost control, reserve analysis is used to monitor the status of contingency and management reserves for the project to determine if these reserves are still needed or if additional reserves need to be requested. As work on the project progresses, these reserves may be used as planned to cover the cost of risk responses or other contingencies. Conversely, when opportunities are captured and resulting in cost savings, funds may be added to the contingency amount, or taken from the project as margin/profit.

If the identified risks do not occur, the unused contingency reserves may be removed from the project budget to free up resources for other projects or operations. Additional risk analysis during the project may reveal a need to request that additional reserves be added to the project budget.

## 7.4.2.3 TO-COMPLETE PERFORMANCE INDEX

The to-complete performance index (TCPI) is a measure of the cost performance that is required to be achieved with the remaining resources in order to meet a specified management goal, expressed as the ratio of the cost to finish the outstanding work to the remaining budget. TCPI is the calculated cost performance index that is achieved on the remaining work to meet a specified management goal, such as the BAC or the EAC. If it becomes obvious that the BAC is no longer viable, the project manager should consider the forecasted EAC. Once approved, the EAC may replace the BAC in the TCPI calculation. The equation for the TCPI based on the BAC: (BAC – EV) / (BAC – AC).

The TCPI is conceptually displayed in Figure 7-13. The equation for the TCPI is shown in the lower left as the work remaining (defined as the BAC minus the EV) divided by the funds remaining (which can be either the BAC minus the AC, or the EAC minus the AC).

If the cumulative CPI falls below the baseline (as shown in Figure 7-13), all future work of the project will need to be performed immediately in the range of the TCPI (BAC) (as reflected in the top line of Figure 7-13) to stay within the authorized BAC. Whether this level of performance is achievable is a judgment call based on a number of considerations, including risk, time remaining in the project, and technical performance. This level of performance is displayed as the TCPI (EAC) line. The equation for the TCPI is based on the EAC: (BAC – EV) / (EAC – AC). The EVM formulas are provided in Table 7-1.

# Table 7-1. Earned Value Calculations Summary Table

| | | | Earned Value Analysis | | | |
|---|---|---|---|---|---|
| **Abbreviation** | **Name** | **Lexicon Definition** | **How Used** | **Equation** | **Interpretation of Result** |
| PV | Planned Value | The authorized budget assigned to scheduled work. | The value of the work planned to be completed to a point in time, usually the data date, or project completion. | | |
| EV | Earned Value | The measure of work performed expressed in terms of the budget authorized for that work. | The planned value of all the work completed (earned) to a point in time, usually the data date, without reference to actual costs. | EV = sum of the planned value of completed work | |
| AC | Actual Cost | The realized cost incurred for the work performed on an activity during a specific time period. | The actual cost of all the work completed to a point in time, usually the data date. | | |
| BAC | Budget at Completion | The sum of all budgets established for the work to be performed. | The value of total planned work, the project cost baseline. | | |
| CV | Cost Variance | The amount of budget deficit or surplus at a given point in time, expressed as the difference between the earned value and the actual cost. | The difference between the value of work completed to a point in time, usually the data date, and the actual costs to the same point in time. | $CV = EV - AC$ | Positive = Under planned cost <br> Neutral = On planned cost <br> Negative = Over planned cost |
| SV | Schedule Variance | The amount by which the project is ahead or behind the planned delivery date, at a given point in time, expressed as the difference between the earned value and the planned value. | The difference between the work completed to a point in time, usually the data date, and the work planned to be completed to the same point in time. | $SV = EV - PV$ | Positive = Ahead of Schedule <br> Neutral = On schedule <br> Negative = Behind Schedule |
| VAC | Variance at Completion | A projection of the amount of budget deficit or surplus, expressed as the difference between the budget at completion and the estimate at completion. | The estimated difference in cost at the completion of the project. | $VAC = BAC - EAC$ | Positive = Under planned cost <br> Neutral = On planned cost <br> Negative = Over planned cost |
| CPI | Cost Performance Index | A measure of the cost efficiency of budgeted resources expressed as the ratio of earned value to actual cost. | A CPI of 1.0 means the project is exactly on budget, that the work actually done so far is exactly the same as the cost so far. Other values show the percentage of how much costs are over or under the budgeted amount for work accomplished. | $CPI = EV/AC$ | Greater than 1.0 = Under planned cost <br> Exactly 1.0 = On planned cost <br> Less than 1.0 = Over planned cost |
| SPI | Schedule Performance Index | A measure of schedule efficiency expressed as the ratio of earned value to planned value. | An SPI of 1.0 means that the project is exactly on schedule, that the work actually done so far is exactly the same as the work planned to be done so far. Other values show the percentage of how much costs are over or under the budgeted amount for work planned. | $SPI = EV/PV$ | Greater than 1.0 = Ahead of schedule <br> Exactly 1.0 = On schedule <br> Less than 1.0 = Behind schedule |
| EAC | Estimate At Completion | The expected total cost of completing all work expressed as the sum of the actual cost to date and the estimate to complete. | If the CPI is expected to be the same for the remainder of the project, EAC can be calculated using: <br><br> If future work will be accomplished at the planned rate, use: <br><br> If the initial plan is no longer valid, use: <br><br> If both the CPI and SPI influence the remaining work, use: | $EAC = BAC/CPI$ <br><br> $EAC = AC + BAC - EV$ <br><br> $EAC = AC + \text{Bottom-up ETC}$ <br><br> $EAC = AC + [(BAC - EV)/(CPI \times SPI)]$ | |
| ETC | Estimate to Complete | The expected cost to finish all the remaining project work. | Assuming work is proceeding on plan, the cost of completing the remaining authorized work can be calculated using: <br><br> Reestimate the remaining work from the bottom up. | $ETC = EAC - AC$ <br><br> $ETC = \text{Reestimate}$ | |
| TCPI | To Complete Performance Index | A measure of the cost performance that must be achieved with the remaining resources in order to meet a specified management goal, expressed as the ratio of the cost to finish the outstanding work to the budget available. | The efficiency that must be maintained in order to complete on plan. <br><br><br> The efficiency that must be maintained in order to complete the current EAC. | $TCPI = (BAC-EV)/(BAC-AC)$ <br><br><br> $TCPI = (BAC-EV)/(EAC-AC)$ | Greater than 1.0 = Harder to complete <br> Exactly 1.0 = Same to complete <br> Less than 1.0 = Easier to complete <br><br> Greater than 1.0 = Harder to complete <br> Exactly 1.0 = Same to complete <br> Less than 1.0 = Easier to complete |

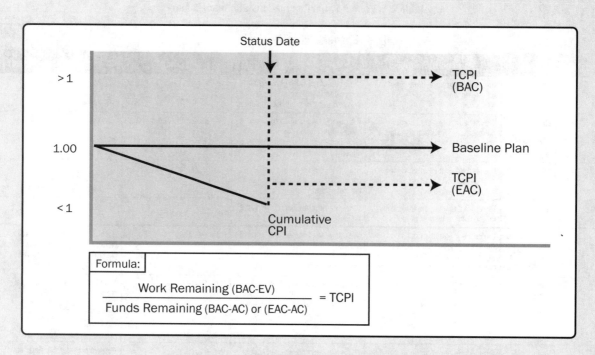

**Figure 7-13. To-Complete Performance Index (TCPI)**

### 7.4.2.4 PROJECT MANAGEMENT INFORMATION SYSTEM (PMIS)

Described in Section 4.3.2.2. Project management information systems are often used to monitor the three EVM dimensions (PV, EV, and AC), to display graphical trends, and to forecast a range of possible final project results.

## 7.4.3 CONTROL COSTS: OUTPUTS

### 7.4.3.1 WORK PERFORMANCE INFORMATION

Described in Section 4.5.1.3. Work performance information includes information on how the project work is performing compared to the cost baseline. Variances in the work performed and the cost of the work are evaluated at the work package level and control account level. For projects using earned value analysis, CV, CPI, EAC, VAC, and TCPI are documented for inclusion in work performance reports (Section 4.5.3.1).

### 7.4.3.2 COST FORECASTS

Either a calculated EAC value or a bottom-up EAC value is documented and communicated to stakeholders.

### 7.4.3.3 CHANGE REQUESTS

Described in Section 4.3.3.4. Analysis of project performance may result in a change request to the cost and schedule baselines or other components of the project management plan. Change requests are processed for review and disposition through the Perform Integrated Change Control process (Section 4.6).

### 7.4.3.4 PROJECT MANAGEMENT PLAN UPDATES

Any change to the project management plan goes through the organization's change control process via a change request. Components that may require a change request for the project management plan include but are not limited to:

◆ **Cost management plan.** Described in Section 7.1.3.1. Changes to the cost management plan, such as changes to control thresholds or specified levels of accuracy required in managing the project's cost, are incorporated in response to feedback from relevant stakeholders.

◆ **Cost baseline.** Described in Section 7.3.3.1. Changes to the cost baseline are incorporated in response to approved changes in scope, resources, or cost estimates. In some cases, cost variances can be so severe that a revised cost baseline is needed to provide a realistic basis for performance measurement.

◆ **Performance measurement baseline.** Described in Section 4.2.3.1. Changes to the performance measurement baseline are incorporated in response to approved changes in scope, schedule performance, or cost estimates. In some cases, the performance variances can be so severe that a change request is put forth to revise the performance measurement baseline to provide a realistic basis for performance measurement.

### 7.4.3.5 PROJECT DOCUMENTS UPDATES

Project documents that may be updated as a result of carrying out this process include but are not limited to:

◆ **Assumption log.** Described in Section 4.1.3.2. Cost performance may indicate the need to revise assumptions on resource productivity and other factors influencing cost performance.

◆ **Basis of estimates.** Described in Section 6.4.3.2. Cost performance may indicate the need to revisit the original basis of estimates.

◆ **Cost estimates.** Described in Section 7.2.3.1. Cost estimates may need to be updated to reflect the actual cost efficiency for the project.

◆ **Lessons learned register.** Described in Section 4.4.3.1. The lessons learned register can be updated with techniques that were effective in maintaining the budget, variance analysis, earned value analysis, forecasting, and corrective actions that were used to respond to cost variances.

◆ **Risk register.** Described in Section 11.2.3.1. The risk register may be updated if the cost variances have crossed, or are likely to cross, the cost threshold.

# 8

## PROJECT QUALITY MANAGEMENT

Project Quality Management includes the processes for incorporating the organization's quality policy regarding planning, managing, and controlling project and product quality requirements in order to meet stakeholders' objectives. Project Quality Management also supports continuous process improvement activities as undertaken on behalf of the performing organization.

The Project Quality Management processes are:

**8.1 Plan Quality Management**—The process of identifying quality requirements and/or standards for the project and its deliverables, and documenting how the project will demonstrate compliance with quality requirements and/or standards.

**8.2 Manage Quality**—The process of translating the quality management plan into executable quality activities that incorporate the organization's quality policies into the project.

**8.3 Control Quality**—The process of monitoring and recording the results of executing the quality management activities to assess performance and ensure the project outputs are complete, correct, and meet customer expectations.

Figure 8-1 provides an overview of the Project Quality Management processes. The Project Quality Management processes are presented as discrete processes with defined interfaces while, in practice, they overlap and interact in ways that cannot be completely detailed in the *PMBOK® Guide*. In addition, these quality processes may differ within industries and companies.

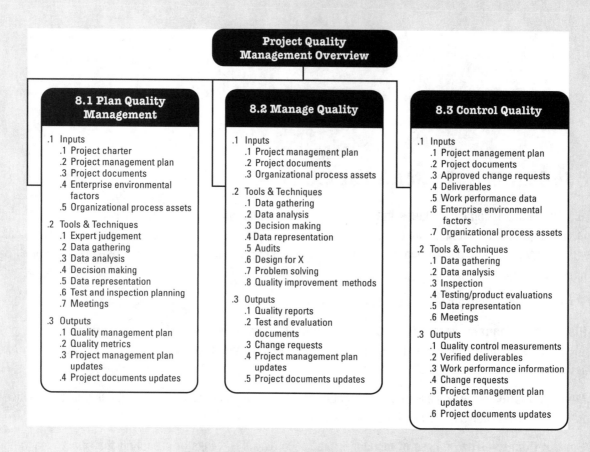

**Figure 8-1. Project Quality Management Overview**

Figure 8-2 provides an overview of the major inputs and outputs of the Project Quality Management processes and the interrelations of these processes in the Project Quality Management Knowledge Area. The Plan Quality Management process is concerned with the quality that the work needs to have. Manage Quality is concerned with managing the quality processes throughout the project. During the Manage Quality process, quality requirements identified during the Plan Quality Management process are turned into test and evaluation instruments, which are then applied during the Control Quality process to verify these quality requirements are met by the project. Control Quality is concerned with comparing the work results with the quality requirements to ensure the result is acceptable. There are two outputs specific to the Project Quality Management Knowledge Area that are used by other Knowledge Areas: verified deliverables and quality reports.

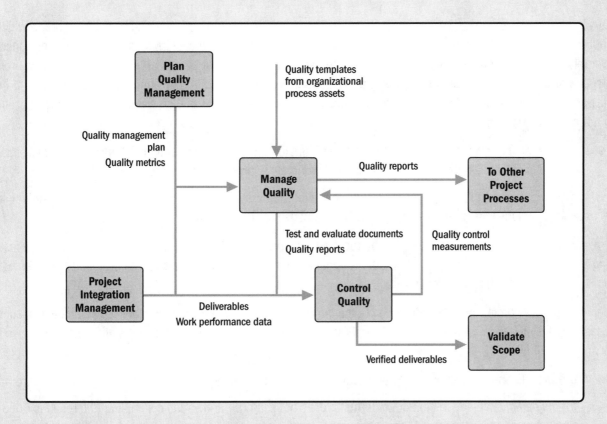

Figure 8-2. Major Project Quality Management Process Interrelations

## KEY CONCEPTS FOR PROJECT QUALITY MANAGEMENT

Project Quality Management addresses the management of the project and the deliverables of the project. It applies to all projects, regardless of the nature of their deliverables. Quality measures and techniques are specific to the type of deliverables being produced by the project. For example, the project quality management of software deliverables may use different approaches and measures from those used when building a nuclear power plant. In either case, failure to meet the quality requirements can have serious negative consequences for any or all of the project's stakeholders. For example:

◆ Meeting customer requirements by overworking the project team may result in decreased profits and increased levels of overall project risks, employee attrition, errors, or rework.

◆ Meeting project schedule objectives by rushing planned quality inspections may result in undetected errors, decreased profits, and increased post-implementation risks.

*Quality* and *grade* are not the same concepts. Quality as a delivered performance or result is "the degree to which a set of inherent characteristics fulfill requirements" (ISO 9000 [18].). Grade as a design intent is a category assigned to deliverables having the same functional use but different technical characteristics. The project manager and the project management team are responsible for managing the trade-offs associated with delivering the required levels of both quality and grade. While a quality level that fails to meet quality requirements is always a problem, a low-grade product may not be a problem. For example:

◆ It may not be a problem if a suitable low-grade product (one with a limited number of features) is of high quality (no obvious defects). In this example, the product would be appropriate for its general purpose of use.

◆ It may be a problem if a high-grade product (one with numerous features) is of low quality (many defects). In essence, a high-grade feature set would prove ineffective and/or inefficient due to low quality.

Prevention is preferred over inspection. It is better to design quality into deliverables, rather than to find quality issues during inspection. The cost of preventing mistakes is generally much less than the cost of correcting mistakes when they are found by inspection or during usage.

Depending on the project and the industry area, the project team may need a working knowledge of statistical control processes to evaluate data contained in the Control Quality outputs. The team should know the differences between the following pairs of terms:

◆ *Prevention* (keeping errors out of the process) and inspection (keeping errors out of the hands of the customer);

◆ *Attribute sampling* (the result either conforms or does not conform) and variable sampling (the result is rated on a continuous scale that measures the degree of conformity); and

◆ *Tolerances* (specified range of acceptable results) and control limits (that identify the boundaries of common variation in a statistically stable process or process performance).

The cost of quality (COQ) includes all costs incurred over the life of the product by investment in preventing nonconformance to requirements, appraising the product or service for conformance to requirements, and failing to meet requirements (rework). Failure costs are often categorized into internal (found by the project team) and external (found by the customer). Failure costs are also called the cost of poor quality. Section 8.1.2.3 provides some examples to consider in each area. Organizations choose to invest in defect prevention because of the benefits over the life of the product. Because projects are temporary, decisions about the COQ over a product's life cycle are often the concern of program management, portfolio management, the PMO, or operations.

There are five levels of increasingly effective quality management as follows:

◆ Usually, the most expensive approach is to let the customer find the defects. This approach can lead to warranty issues, recalls, loss of reputation, and rework costs.

◆ Detect and correct the defects before the deliverables are sent to the customer as part of the quality control process. The control quality process has related costs, which are mainly the appraisal costs and internal failure costs.

◆ Use quality assurance to examine and correct the process itself and not just special defects.

◆ Incorporate quality into the planning and designing of the project and product.

◆ Create a culture throughout the organization that is aware and committed to quality in processes and products.

## TRENDS AND EMERGING PRACTICES IN PROJECT QUALITY MANAGEMENT

Modern quality management approaches seek to minimize variation and to deliver results that meet defined stakeholder requirements. Trends in Project Quality Management include but are not limited to:

◆ **Customer satisfaction.** Understand, evaluate, define, and manage requirements so that customer expectations are met. This requires a combination of conformance to requirements (to ensure the project produces what it was created to produce) and fitness for use (the product or service needs to satisfy the real needs). In agile environments, stakeholder engagement with the team ensures customer satisfaction is maintained throughout the project.

◆ **Continual improvement.** The plan-do-check-act (PDCA) cycle is the basis for quality improvement as defined by Shewhart and modified by Deming. In addition, quality improvement initiatives such as total quality management (TQM), Six Sigma, and Lean Six Sigma may improve both the quality of project management, as well as the quality of the end product, service, or result.

◆ **Management responsibility.** Success requires the participation of all members of the project team. Management retains, within its responsibility for quality, a related responsibility to provide suitable resources at adequate capacities.

◆ **Mutually beneficial partnership with suppliers.** An organization and its suppliers are interdependent. Relationships based on partnership and cooperation with the supplier are more beneficial to the organization and to the suppliers than traditional supplier management. The organization should prefer long-term relationships over short-term gains. A mutually beneficial relationship enhances the ability for both the organization and the suppliers to create value for each other, enhances the joint responses to customer needs and expectations, and optimizes costs and resources.

## TAILORING CONSIDERATIONS

Each project is unique; therefore, the project manager will need to tailor the way Project Quality Management processes are applied. Considerations for tailoring include but are not limited to:

◆ **Policy compliance and auditing.** What quality policies and procedures exist in the organization? What quality tools, techniques, and templates are used in the organization?

◆ **Standards and regulatory compliance.** Are there any specific quality standards in the industry that need to be applied? Are there any specific governmental, legal, or regulatory constraints that need to be taken into consideration?

◆ **Continuous improvement.** How will quality improvement be managed in the project? Is it managed at the organizational level or at the level of each project?

◆ **Stakeholder engagement.** Is there a collaborative environment for stakeholders and suppliers?

## CONSIDERATIONS FOR AGILE/ADAPTIVE ENVIRONMENTS

In order to navigate changes, agile methods call for frequent quality and review steps built in throughout the project rather than toward the end of the project.

Recurring retrospectives regularly check on the effectiveness of the quality processes. They look for the root cause of issues then suggest trials of new approaches to improve quality. Subsequent retrospectives evaluate any trial processes to determine if they are working and should be continued or new adjusting or should be dropped from use.

In order to facilitate frequent, incremental delivery, agile methods focus on small batches of work, incorporating as many elements of project deliverables as possible. Small batch systems aim to uncover inconsistencies and quality issues earlier in the project life cycle when the overall costs of change are lower.

# 8.1 PLAN QUALITY MANAGEMENT

Plan Quality Management is the process of identifying quality requirements and/or standards for the project and its deliverables, and documenting how the project will demonstrate compliance with quality requirements and/or standards. The key benefit of this process is that it provides guidance and direction on how quality will be managed and verified throughout the project. This process is performed once or at predefined points in the project. The inputs and outputs of this process are depicted in Figure 8.3. Figure 8.4 depicts the data flow diagram for the process.

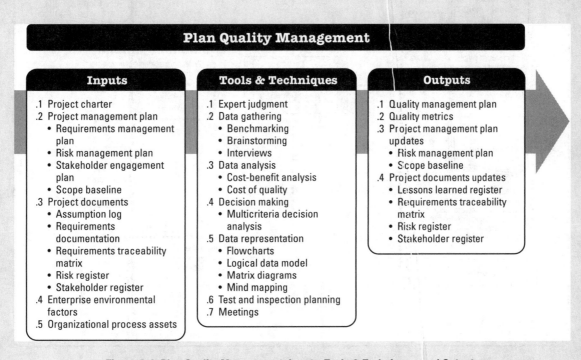

**Figure 8-3. Plan Quality Management: Inputs, Tools & Techniques, and Outputs**

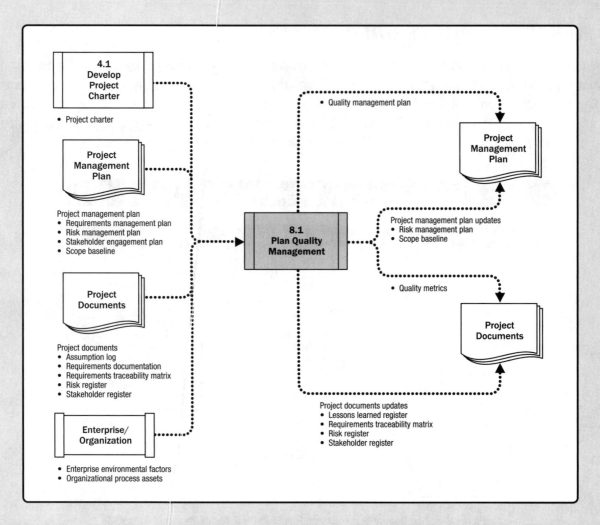

**Figure 8-4. Plan Quality Management: Data Flow Diagram**

Quality planning should be performed in parallel with the other planning processes. For example, changes proposed in the deliverables in order to meet identified quality standards may require cost or schedule adjustments and a detailed risk analysis of the impact to plans.

The quality planning techniques discussed here are those used most frequently on projects. There are many others that may be useful on certain projects or in specific application areas.

### 8.1.1 PLAN QUALITY MANAGEMENT: INPUTS

#### 8.1.1.1 PROJECT CHARTER

Described in Section 4.1.3.1. The project charter provides the high-level project description and product characteristics. It also contains the project approval requirements, measurable project objectives, and related success criteria that will influence the quality management of the project.

#### 8.1.1.2 PROJECT MANAGEMENT PLAN

Described in Section 4.2.3.1. Project management plan components include but are not limited to:

- ◆ **Requirements management plan.** Described in Section 5.1.3.2. The requirements management plan provides the approach for identifying, analyzing, and managing the requirements that the quality management plan and quality metrics will reference.

- ◆ **Risk management plan.** Described in Section 11.1.3.1. The risk management plan provides the approach for identifying, analyzing, and monitoring risks. The information in the risk management plan and quality management plan work together to successfully deliver product and project success.

- ◆ **Stakeholder engagement plan.** Described in Section 13.2.3.1. The stakeholder engagement plan provides the method for documenting the stakeholders' needs and expectations that provide the foundation for quality management.

- ◆ **Scope baseline.** Described in Section 5.4.3.1. The WBS along with the deliverables documented in the project scope statement are considered while determining which quality standards and objectives are suitable for the project, and which project deliverables and processes will be subjected to quality review. The scope statement includes the acceptance criteria for the deliverables. The definition of acceptance criteria may significantly increase or decrease quality costs and, therefore, project costs. Satisfying all acceptance criteria implies the needs of the stakeholders have been met.

### 8.1.1.3 PROJECT DOCUMENTS

Project documents that can be considered as inputs for this process include but are not limited to:

◆ **Assumption log.** Described in Section 4.1.3.2. The assumption log has all the assumptions and constraints regarding quality requirements and standard compliance.

◆ **Requirements documentation.** Described in Section 5.2.3.1. Requirements documentation captures the requirements that the project and product should attain to meet stakeholder expectations. The components of the requirements documentation include but are not limited to project and product quality requirements. Requirements are used by the project team to help plan how quality control will be implemented on the project.

◆ **Requirements traceability matrix.** Described in Section 5.2.3.2. The requirements traceability matrix links product requirements to deliverables and helps to ensure each requirement in the requirements documentation is tested. The matrix provides an overview of the tests required to verify the requirements.

◆ **Risk register.** Described in Section 11.2.3.1. The risk register contains information on threats and opportunities that may impact quality requirements.

◆ **Stakeholder register.** Described in Section 13.1.3.1. The stakeholder register helps to identify stakeholders who have a particular interest in or impact on quality, with the emphasis on the customer and project sponsor needs and expectations.

### 8.1.1.4 ENTERPRISE ENVIRONMENTAL FACTORS

The enterprise environmental factors that can influence the Plan Quality Management process include but are not limited to:

◆ Governmental agency regulations;

◆ Rules, standards, and guidelines specific to the application area;

◆ Geographic distribution;

◆ Organizational structure;

◆ Marketplace conditions;

◆ Working or operating conditions of the project or its deliverables; and

◆ Cultural perceptions.

### 8.1.1.5 ORGANIZATIONAL PROCESS ASSETS

The organizational process assets that can influence the Plan Quality Management process include but are not limited to:

◆ Organizational quality management system including policies, procedures, and guidelines;

◆ Quality templates such as check sheets, traceability matrix, and others; and

◆ Historical databases and lessons learned repository.

### 8.1.2 PLAN QUALITY MANAGEMENT: TOOLS AND TECHNIQUES

#### 8.1.2.1 EXPERT JUDGMENT

Described in Section 4.1.2.1. Expertise should be considered from individuals or groups with specialized knowledge or training in the following topics:

◆ Quality assurance,

◆ Quality control,

◆ Quality measurements,

◆ Quality improvements, and

◆ Quality systems.

#### 8.1.2.2 DATA GATHERING

Data-gathering techniques that can be used for this process include but are not limited to:

◆ **Benchmarking.** Benchmarking involves comparing actual or planned project practices or the project's quality standards to those of comparable projects to identify best practices, generate ideas for improvement, and provide a basis for measuring performance. Benchmarked projects may exist within the performing organization or outside of it, or can be within the same application area or other application area. Benchmarking allows for analogies from projects in a different application area or different industries to be made.

◆ **Brainstorming.** Described in Section 4.1.2.2. Brainstorming can be used to gather data creatively from a group of team members or subject matter experts to develop the quality management plan that best fits the upcoming project.

◆ **Interviews.** Described in Section 5.2.2.2. Project and product quality needs and expectations, implicit and explicit, formal and informal, can be identified by interviewing experienced project participants, stakeholders, and subject matter experts. Interviews should be conducted in an environment of trust and confidentiality to encourage honest and unbiased contributions.

### 8.1.2.3 DATA ANALYSIS

Data analysis techniques that can be used for this process include but are not limited to:

◆ **Cost-benefit analysis.** A cost-benefit analysis is a financial analysis tool used to estimate the strengths and weaknesses of alternatives in order to determine the best alternative in terms of benefits provided. A cost-benefit analysis will help the project manager determine if the planned quality activities are cost effective. The primary benefits of meeting quality requirements include less rework, higher productivity, lower costs, increased stakeholder satisfaction, and increased profitability. A cost-benefit analysis for each quality activity compares the cost of the quality step to the expected benefit.

◆ **Cost of quality.** The cost of quality (COQ) associated with a project consists of one or more of the following costs (Figure 8-5 lists examples for each cost group):

   ▪ *Prevention costs.* Costs related to the prevention of poor quality in the products, deliverables, or services of the specific project.

   ▪ *Appraisal costs.* Costs related to evaluating, measuring, auditing, and testing the products, deliverables, or services of the specific project.

   ▪ *Failure costs (internal/external).* Costs related to nonconformance of the products, deliverables, or services to the needs or expectations of the stakeholders.

The optimal COQ is one that reflects the appropriate balance for investing in the cost of prevention and appraisal to avoid failure costs. Models show that there is an optimal quality cost for projects, where investing in additional prevention/appraisal costs is neither beneficial nor cost effective.

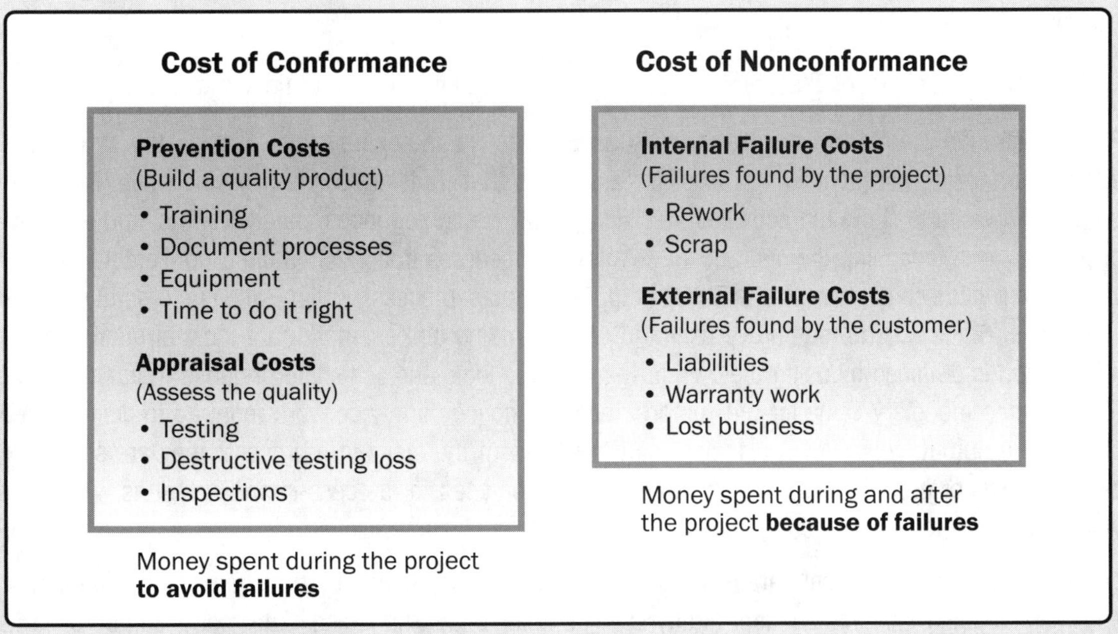

**Cost of Conformance**

**Prevention Costs**
(Build a quality product)

- Training
- Document processes
- Equipment
- Time to do it right

**Appraisal Costs**
(Assess the quality)

- Testing
- Destructive testing loss
- Inspections

Money spent during the project
**to avoid failures**

**Cost of Nonconformance**

**Internal Failure Costs**
(Failures found by the project)

- Rework
- Scrap

**External Failure Costs**
(Failures found by the customer)

- Liabilities
- Warranty work
- Lost business

Money spent during and after
the project **because of failures**

Figure 8-5. Cost of Quality

### 8.1.2.4 DECISION MAKING

A decision-making technique that can be used for this process includes but is not limited to multicriteria decision analysis. Multicriteria decision analysis tools (e.g., prioritization matrix) can be used to identify the key issues and suitable alternatives to be prioritized as a set of decisions for implementation. Criteria are prioritized and weighted before being applied to all available alternatives to obtain a mathematical score for each alternative. The alternatives are then ranked by score. As used in this process, it can help prioritize quality metrics.

### 8.1.2.5 DATA REPRESENTATION

Data representation techniques that can be used for this process include but are not limited to:

◆ **Flowcharts.** Flowcharts are also referred to as process maps because they display the sequence of steps and the branching possibilities that exist for a process that transforms one or more inputs into one or more outputs. Flowcharts show the activities, decision points, branching loops, parallel paths, and the overall order of processing by mapping the operational details of procedures that exist within a horizontal value chain. One version of a value chain, known as a SIPOC (suppliers, inputs, process, outputs, and customers) model, is shown in Figure 8-6. Flowcharts may prove useful in understanding and estimating the cost of quality for a process. Information is obtained by using the workflow branching logic and associated relative frequencies to estimate the expected monetary value for the conformance and nonconformance work required to deliver the expected conforming output. When flowcharts are used to represent the steps in a process, they are sometimes called process flows or process flow diagrams and they can be used for process improvement as well as identifying where quality defects can occur or where to incorporate quality checks.

◆ **Logical data model.** Logical data models are a visual representation of an organization's data, described in business language and independent of any specific technology. The logical data model can be used to identify where data integrity or other quality issues can arise.

◆ **Matrix diagrams.** Matrix diagrams help find the strength of relationships among different factors, causes, and objectives that exist between the rows and columns that form the matrix. Depending on how many factors may be compared, the project manager can use different shapes of matrix diagrams; for example, L, T, Y, X, C, and roof–shaped. In this process they facilitate identifying the key quality metrics that are important for the success of the project.

◆ **Mind mapping.** Described in Section 5.2.2.3. Mind mapping is a diagrammatic method used to visually organize information. A mind map in quality is often created around a single quality concept, drawn as an image in the center of a blank landscape page, to which associated representations of ideas such as images, words, and parts of words are added. The mind-mapping technique may help in the rapid gathering of project quality requirements, constraints, dependencies, and relationships.

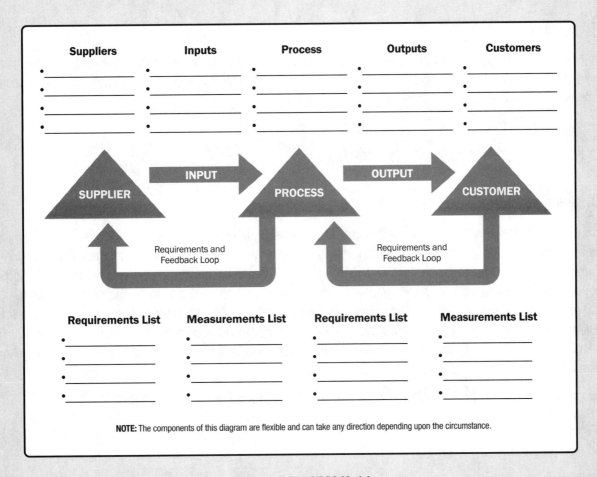

**NOTE:** The components of this diagram are flexible and can take any direction depending upon the circumstance.

**Figure 8-6. The SIPOC Model**

## 8.1.2.6 TEST AND INSPECTION PLANNING

During the planning phase, the project manager and the project team determine how to test or inspect the product, deliverable, or service to meet the stakeholders' needs and expectations, as well as how to meet the goal for the product's performance and reliability. The tests and inspections are industry dependent and can include, for example, alpha and beta tests in software projects, strength tests in construction projects, inspection in manufacturing, and field tests and nondestructive tests in engineering.

### 8.1.2.7 MEETINGS

Project teams may hold planning meetings to develop the quality management plan. Attendees can include the project manager, the project sponsor, selected project team members, selected stakeholders, anyone with responsibility for project quality management activities, and others as needed.

## 8.1.3 PLAN QUALITY MANAGEMENT: OUTPUTS

### 8.1.3.1 QUALITY MANAGEMENT PLAN

The quality management plan is a component of the project management plan that describes how applicable policies, procedures, and guidelines will be implemented to achieve the quality objectives. It describes the activities and resources necessary for the project management team to achieve the quality objectives set for the project. The quality management plan may be formal or informal, detailed, or broadly framed. The style and detail of the quality management plan are determined by the requirements of the project. The quality management plan should be reviewed early in the project to ensure that decisions are based on accurate information. The benefits of this review can include a sharper focus on the project's value proposition, reductions in costs, and less frequent schedule overruns that are caused by rework.

The quality management plan may include but is not limited to the following components:

◆ Quality standards that will be used by the project;

◆ Quality objectives of the project;

◆ Quality roles and responsibilities;

◆ Project deliverables and processes subject to quality review;

◆ Quality control and quality management activities planned for the project;

◆ Quality tools that will be used for the project; and

◆ Major procedures relevant for the project, such as dealing with nonconformance, corrective actions procedures, and continuous improvement procedures.

### 8.1.3.2 QUALITY METRICS

A quality metric specifically describes a project or product attribute and how the Control Quality process will verify compliance to it. Some examples of quality metrics include percentage of tasks completed on time, cost performance measured by CPI, failure rate, number of defects identified per day, total downtime per month, errors found per line of code, customer satisfaction scores, and percentage of requirements covered by the test plan as a measure of test coverage.

### 8.1.3.3 PROJECT MANAGEMENT PLAN UPDATES

Any change to the project management plan goes through the organization's change control process via a change request. Components that may require a change request for the project management plan include but are not limited to:

◆ **Risk management plan.** Described in Section 11.1.3.1. Decisions on the quality management approach may require changes to the agreed-upon approach to managing risk on the project, and these will be recorded in the risk management plan.

◆ **Scope baseline.** Described in Section 5.4.3.1. The scope baseline may change as a result of this process if specific quality management activities need to be added. The WBS dictionary also records quality requirements, which may need updating.

### 8.1.3.4 PROJECT DOCUMENTS UPDATES

Project documents that may be updated as a result of carrying out this process include but are not limited to:

◆ **Lessons learned register.** Described in Section 4.4.3.1. The lessons learned register is updated with information on challenges encountered in the quality planning process.

◆ **Requirements traceability matrix.** Described in Section 5.2.3.2. Where quality requirements are specified by this process, they are recorded in the requirements traceability matrix.

◆ **Risk register.** Described in Section 11.2.3.1. New risks identified during this process are recorded in the risk register and managed using the risk management processes.

◆ **Stakeholder register.** Described in Section 13.1.3.1. Where additional information on existing or new stakeholders is gathered as a result of this process, it is recorded in the stakeholder register.

## 8.2 MANAGE QUALITY

Manage Quality is the process of translating the quality management plan into executable quality activities that incorporate the organization's quality policies into the project. The key benefits of this process are that it increases the probability of meeting the quality objectives as well as identifying ineffective processes and causes of poor quality. Manage Quality uses the data and results from the control quality process to reflect the overall quality status of the project to the stakeholders. This process is performed throughout the project.

The inputs, tools and techniques, and outputs of this process are depicted in Figure 8-7. Figure 8-8 depicts the data flow diagram of the process.

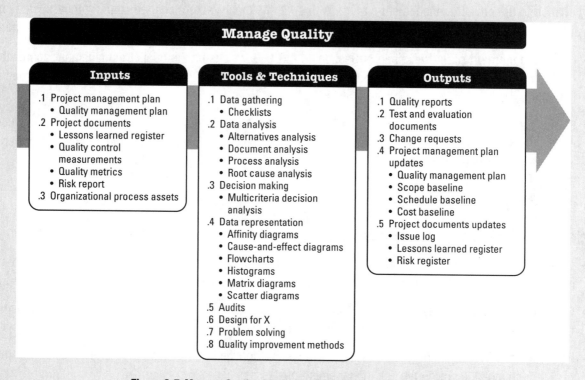

**Figure 8-7. Manage Quality: Inputs, Tools & Techniques, and Outputs**

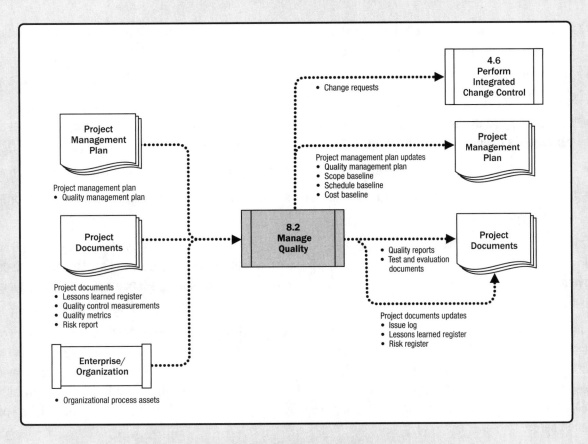

**Figure 8-8. Manage Quality: Data Flow Diagram**

Manage Quality is sometimes called quality assurance, although Manage Quality has a broader definition than quality assurance as it is used in nonproject work. In project management, the focus of quality assurance is on the processes used in the project. Quality assurance is about using project processes effectively. It involves following and meeting standards to assure stakeholders that the final product will meet their needs, expectations, and requirements. Manage Quality includes all the quality assurance activities, and is also concerned with the product design aspects and process improvements. Manage Quality work will fall under the conformance work category in the cost of quality framework.

The Manage Quality process implements a set of planned and systematic acts and processes defined within the project's quality management plan that helps to:

◆ Design an optimal and mature product by implementing specific design guidelines that address specific aspects of the product,

◆ Build confidence that a future output will be completed in a manner that meets the specified requirements and expectations through quality assurance tools and techniques such as quality audits and failure analysis,

◆ Confirm that the quality processes are used and that their use meets the quality objectives of the project, and

◆ Improve the efficiency and effectiveness of processes and activities to achieve better results and performance and enhance stakeholders' satisfaction.

The project manager and project team may use the organization's quality assurance department, or other organizational functions, to execute some of the Manage Quality activities such as failure analysis, design of experiments, and quality improvement. Quality assurance departments usually have cross-organizational experience in using quality tools and techniques and are a good resource for the project.

Manage Quality is considered the work of everybody—the project manager, the project team, the project sponsor, the management of the performing organization, and even the customer. All of these have roles in managing quality in the project, though the roles differ in size and effort. The level of participation in the quality management effort may differ between industries and project management styles. In agile projects, quality management is performed by all team members throughout the project, but in traditional projects, quality management is often the responsibility of specific team members.

## 8.2.1 MANAGE QUALITY: INPUTS

### 8.2.1.1 PROJECT MANAGEMENT PLAN

Described in Section 4.2.3.1. Project management plan components include but are not limited to the quality management plan. Described in Section 8.1.3.1, the quality management plan defines the acceptable level of project and product quality and describes how to ensure this level of quality in its deliverables and processes. The quality management plan also describes what to do with nonconforming products and what corrective action to implement.

## 8.2.1.2 PROJECT DOCUMENTS

Project documents that can be considered as inputs for this process include but are not limited to:

◆ **Lessons learned register.** Described in Section 4.4.3.1. Lessons learned earlier in the project with regard to managing quality can be applied to later phases in the project to improve the efficiency and effectiveness of managing quality.

◆ **Quality control measurements.** Described in Section 8.3.3.1. Quality control measurements are used to analyze and evaluate the quality of the processes and deliverables of the project against the standards of the performing organization or the requirements specified. Quality control measurements can also compare the processes used to create the measurements and validate actual measurements to determine their level of correctness.

◆ **Quality metrics.** Described in Section 8.1.3.2. Quality metrics are verified as part of the Control Quality process. The Manage Quality process uses these quality metrics as a basis for the development of test scenarios for the project and its deliverables and as a basis for improvement initiatives.

◆ **Risk report.** Described in Section 11.2.3.2. Risk report is used in the Manage Quality process to identify sources of overall project risk and the most important drivers of overall risk exposure that can impact the quality objectives of the project.

## 8.2.1.3 ORGANIZATIONAL PROCESS ASSETS

The organizational process assets that can influence the Manage Quality process include but are not limited to:

◆ Organizational quality management system that includes policies, procedures, and guidelines;

◆ Quality templates such as check sheets, traceability matrix, test plans, test documents, and others;

◆ Results from previous audits; and

◆ Lessons learned repository with information from similar projects.

## 8.2.2 MANAGE QUALITY: TOOLS AND TECHNIQUES

### 8.2.2.1 DATA GATHERING

A data-gathering technique that can be used for this process includes but is not limited to checklists (see Section 11.2.2.2). A checklist is a structured tool, usually component-specific, used to verify that a set of required steps has been performed or to check if a list of requirements has been satisfied. Based on the project's requirements and practices, checklists may be simple or complex. Many organizations have standardized checklists available to ensure consistency in frequently performed tasks. In some application areas, checklists are also available from professional associations or commercial service providers. Quality checklists should incorporate the acceptance criteria included in the scope baseline.

### 8.2.2.2 DATA ANALYSIS

Data analysis techniques that can be used for this process include but are not limited to:

◆ **Alternatives analysis.** Described in Section 9.2.2.5. This technique is used to evaluate identified options in order to select which different quality options or approaches are most appropriate to use.

◆ **Document analysis.** Described in Section 5.2.2.3. The analysis of different documents produced as part of the output of project control processes, such as quality reports, test reports, performance reports, and variance analysis, can point to and focus on processes that may be out of control and may jeopardize meeting the specified requirements or stakeholders' expectations.

◆ **Process analysis.** Process analysis identifies opportunities for process improvements. This analysis also examines problems, constraints, and non-value-added activities that occur during a process.

◆ **Root cause analysis (RCA).** Root cause analysis is an analytical technique used to determine the basic underlying reason that causes a variance, defect, or risk. A root cause may underlie more than one variance, defect, or risk. It may also be used as a technique for identifying root causes of a problem and solving them. When all root causes for a problem are removed, the problem does not recur.

## 8.2.2.3 DECISION MAKING

A decision-making technique that can be used for this process includes but is not limited to multicriteria decision analysis. Described in Section 8.1.2.4. Multicriteria decision making is used to evaluate several criteria when discussing alternatives that impact project or product quality. *Project* decisions can include choosing among different implementation scenarios or suppliers. *Product* decisions can include evaluating the life cycle cost, schedule, stakeholder satisfaction, and risks associated with resolving product defects.

## 8.2.2.4 DATA REPRESENTATION

Data representation techniques that can be used for this process include but are not limited to:

◆ **Affinity diagrams.** Described in Section 5.2.2.5. Affinity diagrams can organize potential causes of defects into groups showing areas that should be focused on the most.

◆ **Cause-and-effect diagrams.** Cause-and-effect diagrams are also known as fishbone diagrams, why-why diagrams, or Ishikawa diagrams. This type of diagram breaks down the causes of the problem statement identified into discrete branches, helping to identify the main or root cause of the problem. Figure 8-9 is an example of a cause-and-effect diagram.

◆ **Flowcharts.** Described in Section 8.1.2.5. Flowcharts show a series of steps that lead to a defect.

◆ **Histograms.** Histograms show a graphical representation of numerical data. Histograms can show the number of defects per deliverable, a ranking of the cause of defects, the number of times each process is noncompliant, or other representations of project or product defects.

◆ **Matrix diagrams.** Described in Section 8.1.2.5. The matrix diagram seeks to show the strength of relationships among factors, causes, and objectives that exist between the rows and columns that form the matrix.

◆ **Scatter diagrams.** A scatter diagram is a graph that shows the relationship between two variables. Scatter diagrams can demonstrate a relationship between any element of a process, environment, or activity on one axis and a quality defect on the other axis.

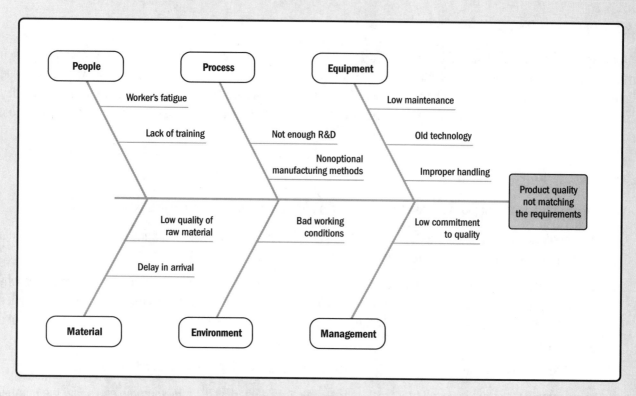

**Figure 8-9. Cause-and-Effect Diagram**

### 8.2.2.5 AUDITS

An audit is a structured, independent process used to determine if project activities comply with organizational and project policies, processes, and procedures. A quality audit is usually conducted by a team external to the project, such as the organization's internal audit department, PMO, or by an auditor external to the organization. Quality audit objectives may include but are not limited to:

◆ Identifying all good and best practices being implemented;

◆ Identifying all nonconformity, gaps, and shortcomings;

◆ Sharing good practices introduced or implemented in similar projects in the organization and/or industry;

◆ Proactively offering assistance in a positive manner to improve the implementation of processes to help raise team productivity; and

◆ Highlighting contributions of each audit in the lessons learned repository of the organization.

The subsequent effort to correct any deficiencies should result in a reduced cost of quality and an increase in sponsor or customer acceptance of the project's product. Quality audits may be scheduled or random, and may be conducted by internal or external auditors.

Quality audits can confirm the implementation of approved change requests including updates, corrective actions, defect repairs, and preventive actions.

### 8.2.2.6 DESIGN FOR X

Design for X (DfX) is a set of technical guidelines that may be applied during the design of a product for the optimization of a specific aspect of the design. DfX can control or even improve the product's final characteristics. The X in DfX can be different aspects of product development, such as reliability, deployment, assembly, manufacturing, cost, service, usability, safety, and quality. Using the DfX may result in cost reduction, quality improvement, better performance, and customer satisfaction.

### 8.2.2.7 PROBLEM SOLVING

Problem solving entails finding solutions for issues or challenges. It can include gathering additional information, critical thinking, creative, quantitative and/or logical approaches. Effective and systematic problem solving is a fundamental element in quality assurance and quality improvement. Problems can arise as a result of the Control Quality process or from quality audits and can be associated with a process or deliverable. Using a structured problem-solving method will help eliminate the problem and develop a long-lasting solution. Problem-solving methods generally include the following elements:

◆ Defining the problem,

◆ Identifying the root-cause,

◆ Generating possible solutions,

◆ Choosing the best solution,

◆ Implementing the solution, and

◆ Verifying solution effectiveness.

### 8.2.2.8 QUALITY IMPROVEMENT METHODS

Quality improvements can occur based on findings and recommendations from quality control processes, the findings of the quality audits, or problem solving in the Manage Quality process. Plan-do-check-act and Six Sigma are two of the most common quality improvement tools used to analyze and evaluate opportunities for improvement.

## 8.2.3 MANAGE QUALITY: OUTPUTS

### 8.2.3.1 QUALITY REPORTS

The quality reports can be graphical, numerical, or qualitative. The information provided can be used by other processes and departments to take corrective actions in order to achieve the project quality expectations. The information presented in the quality reports may include all quality management issues escalated by the team; recommendations for process, project, and product improvements; corrective actions recommendations (including rework, defect/bugs repair, 100% inspection, and more); and the summary of findings from the Control Quality process.

### 8.2.3.2 TEST AND EVALUATION DOCUMENTS

Test and evaluation documents can be created based on industry needs and the organization's templates. They are inputs to the Control Quality process and are used to evaluate the achievement of quality objectives. These documents may include dedicated checklists and detailed requirements traceability matrices as part of the document.

### 8.2.3.3 CHANGE REQUESTS

Described in Section 4.3.3.4. If changes occur during the Manage Quality process that impact any of the components of the project management plan, project documents, or project or product management processes, the project manager should submit a change request and follow the Perform Integrated Change Control process as defined in Section 4.6.

## 8.2.3.4 PROJECT MANAGEMENT PLAN UPDATES

Any change to the project management plan goes through the organization's change control process via a change request. Components that may require a change request for the project management plan include but are not limited to:

◆ **Quality management plan.** Described in Section 8.1.3.1. The agreed-upon approach to managing quality may need to be modified due to the actual results.

◆ **Scope baseline.** Described in Section 5.4.3.1. The scope baseline may change as a result of specific quality management activities.

◆ **Schedule baseline.** Described in Section 6.5.3.1. The schedule baseline may change as a result of specific quality management activities.

◆ **Cost baseline.** Described in Section 7.3.3.1. The cost baseline may change as a result of specific quality management activities.

## 8.2.3.5 PROJECT DOCUMENTS UPDATES

Project documents that may be updated as a result of carrying out this process include but are not limited to:

◆ **Issue log.** Described in Section 4.3.3.3. New issues raised as a result of this process are recorded in the issue log.

◆ **Lessons learned register.** Described in Section 4.4.3.1. The lessons learned register is updated with information on challenges encountered and how they could have been avoided as well as approaches that worked well for the managing quality.

◆ **Risk register.** Described in Section 11.2.3.1. New risks identified during this process are recorded in the risk register and managed using the risk management processes.

# 8.3 CONTROL QUALITY

Control Quality is the process of monitoring and recording results of executing the quality management activities in order to assess performance and ensure the project outputs are complete, correct, and meet customer expectations. The key benefit of this process is verifying that project deliverables and work meet the requirements specified by key stakeholders for final acceptance. The Control Quality process determines if the project outputs do what they were intended to do. Those outputs need to comply with all applicable standards, requirements, regulations, and specifications. This process is performed throughout the project.

The inputs, tools and techniques, and outputs of this process are depicted in Figure 8-10. Figure 8-11 depicts the data flow diagram of the process.

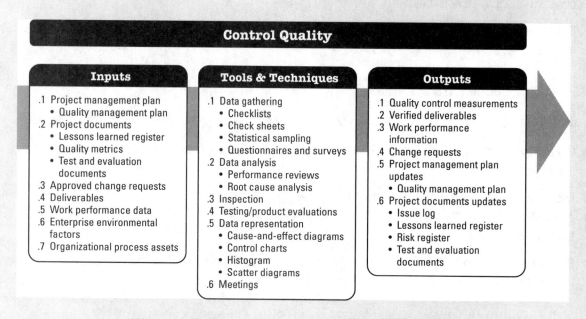

**Figure 8-10. Control Quality: Inputs, Tools & Techniques, and Outputs**

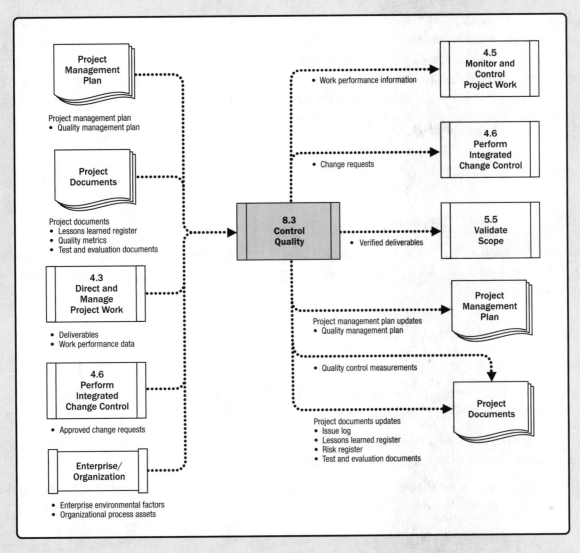

**Figure 8-11. Control Quality: Data Flow Diagram**

The Control Quality process is performed to measure the completeness, compliance, and fitness for use of a product or service prior to user acceptance and final delivery. This is done by measuring all steps, attributes, and variables used to verify conformance or compliance to the specifications stated during the planning stage.

Quality control should be performed throughout the project to formally demonstrate, with reliable data, that the sponsor's and/or customer's acceptance criteria have been met.

The level of effort to control quality and the degree of implementation may differ between industries and project management styles; in pharmaceutical, health, transportation, and nuclear industries, for example, there may be stricter quality control procedures compared to other industries, and the effort needed to meet the standards may be extensive. For example, in agile projects, the Control Quality activities may be performed by all team members throughout the project life cycle. In waterfall model-based projects, the quality control activities are performed at specific times, toward the end of the project or phase, by specified team members.

### 8.3.1 CONTROL QUALITY: INPUTS

#### 8.3.1.1 PROJECT MANAGEMENT PLAN

Described in Section 4.2.3.1. Project management plan components include but are not limited to the quality management plan. Described in Section 8.1.3.1, the quality management plan defines how quality control will be performed within the project.

#### 8.3.1.2 PROJECT DOCUMENTS

Project documents that can be considered as inputs for this process include but are not limited to:

◆ **Lessons learned register.** Described in Section 4.4.3.1. Lessons learned earlier in the project can be applied to later phases in the project to improve quality control.

◆ **Quality metrics.** Described in Section 8.1.3.2. A quality metric specifically describes a project or product attribute and how the Control Quality process will verify compliance to it.

◆ **Test and evaluation documents.** Described in Section 8.2.3.2. Test and evaluation documents are used to evaluate achievement of the quality objectives.

### 8.3.1.3 APPROVED CHANGE REQUESTS

Described in Section 4.6.3.1. As part of the Perform Integrated Change Control process, a change log update indicates that some changes are approved and some are not. Approved change requests may include modifications such as defect repairs, revised work methods, and revised schedules. Partial change completion may result in inconsistencies and later delays due to incomplete steps or corrections. The implementation of approved changes should be verified, confirmed for completeness, retested, and certified as correct.

### 8.3.1.4 DELIVERABLES

A deliverable is any unique and verifiable product, result, or capability to perform a service that is required to be produced to complete a process, phase, or project. Deliverables that are outputs from the Direct and Manage Project Work process are inspected and compared to the acceptance criteria defined in the project scope statement.

### 8.3.1.5 WORK PERFORMANCE DATA

Described in Section 4.3.3.2. Work performance data contains data on product status such as observations, quality metrics, and measurements for technical performance, as well as project quality information on schedule performance and cost performance.

### 8.3.1.6 ENTERPRISE ENVIRONMENTAL FACTORS

The enterprise environmental factors that can influence the Control Quality process include but are not limited to:

- Project management information system; quality management software can be used to track errors and variations in processes or deliverables;
- Governmental agency regulations; and
- Rules, standards, and guidelines specific to the application area.

## 8.3.1.7 ORGANIZATIONAL PROCESS ASSETS

The organizational process assets that can influence the Control Quality process include but are not limited to:

◆ Quality standards and policies;

◆ Quality templates, for example, check sheets, checklists, etc. and;

◆ Issue and defect reporting procedures and communication policies.

## 8.3.2 CONTROL QUALITY: TOOLS AND TECHNIQUES

### 8.3.2.1 DATA GATHERING

Data-gathering techniques that can be used for this process include but are not limited to:

◆ **Checklists.** Described in Section 11.2.2.2. Checklists help in managing the control quality activities in a structured manner.

◆ **Check sheets.** Check sheets are also known as tally sheets and are used to organize facts in a manner that will facilitate the effective collection of useful data about a potential quality problem. They are especially useful for gathering attributes data while performing inspections to identify defects; for example, data about the frequencies or consequences of defects collected. See Figure 8-12.

| Defects/Date | Date 1 | Date 2 | Date 3 | Date 4 | Total |
|---|---|---|---|---|---|
| Small scratch | 1 | 2 | 2 | 2 | 7 |
| Large scratch | 0 | 1 | 0 | 0 | 1 |
| Bent | 3 | 3 | 1 | 2 | 9 |
| Missing component | 5 | 0 | 2 | 1 | 8 |
| Wrong color | 2 | 0 | 1 | 3 | 6 |
| Labeling error | 1 | 2 | 1 | 2 | 6 |

Figure 8-12. Check Sheets

◆ **Statistical sampling.** Statistical sampling involves choosing part of a population of interest for inspection (for example, selecting 10 engineering drawings at random from a list of 75). The sample is taken to measure controls and verify quality. Sample frequency and sizes should be determined during the Plan Quality Management process.

◆ **Questionnaires and Surveys.** Surveys may be used to gather data about customer satisfaction after the deployment of the product or service. The cost regarding defects identified in the surveys may be considered external failure costs in the COQ model and can have extensive cost implications for the organization.

### 8.3.2.2 DATA ANALYSIS

Data analysis techniques that can be used for this process include but are not limited to:

◆ **Performance reviews.** Performance reviews measure, compare, and analyze the quality metrics defined by the Plan Quality Management process against the actual results.

◆ **Root cause analysis (RCA).** Described in Section 8.2.2.2. Root cause analysis is used to identify the source of defects.

### 8.3.2.3 INSPECTION

An inspection is the examination of a work product to determine if it conforms to documented standards. The results of inspections generally include measurements and may be conducted at any level. The results of a single activity can be inspected, or the final product of the project can be inspected. Inspections may be called reviews, peer reviews, audits, or walkthroughs. In some application areas, these terms have narrow and specific meanings. Inspections also are used to verify defect repairs.

### 8.3.2.4 TESTING/PRODUCT EVALUATIONS

Testing is an organized and constructed investigation conducted to provide objective information about the quality of the product or service under test in accordance with the project requirements. The intent of testing is to find errors, defects, bugs, or other nonconformance problems in the product or service. The type, amount, and extent of tests needed to evaluate each requirement are part of the project quality plan and depend on the nature of the project, time, budget, and other constraints. Tests can be performed throughout the project, as different components of the project become available, and at the end of the project on the final deliverables. Early testing helps identify nonconformance problems and helps reduce the cost of fixing the nonconforming components.

Different application areas require different tests. For example, software testing may include unit testing, integration testing, black-box, white-box, interface testing, regression testing, Alpha testing, etc. In construction projects, testing may include cement strength, concrete workability test, nondestructive tests at construction sites for testing the quality of hardened concrete structures, and soil tests. In hardware development, testing may include environmental stress screening, burn-in tests, system testing, and more.

### 8.3.2.5 DATA REPRESENTATION

Data representation techniques that can be used for this process include but are not limited to:

- **Cause-and-effect diagrams.** Described in Section 8.2.2.4. Cause-and-effect diagrams are used to identify the possible effects of quality defects and errors.

- **Control charts.** Control charts are used to determine whether or not a process is stable or has predictable performance. Upper and lower specification limits are based on the requirements and reflect the maximum and minimum values allowed. Upper and lower control limits are different from specification limits. The control limits are determined using standard statistical calculations and principles to ultimately establish the natural capability for a stable process. The project manager and appropriate stakeholders may use the statistically calculated control limits to identify the points at which corrective action will be taken to prevent performance that remains outside the control limits. Control charts can be used to monitor various types of output variables. Although used most frequently to track repetitive activities required for producing manufactured lots, control charts may also be used to monitor cost and schedule variances, volume, frequency of scope changes, or other management results to help determine if the project management processes are in control.

- **Histograms.** Described in Section 8.2.2.4. Histograms can demonstrate the number of defects by source or by component.

- **Scatter diagrams.** Described in Section 8.2.2.4. Scatter diagrams can show the planned performance on one axis and the actual performance on the second axis.

## 8.3.2.6 MEETINGS

The following meetings may be used as part of the Control Quality process:

◆ **Approved change requests review.** All approved change requests should be reviewed to verify that they were implemented as approved. This review should also check that partial changes are completed and all parts have been properly implemented, tested, completed, and certified.

◆ **Retrospectives/lesson learned.** A meeting held by a project team to discuss:

- Successful elements in the project/phase,
- What could be improved,
- What to incorporate in the ongoing project and what in future projects, and
- What to add to the organization process assets.

## 8.3.3 CONTROL QUALITY: OUTPUTS

### 8.3.3.1 QUALITY CONTROL MEASUREMENTS

Quality control measurements are the documented results of Control Quality activities. They should be captured in the format that was specified in the quality management plan.

### 8.3.3.2 VERIFIED DELIVERABLES

A goal of the Control Quality process is to determine the correctness of deliverables. The results of performing the Control Quality process are verified deliverables that become an input to the Validate Scope process (Section 5.5) for formalized acceptance. If there were any change requests or improvements related to the deliverables, they may be changed, inspected, and reverified.

### 8.3.3.3 WORK PERFORMANCE INFORMATION

Described in Section 4.5.1.3. Work performance information includes information on project requirements fulfillment, causes for rejections, rework required, recommendations for corrective actions, lists of verified deliverables, status of the quality metrics, and the need for process adjustments.

### 8.3.3.4 CHANGE REQUESTS

Described in Section 4.3.3.4. If changes occur during the Control Quality process that may impact any of the components of the project management plan or project documents, the project manager should submit a change request. Change requests are processed for review and disposition through the Perform Integrated Change Control process (Section 4.6).

### 8.3.3.5 PROJECT MANAGEMENT PLAN UPDATES

Any change to the project management plan goes through the organization's change control process via a change request. Components that may require a change request for the project management plan include but are not limited to the quality management plan, as described in Section 8.1.3.1.

### 8.3.3.6 PROJECT DOCUMENTS UPDATES

Project documents that may be updated as a result of carrying out this process include but are not limited to:

◆ **Issue log.** Described in Section 4.3.3.3. Many times a deliverable that does not meet the quality requirements is documented as an issue.

◆ **Lessons learned register.** Described in Section 4.4.3.1. The lessons learned register is updated with information on the source of quality defects and how they could have been avoided as well as approaches that worked well.

◆ **Risk register.** Described in Section 11.2.3.1. New risks identified during this process are recorded in the risk register and managed using the risk management processes.

◆ **Test and evaluation documents.** Described in Section 8.2.3.2. Test and evaluation documents may be modified as a result of this process in order to make future tests more effective.

# 9

## PROJECT RESOURCE MANAGEMENT

Project Resource Management includes the processes to identify, acquire, and manage the resources needed for the successful completion of the project. These processes help ensure that the right resources will be available to the project manager and project team at the right time and place.

The Project Resource Management processes are:

**9.1 Plan Resource Management**—The process of defining how to estimate, acquire, manage, and utilize physical and team resources.

**9.2 Estimate Activity Resources**—The process of estimating team resources and the type and quantities of material, equipment, and supplies necessary to perform project work.

**9.3 Acquire Resources**—The process of obtaining team members, facilities, equipment, materials, supplies, and other resources necessary to complete project work.

**9.4 Develop Team**—The process of improving competencies, team member interaction, and the overall team environment to enhance project performance.

**9.5 Manage Team**—The process of tracking team member performance, providing feedback, resolving issues, and managing team changes to optimize project performance.

**9.6 Control Resources**—The process of ensuring that the physical resources assigned and allocated to the project are available as planned, as well as monitoring the planned versus actual use of resources, and performing corrective action as necessary.

Figure 9-1 provides an overview of the Project Resource Management processes. The Project Resource Management processes are presented as discrete processes with defined interfaces while, in practice, they overlap and interact in ways that cannot be completely detailed in the *PMBOK® Guide*.

**Project Resource Management Overview**

**9.1 Plan Resource Management**

.1 Inputs
  .1 Project charter
  .2 Project management plan
  .3 Project documents
  .4 Enterprise environmental factors
  .5 Organizational process assets
.2 Tools & Techniques
  .1 Expert judgment
  .2 Data representation
  .3 Organizational theory
  .4 Meetings
.3 Outputs
  .1 Resource management plan
  .2 Team charter
  .3 Project documents updates

**9.2 Estimate Activity Resources**

.1 Inputs
  .1 Project management plan
  .2 Project documents
  .3 Enterprise environmental factors
  .4 Organizational process assets
.2 Tools & Techniques
  .1 Expert judgment
  .2 Bottom-up estimating
  .3 Analogous estimating
  .4 Parametric estimating
  .5 Data analysis
  .6 Project management information system
  .7 Meetings
.3 Outputs
  .1 Resource requirements
  .2 Basis of estimates
  .3 Resource breakdown structure
  .4 Project documents updates

**9.3 Acquire Resources**

1 Inputs
  .1 Project management plan
  .2 Project documents
  .3 Enterprise environmental factors
  .4 Organizational process assets
.2 Tools & Techniques
  .1 Decision making
  .2 Interpersonal and team skills
  .3 Pre-assignment
  .4 Virtual teams
.3 Outputs
  .1 Physical resource assignments
  .2 Project team assignments
  .3 Resource calendars
  .4 Change requests
  .5 Project management plan updates
  .6 Project documents updates
  .7 Enterprise environmental factors updates
  .8 Organizational process assets updates

**9.4 Develop Team**

.1 Inputs
  .1 Project management plan
  .2 Project documents
  .3 Enterprise environmental factors
  .4 Organizational process assets
.2 Tools & Techniques
  .1 Colocation
  .2 Virtual teams
  .3 Communication technology
  .4 Interpersonal and team skills
  .5 Recognition and rewards
  .6 Training
  .7 Individual and team assessments
  .8 Meetings
.3 Outputs
  .1 Team performance assessments
  .2 Change requests
  .3 Project management plan updates
  .4 Project documents updates
  .5 Enterprise environmental factors updates
  .6 Organizational process assets updates

**9.5 Manage Team**

1 Inputs
  .1 Project management plan
  .2 Project documents
  .3 Work performance reports
  .4 Team performance assessments
  .5 Enterprise environmental factors
  .6 Organizational process assets
.2 Tools & Techniques
  .1 Interpersonal and team skills
  .2 Project management information system
.3 Outputs
  .1 Change requests
  .2 Project management plan updates
  .3 Project documents updates
  .4 Enterprise environmental factors updates

**9.6 Control Resources**

.1 Inputs
  .1 Project management plan
  .2 Project documents
  .3 Work performance data
  .4 Agreements
  .5 Organizational process assets
.2 Tools & Techniques
  .1 Data analysis
  .2 Problem solving
  .3 Interpersonal and team skills
  .4 Project management information system
.3 Outputs
  .1 Work performance information
  .2 Change requests
  .3 Project management plan updates
  .4 Project documents updates

**Figure 9-1. Project Resource Management Overview**

There is a distinction between the skills and competencies needed for the project manager to manage team resources versus physical resources. Physical resources include equipment, materials, facilities, and infrastructure. Team resources or personnel refer to the human resources. Personnel may have varied skill sets, may be assigned full- or part-time, and may be added or removed from the project team as the project progresses. There is some overlap between Project Resource Management and Project Stakeholder Management (Section 13). This section (Section 9) focuses on the subset of stakeholders who make up the project team.

## KEY CONCEPTS FOR PROJECT RESOURCE MANAGEMENT

The project team consists of individuals with assigned roles and responsibilities who work collectively to achieve a shared project goal. The project manager should invest suitable effort in acquiring, managing, motivating, and empowering the project team. Although specific roles and responsibilities for the project team members are assigned, the involvement of all team members in project planning and decision making is beneficial. Participation of team members during planning adds their expertise to the process and strengthens their commitment to the project.

The project manager should be both leader and manager of the project team. In addition to project management activities such as initiating, planning, executing, monitoring and controlling, and closing the various project phases, the project manager is responsible for the team formation as an effective group. The project manager should be aware of different aspects that influence the team, such as:

◆ Team environment,

◆ Geographical locations of team members,

◆ Communications among stakeholders,

◆ Organizational change management,

◆ Internal and external politics,

◆ Cultural issues and organizational uniqueness, and

◆ Other factors that may alter project performance.

As a leader, the project manager is also responsible for proactively developing team skills and competencies while retaining and improving team satisfaction and motivation. The project manager should be aware of, and subscribe to, professional and ethical behavior, and ensure that all team members adhere to these behaviors.

Physical resource management is concentrated in allocating and using the physical resources (material, equipment, and supplies, for example) needed for successful completion of the project in an efficient and effective way. In order to do that, organizations should have data on resource demands (now and in the reasonable future), resource configurations that will be required to meet those demands, and the supply of resources. Failing to manage and control resources efficiently is a source of risk for successful project completion. For example:

◆ Failing to secure critical equipment or infrastructure on time may result in delays in the manufacturing of the final product,

◆ Ordering low-quality material may damage the quality of the product causing a high rate of recalls or rework, and

◆ Keeping too much inventory may result in high operations costs and reduce the organization's profit. Unacceptably low inventory level, on the other hand, may result in not satisfying customer demand and, again, reduce the organization's profit.

## TRENDS AND EMERGING PRACTICES IN PROJECT RESOURCE MANAGEMENT

Project management styles are shifting away from a command and control structure for managing projects and toward a more collaborative and supportive management approach that empowers teams by delegating decision making to the team members. In addition, modern project resource management approaches seek to optimize resource utilization. Trends and emerging practices for Project Resource Management include but are not limited to:

◆ **Resource management methods.** Due to the scarce nature of critical resources, in some industries, several trends have become popular in the past several years. There is extensive literature about lean management, just-in-time (JIT) manufacturing, Kaizen, total productive maintenance (TPM), theory of constraints (TOC), and other methods. A project manager should determine if the performing organization has adopted one or more resource management tools and adapt the project accordingly.

◆ **Emotional intelligence (EI).** The project manager should invest in personal EI by improving inbound (e.g., self-management and self-awareness) and outbound (e.g., relationship management) competencies. Research suggests that project teams that succeed in developing team EI or become an emotionally competent group are more effective. Additionally, there is a reduction in staff turnover.

◆ **Self-organizing teams.** The increase in using agile approaches mainly for the execution of IT projects has given rise to the self-organizing team, where the team functions with an absence of centralized control. In projects that have self-organizing teams, the project manager (who may not be called a project manager) role provides the team with the environment and support needed and trusts the team to get the job done. Successful self-organizing teams usually consist of generalized specialists, instead of subject matter experts, who continuously adapt to the changing environment and embrace constructive feedback.

◆ **Virtual teams/distributed teams.** The globalization of projects has promoted the need for virtual teams that work on the same project, but are not colocated at the same site. The availability of communication technology such as email, audio conferencing, social media, web-based meetings, and video conferencing has made virtual teams feasible. Managing virtual teams has unique advantages, such as being able to use special expertise on a project team even when the expert is not in the same geographic area, incorporating employees who work from home offices, and including people with mobility limitations or disabilities. The challenges of managing virtual teams are mainly in the communication domain, including a possible feeling of isolation, gaps in sharing knowledge and experience between team members, and difficulties in tracking progress and productivity, possible time zone difference and cultural differences.

## TAILORING CONSIDERATIONS

Because each project is unique, the project manager will need to tailor the way Project Resource Management processes are applied. Considerations for tailoring include but are not limited to:

◆ **Diversity.** What is the diversity background of the team?

◆ **Physical location.** What is the physical location of team members and physical resources?

◆ **Industry-specific resources.** What special resources are needed in the industry?

◆ **Acquisition of team members.** How will team members be acquired for the project? Are team resources full-time or part-time on the project?

◆ **Management of team.** How is team development managed for the project? Are there organizational tools to manage team development or will new ones need to be established? Are there team members who have special needs? Will the team need special training to manage diversity?

◆ **Life cycle approaches.** What life cycle approach will be used on the project?

## CONSIDERATIONS FOR AGILE/ADAPTIVE ENVIRONMENTS

Projects with high variability benefit from team structures that maximize focus and collaboration, such as self-organizing teams with generalizing specialists.

Collaboration is intended to boost productivity and facilitate innovative problem solving. Collaborative teams may facilitate accelerated integration of distinct work activities, improve communication, increase knowledge sharing, and provide flexibility of work assignments in addition to other advantages.

Although the benefits of collaboration also apply to other project environments, collaborative teams are often critical to the success of projects with a high degree of variability and rapid changes, because there is less time for centralized tasking and decision making.

Planning for physical and human resources is much less predictable in projects with high variability. In these environments, agreements for fast supply and lean methods are critical to controlling costs and achieving the schedule.

## 9.1 PLAN RESOURCE MANAGEMENT

Plan Resource Management is the process of defining how to estimate, acquire, manage, and use team and physical resources. The key benefit of this process is that it establishes the approach and level of management effort needed for managing project resources based on the type and complexity of the project. This process is performed once or at predefined points in the project. The inputs, tools and techniques, and outputs of the process are depicted in Figure 9-2. Figure 9-3 depicts the data flow diagram for the process.

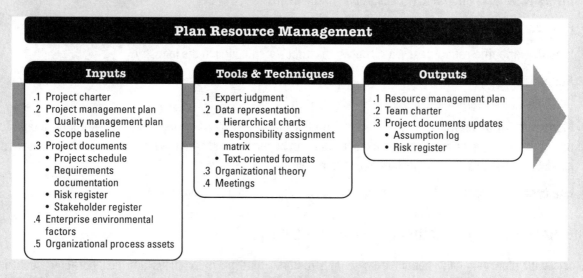

Figure 9-2. Plan Resource Management: Inputs, Tools & Techniques, and Outputs

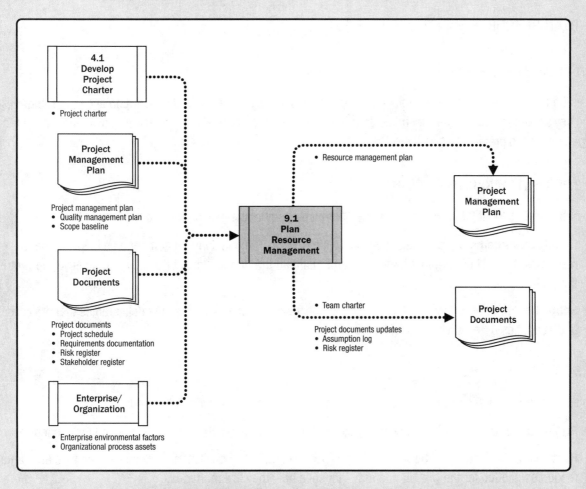

**Figure 9-3. Plan Resource Management: Data Flow Diagram**

Resource planning is used to determine and identify an approach to ensure that sufficient resources are available for the successful completion of the project. Project resources may include team members, supplies, materials, equipment, services and facilities. Effective resource planning should consider and plan for the availability of, or competition for, scarce resources.

Those resources can be obtained from the organization's internal assets or from outside the organization through a procurement process. Other projects may be competing for the same resources required for the project at the same time and location. This may significantly impact project costs, schedules, risks, quality, and other project areas.

# 9.1.1 PLAN RESOURCE MANAGEMENT: INPUTS

## 9.1.1.1 PROJECT CHARTER

Described in Section 4.1.3.1. The project charter provides the high-level project description and requirements. It also has the key stakeholder list, summary milestones, and preapproved financial resources that may influence the resource management of the project.

## 9.1.1.2 PROJECT MANAGEMENT PLAN

Described in Section 4.2.3.1. Project management plan components include but are not limited to:

◆ **Quality management plan.** Described in Section 8.1.3.1. The quality management plan helps define the level of resources that will be required to achieve and maintain the defined level of quality and achieve the metrics for the project.

◆ **Scope baseline.** Described in Section 5.4.3.1. The scope baseline identifies the deliverables that drive the types and quantities of resources that will need to be managed.

## 9.1.1.3 PROJECT DOCUMENTS

Project documents that can be considered as inputs for this process include but are not limited to:

◆ **Project schedule.** Described in Section 6.5.3.2. The project schedule shows the timeline for needed resources.

◆ **Requirements documentation.** Described in Section 5.2.3.1. Requirements will dictate the type and amount of resources needed for the project and may influence how they are managed.

◆ **Risk register.** Described in Section 11.2.3.1. The risk register contains information on threats and opportunities that may impact resource planning.

◆ **Stakeholder register.** Described in Section 13.1.3.1. The stakeholder register aids in identifying those stakeholders who have a particular interest in or an impact on resources needed for the project. It also helps to identify stakeholders who can influence the use of one kind of resource over another.

### 9.1.1.4 ENTERPRISE ENVIRONMENTAL FACTORS

The enterprise environmental factors that can influence the Plan Resource Management include but are not limited to:

◆ Organizational culture and structure,

◆ Geographic distribution of facilities and resources,

◆ Existing resources competencies and availability, and

◆ Marketplace conditions.

### 9.1.1.5 ORGANIZATIONAL PROCESS ASSETS

The organizational process assets that can influence the Plan Resource Management include but are not limited to:

◆ Human resource policies and procedures,

◆ Physical resource management policies and procedures,

◆ Safety policies,

◆ Security policies,

◆ Templates for the resource management plan, and

◆ Historical information for similar projects.

## 9.1.2 PLAN RESOURCE MANAGEMENT: TOOLS AND TECHNIQUES

### 9.1.2.1 EXPERT JUDGMENT

Described in Section 4.1.2.1. Expertise should be considered from individuals or groups with specialized knowledge or training in the following topics:

◆ Negotiating for the best resources within the organization;

◆ Talent management and personnel development;

◆ Determining the preliminary effort level needed to meet project objectives;

◆ Determining reporting requirements based on the organizational culture;

◆ Estimating lead times required for acquisition, based on lessons learned and market conditions;

◆ Identifying risks associated with resource acquisition, retention, and release plans;

◆ Complying with applicable government and union regulations; and

◆ Managing sellers and the logistics effort to ensure materials and supplies are available when needed.

## 9.1.2.2 DATA REPRESENTATION

Data representation techniques that can be used for this process include but are not limited to charts. Various formats exist to document and communicate team member roles and responsibilities. Most fall into hierarchical, matrix, or text-oriented formats. Some project assignments are listed in subsidiary plans, such as the risk, quality, or communications management plans. Regardless of the method used to document team member roles, the objective is to ensure that each work package has an unambiguous owner and that all team members have a clear understanding of their roles and responsibilities. A hierarchical format may be used to represent high-level roles, while a text-based format may be better suited to document the detailed responsibilities.

◆ **Hierarchical charts.** The traditional organizational chart structure can be used to show positions and relationships in a graphical, top-down format.

- *Work breakdown structures (WBS).* The WBS is designed to show how project deliverables are broken down into work packages and provide a way of showing high-level areas of responsibility.

- *Organizational breakdown structure (OBS).* While the WBS shows a breakdown of project deliverables, an OBS is arranged according to an organization's existing departments, units, or teams, with the project activities or work packages listed under each department. An operational department, such as information technology or purchasing, can see all of its project responsibilities by looking at its portion of the OBS.

- *Resource breakdown structure.* The resource breakdown structure is a hierarchical list of team and physical resources related by category and resource type that is used for planning, managing and controlling project work. Each descending (lower) level represents an increasingly detailed description of the resource until the information is small enough to be used in conjunction with the work breakdown structure (WBS) to allow the work to be planned, monitored, and controlled.

◆ **Responsibility Assignment Matrix.** A RAM shows the project resources assigned to each work package. It is used to illustrate the connections between work packages, or activities, and project team members. On larger projects, RAMs can be developed at various levels. For example, a high-level RAM can define the responsibilities of a project team, group, or unit within each component of the WBS. Lower-level RAMs are used within the group to designate roles, responsibilities, and levels of authority for specific activities. The matrix format shows all activities associated with one person and all people associated with one activity. This also ensures that there is only one person accountable for any one task to avoid confusion about who is ultimately in charge or has authority for the work. One example of a RAM is a RACI (responsible, accountable, consult, and inform) chart, shown in Figure 9-4. The sample chart shows the work to be done in the left column as activities. The assigned resources can be shown as individuals or groups. The project manager can select other options, such as "lead" and "resource" designations, as appropriate for the project. A RACI chart is a useful tool to use to ensure clear assignment of roles and responsibilities when the team consists of internal and external resources.

◆ **Text-oriented formats.** Team member responsibilities that require detailed descriptions can be specified in text-oriented formats. Usually in outline form, these documents provide information such as responsibilities, authority, competencies, and qualifications. The documents are known by various names including position descriptions and role-responsibility-authority forms. These documents can be used as templates for future projects, especially when the information is updated throughout the current project by applying lessons learned.

| RACI Chart | Person | | | | |
|---|---|---|---|---|---|
| **Activity** | Ann | Ben | Carlos | Dina | Ed |
| Create charter | A | R | I | I | I |
| Collect requirements | I | A | R | C | C |
| Submit change request | I | A | R | R | C |
| Develop test plan | A | C | I | I | R |
| R = Responsible   A = Accountable   C = Consult   I = Inform | | | | | |

**Figure 9-4. Sample RACI Chart**

### 9.1.2.3 ORGANIZATIONAL THEORY

Organizational theory provides information regarding the way in which people, teams, and organizational units behave. Effective use of common techniques identified in organizational theory can shorten the amount of time, cost, and effort needed to create the Plan Resource Management process outputs and improve planning efficiency. Applicable organizational theories may recommend exercising a flexible leadership style that adapts to the changes in a team's maturity level throughout the project life cycle. It is important to recognize that the organization's structure and culture impacts the project organizational structure.

### 9.1.2.4 MEETINGS

The project team may hold meetings to plan resource management for the project.

### 9.1.3 PLAN RESOURCE MANAGEMENT: OUTPUTS

### 9.1.3.1 RESOURCE MANAGEMENT PLAN

The resource management plan is the component of the project management plan that provides guidance on how project resources should be categorized, allocated, managed, and released. It may be divided between the team management plan and physical resource management plan according to the specifics of the project. The resource management plan may include but is not limited to:

◆ **Identification of resources.** Methods for identifying and quantifying team and physical resources needed.

◆ **Acquiring resources.** Guidance on how to acquire team and physical resources for the project.

◆ **Roles and responsibilities:**

  ▪ *Role.* The function assumed by, or assigned to, a person in the project. Examples of project roles are civil engineer, business analyst, and testing coordinator.

  ▪ *Authority.* The rights to apply project resources, make decisions, sign approvals, accept deliverables, and influence others to carry out the work of the project. Examples of decisions that need clear authority include the selection of a method for completing an activity, quality acceptance criteria, and how to respond to project variances. Team members operate best when their individual levels of authority match their individual responsibilities.

- *Responsibility.* The assigned duties and work that a project team member is expected to perform in order to complete the project's activities.

- *Competence.* The skill and capacity required to complete assigned activities within the project constraints. If project team members do not possess required competencies, performance can be jeopardized. When such mismatches are identified, proactive responses such as training, hiring, schedule changes, or scope changes are initiated.

◆ **Project organization charts.** A project organization chart is a graphic display of project team members and their reporting relationships. It can be formal or informal, highly detailed or broadly framed, based on the needs of the project. For example, the project organization chart for a 3,000-person disaster response team will have greater detail than a project organization chart for an internal, 20-person project.

◆ **Project team resource management.** Guidance on how project team resources should be defined, staffed, managed, and eventually released.

◆ **Training.** Training strategies for team members.

◆ **Team development.** Methods for developing the project team.

◆ **Resource control.** Methods for ensuring adequate physical resources are available as needed and that the acquisition of physical resources is optimized for project needs. Includes information on managing inventory, equipment, and supplies during throughout the project life cycle.

◆ **Recognition plan.** Which recognition and rewards will be given to team members, and when they will be given.

## 9.1.3.2 TEAM CHARTER

The team charter is a document that establishes the team values, agreements, and operating guidelines for the team. The team charter may include but is not limited to:

◆ Team values,

◆ Communication guidelines,

◆ Decision-making criteria and process,

◆ Conflict resolution process,

◆ Meeting guidelines, and

◆ Team agreements.

The team charter establishes clear expectations regarding acceptable behavior by project team members. Early commitment to clear guidelines decreases misunderstandings and increases productivity. Discussing areas such as codes of conduct, communication, decision making, and meeting etiquette allows team members to discover values that are important to one another. The team charter works best when the team develops it, or at least has an opportunity to contribute to it. All project team members share responsibility for ensuring the rules documented in the team charter are followed. The team charter can be reviewed and updated periodically to ensure a continued understanding of the team ground rules and to orient and integrate new team members.

### 9.1.3.3 PROJECT DOCUMENTS UPDATES

Project documents that may be updated as a result of carrying out this process include but are not limited to:

◆ **Assumption log.** Described in Section 4.1.3.2. The assumption log is updated with assumptions regarding the availability, logistics requirements, and location of physical resources as well as the skill sets and availability of team resources.

◆ **Risk register.** Described in Section 11.2.3.1. The risk register is updated with risks associated with team and physical resource availability or other known resource-related risks.

## 9.2 ESTIMATE ACTIVITY RESOURCES

Estimate Activity Resources is the process of estimating team resources and the type and quantities of materials, equipment, and supplies necessary to perform project work. The key benefit of this process is that it identifies the type, quantity, and characteristics of resources required to complete the project. This process is performed periodically throughout the project as needed. The inputs, tools and techniques, and outputs of this process are depicted in Figure 9-5. Figure 9-6 depicts the data flow diagram of the process.

## Estimate Activity Resources

| Inputs | Tools & Techniques | Outputs |
|---|---|---|
| .1 Project management plan<br>• Resource management plan<br>• Scope baseline<br>.2 Project documents<br>• Activity attributes<br>• Activity list<br>• Assumption log<br>• Cost estimates<br>• Resource calendars<br>• Risk register<br>.3 Enterprise environmental factors<br>.4 Organizational process assets | .1 Expert judgment<br>.2 Bottom-up estimating<br>.3 Analogous estimating<br>.4 Parametric estimating<br>.5 Data analysis<br>• Alternatives analysis<br>.6 Project management information system<br>.7 Meetings | .1 Resource requirements<br>.2 Basis of estimates<br>.3 Resource breakdown structure<br>.4 Project documents updates<br>• Activity attributes<br>• Assumption log<br>• Lessons learned register |

Figure 9-5. Estimate Activity Resources: Inputs, Tools & Techniques, and Outputs

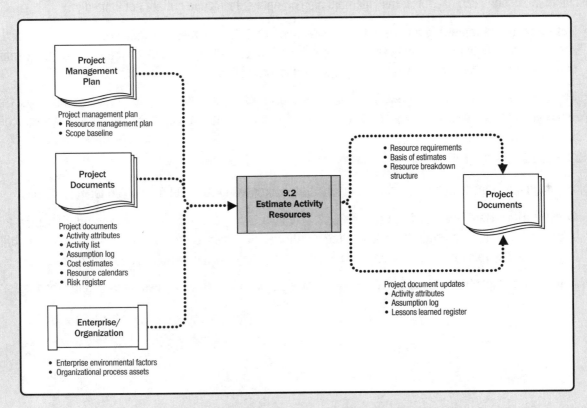

Figure 9-6. Estimate Activity Resources: Data Flow Diagram

The Estimate Activity Resources process is closely coordinated with other processes, such as the Estimate Costs process. For example:

◆ A construction project team will need to be familiar with local building codes. Such knowledge is often readily available from local sellers. If the internal labor pool lacks experience with unusual or specialized construction techniques, the additional cost for a consultant may be the most effective way to secure knowledge of the local building codes.

◆ An automotive design team will need to be familiar with the latest automated assembly techniques. The requisite knowledge could be obtained by hiring a consultant, by sending a designer to a seminar on robotics, or by including someone from manufacturing as a member of the project team.

## 9.2.1 ESTIMATE ACTIVITY RESOURCES: INPUTS

### 9.2.1.1 PROJECT MANAGEMENT PLAN

Described in Section 4.2.3.1. Project management plan components include but are not limited to:

◆ **Resource management plan.** Described in Section 9.1.3.1. The resource management plan defines the approach to identify the different resources needed for the project. It also defines the methods to quantify the resources needed for each activity and aggregates this information.

◆ **Scope baseline.** Described in Section 5.4.3.1. The scope baseline identifies the project and product scope necessary to meet the project objectives. The scope drives the needs for both team and physical resources.

### 9.2.1.2 PROJECT DOCUMENTS

Project documents that can be considered as inputs for this process include but are not limited to:

◆ **Activity attributes.** Described in Section 6.2.3.2. Activity attributes provide the primary data source for use in estimating team and physical resources required for each activity on the activity list. Examples of attributes include the resource requirements, imposed dates, activity location, assumptions, and constraints.

◆ **Activity list.** Described in Section 6.2.3.1. The activity list identifies the activities that will need resources.

◆ **Assumption log.** Described in Section 4.1.3.2. The assumption log may have information on productivity factors, availability, cost estimates, and approaches to work that will influence the nature and number of team and physical resources.

◆ **Cost estimates.** Described in Section 7.2.3.1. The cost of resources may impact resource selection from the quantity and skill level perspectives.

◆ **Resource calendars.** A resource calendar identifies the working days, shifts, start and end of normal business hours, weekends, and public holidays when each specific resource is available. Information on which resources (such as team resource, equipment, and material) are potentially available during a planned activity period is used for estimating resource utilization. Resource calendars also specify when, and for how long, identified team and physical resources will be available during the project. This information may be at the activity or project level. This includes consideration of attributes such as resource experience and/or skill level, as well as various geographical locations.

◆ **Risk register.** Described in Section 11.2.3.1. The risk register describes the individual risks that can impact resource selection and availability.

### 9.2.1.3 ENTERPRISE ENVIRONMENTAL FACTORS

The enterprise environmental factors that can influence the Estimate Activity Resources process include but are not limited to:

◆ Resource location,

◆ Resource availability,

◆ Team resource skills,

◆ Organizational culture,

◆ Published estimating data, and

◆ Marketplace conditions.

### 9.2.1.4 ORGANIZATIONAL PROCESS ASSETS

The organizational process assets that can influence the Estimate Activity Resources process include but are not limited to:

◆ Policies and procedures regarding staffing,

◆ Policies and procedures relating to supplies and equipment, and

◆ Historical information regarding types of resources used for similar work on previous projects.

## 9.2.2 ESTIMATE ACTIVITY RESOURCES: TOOLS AND TECHNIQUES

### 9.2.2.1 EXPERT JUDGMENT

Described in Section 4.1.2.1. Expertise should be considered from individuals or groups with specialized knowledge or training in team and physical resource planning and estimating.

### 9.2.2.2 BOTTOM-UP ESTIMATING

Described in Section 6.4.2.5. Team and physical resources are estimated at the activity level and then aggregated to develop the estimates for work packages, control accounts, and summary project levels.

### 9.2.2.3 ANALOGOUS ESTIMATING

Described in Section 6.4.2.2. Analogous estimating uses information regarding resources from a previous similar project as the basis for estimating a future project. It is used as quick estimating method and can be used when the project manager can only identify a few top levels of the WBS.

### 9.2.2.4 PARAMETRIC ESTIMATING

Described in Section 6.4.2.3. Parametric estimating uses an algorithm or a statistical relationship between historical data and other variables to calculate resource quantities needed for an activity, based on historical data and project parameters. For example, if an activity needs 4,000 hours of coding and it needs to finish it in 1 year, it will require two people to code (each doing 2,000 hours a year). This technique can produce higher levels of accuracy depending on the sophistication and underlying data built into the model.

### 9.2.2.5 DATA ANALYSIS

A data analysis technique used in this process includes but is not limited to alternatives analysis. Alternatives analysis is used to evaluate identified options in order to select the options or approaches to use to execute and perform the work of the project. Many activities have multiple options for accomplishment. They include using various levels of resource capability or skills, different sizes or types of machines, different tools (manual versus automated), and make-rent-or-buy decisions regarding the resources. Alternatives analysis assists in providing the best solution to perform the project activities, within the defined constraints.

### 9.2.2.6 PROJECT MANAGEMENT INFORMATION SYSTEM (PMIS)

Described in Section 4.3.2.2. Project management information systems can include resource management software that can help plan, organize, and manage resource pools and develop resource estimates. Depending on the sophistication of the software, resource breakdown structures, resource availability, resource rates, and various resource calendars can be defined to assist in optimizing resource utilization.

### 9.2.2.7 MEETINGS

The project manager may hold planning meetings with functional managers to estimate the resources needed per activity, level of effort (LoE), skill level of the team resources, and the quantity of the materials needed. Participants at these meetings may include the project manager, the project sponsor, selected project team members, selected stakeholders, and others as needed.

## 9.2.3 ESTIMATE ACTIVITY RESOURCES: OUTPUTS

### 9.2.3.1 RESOURCE REQUIREMENTS

Resource requirements identify the types and quantities of resources required for each work package or activity in a work package and can be aggregated to determine the estimated resources for each work package, each WBS branch, and the project as a whole. The amount of detail and the level of specificity of the resource requirement descriptions can vary by application area. The resource requirements' documentation can include assumptions that were made in determining which types of resources are applied, their availability, and what quantities are needed.

## 9.2.3.2 BASIS OF ESTIMATES

Described in Section 6.4.3.2. The amount and type of additional details supporting the resource estimate vary by application area. Regardless of the level of detail, the supporting documentation should provide a clear and complete understanding of how the resource estimate was derived.

Supporting detail for resource estimates may include:

◆ Method used to develop the estimate,

◆ Resources used to develop the estimate (such as information from previous similar projects),

◆ Assumptions associated with the estimate,

◆ Known constraints,

◆ Range of estimates,

◆ Confidence level of the estimate, and

◆ Documentation of identified risks influencing the estimate.

## 9.2.3.3 RESOURCE BREAKDOWN STRUCTURE

The resource breakdown structure is a hierarchical representation of resources by category and type (see Figure 9-7 for example). Examples of resource categories include but are not limited to labor, material, equipment, and supplies. Resource types may include the skill level, grade level, required certifications, or other information as appropriate to the project. In Plan Resource Management, the resource breakdown structure was used to guide the categorization for the project. In this process it is a completed document that will be used to acquire and monitor resources.

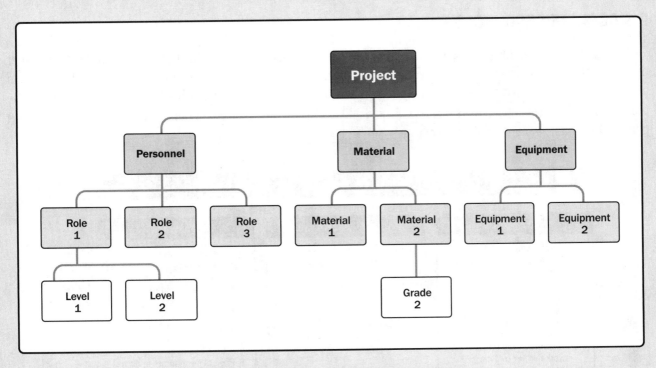

**Figure 9-7. Sample Resource Breakdown Structure**

### 9.2.3.4 PROJECT DOCUMENTS UPDATES

Project documents that may be updated as a result of carrying out this process include but are not limited to:

◆ **Activity attributes.** Described in Section 6.2.3.2. The activity attributes are updated with the resource requirements.

◆ **Assumption log.** Described in Section 4.1.3.2. The assumption log is updated with assumptions regarding the types and quantities of resources required. Additionally, any resource constraints are entered including collective bargaining agreements, continuous hours of operation, planned leave, etc.

◆ **Lessons learned register.** Described in Section 4.4.3.1. The lessons learned register can be updated with techniques that were efficient and effective in developing resource estimates, and information on those techniques that were not efficient or effective.

# 9.3 ACQUIRE RESOURCES

Acquire Resources is the process of obtaining team members, facilities, equipment, materials, supplies, and other resources necessary to complete project work. The key benefit of this process is that it outlines and guides the selection of resources and assigns them to their respective activities. This process is performed periodically throughout the project as needed. The inputs, tools and techniques, and outputs of the process are depicted in Figure 9-8. Figure 9-9 depicts the data flow diagram for the process.

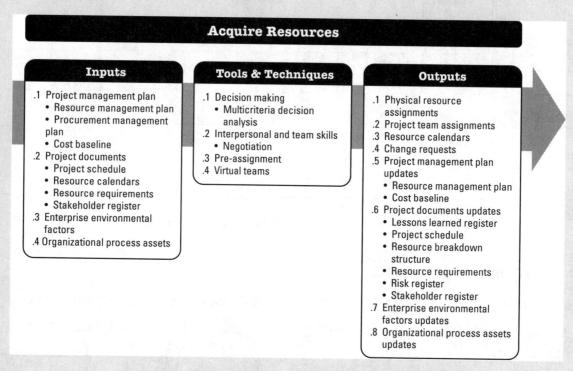

**Figure 9-8. Acquire Resources: Inputs, Tools & Techniques, and Outputs**

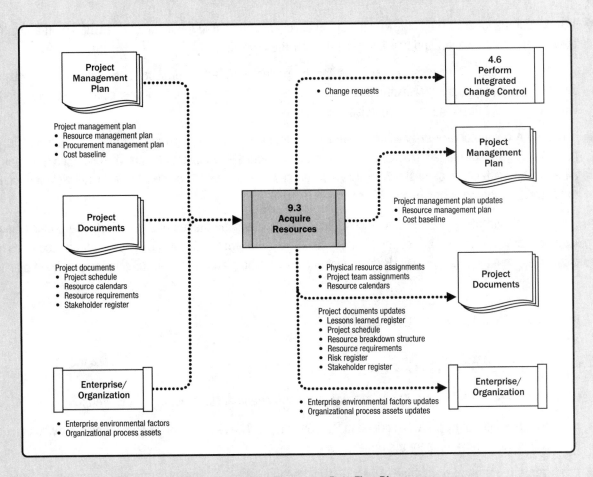

**Figure 9-9. Acquire Resources: Data Flow Diagram**

The resources needed for the project can be internal or external to the project-performing organization. Internal resources are acquired (assigned) from functional or resource managers. External resources are acquired through the procurement processes.

The project management team may or may not have direct control over resource selection because of collective bargaining agreements, use of subcontractor personnel, a matrix project environment, internal or external reporting relationships, or other reasons. It is important that the following factors are considered during the process of acquiring the project resources:

- The project manager or project team should effectively negotiate and influence others who are in a position to provide the required team and physical resources for the project.

- Failure to acquire the necessary resources for the project may affect project schedules, budgets, customer satisfaction, quality, and risks. Insufficient resources or capabilities decrease the probability of success and, in a worst-case scenario, could result in project cancellation.

- If the team resources are not available due to constraints such as economic factors or assignment to other projects, the project manager or project team may be required to assign alternative resources, perhaps with different competencies or costs. Alternative resources are allowed provided there is no violation of legal, regulatory, mandatory, or other specific criteria.

These factors should be considered and accounted for in the planning stages of the project. The project manager or project management team will be required to document the impact of the unavailability of required resources in the project schedule, project budget, project risks, project quality, training plans, and other project management plans.

## 9.3.1 ACQUIRE RESOURCES: INPUTS

### 9.3.1.1 PROJECT MANAGEMENT PLAN

Described in Section 4.2.3.1. Project management plan components include but are not limited to:

- **Resource management plan.** Described in Section 9.1.3.1. The resource management plan provides guidance on how to acquire resources for the project.

- **Procurement management plan.** Described in Section 12.1.3.1. The procurement management plan has information regarding resources that will be acquired from outside the project. This includes information on how procurements will be integrated with other project work and stakeholders involved in procuring resources.

- **Cost baseline.** Described in Section 7.3.3.1. The cost baseline provides the overall budget for the project activities.

### 9.3.1.2 PROJECT DOCUMENTS

Project documents that can be considered as inputs for this process include but are not limited to:

◆ **Project schedule.** Described in Section 6.5.3.2. The project schedule shows the activities and their planned start and end dates to help determine when the resources need to be available and acquired.

◆ **Resource calendars.** Described in Section 9.3.3.3. Resource calendars document the time periods that each resource needed for the project is available for the project. Creating a reliable schedule depends on having a good understanding of each resource's availability and schedule constraints, including time zones, work hours, vacation time, local holidays, maintenance schedule and commitments to other projects. Resource calendars are progressively elaborated and updated throughout the project. Once created as an output of this process, they are used as needed whenever this process is repeated.

◆ **Resource requirements.** Described in Section 9.2.3.1. Resource requirements identify which resources need to be acquired.

◆ **Stakeholder register.** Described in Section 13.1.3.1. The stakeholder register may reveal stakeholders' needs or expectations for specific resources to be used on the project that need to be considered in the Acquire Resources process.

### 9.3.1.3 ENTERPRISE ENVIRONMENTAL FACTORS

The enterprise environmental factors that can influence the Acquire Resources process include but are not limited to:

◆ Existing information on organizational resources including availability, competence levels, and prior experience for team resources and resource costs;

◆ Marketplace conditions;

◆ Organizational structure; and

◆ Geographic locations.

### 9.3.1.4 ORGANIZATIONAL PROCESS ASSETS

The organizational process assets that can influence the Acquire Resources process include but are not limited to:

◆ Policies and procedures for acquiring, allocating, and assigning resources to the project; and

◆ Historical information and lessons learned repository.

## 9.3.2 ACQUIRE RESOURCES: TOOLS AND TECHNIQUES

### 9.3.2.1 DECISION MAKING

Described in Section 5.2.2.4. Decision-making techniques that can be used in the Acquire Resources process include but are not limited to multicriteria decision analysis, as described in Section 8.1.2.4. Selection criteria are often used to select physical project resources, or the project team. Using a multicriteria decision analysis tool, criteria are developed and used to rate or score potential resources (for example, choosing between internal and external team resources). The criteria are weighted according to their relative importance and values can be changed for different types of resources. Some examples of selection criteria that can be used are:

◆ **Availability.** Verify that the resource is available to work on the project within the time period needed.

◆ **Cost.** Verify if the cost of adding the resource is within the prescribed budget.

◆ **Ability.** Verify that the team member provides the capability needed by the project.

Some selection criteria that are unique for team resources are:

◆ **Experience.** Verify that the team member has the relevant experience that will contribute to the project success.

◆ **Knowledge.** Consider if the team member has relevant knowledge of the customer, similar implemented projects, and nuances of the project environment.

◆ **Skills.** Determine if the team member has the relevant skills to use a project tool.

◆ **Attitude.** Determine if the team member has the ability to work with others as a cohesive team.

◆ **International factors.** Consider team member location, time zone, and communication capabilities.

### 9.3.2.2 INTERPERSONAL AND TEAM SKILLS

An interpersonal and team skill that can be used for this process includes but is not limited to negotiation. Described in Section 12.2.2.5. Many projects need to negotiate for required resources. The project management team may need to negotiate with:

◆ **Functional managers.** Ensure that the project receives the best resources possible in the required timeframe and until their responsibilities are complete.

◆ **Other project management teams within the performing organization.** Appropriately assign or share scarce or specialized resources.

◆ **External organizations and suppliers.** Provide appropriate, scarce, specialized, qualified, certified, or other specific team or physical resources. Special consideration should be given to external negotiating policies, practices, processes, guidelines, legal, and other such criteria.

The project management team's ability to influence others plays an important role in negotiating resource allocation, as does the politics of the organizations involved. For example, convincing a functional manager about the high visibility of the project may influence him or her to assign the best resources to this project over competing ones.

### 9.3.2.3 PRE-ASSIGNMENT

When physical or team resources for a project are determined in advance, they are considered pre-assigned. This situation can occur if the project is the result of specific resources being identified as part of a competitive proposal or if the project is dependent upon the expertise of particular persons. Pre-assignment might also include the team members who have already been assigned in Develop Project Charter Process or other processes before the initial Resource Management Plan has been completed.

### 9.3.2.4 VIRTUAL TEAMS

The use of virtual teams creates new possibilities when acquiring project team members. Virtual teams can be defined as groups of people with a shared goal who fulfill their roles with little or no time spent meeting face to face. The availability of communication technology such as email, audio conferencing, social media, web-based meetings, and video conferencing has made virtual teams feasible. The virtual team model makes it possible to:

◆ Form teams of people from the same organization who live in widespread geographic areas;

◆ Add special expertise to a project team even though the expert is not in the same geographic area;

◆ Incorporate employees who work from home offices;

◆ Form teams of people who work different shifts, hours, or days;

◆ Include people with mobility limitations or disabilities;

◆ Move forward with projects that would have been held or canceled due to travel expenses; and

◆ Save the expense of offices and all physical equipment needed for employees.

Communication planning becomes increasingly important in a virtual team environment. Additional time may be needed to set clear expectations, facilitate communications, develop protocols for resolving conflict, include people in decision making, understand cultural differences, and share credit in successes.

### 9.3.3 ACQUIRE RESOURCES: OUTPUTS

### 9.3.3.1 PHYSICAL RESOURCE ASSIGNMENTS

Documentation of the physical resource assignments records the material, equipment, supplies, locations, and other physical resources that will be used during the project.

### 9.3.3.2 PROJECT TEAM ASSIGNMENTS

Documentation of team assignments records the team members and their roles and responsibilities for the project. Documentation can include a project team directory and names inserted into the project management plan, such as the project organization charts and schedules.

### 9.3.3.3 RESOURCE CALENDARS

A resource calendar identifies the working days, shifts, start and end of normal business hours, weekends, and public holidays when each specific resource is available. Information on which resources (such as team resource, equipment, and material) are potentially available during a planned activity period is used for estimating resource utilization. Resource calendars also specify when and for how long identified team and physical resources will be available during the project. This information may be at the activity or project level. This includes consideration of attributes such as resource experience and/or skill level, as well as various geographical locations.

### 9.3.3.4 CHANGE REQUESTS

Described in Section 4.3.3.4. When changes occur as a result of carrying out the Acquire Resources process (for example, impacts to the schedule) or when recommended corrective or preventive actions impact any of the components of the project management plan or project documents, the project manager needs to submit a change request. Change requests are processed for review and disposition through the Perform Integrated Change Control process (Section 4.6).

### 9.3.3.5 PROJECT MANAGEMENT PLAN UPDATES

Any change to the project management plan goes through the organization's change control process via a change request. Components of the project management plan that may be updated as a result of carrying out this process include but are not limited to:

◆ **Resource management plan.** Described in Section 9.1.3.1. The resource management plan may be updated to reflect actual experience in acquiring resources for the project, including lessons learned in acquiring resources early in the project that will impact how resources are acquired later in the project.

◆ **Cost baseline.** Described in Section 7.3.3.1. The cost baseline may change as a result of the acquisition of resources for the project.

### 9.3.3.6 PROJECT DOCUMENTS UPDATES

Project documents that may be updated as a result of carrying out this process include but are not limited to:

◆ **Lessons learned register.** Described in Section 4.4.3.1. The lessons learned register is updated with information on challenges encountered and how they could have been avoided as well as approaches that worked well for acquiring resources.

◆ **Project schedule.** Described in Section 6.5.3.2. Changes to the project schedule may result from the availability of required resources.

◆ **Resource breakdown structure.** Described in Section 9.2.3.3. Resources acquired during this process are recorded in the resource breakdown structure.

◆ **Resource requirements.** Described in Section 9.2.3.1. Resource requirements documentation is updated to reflect resources acquired for the project.

◆ **Risk register.** Described in Section 11.2.3.1. New risks identified during this process are recorded in the risk register and managed using the risk management processes.

◆ **Stakeholder register.** Described in Section 13.1.3.1. The stakeholder register is updated with any new stakeholders and any new information about existing stakeholders that has been gained as a result of this process.

### 9.3.3.7 ENTERPRISE ENVIRONMENTAL FACTORS UPDATES

Enterprise environmental factors that are updated include but are not limited to:

◆ Resource availability within the organization, and

◆ Amount of the organization's consumable resources that have been used.

### 9.3.3.8 ORGANIZATIONAL PROCESS ASSETS UPDATES

Organizational process assets that are updated as a result of the Acquire Resources process include but are not limited to documentation related to acquiring, assigning and allocating resources.

## 9.4 DEVELOP TEAM

Develop Team is the process of improving competencies, team member interaction, and the overall team environment to enhance project performance. The key benefit of this process is that it results in improved teamwork, enhanced interpersonal skills and competencies, motivated employees, reduced attrition, and improved overall project performance. This process is performed throughout the project.

The inputs, tools and techniques, and outputs of the process are depicted in Figure 9-10. Figure 9-11 depicts the data flow diagram for the process.

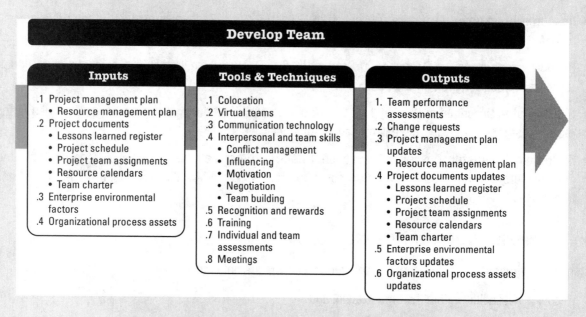

Figure 9-10. Develop Team: Inputs, Tools & Techniques, and Outputs

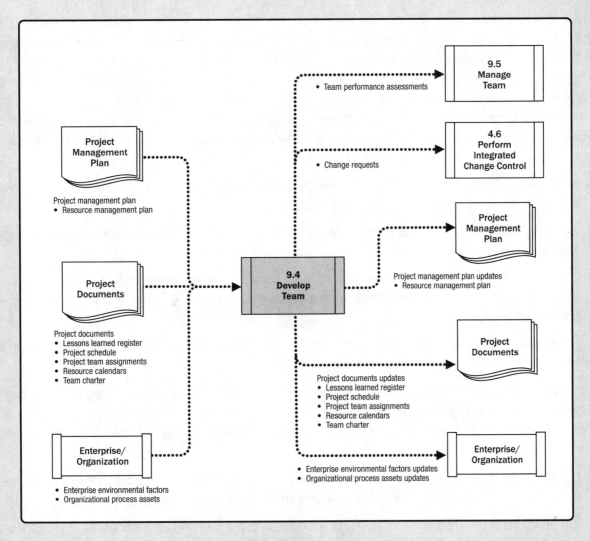

**Figure 9-11. Develop Team: Data Flow Diagram**

Project managers require the skills to identify, build, maintain, motivate, lead, and inspire project teams to achieve high team performance and to meet the project's objectives. Teamwork is a critical factor for project success, and developing effective project teams is one of the primary responsibilities of the project manager. Project managers should create an environment that facilitates teamwork and continually motivates the team by providing challenges and opportunities, providing timely feedback and support as needed, and recognizing and rewarding good performance. High team performance can be achieved by employing these behaviors:

◆ Using open and effective communication,

◆ Creating team-building opportunities,

◆ Developing trust among team members,

◆ Managing conflicts in a constructive manner,

◆ Encouraging collaborative problem solving, and

◆ Encouraging collaborative decision making.

Project managers operate in a global environment and work on projects characterized by cultural diversity. Team members often have diverse industry experience, communicate in multiple languages, and sometimes work with a "team language" or cultural norm that may be different from their native one. The project management team should capitalize on cultural differences, focus on developing and sustaining the project team throughout the project life cycle, and promote working together interdependently in a climate of mutual trust. Developing the project team improves the people skills, technical competencies, and overall team environment and project performance. It requires clear, timely, effective, and efficient communication between team members throughout the life of the project. Objectives of developing a project team include but are not limited to:

◆ Improving the knowledge and skills of team members to increase their ability to complete project deliverables, while lowering costs, reducing schedules, and improving quality;

◆ Improving feelings of trust and agreement among team members to raise morale, lower conflict, and increase teamwork;

◆ Creating a dynamic, cohesive, and collaborative team culture to: (1) improve individual and team productivity, team spirit, and cooperation; and (2) allow cross-training and mentoring between team members to share knowledge and expertise; and

◆ Empowering the team to participate in decision making and take ownership of the provided solutions to improve team productivity for more effective and efficient results.

One of the models used to describe team development is the Tuckman ladder, which includes five stages of development that teams may go through. Although it is common for these stages to occur in order, it is not uncommon for a team to get stuck in a particular stage or regress to an earlier stage. Projects with team members who worked together in the past might skip a stage.

◆ **Forming.** This phase is where the team members meet and learn about the project and their formal roles and responsibilities. Team members tend to be independent and not as open in this phase.

◆ **Storming.** During this phase, the team begins to address the project work, technical decisions, and the project management approach. If team members are not collaborative or open to differing ideas and perspectives, the environment can become counterproductive.

◆ **Norming.** In this phase, team members begin to work together and adjust their work habits and behaviors to support the team. The team members learn to trust each other.

◆ **Performing.** Teams that reach the performing stage function as a well-organized unit. They are interdependent and work through issues smoothly and effectively.

◆ **Adjourning.** In this phase, the team completes the work and moves on from the project. This typically occurs when staff is released from the project as deliverables are completed or as part of the Close Project or Phase process.

The duration of a particular stage depends upon team dynamics, team size, and team leadership. Project managers should have a good understanding of team dynamics in order to move their team members through all stages in an effective manner.

## 9.4.1 DEVELOP TEAM: INPUTS

### 9.4.1.1 PROJECT MANAGEMENT PLAN

Described in Section 4.2.3.1. Project management plan components include but are not limited to the resource management plan. Described in Section 9.1.3.1, the resource management plan provides guidance on providing project team member rewards, feedback, additional training, and disciplinary actions as a result of team performance assessments and other forms of project team management. The resource management plan may include also the team performance assessment criteria.

### 9.4.1.2 PROJECT DOCUMENTS

Project documents that can be considered as inputs for this process include but are not limited to:

◆ **Lessons learned register.** Described in Section 4.4.3.1. Lessons learned earlier in the project with regard to developing the team can be applied to later phases in the project to improve team performance.

◆ **Project schedule.** Described in Section 6.5.3.2. The project schedule defines how and when to provide training to the project team and develop the competencies required at different phases. It identifies the need for team development strategies based on variations, if any, during the project execution.

◆ **Project team assignments.** Described in Section 9.3.3.2. Project team assignments identify the team and member roles and responsibilities.

◆ **Resource calendars.** Described in Section 9.2.1.2. Resource calendars identify times when the project team members can participate in team development activities. It also helps illustrate team availability during the entire project.

◆ **Team charter.** Described in Section 9.1.3.2. The team charter is where the team operating guidelines are documented. The team values and operating guidelines provide the structure that describes how the team will operate together.

### 9.4.1.3 ENTERPRISE ENVIRONMENTAL FACTORS

The enterprise environmental factors that can influence the Develop Team process include but are not limited to:

◆ Human resource management policies regarding hiring and termination, employee performance reviews, employee development and training records, and recognition and rewards;

◆ Team member skills, competencies, and specialized knowledge; and

◆ Geographic distribution of team members.

### 9.4.1.4 ORGANIZATIONAL PROCESS ASSETS

The organizational process assets that can influence the Develop Team process include but are not limited to historical information and the lessons learned repository.

## 9.4.2 DEVELOP TEAM: TOOLS AND TECHNIQUES

### 9.4.2.1 COLOCATION

Colocation involves placing many or all of the most active project team members in the same physical location to enhance their ability to perform as a team. Colocation can be temporary, such as at strategically important times during the project, or can continue for the entire project. Colocation strategies can include a team meeting room, common places to post schedules, and other conveniences that enhance communication and a sense of community.

### 9.4.2.2 VIRTUAL TEAMS

The use of virtual teams can bring benefits such as the use of more skilled resources, reduced costs, less travel and relocation expenses, and the proximity of team members to suppliers, customers, or other key stakeholders. Virtual teams can use technology to create an online team environment where the team can store files, use conversations threads to discuss issues, and keep a team calendar.

### 9.4.2.3 COMMUNICATION TECHNOLOGY

Described in Section 10.1.2.3. Communication technology is important in addressing the team development issues in colocated and virtual teams. It helps build a harmonious environment for the colocated team and a better understanding for the virtual team, especially those working in different time zones. Examples of communication technology that may be used are:

- ◆ **Shared portal.** A shared repository for information sharing (e.g., website, collaboration software or intranet) is effective for virtual project teams.

- ◆ **Video conferencing.** Video conferencing is an important technique for effective communication with virtual teams.

- ◆ **Audio conferencing.** Communication within a team using audio conferencing is another technique to build rapport and confidence within virtual teams.

- ◆ **Email/chat.** Regular communications using email and chat is also an effective technique.

## 9.4.2.4 INTERPERSONAL AND TEAM SKILLS

Interpersonal and team skills that can be used for this process include but are not limited to:

◆ **Conflict management.** Described in Section 9.5.2.1. The project manager needs to resolve conflicts in a timely manner and in a constructive way in order to achieve a high-performing team.

◆ **Influencing.** Described in Section 9.5.2.1. An influencing skill used in this process is gathering relevant and critical information to address important issues and reach agreements while maintaining mutual trust.

◆ **Motivation.** Motivation is providing a reason for someone to act. Teams are motivated by empowering them to participate in decision making and encouraging them to work independently.

◆ **Negotiation.** Described in Section 12.2.2.5. Negotiation among team members is used to reach consensus on project needs. Negotiation can build trust and harmony among the team members.

◆ **Team building.** Team building is conducting activities that enhance the team's social relations and build a collaborative and cooperative working environment. Team building activities can vary from a 5-minute agenda item in a status review meeting to an offsite, professionally facilitated event designed to improve interpersonal relationships. The objective of team-building activities is to help individual team members work together effectively. Team-building strategies are particularly valuable when team members operate from remote locations without the benefit of face-to-face contact. Informal communication and activities can help in building trust and establishing good working relationships. While team building is essential during the initial stages of a project, it should be a continuous process. Changes in a project environment are inevitable, and to manage them effectively, a continuous or renewed team-building effort may be applied. The project manager should continually monitor team functionality and performance to determine if any actions are needed to prevent or correct various team problems.

## 9.4.2.5 RECOGNITION AND REWARDS

Part of the team development process involves recognizing and rewarding desirable behavior. The original plan for rewarding people is developed during the Plan Resource Management process. Rewards will be effective only if they satisfy a need that is valued by that individual. Reward decisions are made, formally or informally, during the process of managing the project team. Cultural differences should be considered when determining recognition and rewards.

People are motivated when they feel they are valued in the organization and this value is demonstrated by the rewards given to them. Generally, money is viewed as a tangible aspect of any reward system, but intangible rewards could be equally or even more effective. Most project team members are motivated by an opportunity to grow, accomplish, be appreciated, and apply their professional skills to meet new challenges. A good strategy for project managers is to give the team recognition throughout the life cycle of the project rather than waiting until the project is completed.

### 9.4.2.6 TRAINING

Training includes all activities designed to enhance the competencies of the project team members. Training can be formal or informal. Examples of training methods include classroom, online, computer-based, on-the-job training from another project team member, mentoring, and coaching. If project team members lack the necessary management or technical skills, such skills can be developed as part of the project work. Scheduled training takes place as stated in the resource management plan. Unplanned training takes place as a result of observation, conversation, and project performance appraisals conducted during management of the project team. Training costs could be included in the project budget or supported by the performing organization if the added skills may be useful for future projects. It may be performed by in-house or by external trainers.

### 9.4.2.7 INDIVIDUAL AND TEAM ASSESSMENTS

Individual and team assessment tools give the project manager and the project team insight into areas of strengths and weaknesses. These tools help project managers assess team members' preferences, aspirations, how they process and organize information, how they make decisions, and how they interact with people. Various tools are available such as attitudinal surveys, specific assessments, structured interviews, ability tests, and focus groups. These tools can provide improved understanding, trust, commitment, and communications among team members and facilitate more productive teams throughout the project.

### 9.4.2.8 MEETINGS

Meetings are used to discuss and address pertinent topics for developing the team. Attendees include the project manager and the project team. Types of meetings include but are not limited to project orientation meetings, team-building meetings, and team development meetings.

## 9.4.3 DEVELOP TEAM: OUTPUTS

### 9.4.3.1 TEAM PERFORMANCE ASSESSMENTS

As project team development efforts such as training, team building, and colocation are implemented, the project management team makes formal or informal assessments of the project team's effectiveness. Effective team development strategies and activities are expected to increase the team's performance, which increases the likelihood of meeting project objectives.

The evaluation of a team's effectiveness may include indicators such as:

◆ Improvements in skills that allow individuals to perform assignments more effectively,

◆ Improvements in competencies that help team members perform better as a team,

◆ Reduced staff turnover rate, and

◆ Increased team cohesiveness where team members share information and experiences openly and help each other to improve the overall project performance.

As a result of conducting an evaluation of the team's overall performance, the project management team can identify the specific training, coaching, mentoring, assistance, or changes required to improve the team's performance. This should also include identifying the appropriate or required resources necessary to achieve and implement the improvements identified in the assessment.

### 9.4.3.2 CHANGE REQUESTS

Described in Section 4.3.3.4. If change requests occur as a result of carrying out the Develop Team process or if recommended corrective or preventive actions impact any of the components of the project management plan or project documents, the project manager needs to submit a change request and follow the Perform Integrated Change Control process as defined in Section 4.6.

### 9.4.3.3 PROJECT MANAGEMENT PLAN UPDATES

Any change to the project management plan goes through the organization's change control process via a change request. Components that may require a change request for the project management plan include but are not limited to the resource management plan, as described in Section 9.1.3.1.

### 9.4.3.4 PROJECT DOCUMENTS UPDATES

Project documents that may be updated as a result of carrying out this process include but are not limited to:

◆ **Lessons learned register.** Described in Section 4.4.3.1. The lessons learned register is updated with information on challenges encountered and how they could have been avoided as well as approaches that worked well for the development of the team.

◆ **Project schedule.** Described in Section 6.5.3.2. Activities to develop the project team may result in changes to the project schedule.

◆ **Project team assignments.** Described in Section 9.3.3.2. When team development results in changes to agreed-upon assignments, these changes are recorded in the project team assignments documentation.

◆ **Resource calendars.** Described in Section 9.2.1.2. Resource calendars are updated to reflect the availability of resources for the project.

◆ **Team charter.** Described in Section 9.1.3.2. The team charter may be updated to reflect changes to agreed-upon team operating guidelines that result from team development.

### 9.4.3.5 ENTERPRISE ENVIRONMENTAL FACTORS UPDATES

Enterprise environmental factors that are updated as a result of the Develop Project Team process include but are not limited to:

◆ Employee development plan records, and

◆ Skill assessments.

### 9.4.3.6 ORGANIZATIONAL PROCESS ASSETS UPDATES

Organizational process assets that are updated as a result of the Develop Team process include but are not limited to:

◆ Training requirements, and

◆ Personnel assessment.

# 9.5 MANAGE TEAM

Manage Team is the process of tracking team member performance, providing feedback, resolving issues, and managing team changes to optimize project performance. The key benefit of this process is that it influences team behavior, manages conflict, and resolves issues. This process is performed throughout the project.

The inputs, tools and techniques, and outputs of the process are depicted in Figure 9-12. Figure 9-13 depicts the data flow diagram for the process.

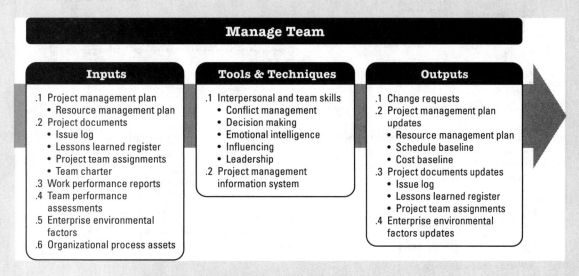

**Figure 9-12. Manage Team: Inputs, Tools & Techniques, and Outputs**

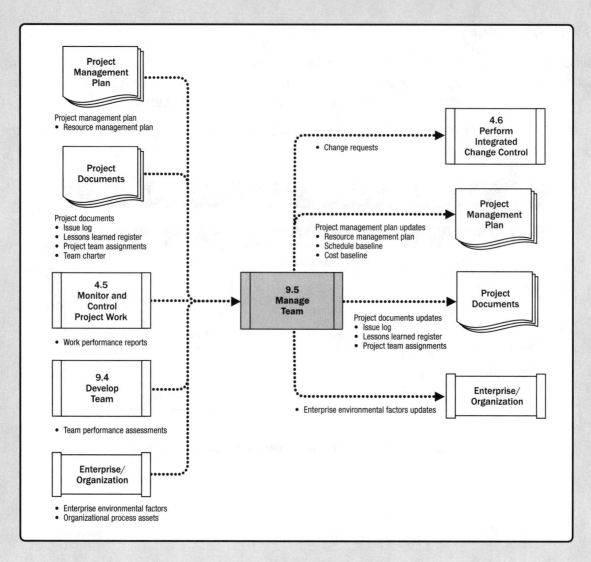

**Figure 9-13. Manage Team: Data Flow Diagram**

Managing the project team requires a variety of management and leadership skills for fostering teamwork and integrating the efforts of team members to create high-performance teams. Team management involves a combination of skills with special emphasis on communication, conflict management, negotiation, and leadership. Project managers should provide challenging assignments to team members and provide recognition for high performance.

The project manager needs to be sensitive to both the willingness and the ability of team members to perform their work and adjust their management and leadership styles accordingly. Team members with low-skill abilities will require more intensive oversight than those who have demonstrated ability and experience.

## 9.5.1 MANAGE TEAM: INPUTS

### 9.5.1.1 PROJECT MANAGEMENT PLAN

Described in Section 4.2.3.1. Project management plan components include but are not limited to the resource management plan. Described in Section 9.1.3.1, the resource management plan provides guidance on how project team resources should be managed and eventually released.

### 9.5.1.2 PROJECT DOCUMENTS

Project documents that can be considered as inputs for this process include but are not limited to:

◆ **Issue log.** Described in Section 4.3.3.3. Issues arise in the course of managing the project team. An issue log can be used to document and monitor who is responsible for resolving specific issues by a target date.

◆ **Lessons learned register.** Described in Section 4.4.3.1. Lessons learned earlier in the project can be applied to later phases in the project to improve the efficiency and effectiveness of managing the team.

◆ **Project team assignments.** Described in Section 9.3.3.2. Project team assignments identify the team member roles and responsibilities.

◆ **Team charter.** Described in Section 9.1.3.2. The team charter provides guidance for how the team will make decisions, conduct meetings, and resolve conflict.

### 9.5.1.3 WORK PERFORMANCE REPORTS

Described in Section 4.5.3.1. Work performance reports are the physical or electronic representation of work performance information intended to generate decisions, actions, or awareness. Performance reports that can help with project team management include results from schedule control, cost control, quality control, and scope validation. The information from performance reports and related forecasts assists in determining future team resource requirements, recognition and rewards, and updates to the resource management plan.

### 9.5.1.4 TEAM PERFORMANCE ASSESSMENTS

Described in Section 9.4.3.1. The project management team makes ongoing formal or informal assessments of the project team's performance. By continually assessing the project team's performance, actions can be taken to resolve issues, modify communication, address conflict, and improve team interaction.

### 9.5.1.5 ENTERPRISE ENVIRONMENTAL FACTORS

The enterprise environmental factors that can influence the Manage Team process include but are not limited to human resource management policies.

### 9.5.1.6 ORGANIZATIONAL PROCESS ASSETS

The organizational process assets that can influence the Manage Team process include but are not limited to:

◆ Certificates of appreciation,

◆ Corporate apparel, and

◆ Other organizational perquisites.

## 9.5.2 MANAGE TEAM: TOOLS AND TECHNIQUES

### 9.5.2.1 INTERPERSONAL AND TEAM SKILLS

Interpersonal and team skills that can be used for this process include but are not limited to:

◆ **Conflict management.** Conflict is inevitable in a project environment. Sources of conflict include scarce resources, scheduling priorities, and personal work styles. Team ground rules, group norms, and solid project management practices, like communication planning and role definition, reduce the amount of conflict.

Successful conflict management results in greater productivity and positive working relationships. When managed properly, differences of opinion can lead to increased creativity and better decision making. If the differences become a negative factor, project team members are initially responsible for their resolution. If conflict escalates, the project manager should help facilitate a satisfactory resolution. Conflict should be addressed early and usually in private, using a direct, collaborative approach. If disruptive conflict continues, formal procedures may be used, including disciplinary actions.

The success of project managers in managing their project teams often depends on their ability to resolve conflict. Different project managers may use different conflict resolution methods. Factors that influence conflict resolution methods include:

■ Importance and intensity of the conflict,

■ Time pressure for resolving the conflict,

■ Relative power of the people involved in the conflict,

■ Importance of maintaining a good relationship, and

■ Motivation to resolve conflict on a long-term or short-term basis.

There are five general techniques for resolving conflict. Each technique has its place and use:

- *Withdraw/avoid.* Retreating from an actual or potential conflict situation; postponing the issue to be better prepared or to be resolved by others.

- *Smooth/accommodate.* Emphasizing areas of agreement rather than areas of difference; conceding one's position to the needs of others to maintain harmony and relationships.

- *Compromise/reconcile.* Searching for solutions that bring some degree of satisfaction to all parties in order to temporarily or partially resolve the conflict. This approach occasionally results in a lose-lose situation.

- *Force/direct.* Pushing one's viewpoint at the expense of others; offering only win-lose solutions, usually enforced through a power position to resolve an emergency. This approach often results to a win-lose situation.

- *Collaborate/problem solve.* Incorporating multiple viewpoints and insights from differing perspectives; requires a cooperative attitude and open dialogue that typically leads to consensus and commitment. This approach can result in a win-win situation.

◆ **Decision making.** Decision making, in this context, involves the ability to negotiate and influence the organization and the project management team, rather than the set of tools described in the decision making tool set. Some guidelines for decision making include:

- Focus on goals to be served,

- Follow a decision-making process,

- Study the environmental factors,

- Analyze available information,

- Stimulate team creativity, and

- Account for risk.

◆ **Emotional intelligence.** Emotional intelligence is the ability to identify, assess, and manage the personal emotions of oneself and other people, as well as the collective emotions of groups of people. The team can use emotional intelligence to reduce tension and increase cooperation by identifying, assessing, and controlling the sentiments of project team members, anticipating their actions, acknowledging their concerns, and following up on their issues.

◆ **Influencing.** Because project managers often have little or no direct authority over team members in a matrix environment, their ability to influence stakeholders on a timely basis is critical to project success. Key influencing skills include:

- Ability to be persuasive;
- Clearly articulating points and positions;
- High levels of active and effective listening skills;
- Awareness of, and consideration for, the various perspectives in any situation; and
- Gathering relevant information to address issues and reach agreements while maintaining mutual trust.

◆ **Leadership.** Successful projects require leaders with strong leadership skills. Leadership is the ability to lead a team and inspire them to do their jobs well. It encompasses a wide range of skills, abilities and actions. Leadership is important through all phases of the project life cycle. There are multiple leadership theories defining leadership styles that should be used as needed for each situation or team. It is especially important to communicate the vision and inspire the project team to achieve high performance.

### 9.5.2.2 PROJECT MANAGEMENT INFORMATION SYSTEM (PMIS)

Described in Section 4.3.2.2. Project management information systems can include resource management or scheduling software that can be used for managing and coordinating team members across project activities.

### 9.5.3 MANAGE TEAM: OUTPUTS

### 9.5.3.1 CHANGE REQUESTS

Described in Section 4.3.3.4. When change requests occur as a result of carrying out the Manage Team process or when recommended corrective or preventive actions impact any of the components of the project management plan or project documents, the project manager needs to submit a change request. Change requests are processed for review and disposition through the Perform Integrated Change Control process (Section 4.6).

For example, staffing changes, whether made by choice or by uncontrollable events, can disrupt the project team. This disruption can cause the schedule to slip or the budget to be exceeded. Staffing changes include moving people to different assignments, outsourcing some of the work, or replacing team members who leave.

### 9.5.3.2 PROJECT MANAGEMENT PLAN UPDATES

Any change to the project management plan goes through the organization's change control process via a change request. Components of the project management plan that may require a change request for the project management plan include but are not limited to:

◆ **Resource management plan.** Described in Section 9.1.3.1. The resource management plan is updated to reflect actual experience in managing the project team.

◆ **Schedule baseline.** Described in Section 6.5.3.1. Changes to the project schedule may be required to reflect the way the team is performing.

◆ **Cost baseline.** Described in Section 7.3.3.1. Changes to the project cost baseline may be required to reflect the way the team is performing.

### 9.5.3.3 PROJECT DOCUMENTS UPDATES

Project documents that may be updated as a result of carrying out this process include but are not limited to:

◆ **Issue log.** Described in Section 4.3.3.3. New issues raised as a result of this process are recorded in the issue log.

◆ **Lessons learned register.** Described in Section 4.4.3.1. The lessons learned register is updated with information on challenges encountered and how they could have been avoided as well as approaches that worked well for the managing the team.

◆ **Project team assignments.** Described in Section 9.3.3.2. If changes to the team are required, those changes are recorded in the project team assignments documentation.

### 9.5.3.4 ENTERPRISE ENVIRONMENTAL FACTORS UPDATES

Enterprise environmental factors that are updated as a result of the Manage Team process include but are not limited to:

◆ Input to organizational performance appraisals, and

◆ Personnel skill.

# 9.6 CONTROL RESOURCES

Control Resources is the process of ensuring that the physical resources assigned and allocated to the project are available as planned, as well as monitoring the planned versus actual utilization of resources and taking corrective action as necessary. The key benefit of this process is ensuring that the assigned resources are available to the project at the right time and in the right place and are released when no longer needed. This process is performed throughout the project. The inputs and outputs of this process are depicted in Figure 9-14. Figure 9-15 depicts the data flow diagram for the process.

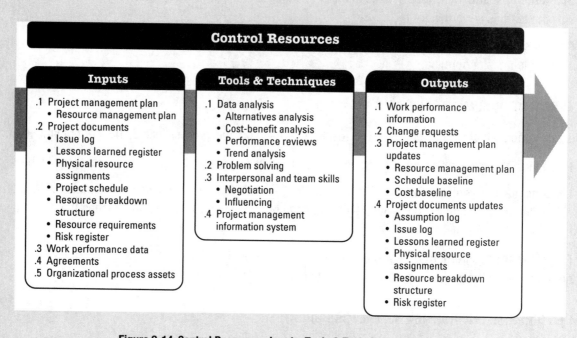

**Figure 9-14. Control Resources: Inputs, Tools & Techniques, and Outputs**

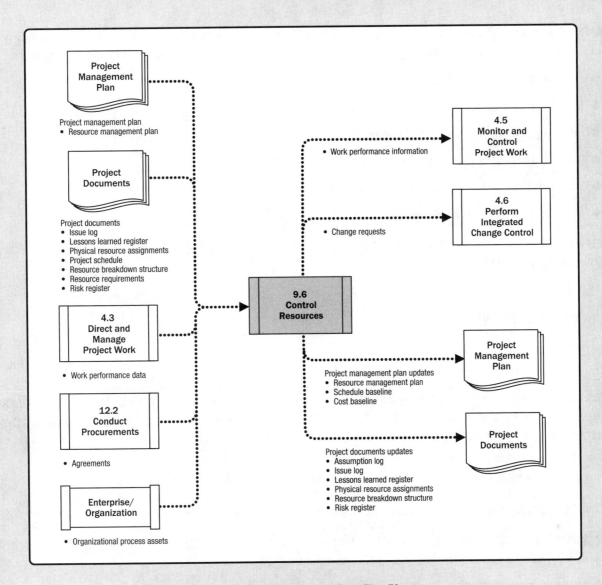

**Figure 9-15. Control Resources: Data Flow Diagram**

The Control Resources process should be performed continuously in all project phases and throughout the project life cycle. The resources needed for the project should be assigned and released at the right time, right place, and right amount for the project to continue without delays. The Control Resources process is concerned with physical resources such as equipment, materials, facilities, and infrastructure. Team members are addressed in the Manage Team process.

The Control Resources techniques discussed here are those used most frequently on projects. There are many others that may be useful on certain projects or in some application areas.

Updating resource allocation requires knowing what actual resources have been used to date and what is still needed. This is done mainly by reviewing the performance usage to date. Control Resources is concerned with:

◆ Monitoring resource expenditures,

◆ Identifying and dealing with resource shortage/surplus in a timely manner,

◆ Ensuring that resources are used and released according to the plan and project needs,

◆ Informing appropriate stakeholders if any issues arise with relevant resources,

◆ Influencing the factors that can create resources utilization change, and

◆ Managing the actual changes as they occur.

Any changes needed to the schedule or cost baselines can be approved only through the Perform Integrated Change Control process (Section 4.6).

## 9.6.1 CONTROL RESOURCES: INPUTS

### 9.6.1.1 PROJECT MANAGEMENT PLAN

Described in Section 4.2.3.1. Project management plan components include but are not limited to the resource management plan. Described in Section 9.1.3.1, the resource management plan provides guidance on how physical resources should be used, controlled, and eventually released.

### 9.6.1.2 PROJECT DOCUMENTS

Project documents that can be considered as inputs for this process include but are not limited to:

◆ **Issue log.** Described in Section 4.3.3.3. The issue log is used to identify issues such as lack of resources, delays in raw material supplies, or low grades of raw material.

◆ **Lessons learned register.** Described in Section 4.4.3.1. Lessons learned earlier in the project can be applied to later phases in the project to improve physical resource control.

◆ **Physical resource assignments.** Described in Section 9.3.3.1. The physical resource assignments describe the expected resource utilization along with details such as type, amount, location, and whether the resource is internal to the organization or outsourced.

- **Project schedule.** Described in Section 6.5.3.2. The project schedule shows the resources that are needed, when they are needed, and the location where they are needed.

- **Resource breakdown structure.** Described in Section 9.2.3.3. The resource breakdown structure provides a reference in case any resource needs to be replaced or reacquired during the course of the project.

- **Resource requirements.** Described in Section 9.2.3.1. Resource requirements identify the needed material, equipment, supplies, and other resources.

- **Risk register.** Described in Section 11.2.3.1. The risk register identifies individual risks that can impact equipment, materials, or supplies.

## 9.6.1.3 WORK PERFORMANCE DATA

Described in Section 4.3.3.2. Work performance data contains data on project status such as the number and type of resources that have been used.

## 9.6.1.4 AGREEMENTS

Described in Section 12.2.3.2. Agreements made within the context of the project are the basis for all resources external to the organization and should define procedures when new, unplanned resources are needed or when issues arise with the current resources.

## 9.6.1.5 ORGANIZATIONAL PROCESS ASSETS

The organizational process assets that can influence the Control Resources process include but are not limited to:

- Policies regarding resource control and assignment,
- Escalation procedures for handling issues within the performing organization, and
- Lessons learned repository from previous similar projects.

## 9.6.2 CONTROL RESOURCES: TOOLS AND TECHNIQUES

### 9.6.2.1 DATA ANALYSIS

Data analysis techniques that can be used in this process include but are not limited to:

◆ **Alternatives analysis.** Described in Section 9.2.2.5. Alternatives can be analyzed to select the best resolution for correcting variances in resource utilization. Alternatives such as paying additional for overtime or additional team resources can be weighed against a late delivery or phased deliveries.

◆ **Cost-benefit analysis.** Described in Section 8.1.2.3. This analysis helps to determine the best corrective action in terms of cost in case of project deviations.

◆ **Performance reviews.** Performance reviews measure, compare, and analyze planned resource utilization to actual resource utilization. Cost and schedule work performance information can also be analyzed to help pinpoint issues that can influence resource utilization.

◆ **Trend analysis.** Described in Section 4.5.2.2. As the project progresses, the project team may use trend analysis, based on current performance information, to determine the resources needed at upcoming stages of the project. Trend analysis examines project performance over time and can be used to determine whether performance is improving or deteriorating.

### 9.6.2.2 PROBLEM SOLVING

Described in Section 8.2.2.7. Problem solving may use a set of tools that helps the project manager to solve problems that arise during the control resource process. The problem can come from inside the organization (machines or infrastructure used by another department in the organization and not released in time, materials that have been damaged because of unsuitable storage conditions, etc.) or from outside the organization (major supplier that has gone bankrupt or bad weather that has damaged resources). The project manager should use methodical steps to deal with problem solving, which can include:

◆ **Identify the problem.** Specify the problem.

◆ **Define the problem.** Break it into smaller, manageable problems.

◆ **Investigate.** Collect data.

◆ **Analyze.** Find the root cause of the problem.

◆ **Solve.** Choose the suitable solution from a variety of available ones.

◆ **Check the solution.** Determine if the problem has been fixed.

### 9.6.2.3 INTERPERSONAL AND TEAM SKILLS

Interpersonal and team skills, sometimes known as "soft skills," are personal competencies. The interpersonal and team skills used in this process include:

◆ **Negotiation.** Described in Section 12.2.2.5. The project manager may need to negotiate for additional physical resources, changes in physical resources, or costs associated with the resources.

◆ **Influencing**. Described in Section 9.5.2.1. Influencing can help the project manager solve problems and obtain the resources needed in a timely manner.

### 9.6.2.4 PROJECT MANAGEMENT INFORMATION SYSTEM (PMIS)

Described in Section 4.3.2.2. Project management information systems can include resource management or scheduling software that can be used to monitor the resource utilization which helps ensure that the right resources are working on the right activities at the right time and place.

## 9.6.3 CONTROL RESOURCES: OUTPUTS

### 9.6.3.1 WORK PERFORMANCE INFORMATION

Described in Section 4.5.1.3. Work performance information includes information on how the project work is progressing by comparing resource requirements and resource allocation to resource utilization across the project activities. This comparison can show gaps in resource availability that need to be addressed.

### 9.6.3.2 CHANGE REQUESTS

Described in Section 4.3.3.4. When change requests occur as a result of carrying out the Control Resources process or when recommended, corrective, or preventive actions impact any of the components of the project management plan or project documents, the project manager needs to submit a change request. Change requests are processed for review and disposition through the Perform Integrated Change Control process (Section 4.6).

### 9.6.3.3 PROJECT MANAGEMENT PLAN UPDATES

Any change to the project management plan goes through the organization's change control process via a change request. Components that may require a change request for the project management plan include but are not limited to:

◆ **Resource management plan.** Described in Section 9.1.3.1. The resource management plan is updated to reflect actual experience in managing project resources.

◆ **Schedule baseline.** Described in Section 6.5.3.1. Changes to the project schedule may be required to reflect the way project resources are being managed.

◆ **Cost baseline.** Described in Section 7.3.3.1. Changes to the project cost baseline may be required to reflect the way project resources are being managed.

### 9.6.3.4 PROJECT DOCUMENTS UPDATES

Project documents that may be updated as a result of performing this process include but are not limited to:

◆ **Assumption log.** Described in Section 4.1.3.2. The assumption log may be updated with new assumptions regarding equipment, materials, supplies, and other physical resources.

◆ **Issue log.** Described in Section 4.3.3.3. New issues raised as a result of this process are recorded in the issue log.

◆ **Lessons learned register.** Described in Section 4.4.3.1. The lessons learned register can be updated with techniques that were effective in managing resource logistics, scrap, utilization variances, and corrective actions that were used to respond to resource variances.

◆ **Physical resource assignments.** Described in Section 9.3.3.1. Physical resource assignments are dynamic and subject to change due to availability, the project, organization, environment, or other factors.

◆ **Resource breakdown structure.** Described in Section 9.2.3.3. Changes to the resource breakdown structure may be required to reflect the way project resources are being used.

◆ **Risk register.** Described in Section 11.2.3.1. The risk register is updated with any new risks associated with resource availability, utilization, or other physical resource risks.

# 10

## PROJECT COMMUNICATIONS MANAGEMENT

Project Communications Management includes the processes necessary to ensure that the information needs of the project and its stakeholders are met through development of artifacts and implementation of activities designed to achieve effective information exchange. Project Communications Management consists of two parts. The first part is developing a strategy to ensure communication is effective for stakeholders. The second part is carrying out the activities necessary to implement the communication strategy.

The Project Communications Management processes are:

**10.1 Plan Communications Management**—The process of developing an appropriate approach and plan for project communication activities based on the information needs of each stakeholder or group, available organizational assets, and the needs of the project.

**10.2 Manage Communications**—The process of ensuring timely and appropriate collection, creation, distribution, storage, retrieval, management, monitoring, and the ultimate disposition of project information.

**10.3 Monitor Communications**—The process of ensuring the information needs of the project and its stakeholders are met.

Figure 10-1 provides an overview of the Project Communications Management processes. The Project Communications Management processes are presented as discrete processes with defined interfaces while, in practice, they overlap and interact in ways that cannot be completely detailed in the *PMBOK® Guide*.

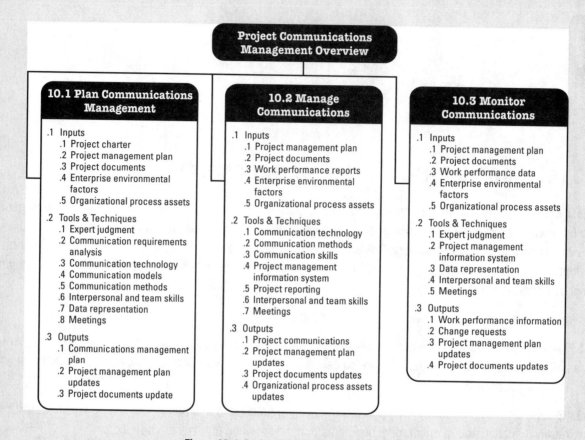

**Figure 10-1. Project Communications Overview**

## KEY CONCEPTS FOR PROJECT COMMUNICATIONS MANAGEMENT

Communication is the exchange of information, intended or involuntary. The information exchanged can be in the form of ideas, instructions, or emotions. The mechanisms by which information is exchanged can be in:

◆ **Written form.** Either physical or electronic.

◆ **Spoken.** Either face-to-face or remote.

◆ **Formal or informal** (as in formal papers or social media).

◆ **Through gestures.** Tone of voice and facial expressions.

◆ **Through media**. Pictures, actions, or even just the choice of words.

◆ **Choice of words.** There is often more than one word to express an idea; there can be subtle differences in the meaning of each of these words and phrases.

Communications describe the possible means by which the information can be sent or received, either through communication activities, such as meetings and presentations, or artifacts, such as emails, social media, project reports, or project documentation.

Project managers spend most of their time communicating with team members and other project stakeholders, both internal (at all organizational levels) and external to the organization. Effective communication builds a bridge between diverse stakeholders who may have different cultural and organizational backgrounds as well as different levels of expertise, perspectives, and interests.

Communication activities have many dimensions, including but not limited to:

◆ **Internal.** Focus on stakeholders within the project and within the organization.

◆ **External.** Focus on external stakeholders such as customers, vendors, other projects, organizations, government, the public, and environmental advocates.

◆ **Formal.** Reports, formal meetings (both regular and ad hoc), meeting agendas and minutes, stakeholder briefings, and presentations.

◆ **Informal.** General communications activities using emails, social media, websites, and informal ad hoc discussions.

◆ **Hierarchical focus.** The position of the stakeholder or group with respect to the project team will affect the format and content of the message, in the following ways:

  ■ *Upward.* Senior management stakeholders.

  ■ *Downward.* The team and others who will contribute to the work of the project.

  ■ *Horizontal.* Peers of the project manager or team.

◆ **Official.** Annual reports; reports to regulators or government bodies.

◆ **Unofficial.** Communications that focus on establishing and maintaining the profile and recognition of the project and building strong relationships between the project team and its stakeholders using flexible and often informal means.

◆ **Written and oral.** Verbal (words and voice inflections) and nonverbal (body language and actions), social media and websites, media releases.

Communication develops the relationships necessary for successful project and program outcomes. Communication activities and artifacts to support communication vary widely, ranging from emails and informal conversations to formal meetings and regular project reports. The act of sending and receiving information takes place consciously or unconsciously through words, facial expressions, gestures and other actions. In the context of successfully managing project relationships with stakeholders, communication includes developing strategies and plans for suitable communications artifacts and activities with the stakeholder community and the application of skills to enhance the effectiveness of the planned and other ad hoc communications.

There are two parts to successful communication. The first part involves developing an appropriate communication strategy based on both the needs of the project and the project's stakeholders. From that strategy, a communications management plan is developed to ensure that the appropriate messages are communicated to stakeholders in various formats and various means as defined by the communication strategy. These messages constitute the project's communications—the second part of successful communication. Project communications are the products of the planning process, addressed by the communications management plan that defines the collection, creation, dissemination, storage, retrieval, management, tracking, and disposition of these communications artifacts. Finally, the communication strategy and communications management plan will form the foundation to monitor the effect of the communication.

The project's communications are supported by efforts to prevent misunderstandings and miscommunication and by careful selection of the methods, messengers, and messages developed from the planning process.

Misunderstandings can be reduced but not eliminated through using the 5Cs of written communications in composing a traditional (non-social media) written or spoken message:

◆ **Correct grammar and spelling.** Poor use of grammar or inaccurate spelling can be distracting and can also introduce distortions in the message, diminishing credibility.

◆ **Concise expression and elimination of excess words.** A concise, well-crafted message reduces the opportunities for misunderstanding the intent of the message.

◆ **Clear purpose and expression directed to the needs of the reader.** Ensure that the needs and interests of the audience are factored into the message.

◆ **Coherent logical flow of ideas.** A coherent logical flow of ideas and using "markers" such as introduction and summaries of the ideas throughout the writing.

◆ **Controlling flow of words and ideas.** Controlling the flow of words and ideas may involve graphics or just summaries.

The 5Cs of written communications are supported by communication skills, such as:

◆ **Listening actively.** Staying engaged with the speaker and summarizing conversations to ensure effective information exchange.

◆ **Awareness of cultural and personal differences.** Developing the team's awareness of cultural and personal differences to reduce misunderstandings and enhance communication capability.

◆ **Identifying, setting, and managing stakeholder expectations.** Negotiating with stakeholders reduces the existence of conflicting expectations among the stakeholder community.

◆ **Enhancement of skills.** Enhancing the skills of all team members in the following activities:

■ Persuading a person, a team, or an organization to perform an action;

■ Motivating people and providing encouragement or reassurance;

■ Coaching to improve performance and achieve desired results;

■ Negotiating to achieve mutually acceptable agreements between parties and reduce approval or decision delays; and

■ Resolving conflict to prevent disruptive impacts.

The fundamental attributes of effective communication activities and developing effective communication artifacts are:

■ Clarity on the purpose of the communication—defining its purpose;

■ Understanding as much as possible about the receiver of the communications, meeting needs, and preferences; and

■ Monitoring and measuring the effectiveness of the communications.

# TRENDS AND EMERGING PRACTICES IN PROJECT COMMUNICATIONS MANAGEMENT

Along with a focus on stakeholders and recognition of the value to projects and organizations of effective stakeholder engagement comes the recognition that developing and implementing appropriate communication strategies is vital to maintaining effective relationships with stakeholders. Trends and emerging practices for Project Communications Management include but are not limited to:

◆ **Inclusion of stakeholders in project reviews.** The stakeholder community of each project includes individuals, groups, and organizations that the project team has identified as essential to the successful delivery of project objectives and organizational outcomes. An effective communication strategy requires regular and timely reviews of the stakeholder community and updates to manage changes in its membership and attitudes.

◆ **Inclusion of stakeholders in project meetings.** Project meetings should include stakeholders from outside the project and even the organization, where appropriate. Practices inherent in the agile approaches can be applied to all types of projects. Practices often include short, daily standup meetings, where the achievements and issues of the previous day, and plans for the current day's work, are discussed with the project team and key stakeholders.

◆ **Increased use of social computing.** Social computing in the form of infrastructure, social media services, and personal devices has changed how organizations and their people communicate and do business. Social computing incorporates different approaches to collaboration supported by public IT infrastructure. Social networking refers to how users build networks of relationships to explore their interests and activities with others. Social media tools can not only support information exchange, but also build relationships accompanied by deeper levels of trust and community.

◆ **Multifaceted approaches to communication.** The standard communication strategy for project stakeholder communications embraces and selects from all technologies and respects cultural, practical, and personal preferences for language, media, content, and delivery. When appropriate, social media and other advanced computing technologies may be included. Multifaceted approaches such as these are more effective for communicating to stakeholders from different generations and cultures.

## TAILORING CONSIDERATIONS

Because each project is unique, the project team will need to tailor the way that Project Communications Management processes are applied. Considerations for tailoring include but are not limited to:

◆ **Stakeholders.** Are the stakeholders internal or external to the organization, or both?

◆ **Physical location.** What is the physical location of team members? Is the team colocated? Is the team in the same geographical area? Is the team distributed across multiple time zones?

◆ **Communications technology.** What technology is available to develop, record, transmit, retrieve, track, and store communication artifacts? What technologies are most appropriate and cost effective for communicating to stakeholders?

◆ **Language.** Language is a main factor to consider in communication activities. Is one language used? Or are many languages used? Have allowances been made to adjust to the complexity of team members from diverse language groups?

◆ **Knowledge management.** Does the organization have a formal knowledge management repository? Is the repository used?

## CONSIDERATIONS FOR AGILE/ADAPTIVE ENVIRONMENTS

Project environments subject to various elements of ambiguity and change have an inherent need to communicate evolving and emerging details more frequently and quickly. This motivates streamlining team member access to information, frequent team checkpoints, and colocating team members as much as possible.

In addition, posting project artifacts in a transparent fashion, and holding regular stakeholder reviews are intended to promote communication with management and stakeholders.

# 10.1 PLAN COMMUNICATIONS MANAGEMENT

Plan Communications Management is the process of developing an appropriate approach and plan for project communications activities based on the information needs of each stakeholder or group, available organizational assets, and the needs of the project. The key benefit of this process is a documented approach to effectively and efficiently engage stakeholders by presenting relevant information in a timely manner. This process is performed periodically throughout the project as needed. The inputs, tools and techniques, and outputs of the process are depicted in Figure 10-2. Figure 10-3 depicts the data flow diagram for the process.

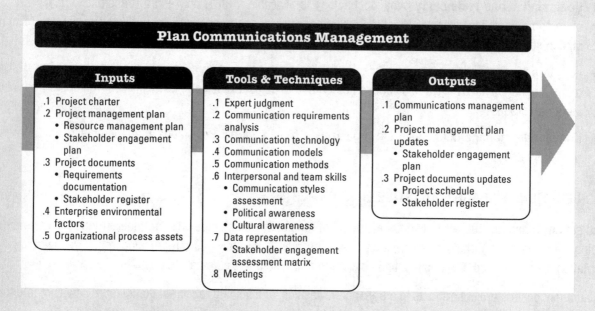

**Figure 10-2. Plan Communications Management: Inputs, Tools & Techniques, and Outputs**

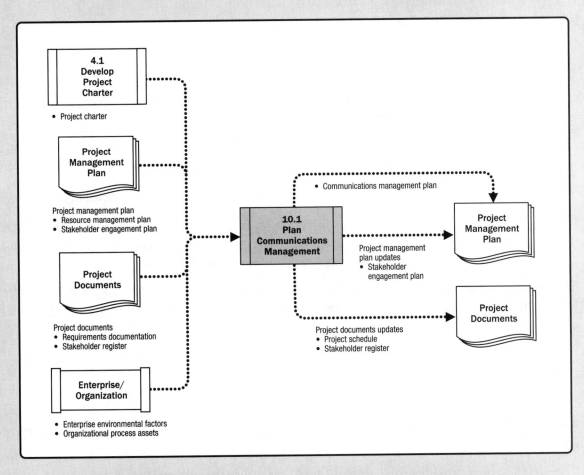

**Figure 10-3. Plan Communications Management: Data Flow Diagram**

An effective communications management plan that recognizes the diverse information needs of the project's stakeholders is developed early in the project life cycle. It should be reviewed regularly and modified when necessary, when the stakeholder community changes or at the start of each new project phase.

On most projects, communications planning is performed very early, during stakeholder identification and project management plan development.

While all projects share the need to communicate project information, the information needs and methods of distribution may vary widely. In addition, the methods of storage, retrieval, and ultimate disposition of the project information need to be considered and documented during this process. The results of the Plan Communications Management process should be reviewed regularly throughout the project and revised as needed to ensure continued applicability.

## 10.1.1 PLAN COMMUNICATIONS MANAGEMENT: INPUTS

### 10.1.1.1 PROJECT CHARTER

Described in Section 4.1.3.1. The project charter identifies the key stakeholder list. It may also contain information about the roles and responsibilities of the stakeholders.

### 10.1.1.2 PROJECT MANAGEMENT PLAN

Described in Section 4.2.3.1. Project management plan components include but are not limited to:

◆ **Resource management plan.** Described in Section 9.1.3.1. Provides guidance on how team resources will be categorized, allocated, managed, and released. Team members and groups may have communication requirements that should be identified in the communications management plan.

◆ **Stakeholder engagement plan.** Described in Section 13.2.3.1. The stakeholder engagement plan identifies the management strategies required to effectively engage stakeholders. These strategies are often fulfilled via communications.

### 10.1.1.3 PROJECT DOCUMENTS

Project documents that can be considered as inputs for this process include but are not limited to:

◆ **Requirements documentation.** Described in Section 5.2.3.1. Requirements documentation can include project stakeholder communications.

◆ **Stakeholder register.** Described in Section 13.1.3.1. The stakeholder register is used to plan communications activities with stakeholders.

### 10.1.1.4 ENTERPRISE ENVIRONMENTAL FACTORS

The enterprise environmental factors that can influence the Plan Communications Management process include but are not limited to:

◆ Organizational culture, political climate, and governance framework;

◆ Personnel administration policies;

◆ Stakeholder risk thresholds;

◆ Established communication channels, tools, and systems;

◆ Global, regional, or local trends, practices, or habits; and

◆ Geographic distribution of facilities and resources.

### 10.1.1.5 ORGANIZATIONAL PROCESS ASSETS

The organizational process assets that can influence the Plan Communications Management process include but are not limited to:

◆ Organizational policies and procedures for social media, ethics, and security;

◆ Organizational policies and procedures for issue, risk, change, and data management;

◆ Organizational communication requirements;

◆ Standardized guidelines for development, exchange, storage, and retrieval of information;

◆ Historical information and lessons learned repository; and

◆ Stakeholder and communications data and information from previous projects.

## 10.1.2 PLAN COMMUNICATIONS MANAGEMENT: TOOLS AND TECHNIQUES

### 10.1.2.1 EXPERT JUDGMENT

Described in Section 4.1.2.1. Expertise should be considered from individuals or groups with specialized knowledge or training in the following topics:

◆ Politics and power structures in the organization;

◆ Environment and culture of the organization and other customer organizations;

◆ Organizational change management approach and practices;

◆ Industry or type of project deliverables;

◆ Organizational communications technologies;

◆ Organizational policies and procedures regarding legal requirements of corporate communications;

◆ Organizational policies and procedures regarding security; and

◆ Stakeholders, including customers or sponsors.

### 10.1.2.2 COMMUNICATION REQUIREMENTS ANALYSIS

Analysis of communication requirements determines the information needs of the project stakeholders. These requirements are defined by combining the type and format of information needed with an analysis of the value of that information.

Sources of information typically used to identify and define project communication requirements include but are not limited to:

◆ Stakeholder information and communication requirements from within the stakeholder register and stakeholder engagement plan;

◆ Number of potential communication channels or paths, including one-to-one, one-to-many, and many-to-many communications;

◆ Organizational charts;

◆ Project organization and stakeholder responsibility, relationships, and interdependencies;

◆ Development approach;

◆ Disciplines, departments, and specialties involved in the project;

◆ Logistics of how many persons will be involved with the project and at which locations;

◆ Internal information needs (e.g., when communicating within organizations);

◆ External information needs (e.g., when communicating with the media, public, or contractors); and

◆ Legal requirements.

### 10.1.2.3 COMMUNICATION TECHNOLOGY

The methods used to transfer information among project stakeholders may vary significantly. Common methods used for information exchange and collaboration include conversations, meetings, written documents, databases, social media, and websites.

Factors that can affect the choice of communication technology include:

◆ **Urgency of the need for information.** The urgency, frequency, and format of the information to be communicated may vary from project to project and also within different phases of a project.

◆ **Availability and reliability of technology.** The technology that is required for distribution of project communications artifacts should be compatible, available, and accessible for all stakeholders throughout the project.

◆ **Ease of use.** The choice of communication technologies should be suitable for project participants and proper training events should be planned, where appropriate.

- ◆ **Project environment.** Whether the team will meet and operate on a face-to-face basis or in a virtual environment; whether they will be located in one or multiple time zones; whether they will use multiple languages for communication; and finally, whether there are any other project environmental factors, such as various aspects of culture, which may constrain the efficiency of the communication.

- ◆ **Sensitivity and confidentiality of the information.** Some aspects to consider are:

  - Whether information to be communicated is sensitive or confidential. If so, additional security measures may be required.

  - Social media policies for employees to ensure appropriate behavior, security, and the protection of proprietary information.

## 10.1.2.4 COMMUNICATION MODELS

Communication models can represent the communication process in its most basic linear form (sender and receiver), in a more interactive form that encompasses the additional element of feedback (sender, receiver, and feedback), or in a more complex model that incorporates the human elements of the sender(s) or receiver(s) and attempts to show the complexity of any communication that involves people.

- ◆ **Sample basic sender/receiver communication model.** This model describes communication as a process and consists of two parties, defined as the sender and receiver. This model is concerned with ensuring that the message is delivered, rather than understood. The sequence of steps in a basic communication model is:

  - *Encode.* The message is coded into symbols, such as text, sound or some other medium for transmission (sending).

  - *Transmit message.* The message is sent via a communication channel. The transmission of this message may be compromised by various physical factors such as unfamiliar technology or inadequate infrastructure. Noise and other factors may be present and contribute to loss of information in transmission and/or reception of the message.

  - *Decode.* The data received is translated by the receiver back into a form useful to the receiver.

◆ **Sample interactive communication model.** This model also describes communication as a process consisting of two parties, the sender and receiver, but recognizes the need to ensure that the message has been understood. In this model, noise includes any interference or barriers that might compromise the understanding of the message, such as the distraction of the receiver, variations in the perceptions of receivers, or lack of appropriate knowledge or interest. The additional steps in an interactive communication model are:

- *Acknowledge.* Upon receipt of a message, the receiver may signal (acknowledge) receipt of the message, but this does not necessarily mean agreement with or comprehension of the message—merely that it has been received.

- *Feedback/response.* When the received message has been decoded and understood, the receiver encodes thoughts and ideas into a message and then transmits this message to the original sender. If the sender perceives that the feedback matches the original message, the communication has been successful. In communication between people, feedback can be achieved through active listening, described in Section 10.2.2.6.

As part of the communication process, the sender is responsible for the transmission of the message, ensuring the information being communicated is clear and complete, and confirming the message is correctly interpreted. The receiver is responsible for ensuring that the information is received in its entirety, interpreted correctly, and acknowledged or responded to appropriately. These components take place in an environment where there will likely be noise and other barriers to effective communication.

Cross-cultural communication presents challenges to ensuring that the meaning of the message has been understood. Differences in communication styles can arise from differences in working methods, age, nationality, professional discipline, ethnicity, race, or gender. People from different cultures communicate using different languages (e.g., technical design documents, different styles) and expect different processes and protocols.

The communication model shown in Figure 10-4 incorporates the idea that the message itself and how it is transmitted are influenced by the sender's current emotional state, knowledge, background, personality, culture, and biases. Similarly, the receiver's emotional state knowledge, background, personality, culture, and biases will influence how the message is received and interpreted, and will contribute to the barriers or noise.

This communication model and its enhancements can assist in developing communication strategies and plans for person-to-person or even small group to small group communications. It is not useful for other communications artifacts such as emails, broadcast messages, or social media.

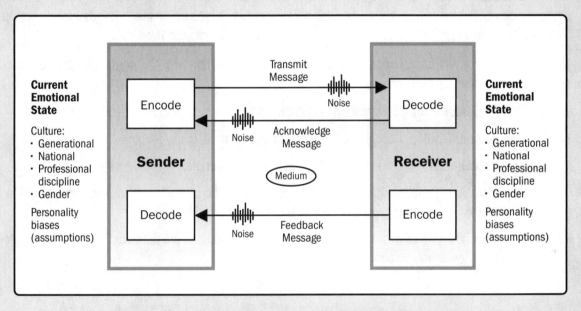

Figure 10-4. Communication Model for Cross-Cultural Communication

## 10.1.2.5 COMMUNICATION METHODS

There are several communication methods that are used to share information among project stakeholders. These methods are broadly classified as follows:

◆ **Interactive communication.** Between two or more parties performing a multidirectional exchange of information in real time. It employs communications artifacts such as meetings, phone calls, instant messaging, some forms of social media, and videoconferencing.

◆ **Push communication.** Sent or distributed directly to specific recipients who need to receive the information. This ensures that the information is distributed but does not ensure that it actually reached or was understood by the intended audience. Push communications artifacts include letters, memos, reports, emails, faxes, voice mails, blogs, and press releases.

◆ **Pull communication.** Used for large complex information sets, or for large audiences, and requires the recipients to access content at their own discretion subject to security procedures. These methods include web portals, intranet sites, e-learning, lessons learned databases, or knowledge repositories.

Different approaches should be applied to meet the needs of the major forms of communication defined in the communications management plan:

◆ **Interpersonal communication.** Information is exchanged between individuals, typically face-to-face.

◆ **Small group communication.** Occurs within groups of around three to six people.

◆ **Public communication.** A single speaker addressing a group of people.

◆ **Mass communication.** There is a minimal connection between the person or group sending the message and the large, sometimes anonymous groups for whom the information is intended.

◆ **Networks and social computing communication.** Supports emerging communication trends of many-to-many supported by social computing technology and media.

Possible communications artifacts and methods include but are not limited to:

◆ Notice boards,

◆ Newsletters/in-house magazines/e-magazines,

◆ Letters to staff/volunteers,

◆ Press releases,

◆ Annual reports,

◆ Emails and intranets,

◆ Web portals and other information repositories (for pull communication)

◆ Phone conversations,

◆ Presentations,

◆ Team briefings/group meetings,

◆ Focus groups,

◆ Face-to-face formal or informal meetings between various stakeholders,

◆ Consultation groups or staff forums, and

◆ Social computing technology and media.

## 10.1.2.6 INTERPERSONAL AND TEAM SKILLS

Interpersonal and team skills that can be used for this process include but are not limited to:

◆ **Communication styles assessment.** A technique used to assess communication styles and identify the preferred communication method, format, and content for planned communication activities. Often used with unsupportive stakeholders, this assessment may follow a stakeholder engagement assessment (described in Section 13.2.2.5) to identify gaps in stakeholder engagement that require additional tailored communication activities and artifacts.

◆ **Political awareness.** Political awareness helps the project manager to plan communications based on the project environment as well as the organization's political environment. Political awareness concerns the recognition of power relationships, both formal and informal, and also the willingness to operate within these structures. An understanding of the strategies of the organization, knowing who wields power and influence in this arena, and developing an ability to communicate with these stakeholders are all aspects of political awareness.

◆ **Cultural awareness.** Cultural awareness is an understanding of the differences between individuals, groups, and organizations and adapting the project's communication strategy in the context of these differences. This awareness and any consequent actions minimize misunderstandings and miscommunication that may result from cultural differences within the project's stakeholder community. Cultural awareness and cultural sensitivity help the project manager to plan communications based on the cultural differences and requirements of stakeholders and team members.

### 10.1.2.7 DATA REPRESENTATION

A data representation technique that can be used for this process includes but is not limited to a stakeholder engagement assessment matrix. Described in Section 13.2.2.5. The stakeholder engagement assessment matrix, shown in Figure 13-6, displays gaps between current and desired engagement levels of individual stakeholders, it can be further analyzed in this process to identify additional communication requirements (beyond the regular reports) as a method to close any engagement level gaps.

### 10.1.2.8 MEETINGS

Project meetings can include virtual (e-meetings) or face-to-face meetings, and can be supported with document collaboration technologies, including email messages and project websites. The Plan Communications Management process requires discussion with the project team to determine the most appropriate way to update and communicate project information, and to respond to requests from various stakeholders for information.

## 10.1.3 PLAN COMMUNICATIONS MANAGEMENT: OUTPUTS

### 10.1.3.1 COMMUNICATIONS MANAGEMENT PLAN

The communications management plan is a component of the project management plan that describes how project communications will be planned, structured, implemented, and monitored for effectiveness. The plan contains the following information:

◆ Stakeholder communication requirements;

◆ Information to be communicated, including language, format, content, and level of detail;

◆ Escalation processes;

◆ Reason for the distribution of that information;

◆ Timeframe and frequency for the distribution of required information and receipt of acknowledgment or response, if applicable;

◆ Person responsible for communicating the information;

◆ Person responsible for authorizing release of confidential information;

◆ Person or groups who will receive the information, including information about their needs, requirements, and expectations;

◆ Methods or technologies used to convey the information, such as memos, email, press releases, or social media;

◆ Resources allocated for communication activities, including time and budget;

◆ Method for updating and refining the communications management plan as the project progresses and develops, such as when the stakeholder community changes as the project moves through different phases;

◆ Glossary of common terminology;

◆ Flow charts of the information flow in the project, workflows with possible sequence of authorization, list of reports, meeting plans, etc.; and

◆ Constraints derived from specific legislation or regulation, technology, organizational policies, etc.

The communications management plan can include guidelines and templates for project status meetings, project team meetings, e-meetings, and email messages. The use of a project website and project management software can be included if these are to be used in the project.

## 10.1.3.2 PROJECT MANAGEMENT PLAN UPDATES

Any change to the project management plan goes through the organization's change control process via a change request. Components that may require a change request for the project management plan include but are not limited to the stakeholder engagement plan, which is described in Section 13.2.3.1. The stakeholder engagement plan is updated to reflect any processes, procedures, tools, or techniques that affect the engagement of stakeholders in project decisions and execution.

## 10.1.3.3 PROJECT DOCUMENTS UPDATES

Project documents that may be updated as a result of carrying out this process include but are not limited to:

◆ **Project schedule.** Described in Section 6.5.3.2. The project schedule may be updated to reflect communication activities.

◆ **Stakeholder register.** Described in Section 13.1.3.1. The stakeholder register may be updated to reflect communications planned.

## 10.2 MANAGE COMMUNICATIONS

Manage Communications is the process of ensuring timely and appropriate collection, creation, distribution, storage, retrieval, management, monitoring, and the ultimate disposition of project information. The key benefit of this process is that it enables an efficient and effective information flow between the project team and the stakeholders. This process is performed throughout the project.

The Manage Communications process identifies all aspects of effective communication, including choice of appropriate technologies, methods, and techniques. In addition, it should allow for flexibility in the communications activities, allowing adjustments in the methods and techniques to accommodate the changing needs of stakeholders and the project. The inputs, tools, techniques, and outputs of this process are depicted in Figure 10-5. Figure 10-6 depicts the data flow diagram of the Manage Communications process.

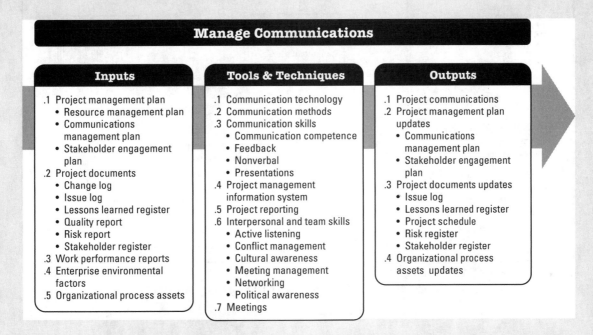

**Figure 10-5. Manage Communications: Inputs, Tools & Techniques, and Outputs**

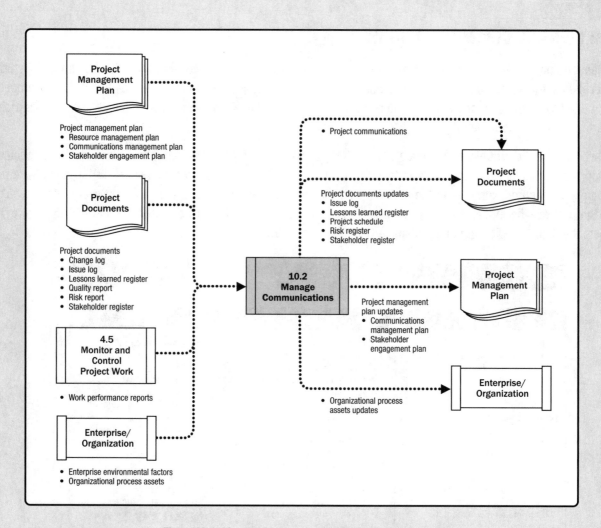

**Figure 10-6. Manage Communications: Data Flow Diagram**

This process goes beyond the distribution of relevant information and seeks to ensure that the information being communicated to project stakeholders has been appropriately generated and formatted, and received by the intended audience. It also provides opportunities for stakeholders to make requests for further information, clarification, and discussion. Techniques and considerations for effective communications management include but are not limited to:

◆ **Sender-receiver models.** Incorporating feedback loops to provide opportunities for interaction/participation and remove barriers to effective communication.

◆ **Choice of media.** Decisions about application of communications artifacts to meet specific project needs, such as when to communicate in writing versus orally, when to prepare an informal memo versus a formal report, and when to use push/pull options and the choice of appropriate technology.

◆ **Writing style.** Appropriate use of active versus passive voice, sentence structure, and word choice.

◆ **Meeting management.** Described in Section 10.2.2.6. Preparing an agenda, inviting essential participants, and ensuring they attend. Dealing with conflicts within the meeting or resulting from inadequate follow-up of minutes and actions, or attendance of the wrong people.

◆ **Presentations.** Awareness of the impact of body language and design of visual aids.

◆ **Facilitation.** Described in Section 4.1.2.3. Building consensus and overcoming obstacles such as difficult group dynamics, and maintaining interest and enthusiasm among group members.

◆ **Active listening.** Described in Section 10.2.2.6. Listening actively involves acknowledging, clarifying and confirming, understanding, and removing barriers that adversely affect comprehension.

## 10.2.1 MANAGE COMMUNICATIONS: INPUTS

### 10.2.1.1 PROJECT MANAGEMENT PLAN

Described in Section 4.2.3.1. Project management plan components include but are not limited to:

◆ **Resource management plan.** Described in Section 9.1.3.1. The resource management plan describes the communications that are needed for management of team or physical resources.

◆ **Communications management plan.** Described in Section 10.1.3.1. The communications management plan describes how project communications will be planned, structured, monitored, and controlled.

◆ **Stakeholder engagement plan.** Described in detail in Section 13.2.3.1. The stakeholder engagement plan describes how stakeholders will be engaged through appropriate communication strategies.

## 10.2.1.2 PROJECT DOCUMENTS

Project documents that can be considered as inputs for this process include but are not limited to

◆ **Change log.** Described in Section 4.6.3.3. The change log is used to communicate changes and approved, deferred, and rejected change requests to the impacted stakeholders.

◆ **Issue log.** Described in Section 4.6.3.3. Information about issues is communicated to impacted stakeholders.

◆ **Lessons learned register.** Described in Section 4.4.3.1. Lessons learned earlier in the project with regard to managing communications can be applied to later phases in the project to improve the efficiency and effectiveness of communications and the communication process.

◆ **Quality report.** Described in Section 8.2.3.1. Information in the quality report includes quality issues, project and product improvements, and process improvements. This information is forwarded to those who can take corrective actions in order to achieve the project quality expectations.

◆ **Risk report.** Described in Section 11.2.3.2. The risk report presents information on sources of overall project risk, together with summary information on identified individual project risks. This information is communicated to risk owners and other impacted stakeholders.

◆ **Stakeholder register.** Described in Section 13.1.3.1. The stakeholder register identifies the individuals, groups, or organizations that will need various types of information.

## 10.2.1.3 WORK PERFORMANCE REPORTS

Described in Section 4.5.3.1. Work performance reports are circulated to the project stakeholders through this process as defined in the communications management plan. Examples of work performance reports include status reports and progress reports. Work performance reports can contain earned value graphs and information, trend lines and forecasts, reserve burndown charts, defect histograms, contract performance information, and risk summaries. They can be presented as dashboards, heat reports, stop light charts, or other representations useful for creating awareness and generating decisions and actions.

## 10.2.1.4 ENTERPRISE ENVIRONMENTAL FACTORS

The enterprise environmental factors that can influence this process include but are not limited to:

◆ Organizational culture, political climate, and governance framework;

◆ Personnel administration policies;

◆ Stakeholder risk thresholds;

◆ Established communication channels, tools, and systems;

◆ Global, regional, or local trends and practices or habits; and

◆ Geographic distribution of facilities and resources.

## 10.2.1.5 ORGANIZATIONAL PROCESS ASSETS

The organizational process assets that can influence this process include but are not limited to:

◆ Corporate policies and procedures for social media, ethics, and security;

◆ Corporate policies and procedures for issue, risk, change, and data management;

◆ Organizational communication requirements;

◆ Standardized guidelines for development, exchange, storage, and retrieval of information; and

◆ Historical information from previous projects, including the lessons learned repository.

## 10.2.2 MANAGE COMMUNICATIONS: TOOLS AND TECHNIQUES

### 10.2.2.1 COMMUNICATION TECHNOLOGY

Described in Section 10.1.2.3. Factors that influence the technology include whether the team is colocated, the confidentiality of any information that needs to be shared, resources available to the team members, and how the organization's culture influences the way in which meetings and discussions are normally conducted.

### 10.2.2.2 COMMUNICATION METHODS

Described in Section 10.1.2.5. The choice of communication methods should allow flexibility in the event that the membership of the stakeholder community changes or their needs and expectations change.

## 10.2.2.3 COMMUNICATION SKILLS

Communication techniques that can be used for this process include but are not limited to:

◆ **Communication competence.** A combination of tailored communication skills that considers factors such as clarity of purpose in key messages, effective relationships and information sharing, and leadership behaviors.

◆ **Feedback.** Feedback is information about reactions to communications, a deliverable, or a situation. Feedback supports interactive communication between the project manager, team and all other project stakeholders. Examples include coaching, mentoring, and negotiating.

◆ **Nonverbal.** Examples of nonverbal communication include appropriate body language to transmit meaning through gestures, tone of voice, and facial expressions. Mirroring and eye contact are also important techniques. The team members should be aware of how they are expressing themselves both through what they say and what they don't say.

◆ **Presentations.** A presentation is the formal delivery of information and/or documentation. Clear and effective presentations of project information to relevant stakeholders can include but are not limited to:

■ Progress reports and information updates to stakeholders;

■ Background information to support decision making;

■ General information about the project and its objectives, for the purposes of raising the profile of the work of the project and the team; and

■ Specific information aimed at increasing understanding and support of the work and objectives of the project.

Presentations will be successful when the content and delivery take the following into account:

■ The audience, their expectations, and needs; and

■ The needs and objectives of the project and project team.

## 10.2.2.4 PROJECT MANAGEMENT INFORMATION SYSTEM (PMIS)

Described in Section 4.3.2.2. Project management information systems can ensure that stakeholders can easily retrieve the information they need in a timely way. Project information is managed and distributed using a variety of tools, including:

- ◆ **Electronic project management tools.** Project management software, meeting and virtual office support software, web interfaces, specialized project portals and dashboards, and collaborative work management tools.

- ◆ **Electronic communications management.** Email, fax, and voice mail; audio, video and web conferencing; and websites and web publishing.

- ◆ **Social media management.** Websites and web publishing; and blogs and applications, which offer the opportunity to engage with stakeholders and form online communities.

## 10.2.2.5 PROJECT REPORTING

Project reporting is the act of collecting and distributing project information. Project information is distributed to many groups of stakeholders and should be adapted to provide information at an appropriate level, format, and detail for each type of stakeholder. The format may range from a simple communication to more elaborate custom reports and presentations. Information may be prepared regularly or on an exception basis. While work performance reports are the output of the Monitor and Control Project Work process, this process develops ad hoc reports, project presentations, blogs, and other types of communication about the project.

## 10.2.2.6 INTERPERSONAL AND TEAM SKILLS

Interpersonal and team skills that can be used for this process include but are not limited to:

◆ **Active listening.** Techniques of active listening involve acknowledging, clarifying and confirming, understanding, and removing barriers that adversely affect comprehension.

◆ **Conflict management.** Described in Section 9.5.2.1.

◆ **Cultural awareness.** Described in Section 10.1.2.6.

◆ **Meeting management.** Meeting management is taking steps to ensure meetings meet their intended objectives effectively and efficiently. The following steps should be used for meeting planning:

- Prepare and distribute the agenda stating the objectives of the meeting.
- Ensure that the meetings start and finish at the published time.
- Ensure the appropriate participants are invited and attend.
- Stay on topic.
- Manage expectations, issues, and conflicts during the meeting.
- Record all actions and those who have been allocated the responsibility for completing the action.

◆ **Networking.** Networking is interacting with others to exchange information and develop contacts. Networks provide project managers and their teams with access to informal organizations to solve problems, influence actions of their stakeholders, and increase stakeholder support for the work and outcomes of the project, thus improving performance.

◆ **Political awareness.** Described in Section 10.1.2.6. Political awareness assists the project manager in engaging stakeholders appropriately to maintain their support throughout the project.

## 10.2.2.7 MEETINGS

Meetings support the actions defined in the communication strategy and communications plan.

## 10.2.3 MANAGE COMMUNICATIONS: OUTPUTS

### 10.2.3.1 PROJECT COMMUNICATIONS

Project communications artifacts may include but are not limited to: performance reports, deliverable status, schedule progress, cost incurred, presentations, and other information required by stakeholders.

### 10.2.3.2 PROJECT MANAGEMENT PLAN UPDATES

Any change to the project management plan goes through the organization's change control process via a change request. Components of the project management plan that may be updated as a result of carrying out this process include but are not limited to:

◆ **Communications management plan.** Described in Section 10.1.3.1. When changes are made to the project communications approach as a result of this process, these changes are reflected in the project communications plan.

◆ **Stakeholder engagement plan.** Described in Section 13.2.3.1. Stakeholder communication requirements and agreed-upon communications strategies are updated as a result of this process.

### 10.2.3.3 PROJECT DOCUMENTS UPDATES

Project documents that may be updated as a result of carrying out this process include but are not limited to:

◆ **Issue log.** Described in Sections 4.3.3.3. The issue log is updated to reflect any communication issues on the project, or how any communications have been used to impact active issues.

◆ **Lessons learned register.** Described in Section 4.4.3.1. The lessons learned register is updated with information on challenges encountered and how they could have been avoided as well as approaches that worked well and what did not work well for managing communications.

◆ **Project schedule.** Described in Section 6.5.3.2. The project schedule may be updated to reflect the status of communication activities.

◆ **Risk register.** Described in Section 11.2.3.1. The risk register is updated to capture risks associated with managing communications.

◆ **Stakeholder register.** Described in Section 13.1.3.1. The stakeholder register can be updated to include information regarding communications activities with project stakeholders.

### 10.2.3.4 ORGANIZATIONAL PROCESS ASSETS UPDATES

Organizational process assets that may be updated as a result of this process include but are not limited to:

◆ Project records such as correspondence, memos, meeting minutes and other documents used on the project; and

◆ Planned and ad hoc project reports and presentations.


## 10.3 MONITOR COMMUNICATIONS

Monitor Communications is the process of ensuring the information needs of the project and its stakeholders are met. The key benefit of this process is the optimal information flow as defined in the communications management plan and the stakeholder engagement plan. This process is performed throughout the project. The inputs, tools and techniques, and outputs of the process are depicted in Figure 10-7. Figure 10-8 depicts the data flow diagram for the process.

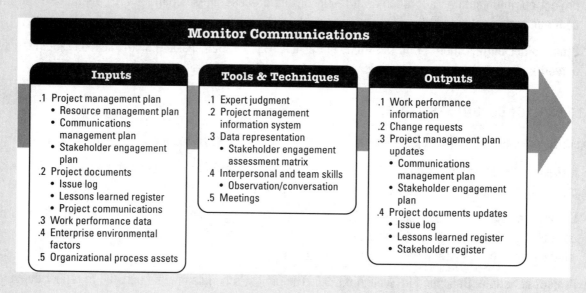

**Figure 10-7. Monitor Communications: Inputs, Tools & Techniques, and Outputs**

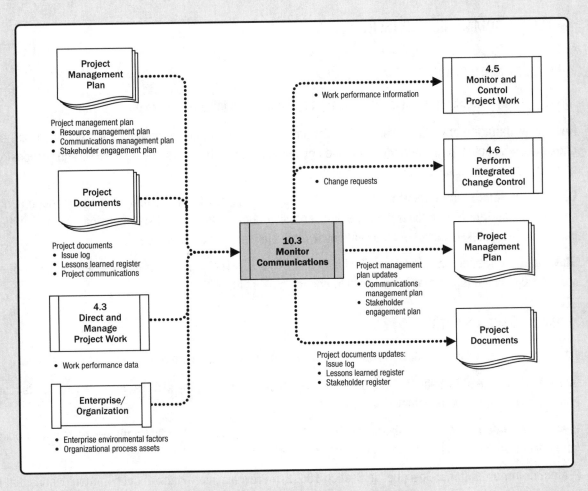

**Figure 10-8. Monitor Communications: Data Flow Diagram**

Monitor Communications determines if the planned communications artifacts and activities have had the desired effect of increasing or maintaining stakeholders' support for the project's deliverables and expected outcomes. The impact and consequences of project communications should be carefully evaluated and monitored to ensure that the right message with the right content (the same meaning for sender and receiver) is delivered to the right audience, through the right channel, and at the right time. Monitor Communications may require a variety of methods, such as customer satisfaction surveys, collecting lessons learned, observations of the team, reviewing data from the issue log, or evaluating changes in the stakeholder engagement assessment matrix described in Section 13.2.2.5.

The Monitor Communications process can trigger an iteration of the Plan Communications Management and/or Manage Communications processes to improve effectiveness of communication through additional and possibly amended communications plans and activities. Such iterations illustrate the continuous nature of the Project Communications Management processes. Issues or key performance indicators, risks, or conflicts may trigger an immediate revision.

# 10.3.1 MONITOR COMMUNICATIONS: INPUTS

## 10.3.1.1 PROJECT MANAGEMENT PLAN

Described in Section 4.2.3.1. Project management plan components include but are not limited to:

◆ **Resource management plan.** Described in Section 9.1.3.1. The resource management plan can be used to understand the actual project organization and any changes through understanding of roles and responsibilities and the project organization charts.

◆ **Communications management plan.** Described in Section 10.1.3.1. The communications management plan contains the current plan for collecting, creating, and distributing information in a timely manner. It identifies the team members, stakeholders, and the work involved in the communication process.

◆ **Stakeholder engagement plan.** Described in Section 13.2.3.1. The stakeholder engagement plan identifies the communication strategies that are planned to engage stakeholders.

## 10.3.1.2 PROJECT DOCUMENTS

Project documents that can be considered as inputs for this process include but are not limited to:

◆ **Issue log.** Described in Section 4.3.3.3. The issue log provides the project's history, a record of stakeholder engagement issues, and how they were resolved.

◆ **Lessons learned register.** Described in Section 4.4.3.1. Lessons learned earlier in the project can be applied to later phases in the project to improve communication effectiveness.

◆ **Project communications.** Described in Section 10.2.3.1. Provides information about communications that have been distributed.

## 10.3.1.3 WORK PERFORMANCE DATA

Described in Section 4.3.3.2. Work performance data contains data on the types and quantities of communications that have actually been distributed.

### 10.3.1.4 ENTERPRISE ENVIRONMENTAL FACTORS

The enterprise environmental factors that can influence the Monitor Communications process include but are not limited to:

◆ Organizational culture, political climate, and governance framework;

◆ Established communication channels, tools, and systems;

◆ Global, regional, or local trends, practices, or habits; and

◆ Geographic distribution of facilities and resources.

### 10.3.1.5 ORGANIZATIONAL PROCESS ASSETS

The organizational process assets that may influence the Monitor Communications process include but are not limited to:

◆ Corporate policies and procedures for social media, ethics, and security;

◆ Organizational communication requirements;

◆ Standardized guidelines for development, exchange, storage, and retrieval of information;

◆ Historical information and lessons learned repository from previous projects; and

◆ Stakeholder and communications data and information from previous projects.

## 10.3.2 MONITOR COMMUNICATIONS: TOOLS AND TECHNIQUES

### 10.3.2.1 EXPERT JUDGMENT

Described in Section 4.1.2.1. Expertise should be considered from individuals or groups with specialized knowledge or training in the following topics:

◆ Communications with the public, the community, and the media, and, in an international environment, between virtual groups; and

◆ Communications and project management systems.

### 10.3.2.2 PROJECT MANAGEMENT INFORMATION SYSTEM (PMIS)

Described in Section 4.3.2.2. Project management information systems provides a set of standard tools for the project manager to capture, store, and distribute information to internal and external stakeholders with the information they need according the communications plan. The information contained in the system is monitored to assess its validity and effectiveness.

### 10.3.2.3 DATA REPRESENTATION

A data representation technique that can be used includes but is not limited to the stakeholder engagement assessment matrix (Section 13.2.2.5), which can provide information about the effectiveness of the communications activities. This is achieved by reviewing changes between desired and current engagement and adjusting communications as necessary.

### 10.3.2.4 INTERPERSONAL AND TEAM SKILLS

Interpersonal and team skills that can be used for this process include but are not limited to observation/conversation as described in Section 5.2.2.6. Discussion and dialogue with the project team helps determine the most appropriate way to update and communicate project performance, and to respond to requests from stakeholders for information. Observation and conversation enables the project manager to identify issues within the team, conflicts between people, or individual performance issues.

### 10.3.2.5 MEETINGS

Face-to-face or virtual meetings are used for decision making; responding to stakeholder requests; and having discussions with suppliers, vendors, and other project stakeholders.

## 10.3.3 MONITOR COMMUNICATIONS: OUTPUTS

### 10.3.3.1 WORK PERFORMANCE INFORMATION

Described in Section 4.5.1.3. Work performance information includes information on how project communication is performing by comparing the communications that were implemented compared to those that were planned. It also considers feedback on communications, such as survey results on communication effectiveness.

### 10.3.3.2 CHANGE REQUESTS

Described in Section 4.3.3.4. The Monitor Communications process often results in the need for adjustment, action, and intervention on communications activities defined in the communications management plan. Change requests are processed through the Perform Integrated Change Control process (Section 4.6).

These change requests may result in:

◆ Revision of stakeholder communication requirements, including stakeholders' information distribution, content or format, and distribution method; and

◆ New procedures to eliminate bottlenecks.

### 10.3.3.3 PROJECT MANAGEMENT PLAN UPDATES

Any change to the project management plan goes through the organization's change control process via a change request. Components that may require a change request for the project management plan include but are not limited to:

◆ **Communications management plan.** Described in Section 10.1.3.1. The communications management plan is updated with new information to make communication more effective.

◆ **Stakeholder engagement plan.** Described in Section 13.2.3.1. The stakeholder engagement plan is updated to reflect the actual situation of stakeholders, their communication needs, and their importance.

### 10.3.3.4 PROJECT DOCUMENTS UPDATES

Project documents that may be updated as a result of carrying out this process include but are not limited to:

◆ **Issue log.** Described in Section 4.3.3.3. The issue log may be updated with new information on issues raised, their progress, and resolution.

◆ **Lessons learned register.** Described in Section 4.4.3.1. The lessons learned register may be updated with causes of issues, reasons behind the corrective actions chosen, and other communication lessons learned as appropriate.

◆ **Stakeholder register.** Described in Section 13.1.3.1. The stakeholder register may be updated with revised stakeholder communication requirements.

# 11

# PROJECT RISK MANAGEMENT

Project Risk Management includes the processes of conducting risk management planning, identification, analysis, response planning, response implementation, and monitoring risk on a project. The objectives of project risk management are to increase the probability and/or impact of positive risks and to decrease the probability and/or impact of negative risks, in order to optimize the chances of project success.

The Project Risk Management processes are:

**11.1 Plan Risk Management**—The process of defining how to conduct risk management activities for a project.

**11.2 Identify Risks**—The process of identifying individual project risks as well as sources of overall project risk, and documenting their characteristics.

**11.3 Perform Qualitative Risk Analysis**—The process of prioritizing individual project risks for further analysis or action by assessing their probability of occurrence and impact as well as other characteristics.

**11.4 Perform Quantitative Risk Analysis**—The process of numerically analyzing the combined effect of identified individual project risks and other sources of uncertainty on overall project objectives.

**11.5 Plan Risk Responses**—The process of developing options, selecting strategies, and agreeing on actions to address overall project risk exposure, as well as to treat individual project risks.

**11.6 Implement Risk Responses**—The process of implementing agreed-upon risk response plans.

**11.7 Monitor Risks**—The process of monitoring the implementation of agreed-upon risk response plans, tracking identified risks, identifying and analyzing new risks, and evaluating risk process effectiveness throughout the project.

Figure 11-1 provides an overview of the Project Risk Management processes. The Project Management Risk processes are presented as discrete processes with defined interfaces while, in practice, they overlap and interact in ways that cannot be completely detailed in this *PMBOK® Guide*.

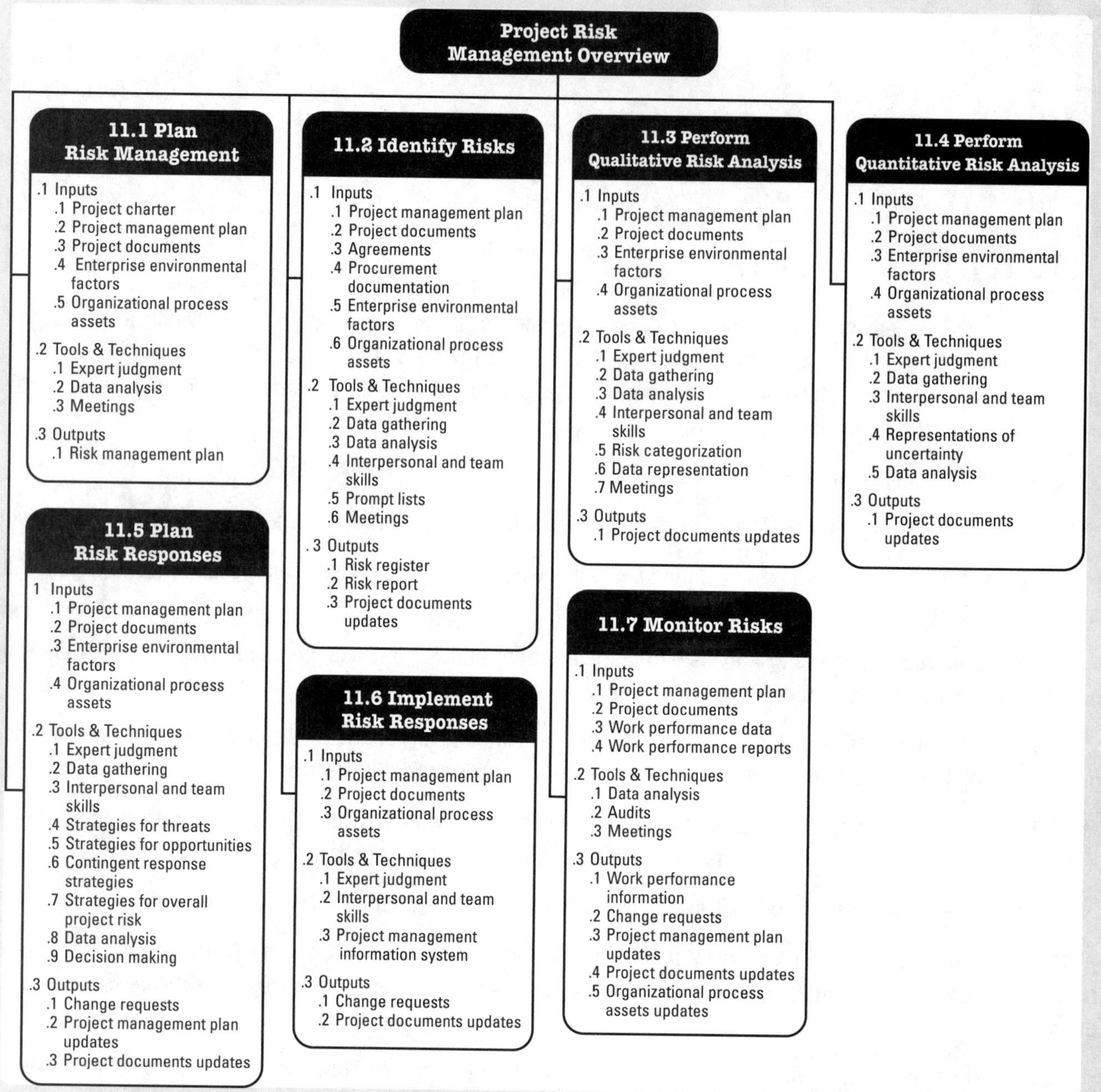

## Project Risk Management Overview

**11.1 Plan Risk Management**

.1 Inputs
   .1 Project charter
   .2 Project management plan
   .3 Project documents
   .4 Enterprise environmental factors
   .5 Organizational process assets

.2 Tools & Techniques
   .1 Expert judgment
   .2 Data analysis
   .3 Meetings

.3 Outputs
   .1 Risk management plan

**11.2 Identify Risks**

.1 Inputs
   .1 Project management plan
   .2 Project documents
   .3 Agreements
   .4 Procurement documentation
   .5 Enterprise environmental factors
   .6 Organizational process assets

.2 Tools & Techniques
   .1 Expert judgment
   .2 Data gathering
   .3 Data analysis
   .4 Interpersonal and team skills
   .5 Prompt lists
   .6 Meetings

.3 Outputs
   .1 Risk register
   .2 Risk report
   .3 Project documents updates

**11.3 Perform Qualitative Risk Analysis**

.1 Inputs
   .1 Project management plan
   .2 Project documents
   .3 Enterprise environmental factors
   .4 Organizational process assets

.2 Tools & Techniques
   .1 Expert judgment
   .2 Data gathering
   .3 Data analysis
   .4 Interpersonal and team skills
   .5 Risk categorization
   .6 Data representation
   .7 Meetings

.3 Outputs
   .1 Project documents updates

**11.4 Perform Quantitative Risk Analysis**

.1 Inputs
   .1 Project management plan
   .2 Project documents
   .3 Enterprise environmental factors
   .4 Organizational process assets

.2 Tools & Techniques
   .1 Expert judgment
   .2 Data gathering
   .3 Interpersonal and team skills
   .4 Representations of uncertainty
   .5 Data analysis

.3 Outputs
   .1 Project documents updates

**11.5 Plan Risk Responses**

1 Inputs
   .1 Project management plan
   .2 Project documents
   .3 Enterprise environmental factors
   .4 Organizational process assets

.2 Tools & Techniques
   .1 Expert judgment
   .2 Data gathering
   .3 Interpersonal and team skills
   .4 Strategies for threats
   .5 Strategies for opportunities
   .6 Contingent response strategies
   .7 Strategies for overall project risk
   .8 Data analysis
   .9 Decision making

.3 Outputs
   .1 Change requests
   .2 Project management plan updates
   .3 Project documents updates

**11.6 Implement Risk Responses**

.1 Inputs
   .1 Project management plan
   .2 Project documents
   .3 Organizational process assets

.2 Tools & Techniques
   .1 Expert judgment
   .2 Interpersonal and team skills
   .3 Project management information system

.3 Outputs
   .1 Change requests
   .2 Project documents updates

**11.7 Monitor Risks**

.1 Inputs
   .1 Project management plan
   .2 Project documents
   .3 Work performance data
   .4 Work performance reports

.2 Tools & Techniques
   .1 Data analysis
   .2 Audits
   .3 Meetings

.3 Outputs
   .1 Work performance information
   .2 Change requests
   .3 Project management plan updates
   .4 Project documents updates
   .5 Organizational process assets updates

**Figure 11-1. Project Risk Management Overview**

## KEY CONCEPTS FOR PROJECT RISK MANAGEMENT

All projects are risky since they are unique undertakings with varying degrees of complexity that aim to deliver benefits. They do this in a context of constraints and assumptions, while responding to stakeholder expectations that may be conflicting and changing. Organizations should choose to take project risk in a controlled and intentional manner in order to create value while balancing risk and reward.

Project Risk Management aims to identify and manage risks that are not addressed by the other project management processes. When unmanaged, these risks have the potential to cause the project to deviate from the plan and fail to achieve the defined project objectives. Consequently, the effectiveness of Project Risk Management is directly related to project success.

Risk exists at two levels within every project. Each project contains individual risks that can affect the achievement of project objectives. It is also important to consider the riskiness of the overall project, which arises from the combination of individual project risks and other sources of uncertainty. Project Risk Management processes address both levels of risk in projects, and these are defined as follows:

◆ **Individual project risk** is an uncertain event or condition that, if it occurs, has a positive or negative effect on one or more project objectives.

◆ **Overall project risk** is the effect of uncertainty on the project as a whole, arising from all sources of uncertainty including individual risks, representing the exposure of stakeholders to the implications of variations in project outcome, both positive and negative.

Individual project risks can have a positive or negative effect on project objectives if they occur. Project Risk Management aims to exploit or enhance positive risks (opportunities) while avoiding or mitigating negative risks (threats). Unmanaged threats may result in issues or problems such as delay, cost overruns, performance shortfall, or loss of reputation. Opportunities that are captured can lead to benefits such as reduced time and cost, improved performance, or reputation.

Overall project risk can also be positive or negative. Management of overall project risk aims to keep project risk exposure within an acceptable range by reducing drivers of negative variation, promoting drivers of positive variation, and maximizing the probability of achieving overall project objectives.

Risks will continue to emerge during the lifetime of the project, so Project Risk Management processes should be conducted iteratively. Risk is initially addressed during project planning by shaping the project strategy. Risk should also be monitored and managed as the project progresses to ensure that the project stays on track and emergent risks are addressed.

In order to manage risk effectively on a particular project, the project team needs to know what level of risk exposure is acceptable in pursuit of the project objectives. This is defined by measurable risk thresholds that reflect the risk appetite of the organization and project stakeholders. Risk thresholds express the degree of acceptable variation around a project objective. They are explicitly stated and communicated to the project team and reflected in the definitions of risk impact levels for the project.

## TRENDS AND EMERGING PRACTICES IN PROJECT RISK MANAGEMENT

The focus of project risk management is broadening to ensure that all types of risk are considered, and that project risks are understood in a wider context. Trends and emerging practices for Project Risk Management include but are not limited to:

◆ **Non-event risks.** Most projects focus only on risks that are uncertain future events that may or may not occur. Examples of event-based risks include: a key seller may go out of business during the project, the customer may change the requirement after design is complete, or a subcontractor may propose enhancements to the standard operating processes.

There is an increasing recognition that non-event risks need to be identified and managed. There are two main types of non-event risks:

   ■ *Variability risk.* Uncertainty exists about some key characteristics of a planned event or activity or decision. Examples of variability risks include: productivity may be above or below target, the number of errors found during testing may be higher or lower than expected, or unseasonal weather conditions may occur during the construction phase.

   ■ *Ambiguity risk.* Uncertainty exists about what might happen in the future. Areas of the project where imperfect knowledge might affect the project's ability to achieve its objectives include: elements of the requirement or technical solution, future developments in regulatory frameworks, or inherent systemic complexity in the project.

Variability risks can be addressed using Monte Carlo analysis, with the range of variation reflected in probability distributions, followed by actions to reduce the spread of possible outcomes. Ambiguity risks are managed by defining those areas where there is a deficit of knowledge or understanding, then filling the gap by obtaining expert external input or benchmarking against best practices. Ambiguity is also addressed through incremental development, prototyping, or simulation.

◆ **Project resilience.** The existence of emergent risk is becoming clear, with a growing awareness of so-called unknowable-unknowns. These are risks that can only be recognized after they have occurred. Emergent risks can be tackled through developing project resilience. This requires each project to have:

■ Right level of budget and schedule contingency for emergent risks, in addition to a specific risk budget for known risks;

■ Flexible project processes that can cope with emergent risk while maintaining overall direction toward project goals, including strong change management;

■ Empowered project team that has clear objectives and that is trusted to get the job done within agreed-upon limits;

■ Frequent review of early warning signs to identify emergent risks as early as possible; and

■ Clear input from stakeholders to clarify areas where the project scope or strategy can be adjusted in response to emergent risks.

◆ **Integrated risk management.** Projects exist in an organizational context, and they may form part of a program or portfolio. Risk exists at each of these levels, and risks should be owned and managed at the appropriate level. Some risks identified at higher levels will be delegated to the project team for management, and some project risks may be escalated to higher levels if they are best managed outside the project. A coordinated approach to enterprise-wide risk management ensures alignment and coherence in the way risk is managed across all levels. This builds risk efficiency into the structure of programs and portfolios, providing the greatest overall value for a given level of risk exposure.

## TAILORING CONSIDERATIONS

Because each project is unique, it is necessary to tailor the way Project Risk Management processes are applied. Considerations for tailoring include but are not limited to:

◆ **Project size.** Does the project's size in terms of budget, duration, scope, or team size require a more detailed approach to risk management? Or is it small enough to justify a simplified risk process?

◆ **Project complexity.** Is a robust risk approach demanded by high levels of innovation, new technology, commercial arrangements, interfaces, or external dependencies that increase project complexity? Or is the project simple enough that a reduced risk process will suffice?

◆ **Project importance.** How strategically important is the project? Is the level of risk increased for this project because it aims to produce breakthrough opportunities, addresses significant blocks to organizational performance, or involves major product innovation?

◆ **Development approach.** Is this a waterfall project, where risk processes can be followed sequentially and iteratively, or does the project follow an agile approach where risk is addressed at the start of each iteration as well as during its execution?

Tailoring of the Project Risk Management processes to meet these considerations is part of the Plan Risk Management process, and the outcomes of tailoring decisions are recorded in the risk management plan.

## CONSIDERATIONS FOR AGILE/ADAPTIVE ENVIRONMENTS

High-variability environments, by definition, incur more uncertainty and risk. To address this, projects managed using adaptive approaches make use of frequent reviews of incremental work products and cross-functional project teams to accelerate knowledge sharing and ensure that risk is understood and managed. Risk is considered when selecting the content of each iteration, and risks will also be identified, analyzed, and managed during each iteration.

Additionally, the requirements are kept as a living document that is updated regularly, and work may be reprioritized as the project progresses, based on an improved understanding of current risk exposure.

## 11.1 PLAN RISK MANAGEMENT

Plan Risk Management is the process of defining how to conduct risk management activities for a project. The key benefit of this process is that it ensures that the degree, type, and visibility of risk management are proportionate to both risks and the importance of the project to the organization and other stakeholders. This process is performed once or at predefined points in the project. The inputs, tools and techniques, and outputs of the process are depicted in Figure 11-2. Figure 11-3 depicts the data flow diagram for the process.

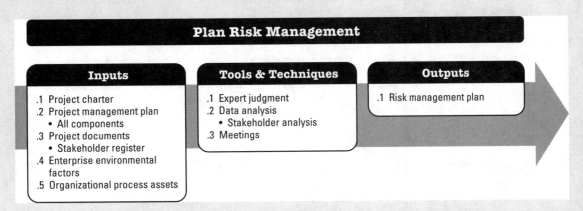

Figure 11-2. Plan Risk Management: Inputs, Tools & Techniques, and Outputs

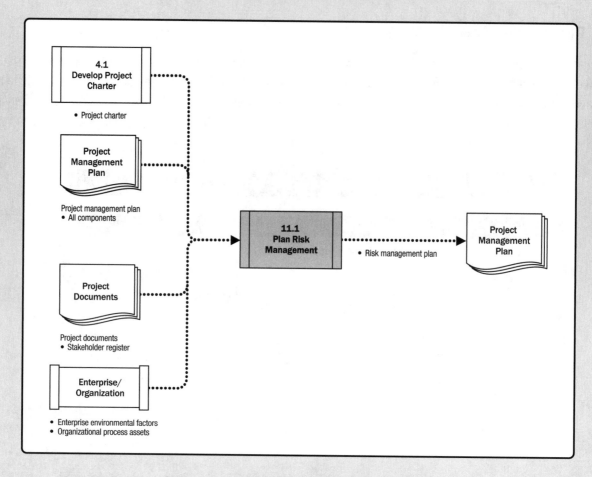

**Figure 11-3. Plan Risk Management: Data Flow Diagram**

The Plan Risk Management process should begin when a project is conceived and should be completed early in the project. It may be necessary to revisit this process later in the project life cycle, for example at a major phase change, or if the project scope changes significantly, or if a subsequent review of risk management effectiveness determines that the Project Risk Management process requires modification.

### 11.1.1 PLAN RISK MANAGEMENT: INPUTS

#### 11.1.1.1 PROJECT CHARTER

Described in Section 4.1.3.1. The project charter documents the high-level project description and boundaries, high-level requirements, and risks.

## 11.1.1.2 PROJECT MANAGEMENT PLAN

Described in Section 4.2.3.1. In planning Project Risk Management, all approved subsidiary management plans should be taken into consideration in order to make the risk management plan consistent with them. The methodology outlined in other project management plan components might influence the Plan Risk Management process.

## 11.1.1.3 PROJECT DOCUMENTS

Project documents that can be considered as inputs for this process include but are not limited to the stakeholder register as described in Section 13.1.3.1. The stakeholder register contains details of the project's stakeholders and provides an overview of their project roles and their attitude toward risk on this project. This is useful in determining roles and responsibilities for managing risk on the project, as well as setting risk thresholds for the project.

## 11.1.1.4 ENTERPRISE ENVIRONMENTAL FACTORS

The enterprise environmental factors that can influence the Plan Risk Management process include but are not limited to overall risk thresholds set by the organization or key stakeholders.

## 11.1.1.5 ORGANIZATIONAL PROCESS ASSETS

The organizational process assets that can influence the Plan Risk Management process include but are not limited to:

◆ Organizational risk policy;

◆ Risk categories, possibly organized into a risk breakdown structure;

◆ Common definitions of risk concepts and terms;

◆ Risk statement formats;

◆ Templates for the risk management plan, risk register, and risk report;

◆ Roles and responsibilities;

◆ Authority levels for decision making; and

◆ Lessons learned repository from previous similar projects.

## 11.1.2 PLAN RISK MANAGEMENT: TOOLS AND TECHNIQUES

### 11.1.2.1 EXPERT JUDGMENT

Described in Section 4.1.2.1. Expertise should be considered from individuals or groups with specialized knowledge or training in the following topics:

◆ Familiarity with the organization's approach to managing risk, including enterprise risk management where this is performed;

◆ Tailoring risk management to the specific needs of a project; and

◆ Types of risk that are likely to be encountered on projects in the same area.

### 11.1.2.2 DATA ANALYSIS

Data analysis techniques that can be used for this process includes but are not limited to a stakeholder analysis (Section 13.1.2.3) to determine the risk appetite of project stakeholders.

### 11.1.2.3 MEETINGS

The risk management plan may be developed as part of the project kick-off meeting or a specific planning meeting may be held. Attendees may include the project manager, selected project team members, key stakeholders, or team members who are responsible to manage the risk management process on the project. Others outside the organization may also be invited, as needed, including customers, sellers, and regulators. A skilled facilitator can help participants remain focused on the task, agree on key aspects of the risk approach, identify and overcome sources of bias, and resolve any disagreements that may arise.

Plans for conducting risk management activities are defined in these meetings and documented in the risk management plan (see Section 11.1.3.1).

## 11.1.3 PLAN RISK MANAGEMENT: OUTPUTS

### 11.1.3.1 RISK MANAGEMENT PLAN

The risk management plan is a component of the project management plan that describes how risk management activities will be structured and performed. The risk management plan may include some or all of the following elements:

◆ **Risk strategy.** Describes the general approach to managing risk on this project.

◆ **Methodology.** Defines the specific approaches, tools, and data sources that will be used to perform risk management on the project.

◆ **Roles and responsibilities.** Defines the lead, support, and risk management team members for each type of activity described in the risk management plan, and clarifies their responsibilities.

◆ **Funding.** Identifies the funds needed to perform activities related to Project Risk Management. Establishes protocols for the application of contingency and management reserves.

◆ **Timing.** Defines when and how often the Project Risk Management processes will be performed throughout the project life cycle, and establishes risk management activities for inclusion into the project schedule.

◆ **Risk categories.** Provide a means for grouping individual project risks. A common way to structure risk categories is with a risk breakdown structure (RBS), which is a hierarchical representation of potential sources of risk (see example in Figure 11-4). An RBS helps the project team consider the full range of sources from which individual project risks may arise. This can be useful when identifying risks or when categorizing identified risks. The organization may have a generic RBS to be used for all projects, or there may be several RBS frameworks for different types of projects, or the project may develop a tailored RBS. Where an RBS is not used, an organization may use a custom risk categorization framework, which may take the form of a simple list of categories or a structure based on project objectives.

| RBS LEVEL 0 | RBS LEVEL 1 | RBS LEVEL 2 | |
|---|---|---|---|
| 0. ALL SOURCES OF PROJECT RISK | 1. TECHNICAL RISK | 1.1 | Scope definition |
| | | 1.2 | Requirements definition |
| | | 1.3 | Estimates, assumptions, and constraints |
| | | 1.4 | Technical processes |
| | | 1.5 | Technology |
| | | 1.6 | Technical interfaces |
| | | Etc. | |
| | 2. MANAGEMENT RISK | 2.1 | Project management |
| | | 2.2 | Program/portfolio management |
| | | 2.3 | Operations management |
| | | 2.4 | Organization |
| | | 2.5 | Resourcing |
| | | 2.6 | Communication |
| | | Etc. | |
| | 3. COMMERCIAL RISK | 3.1 | Contractual terms and conditions |
| | | 3.2 | Internal procurement |
| | | 3.3 | Suppliers and vendors |
| | | 3.4 | Subcontracts |
| | | 3.5 | Client/customer stability |
| | | 3.6 | Partnerships and joint ventures |
| | | Etc. | |
| | 4. EXTERNAL RISK | 4.1 | Legislation |
| | | 4.2 | Exchange rates |
| | | 4.3 | Site/facilities |
| | | 4.4 | Environmental/weather |
| | | 4.5 | Competition |
| | | 4.6 | Regulatory |
| | | Etc. | |

Figure 11-4. Extract from Sample Risk Breakdown Structure (RBS)

◆ **Stakeholder risk appetite.** The risk appetites of key stakeholders on the project are recorded in the risk management plan, as they inform the details of the Plan Risk Management process. In particular, stakeholder risk appetite should be expressed as measurable risk thresholds around each project objective. These thresholds will determine the acceptable level of overall project risk exposure, and they are also used to inform the definitions of probability and impacts to be used when assessing and prioritizing individual project risks.

◆ **Definitions of risk probability and impacts.** Definitions of risk probability and impact levels are specific to the project context and reflect the risk appetite and thresholds of the organization and key stakeholders. The project may generate specific definitions of probability and impact levels or it may start with general definitions provided by the organization. The number of levels reflects the degree of detail required for the Project Risk Management process, with more levels used for a more detailed risk approach (typically five levels), and fewer for a simple process (usually three). Table 11-1 provides an example of definitions of probability and impacts against three project objectives. These scales can be used to evaluate both threats and opportunities by interpreting the impact definitions as negative for threats (delay, additional cost, and performance shortfall) and positive for opportunities (reduced time or cost, and performance enhancement).

Table 11-1. Example of Definitions for Probability and Impacts

| SCALE | PROBABILITY | +/− IMPACT ON PROJECT OBJECTIVES | | |
|-------|-------------|------|------|---------|
| | | TIME | COST | QUALITY |
| Very High | >70% | >6 months | >$5M | Very significant impact on overall functionality |
| High | 51-70% | 3-6 months | $1M-$5M | Significant impact on overall functionality |
| Medium | 31-50% | 1-3 months | $501K-$1M | Some impact in key functional areas |
| Low | 11-30% | 1-4 weeks | $100K-$500K | Minor impact on overall functionality |
| Very Low | 1-10% | 1 week | <$100K | Minor impact on secondary functions |
| Nil | <1% | No change | No change | No change in functionality |

◆ **Probability and impact matrix.** Described in Section 11.3.2.6. Prioritization rules may be specified by the organization in advance of the project and be included in organizational process assets, or they may be tailored to the specific project. Opportunities and threats are represented in a common probability and impact matrix using positive definitions of impact for opportunities and negative impact definitions for threats. Descriptive terms (such as very high, high, medium, low, and very low) or numeric values can be used for probability and impact. Where numeric values are used, these can be multiplied to give a probability-impact score for each risk, which allows the relative priority of individual risks to be evaluated within each priority level. An example probability and impact matrix is presented in Figure 11-5, which also shows a possible numeric risk scoring scheme.

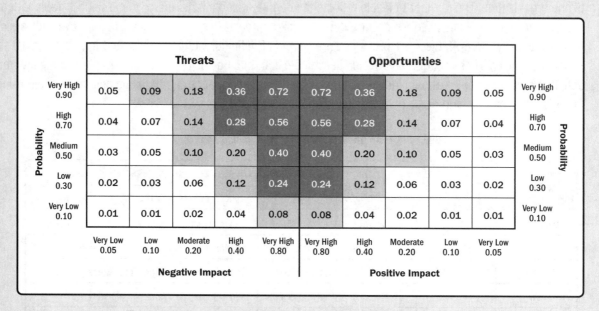

Figure 11-5. Example Probability and Impact Matrix with Scoring Scheme

◆ **Reporting formats.** Reporting formats define how the outcomes of the Project Risk Management process will be documented, analyzed, and communicated. This section of the risk management plan describes the content and format of the risk register and the risk report, as well as any other required outputs from the Project Risk Management processes.

◆ **Tracking.** Tracking documents how risk activities will be recorded and how risk management processes will be audited.

## 11.2 IDENTIFY RISKS

Identify Risks is the process of identifying individual project risks as well as sources of overall project risk, and documenting their characteristics. The key benefit of this process is the documentation of existing individual project risks and the sources of overall project risk. It also brings together information so the project team can respond appropriately to identified risks. This process is performed throughout the project. The inputs, tools and techniques, and outputs of the process are depicted in Figure 11-6. Figure 11-7 depicts the data flow diagram for the process.

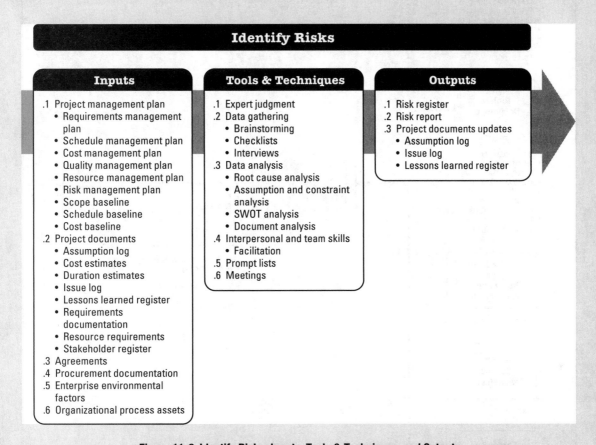

**Figure 11-6. Identify Risks: Inputs, Tools & Techniques, and Outputs**

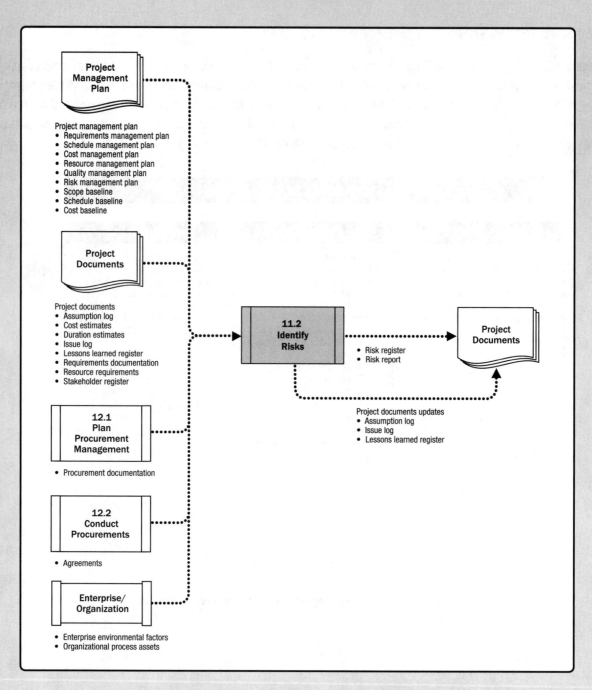

Project management plan
- Requirements management plan
- Schedule management plan
- Cost management plan
- Resource management plan
- Quality management plan
- Risk management plan
- Scope baseline
- Schedule baseline
- Cost baseline

Project documents
- Assumption log
- Cost estimates
- Duration estimates
- Issue log
- Lessons learned register
- Requirements documentation
- Resource requirements
- Stakeholder register

- Procurement documentation

- Agreements

- Enterprise environmental factors
- Organizational process assets

- Risk register
- Risk report

Project documents updates
- Assumption log
- Issue log
- Lessons learned register

**Figure 11-7. Identify Risks: Data Flow Diagram**

Identify Risks considers both individual project risks and sources of overall project risk. Participants in risk identification activities may include the following: project manager, project team members, project risk specialist (if assigned), customers, subject matter experts from outside the project team, end users, other project managers, operations managers, stakeholders, and risk management experts within the organization. While these personnel are often key participants for risk identification, all project stakeholders should be encouraged to identify individual project risks. It is particularly important to involve the project team so they can develop and maintain a sense of ownership and responsibility for identified individual project risks, the level of overall project risk, and associated risk response actions.

When describing and recording individual project risks, a consistent format should be used for risk statements to ensure that each risk is understood clearly and unambiguously in order to support effective analysis and risk response development. Risk owners for individual project risks may be nominated as part of the Identify Risks process, and will be confirmed during the Perform Qualitative Risk Analysis process. Preliminary risk responses may also be identified and recorded and will be reviewed and confirmed as part of the Plan Risk Responses process.

Identify Risks is an iterative process, since new individual project risks may emerge as the project progresses through its life cycle and the level of overall project risk will also change. The frequency of iteration and participation in each risk identification cycle will vary by situation, and this will be defined in the risk management plan.

## 11.2.1 IDENTIFY RISKS: INPUTS

### 11.2.1.1 PROJECT MANAGEMENT PLAN

Described in Section 4.2.3.1. Project management plan components include but are not limited to:

◆ **Requirements management plan.** Described in Section 5.1.3.2. The requirements management plan may indicate project objectives that are particularly at risk.

◆ **Schedule management plan.** Described in Section 6.1.3.1. The schedule management plan may identify areas that are subject to uncertainty or ambiguity.

◆ **Cost management plan.** Described in Section 7.1.3.1. The cost management plan may identify areas that are subject to uncertainty or ambiguity.

◆ **Quality management plan**. Described in Section 8.1.3.1. The quality management plan may identify areas that are subject to uncertainty or ambiguity, or where key assumptions have been made that might give rise to risk.

◆ **Resource management plan**. Described in Section 9.1.3.1. The resource management plan may identify areas that are subject to uncertainty or ambiguity, or where key assumptions have been made that might give rise to risk.

- **Risk management plan.** Described in Section 11.1.3.1. The risk management plan provides information on risk-related roles and responsibilities, indicates how risk management activities are included in the budget and schedule, and describes categories of risk, which may be expressed as a risk breakdown structure (Figure 11-4).

- **Scope baseline.** Described in Section 5.4.3.1. The scope baseline includes deliverables and criteria for their acceptance, some of which might give rise to risk. It also contains the WBS, which can be used as a framework to structure risk identification techniques.

- **Schedule baseline.** Described in Section 6.5.3.1. The schedule baseline may be reviewed to identify milestones and deliverable due dates that are subject to uncertainty or ambiguity, or where key assumptions have been made that might give rise to risk.

- **Cost baseline.** Described in Section 7.3.3.1. The cost baseline may be reviewed to identify costs or funding requirements that are subject to uncertainty or ambiguity, or where key assumptions have been made that might give rise to risk.

## 11.2.1.2 PROJECT DOCUMENTS

Project documents that can be considered as inputs for this process include but are not limited to:

- **Assumption log.** Described in Section 4.1.3.2. Assumptions and constraints recorded in the assumption log may give rise to individual project risks and may also influence the level of overall project risk.

- **Cost estimates.** Described in Section 7.2.3.1. Cost estimates provide quantitative assessments of project costs, ideally expressed as a range, indicating the degree of risk, where a structured review of the documents may indicate that the current estimate is insufficient and poses a risk to the project.

- **Duration estimates.** Described in Section 6.4.3.1. Duration estimates provide quantitative assessments of project durations, ideally expressed as a range, indicating the degree of risk, where a structured review of the documents may indicate that the current estimate is insufficient and poses a risk to the project.

- **Issue log.** Described in Section 4.3.3.3. Issues recorded in the issue log may give rise to individual project risks and may also influence the level of overall project risk.

- **Lessons learned register.** Described in Section 4.4.3.1. Lessons learned about risk identified from earlier phases of the project are reviewed to determine whether similar risks might recur during the remainder of the project.

- **Requirements documentation.** Described in Section 5.2.3.1. Requirements documentation lists the project requirements and allows the team to identify those that could be at risk.

◆ **Resource requirements.** Described in Section 9.2.3.1. Resource requirements provide quantitative assessments of project resource requirements, ideally expressed as a range, indicating the degree of risk, where a structured review of the documents may indicate that the current estimate is insufficient and poses a risk to the project.

◆ **Stakeholder register.** Described in Section 13.1.3.1. The stakeholder register indicates which individuals or groups might participate in identifying risks to the project. It also details those individuals who are available to act as risk owners.

## 11.2.1.3 AGREEMENTS

Described in Section 12.2.3.2. If the project requires external procurement of resources, the agreements may have information such as milestone dates, contract type, acceptance criteria, and awards and penalties that can present threats or opportunities.

## 11.2.1.4 PROCUREMENT DOCUMENTATION

Described in Section 12.3.1.4. If the project requires external procurement of resources, the initial procurement documentation should be reviewed as procuring goods and services from outside the organization may increase or decrease overall project risk and may introduce additional individual project risks. As the procurement documentation is updated throughout the project, the most up to date documentation can be reviewed for risks. For example, seller performance reports, approved change requests and information on inspections.

## 11.2.1.5 ENTERPRISE ENVIRONMENTAL FACTORS

The enterprise environmental factors that can influence the Identify Risks process include but are not limited to:

◆ Published material, including commercial risk databases or checklists,

◆ Academic studies,

◆ Benchmarking results, and

◆ Industry studies of similar projects.

## 11.2.1.6 ORGANIZATIONAL PROCESS ASSETS

The organizational process assets that can influence the Identify Risks process include but are not limited to:

◆ Project files, including actual data,

◆ Organizational and project process controls,

◆ Risk statement formats, and

◆ Checklists from previous similar projects.

## 11.2.2 IDENTIFY RISKS: TOOLS AND TECHNIQUES

### 11.2.2.1 EXPERT JUDGMENT

Described in Section 4.1.2.1. Expertise should be considered from individuals or groups with specialized knowledge of similar projects or business areas. Such experts should be identified by the project manager and invited to consider all aspects of individual project risks as well as sources of overall project risk, based on their previous experience and areas of expertise. The experts' bias should be taken into account in this process.

### 11.2.2.2 DATA GATHERING

Data-gathering techniques that can be used for this process include but are not limited to:

◆ **Brainstorming.** The goal of brainstorming (see Section 4.1.2.2) is to obtain a comprehensive list of individual project risks and sources of overall project risk. The project team usually performs brainstorming, often with a multidisciplinary set of experts who are not part of the team. Ideas are generated under the guidance of a facilitator, either in a free-form brainstorm session or one that uses more structured techniques. Categories of risk, such as in a risk breakdown structure, can be used as a framework. Particular attention should be paid to ensuring that risks identified through brainstorming are clearly described, since the technique can result in ideas that are not fully formed.

◆ **Checklists.** A checklist is a list of items, actions, or points to be considered. It is often used as a reminder. Risk checklists are developed based on historical information and knowledge that has been accumulated from similar projects and from other sources of information. They are an effective way to capture lessons learned from similar completed projects, listing specific individual project risks that have occurred previously and that may be relevant to this project. The organization may maintain a risk checklist based on its own completed projects or may use generic risk checklists from the industry. While a checklist may be quick and simple to use, it is impossible to build an exhaustive one, and care should be taken to ensure the checklist is not used to avoid the effort of proper risk identification. The project team should also explore items that do not appear on the checklist. Additionally, the checklist should be reviewed from time to time to update new information as well as remove or archive obsolete information.

◆ **Interviews.** Individual project risks and sources of overall project risk can be identified by interviewing experienced project participants, stakeholders, and subject matter experts. Interviews (see Section 5.2.2.2) should be conducted in an environment of trust and confidentiality to encourage honest and unbiased contributions.

## 11.2.2.3 DATA ANALYSIS

Data analysis techniques that can be used for this process include but are not limited to:

◆ **Root cause analysis.** Root cause analysis (see Section 8.2.2.2) is typically used to discover the underlying causes that lead to a problem, and develop preventive action. It can be used to identify threats by starting with a problem statement (for example, the project might be delayed or over budget) and exploring which threats might result in that problem occurring. The same technique can be used to find opportunities by starting with a benefit statement (for example, early delivery or under budget) and exploring which opportunities might result in that benefit being realized.

◆ **Assumption and constraint analysis.** Every project and its project management plan are conceived and developed based on a set of assumptions and within a series of constraints. These are often already incorporated in the scope baseline and project estimates. Assumption and constraint analysis explores the validity of assumptions and constraints to determine which pose a risk to the project. Threats may be identified from the inaccuracy, instability, inconsistency, or incompleteness of assumptions. Constraints may give rise to opportunities through removing or relaxing a limiting factor that affects the execution of a project or process.

◆ **SWOT analysis.** This technique examines the project from each of the strengths, weaknesses, opportunities, and threats (SWOT) perspectives. For risk identification, it is used to increase the breadth of identified risks by including internally generated risks. The technique starts with the identification of strengths and weaknesses of the organization, focusing on either the project, organization, or the business area in general. SWOT analysis then identifies any opportunities for the project that may arise from strengths, and any threats resulting from weaknesses. The analysis also examines the degree to which organizational strengths may offset threats and determines if weaknesses might hinder opportunities.

◆ **Document analysis.** Described in Section 5.2.2.3. Risks may be identified from a structured review of project documents, including, but not limited to, plans, assumptions, constraints, previous project files, contracts, agreements, and technical documentation. Uncertainty or ambiguity in project documents, as well as inconsistencies within a document or between different documents, may be indicators of risk on the project.

### 11.2.2.4 INTERPERSONAL AND TEAM SKILLS

Interpersonal and team skills that can be used for this process includes but are not limited to facilitation (see Section 4.1.2.3). Facilitation improves the effectiveness of many of the techniques used to identify individual project risks and sources of overall project risk. A skilled facilitator can help participants remain focused on the risk identification task, follow the method associated with the technique accurately, ensure clear risk descriptions, identify and overcome sources of bias, and resolve any disagreements that may arise.

### 11.2.2.5 PROMPT LISTS

A prompt list is a predetermined list of risk categories that might give rise to individual project risks and that could also act as sources of overall project risk. The prompt list can be used as a framework to aid the project team in idea generation when using risk identification techniques. The risk categories in the lowest level of the risk breakdown structure can be used as a prompt list for individual project risks. Some common strategic frameworks are more suitable for identifying sources of overall project risk, for example PESTLE (political, economic, social, technological, legal, environmental), TECOP (technical, environmental, commercial, operational, political), or VUCA (volatility, uncertainty, complexity, ambiguity).

### 11.2.2.6 MEETINGS

To undertake risk identification, the project team may conduct a specialized meeting (often called a risk workshop). Most risk workshops include some form of brainstorming (see Section 4.1.2.2), but other risk identification techniques may be included depending on the level of the risk process defined in the risk management plan. Use of a skilled facilitator will increase the effectiveness of the meeting. It is also essential to ensure that the right people participate in the risk workshop. On larger projects, it may be appropriate to invite the project sponsor, subject matter experts, sellers, representatives of the customer, or other project stakeholders. Risk workshops for smaller projects may be restricted to a subset of the project team.

## 11.2.3 IDENTIFY RISKS: OUTPUTS

### 11.2.3.1 RISK REGISTER

The risk register captures details of identified individual project risks. The results of Perform Qualitative Risk Analysis, Plan Risk Responses, Implement Risk Responses, and Monitor Risks are recorded in the risk register as those processes are conducted throughout the project. The risk register may contain limited or extensive risk information depending on project variables such as size and complexity.

On completion of the Identify Risks process, the content of the risk register may include but is not limited to:

◆ **List of identified risks.** Each individual project risk is given a unique identifier in the risk register. Identified risks are described in as much detail as required to ensure unambiguous understanding. A structured risk statement may be used to distinguish risks from their cause(s) and their effect(s).

◆ **Potential risk owners.** Where a potential risk owner has been identified during the Identify Risks process, the risk owner is recorded in the risk register. This will be confirmed during the Perform Qualitative Risk Analysis process.

◆ **List of potential risk responses.** Where a potential risk response has been identified during the Identify Risks process, it is recorded in the risk register. This will be confirmed during the Plan Risk Responses process.

Additional data may be recorded for each identified risk, depending on the risk register format specified in the risk management plan. This may include: a short risk title, risk category, current risk status, one or more causes, one or more effects on objectives, risk triggers (events or conditions that indicate that a risk is about to occur), WBS reference of affected activities, and timing information (when was the risk identified, when might the risk occur, when might it no longer be relevant, and what is the deadline for taking action).

## 11.2.3.2 RISK REPORT

The risk report presents information on sources of overall project risk, together with summary information on identified individual project risks. The risk report is developed progressively throughout the Project Risk Management process. The results of Perform Qualitative Risk Analysis, Perform Quantitative Risk Analysis, Plan Risk Responses, Implement Risk Responses, and Monitor Risks are also included in the risk report as those processes are completed. On completion of the Identify Risks process, information in the risk report may include but is not limited to:

◆ Sources of overall project risk, indicating which are the most important drivers of overall project risk exposure; and

◆ Summary information on identified individual project risks, such as number of identified threats and opportunities, distribution of risks across risk categories, metrics and trends, etc.

Additional information may be included in the risk report, depending on the reporting requirements specified in the risk management plan.

## 11.2.3.3 PROJECT DOCUMENTS UPDATES

Project documents that may be updated as a result of this process include but are not limited to:

◆ **Assumption log.** Described in Section 4.1.3.2. During the Identify Risks process, new assumptions may be made, new constraints may be identified, and existing assumptions or constraints may be revisited and changed. The assumption log should be updated with this new information.

◆ **Issue log.** Described in Section 4.3.3.3. The issue log should be updated to capture any new issues uncovered or changes in currently logged issues.

◆ **Lessons learned register.** Described in Section 4.4.3.1. The lessons learned register can be updated with information on techniques that were effective in identifying risks to improve performance in later phases or other projects.

# 11.3 PERFORM QUALITATIVE RISK ANALYSIS

Perform Qualitative Risk Analysis is the process of prioritizing individual project risks for further analysis or action by assessing their probability of occurrence and impact as well as other characteristics. The key benefit of this process is that it focuses efforts on high-priority risks. This process is performed throughout the project. The inputs, tools and techniques, and outputs of the process are depicted in Figure 11-8. Figure 11-9 depicts the data flow diagram for the process.

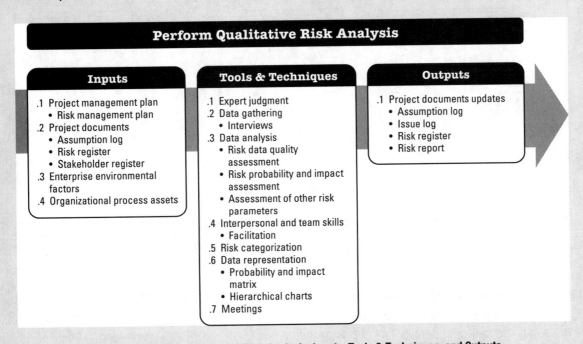

**Perform Qualitative Risk Analysis**

| Inputs | Tools & Techniques | Outputs |
|---|---|---|
| .1 Project management plan<br>  • Risk management plan<br>.2 Project documents<br>  • Assumption log<br>  • Risk register<br>  • Stakeholder register<br>.3 Enterprise environmental factors<br>.4 Organizational process assets | .1 Expert judgment<br>.2 Data gathering<br>  • Interviews<br>.3 Data analysis<br>  • Risk data quality assessment<br>  • Risk probability and impact assessment<br>  • Assessment of other risk parameters<br>.4 Interpersonal and team skills<br>  • Facilitation<br>.5 Risk categorization<br>.6 Data representation<br>  • Probability and impact matrix<br>  • Hierarchical charts<br>.7 Meetings | .1 Project documents updates<br>  • Assumption log<br>  • Issue log<br>  • Risk register<br>  • Risk report |

Figure 11-8. Perform Qualitative Risk Analysis: Inputs, Tools & Techniques, and Outputs

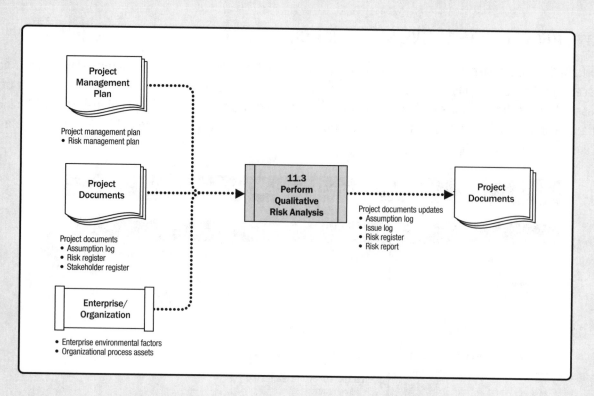

**Figure 11-9. Perform Qualitative Risk Analysis: Data Flow Diagram**

Perform Qualitative Risk Analysis assesses the priority of identified individual project risks using their probability of occurrence, the corresponding impact on project objectives if the risks occur, and other factors. Such assessments are subjective as they are based on perceptions of risk by the project team and other stakeholders. Effective assessment therefore requires explicit identification and management of the risk attitudes of key participants in the Perform Qualitative Risk Analysis process. Risk perception introduces bias into the assessment of identified risks, so attention should be paid to identifying bias and correcting for it. Where a facilitator is used to support the Perform Qualitative Risk Analysis process, addressing bias is a key part of the facilitator's role. An evaluation of the quality of the available information on individual project risks also helps to clarify the assessment of each risk's importance to the project.

Perform Qualitative Risk Analysis establishes the relative priorities of individual project risks for Plan Risk Responses. It identifies a risk owner for each risk who will take responsibility for planning an appropriate risk response and ensuring that it is implemented. Perform Qualitative Risk Analysis also lays the foundation for Perform Quantitative Risk Analysis if this process is required.

The Perform Qualitative Risk Analysis process is performed regularly throughout the project life cycle, as defined in the risk management plan. Often, in an agile development environment, the Perform Qualitative Risk Analysis process is conducted before the start of each iteration.

## 11.3.1 PERFORM QUALITATIVE RISK ANALYSIS: INPUTS

### 11.3.1.1 PROJECT MANAGEMENT PLAN

Described in Section 4.2.3.1. Project management plan components include the risk management plan as described in Section 11.1.3.1. Of particular interest in this process are the roles and responsibilities for conducting risk management, budgets for risk management, schedule activities for risk management, risk categories (often defined in a risk breakdown structure), definitions of probability and impact, the probability and impact matrix, and stakeholders' risk thresholds. These inputs are usually tailored to the project during the Plan Risk Management process. If they are not available, they may be developed during the Perform Qualitative Risk Analysis process and presented to the project sponsor for approval before use.

### 11.3.1.2 PROJECT DOCUMENTS

Project documents that can be considered as inputs for this process include but are not limited to:

◆ **Assumption log.** Described in Section 4.1.3.2. The assumption log is used for identifying, managing, and monitoring key assumptions and constraints that may affect the project. These may inform the assessment of the priority of individual project risks.

◆ **Risk register.** Described in Section 11.2.3.1. The risk register contains details of each identified individual project risk that will be assessed during the Perform Qualitative Risk Analysis process.

◆ **Stakeholder register.** Described in Section 13.1.3.1. This includes details of project stakeholders who may be nominated as risk owners.

### 11.3.1.3 ENTERPRISE ENVIRONMENTAL FACTORS

The enterprise environmental factors that can influence Perform Qualitative Risk Analysis include but are not limited to:

◆ Industry studies of similar projects, and

◆ Published material, including commercial risk databases or checklists.

### 11.3.1.4 ORGANIZATIONAL PROCESS ASSETS

The organizational process assets that can influence Perform Qualitative Risk Analysis include but are not limited to information from similar completed projects.

## 11.3.2 PERFORM QUALITATIVE RISK ANALYSIS: TOOLS AND TECHNIQUES

### 11.3.2.1 EXPERT JUDGMENT

Described in Section 4.1.2.1. Expertise should be considered from individuals or groups with specialized knowledge or training in the following topics:

◆ Previous similar projects, and

◆ Qualitative risk analysis.

Expert judgment is often obtained through facilitated risk workshops or interviews. The possibility of expert views being biased should be taken into account in this process.

### 11.3.2.2 DATA GATHERING

Data-gathering techniques that can be used for this process include but are not limited to interviews. Structured or semi-structured interviews (Section 5.2.2.2) can be used to assess the probability and impacts of individual project risks, as well as other factors. The interviewer should promote an environment of trust and confidentiality in the interview setting to encourage honest and unbiased assessments.

## 11.3.2.3 DATA ANALYSIS

Data analysis techniques that can be used during this process include but are not limited to:

◆ **Risk data quality assessment.** Risk data quality assessment evaluates the degree to which the data about individual project risks is accurate and reliable as a basis for qualitative risk analysis. The use of low-quality risk data may lead to a qualitative risk analysis that is of little use to the project. If data quality is unacceptable, it may be necessary to gather better data. Risk data quality may be assessed via a questionnaire measuring the project's stakeholder perceptions of various characteristics, which may include completeness, objectivity, relevancy, and timeliness. A weighted average of selected data quality characteristics can then be generated to give an overall quality score.

◆ **Risk probability and impact assessment.** Risk probability assessment considers the likelihood that a specific risk will occur. Risk impact assessment considers the potential effect on one or more project objectives such as schedule, cost, quality, or performance. Impacts will be negative for threats and positive for opportunities. Probability and impact are assessed for each identified individual project risk. Risks can be assessed in interviews or meetings with participants selected for their familiarity with the types of risk recorded in the risk register. Project team members and knowledgeable persons external to the project are included. The level of probability for each risk and its impact on each objective are evaluated during the interview or meeting. Differences in the levels of probability and impact perceived by stakeholders are to be expected, and such differences should be explored. Explanatory detail, including assumptions justifying the levels assigned, are also recorded. Risk probabilities and impacts are assessed using the definitions given in the risk management plan (see Table 11-1). Risks with low probability and impact may be included within the risk register as part of a watch list for future monitoring.

◆ **Assessment of other risk parameters.** The project team may consider other characteristics of risk (in addition to probability and impact) when prioritizing individual project risks for further analysis and action. These characteristics may include but are not limited to:

- *Urgency.* The period of time within which a response to the risk is to be implemented in order to be effective. A short period indicates high urgency.

- *Proximity.* The period of time before the risk might have an impact on one or more project objectives. A short period indicates high proximity.

- *Dormancy.* The period of time that may elapse after a risk has occurred before its impact is discovered. A short period indicates low dormancy.

- *Manageability.* The ease with which the risk owner (or owning organization) can manage the occurrence or impact of a risk. Where management is easy, manageability is high.

- *Controllability.* The degree to which the risk owner (or owning organization) is able to control the risk's outcome. Where the outcome can be easily controlled, controllability is high.

- *Detectability.* The ease with which the results of the risk occurring, or being about to occur, can be detected and recognized. Where the risk occurrence can be detected easily, detectability is high.

- *Connectivity.* The extent to which the risk is related to other individual project risks. Where a risk is connected to many other risks, connectivity is high.

- *Strategic impact.* The potential for the risk to have a positive or negative effect on the organization's strategic goals. Where the risk has a major effect on strategic goals, strategic impact is high.

- *Propinquity.* The degree to which a risk is perceived to matter by one or more stakeholders. Where a risk is perceived as very significant, propinquity is high.

The consideration of some of these characteristics can provide a more robust prioritization of risks than is possible by only assessing probability and impact.

## 11.3.2.4 INTERPERSONAL AND TEAM SKILLS

Interpersonal and team skills that can be used for this process include but are not limited to facilitation (see Section 4.1.2.3). Facilitation improves the effectiveness of the qualitative analysis of individual project risks. A skilled facilitator can help participants remain focused on the risk analysis task, follow the method associated with the technique accurately, reach consensus on assessments of probability and impacts, identify and overcome sources of bias, and resolve any disagreements that may arise.

## 11.3.2.5 RISK CATEGORIZATION

Risks to the project can be categorized by sources of risk (e.g., using the risk breakdown structure (RBS); see Figure 11-4), the area of the project affected (e.g., using the work breakdown structure (WBS); see Figures 5-12, 5-13, and 5-14), or other useful categories (e.g., project phase, project budget, and roles and responsibilities) to determine the areas of the project most exposed to the effects of uncertainty. Risks can also be categorized by common root causes. Risk categories that may be used for the project are defined in the risk management plan.

Grouping risks into categories can lead to the development of more effective risk responses by focusing attention and effort on the areas of highest risk exposure, or by developing generic risk responses to address groups of related risks.

## 11.3.2.6 DATA REPRESENTATION

Data representation techniques that can be used during this process include but are not limited to:

◆ **Probability and impact matrix.** A probability and impact matrix is a grid for mapping the probability of each risk occurrence and its impact on project objectives if that risk occurs. This matrix specifies combinations of probability and impact that allow individual project risks to be divided into priority groups (see Figure 11-5). Risks can be prioritized for further analysis and planning of risk responses based on their probability and impacts. The probability of occurrence for each individual project risk is assessed as well as its impact on one or more project objectives if it does occur, using definitions of probability and impact for the project as specified in the risk management plan. Individual project risks are assigned to a priority level based on the combination of their assessed probability and impact, using a probability and impact matrix.

An organization can assess a risk separately for each objective (e.g., cost, time, and scope) by having a separate probability and impact matrix for each. Alternatively, it may develop ways to determine one overall priority level for each risk, either by combining assessments for different objectives, or by taking the highest priority level regardless of which objective is affected.

◆ **Hierarchical charts.** Where risks have been categorized using more than two parameters, the probability and impact matrix cannot be used and other graphical representations are required. For example, a bubble chart displays three dimensions of data, where each risk is plotted as a disk (bubble), and the three parameters are represented by the x-axis value, the y-axis value, and the bubble size. An example bubble chart is shown in Figure 11-10, with detectability and proximity plotted on the x and y axes, and impact value represented by bubble size.

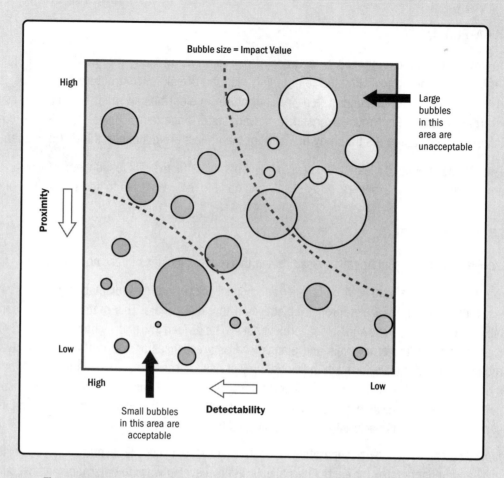

**Figure 11-10. Example Bubble Chart Showing Detectability, Proximity, and Impact Value**

### 11.3.2.7 MEETINGS

To undertake qualitative risk analysis, the project team may conduct a specialized meeting (often called a risk workshop) dedicated to the discussion of identified individual project risks. The goals of this meeting include the review of previously identified risks, assessment of probability and impacts (and possibly other risk parameters), categorization, and prioritization. A risk owner, who will be responsible for planning an appropriate risk response and for reporting progress on managing the risk, will be allocated to each individual project risk as part of the Perform Qualitative Risk Analysis process. The meeting may start by reviewing and confirming the probability and impact scales to be used for the analysis. The meeting may also identify additional risks during the discussion, and these should be recorded for analysis. Use of a skilled facilitator will increase the effectiveness of the meeting.

## 11.3.3 PERFORM QUALITATIVE RISK ANALYSIS: OUTPUTS

### 11.3.3.1 PROJECT DOCUMENTS UPDATES

Project documents that may be updated as a result of carrying out this process include but are not limited to:

◆ **Assumption log.** Described in Section 4.1.3.2. During the Perform Qualitative Risk Analysis process, new assumptions may be made, new constraints may be identified, and existing assumptions or constraints may be revisited and changed. The assumption log should be updated with this new information.

◆ **Issue log.** Described in Section 4.3.3.3. The issue log should be updated to capture any new issues uncovered or changes in currently logged issues.

◆ **Risk register.** Described in Section 11.2.3.1. The risk register is updated with new information generated during the Perform Qualitative Risk Analysis process. Updates to the risk register may include assessments of probability and impacts for each individual project risk, its priority level or risk score, the nominated risk owner, risk urgency information or risk categorization, and a watch list for low-priority risks or risks requiring further analysis.

◆ **Risk report.** Described in Section 11.2.3.2. The risk report is updated to reflect the most important individual project risks (usually those with the highest probability and impact), as well as a prioritized list of all identified risks on the project and a summary conclusion.

# 11.4 PERFORM QUANTITATIVE RISK ANALYSIS

Perform Quantitative Risk Analysis is the process of numerically analyzing the combined effect of identified individual project risks and other sources of uncertainty on overall project objectives. The key benefit of this process is that it quantifies overall project risk exposure, and it can also provide additional quantitative risk information to support risk response planning. This process is not required for every project, but where it is used, it is performed throughout the project. The inputs and outputs of this process are depicted in Figure 11-11. Figure 11-12 depicts the data flow diagram for the process.

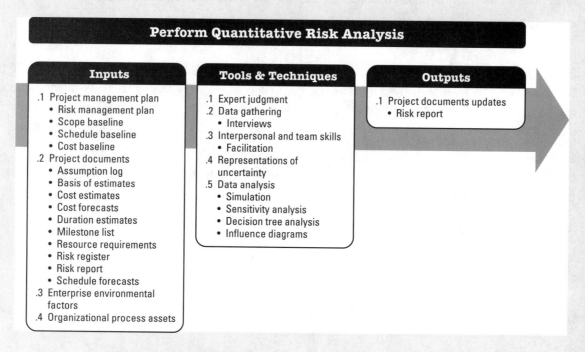

Figure 11-11. Perform Quantitative Risk Analysis: Inputs, Tools & Techniques, and Outputs

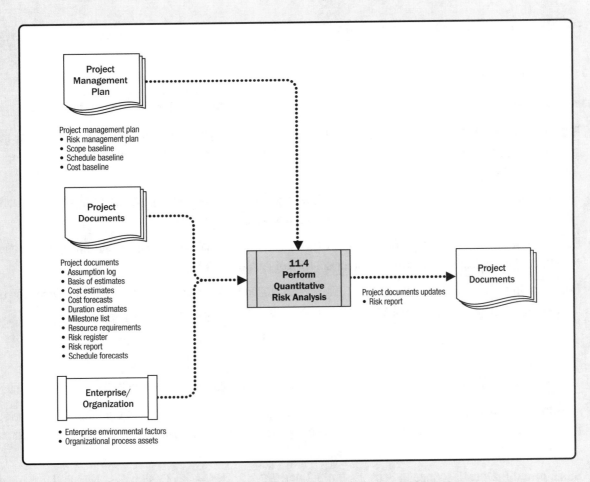

**Figure 11-12. Perform Quantitative Risk Analysis: Data Flow Diagram**

Perform Quantitative Risk Analysis is not required for all projects. Undertaking a robust analysis depends on the availability of high-quality data about individual project risks and other sources of uncertainty, as well as a sound underlying project baseline for scope, schedule, and cost. Quantitative risk analysis usually requires specialized risk software and expertise in the development and interpretation of risk models. It also consumes additional time and cost. The use of quantitative risk analysis for a project will be specified in the project's risk management plan. It is most likely appropriate for large or complex projects, strategically important projects, projects for which it is a contractual requirement, or projects in which a key stakeholder requires it. Quantitative risk analysis is the only reliable method to assess overall project risk through evaluating the aggregated effect on project outcomes of all individual project risks and other sources of uncertainty.

Perform Quantitative Risk Analysis uses information on individual project risks that have been assessed by the Perform Qualitative Risk Analysis process as having a significant potential to affect the project's objectives.

Outputs from Perform Quantitative Risk Analysis are used as inputs to the Plan Risk Responses process, particularly in recommending responses to the level of overall project risk and key individual risks. A quantitative risk analysis may also be undertaken following the Plan Risk Responses process, to determine the likely effectiveness of planned responses in reducing overall project risk exposure.

## 11.4.1 PERFORM QUANTITATIVE RISK ANALYSIS: INPUTS

### 11.4.1.1 PROJECT MANAGEMENT PLAN

Described in Section 4.2.3.1. Project management plan components include but are not limited to:

◆ **Risk management plan.** Described in Section 11.1.3.1. The risk management plan specifies whether quantitative risk analysis is required for the project. It also details the resources available for the analysis and the expected frequency of analyses.

◆ **Scope baseline.** Described in Section 5.4.3.1. The scope baseline describes the starting point from which the effect of individual project risks and other sources of uncertainty are evaluated.

◆ **Schedule baseline.** Described in Section 6.5.3.1. The schedule baseline describes the starting point from which the effect of individual project risks and other sources of uncertainty can be evaluated.

◆ **Cost baseline.** Described in Section 7.3.3.1. The cost baseline describes the starting point from which the effect of individual project risks and other sources of uncertainty can be evaluated.

### 11.4.1.2 PROJECT DOCUMENTS

Project documents that can be considered as inputs for this process include but are not limited to:

◆ **Assumption log.** Described in Section 4.1.3.2. Assumptions may form inputs to the quantitative risk analysis if they are assessed as posing a risk to project objectives. The effect of constraints may also be modeled during a quantitative risk analysis.

◆ **Basis of estimates.** Described in Sections 6.4.3.2 and 7.2.3.2. The basis of estimates used in the planning of the project may be reflected in variability modeled during a quantitative risk analysis process. This may include information on the estimate's purpose, classification, assumed accuracy, methodology, and source.

◆ **Cost estimates.** Described in Section 7.2.3.1. Cost estimates provide the starting point from which cost variability is evaluated.

◆ **Cost forecasts.** Described in Section 7.4.3.2. Forecasts such as the project's estimate to complete (ETC), estimate at completion (EAC), budget at completion (BAC), and to-complete performance index (TCPI) may be compared to the results of a quantitative cost risk analysis to determine the confidence level associated with achieving these targets.

◆ **Duration estimates.** Described in Section 6.4.3.1. Duration estimates provide the starting point from which schedule variability is evaluated.

◆ **Milestone list.** Described in Section 6.2.3.3. Significant events in the project define the schedule targets against which the results of a quantitative schedule risk analysis are compared, in order to determine the confidence level associated with achieving these targets.

- **Resource requirements.** Described in Section 9.2.3.1. Resource requirements provide the starting point from which variability is evaluated.

- **Risk register.** Described in Section 11.2.3.1. The risk register contains details of individual project risks to be used as input for quantitative risk analysis.

- **Risk report.** Described in Section 11.2.3.2. The risk report describes sources of overall project risk and the current overall project risk status.

- **Schedule forecasts.** Described in Section 6.6.3.2. Forecasts may be compared to the results of a quantitative schedule risk analysis to determine the confidence level associated with achieving these targets.

### 11.4.1.3 ENTERPRISE ENVIRONMENTAL FACTORS

The enterprise environmental factors that can influence the Perform Quantitative Risk Analysis process include but are not limited to:

- Industry studies of similar projects, and

- Published material, including commercial risk databases or checklists.

### 11.4.1.4 ORGANIZATIONAL PROCESS ASSETS

The organizational process assets that can influence the Perform Quantitative Risk Analysis process include information from similar completed projects.

## 11.4.2 PERFORM QUANTITATIVE RISK ANALYSIS: TOOLS AND TECHNIQUES

### 11.4.2.1 EXPERT JUDGMENT

Described in Section 4.1.2.1. Expertise should be considered from individuals or groups with specialized knowledge or training in the following topics:

- Translating information on individual project risks and other sources of uncertainty into numeric inputs for the quantitative risk analysis model,

- Selecting the most appropriate representation of uncertainty to model particular risks or other sources of uncertainty,

- Modeling techniques that are appropriate in the context of the project,

- Identifying which tools would be most suitable for the selected modeling techniques, and

- Interpreting the outputs of quantitative risk analysis.

### 11.4.2.2 DATA GATHERING

Interviews (see Section 5.2.2.2) may be used to generate inputs for the quantitative risk analysis, drawing on inputs that include individual project risks and other sources of uncertainty. This is particularly useful where information is required from experts. The interviewer should promote an environment of trust and confidentiality during the interview to encourage honest and unbiased contributions.

### 11.4.2.3 INTERPERSONAL AND TEAM SKILLS

Interpersonal and team skills that can be used for this process include but are not limited to facilitation (see Section 4.1.2.3). A skilled facilitator is useful for gathering input data during a dedicated risk workshop involving project team members and other stakeholders. Facilitated workshops can improve effectiveness by establishing a clear understanding of the purpose of the workshop, building consensus among participants, ensuring continued focus on the task, and using creative approaches to deal with interpersonal conflict or sources of bias.

### 11.4.2.4 REPRESENTATIONS OF UNCERTAINTY

Quantitative risk analysis requires inputs to a quantitative risk analysis model that reflect individual project risks and other sources of uncertainty.

Where the duration, cost, or resource requirement for a planned activity is uncertain, the range of possible values can be represented in the model as a probability distribution. This may take several forms. The most commonly used are triangular, normal, lognormal, beta, uniform, or discrete distributions. Care should be taken when selecting an appropriate probability distribution to reflect the range of possible values for the planned activity.

Individual project risks may be covered by probability distributions. Alternatively, risks may be included in the model as probabilistic branches, where optional activities are added to the model to represent the time and/or cost impact of the risk should it occur, and the chance that these activities actually occur in a particular simulation run matches the risk's probability. Branches are most useful for risks that might occur independently of any planned activity. Where risks are related, for example, with a common cause or a logical dependency, correlation is used in the model to indicate this relationship.

Other sources of uncertainty may also be represented using branches to describe alternative paths through the project.

## 11.4.2.5 DATA ANALYSIS

Data analysis techniques that can be used during this process include but are not limited to:

◆ **Simulation.** Quantitative risk analysis uses a model that simulates the combined effects of individual project risks and other sources of uncertainty to evaluate their potential impact on achieving project objectives. Simulations are typically performed using a Monte Carlo analysis. When running a Monte Carlo analysis for cost risk, the simulation uses the project cost estimates. When running a Monte Carlo analysis for schedule risk, the schedule network diagram and duration estimates are used. An integrated quantitative cost-schedule risk analysis uses both inputs. The output is a quantitative risk analysis model.

Computer software is used to iterate the quantitative risk analysis model several thousand times. The input values (e.g., cost estimates, duration estimates, or occurrence of probabilistic branches) are chosen at random for each iteration. Outputs represent the range of possible outcomes for the project (e.g., project end date, project cost at completion). Typical outputs include a histogram presenting the number of iterations where a particular outcome resulted from the simulation, or a cumulative probability distribution (S-curve) representing the probability of achieving any particular outcome or less. An example S-curve from a Monte Carlo cost risk analysis is shown in Figure 11-13.

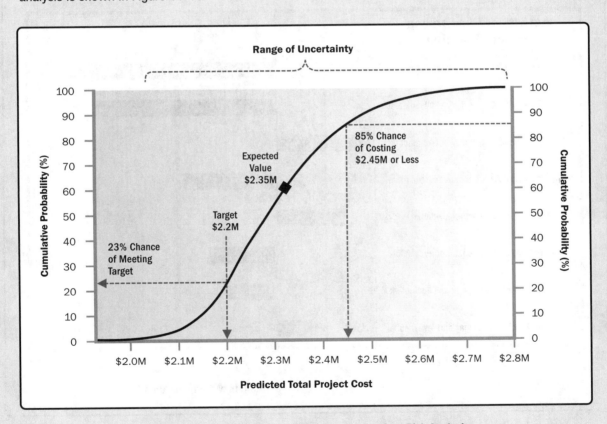

**Figure 11-13. Example S-Curve from Quantitative Cost Risk Analysis**

For a quantitative schedule risk analysis, it is also possible to conduct a criticality analysis that determines which elements of the risk model have the greatest effect on the project critical path. A criticality index is calculated for each element in the risk model, which gives the frequency with which that element appears on the critical path during the simulation, usually expressed as a percentage. The output from a criticality analysis allows the project team to focus risk response planning efforts on those activities with the highest potential effect on the overall schedule performance of the project.

◆ **Sensitivity analysis.** Sensitivity analysis helps to determine which individual project risks or other sources of uncertainty have the most potential impact on project outcomes. It correlates variations in project outcomes with variations in elements of the quantitative risk analysis model.

One typical display of sensitivity analysis is the tornado diagram, which presents the calculated correlation coefficient for each element of the quantitative risk analysis model that can influence the project outcome. This can include individual project risks, project activities with high degrees of variability, or specific sources of ambiguity. Items are ordered by descending strength of correlation, giving the typical tornado appearance. An example tornado diagram is shown in Figure 11-14.

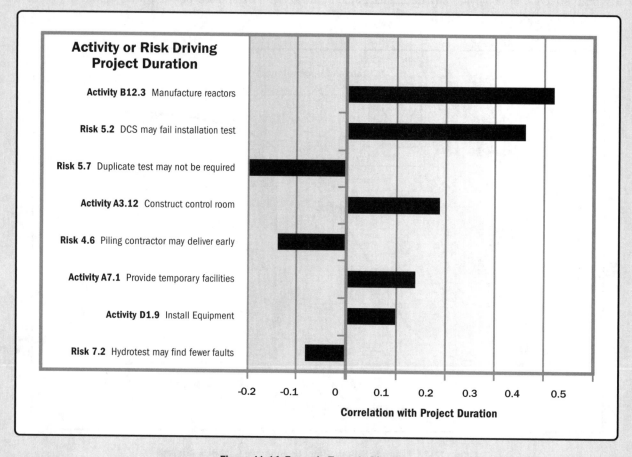

Figure 11-14. Example Tornado Diagram

◆ **Decision tree analysis.** Decision trees are used to support selection of the best of several alternative courses of action. Alternative paths through the project are shown in the decision tree using branches representing different decisions or events, each of which can have associated costs and related individual project risks (including both threats and opportunities). The end-points of branches in the decision tree represent the outcome from following that particular path, which can be negative or positive.

The decision tree is evaluated by calculating the expected monetary value of each branch, allowing the optimal path to be selected. An example decision tree is shown in Figure 11-15.

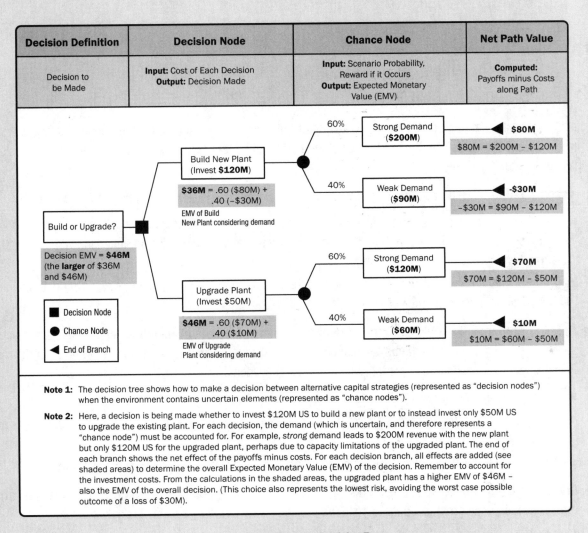

| Decision Definition | Decision Node | Chance Node | Net Path Value |
|---|---|---|---|
| Decision to be Made | **Input:** Cost of Each Decision <br> **Output:** Decision Made | **Input:** Scenario Probability, Reward if it Occurs <br> **Output:** Expected Monetary Value (EMV) | **Computed:** Payoffs minus Costs along Path |

60% → Strong Demand (**$200M**) → ◄ **$80M**
$80M = $200M − $120M

Build New Plant (Invest **$120M**)

**$36M** = .60 ($80M) + .40 (−$30M)
EMV of Build New Plant considering demand

40% → Weak Demand (**$90M**) → ◄ **−$30M**
−$30M = $90M − $120M

Build or Upgrade?

Decision EMV = **$46M** (the **larger** of $36M and $46M)

■ Decision Node
● Chance Node
◄ End of Branch

60% → Strong Demand (**$120M**) → ◄ **$70M**
$70M = $120M − $50M

Upgrade Plant (Invest $50M)

**$46M** = .60 ($70M) + .40 ($10M)
EMV of Upgrade Plant considering demand

40% → Weak Demand (**$60M**) → ◄ **$10M**
$10M = $60M − $50M

**Note 1:** The decision tree shows how to make a decision between alternative capital strategies (represented as "decision nodes") when the environment contains uncertain elements (represented as "chance nodes").

**Note 2:** Here, a decision is being made whether to invest $120M US to build a new plant or to instead invest only $50M US to upgrade the existing plant. For each decision, the demand (which is uncertain, and therefore represents a "chance node") must be accounted for. For example, *strong* demand leads to $200M revenue with the new plant but only $120M US for the upgraded plant, perhaps due to capacity limitations of the upgraded plant. The end of each branch shows the net effect of the payoffs minus costs. For each decision branch, all effects are added (see shaded areas) to determine the overall Expected Monetary Value (EMV) of the decision. Remember to account for the investment costs. From the calculations in the shaded areas, the upgraded plant has a higher EMV of $46M – also the EMV of the overall decision. (This choice also represents the lowest risk, avoiding the worst case possible outcome of a loss of $30M).

**Figure 11-15. Example Decision Tree**

◆ **Influence diagrams.** Influence diagrams are graphical aids to decision making under uncertainty. An influence diagram represents a project or situation within the project as a set of entities, outcomes, and influences, together with the relationships and effects between them. Where an element in the influence diagram is uncertain as a result of the existence of individual project risks or other sources of uncertainty, this can be represented in the influence diagram using ranges or probability distributions. The influence diagram is then evaluated using a simulation technique, such as Monte Carlo analysis, to indicate which elements have the greatest influence on key outcomes. Outputs from an influence diagram are similar to other quantitative risk analysis methods, including S-curves and tornado diagrams.

## 11.4.3 PERFORM QUANTITATIVE RISK ANALYSIS: OUTPUTS

### 11.4.3.1 PROJECT DOCUMENTS UPDATES

Project documents that can be considered as outputs for this process include but are not limited to the risk report described in Section 11.2.3.2. The risk report will be updated to reflect the results of the quantitative risk analysis. This will typically include:

◆ **Assessment of overall project risk exposure.** Overall project risk is reflected in two key measures:

■ Chances of project success, indicated by the probability that the project will achieve its key objectives (e.g., required end date or interim milestones, required cost target, etc.) given the identified individual project risks and other sources of uncertainty; and

■ Degree of inherent variability remaining within the project at the time the analysis was conducted, indicated by the range of possible project outcomes.

◆ **Detailed probabilistic analysis of the project.** Key outputs from the quantitative risk analysis are presented, such as S-curves, tornado diagrams, and criticality analysis, together with a narrative interpretation of the results. Possible detailed results of a quantitative risk analysis may include:

■ Amount of contingency reserve needed to provide a specified level of confidence;

■ Identification of individual project risks or other sources of uncertainty that have the greatest effect on the project critical path; and

■ Major drivers of overall project risk, with the greatest influence on uncertainty in project outcomes.

◆ **Prioritized list of individual project risks.** This list includes those individual project risks that pose the greatest threat or present the greatest opportunity to the project, as indicated by sensitivity analysis.

◆ **Trends in quantitative risk analysis results.** As the analysis is repeated at different times during the project life cycle, trends may become apparent that inform the planning of risk responses.

◆ **Recommended risk responses.** The risk report may present suggested responses to the level of overall project risk exposure or key individual project risks, based on the results of the quantitative risk analysis. These recommendations will form inputs to the Plan Risk Responses process.

# 11.5 PLAN RISK RESPONSES

Plan Risk Responses is the process of developing options, selecting strategies, and agreeing on actions to address overall project risk exposure, as well as to treat individual project risks. The key benefit of this process is that it identifies appropriate ways to address overall project risk and individual project risks. This process also allocates resources and inserts activities into project documents and the project management plan as needed. This process is performed throughout the project. The inputs, tools and techniques, and outputs of the process are depicted in Figure 11-16. Figure 11-17 depicts the data flow diagram for the process.

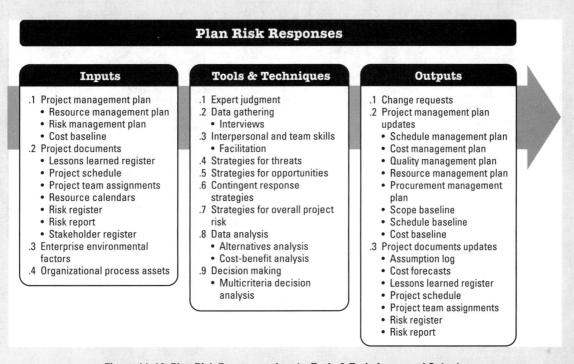

**Plan Risk Responses**

| Inputs | Tools & Techniques | Outputs |
|---|---|---|
| .1 Project management plan<br>  • Resource management plan<br>  • Risk management plan<br>  • Cost baseline<br>.2 Project documents<br>  • Lessons learned register<br>  • Project schedule<br>  • Project team assignments<br>  • Resource calendars<br>  • Risk register<br>  • Risk report<br>  • Stakeholder register<br>.3 Enterprise environmental factors<br>.4 Organizational process assets | .1 Expert judgment<br>.2 Data gathering<br>  • Interviews<br>.3 Interpersonal and team skills<br>  • Facilitation<br>.4 Strategies for threats<br>.5 Strategies for opportunities<br>.6 Contingent response strategies<br>.7 Strategies for overall project risk<br>.8 Data analysis<br>  • Alternatives analysis<br>  • Cost-benefit analysis<br>.9 Decision making<br>  • Multicriteria decision analysis | .1 Change requests<br>.2 Project management plan updates<br>  • Schedule management plan<br>  • Cost management plan<br>  • Quality management plan<br>  • Resource management plan<br>  • Procurement management plan<br>  • Scope baseline<br>  • Schedule baseline<br>  • Cost baseline<br>.3 Project documents updates<br>  • Assumption log<br>  • Cost forecasts<br>  • Lessons learned register<br>  • Project schedule<br>  • Project team assignments<br>  • Risk register<br>  • Risk report |

**Figure 11-16. Plan Risk Responses: Inputs, Tools & Techniques, and Outputs**

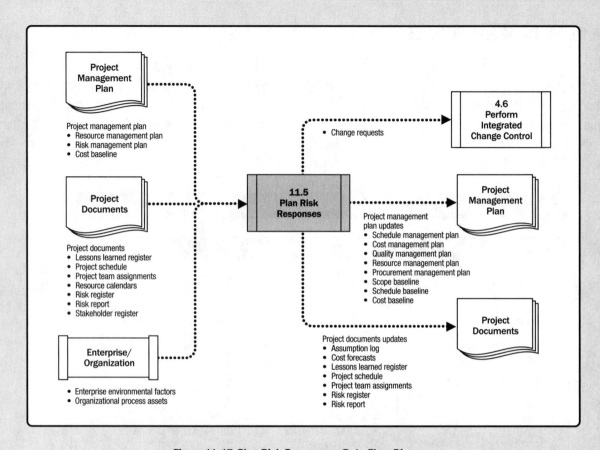

**Figure 11-17. Plan Risk Responses: Data Flow Diagram**

Effective and appropriate risk responses can minimize individual threats, maximize individual opportunities, and reduce overall project risk exposure. Unsuitable risk responses can have the converse effect. Once risks have been identified, analyzed, and prioritized, plans should be developed by the nominated risk owner for addressing every individual project risk the project team considers to be sufficiently important, either because of the threat it poses to the project objectives or the opportunity it offers. The project manager should also consider how to respond appropriately to the current level of overall project risk.

Risk responses should be appropriate for the significance of the risk, cost-effective in meeting the challenge, realistic within the project context, agreed upon by all parties involved, and owned by a responsible person. Selecting the optimal risk response from several options is often required. The strategy or mix of strategies most likely to be effective should be selected for each risk. Structured decision-making techniques may be used to choose the most appropriate response. For large or complex projects, it may be appropriate to use a mathematical optimization model or real options analysis as a basis for a more robust economic analysis of alternative risk response strategies.

Specific actions are developed to implement the agreed-upon risk response strategy, including primary and backup strategies, as necessary. A contingency plan (or fallback plan) can be developed for implementation if the selected strategy turns out not to be fully effective or if an accepted risk occurs. Secondary risks should also be identified. Secondary risks are risks that arise as a direct result of implementing a risk response. A contingency reserve is often allocated for time or cost. If developed, it may include identification of the conditions that trigger its use.

## 11.5.1 PLAN RISK RESPONSES: INPUTS

### 11.5.1.1 PROJECT MANAGEMENT PLAN

Described in Section 4.2.3.1. Project management plan components include but are not limited to:

◆ **Resource management plan.** Described in Section 9.1.3.1. The resource management plan is used to help determine how resources allocated to agreed-upon risk responses will be coordinated with other project resources.

◆ **Risk management plan.** Described in Section 11.1.3.1. Risk management roles and responsibilities and risk thresholds are used in this process.

◆ **Cost baseline.** Described in Section 7.3.3.1. The cost baseline has information on the contingency fund that is allocated to respond to risks.

## 11.5.1.2 PROJECT DOCUMENTS

Project documents that can be considered as inputs for this process include but are not limited to:

◆ **Lessons learned register.** Described in Section 4.4.3.1. Lessons learned about effective risk responses used in earlier phases of the project are reviewed to determine if similar responses might be useful during the remainder of the project.

◆ **Project schedule.** Described in Section 6.5.3.2. The schedule is used to determine how agreed-upon risk responses will be scheduled alongside other project activities.

◆ **Project team assignments.** Described in Section 9.3.3.2. Project team assignments can show the resources that can be allocated to agreed-upon risk responses.

◆ **Resource calendars.** Described in Section 9.2.1.2. Resource calendars identify when potential resources are available to be allocated to agreed-upon risk responses.

◆ **Risk register.** Described in Section 11.2.3.1. The risk register contains details of individual project risks that have been identified and prioritized, and for which risk responses are required. The priority level for each risk can help to guide the selection of appropriate risk responses. For example, high-priority threats or opportunities may require priority action and highly proactive response strategies. Threats and opportunities in the low-priority zone may not require proactive management action beyond being placed in the risk register as part of the watch list or adding a contingency reserve.

The risk register identifies the nominated risk owner for each risk. It may also contain preliminary risk responses identified earlier in the Project Risk Management process. The risk register may provide other data on identified risks that can assist in planning risk responses, including root causes, risk triggers and warning signs, risks requiring responses in the near term, and risks where a need for additional analysis has been identified.

◆ **Risk report.** Described in Section 11.2.3.2. The risk report presents the current level of overall risk exposure of the project that will inform selection of the risk response strategy. The risk report may also list individual project risks in priority order and provide additional analysis of the distribution of individual project risks that may inform risk response selection.

◆ **Stakeholder register.** Described in Section 13.1.3.1. The stakeholder register identifies potential owners for risk responses.

### 11.5.1.3 ENTERPRISE ENVIRONMENTAL FACTORS

The enterprise environmental factors that can influence the Plan Risk Responses process include but are not limited to the risk appetite and thresholds of key stakeholders.

### 11.5.1.4 ORGANIZATIONAL PROCESS ASSETS

The organizational process assets that can influence the Plan Risk Responses process include but are not limited to:

◆ Templates for the risk management plan, risk register, and risk report;

◆ Historical databases; and

◆ Lessons learned repositories from similar projects.

## 11.5.2 PLAN RISK RESPONSES: TOOLS AND TECHNIQUES

### 11.5.2.1 EXPERT JUDGMENT

Described in Section 4.1.2.1. Expertise should be considered from individuals or groups with specialized knowledge in the following topics:

◆ Threat response strategies,

◆ Opportunity response strategies,

◆ Contingent response strategies, and

◆ Overall project risk response strategies.

Expert input may be sought from individuals with particular subject matter expertise relevant to a specific individual project risk, for example, where specialist technical knowledge is required.

## 11.5.2.2 DATA GATHERING

Data-gathering techniques that can be used for this process include but are not limited to interviews (see Section 5.2.2.2). Development of responses to individual project risks and overall project risk may be undertaken during structured or semi-structured interviews (see Section 5.2.2.2) with risk owners. Other stakeholders may also be interviewed if necessary. The interviewer should promote an environment of trust and confidentiality in the interview setting to encourage honest and unbiased decisions.

## 11.5.2.3 INTERPERSONAL AND TEAM SKILLS

Interpersonal and team skills that can be used for this process includes but are not limited to facilitation (see Section 4.1.2.3). The use of facilitation improves the effectiveness of developing responses to individual project risks and overall project risk. A skilled facilitator can help risk owners understand the risk, identify and compare alternative possible risk response strategies, choose an appropriate response strategy, and identify and overcome sources of bias.

## 11.5.2.4 STRATEGIES FOR THREATS

Five alternative strategies may be considered for dealing with threats, as follows:

◆ **Escalate.** Escalation is appropriate when the project team or the project sponsor agrees that a threat is outside the scope of the project or that the proposed response would exceed the project manager's authority. Escalated risks are managed at the program level, portfolio level, or other relevant part of the organization, and not on the project level. The project manager determines who should be notified about the threat and communicates the details to that person or part of the organization. It is important that ownership of escalated threats is accepted by the relevant party in the organization. Threats are usually escalated to the level that matches the objectives that would be affected if the threat occurred. Escalated threats are not monitored further by the project team after escalation, although they may be recorded in the risk register for information.

◆ **Avoid.** Risk avoidance is when the project team acts to eliminate the threat or protect the project from its impact. It may be appropriate for high-priority threats with a high probability of occurrence and a large negative impact. Avoidance may involve changing some aspect of the project management plan or changing the objective that is in jeopardy in order to eliminate the threat entirely, reducing its probability of occurrence to zero. The risk owner may also take action to isolate the project objectives from the risk's impact if it were to occur. Examples of avoidance actions may include removing the cause of a threat, extending the schedule, changing the project strategy, or reducing scope. Some risks can be avoided by clarifying requirements, obtaining information, improving communication, or acquiring expertise.

◆ **Transfer.** Transfer involves shifting ownership of a threat to a third party to manage the risk and to bear the impact if the threat occurs. Risk transfer often involves payment of a risk premium to the party taking on the threat. Transfer can be achieved by a range of actions, which include but are not limited to the use of insurance, performance bonds, warranties, guarantees, etc. Agreements may be used to transfer ownership and liability for specified risks to another party.

◆ **Mitigate.** In risk mitigation, action is taken to reduce the probability of occurrence and/or impact of a threat. Early mitigation action is often more effective than trying to repair the damage after the threat has occurred. Adopting less complex processes, conducting more tests, or choosing a more stable seller are examples of mitigation actions. Mitigation may involve prototype development (see Section 5.2.2.8) to reduce the risk of scaling up from a bench-scale model of a process or product. Where it is not possible to reduce probability, a mitigation response might reduce the impact by targeting factors that drive the severity. For example, designing redundancy into a system may reduce the impact from a failure of the original component.

◆ **Accept.** Risk acceptance acknowledges the existence of a threat, but no proactive action is taken. This strategy may be appropriate for low-priority threats, and it may also be adopted where it is not possible or cost-effective to address a threat in any other way. Acceptance can be either active or passive. The most common active acceptance strategy is to establish a contingency reserve, including amounts of time, money, or resources to handle the threat if it occurs. Passive acceptance involves no proactive action apart from periodic review of the threat to ensure that it does not change significantly.

## 11.5.2.5 STRATEGIES FOR OPPORTUNITIES

Five alternative strategies may be considered for dealing with opportunities, as follows:

◆ **Escalate.** This risk response strategy is appropriate when the project team or the project sponsor agrees that an opportunity is outside the scope of the project or that the proposed response would exceed the project manager's authority. Escalated opportunities are managed at the program level, portfolio level, or other relevant part of the organization, and not on the project level. The project manager determines who should be notified about the opportunity and communicates the details to that person or part of the organization. It is important that ownership of escalated opportunities is accepted by the relevant party in the organization. Opportunities are usually escalated to the level that matches the objectives that would be affected if the opportunity occurred. Escalated opportunities are not monitored further by the project team after escalation, although they may be recorded in the risk register for information.

◆ **Exploit.** The exploit strategy may be selected for high-priority opportunities where the organization wants to ensure that the opportunity is realized. This strategy seeks to capture the benefit associated with a particular opportunity by ensuring that it definitely happens, increasing the probability of occurrence to 100%. Examples of exploiting responses may include assigning an organization's most talented resources to the project to reduce the time to completion, or using new technologies or technology upgrades to reduce cost and duration.

◆ **Share.** Sharing involves transferring ownership of an opportunity to a third party so that it shares some of the benefit if the opportunity occurs. It is important to select the new owner of a shared opportunity carefully so they are best able to capture the opportunity for the benefit of the project. Risk sharing often involves payment of a risk premium to the party taking on the opportunity. Examples of sharing actions include forming risk-sharing partnerships, teams, special-purpose companies, or joint ventures.

◆ **Enhance.** The enhance strategy is used to increase the probability and/or impact of an opportunity. Early enhancement action is often more effective than trying to improve the benefit after the opportunity has occurred. The probability of occurrence of an opportunity may be increased by focusing attention on its causes. Where it is not possible to increase probability, an enhancement response might increase the impact by targeting factors that drive the size of the potential benefit. Examples of enhancing opportunities include adding more resources to an activity to finish early.

◆ **Accept.** Accepting an opportunity acknowledges its existence but no proactive action is taken. This strategy may be appropriate for low-priority opportunities, and it may also be adopted where it is not possible or cost-effective to address an opportunity in any other way. Acceptance can be either active or passive. The most common active acceptance strategy is to establish a contingency reserve, including amounts of time, money, or resources to take advantage of the opportunity if it occurs. Passive acceptance involves no proactive action apart from periodic review of the opportunity to ensure that it does not change significantly.

### 11.5.2.6 CONTINGENT RESPONSE STRATEGIES

Some responses are designed for use only if certain events occur. For some risks, it is appropriate for the project team to make a response plan that will only be executed under certain predefined conditions, if it is believed that there will be sufficient warning to implement the plan. Events that trigger the contingency response, such as missing intermediate milestones or gaining higher priority with a seller, should be defined and tracked. Risk responses identified using this technique are often called contingency plans or fallback plans and include identified triggering events that set the plans in effect.

### 11.5.2.7 STRATEGIES FOR OVERALL PROJECT RISK

Risk responses should be planned and implemented not only for individual project risks but also to address overall project risk. The same risk response strategies that are used to deal with individual project risks can also be applied to overall project risk:

◆ **Avoid.** Where the level of overall project risk is significantly negative and outside the agreed-upon risk thresholds for the project, an avoid strategy may be adopted. This involves taking focused action to reduce the negative effect of uncertainty on the project as a whole and bring the project back within the thresholds. An example of avoidance at the overall project level would include removal of high-risk elements of scope from the project. Where it is not possible to bring the project back within the thresholds, the project may be canceled. This represents the most extreme degree of risk avoidance and it should be used only if the overall level of threat is, and will remain, unacceptable.

◆ **Exploit.** Where the level of overall project risk is significantly positive and outside the agreed-upon risk thresholds for the project, an exploit strategy may be adopted. This involves taking focused action to capture the positive effect of uncertainty on the project as a whole. An example of exploiting at the overall project level would include addition of high-benefit elements of scope to the project to add value or benefits to stakeholders. Alternatively the risk thresholds for the project may be modified with the agreement of key stakeholders in order to embrace the opportunity.

◆ **Transfer/share.** If the level of overall project risk is high but the organization is unable to address it effectively, a third party may be involved to manage the risk on behalf of the organization. Where overall project risk is negative, a transfer strategy is required, which may involve payment of a risk premium. In the case of high positive overall project risk, ownership may be shared in order to reap the associated benefits. Examples of both transfer and share strategies for overall project risk include but are not limited to setting up a collaborative business structure in which the buyer and the seller share the overall project risk, launching a joint venture or special-purpose company, or subcontracting key elements of the project.

◆ **Mitigate/enhance.** These strategies involve changing the level of overall project risk to optimize the chances of achieving the project's objectives. The mitigation strategy is used where overall project risk is negative, and enhancement applies when it is positive. Examples of mitigation or enhancement strategies include replanning the project, changing the scope and boundaries of the project, modifying project priority, changing resource allocations, adjusting delivery times, etc.

◆ **Accept.** Where no proactive risk response strategy is possible to address overall project risk, the organization may choose to continue with the project as currently defined, even if overall project risk is outside the agreed-upon thresholds. Acceptance can be either active or passive. The most common active acceptance strategy is to establish an overall contingency reserve for the project, including amounts of time, money, or resources to be used if the project exceeds its thresholds. Passive acceptance involves no proactive action apart from periodic review of the level of overall project risk to ensure that it does not change significantly.

## 11.5.2.8 DATA ANALYSIS

A number of alternative risk response strategies may be considered. Data analysis techniques that can be used to select a preferred risk response strategy include but are not limited to:

◆ **Alternatives analysis.** A simple comparison of the characteristics and requirements of alternative risk response options can lead to a decision on which response is most appropriate.

◆ **Cost-benefit analysis.** If the impact of an individual project risk can be quantified in monetary terms, then the cost-effectiveness of alternative risk response strategies can be determined using cost-benefit analysis (see Section 8.1.2.3). The ratio of (change in impact level) divided by (implementation cost) gives the cost effectiveness of the response strategy, with a higher ratio indicating a more effective response.

## 11.5.2.9 DECISION MAKING

Decision-making techniques that can be used to select a risk response strategy include but are not limited to multicriteria decision analysis (described in Section 8.1.2.4). One or more risk response strategies may be under consideration. Decision-making techniques can help prioritize risk response strategies. Multicriteria decision analysis uses a decision matrix to provide a systematic approach for establishing key decision criteria, evaluating and ranking alternatives, and selecting a preferred option. Criteria for risk response selection may include but are not limited to cost of response, likely effectiveness of response in changing probability and/or impact, resource availability, timing constraints (urgency, proximity, and dormancy), level of impact if the risk occurs, effect of response on related risks, introduction of secondary risks, etc. Different strategies may be selected later in the project if the original choice proves to be ineffective.

## 11.5.3 PLAN RISK RESPONSES: OUTPUTS

### 11.5.3.1 CHANGE REQUESTS

Described in Section 4.3.3.4. Planned risk responses may result in a change request to the cost and schedule baselines or other components of the project management plan. Change requests are processed for review and disposition through the Perform Integrated Change Control process (Section 4.6).

### 11.5.3.2 PROJECT MANAGEMENT PLAN UPDATES

Any change to the project management plan goes through the organization's change control process via a change request. Components that may require a change request for the project management plan include but are not limited to:

◆ **Schedule management plan.** Described in Section 6.1.3.1. Changes to the schedule management plan, such as changes to resource loading and leveling, or updates to the schedule strategy, are incorporated.

◆ **Cost management plan.** Described in Section 7.1.3.1. Changes to the cost management plan, such as changes to cost accounting, tracking, and reports, as well as updates to the budget strategy and how contingency reserves are consumed, are incorporated.

◆ **Quality management plan.** Described in Section 8.1.3.1. Changes to the quality management plan, such as changes to approaches for meeting requirements, quality management approaches, or quality control processes, are incorporated.

◆ **Resource management plan.** Described in Section 9.1.3.1. Changes to the resource management plan, such as changes to resource allocation, as well as updates to the resource strategy, are incorporated.

◆ **Procurement management plan.** Described in Section 12.1.3.1. Changes to the procurement management plan, such as alterations in the make-or-buy decision or contract type(s), are incorporated.

◆ **Scope baseline.** Described in Section 5.4.3.1. Changes in the scope baseline are incorporated in response to approved changes in scope that may arise from agreed-upon risk responses.

◆ **Schedule baseline.** Described in Section 6.5.3.1. Changes in the schedule baseline are incorporated in response to approved changes in schedule estimates that may arise from agreed-upon risk responses.

◆ **Cost baseline.** Described in Section 7.3.3.1. Changes in the cost baseline are incorporated in response to approved changes in cost estimates that may arise from agreed-upon risk responses.

## 11.5.3.3 PROJECT DOCUMENTS UPDATES

Project documents that may be updated as a result of carrying out this process include but are not limited to:

◆ **Assumption log.** Described in Section 4.1.3.2. During the Plan Risk Responses process, new assumptions may be made, new constraints may be identified, and existing assumptions or constraints may be revisited and changed. The assumption log should be updated with this new information.

◆ **Cost forecasts.** Described in Section 7.4.3.2. Cost forecasts may change as a result of planned risk responses.

◆ **Lessons learned register.** Described in Section 4.4.3.1. The lessons learned register is updated with information about risk responses that may be useful for future phases of the project or future projects.

◆ **Project schedule.** Described in Section 6.5.3.2. Activities relating to agreed-upon risk responses may be added to the project schedule.

◆ **Project team assignments.** Described in Section 9.3.3.2. Once the responses are confirmed, the necessary resources should be allocated to each action associated with a risk response plan. These resources include suitably qualified and experienced personnel to execute the agreed-upon action (usually within the project team) a specific budget and time allowance for the action, and any required technical resources to complete the action.

◆ **Risk register.** Described in Section 11.2.3.1. The risk register is updated when appropriate risk responses are chosen and agreed upon. Updates to the risk register may include but are not limited to:

- Agreed-upon response strategies;
- Specific actions to implement the chosen response strategy;
- Trigger conditions, symptoms, and warning signs of a risk occurrence;
- Budget and schedule activities required to implement the chosen responses;
- Contingency plans and risk triggers that call for their execution;
- Fallback plans for use when a risk that has occurred and the primary response proves to be inadequate;
- Residual risks that are expected to remain after planned responses have been taken, as well as those that have been deliberately accepted; and
- Secondary risks that arise as a direct outcome of implementing a risk response.

◆ **Risk report.** Described in Section 11.2.3.2. The risk report may be updated to present agreed-upon responses to the current overall project risk exposure and high-priority risks, together with the expected changes that may be expected as a result of implementing these responses.

# 11.6 IMPLEMENT RISK RESPONSES

Implement Risk Responses is the process of implementing agreed-upon risk response plans. The key benefit of this process is that it ensures that agreed-upon risk responses are executed as planned in order to address overall project risk exposure, minimize individual project threats, and maximize individual project opportunities. This process is performed throughout the project. The inputs, tools and techniques, and outputs of the process are depicted in Figure 11-18. Figure 11-19 depicts the data flow diagram for the process.

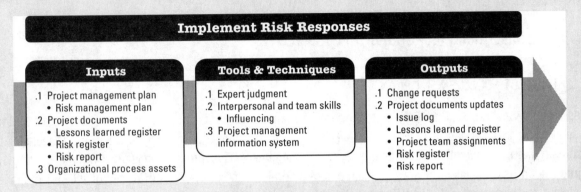

**Implement Risk Responses**

| Inputs | Tools & Techniques | Outputs |
|---|---|---|
| .1 Project management plan<br>• Risk management plan<br>.2 Project documents<br>• Lessons learned register<br>• Risk register<br>• Risk report<br>.3 Organizational process assets | .1 Expert judgment<br>.2 Interpersonal and team skills<br>• Influencing<br>.3 Project management information system | .1 Change requests<br>.2 Project documents updates<br>• Issue log<br>• Lessons learned register<br>• Project team assignments<br>• Risk register<br>• Risk report |

Figure 11-18. Implement Risk Responses: Inputs, Tools & Techniques, and Outputs

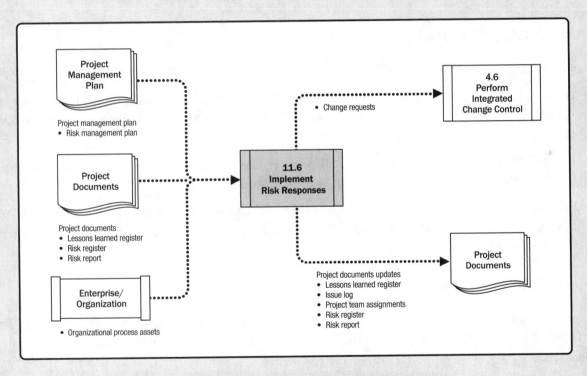

Figure 11-19. Implement Risk Responses: Data Flow Diagram

Proper attention to the Implement Risk Responses process will ensure that agreed-upon risk responses are actually executed. A common problem with Project Risk Management is that project teams spend effort in identifying and analyzing risks and developing risk responses, then risk responses are agreed upon and documented in the risk register and risk report, but no action is taken to manage the risk.

Only if risk owners give the required level of effort to implementing the agreed-upon responses will the overall risk exposure of the project and individual threats and opportunities be managed proactively.

## 11.6.1 IMPLEMENT RISK RESPONSES: INPUTS

### 11.6.1.1 PROJECT MANAGEMENT PLAN

Described in Section 4.2.3.1. Project management plan components include but are not limited to the risk management plan. Described in Section 11.1.3.1, the risk management plan lists the roles and responsibilities of project team members and other stakeholders for risk management. This information is used when allocating owners for agreed-upon risk responses. The risk management plan also defines the level of detail for the risk management methodology for the project. It also specifies risk thresholds for the project based on the risk appetite of key stakeholders, which define the acceptable target that the implementation of risk responses is required to achieve.

### 11.6.1.2 PROJECT DOCUMENTS

Project documents that can be considered as inputs for this process include but are not limited to:

◆ **Lessons learned register.** Described in Section 4.4.3.1. Lessons learned earlier in the project with regard to implementing risk responses can be applied to later phases in the project to improve the effectiveness of this process.

◆ **Risk register.** Described in Section 11.2.3.1. The risk register records the agreed-upon risk responses for each individual risk and the nominated owners for each response plan.

◆ **Risk report.** Described in Section 11.2.3.2. The risk report includes an assessment of the current overall project risk exposure, as well as the agreed-upon risk response strategy. It also describes the major individual project risks with their planned responses.

### 11.6.1.3 ORGANIZATIONAL PROCESS ASSETS

The organizational process assets that can influence the Implement Risk Responses process include but are not limited to the lessons learned repository from similar completed projects that indicate the effectiveness of particular risk responses.

## 11.6.2 IMPLEMENT RISK RESPONSES: TOOLS AND TECHNIQUES

### 11.6.2.1 EXPERT JUDGMENT

Described in Section 4.1.2.1. Expertise should be considered from individuals or groups with specialized knowledge to validate or modify risk responses if necessary, and decide how to implement them in the most efficient and effective manner.

### 11.6.2.2 INTERPERSONAL AND TEAM SKILLS

Interpersonal and team skills that can be used for this process include but are not limited to influencing. Some risk response actions may be owned by people outside the immediate project team or who have other competing demands. The project manager or person responsible for facilitating the risk process may need to exercise influencing (see Section 9.5.2.1) to encourage nominated risk owners to take necessary action where required.

### 11.6.2.3 PROJECT MANAGEMENT INFORMATION SYSTEM (PMIS)

Described in Section 4.3.2.2. Project management information systems can include schedule, resource, and cost software to ensure that agreed-upon risk response plans and their associated activities are integrated into the project alongside other project activities.

## 11.6.3 IMPLEMENT RISK RESPONSES: OUTPUTS

### 11.6.3.1 CHANGE REQUESTS

Described in Section 4.3.3.4. Implementation of risk responses may result in a change request to the cost and schedule baselines or other components of the project management plan. Change requests are processed for review and disposition through the Perform Integrated Change Control process (Section 4.6).

## 11.6.3.2 PROJECT DOCUMENTS UPDATES

Project documents that may be updated as a result of carrying out this process include but are not limited to:

◆ **Issue log.** Described in Section 4.3.3.3. Where issues are identified as part of the Implement Risk Responses process, they are recorded in the issue log.

◆ **Lessons learned register.** Described in Section 4.4.3.1. The lessons learned register is updated with information on challenges encountered when implementing risk responses and how they could have been avoided, as well as approaches that worked well for implementing risk responses.

◆ **Project team assignments.** Described in Section 9.3.3.2. Once the risk responses are confirmed, the necessary resources should be allocated to each action associated with a risk response plan. These resources include suitably qualified and experienced personnel to execute the agreed-upon action (usually within the project team), a specific budget and time allowance for the action, and any required technical resources to complete the action.

◆ **Risk register.** Described in Section 11.2.3.1. The risk register may be updated to reflect any changes to the previously agreed-upon risk responses for individual project risks that are subsequently made as a result of the Implement Risk Responses process.

◆ **Risk report.** Described in Section 11.2.3.2. The risk report may be updated to reflect any changes to the previously agreed-upon risk response to overall project risk exposure that are subsequently made as a result of the Implement Risk Responses process.

# 11.7 MONITOR RISKS

Monitor Risks is the process of monitoring the implementation of agreed-upon risk response plans, tracking identified risks, identifying and analyzing new risks, and evaluating risk process effectiveness throughout the project. The key benefit of this process is that it enables project decisions to be based on current information about overall project risk exposure and individual project risks. This process is performed throughout the project. The inputs, tools and techniques, and outputs of the process are depicted in Figure 11-20. Figure 11-21 depicts the data flow diagram for the process.

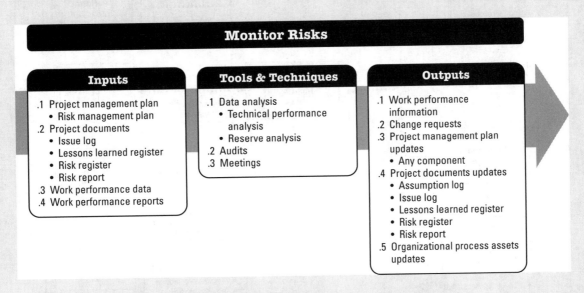

**Monitor Risks**

| Inputs | Tools & Techniques | Outputs |
|---|---|---|
| .1 Project management plan<br>• Risk management plan<br>.2 Project documents<br>• Issue log<br>• Lessons learned register<br>• Risk register<br>• Risk report<br>.3 Work performance data<br>.4 Work performance reports | .1 Data analysis<br>• Technical performance analysis<br>• Reserve analysis<br>.2 Audits<br>.3 Meetings | .1 Work performance information<br>.2 Change requests<br>.3 Project management plan updates<br>• Any component<br>.4 Project documents updates<br>• Assumption log<br>• Issue log<br>• Lessons learned register<br>• Risk register<br>• Risk report<br>.5 Organizational process assets updates |

Figure 11-20. Monitor Risks: Inputs, Tools & Techniques, and Outputs

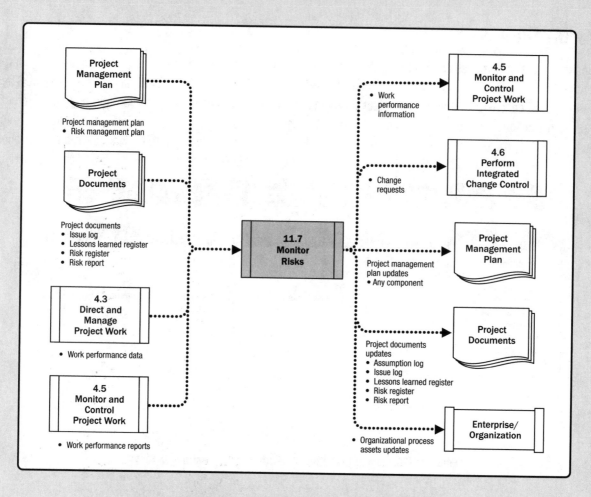

**Figure 11-21. Monitor Risks: Data Flow Diagram**

In order to ensure that the project team and key stakeholders are aware of the current level of risk exposure, project work should be continuously monitored for new, changing, and outdated individual project risks and for changes in the level of overall project risk by applying the Monitor Risks process. The Monitor Risks process uses performance information generated during project execution to determine if:

◆ Implemented risk responses are effective,

◆ Level of overall project risk has changed,

◆ Status of identified individual project risks has changed,

◆ New individual project risks have arisen,

◆ Risk management approach is still appropriate,

◆ Project assumptions are still valid,

◆ Risk management policies and procedures are being followed,

◆ Contingency reserves for cost or schedule require modification, and

◆ Project strategy is still valid.

## 11.7.1 MONITOR RISKS: INPUTS

### 11.7.1.1 PROJECT MANAGEMENT PLAN

Described in Section 4.2.3.1. Project management plan components include but are not limited to the risk management plan. Described in Section 11.3.1.1. The risk management plan provides guidance on how and when risks should be reviewed, which policies and procedures should be followed, the roles and responsibilities in the monitoring process, and reporting formats.

### 11.7.1.2 PROJECT DOCUMENTS

Project documents that should be considered as inputs for this process include but are not limited to:

◆ **Issue log.** Described in Section 4.3.3.3. The issue log is used to see if any of the open issues have been updated and necessitate an update to the risk register.

◆ **Lessons learned register.** Described in Section 4.4.3.1. Risk-related lessons from earlier in the project can be applied to later phases in the project.

◆ **Risk register.** Described in Section 11.2.3.1. The risk register has key inputs that include identified individual project risks, risk owners, agreed-upon risk responses, and specific implementation actions. It may also provide other details including control actions for assessing the effectiveness of response plans, symptoms and warning signs of risk, residual and secondary risks, and a watch list of low-priority risks.

◆ **Risk report.** Described in Section 11.2.3.2. The risk report includes an assessment of the current overall project risk exposure as well as the agreed-upon risk response strategy. It also describes the major individual risks with planned responses and risk owners.

### 11.7.1.3 WORK PERFORMANCE DATA

Described in Section 4.3.3.2. Work performance data contains data on project status such as risk responses that have been implemented, risks that have occurred, risks that are active and those that have been closed out.

### 11.7.1.4 WORK PERFORMANCE REPORTS

Described in Section 4 5.3.1. Work performance reports provide information from performance measurements that can be analyzed to provide project work performance information including variance analysis, earned value data, and forecasting data. This information could be relevant when monitoring performance-related risks.

## 11.7.2 MONITOR RISKS: TOOLS AND TECHNIQUES

### 11.7.2.1 DATA ANALYSIS

Data analysis techniques that can be used for this process include but are not limited to:

◆ **Technical performance analysis.** Technical performance analysis compares technical accomplishments during project execution to the schedule of technical achievement. It requires the definition of objective, quantifiable measures of technical performance, which can be used to compare actual results against targets. Such technical performance measures may include weight, transaction times, number of delivered defects, storage capacity, etc. Deviation can indicate the potential impact of threats or opportunities.

◆ **Reserve analysis.** Described in Section 7.2.2.6. Throughout execution of the project, some individual project risks may occur with positive or negative impacts on budget or schedule contingency reserves. Reserve analysis compares the amount of the contingency reserves remaining to the amount of risk remaining at any time in the project in order to determine if the remaining reserve is adequate. This may be communicated using various graphical representations, including a burndown chart.

### 11.7.2.2 AUDITS

Described in Section 8.2.2.5. Risk audits are a type of audit that may be used to consider the effectiveness of the risk management process. The project manager is responsible for ensuring that risk audits are performed at an appropriate frequency, as defined in the project's risk management plan. Risk audits may be included during routine project review meetings or may form part of a risk review meeting, or the team may choose to hold separate risk audit meetings. The format for the risk audit and its objectives should be clearly defined before the audit is conducted.

### 11.7.2.3 MEETINGS

Meetings that can be used during this process include but are not limited to risk reviews. Risk reviews are scheduled regularly and should examine and document the effectiveness of risk responses in dealing with overall project risk and with identified individual project risks. Risk reviews may also result in identification of new individual project risks, (including secondary risks that arise from agreed-upon risk responses), reassessment of current risks, the closing of risks that are outdated, issues that have arisen as the result of risks that have occurred, and identification of lessons to be learned for implementation in ongoing phases in the current project or in similar projects in the future. The risk review may be conducted as part of a periodic project status meeting or a dedicated risk review meeting may be held, as specified in the risk management plan.

## 11.7.3 MONITOR RISKS: OUTPUTS

### 11.7.3.1 WORK PERFORMANCE INFORMATION

Described in Section 4.5.1.3. Work performance information includes information on how project risk management is performing by comparing the individual risks that have occurred with the expectation of how they would occur. This information indicates the effectiveness of the response planning and response implementation processes.

### 11.7.3.2 CHANGE REQUESTS

Described in Section 4.3.3.4. The Monitor Risks process may result in a change request to the cost and schedule baselines or other components of the project management plan. Change requests are processed for review and disposition through the Perform Integrated Change Control process (Section 4.6).

Change requests can include recommended corrective and preventive actions to address the current level of overall project risk or to address individual project risks.

### 11.7.3.3 PROJECT MANAGEMENT PLAN UPDATES

Any change to the project management plan goes through the organization's change control process via a change request. This may affect any component of the project management plan.

### 11.7.3.4 PROJECT DOCUMENTS UPDATES

Project documents that may be updated as a result of carrying out this process include but are not limited to:

◆ **Assumption log.** Described in Section 4.1.3.2. During the Monitor Risks process, new assumptions may be made, new constraints may be identified, and existing assumptions or constraints may be revisited and changed. The assumption log is updated with this new information.

◆ **Issue log.** Described in Section 4.3.3.3. Where issues are identified as part of the Monitor Risks process, these are recorded in the issue log.

◆ **Lessons learned register.** Described in Section 4.4.3.1. The lessons learned register is updated with any risk-related lessons learned during risk reviews so these can be used on later phases of the project or in future projects.

◆ **Risk register.** Described in Section 11.2.3.1. The risk register is updated with information on individual project risks generated during the Monitor Risks process. This may include adding new risks, updating outdated risks or risks that were realized, updating risk responses, and so forth.

◆ **Risk report**. Described in Section 11.2.3.2. As new information becomes available through the Monitor Risks process, the risk report is updated to reflect the current status of major individual project risks and the current level of overall project risk. The risk report may also include details of the top individual project risks, agreed-upon responses and owners, and conclusions and recommendations. It may also include conclusions from risk audits on the effectiveness of the risk management process.

### 11.7.3.5 ORGANIZATIONAL PROCESS ASSETS UPDATES

Organizational process assets that are updated as a result of the Monitor Risks process include but are not limited to:

◆ Templates for the risk management plan, risk register, and risk report; and

◆ Risk breakdown structure.

# 12

## PROJECT PROCUREMENT MANAGEMENT

Project Procurement Management includes the processes necessary to purchase or acquire products, services, or results needed from outside the project team. Project Procurement Management includes the management and control processes required to develop and administer agreements such as contracts, purchase orders, memoranda of agreements (MOAs), or internal service level agreements (SLAs). The personnel authorized to procure the goods and/or services required for the project may be members of the project team, management, or part of the organization's purchasing department if applicable.

Project Procurement Management processes include the following:

**12.1 Plan Procurement Management**—The process of documenting project procurement decisions, specifying the approach, and identifying potential sellers.

**12.2 Conduct Procurements**—The process of obtaining seller responses, selecting a seller, and awarding a contract.

**12.3 Control Procurements**—The process of managing procurement relationships, monitoring contract performance, making changes and corrections as appropriate, and closing out contracts.

The procurement processes are presented as discrete processes with defined interfaces. In practice, procurement processes can be complex and can interact with each other and with processes in other Knowledge Areas in ways that cannot be completely detailed in the *PMBOK® Guide.* The processes described in this section are written from the viewpoint where goods or services are obtained from outside of the project.

Figure 12-1 provides an overview of the Project Procurement Management processes. The Project Procurement Management processes are presented as discrete processes with defined interfaces while, in practice, they overlap and interact in ways that cannot be completely detailed in the *PMBOK® Guide.*

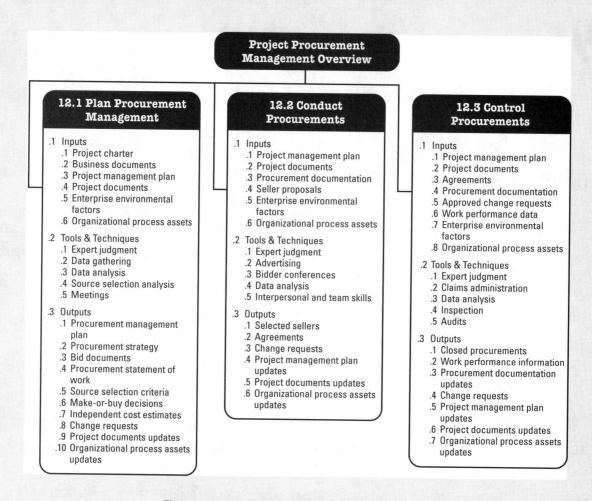

**Figure 12-1. Project Procurement Management Overview**

## KEY CONCEPTS FOR PROJECT PROCUREMENT MANAGEMENT

More than most other project management processes, there can be significant legal obligations and penalties tied to the procurement process. The project manager does not have to be a trained expert in procurement management laws and regulations but should be familiar enough with the procurement process to make intelligent decisions regarding contracts and contractual relationships. The project manager is typically not authorized to sign legal agreements binding the organization; this is reserved for those who have the authority to do so.

The Project Procurement Management processes involve agreements that describe the relationship between two parties—a buyer and a seller. Agreements can be as simple as the purchase of a defined quantity of labor hours at a specified labor rate, or they can be as complex as multiyear international construction contracts. The contracting approach and the contract itself should reflect the simplicity or complexity of the deliverables or required effort and should be written in a manner that complies with local, national, and international laws regarding contracts.

A contract should clearly state the deliverables and results expected, including any knowledge transfer from the seller to the buyer. Anything not in the contract cannot be legally enforced. When working internationally, project managers should keep in mind the effect that culture and local law have upon contracts and their enforceability, no matter how clearly a contract is written.

A purchasing contract includes terms and conditions and may incorporate other buyer specifics as to what the seller is to perform or provide. It is the project management team's responsibility to make certain that all procurements meet the specific needs of the project while working with the procurement office to ensure organizational procurement policies are followed. Depending on the application area, an agreement can be a contract, an SLA, an understanding, an MOA, or a purchase order.

Most organizations document policies and procedures specifically defining procurement rules and specifying who has authority to sign and administer such agreements on behalf of the organization. Across the world, organizations use different names for departments or divisions that deal with procurement, such as purchasing, contracting, procurement, or acquisitions; however, the responsibilities are likely to be similar.

Although all project documents may be subject to some form of review and approval, the legally binding nature of a contract means it will be subjected to a more extensive approval process, often involving the legal department. In all cases, the primary focus of the review and approval process is to ensure that the contract adequately describes the products, services, or results that the seller is agreeing to provide, while being in compliance with the laws and regulations regarding procurements. These sections are often separate appendices or annexes, allowing standardized legal contract language to be used.

A complex project may involve managing multiple contracts simultaneously or in sequence. In such cases, each contract life cycle may begin and end during any phase of the project life cycle. The buyer-seller relationship may exist at many levels on any one project, and between organizations internal to and external to the acquiring organization.

Depending on the application area, the seller may be identified as a contractor, vendor, service provider, or supplier. The buyer may be the owner of the final product, a subcontractor, the acquiring organization, a service requestor, or the purchaser. The seller can be viewed during the contract life cycle first as a bidder, then as the selected source, and then as the contracted supplier or vendor.

The winning bidder may manage the work as a project. In such cases:

◆ The buyer becomes the customer to subcontractors, suppliers, and service providers and is therefore a key project stakeholder from the seller's perspective.

◆ The seller's project management team may be concerned with all the processes involved in performing the work or providing the services.

◆ Terms and conditions of the contract and the procurement statement of work (SOW) become key inputs to many of the seller's management processes. The contract can actually contain the inputs (e.g., major deliverables, key milestones, cost objectives) or it can limit the project team's options (for example, buyer approval of staffing decisions is often required on IT integration projects). The procurement SOW may have other names, such as the technical statement of work.

◆ The seller itself may become a buyer of lower-tiered products, services, and materials from subcontractors and suppliers.

In this section, it is assumed that the buyer of an item for the project is assigned to the project team and/or is part of the larger organization. The seller is assumed to be providing services and/or materials to the project and is usually outside the performing organization. For some projects, the seller role may be filled by a group or function that is part of the performing organization but external to the project. For larger, more complex projects, the seller may become part of an integrated project team after the contract is awarded.

For smaller organizations or startup companies and those without a purchasing, contracting, or procurement department, the project manager may assume the purchasing authority role to negotiate and sign contracts directly (decentralized purchasing). For more mature organizations, the actual procurement and contracting functions will be carried out by a separate department with the specific role to purchase, negotiate, and sign contracts (centralized purchasing).

In international contracting, the legal jurisdictions under which the contracts will be administered are clearly spelled out in the contract. In most cases, the seller is an external contractor who is bound by a formal contractual relationship.

# TRENDS AND EMERGING PRACTICES IN PROCUREMENT MANAGEMENT

There are a number of major trends in software tools, risk, processes, logistics, and technology with different industries that can affect the success rate of projects. Trends and emerging practices for Project Procurement Management include but are not limited to:

◆ **Advances in tools.** There has been significant improvement in the development of tools to manage the procurement and implementation phases of a project. Online tools for procurement now give the buyers a single point where procurements can be advertised and provide sellers with a single source to find bid documents and complete them directly online. In the construction/engineering/infrastructure field, the increasing use of the building information model (BIM) in software tools has been shown to save significant amounts of time and money on projects using it. This approach can substantially reduce construction claims, thereby reducing both costs and schedule. Major companies and governments worldwide are beginning to mandate the use of BIM on large projects.

◆ **More advanced risk management.** An increasing trend in risk management is to write contracts that accurately allocate specific risks to those entities most capable of managing them. No contractor is capable of managing all the possible major risks on a project. The buyer will be required to accept the risks that the contractors do not have control over, such as changing corporate policies in the buying organization, changing regulatory requirements, and other risks from outside the project. Contracts may specify that risk management be performed as part of the contract.

◆ **Changing contracting processes.** There has been a significant growth in megaprojects in the past several years, particularly in the areas of infrastructure development and engineering projects. Multibillion-dollar projects are now common. A large proportion of these involve international contracts with multiple contractors from many countries and are inherently more risky than projects using only local contractors. Increasingly, the contractor works closely with the client in the procurement process to take advantage of discounts through quantity purchases or other special considerations. For these projects, the use of internationally recognized standard contract forms is increasing in order to reduce problems and claims during execution.

◆ **Logistics and supply chain management.** Because so many large engineering, construction infrastructure projects are done through multiple international contractors, the management of the flow of materials becomes critical to successful completion. For long-lead items, both the manufacture of the items and their transportation to the project site become schedule-drivers. In the IT field, a long-lead item may require ordering 2 to 3 months in advance. In complex construction projects, long-lead items may require ordering 1 to 2 years in advance or longer. For these projects, long-lead items may be procured in advance of other procurement contracts to meet the planned project completion date. It is possible to begin contracting for these long-lead materials, supplies, or equipment before the final design of the end product itself is completed based on the known requirements identified in the top-level design. The management of the supply chain is an area of increasing emphasis by the contractor's project team. Not only are primary sources of supplies identified early in the project, but secondary, back-up sources are also generally identified. Many countries around the world require international contractors to purchase certain minimum percentages of material and supplies from local vendors.

◆ **Technology and stakeholder relations.** Publicly funded projects are under increasing scrutiny. A trend in infrastructure and commercial construction projects is the use of technology including web cameras (webcams) to improve stakeholder communications and relations. During construction, one or more webcams are installed on the site, with periodic updates to a publicly available website. The progress on the project can be viewed on the Internet by all stakeholders. Video data can also be stored, allowing analysis if a claim arises. Some projects have discovered that the use of webcams minimizes disputes relating to the construction work on site, as the webcam has recorded the events, so there should be no disagreement about the facts of the matter.

◆ **Trial engagements.** Not every seller is well suited for an organization's environment. Therefore, some projects will engage several candidate sellers for initial deliverables and work products on a paid basis before making the full commitment to a larger portion of the project scope. This accelerates momentum by allowing the buyer to evaluate potential partners, while simultaneously making progress on project work.

## TAILORING CONSIDERATIONS

Because each project is unique, the project manager may need to tailor the way that Project Procurement Management processes are applied. Considerations for tailoring include but are not limited to:

◆ **Complexity of procurement.** Is there one main procurement or are there multiple procurements at different times with different sellers that add to the complexity of the procurements?

◆ **Physical location.** Are the buyers and sellers in the same location, or reasonably close, or in different time zones, countries, or continents?

◆ **Governance and regulatory environment.** Are local laws and regulations regarding procurement activities integrated with the organization's procurement policies? How does this affect contract auditing requirements?

◆ **Availability of contractors.** Are there available contractors who are capable of performing the work?

## CONSIDERATIONS FOR AGILE/ADAPTIVE ENVIRONMENTS

In agile environments, specific sellers may be used to extend the team. This collaborative working relationship can lead to a shared risk procurement model where both the buyer and the seller share in the risk and rewards associated with a project.

Larger projects may use an adaptive approach for some deliverables and a more stable approach for other parts. In these cases, a governing agreement such as a master services agreement (MSA) may be used for the overall engagement, with the adaptive work being placed in an appendix or supplement. This allows changes to occur on the adaptive scope without impacting the overall contract.

# 12.1 PLAN PROCUREMENT MANAGEMENT

Plan Procurement Management is the process of documenting project procurement decisions, specifying the approach and identifying potential sellers. The key benefit of this process is that it determines whether to acquire goods and services from outside the project and, if so, what to acquire as well as how and when to acquire it. Goods and services may be procured from other parts of the performing organization or from external sources. This process is performed once or at predefined points in the project. The inputs, tools and techniques, and outputs of this process are depicted in Figure 12-2. Figure 12-3 depicts the data flow diagram of the process.

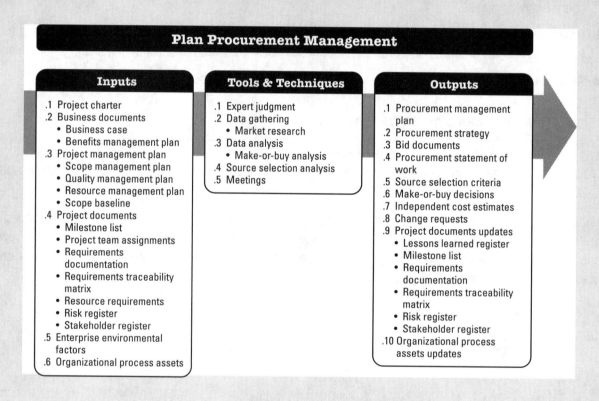

**Figure 12-2. Plan Procurement Management: Inputs, Tools & Techniques, and Outputs**

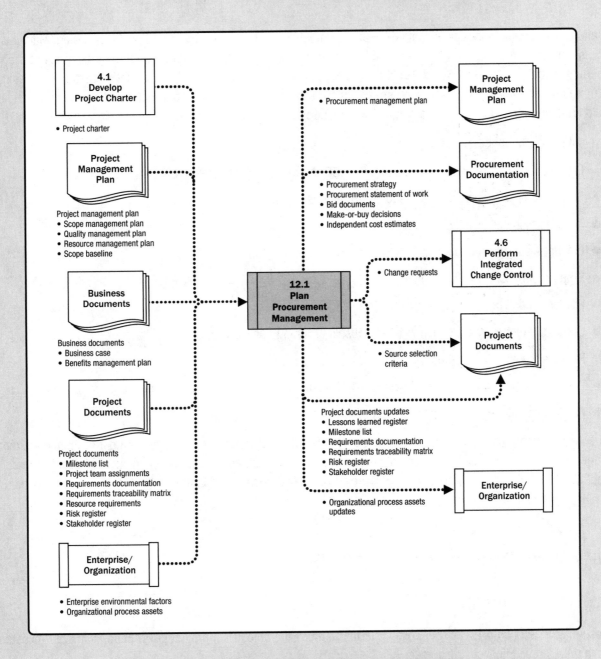

Figure 12-3. Plan Procurement Management: Data Flow Diagram

Defining roles and responsibilities related to procurement should be done early in the Plan Procurement Management process. The project manager should ensure that the project team is staffed with procurement expertise at the level required for the project. Participants in the procurement process may include personnel from the purchasing or procurement department as well as personnel from the buying organization's legal department. These responsibilities should be documented in the procurement management plan.

Typical steps might be:

◆ Prepare the procurement statement of work (SOW) or terms of reference (TOR).

◆ Prepare a high-level cost estimate to determine the budget.

◆ Advertise the opportunity.

◆ Identify a short list of qualified sellers.

◆ Prepare and issue bid documents.

◆ Prepare and submit proposals by the seller.

◆ Conduct a technical evaluation of the proposals including quality.

◆ Perform a cost evaluation of the proposals.

◆ Prepare the final combined quality and cost evaluation to select the winning proposal.

◆ Finalize negotiations and sign contract between the buyer and the seller.

The requirements of the project schedule can significantly influence the strategy during the Plan Procurement Management process. Decisions made in developing the procurement management plan can also influence the project schedule and are integrated with the Develop Schedule process, the Estimate Activity Resources process, and make-or-buy decisions.

## 12.1.1 PLAN PROCUREMENT MANAGEMENT: INPUTS

### 12.1.1.1 PROJECT CHARTER

Described in Section 4.1.3.1. The project charter contains the objectives, project description, summary milestones, and the preapproved financial resources.

### 12.1.1.2 BUSINESS DOCUMENTS

Described in Section 1.2.6. The business documents include the following:

◆ **Business case.** The procurement strategy and business case need to be aligned to ensure the business case remains valid.

◆ **Benefits management plan.** The benefits management plan describes when specific project benefits are expected to be available, which will drive procurement dates and contract language.

### 12.1.1.3 PROJECT MANAGEMENT PLAN

Described in Section 4.2.3.1. Project management plan components include but are not limited to:

◆ **Scope management plan.** Described in Section 5.1.3.1. The scope management plan describes how the scope of work by the contractors will be managed through the execution phase of the project.

◆ **Quality management plan.** Described in Section 8.1.3.1. The quality management plan contains the applicable industry standards and codes the project is required to follow. This information is used in bidding documents such as the RFP and will eventually be referenced in the contract. This information may be used in supplier prequalification or as part of the selection criteria.

◆ **Resource management plan.** Described in Section 9.1.3.1. The resource management plan has information on which resources will be purchased or leased, along with any assumptions or constraints that would influence the procurement.

◆ **Scope baseline.** Described in Section 5.4.3.1. The scope baseline contains the scope statement, WBS, and WBS dictionary. Early in the project, the project scope may still be evolving. The elements of the scope that are known are used to develop the statement of work (SOW) and the terms of reference (TOR).

### 12.1.1.4 PROJECT DOCUMENTS

Project documents that can be considered as inputs for this process include but are not limited to:

◆ **Milestone list.** Described in Section 6.2.3.3. This list of major milestones show when the sellers are required to deliver their results.

◆ **Project team assignments.** Described in Section 9.3.3.2. The project team assignments contain information on the skills and abilities of the project team and their availability to support the procurement activities. If the project team does not have the skills to perform the procurement activities for which they are responsible, additional resources will need to be acquired or training will need to be provided, or both.

- **Requirements documentation.** Described in Section 5.2.3.1. Requirements documentation may include:

  - Technical requirements that the seller is required to satisfy, and

  - Requirements with contractual and legal implications that may include health, safety, security, performance, environmental, insurance, intellectual property rights, equal employment opportunity, licenses, permits, and other nontechnical requirements.

- **Requirements traceability matrix.** Described in Section 5.2.3.2. The requirements traceability matrix links product requirements from their origin to the deliverables that satisfy them.

- **Resource requirements.** Described in Section 9.2.3.1. Resource requirements contain information on specific needs such as team and physical resources that may need to be acquired.

- **Risk register.** Described in Section 11.2.3.1. The risk register provides the list of risks, along with the results of risk analysis and risk response planning. Some risks are transferred via a procurement agreement.

- **Stakeholder register.** Described in Section 13.1.3.1. The stakeholder register provides details on the project participants and their interests in the project, including regulatory agencies, contracting personnel, and legal personnel.

## 12.1.1.5 ENTERPRISE ENVIRONMENTAL FACTORS

The enterprise environmental factors that can influence the Plan Procurement Management process include but are not limited to:

- Marketplace conditions;

- Products, services, and results that are available in the marketplace;

- Sellers, including their past performance or reputation;

- Typical terms and conditions for products, services, and results or for the specific industry;

- Unique local requirements, such as regulatory requirements for local labor or sellers;

- Legal advice regarding procurements;

- Contract management systems, including procedures for contract change control;

- Established multi-tier supplier system of prequalified sellers based on prior experience; and

- Financial accounting and contract payments system.

## 12.1.1.6 ORGANIZATIONAL PROCESS ASSETS

The various types of contractual agreements used by the organization also influence decisions for the Plan Procurement Management process. The organizational process assets that can influence the Plan Procurement Management process include but are not limited to:

◆ **Preapproved seller lists.** Lists of sellers that have been properly vetted can streamline the steps needed to advertise the opportunity and shorten the timeline for the seller selection process.

◆ **Formal procurement policies, procedures, and guidelines.** Most organizations have formal procurement policies and buying organizations. When such procurement support is not available, the project team should supply both the resources and the expertise to perform such procurement activities.

◆ **Contract types.** All legal contractual relationships generally fall into one of two broad families: either fixed-price or cost-reimbursable. Also, there is a third hybrid type commonly used called the time and materials contract. The more popular contract types in use are discussed below as discrete types, but, in practice, it is not unusual to combine one or more types into a single procurement.

  ■ *Fixed-price contracts.* This category of contracts involves setting a fixed total price for a defined product, service, or result to be provided. These contracts should be used when the requirements are well defined and no significant changes to the scope are expected. Types of fixed-price contract include:

    ○ *Firm fixed price (FFP).* The most commonly used contract type is the FFP. It is favored by most buying organizations because the price for goods is set at the outset and not subject to change unless the scope of work changes.

    ○ *Fixed price incentive fee (FPIF).* This fixed-price arrangement gives the buyer and seller some flexibility in that it allows for deviation from performance, with financial incentives tied to achieving agreed-upon metrics. Typically, such financial incentives are related to cost, schedule, or technical performance of the seller. Under FPIF contracts, a price ceiling is set, and all costs above the price ceiling are the responsibility of the seller.

    ○ *Fixed price with economic price adjustments (FPEPA).* This type is used whenever the seller's performance period spans a considerable period of years, or if the payments are made in a different currency. It is a fixed-price contract, but with a special provision allowing for predefined final adjustments to the contract price due to changed conditions, such as inflation changes or cost increases (or decreases) for specific commodities.

◆ **Cost-reimbursable contracts.** This category of contract involves payments (cost reimbursements) to the seller for all legitimate actual costs incurred for completed work, plus a fee representing seller profit. This type should be used if the scope of work is expected to change significantly during the execution of the contract. Variations can include:

  ■ *Cost plus fixed fee (CPFF).* The seller is reimbursed for all allowable costs for performing the contract work and receives a fixed-fee payment calculated as a percentage of the initial estimated project costs. Fee amounts do not change unless the project scope changes.

  ■ *Cost plus incentive fee (CPIF).* The seller is reimbursed for all allowable costs for performing the contract work and receives a predetermined incentive fee based on achieving certain performance objectives as set forth in the contract. In CPIF contracts, if the final costs are less or greater than the original estimated costs, then both the buyer and seller share costs from the departures based upon a prenegotiated cost-sharing formula, for example, an 80/20 split over/under target costs based on the actual performance of the seller.

  ■ *Cost plus award fee (CPAF).* The seller is reimbursed for all legitimate costs, but the majority of the fee is earned based on the satisfaction of certain broad subjective performance criteria that are defined and incorporated into the contract. The determination of fee is based solely on the subjective determination of seller performance by the buyer and is generally not subject to appeals.

◆ **Time and material contracts (T&M).** Time and material contracts (also called time and means) are a hybrid type of contractual arrangement with aspects of both cost-reimbursable and fixed-price contracts. They are often used for staff augmentation, acquisition of experts, and any outside support when a precise statement of work cannot be quickly prescribed.

## 12.1.2 PLAN PROCUREMENT MANAGEMENT: TOOLS AND TECHNIQUES

### 12.1.2.1 EXPERT JUDGMENT

Described in Section 4.1.2.1. Expertise should be considered from individuals or groups with specialized knowledge or training in the following topics:

◆ Procurement and purchasing,

◆ Contract types and contract documents, and

◆ Regulations and compliance topics.

### 12.1.2.2 DATA GATHERING

A data-gathering technique that can be used for this process includes but is not limited to market research. Market research includes examination of industry and specific seller capabilities. Procurement teams may leverage information gained at conferences, online reviews, and a variety of sources to identify market capabilities. The team may also refine specific procurement objectives to leverage maturing technologies while balancing risks associated with the breadth of sellers who can provide the desired materials or services.

### 12.1.2.3 DATA ANALYSIS

Data analysis techniques that can be used for this process include but are not limited to make-or-buy analysis. A make-or-buy analysis is used to determine whether work or deliverables can best be accomplished by the project team or should be purchased from outside sources. Factors to consider in the make-or-buy decision include the organization's current resource allocation and their skills and abilities, the need for specialized expertise, the desire to not expand permanent employment obligations, and the need for independent expertise. It also includes evaluating the risks involved with each make-or-buy decision.

Make-or-buy analysis may use payback period, return on investment (ROI), internal rate of return (IRR), discounted cash flow, net present value (NPV), benefit/cost analysis (BCA), or other techniques in order to decide whether to include something as part of the project or purchase it externally.

### 12.1.2.4 SOURCE SELECTION ANALYSIS

It is necessary to review the prioritization of the competing demands for the project before deciding on the selection method. Since competitive selection methods may require sellers to invest a large amount of time and resources upfront, it is a good practice to include the evaluation method in the bid documents so bidders know how they will be evaluated. Commonly used selection methods include the following:

◆ **Least cost.** The least cost method may be appropriate for procurements of a standard or routine nature where well-established practices and standards exist and from which a specific and well-defined outcome is expected, which can be executed at different costs.

◆ **Qualifications only.** The qualifications only selection method applies when the time and cost of a full selection process would not make sense because the value of the procurement is relatively small. The buyer establishes a short list and selects the bidder with the best credibility, qualifications, experience, expertise, areas of specialization, and references.

◆ **Quality-based/highest technical proposal score.** The selected firm is asked to submit a proposal with both technical and cost details and is then invited to negotiate the contract if the technical proposal proves acceptable. Using this method, technical proposals are first evaluated based on the quality of the technical solution offered. The seller who submitted the highest-ranked technical proposal is selected if their financial proposal can be negotiated and accepted.

◆ **Quality and cost-based.** The quality and cost-based method allows cost to be included as a factor in the seller selection process. In general, when risk and/or uncertainty are greater for the project, quality should be a key element when compared to cost.

◆ **Sole source.** The buyer asks a specific seller to prepare technical and financial proposals, which are then negotiated. Since there is no competition, this method is acceptable only when properly justified and should be viewed as an exception.

◆ **Fixed budget.** The fixed-budget method requires disclosing the available budget to invited sellers in the RFP and selecting the highest-ranking technical proposal within the budget. Because sellers are subject to a cost constraint, they will adapt the scope and quality of their offer to that budget. The buyer should therefore ensure that the budget is compatible with the SOW and that the seller will be able to perform the tasks within the budget. This method is appropriate only when the SOW is precisely defined, no changes are anticipated, and the budget is fixed and cannot be exceeded.

## 12.1.2.5 MEETINGS

Research alone may not provide specific information to formulate a procurement strategy without additional information interchange meetings with potential bidders. By collaborating with potential bidders, the organization purchasing the material or service may benefit while the seller can influence a mutually beneficial approach or product. Meetings can be used to determine the strategy for managing and monitoring the procurement.

### 12.1.3 PLAN PROCUREMENT MANAGEMENT: OUTPUTS

#### 12.1.3.1 PROCUREMENT MANAGEMENT PLAN

The procurement management plan contains the activities to be undertaken during the procurement process. It should document whether international competitive bidding, national competitive bidding, local bidding, etc., should be done. If the project is financed externally, the sources and availability of funding should be aligned with the procurement management plan and the project schedule.

The procurement management plan can include guidance for:

◆ How procurement will be coordinated with other project aspects, such as project schedule development and control processes;

◆ Timetable of key procurement activities;

◆ Procurement metrics to be used to manage contracts;

◆ Stakeholder roles and responsibilities related to procurement, including authority and constraints of the project team when the performing organization has a procurement department;

◆ Constraints and assumptions that could affect planned procurements;

◆ The legal jurisdiction and the currency in which payments will be made;

◆ Determination of whether independent estimates will be used and whether they are needed as evaluation criteria;

◆ Risk management issues including identifying requirements for performance bonds or insurance contracts to mitigate some forms of project risk; and

◆ Prequalified sellers, if any, to be used.

A procurement management plan can be formal or informal, can be highly detailed or broadly framed, and is based upon the needs of each project.

### 12.1.3.2 PROCUREMENT STRATEGY

Once the make-or-buy analysis is complete and the decision is made to acquire from outside the project, a procurement strategy should be identified. The objective of the procurement strategy is to determine the project delivery method, the type of legally binding agreement(s), and how the procurement will advance through the procurement phases.

◆ **Delivery methods.** Delivery methods are different for professional services versus construction projects.

  ■ For professional services, delivery methods include: buyer/services provider with no subcontracting, buyer/ services provider with subcontracting allowed, joint venture between buyer and services provider, and buyer/ services provider acts as the representative.

  ■ For industrial or commercial construction, project delivery methods include but are not limited to: turnkey, design build (DB), design bid build (DBB), design build operate (DBO), build own operate transfer (BOOT), and others.

◆ **Contract payment types.** Contract payment types are separate from the project delivery methods and are coordinated with the buying organization's internal financial systems. They include but are not limited to these contract types plus variations: lump sum, firm fixed price, cost plus award fees, cost plus incentive fees, time and materials, target cost, and others.

  ■ Fixed-price contracts are suitable when the type of work is predictable and the requirements are well defined and not likely to change.

  ■ Cost plus contracts are suitable when the work is evolving, likely to change, or not well defined.

  ■ Incentives and awards may be used to align the objectives of buyer and seller.

◆ **Procurement phases.** The procurement strategy can also include information on procurement phases. Information may include:

  ■ Sequencing or phasing of the procurement, a description of each phase and the specific objectives of each phase;

  ■ Procurement performance indicators and milestones to be used in monitoring;

  ■ Criteria for moving from phase to phase;

  ■ Monitoring and evaluation plan for tracking progress; and

  ■ Process for knowledge transfer for use in subsequent phases.

### 12.1.3.3 BID DOCUMENTS

Bid documents are used to solicit proposals from prospective sellers. Terms such as bid, tender, or quotation are generally used when the seller selection decision is based on price (as when buying commercial or standard items), while a term such as proposal is generally used when other considerations such as technical capability or technical approach are the most important. Specific procurement terminology used may vary by industry and location of the procurement.

Depending on the goods or services needed, the bidding documents can include a request for information, request for quotation, request for proposal, or other appropriate documents. The conditions involving their use are presented below:

◆ **Request for information (RFI).** An RFI is used when more information on the goods and services to be acquired is needed from the sellers. It will typically be followed by an RFQ or RFP.

◆ **Request for quotation (RFQ).** An RFQ is commonly used when more information is needed on how vendors would satisfy the requirements and/or how much it will cost.

◆ **Request for proposal (RFP).** An RFP is used when there is a problem in the project and the solution is not easy to determine. This is the most formal of the "request for" documents and has strict procurement rules for content, timeline, and seller responses.

The buyer structures bid documents to facilitate an accurate and complete response from each prospective seller and to facilitate easy evaluation of the responses. These documents include a description of the desired form of the response, the relevant procurement SOW, and any required contractual provisions.

The complexity and level of detail of the bid documents should be consistent with the value of, and risks associated with, the planned procurement. Bid documents are required to be sufficiently detailed to ensure consistent, appropriate responses, but flexible enough to allow consideration of any seller suggestions for better ways to satisfy the same requirements.

### 12.1.3.4 PROCUREMENT STATEMENT OF WORK

The statement of work (SOW) for each procurement is developed from the project scope baseline and defines only that portion of the project scope that is to be included within the related contract. The SOW describes the procurement item in sufficient detail to allow prospective sellers to determine if they are capable of providing the products, services, or results. Sufficient detail can vary based on the nature of the item, the needs of the buyer, or the expected contract form. Information included in a SOW can include specifications, quantity desired, quality levels, performance data, period of performance, work location, and other requirements.

The procurement SOW should be clear, complete, and concise. It includes a description of any collateral services required, such as performance reporting or post-project operational support for the procured item. The SOW can be revised as required as it moves through the procurement process until incorporated into a signed agreement.

The phrase *terms of reference* (TOR) is sometimes used when contracting for services. Similar to the procurement SOW, a TOR typically includes these elements:

◆ Tasks the contractor is required to perform as well as specified coordination requirements;

◆ Standards the contractor will fulfill that are applicable to the project;

◆ Data that needs to be submitted for approval;

◆ Detailed list of all data and services that will be provided to the contractor by the buyer for use in performing the contract, if applicable; and

◆ Definition of the schedule for initial submission and the review/approval time required.

## 12.1.3.5 SOURCE SELECTION CRITERIA

In choosing evaluation criteria, the buyer seeks to ensure that the proposal selected will offer the best quality for the services required. The source selection criteria may include but are not limited to:

◆ Capability and capacity;

◆ Product cost and life cycle cost;

◆ Delivery dates;

◆ Technical expertise and approach;

◆ Specific relevant experience;

◆ Adequacy of the proposed approach and work plan in responding to the SOW;

◆ Key staff's qualifications, availability, and competence;

◆ Financial stability of the firm;

◆ Management experience; and

◆ Suitability of the knowledge transfer program, including training.

For international projects, evaluation criteria may include "local content" requirements, for example, participation by nationals among proposed key staff.

The specific criteria may be a numerical score, color-code, or a written description of how well the seller satisfies the buying organization's needs. The criteria will be part of a weighting system that can be used to select a single seller that will be asked to sign a contract and establish a negotiating sequence by ranking all the proposals by the weighted evaluation scores assigned to each proposal.

### 12.1.3.6 MAKE-OR-BUY DECISIONS

A make-or-buy analysis results in a decision as to whether particular work can best be accomplished by the project team or needs to be purchased from outside sources.

### 12.1.3.7 INDEPENDENT COST ESTIMATES

For large procurements, the procuring organization may elect to either prepare its own independent estimate or have a cost estimate prepared by an outside professional estimator to serve as a benchmark on proposed responses. Significant differences in cost estimates can be an indication that the procurement SOW was deficient or ambiguous, or that the prospective sellers either misunderstood or failed to respond fully to the procurement SOW.

### 12.1.3.8 CHANGE REQUESTS

Described in Section 4.3.3.4. A decision that involves procuring goods, services, or resources may require a change request. Other decisions during procurement planning can also create the need for additional change requests. Changes to the project management plan, its subsidiary plans, and other components may result in change requests that impact procurement actions. Change requests are processed for review and disposition through the Perform Integrated Change Control process (Section 4.6).

## 12.1.3.9 PROJECT DOCUMENTS UPDATES

Project documents that may be updated as a result of carrying out this process include but are not limited to:

◆ **Lessons learned register.** Described in Section 4.4.3.1. The lessons learned register is updated with any relevant lessons regarding regulations and compliance, data gathering, data analysis, and source selection analysis.

◆ **Milestone list.** Described in Section 6.2.3.3. This list of major milestones shows when the sellers are expected to deliver their results.

◆ **Requirements documentation.** Described in Section 5.2.3.1. Requirements documentation may include:

  ■ Technical requirements that the seller is required to satisfy, and

  ■ Requirements with contractual and legal implications that may include health, safety, security, performance, environmental, insurance, intellectual property rights, equal employment opportunity, licenses, permits, and other nontechnical requirements.

◆ **Requirements traceability matrix.** Described in Section 5.2.3.2. The requirements traceability matrix links product requirements from their origin to the deliverables that satisfy them.

◆ **Risk register.** Described in Section 11.2.3.1. Each approved seller comes with its own unique set of risks, depending on the seller's organization, the duration of the contract, the external environment, the project delivery method, the type of contracting vehicle chosen, and the final agreed-upon price.

◆ **Stakeholder register.** Described in Section 13.1.3.1. The stakeholder register is updated with any additional information on stakeholders, particularly regulatory agencies, contracting personnel, and legal personnel.

## 12.1.3.10 ORGANIZATIONAL PROCESS ASSETS UPDATES

Organizational process assets that are updated as a result of the Plan Procurement Management process include but are not limited to information on qualified sellers.

For projects with few procurements and relatively simple procurements, some of these outputs may be combined. However, for projects with large, complex procurements and where much of the work is done by contractors, there are several different types of documentation. Table 12-1 is a representative list of common types of documents used in procurements and some of their contents. Given the legal nature of procurements, this list should not be considered prescriptive, but rather it should be used as a general outline of types of documents and contents needed to conduct procurement. The organization, environment, and legal constraints dictate the required bid documents and information needed for the project.

Table 12-1. Comparison of Procurement Documentation

| Procurement Management Plan | Procurement Strategy | Statement of Work | Bid Documents |
|---|---|---|---|
| How procurement work will be coordinated and integrated with other project work, particularly with resources, schedule, and budget | Procurement delivery methods | Description of the procurement item | Request for information (RFI), Request for quote (RFQ), Request for proposal (RFP) |
| Timetable for key procurement activities | Type of agreements | Specifications, quality requirements and performance metrics | |
| Procurement metrics to manage the contract | Procurement phases | Description of collateral services required | |
| Responsibilities of all stakeholders | | Acceptance methods and criteria | |
| Procurement assumptions and constraints | | Performance data and other reports required | |
| Legal jurisdiction and currency used for payment | | Quality | |
| Information on independent estimates | | Period and place of performance | |
| Risk management issues | | Currency; payment schedule | |
| Prequalified sellers, if applicable | | Warranty | |

# 12.2 CONDUCT PROCUREMENTS

Conduct Procurements is the process of obtaining seller responses, selecting a seller, and awarding a contract. The key benefit of this process is that it selects a qualified seller and implements the legal agreement for delivery. The end results of the process are the established agreements including formal contracts. This process is performed periodically throughout the project as needed. The inputs, tools and techniques, and outputs of the Conduct Procurements process are depicted in Figure 12-4. Figure 12-5 depicts the data flow diagram for the process.

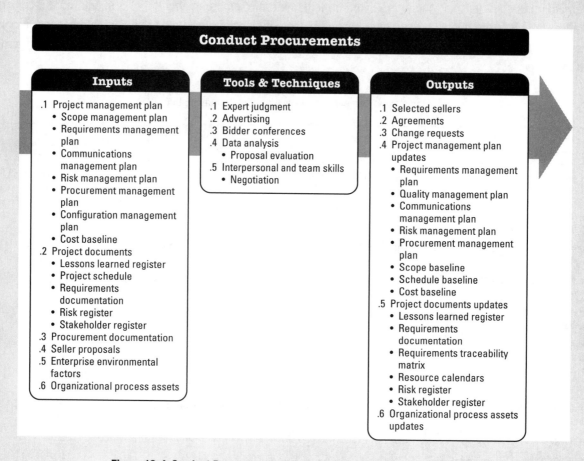

Figure 12-4. Conduct Procurements: Inputs, Tools & Techniques, and Outputs

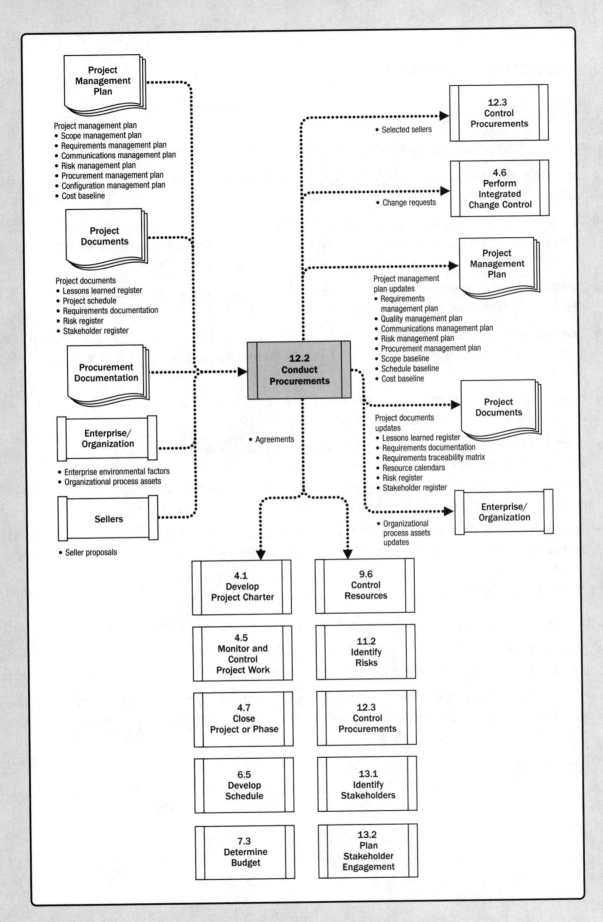

**Figure 12-5. Conduct Procurements: Data Flow Diagram**

## 12.2.1 CONDUCT PROCUREMENTS: INPUTS

### 12.2.1.1 PROJECT MANAGEMENT PLAN

Described in Section 4.2.3.1. Project management plan components include but are not limited to:

◆ **Scope management plan.** Described in Section 5.1.3.1. The scope management plan describes how the overall scope of work will be managed, including the scope performed by sellers.

◆ **Requirements management plan.** Described in Section 5.1.3.2. The requirements management plan describes how requirements will be analyzed, documented, and managed. The requirements management plan may include how sellers will manage the requirements they are under agreement to satisfy.

◆ **Communications management plan.** Described in Section 10.1.3.1. The communications management plan describes how communications between buyers and sellers will be conducted.

◆ **Risk management plan.** Described in Section 11.1.3.1. The risk management plan is a component of the project management plan and describes how risk management activities will be structured and performed for the project.

◆ **Procurement management plan.** Described in Section 12.1.3.1. The procurement management plan contains the activities to be undertaken during the Conduct Procurements process.

◆ **Configuration management plan.** Described in Section 5.6.1.1. The configuration management plan defines those items that are configurable, those items that require formal change control, and the process for controlling changes to such items. It includes formats and processes for how sellers will provide configuration management in a way that is consistent with the buyer's approach.

◆ **Cost baseline.** Described in Section 7.3.3.1. The cost baseline includes the budget for the procurement as well as costs associated with managing the procurement process and sellers.

### 12.2.1.2 PROJECT DOCUMENTS

Project documents that can be considered as inputs for this process include but are not limited to:

◆ **Lessons learned register.** Described in Section 4.4.3.1. Lessons learned earlier in the project with regard to conducting procurements can be applied to later phases in the project to improve the efficiency of this process.

◆ **Project schedule.** Described in Section 6.5.3.2. The project schedule identifies the start and end dates of project activities, including procurement activities. It also defines when contractor deliverables are due.

- **Requirements documentation.** Described in Section 5.2.3.1. Requirements documentation may include:
    - Technical requirements the seller is required to satisfy, and
    - Requirements with contractual and legal implications that may include health, safety, security, performance, environmental, insurance, intellectual property rights, equal employment opportunity, licenses, permits, and other nontechnical requirements.

- **Risk register.** Described in Section 11.2.3.1. Each approved seller comes with its own unique set of risks, depending on the seller's organization, the duration of the contract, the external environment, the project delivery method, the type of contracting vehicle chosen, and the final agreed-upon price.

- **Stakeholder register.** Described in Section 13.1.3.1. This document contains all of the details about the identified stakeholders.

### 12.2.1.3 PROCUREMENT DOCUMENTATION

Procurement documentation provides a written record used in reaching the legal agreement, and may include older documents predating the current project. Procurement documentation can include:

- **Bid documents.** Described in Section 12.1.3.3. Bid documents include the RFI, RFP, RFQ, or other documents sent to sellers so they can develop a bid response.

- **Procurement statement of work.** Described in Section 12.1.3.4. The procurement statement of work (SOW) provides sellers with a clearly stated set of goals, requirements, and outcomes from which they can provide a quantifiable response.

- **Independent cost estimates.** Described in Section 12.1.3.7. Independent cost estimates are developed either internally or by using external resources and provide a reasonableness check against the proposals submitted by bidders.

- **Source selection criteria.** Described in Section 12.1.3.5. These criteria describe how bidder proposals will be evaluated, including evaluation criteria and weights. For risk mitigation, the buyer may decide to sign agreements with more than one seller to mitigate damage caused by a single seller having problems that impact the overall project.

### 12.2.1.4 SELLER PROPOSALS

Seller proposals, prepared in response to a bid document package, form the basic information that will be used by an evaluation body to select one or more successful bidders (sellers). If the seller is going to submit a price proposal, good practice is to require that it be separate from the technical proposal. The evaluation body reviews each submitted proposal according to the source selection criteria and selects the seller that can best satisfy the buying organization's requirements.

### 12.2.1.5 ENTERPRISE ENVIRONMENTAL FACTORS

The enterprise environmental factors that can influence the Conduct Procurements Process include:

◆ Local laws and regulations regarding procurements;

◆ Local laws and regulations ensuring that the major procurements involve local sellers;

◆ External economic environment constraining procurement processes;

◆ Marketplace conditions;

◆ Information on relevant past experience with sellers, both good and bad;

◆ Prior agreements already in place; and

◆ Contract management systems.

### 12.2.1.6 ORGANIZATIONAL PROCESS ASSETS

The organizational process assets that can influence the Conduct Procurements process include but are not limited to:

◆ List of preferred sellers that have been prequalified,

◆ Organizational policies that influence the selection of a seller,

◆ Specific organizational templates or guidelines that will determine the way agreements are drafted and built, and

◆ Financial policies and procedures regarding invoicing and payment processes.

## 12.2.2 CONDUCT PROCUREMENTS: TOOLS AND TECHNIQUES

### 12.2.2.1 EXPERT JUDGMENT

Described in Section 4.1.2.1 Expertise should be considered from individuals or groups with specialized knowledge or training in the following topics:

◆ Proposal evaluation;

◆ Technical or subject matter;

◆ Relevant functional areas such as finance, engineering, design, development, supply chain management, etc.;

◆ Industry regulatory environment;

◆ Laws, regulations, and compliance requirements; and

◆ Negotiation.

### 12.2.2.2 ADVERTISING

Advertising is communicating with users or potential users of a product, service, or result. Existing lists of potential sellers often can be expanded by placing advertisements in general circulation publications such as selected newspapers or in specialty trade publications. Most government jurisdictions require public advertising or online posting of pending government contracts.

### 12.2.2.3 BIDDER CONFERENCES

Bidder conferences (also called contractor conferences, vendor conferences, and pre-bid conferences) are meetings between the buyer and prospective sellers prior to proposal submittal. They are used to ensure that all prospective bidders have a clear and common understanding of the procurement and no bidders receive preferential treatment.

### 12.2.2.4 DATA ANALYSIS

A data analysis technique that can be used for this process includes but is not limited to proposal evaluation. Proposals are evaluated to ensure they are complete and respond in full to the bid documents, procurement statement of work, source selection criteria, and any other documents that went out in the bid package.

### 12.2.2.5 INTERPERSONAL AND TEAM SKILLS

Interpersonal and team skills that can be used for this process include negotiation. Negotiation is a discussion aimed at reaching an agreement. Procurement negotiation clarifies the structure, rights, and obligations of the parties and other terms of the purchases so that mutual agreement can be reached prior to signing the contract. Final document language reflects all agreements reached. Negotiation concludes with a signed contract document or other formal agreement that can be executed by both buyer and seller.

The negotiation should be led by a member of the procurement team that has the authority to sign contracts. The project manager and other members of the project management team may be present during negotiation to provide assistance as needed.

## 12.2.3 CONDUCT PROCUREMENTS: OUTPUTS

### 12.2.3.1 SELECTED SELLERS

The selected sellers are those who have been judged to be in a competitive range based on the outcome of the proposal or bid evaluation. Final approval of complex, high-value, high-risk procurements will generally require organizational senior management approval prior to award.

## 12.2.3.2 AGREEMENTS

A contract is a mutually binding agreement that obligates the seller to provide the specified products, services, or results; obligates the buyer to compensate the seller; and represents a legal relationship that is subject to remedy in the courts. The major components in an agreement document will vary, and may include but are not limited to:

◆ Procurement statement of work or major deliverables;

◆ Schedule, milestones, or date by which a schedule is required;

◆ Performance reporting;

◆ Pricing and payment terms;

◆ Inspection, quality, and acceptance criteria;

◆ Warranty and future product support;

◆ Incentives and penalties;

◆ Insurance and performance bonds;

◆ Subordinate subcontractor approvals;

◆ General terms and conditions;

◆ Change request handling; and

◆ Termination clause and alternative dispute resolution mechanisms.

## 12.2.3.3 CHANGE REQUESTS

Described in Section 4.3.3.4. Change requests to the project management plan, its subsidiary plans, and other components are processed for review and disposition through the Perform Integrated Change Control process (Section 4.6).

## 12.2.3.4 PROJECT MANAGEMENT PLAN UPDATES

Any change to the project management plan goes through the organization's change control process via a change request. Components of the project management plan that may require a change request for the project management plan include but are not limited to:

◆ **Requirements management plan.** Described in Section 5.1.3.2. There may be changes to project requirements due to changes identified by sellers.

◆ **Quality management plan.** Described in Section 8.1.3.1. Sellers may offer alternative quality standards or alternative solutions that impact the quality approaches defined in the quality management plan.

◆ **Communications management plan.** Described in Section 10.1.3.1. As sellers are hired, the communications management plan is updated to incorporate their communications needs and approaches.

◆ **Risk management plan.** Described in Section 11.1.3.1. Each agreement and seller has its own set of risks that may require updates to the risk management plan. Specific risks are incorporated into the risk register.

◆ **Procurement management plan.** Described in Section 12.1.3.1. Updates may be required depending on the results of the contracting and negotiations processes.

◆ **Scope baseline.** Described in Section 5.4.3.1. The project WBS and deliverables documented in the scope baseline are considered when performing procurement activities. Any one or all of these may change during the procurement process.

◆ **Schedule baseline.** Described in Section 6.5.3.1. If there are delivery changes created by sellers that impact overall project schedule performance, the baseline schedule may need to be updated and approved to reflect the current expectations.

◆ **Cost baseline.** Described in Section 7.3.3.1. Contractor and materials prices can change frequently during the delivery of a project. These changes can occur because of fluctuating materials and labor prices created by the external economic environment and need to be incorporated into the cost baseline.

## 12.2.3.5 PROJECT DOCUMENTS UPDATES

Project documents that may be updated as a result of carrying out this process include but are not limited to:

◆ **Lessons learned register.** Described in Section 4.4.3.1. The lessons learned register is updated with information on challenges encountered while conducting procurements and how they could have been avoided as well as approaches that worked well.

◆ **Requirements documentation.** Described in Section 5.2.3.1. Requirements documentation may include:

■ Technical requirements that the seller is required to satisfy, and

■ Requirements with contractual and legal implications that may include health, safety, security, performance, environmental, insurance, intellectual property rights, equal employment opportunity, licenses, permits, and other nontechnical requirements.

◆ **Requirements traceability matrix.** Described in Section 5.2.3.2. As sellers are incorporated into the project's plan, the requirements register and the traceability matrix may change depending on the capabilities of the specific seller.

◆ **Resource calendars.** Described in Section 9.2.1.2. Schedule resource calendars may need to be updated depending on the availabilities of the sellers.

◆ **Risk register.** Described in Section 11.2.3.1. Each approved seller comes with its own unique set of risks, depending on the seller's organization, the duration of the contract, the external environment, the project delivery method, the type of contracting vehicle chosen, and the final agreed-upon price. Changes are made to the risk register during the contracting process, which reflect the specific risks of each seller.

◆ **Stakeholder register.** Described in Section 13.1.3.1. This document contains all the details about the identified stakeholders. The stakeholder register is updated as agreements are made with specific sellers.

## 12.2.3.6 ORGANIZATIONAL PROCESS ASSETS UPDATES

Elements of the organizational process assets that can be updated as a result of the Conduct Procurements process can include:

◆ Listings of prospective and prequalified sellers; and

◆ Information on relevant experience with sellers, both good and bad.

## 12.3 CONTROL PROCUREMENTS

Control Procurements is the process of managing procurement relationships; monitoring contract performance, and making changes and corrections as appropriate; and closing out contracts. The key benefit of this process is that it ensures that both the seller's and buyer's performance meet the project's requirements according to the terms of the legal agreement. This process is performed throughout the project as needed. The inputs, tools and techniques, and outputs of this process are depicted in Figure 12-6. Figure 12-7 depicts the data flow diagram of the process.

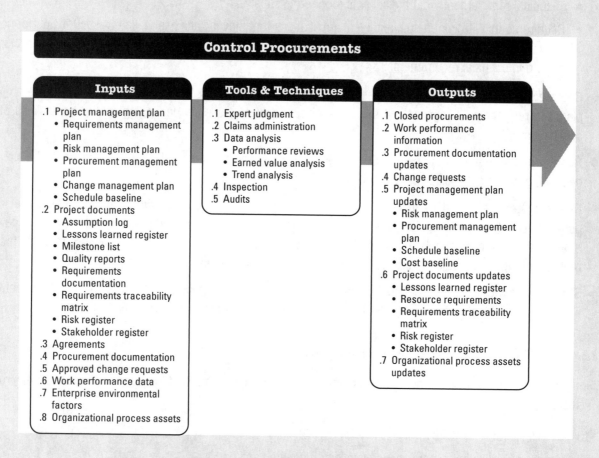

**Control Procurements**

| Inputs | Tools & Techniques | Outputs |
|---|---|---|
| .1 Project management plan<br>  • Requirements management plan<br>  • Risk management plan<br>  • Procurement management plan<br>  • Change management plan<br>  • Schedule baseline<br>.2 Project documents<br>  • Assumption log<br>  • Lessons learned register<br>  • Milestone list<br>  • Quality reports<br>  • Requirements documentation<br>  • Requirements traceability matrix<br>  • Risk register<br>  • Stakeholder register<br>.3 Agreements<br>.4 Procurement documentation<br>.5 Approved change requests<br>.6 Work performance data<br>.7 Enterprise environmental factors<br>.8 Organizational process assets | .1 Expert judgment<br>.2 Claims administration<br>.3 Data analysis<br>  • Performance reviews<br>  • Earned value analysis<br>  • Trend analysis<br>.4 Inspection<br>.5 Audits | .1 Closed procurements<br>.2 Work performance information<br>.3 Procurement documentation updates<br>.4 Change requests<br>.5 Project management plan updates<br>  • Risk management plan<br>  • Procurement management plan<br>  • Schedule baseline<br>  • Cost baseline<br>.6 Project documents updates<br>  • Lessons learned register<br>  • Resource requirements<br>  • Requirements traceability matrix<br>  • Risk register<br>  • Stakeholder register<br>.7 Organizational process assets updates |

**Figure 12-6. Control Procurements: Inputs, Tools & Techniques, and Outputs**

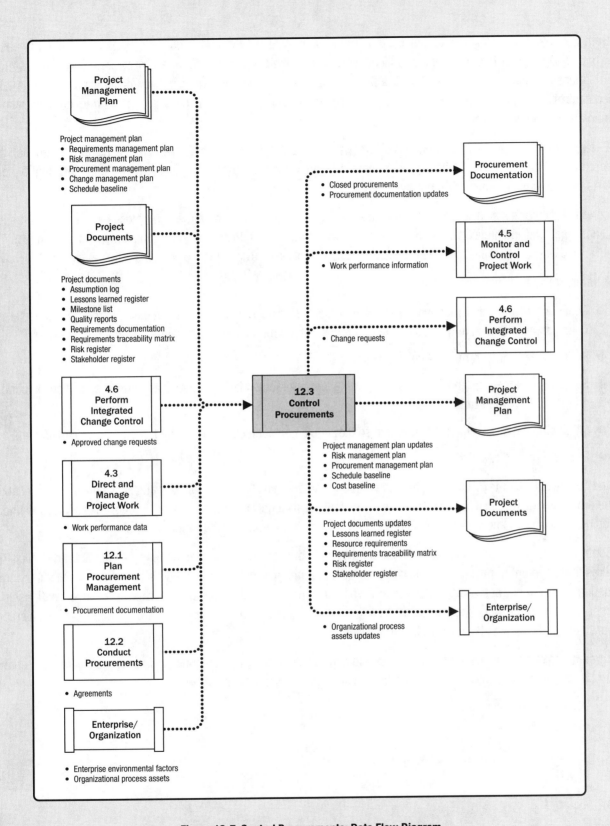

**Figure 12-7. Control Procurements: Data Flow Diagram**

Both the buyer and the seller administer the procurement contract for similar purposes. Each is required to ensure that both parties meet their contractual obligations and that their own legal rights are protected. The legal nature of the relationship makes it imperative that the project management team is aware of the implications of actions taken when controlling any procurement. On larger projects with multiple providers, a key aspect of contract administration is managing communication among the various providers.

Because of the legal aspect, many organizations treat contract administration as an organizational function that is separate from the project. While a procurement administrator may be on the project team, this individual typically reports to a supervisor from a different department.

Control Procurements includes application of the appropriate project management processes to the contractual relationship(s) and integration of the outputs from these processes into the overall management of the project. This integration often occurs at multiple levels when there are multiple sellers and multiple products, services, or results involved.

Administrative activities may include:

◆ Collection of data and managing project records, including maintenance of detailed records of physical and financial performance and establishment of measurable procurement performance indicators;

◆ Refinement of procurement plans and schedules;

◆ Set up for gathering, analyzing, and reporting procurement-related project data and preparation of periodic reports to the organization;

◆ Monitoring the procurement environment so that implementation can be facilitated or adjustments made; and

◆ Payment of invoices.

The quality of the controls, including the independence and credibility of procurement audits, is critical to the reliability of the procurement system. The organization's code of ethics, its legal counsel, and external legal advisory arrangements including any ongoing anti-corruption initiatives can contribute to proper procurement controls.

Control Procurements has a financial management component that involves monitoring payments to the seller. This ensures that payment terms defined within the contract are met and that compensation is linked to the seller's progress as defined in the contract. A principal concern when making payments is to ensure there is a close relationship of payments made to the work accomplished. A contract that requires payments linked to project output and deliverables rather than inputs such as labor hours has better controls.

Agreements can be amended at any time prior to contract closure by mutual consent, in accordance with the change control terms of the agreement. Such amendments are typically captured in writing.

## 12.3.1 CONTROL PROCUREMENTS: INPUTS

### 12.3.1.1 PROJECT MANAGEMENT PLAN

Described in Section 4.2.3.1. Project management plan components include but are not limited to:

◆ **Requirements management plan.** Described in Section 5.1.3.2. The requirements management plan describes how contractor requirements will be analyzed, documented, and managed.

◆ **Risk management plan.** Described in Section 11.1.3.1. The risk management plan describes how risk activities created by sellers will be structured and performed for the project.

◆ **Procurement management plan.** Described in Section 12.1.3.2. The procurement management plan contains the activities to be performed during the Control Procurement process.

◆ **Change management plan**. Described in Section 4.2.3.1. The change management plan contains information about how seller-created changes will be processed.

◆ **Schedule baseline.** Described in Section 6.5.3.1. If there are slippages created by sellers that impact overall project performance, the schedule may need to be updated and approved to reflect the current expectations.

### 12.3.1.2 PROJECT DOCUMENTS

Project documents that can be considered as inputs to this process include but are not limited to:

◆ **Assumption log.** Described in Section 4.1.3.2. The assumption log documents the assumptions that have been made during the procurement process.

◆ **Lessons learned register.** Described in Section 4.4.3.1. Lessons learned earlier in the project can be applied further along in the project to improve contractor performance and the procurement process.

◆ **Milestone list.** Described in Section 6.2.3.3. This list of major milestones shows when the sellers are expected to deliver their results.

◆ **Quality reports.** Described in Section 8.2.3.1. The quality reports can identify seller processes, procedures, or products that are out of compliance.

◆ **Requirements documentation.** Described in Section 5.2.3.1. Requirements documentation may include:

   ■ Technical requirements the seller is required to satisfy, and

   ■ Requirements with contractual and legal implications that may include health, safety, security, performance, environmental, insurance, intellectual property rights, equal employment opportunity, licenses, permits, and other nontechnical requirements.

◆ **Requirements traceability matrix.** Described in Section 5.2.3.2. The requirements traceability matrix links product requirements from their origin to the deliverables that satisfy them.

◆ **Risk register.** Described in Section 11.2.3.1. Each approved seller comes with its own unique set of risks, depending on the seller's organization, the duration of the contract, the external environment, the project delivery method, the type of contracting vehicle chosen, and the final agreed-upon price.

◆ **Stakeholder register.** Described in Section 13.1.3.1. The stakeholder register includes information about identified stakeholders, including contracted team members, selected sellers, contracting officers, and other stakeholders who are involved in procurements.

### 12.3.1.3 AGREEMENTS

Described in Section 12.2.3.2. Agreements are understandings between parties, including understanding of the duties of each party. The relevant agreements are reviewed to verify terms and conditions are met.

### 12.3.1.4 PROCUREMENT DOCUMENTATION

Procurement documentation contains complete supporting records for administration of the procurement processes. Procurement documentation includes the statement of work, payment information, contractor work performance information, plans, drawings, and other correspondence.

### 12.3.1.5 APPROVED CHANGE REQUESTS

Described in Section 4.6.3.1. Approved change requests can include modifications to the terms and conditions of the contract, including the procurement statement of work (SOW), pricing, and descriptions of the products, services, or results to be provided. All procurement-related changes are formally documented in writing and approved before being implemented through the Control Procurements process. In complex projects and programs, change requests may come from sellers involved with the project that can influence other involved sellers. The project should have the capability of identifying, communicating, and resolving changes that impact the work of multiple sellers.

### 12.3.1.6 WORK PERFORMANCE DATA

Described in Section 4.3.3.2. Work performance data contains seller data on project status such as technical performance; activities that have started, are in progress, or have completed; and costs that have been incurred or committed. Work performance data can also include information on the seller invoices that have been paid.

### 12.3.1.7 ENTERPRISE ENVIRONMENTAL FACTORS

The enterprise environmental factors that can influence the Control Procurements process include but are not limited to:

◆ Contract change control system,

◆ Marketplace conditions,

◆ Financial management and accounts payable system, and

◆ Buying organization's code of ethics.

### 12.3.1.8 ORGANIZATIONAL PROCESS ASSETS

The organizational process assets that can influence the Control Procurements process include but are not limited to, procurement policies.

## 12.3.2 CONTROL PROCUREMENTS: TOOLS AND TECHNIQUES

### 12.3.2.1 EXPERT JUDGMENT

Described in Section 4.1.2.1 Expertise should be considered from individuals or groups with specialized knowledge or training in the following topics:

◆ Relevant functional areas such as finance, engineering, design, development, supply chain management, etc.;

◆ Laws, regulations, and compliance requirements; and

◆ Claims administration.

### 12.3.2.2 CLAIMS ADMINISTRATION

Contested changes and potential constructive changes are those requested changes where the buyer and seller cannot reach an agreement on compensation for the change or cannot agree that a change has occurred. These contested changes are called claims. When they cannot be resolved, they become disputes and finally appeals. Claims are documented, processed, monitored, and managed throughout the contract life cycle, usually in accordance with the terms of the contract. If the parties themselves do not resolve a claim, it may have to be handled in accordance with alternative dispute resolution (ADR) typically following procedures established in the contract. Settlement of all claims and disputes through negotiation is the preferred method.

### 12.3.2.3 DATA ANALYSIS

Data analysis techniques that can be used to monitor and control procurements include but are not limited to:

◆ **Performance Reviews.** Performance reviews for contracts measure, compare, and analyze quality, resource, schedule, and cost performance against the agreement. This includes identifying work packages that are ahead or behind schedule, over or under budget, or have resource or quality issues.

◆ **Earned Value Analysis (EVA).** Described in Section 7.4.2.2. Schedule and cost variances along with schedule and cost performance indexes are calculated to determine the degree of variance from target.

◆ **Trend Analysis.** Described in Section 4.5.2.2. Trend analysis can develop a forecast estimate at completion (EAC) for cost performance to see if performance is improving or deteriorating. See 7.4.2.2 for more detail on EAC methods.

### 12.3.2.4 INSPECTION

An inspection is a structured review of the work being performed by the contractor. This may involve a simple review of the deliverables or an actual physical review of the work itself. On a construction/engineering/infrastructure project, inspections involve walkthroughs of the site by both the buyer and the contractor to ensure a mutual understanding of the work in progress.

### 12.3.2.5 AUDITS

Audits are described in Section 8.2.2.5. Audits are a structured review of the procurement process. Rights and obligations related to audits should be described in the procurement contract. Resulting audit observations should be brought to the attention of the buyer's project manager and the seller's project manager for adjustments to the project, when necessary.

### 12.3.3 CONTROL PROCUREMENTS: OUTPUTS

#### 12.3.3.1 CLOSED PROCUREMENTS

The buyer, usually through its authorized procurement administrator, provides the seller with formal written notice that the contract has been completed. Requirements for formal procurement closure are usually defined in the terms and conditions of the contract and are included in the procurement management plan. Typically, all deliverables should have been provided on time and meet technical and quality requirements, there should be no outstanding claims or invoices, and all final payments should have been made. The project management team should have approved all deliverables prior to closure.

#### 12.3.3.2 WORK PERFORMANCE INFORMATION

Described in Section 4.5.1.3. Work performance information includes information on how a seller is performing by comparing the deliverables received, the technical performance achieved, and the costs incurred and accepted against the SOW budget for the work performed.

#### 12.3.3.3 PROCUREMENT DOCUMENTATION UPDATES

Procurement documentation that may be updated includes the contract with all supporting schedules, requested unapproved contract changes, and approved change requests. Procurement documentation also includes any seller-developed technical documentation and other work performance information such as deliverables, seller performance reports and warranties, financial documents including invoices and payment records, and the results of contract-related inspections.

#### 12.3.3.4 CHANGE REQUESTS

Described in Section 4.3.3.4. Change requests to the project management plan, its subsidiary plans, and other components such as the cost baseline, schedule baseline, and procurement management plan, may result from the Control Procurements process. Change requests are processed for review and disposition through the Perform Integrated Change Control process (Section 4.6).

Requested but unresolved changes can include direction provided by the buyer or actions taken by the seller, which the other party considers a constructive change to the contract. Since any of these constructive changes may be disputed by one party and can lead to a claim against the other party, such changes are uniquely identified and documented by project correspondence.

### 12.3.3.5 PROJECT MANAGEMENT PLAN UPDATES

Any change to the project management plan goes through the organization's change control process via a change request. Components that may require a change request for the project management plan include but are not limited to:

◆ **Risk management plan.** Described in Section 11.1.3.1. Each agreement and seller has its own set of risks that may require updates to the risk management plan. If significant unexpected risks occur during the execution of the contract, the risk management plan may require updating. Specific risks are incorporated into the risk register.

◆ **Procurement management plan.** Described in Section 12.1.3.1. The procurement management plan contains the activities to be undertaken during the procurement process. Updates may be required depending on the results of the performance of the sellers during execution of the work.

◆ **Schedule baseline.** Described in Section 6.5.3.1. If there are significant schedule changes created by sellers that impact overall project schedule performance, the baseline schedule may need to be updated and approved to reflect the current expectations. The buyer should be aware of any cascading impacts of schedule delays created by a seller that impact other sellers.

◆ **Cost baseline.** Described in Section 7.3.3.1. Contractor and material costs can change frequently during the delivery of a project. These changes can occur because of fluctuating materials and labor prices created by the external economic environment and need to be incorporated into the cost baseline.

### 12.3.3.6 PROJECT DOCUMENTS UPDATES

Project documents that may be updated as a result of carrying out this process include but are not limited to:

◆ **Lessons learned register.** Described in Section 4.4.3.1. The lessons learned register can be updated with techniques that were effective in maintaining the scope, schedule, and cost of the procured items. Where variances occurred, the register should show the corrective actions that were used to respond to variances and how effective those actions were. If there are any claims, information should be documented to avoid recurrences. Additional information on how to improve the procurement process can also be recorded.

◆ **Resource requirements.** Described in Section 9.2.3.1. As the work progresses by the contractors, there may be changes to the resource requirements resulting from work being done that is not in accordance with the planned work schedule.

◆ **Requirements traceability matrix.** Described in Section 5.2.3.2. The requirements traceability matrix is updated with information on requirements that have been satisfied.

◆ **Risk register.** Described in Section 11.2.3.1. Each approved seller comes with its own unique set of risks, depending on the seller's organization, the duration of the contract, the external environment, the project delivery method, the type of contracting vehicle chosen, and the final agreed-upon price. Changes are made to the risk register during the execution of the project, as early risks may no longer be applicable and new risks occur.

◆ **Stakeholder register.** Described in Section 13.1.3.1. As the work progresses through the execution phase, the contractors and suppliers may change. These changes should be reflected in the stakeholder register.

## 12.3.3.7 ORGANIZATIONAL PROCESS ASSETS UPDATES

Organizational process assets that can be updated as a result of the Control Procurements process include but are not limited to:

◆ **Payment schedules and requests.** All payments should be made in accordance with the procurement contract terms and conditions.

◆ **Seller performance evaluation documentation.** Seller performance evaluation documentation is prepared by the buyer and documents the seller's ability to continue to perform work on the current contract, indicates whether the seller can be allowed to perform work on future projects, or rates how well the seller is performing the project work or has performed in the past.

◆ **Prequalified seller lists updates.** Prequalified seller lists are lists of potential sellers who are previously qualified (approved). These lists will be updated according to the Procurement Control process outcomes because sellers could be disqualified and removed from the lists based on poor performance.

◆ **Lessons learned repository.** Lessons learned should be archived in the lessons learned repository to improve procurements on future projects. At the end of a contract, the actual results of the procurement are compared with the projected results in the original procurement management plan. These lessons learned state whether the project objectives were achieved and, if not, provides the reasons they were not.

◆ **Procurement file.** A complete set of indexed contract documentation, including the closed contract, is prepared for inclusion with the final project files.

# 13

## PROJECT STAKEHOLDER MANAGEMENT

Project Stakeholder Management includes the processes required to identify the people, groups, or organizations that could impact or be impacted by the project, to analyze stakeholder expectations and their impact on the project, and to develop appropriate management strategies for effectively engaging stakeholders in project decisions and execution. The processes support the work of the project team to analyze stakeholder expectations, assess the degree to which they impact or are impacted by the project, and develop strategies to effectively engage stakeholders in support of project decisions and the planning and execution of the work of the project.

The Project Stakeholder Management processes are:

**13.1 Identify Stakeholders**—The process of identifying project stakeholders regularly and analyzing and documenting relevant information regarding their interests, involvement, interdependencies, influence, and potential impact on project success.

**13.2 Plan Stakeholder Engagement**—The process of developing approaches to involve project stakeholders based on their needs, expectation, interests, and potential impact on the project.

**13.3 Manage Stakeholder Engagement**—The process of communicating and working with stakeholders to meet their needs and expectations, address issues, and foster appropriate stakeholder engagement involvement.

**13.4 Monitor Stakeholder Engagement**—The process of monitoring project stakeholder relationships and tailoring strategies for engaging stakeholders through the modification of engagement strategies and plans.

Figure 13-1 provides an overview of the Project Stakeholder Management processes. The Project Stakeholder Management processes are presented as discrete processes with defined interfaces while, in practice, they overlap and interact in ways that cannot be completely detailed in the *PMBOK® Guide*.

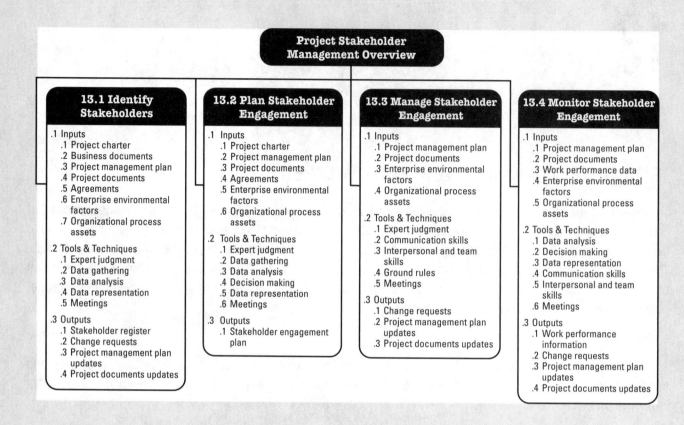

**Figure 13-1. Project Stakeholder Management Overview**

## KEY CONCEPTS FOR PROJECT STAKEHOLDER MANAGEMENT

Every project has stakeholders who are impacted by or can impact the project in a positive or negative way. Some stakeholders may have a limited ability to influence the project's work or outcomes; others may have significant influence on the project and its expected outcomes. Academic research and analyses of high-profile project disasters highlight the importance of a structured approach to the identification, prioritization, and engagement of all stakeholders. The ability of the project manager and team to correctly identify and engage all stakeholders in an appropriate way can mean the difference between project success and failure. To increase the chances of success, the process of stakeholder identification and engagement should commence as soon as possible after the project charter has been approved, the project manager has been assigned and the team begins to form.

Stakeholder satisfaction should be identified and managed as a project objective. The key to effective stakeholder engagement is a focus on continuous communication with all stakeholders, including team members, to understand their needs and expectations, address issues as they occur, manage conflicting interests, and foster appropriate stakeholder engagement in project decisions and activities.

The process of identifying and engaging stakeholders for the benefit of the project is iterative. Although the processes in Project Stakeholder Management are described only once, the activities of identification, prioritization, and engagement should be reviewed and updated routinely, and at least at the following times when:

◆ The project moves through different phases in its life cycle,

◆ Current stakeholders are no longer involved in the work of the project or new stakeholders become members of the project's stakeholder community, or

◆ There are significant changes in the organization or the wider stakeholder community.

## TRENDS AND EMERGING PRACTICES IN PROJECT STAKEHOLDER ENGAGEMENT

Broader definitions of stakeholders are being developed that expand the traditional categories of employees, suppliers, and shareholders to include groups such as regulators, lobby groups, environmentalists, financial organizations, the media, and those who simply believe they are stakeholders—they perceive that they will be affected by the work or outcomes of the project.

Trends and emerging practices for Project Stakeholder Management include but are not limited to:

◆ Identifying all stakeholders, not just a limited set;

◆ Ensuring that all team members are involved in stakeholder engagement activities;

◆ Reviewing the stakeholder community regularly, often in parallel with reviews of individual project risks;

◆ Consulting with stakeholders who are most affected by the work or outcomes of the project through the concept of co-creation. Co-creation places greater emphasis on including affected stakeholders in the team as partners; and

◆ Capturing the value of effective stakeholder engagement, both positive and negative. Positive value can be based on the consideration of benefits derived from higher levels of active support from stakeholders, particularly powerful stakeholders. Negative value can be derived by measuring the true costs of not engaging stakeholders effectively, leading to product recalls or loss of organizational or project reputation.

## TAILORING CONSIDERATIONS

Because each project is unique, the project manager may need to tailor the way Project Stakeholder Management processes are applied. Considerations for tailoring include but are not limited to:

◆ **Stakeholder diversity.** How many stakeholders are there? How diverse is the culture within the stakeholder community?

◆ **Complexity of stakeholder relationships.** How complex are the relationships within the stakeholder community? The more networks a stakeholder or stakeholder group participates in, the more complex the networks of information and misinformation the stakeholder may receive.

◆ **Communication technology.** What communication technology is available? What support mechanisms are in place to ensure that best value is achieved from the technology?

## CONSIDERATIONS FOR AGILE/ADAPTIVE ENVIRONMENTS

Projects experiencing a high degree of change require active engagement and participation with project stakeholders. To facilitate timely, productive discussion and decision making, adaptive teams engage with stakeholders directly rather than going through layers of management. Often the client, user, and developer exchange information in a dynamic co-creative process that leads to more stakeholder involvement and higher satisfaction. Regular interactions with the stakeholder community throughout the project mitigate risk, build trust, and support adjustments earlier in the project cycle, thus reducing costs and increasing the likelihood of success for the project.

In order to accelerate the sharing of information within and across the organization, agile methods promote aggressive transparency. The intent of inviting any stakeholders to project meetings and reviews or posting project artifacts in public spaces is to surface as quickly as possible any misalignment, dependency, or other issue related to the changing project.

# 13.1 IDENTIFY STAKEHOLDERS

Identify Stakeholders is the process of identifying project stakeholders regularly and analyzing and documenting relevant information regarding their interests, involvement, interdependencies, influence, and potential impact on project success. The key benefit of this process is that it enables the project team to identify the appropriate focus for engagement of each stakeholder or group of stakeholders. This process is performed periodically throughout the project as needed. The inputs, tools and techniques, and outputs of the process are depicted in Figure 13-2. Figure 13-3 depicts the data flow diagram for the process.

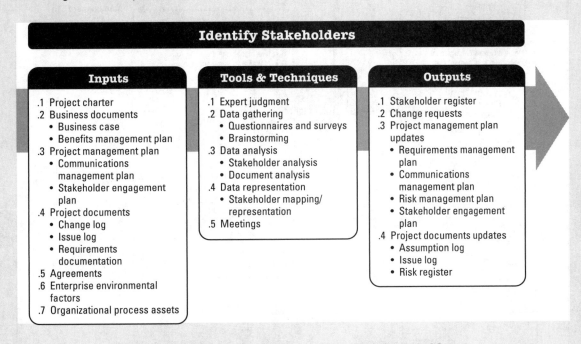

**Figure 13-2. Identify Stakeholders: Inputs, Tools & Techniques, and Outputs**

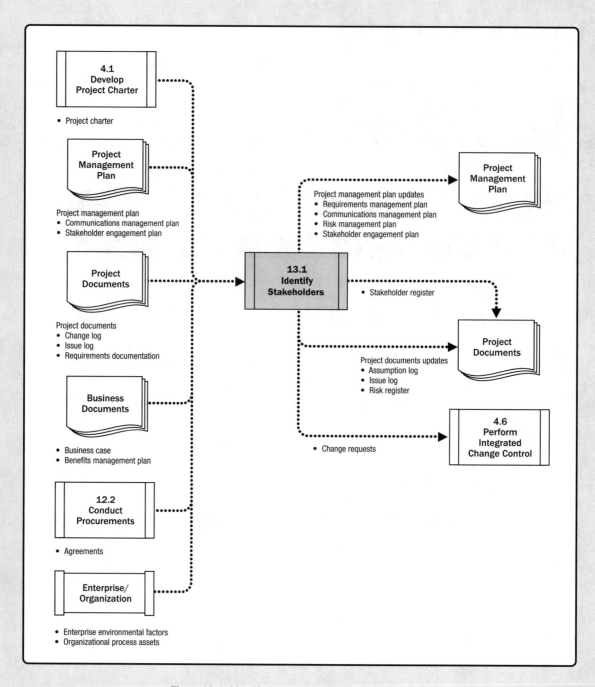

**Figure 13-3. Identify Stakeholders: Data Flow Diagram**

This process frequently occurs for the first time in a project either prior to or at the same time the project charter is developed and approved. It is repeated as necessary, but should be performed at the start of each phase and when a significant change in the project or the organization occurs. Each time the identification process is repeated, the project management plan components and project documents should be consulted to identify relevant project stakeholders.

## 13.1.1 IDENTIFY STAKEHOLDERS: INPUTS

### 13.1.1.1 PROJECT CHARTER

Described in Section 4.1.3.1. The project charter identifies the key stakeholder list. It may also contain information about the responsibilities of the stakeholders.

### 13.1.1.2 BUSINESS DOCUMENTS

In the first iteration of the Identify Stakeholders process, the business case and the benefits management plan are sources of information about the project's stakeholders.

◆ **Business case.** Described in Section 1.2.6.1. The business case identifies the project objectives and identifies an initial list of stakeholders affected by the project.

◆ **Benefits management plan.** Described in Section 1.2.6.2. The benefits management plan describes the expected plan for realizing the benefits claimed in the business case. It may identify the individuals and groups that will benefit from the delivery of the outcomes of the project and are thus considered as stakeholders.

### 13.1.1.3 PROJECT MANAGEMENT PLAN

Described in Section 4.2.3.1. The project management plan is not available when initially identifying stakeholders; however, once it has been developed, project management plan components include but are not limited to:

◆ **Communications management plan.** Described in Section 10.1.3.1. Communications and stakeholder engagement are strongly linked. Information included in the communications management plan is a source of knowledge about the project's stakeholders.

◆ **Stakeholder engagement plan.** Described in Section 13.2.3.1. The stakeholder engagement plan identifies the management strategies and actions required to effectively engage stakeholders.

### 13.1.1.4 PROJECT DOCUMENTS

It is unlikely that any project documents will be an input for the initial stakeholder identification. However, stakeholder identification occurs throughout the project. Once the project is past the startup phase, more documents become available and are used throughout the project. Project documents that can be considered as inputs for this process include but are not limited to:

◆ **Change log.** Described in Section 4.6.3.3. The change log may introduce a new stakeholder or change the nature of an existing stakeholder's relationship to the project.

◆ **Issue log.** Described in Section 4.3.3.3. The issue log records issues that may introduce new stakeholders to the project or change the type of participation of existing stakeholders.

◆ **Requirements documentation.** Described in Section 5.2.3.1. Requirements can provide information on potential stakeholders.

### 13.1.1.5 AGREEMENTS

Described in Section 12.2.3.2. The parties of an agreement are project stakeholders. The agreement can contain references to additional stakeholders.

### 13.1.1.6 ENTERPRISE ENVIRONMENTAL FACTORS

The enterprise environmental factors that can influence the Identify Stakeholders process include but are not limited to:

◆ Organizational culture, political climate, and governance framework;

◆ Government or industry standards (regulations, product standards, and codes of conduct);

◆ Global, regional, or local trends and practices or habits; and

◆ Geographic distribution of facilities and resources.

### 13.1.1.7 ORGANIZATIONAL PROCESS ASSETS

The organizational process assets that can influence the Identify Stakeholders process include but are not limited to:

◆ Stakeholder register templates and instructions,

◆ Stakeholder registers from previous projects, and

◆ Lessons learned repository with information about the preferences, actions, and involvement of stakeholders.

## 13.1.2 IDENTIFY STAKEHOLDERS: TOOLS AND TECHNIQUES

### 13.1.2.1 EXPERT JUDGMENT

Described in Section 4.1.2.1. Expertise should be considered from individuals or groups with specialized knowledge or training in the following topics:

◆ Understanding the politics and power structures in the organization,

◆ Knowledge of the environment and culture of the organization and other affected organizations including customers and the wider environment,

◆ Knowledge of the industry or type of project deliverable, and

◆ Knowledge of individual team member contributions and expertise.

### 13.1.2.2 DATA GATHERING

Data-gathering techniques that can be used for this process include but are not limited to:

◆ **Questionnaires and surveys.** Described in Section 5.2.2.2. Questionnaires and surveys can include one-on-one reviews, focus group sessions, or other mass information collection techniques.

◆ **Brainstorming.** Described in Section 4.1.2.2. Brainstorming as used to identify stakeholders can include both brainstorming and brain writing.

■ *Brainstorming.* A general data-gathering and creativity technique that elicits input from groups such as team members or subject matter experts.

■ *Brain writing.* A refinement of brainstorming that allows individual participants time to consider the question(s) individually before the group creativity session is held. The information can be gathered in face-to-face groups or using virtual environments supported by technology.

### 13.1.2.3 DATA ANALYSIS

Data analysis techniques that can be used for this process include but are not limited to:

◆ **Stakeholder analysis.** Stakeholder analysis results in a list of stakeholders and relevant information such as their positions in the organization, roles on the project, "stakes," expectations, attitudes (their levels of support for the project), and their interest in information about the project. Stakeholders' stakes can include but are not limited to a combination of:

  ■ *Interest.* A person or group can be affected by a decision related to the project or its outcomes.

  ■ *Rights (legal or moral rights).* Legal rights, such as occupational health and safety, may be defined in the legislation framework of a country. Moral rights may involve concepts of protection of historical sites or environmental sustainability.

  ■ *Ownership.* A person or group has a legal title to an asset or a property.

  ■ *Knowledge.* Specialist knowledge, which can benefit the project through more effective delivery of project objectives, organizational outcomes, or knowledge of the power structures of the organization.

  ■ *Contribution.* Provision of funds or other resources, including human resources, or providing support for the project in more intangible ways, such as advocacy in the form of promoting the objectives of the project or acting as a buffer between the project and the power structures of the organization and its politics.

◆ **Document analysis.** Described in Section 5.2.2.3. Assessing the available project documentation and lessons learned from previous projects to identify stakeholders and other supporting information.

### 13.1.2.4 DATA REPRESENTATION

A data representation technique that may be used in this process includes but is not limited to stakeholder mapping/representation. Stakeholder mapping and representation is a method of categorizing stakeholders using various methods. Categorizing stakeholders assists the team in building relationships with the identified project stakeholders. Common methods include:

◆ **Power/interest grid, power/influence grid, or impact/influence grid.** Each of these techniques supports a grouping of stakeholders according to their level of authority (power), level of concern about the project's outcomes (interest), ability to influence the outcomes of the project (influence), or ability to cause changes to the project's planning or execution. These classification models are useful for small projects or for projects with simple relationships between stakeholders and the project, or within the stakeholder community itself.

◆ **Stakeholder cube.** This is a refinement of the grid models previously mentioned. This model combines the grid elements into a three-dimensional model that can be useful to project managers and teams in identifying and engaging their stakeholder community. It provides a model with multiple dimensions that improves the depiction of the stakeholder community as a multidimensional entity and assists with the development of communication strategies.

◆ **Salience model.** Describes classes of stakeholders based on assessments of their power (level of authority or ability to influence the outcomes of the project), urgency (need for immediate attention, either time-constrained or relating to the stakeholders' high stake in the outcome), and legitimacy (their involvement is appropriate). There is an adaptation of the salience model that substitutes proximity for legitimacy (applying to the team and measuring their level of involvement with the work of the project). The salience model is useful for large complex communities of stakeholders or where there are complex networks of relationships within the community. It is also useful in determining the relative importance of the identified stakeholders.

◆ **Directions of influence.** Classifies stakeholders according to their influence on the work of the project or the project team itself. Stakeholders can be classified in the following ways:

  ■ *Upward* (senior management of the performing organization or customer organization, sponsor, and steering committee),

  ■ *Downward* (the team or specialists contributing knowledge or skills in a temporary capacity),

  ■ *Outward* (stakeholder groups and their representatives outside the project team, such as suppliers, government departments, the public, end-users, and regulators), or

  ■ *Sideward* (the peers of the project manager, such as other project managers or middle managers who are in competition for scarce project resources or who collaborate with the project manager in sharing resources or information).

◆ **Prioritization.** Prioritizing stakeholders may be necessary for projects with a large number of stakeholders, where the membership of the stakeholder community is changing frequently, or when the relationships between stakeholders and the project team or within the stakeholder community are complex.

### 13.1.2.5 MEETINGS

Meetings are used to develop an understanding of significant project stakeholders. They can take the form of facilitation workshops, small group guided discussions, and virtual groups using electronics or social media technologies to share ideas and analyze data.

## 13.1.3 IDENTIFY STAKEHOLDERS: OUTPUTS

### 13.1.3.1 STAKEHOLDER REGISTER

The main output of the Identify Stakeholders process is the stakeholder register. This document contains information about identified stakeholders that includes but is not limited to:

◆ **Identification information.** Name, organizational position, location and contact details, and role on the project.

◆ **Assessment information.** Major requirements, expectations, potential for influencing project outcomes, and the phase of the project life cycle where the stakeholder has the most influence or impact.

◆ **Stakeholder classification.** Internal/external, impact/influence/power/interest, upward/downward/outward/ sideward, or any other classification model chosen by the project manager.

### 13.1.3.2 CHANGE REQUESTS

Described in Section 4.3.3.4. During the first iteration of identifying stakeholders, there will not be any change requests. As stakeholder identification continues throughout the project, new stakeholders, or new information about stakeholders, may result in a change request to the product, project management plan, or project documents.

Change requests are processed for review and disposition through the Perform Integrated Change Control (Section 4.6) process.

### 13.1.3.3 PROJECT MANAGEMENT PLAN UPDATES

When stakeholders are identified at the very beginning of a project, there will not be updates to the project management plan. As the project progresses, any change to the project management plan goes through the organization's change control process via a change request. Components that may require a change request for the project management plan include but are not limited to:

◆ **Requirements management plan.** Described in Section 5.1.3.2. Newly identified stakeholders can impact how requirements activities will be planned, tracked, and reported.

◆ **Communications management plan.** Described in Section 10.1.3.1. Stakeholder communication requirements and agreed-upon communications strategies are recorded in the communications management plan.

◆ **Risk management plan.** Described in Section 11.1.3.1. Where stakeholder communication requirements and agreed-upon communications strategies affect the approach to managing risk on the project, this is reflected in the risk management plan.

◆ **Stakeholder engagement plan.** Described in Section 13.2.3.1. Agreed-upon communications strategies for identified stakeholders are recorded in the stakeholder engagement plan.

### 13.1.3.4 PROJECT DOCUMENTS UPDATES

Project documents that may be updated as a result of carrying out this process include but are not limited to:

◆ **Assumption log.** Described in Section 4.1.3.2. Much of the information about the relative power, interest, and engagement of stakeholders is based on assumptions. This information is entered into the assumption log. Additionally, any constraints associated with interacting with specific stakeholders are entered as well.

◆ **Issue log.** Described in Section 4.3.3.3. New issues raised as a result of this process are recorded in the issue log.

◆ **Risk register.** Described in Section 11.2.3.1. New risks identified during this process are recorded in the risk register and managed using the risk management processes.

## 13.2 PLAN STAKEHOLDER ENGAGEMENT

Plan Stakeholder Engagement is the process of developing approaches to involve project stakeholders based on their needs, expectations, interests, and potential impact on the project. The key benefit is that it provides an actionable plan to interact effectively with stakeholders. This process is performed periodically throughout the project as needed.

The inputs, tools and techniques, and outputs of the process are depicted in Figure 13-4. Figure 13-5 depicts the data flow diagram for the process.

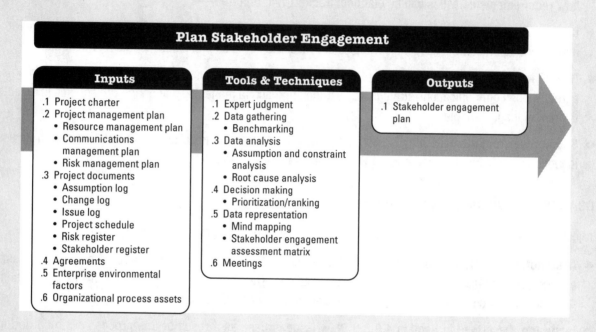

Figure 13-4. Plan Stakeholder Engagement: Inputs, Tools & Techniques, and Outputs

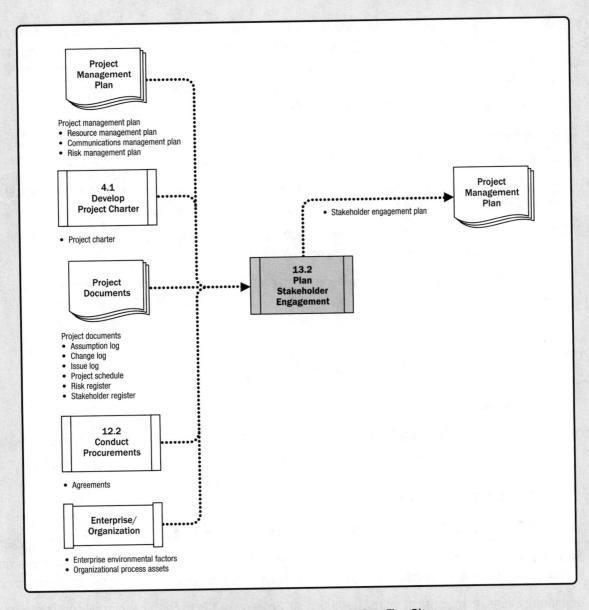

Figure 13-5. Plan Stakeholder Engagement: Data Flow Diagram

An effective plan that recognizes the diverse information needs of the project's stakeholders is developed early in the project life cycle and is reviewed and updated regularly as the stakeholder community changes. The first version of the stakeholder engagement plan is developed after the initial stakeholder community has been identified by the Identify Stakeholder process. The stakeholder engagement plan is updated regularly to reflect changes to the stakeholder community. Typical trigger situations requiring updates to the plan include but are not limited to:

◆ When it is the start of a new phase of the project;

◆ When there are changes to the organization structure or within the industry;

◆ When new individuals or groups become stakeholders, current stakeholders are no longer part of the stakeholder community, or the importance of particular stakeholders to the project's success changes; and

◆ When outputs of other project process areas, such as change management, risk management, or issue management, require a review of stakeholder engagement strategies.

The results of these adjustments may be changes to the relative importance of the stakeholders who have been identified.

## 13.2.1 PLAN STAKEHOLDER ENGAGEMENT: INPUTS

### 13.2.1.1 PROJECT CHARTER

Described in Section 4.1.3.1. The project charter contains information on the project purpose, objectives, and success criteria that can be taken into consideration when planning how to engage stakeholders.

### 13.2.1.2 PROJECT MANAGEMENT PLAN

Described in Section 4.2.3.1. Project management plan components include but are not limited to:

◆ **Resource management plan.** Described in Section 9.1.3.1. The resource management plan may contain information regarding roles and responsibilities of the team and other stakeholders listed in the stakeholder register.

◆ **Communications management plan.** Described in Section 10.1.3.1. The communications strategies for stakeholder management and their implementation plans are both inputs to, and recipients of, information from processes in Project Stakeholder Management.

◆ **Risk management plan.** Described in Section 11.1.3.1. The risk management plan may contain risk thresholds or risk attitudes that can assist in the selection of the optimal stakeholder engagement strategy mix.

### 13.2.1.3 PROJECT DOCUMENTS

Project documents that can be considered as inputs for this process, especially after initial planning has taken place, include but are not limited to:

◆ **Assumption log.** Described in Section 4.1.3.2. The assumption log contains information about assumptions and constraints and may be linked to specific stakeholders.

◆ **Change log.** Described in Section 4.6.3.3. The change log contains changes to the original scope of the project. It usually links to specific stakeholders because they fall into categories of requesting certain changes, making decisions about change requests, or being impacted by the implementation of approved changes.

◆ **Issue log.** Described in Section 4.3.3.3. Managing and resolving issues contained in the issue log will require additional communications with the stakeholders affected.

◆ **Project schedule.** Described in Section 6.5.3.2. The schedule contains activities that may be linked to specific stakeholders as owners or executors.

◆ **Risk register.** Described in Section 11.2.3.1. The risk register contains the identified risks of the project and usually links them to the specific stakeholders as either risk owners or as subject to risk impact.

◆ **Stakeholder register.** Described in Section 13.1.3.1. The stakeholder register provides the list of project stakeholders including additional classification data and other information.

### 13.2.1.4 AGREEMENTS

Described in Section 12.2.3.2. When planning for the engagement of contractors and suppliers, coordination usually involves working with the procurement/contracting group in the organization to ensure contractors and suppliers are effectively managed.

### 13.2.1.5 ENTERPRISE ENVIRONMENTAL FACTORS

The enterprise environmental factors that can influence Plan Stakeholder Engagement include but are not limited to:

◆ Organizational culture, political climate, and governance framework;

◆ Personnel administration policies;

◆ Stakeholder risk appetites;

◆ Established communication channels;

◆ Global regional or local trends, practices, or habits; and

◆ Geographic distribution of facilities and resources.

### 13.2.1.6 ORGANIZATIONAL PROCESS ASSETS

The organizational process assets that can influence the Plan Stakeholder Engagement process include but are not limited to:

◆ Corporate policies and procedures for social media, ethics, and security;

◆ Corporate policies and procedures for issue, risk, change, and data management;

◆ Organizational communication requirements;

◆ Standardized guidelines for development, exchange, storage, and retrieval of information;

◆ Lessons learned repository with information about the preferences, actions, and involvement of stakeholders; and

◆ Software tools needed to support effective stakeholder engagement.


## 13.2.2 PLAN STAKEHOLDER ENGAGEMENT: TOOLS AND TECHNIQUES

### 13.2.2.1 EXPERT JUDGMENT

Described in Section 4.1.2.1. Expertise should be considered from individuals or groups with specialized knowledge or training in the following topics:

◆ Politics and power structures in the organization and outside the organization,

◆ Environment and culture of the organization and outside the organization,

◆ Analytical and assessment techniques to be used for stakeholder engagement processes,

◆ Communication means and strategies, and

◆ Knowledge from previous projects of the characteristics of stakeholders and stakeholder groups and organizations involved in the current project that may have been involved in previous similar projects.

### 13.2.2.2 DATA GATHERING

A data-gathering technique that can be used for this process includes but is not limited to benchmarking. Described in Section 8.1.2.2. The results of stakeholder analysis are compared with information from other organizations or other projects that are considered to be world class.

### 13.2.2.3 DATA ANALYSIS

Data analysis techniques that can be used for this process include but are not limited to:

◆ **Assumption and constraint analysis.** Described in Section 11.2.2.3. Analysis of current assumptions and constraints may be conducted in order to tailor appropriate engagement strategies.

◆ **Root cause analysis.** Described in Section 8.2.2.2. Root cause analysis identifies underlying reasons for the level of support of project stakeholders in order to select the appropriate strategy to improve their level of engagement.

### 13.2.2.4 DECISION MAKING

Decision-making techniques that can be used for this process include but are not limited to prioritization/ranking. Stakeholder requirements need to be prioritized and ranked, as do the stakeholders themselves. Stakeholders with the most interest and the highest influence are often prioritized at the top of the list.

### 13.2.2.5 DATA REPRESENTATION

Data representation techniques that may be used in this process include but are not limited to:

◆ **Mind mapping.** Described in Section 5.2.2.3. Mind mapping is used to visually organize information about stakeholders and their relationship to each other and the organization.

◆ **Stakeholder engagement assessment matrix.** A stakeholder engagement assessment matrix supports comparison between the current engagement levels of stakeholders and the desired engagement levels required for successful project delivery. One way to classify the engagement level of stakeholders is shown in Figure 13-6. The engagement level of stakeholders can be classified as follows:

  - *Unaware.* Unaware of the project and potential impacts.
  - *Resistant.* Aware of the project and potential impacts but resistant to any changes that may occur as a result of the work or outcomes of the project. These stakeholders will be unsupportive of the work or outcomes of the project.
  - *Neutral.* Aware of the project, but neither supportive nor unsupportive.
  - *Supportive.* Aware of the project and potential impacts and supportive of the work and its outcomes.
  - *Leading.* Aware of the project and potential impacts and actively engaged in ensuring that the project is a success.

In Figure 13-6, C represents the current engagement level of each stakeholder and D indicates the level that the project team has assessed as essential to ensure project success (desired). The gap between current and desired for each stakeholder will direct the level of communications necessary to effectively engage the stakeholder. The closing of this gap between current and desired is an essential element of monitoring stakeholder engagement.

| Stakeholder | Unaware | Resistant | Neutral | Supportive | Leading |
|---|---|---|---|---|---|
| Stakeholder 1 | C | | | D | |
| Stakeholder 2 | | | C | D | |
| Stakeholder 3 | | | | D C | |

Figure 13-6. Stakeholder Engagement Assessment Matrix

### 13.2.2.6 MEETINGS

Meetings are used to discuss and analyze the input data of the stakeholder engagement planning process and to develop a sound stakeholder engagement plan.

## 13.2.3 PLAN STAKEHOLDER ENGAGEMENT: OUTPUTS

### 13.2.3.1 STAKEHOLDER ENGAGEMENT PLAN

The stakeholder engagement plan is a component of the project management plan that identifies the strategies and actions required to promote productive involvement of stakeholders in decision making and execution. It can be formal or informal and highly detailed or broadly framed, based on the needs of the project and the expectations of stakeholders.

The stakeholder engagement plan may include but is not limited to specific strategies or approaches for engaging with individuals or groups of stakeholders.

## 13.3 MANAGE STAKEHOLDER ENGAGEMENT

Manage Stakeholder Engagement is the process of communicating and working with stakeholders to meet their needs and expectations, address issues, and foster appropriate stakeholder involvement. The key benefit of this process is that it allows the project manager to increase support and minimize resistance from stakeholders. This process is performed throughout the project. The inputs, tools and techniques, and outputs of the process are depicted in Figure 13-7. Figure 13-8 depicts the data flow diagram for the process.

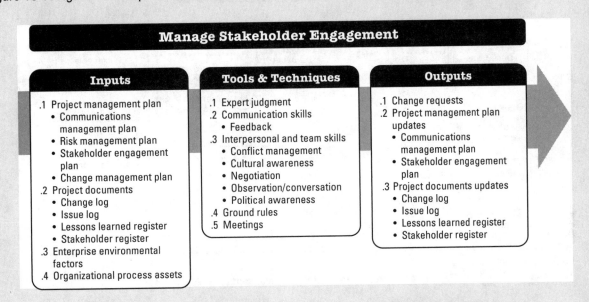

Figure 13-7. Manage Stakeholder Engagement: Inputs, Tools & Techniques, and Outputs

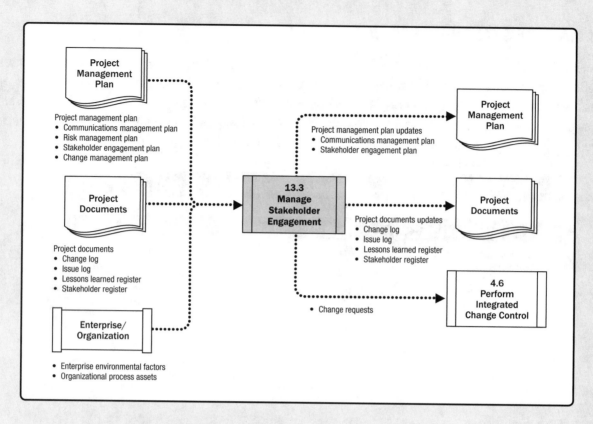

**Figure 13-8. Manage Stakeholder Engagement: Data Flow Diagram**

Manage Stakeholder Engagement involves activities such as:

◆ Engaging stakeholders at appropriate project stages to obtain, confirm, or maintain their continued commitment to the success of the project;

◆ Managing stakeholder expectations through negotiation and communication;

◆ Addressing any risks or potential concerns related to stakeholder management and anticipating future issues that may be raised by stakeholders; and

◆ Clarifying and resolving issues that have been identified.

Managing stakeholder engagement helps to ensure that stakeholders clearly understand the project goals, objectives, benefits, and risks for the project, as well as how their contribution will enhance project success.

## 13.3.1 MANAGE STAKEHOLDER ENGAGEMENT: INPUTS

### 13.3.1.1 PROJECT MANAGEMENT PLAN

Described in Section 4.2.3.1. Project management plan components include but are not limited to:

◆ **Communications management plan.** Described in Section 10.1.3.1. The communications management plan describes the methods, formats, and technologies used for stakeholder communication.

◆ **Risk management plan.** Described in Section 11.1.3.1. The risk management plan describes the risk categories, risk appetites, and reporting formats that can be used to manage stakeholder engagement.

◆ **Stakeholder engagement plan.** Described in Section 13.2.3.1. The stakeholder engagement plan provides guidance and information on managing stakeholder expectations.

◆ **Change management plan.** Described in Section 4.2.3.1. The change management plan describes the process for submitting, evaluating and implementing changes to the project.

### 13.3.1.2 PROJECT DOCUMENTS

Project documents that can be considered as inputs to this process include but are not limited to:

◆ **Change log.** Described in Section 4.6.3.3. Change requests and their status are documented in the change log and communicated to the appropriate stakeholders.

◆ **Issue log.** Described in Section 4.3.3.3. Any project or stakeholder concerns are documented in the issue log, as well as any assigned action items associated with managing the issue.

◆ **Lessons learned register.** Described in Section 4.4.3.1. Lessons learned earlier in the project with regard to managing stakeholder engagement can be applied to later phases in the project to improve the efficiency and effectiveness of this process.

◆ **Stakeholder register.** Described in Section 13.1.3.1. The stakeholder register provides the list of project stakeholders and any information needed to execute the stakeholder engagement plan.

### 13.3.1.3 ENTERPRISE ENVIRONMENTAL FACTORS

The enterprise environmental factors that can influence the Manage Stakeholder Engagement include but are not limited to:

◆ Organizational culture, political climate, and governance structure of the organization;

◆ Personnel administration policies;

◆ Stakeholder risk thresholds;

◆ Established communication channels;

◆ Global, regional, or local trends, practices, or habits; and

◆ Geographic distribution of facilities and resources.

### 13.3.1.4 ORGANIZATIONAL PROCESS ASSETS

The organizational process assets that can influence the Manage Stakeholder Engagement process include but are not limited to:

◆ Corporate policies and procedures for social media, ethics, and security;

◆ Corporate policies and procedures for issue, risk, change, and data management;

◆ Organizational communication requirements;

◆ Standardized guidelines for development, exchange, storage, and retrieval of information; and

◆ Historical information from previous similar projects.

### 13.3.2 MANAGE STAKEHOLDER ENGAGEMENT: TOOLS AND TECHNIQUES

### 13.3.2.1 EXPERT JUDGMENT

Described in Section 4.1.2.1. Expertise should be considered from individuals or groups with specialized knowledge or training in the following topics:

◆ Politics and power structures in the organization and outside the organization;

◆ Environment and culture of the organization and outside the organization;

◆ Analytical and assessment techniques to be used for stakeholder engagement processes;

◆ Communication methods and strategies;

◆ Characteristics of stakeholders, stakeholder groups, and organizations involved in the current project that may have been involved in previous projects; and

◆ Requirements management, vendor management, and change management.

### 13.3.2.2 COMMUNICATION SKILLS

The methods of communication identified for each stakeholder in the communications management plan are applied during stakeholder engagement management. The project management team uses feedback to assist in understanding stakeholder reaction to the various project management activities and key decisions. Feedback may be collected in the following ways, but not limited to:

◆ Conversations; both formal and informal,

◆ Issue identification and discussion,

◆ Meetings,

◆ Progress reporting, and

◆ Surveys.

### 13.3.2.3 INTERPERSONAL AND TEAM SKILLS

Interpersonal and team skills that can be used for this process include but are not limited to:

◆ **Conflict management.** Described in Section 9.5.2.1. The project manager should ensure that conflicts are resolved in a timely manner.

◆ **Cultural awareness.** Described in Section 10.1.2.6. Cultural awareness is used to help the project manager and team to communicate effectively by considering cultural differences and the requirements of stakeholders.

◆ **Negotiation.** Described in Section 12.2.2.5. Negotiation is used to achieve support or agreement that supports the work of the project or its outcomes and to resolve conflicts within the team or with other stakeholders.

◆ **Observation/conversation.** Described in Section 5.2.2.6. Observation/conversation is used to stay in touch with the work and attitudes of project team members and other stakeholders.

◆ **Political awareness.** Described in Section 10.1.2.6. Political awareness is achieved through understanding the power relationships within and around the project.

### 13.3.2.4 GROUND RULES

Ground rules, defined in the team charter set the expected behavior for project team members, as well as other stakeholders, with regard to stakeholder engagement.

### 13.3.2.5 MEETINGS

Described in Section 10.1.2.8. Meetings are used to discuss and address any issue or concern regarding stakeholder engagement. Types of meetings that are beneficial as part of this process include but are not limited to:

◆ Decision making,

◆ Issue resolution,

◆ Lessons learned and retrospectives,

◆ Project kick-off,

◆ Sprint planning, and

◆ Status updates.

## 13.3.3 MANAGE STAKEHOLDER ENGAGEMENT: OUTPUTS

### 13.3.3.1 CHANGE REQUESTS

Described in Section 4.3.3.4. As a result of managing stakeholder engagement, changes to the project scope or product scope may emerge. All change requests are processed for review and disposition through the Perform Integrated Change Control process (Section 4.6).

## 13.3.3.2 PROJECT MANAGEMENT PLAN UPDATES

Any change to the project management plan goes through the organization's change control process via a change request. Components of the project management plan that may require a change request for the project management plan include but are not limited to:

◆ **Communications management plan.** Described in Section 10.1.3.1. The communications management plan is updated to reflect new or changed stakeholder requirements.

◆ **Stakeholder engagement plan.** Described in Section 13.2.3.1. The stakeholder engagement plan is updated to reflect new or changed management strategies required to effectively engage stakeholders.

## 13.3.3.3 PROJECT DOCUMENTS UPDATES

Project documents that may be updated as a result of carrying out this process include but are not limited to:

◆ **Change log.** Described in Section 4.6.3.3. The change log may be updated based on any change requests.

◆ **Issue log.** Described in Section 4.3.3.3. The issue log may be updated to reflect an update to, or the development of, an issue log entry.

◆ **Lessons learned register.** Described in Section 4.4.3.1. The lessons learned register is updated with effective or ineffective approaches to managing stakeholder engagement so that information can be used in the current project or future projects.

◆ **Stakeholder register.** Described in Section 13.1.3.1. The stakeholder register may be updated based on new information provided to stakeholders about resolved issues, approved changes, and general project status.

# 13.4 MONITOR STAKEHOLDER ENGAGEMENT

Monitor Stakeholder Engagement is the process of monitoring project stakeholder relationships and tailoring strategies for engaging stakeholders through modification of engagement strategies and plans. The key benefit of this process is that it maintains or increases the efficiency and effectiveness of stakeholder engagement activities as the project evolves and its environment changes. This process is performed throughout the project. The inputs, tools and techniques, and outputs of the process are depicted in Figure 13-9. Figure 13-10 depicts the data flow diagram for the process.

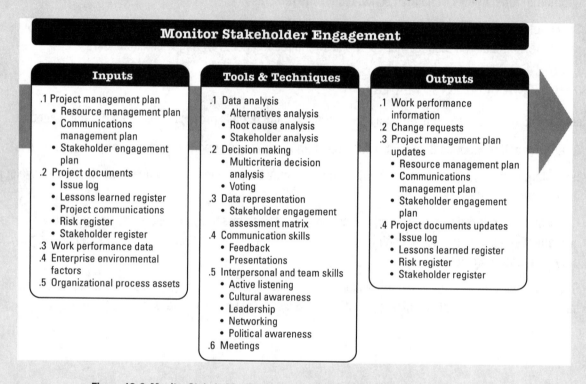

Figure 13-9. Monitor Stakeholder Engagement: Inputs, Tools & Techniques, and Outputs

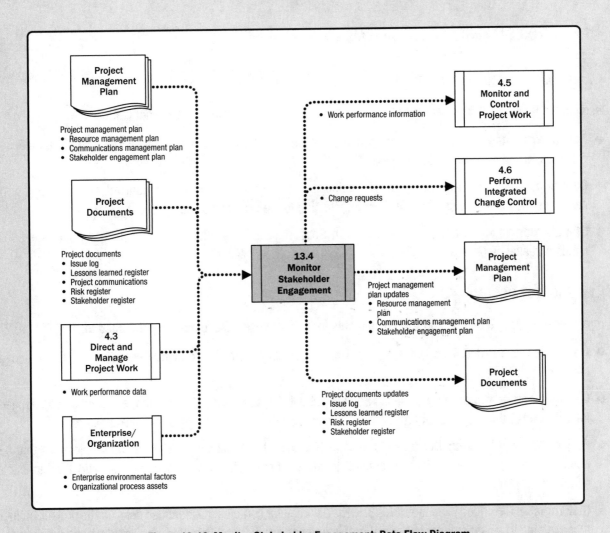

**Figure 13-10. Monitor Stakeholder Engagement: Data Flow Diagram**

### 13.4.1 MONITOR STAKEHOLDER ENGAGEMENT: INPUTS

#### 13.4.1.1 PROJECT MANAGEMENT PLAN

Described in Section 4.2.3.1. Project management plan components include but are not limited to:

◆ **Resource management plan.** Described in Section 9.1.3.1. The resource management plan identifies the methods for team member management.

◆ **Communications management plan.** Described in Section 10.1.3.1. The communications management plan describes the plans and strategies for communication to the project's stakeholders.

◆ **Stakeholder engagement plan.** Described in Section 13.2.3.1. Defines the plan for managing stakeholder needs and expectations.

#### 13.4.1.2 PROJECT DOCUMENTS

Project documents that can be considered as inputs for this process include but are not limited to:

◆ **Issue log.** Described in Section 4.3.3.3. The issue log documents all the known issues related to the project and stakeholders.

◆ **Lessons learned register.** Described in Section 4.4.3.1. Lessons learned earlier in the project can be applied in later phases of the project to improve the efficiency and effectiveness of engaging stakeholders.

◆ **Project communications.** Described in Section 10.2.3.1. These include the project communications that have been distributed to stakeholders as defined in the communications management plan and the stakeholder engagement plan.

◆ **Risk register.** Described in Section 11.2.3.1. The risk register contains the identified risks for the project, including those related to stakeholder engagement and interactions, their categorization, and list of potential responses.

◆ **Stakeholder register.** Described in Section 13.1.3.1. The stakeholder register contains stakeholder information that includes but is not limited to stakeholder identification, assessment, and classification.

#### 13.4.1.3 WORK PERFORMANCE DATA

Described in Section 4.3.3.2. Work performance data contains data on project status such as which stakeholders are supportive of the project, and their level and type of engagement.

### 13.4.1.4 ENTERPRISE ENVIRONMENTAL FACTORS

The enterprise environmental factors that can influence the Monitor Stakeholder Engagement process include but are not limited to:

◆ Organizational culture, political climate, and governance framework;

◆ Personnel administration policies;

◆ Stakeholder risk thresholds;

◆ Established communication channels;

◆ Global, regional, or local trends, practices, or habits; and

◆ Geographic distribution of facilities and resources.

### 13.4.1.5 ORGANIZATIONAL PROCESS ASSETS

The organizational process assets that can influence the Monitor Stakeholder Engagement process include but are not limited to:

◆ Corporate policies and procedures for social media, ethics, and security;

◆ Corporate policies and procedures for issue, risk, change, and data management;

◆ Organizational communication requirement;

◆ Standardized guidelines for development, exchange, storage, and retrieval of information; and

◆ Historical information from previous projects.

## 13.4.2 MONITOR STAKEHOLDER ENGAGEMENT: TOOLS AND TECHNIQUES

### 13.4.2.1 DATA ANALYSIS

Data analysis techniques that can be used for this process include but are not limited to:

◆ **Alternatives analysis.** Described in Section 9.2.2.5. Alternatives analysis can be used to evaluate options to respond to variances in the desired results of stakeholder engagement.

◆ **Root cause analysis.** Described in Section 8.2.2.2. A root cause analysis can be used to determine the basic underlying reason that stakeholder engagement is not having the planned effect.

◆ **Stakeholder analysis.** Described in Section 13.1.2.3. The stakeholder analysis helps to determine the position of stakeholder groups and individuals at any particular time in the project.

## 13.4.2.2 DECISION MAKING

Decision-making techniques that can be used for this process include but are not limited to:

◆ **Multicriteria decision analysis.** Described in Section 8.1.2.4. Criteria for successful stakeholder engagement are prioritized and weighted to identify the most appropriate choice.

◆ **Voting.** Described in Section 5.2.2.4. Voting can be used to select the best response for a variance in stakeholder engagement.

## 13.4.2.3 DATA REPRESENTATION

A data representation technique used in this process includes but is not limited to a stakeholder engagement assessment matrix. Described in Section 13.2.2.3. The stakeholder engagement assessment matrix monitors stakeholder engagement through tracking changes in level of engagement for each stakeholder.

## 13.4.2.4 COMMUNICATION SKILLS

Communication techniques that can be used for this process include but are not limited to:

◆ **Feedback.** Described in Section 10.2.2.3. Feedback is used to ensure that the information to stakeholders is received and understood.

◆ **Presentations.** Described in Section 10.2.2.3. Presentations provide clear information to stakeholders.

## 13.4.2.5 INTERPERSONAL AND TEAM SKILLS

Interpersonal skills to that can be used for this process include but are not limited to:

◆ **Active listening.** Described in Section 10.2.2.6. Active listening is used to reduce misunderstandings and other miscommunication.

◆ **Cultural awareness**. Described in Section 10.1.2.6. Cultural awareness and cultural sensitivity help the project manager to plan communications based on the cultural differences and requirements of stakeholders and team members.

◆ **Leadership.** Described in Section 3.4.4. Successful stakeholder engagement requires strong leadership skills to communicate the vision and inspire stakeholders to support the work and outcomes of the project.

◆ **Networking.** Described in Section 10.2.2.6. Networking ensures access to information about levels of engagement of stakeholders.

◆ **Political awareness.** Described in Section 10.1.2.6. Political awareness is used to understand the strategies of the organization, understand who wields power and influence in this arena, and to develop an ability to communicate with these stakeholders.

### 13.4.2.6 MEETINGS

Types of meetings include status meetings, standup meetings, retrospectives, and any other meetings as agreed upon in the stakeholder engagement plan to monitor and assess stakeholder engagement levels. Meetings are no longer limited by face-to-face or voice-to-voice interactions. While face-to-face interactions are ideal, they can be expensive. Teleconferencing and technology bridge the gap and provide numerous ways to connect and conduct a meeting.

## 13.4.3 MONITOR STAKEHOLDER ENGAGEMENT: OUTPUTS

### 13.4.3.1 WORK PERFORMANCE INFORMATION

Described in Section 4.5.1.3. Work performance information includes information about the status of stakeholder engagement, such as the level of current project support and compared to the desired levels of engagement as defined in the stakeholder engagement assessment matrix, stakeholder cube, or other tool.

### 13.4.3.2 CHANGE REQUESTS

Described in Section 4.3.3.4. A change request may include corrective and preventive actions to improve the current level of stakeholder engagement. Change requests are processed for review and disposition through the Perform Integrated Change Control process (Section 4.6).

### 13.4.3.3 PROJECT MANAGEMENT PLAN UPDATES

Any change to the project management plan goes through the organization's change control process via a change request. Components of the project management plan that may require a change request include but are not limited to:

◆ **Resource management plan.** Described in Section 9.1.3.1. Team responsibilities for stakeholder engagement activities may need to be updated.

◆ **Communications management plan.** Described in Section 10.1.3.1. The project's communication strategies may need to be updated.

◆ **Stakeholder engagement plan.** Described in Section 13.2.3.1. Information about the project's stakeholder community may need to be updated.

### 13.4.3.4 PROJECT DOCUMENTS UPDATES

Project documents that may be updated as a result of carrying out this process include but are not limited to:

◆ **Issue log.** Described in Section 4.3.3.3. Information in the issue log indicates stakeholder attitudes and may need to be updated.

◆ **Lessons learned register.** Described in Section 4.4.3.1. The lessons learned register is updated with information on challenges and how they could have been avoided. It is also updated with approaches that worked well for engaging stakeholders optimally, and those that did not work well.

◆ **Risk register.** Described in Section 11.2.3.1. The risk register may need to be updated with responses to stakeholder risks.

◆ **Stakeholder register.** Described in Section 13.1.3.1. The stakeholder register is updated with information as a result of monitoring stakeholder engagement.

# REFERENCES

[1]     Project Management Institute. 2017. *The Standard for Project Management.* Newtown Square, PA: Author.

[2]     Project Management Institute. 2013. *The Standard for Portfolio Management* – Third Edition. Newtown Square, PA: Author.

[3]     Project Management Institute. 2017. *The Standard for Program Management* – Fourth Edition. Newtown Square, PA: Author.

[4]     Project Management Institute. 2016. *The PMI Lexicon of Project Management Terms.* Available from http://www.pmi.org/lexiconterms

[5]     Project Management Institute. *Code of Ethics and Professional Conduct.* Available from http://www.pmi.org/codeofethics

[6]     Project Management Institute. 2013. *Managing Change in Organizations: A Practice Guide.* Newtown Square, PA: Author.

[7]     Project Management Institute. 2015. *Business Analysis for Practitioners: A Practice Guide.* Newtown Square, PA: Author.

[8]     Project Management Institute. 2014. *Implementing Organizational Project Management: A Practice Guide.* Newtown Square, PA: Author.

[9]     Project Management Institute. 2014. Project Management Institute Excellence in Practice-Research Collaboration, PMI-RI Standards Program: Making Sense of PPP Governance, December 19, 2014. Newtown Square, PA: Author

[10]    Project Management Institute. 2016. *Governance of Portfolios, Programs, and Projects: A Practice Guide.* Newtown Square, PA: Author.

[11]    Project Management Institute. (2013). *PMI's Pulse of the Profession® In-Depth Report: The Competitive Advantage of Effective Talent Management.* Available from http://www.pmi.org

[12]    Project Management Institute. 2015. White Paper, Complexity Management for Projects, Programmes, and Portfolios: An Engineering Systems Perspective, March 2015. Newtown Square, PA: Author.

[13]    Project Management Institute. 2014. *Navigating Complexity: A Practice Guide.* Newtown Square, PA: Author.

[14]    Project Management Institute. 2016. *Requirements Management: A Practice Guide.* Newtown Square, PA: Author.

[15]    Project Management Institute. 2006. *Practice Standard for Work Breakdown Structures (WBS).* Newtown Square, PA: Author.

[16]    Project Management Institute. 2011. *Practice Standard for Scheduling* – Second Edition. Newtown Square, PA: Author.

[17]    Project Management Institute. 2011. *Practice Standard for Earned Value Management* – Second Edition

[18]    International Standards Organization. 2015. ISO 9000:2015 *Quality Management Systems—Fundamentals and Vocabulary.* Geneva: Author.

# Part 2

# The Standard for Project Management

Approved American National Standard

ANSI/PMI 99-001-2017

# 1

## INTRODUCTION

A standard is a document established by an authority, custom, or general consent as a model or example. This standard was developed using a process based on the concepts of consensus, openness, due process, and balance. This standard describes the processes considered to be good practice on most projects most of the time. These processes are organized by Process Group. It further defines key project management concepts including the relationship of project management to organizational strategy and objectives, governance, portfolio management, program management, the project environment, and project success. It also covers information on project life cycles, project stakeholders, and the role of the project manager. Section 1 discusses key concepts and provides contextual information about project management. Sections 2 through 6 provide definitions for each of the five Process Groups and describe the processes within those Process Groups. Sections 2 through 6 also describe the key benefits, inputs, and outputs for each project management process. This standard serves as the foundation and framework for *A Guide to the Project Management Body of Knowledge* (*PMBOK® Guide*).[1] *PMBOK® Guide* expands on the information in this standard by providing a more in-depth description of the context, environment and influences on project management. In addition, the *PMBOK® Guide* provides descriptions of the project management process inputs and outputs, identifies tools and techniques, and discusses key concepts and emerging trends associated with each Knowledge Area.

---

[1] Project Management Institute. 2017. *A Guide to the Project Management Body of Knowledge (PMBOK® Guide).* Newtown Square, PA: Author.

# 1.1 PROJECTS AND PROJECT MANAGEMENT

A project is a temporary endeavor undertaken to create a unique product, service, or result. The temporary nature of projects indicates a definite beginning and end. Temporary does not necessarily mean a project has a short duration. A project's end is reached when the objectives have been achieved or when the project is terminated because its objectives will not or cannot be met, or when the need for the project no longer exists. The decision to terminate a project requires approval and authorization by an appropriate authority.

Project management is the application of knowledge, skills, tools, and techniques to project activities to meet project requirements. Project management is accomplished through the appropriate application and integration of the project management processes identified for the project.

Managing a project typically includes but is not limited to:

◆ Identifying project requirements;

◆ Addressing the various needs, concerns, and expectations of stakeholders;

◆ Establishing and maintaining active communication with stakeholders;

◆ Managing resources; and

◆ Balancing the competing project constraints, which include but are not limited to:

- Scope,

- Schedule,

- Cost,

- Quality,

- Resources, and

- Risk.

Project circumstances will influence how each project management process is implemented and how the project constraints are prioritized.

## 1.2 RELATIONSHIPS AMONG PORTFOLIOS, PROGRAMS, AND PROJECTS

A portfolio is defined as projects, programs, subsidiary portfolios, and operations managed in a coordinated manner to achieve strategic objectives. Portfolio management is the centralized management of one or more portfolios to achieve strategic objectives. Portfolio management focuses on ensuring the portfolio is performing consistent with the organization's objectives and evaluating portfolio components to optimize resource allocation. Portfolios may include work that is operational in nature.

A program is defined as related projects, subsidiary programs, and program activities managed in a coordinated manner to obtain benefits not available from managing them individually. Programs include program related work outside the scope of the discrete projects in the program. Program management is the application of knowledge, skills, and principles to a program to achieve the program objectives and to obtain benefits and control not available by managing related program components individually. Programs may also include work that is operational in nature.

Program management supports organizational strategies by authorizing, changing, or terminating projects and managing their interdependencies. Managing project interdependencies may include, among other actions, the following:

◆ Resolving resource constraints and/or conflicts that affect components within the program;

◆ Aligning with the organization's strategies that impact and affect program goals and objectives

◆ Managing issues and employing change management within a shared governance structure;

◆ Addressing project and program risks that can impact one or more components; and

◆ Managing program benefits realization by effectively analyzing, sequencing and monitoring component interdependencies.

A project may be managed in three separate scenarios: as a stand-alone project (outside a portfolio or program); within a program; or within a portfolio. Project management has interactions with portfolio and program management when a project is within a portfolio or program.

Figure 1-1 illustrates a sample portfolio structure indicating relationships of the components, shared resources and stakeholders. The portfolio components are grouped together in order to facilitate the effective governance and management of that work and to achieve organizational strategies and priorities. Organizational and portfolio planning impact the components by means of prioritization based on risk, funding, and other considerations. This allows organizations to have an overall view of how the strategic goals are reflected in the portfolio; institute appropriate portfolio, program, and project governance; and authorize human, financial, or physical resources. These resources will be allocated based on expected performance and benefits. Figure 1-1 illustrates that organizational strategies and priorities are linked and have relationships between portfolios and programs, between portfolios and projects, and between programs and individual projects. These relationships are not always strictly hierarchical.

Organizational project management (OPM) is a strategy execution framework utilizing portfolio, program, and project management. It provides a framework that enables organizations to consistently and predictably deliver on organizational strategy, producing better performance, better results, and a sustainable competitive advantage.

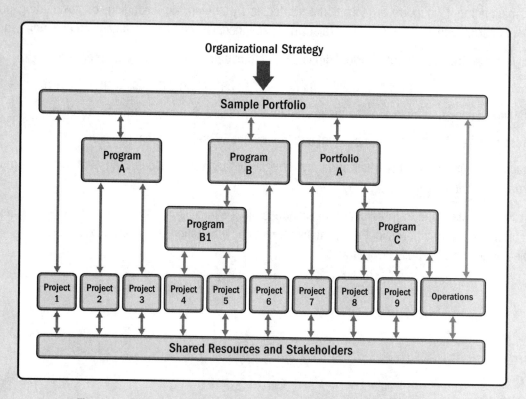

**Figure 1-1. Example of Portfolio, Program, and Project Management Interfaces**

# 1.3 LINKING ORGANIZATIONAL GOVERNANCE AND PROJECT GOVERNANCE

There are various types of governance including organizational governance; organizational project management (OPM) governance; and portfolio, program, and project governance. Organizational governance is a structured way to provide direction and control through policies, and processes, to meet strategic and operational goals. Organizational governance is typically conducted by a board of directors to ensure accountability, fairness, and transparency to its stakeholders. Organizational governance principles, decisions, and processes may influence and impact the governance of portfolios, programs, and projects in the following ways:

◆ Enforcing legal, regulatory, standards, and compliance requirements,

◆ Defining ethical, social, and environmental responsibilities, and

◆ Specifying operational, legal, and risk policies.

Project governance is the framework, functions, and processes that guide project management activities in order to create a unique product, service, or result to meet organizational, strategic, and operational goals. Governance at the project level includes:

◆ Guiding and overseeing the management of project work;

◆ Ensuring adherence to policies, standards, and guidelines;

◆ Establishing governance roles, responsibilities, and authorities;

◆ Decision-making regarding risk escalations, changes, and resources (e.g. team, financial, physical, facilities);

◆ Ensuring appropriate stakeholder engagement; and

◆ Monitoring performance.

The project governance framework provides the project stakeholders with structure, processes, roles, responsibilities, accountabilities, and decision-making models for managing the project. Elements of a project governance framework include but are not limited to principles or processes for:

◆ Stage gate or phase reviews;

◆ Identifying, escalating, and resolving risks and issues;

◆ Defining roles, responsibilities, and authorities;

◆ Process for project knowledge management and capturing lessons learned;

◆ Decision making, problem solving and escalating topics that are beyond the project manager's authority; and

◆ Reviewing and approving changes to project, and product changes that are beyond the authority of the project manager.

# 1.4 PROJECT SUCCESS AND BENEFITS MANAGEMENT

Projects are initiated to realize business opportunities that are aligned with an organization's strategic goals. Prior to initiating a project, a business case is often developed to outline the project objectives, the required investment, and financial and qualitative criteria for project success. The business case provides the basis to measure success and progress throughout the project life cycle by comparing the results with the objectives and the identified success criteria.

Projects are typically initiated as a result of one or more of the following strategic considerations:

◆ Market demand,

◆ Strategic opportunity/business need,

◆ Social need,

◆ Environmental consideration,

◆ Customer request,

◆ Technological advancement,

◆ Legal or regulatory requirement, and

◆ Existing or forecasted problem.

A benefits management plan describes how and when the benefits of the project will be delivered and how they will be measured. The benefits management plan may include the following:

◆ **Target benefits.** The expected tangible and intangible business value to be gained by the implementation of the product, service, or result.

◆ **Strategic alignment.** How the project benefits support and align with the business strategies of the organization.

◆ **Timeframe for realizing benefits.** Benefits by phase: short term, long term, and ongoing.

◆ **Benefits owner.** The accountable person or group that monitors, records, and reports realized benefits throughout the timeframe established in the plan.

◆ **Metrics.** The direct and indirect measurements used to show the benefits realized.

◆ **Risks.** Risks associated with achieving target benefits.

The success of the project is measured against the project objectives and success criteria. In many cases, the success of the product, service, or result is not known until sometime after the project is complete. For example, an increase in market share, a decrease in operating expenses, or the success of a new product may not be known when the project is transitioned to operations. In these circumstances, the project management office (PMO), portfolio steering committee, or some other business function within the organization should evaluate the success at a later date to determine if the outcomes met the business objectives.

Both the business case and the benefits management plan are developed prior to the project being initiated. Additionally, both documents are referenced after the project has been completed. Therefore, they are considered business documents rather than project documents or components of the project management plan. As appropriate, these business documents may be inputs to some of the processes involved in managing the project, such as developing the project charter.

## 1.5 THE PROJECT LIFE CYCLE

A project life cycle is the series of phases that a project passes through from its start to its completion. A project phase is a collection of logically related project activities that culminates in the completion of one or more deliverables. The phases can be sequential, iterative, or overlapping. The names, number, and duration of the project phases are determined by the management and control needs of the organization(s) involved in the project, the nature of the project itself, and its area of application. Phases are time bound, with a start and end or control point (sometimes referred to as a phase review, phase gate, control gate, or other similar term). At the control point, the project charter and business documents are reexamined based on the current environment. At that time, the project's performance is compared to the project management plan to determine if the project should be changed, terminated, or continue as planned.

The project life cycle can be influenced by the unique aspects of the organization, industry, development method, or technology employed. While every project has a start and end, the specific deliverables and work that take place vary widely depending on the project. The life cycle provides the basic framework for managing the project, regardless of the specific work involved.

Though projects vary in size and the amount of complexity they contain, a typical project can be mapped to the following project life cycle structure (see Figure 1-2):

◆ Starting the project,

◆ Organizing and preparing,

◆ Carrying out the work, and

◆ Closing the project.

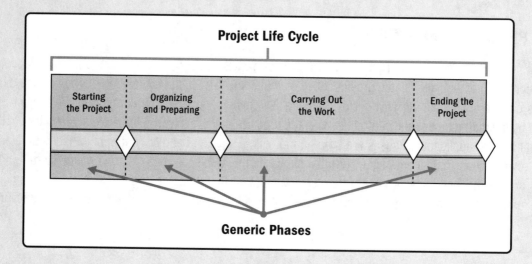

Figure 1-2. Generic Depiction of a Project Life Cycle

A generic life cycle structure typically displays the following characteristics:

◆ Cost and staffing levels are low at the start, increase as the work is carried out, and drop rapidly as the project draws to a close.

◆ Risk is greatest at the start of the project as illustrated by Figure 1-3. These factors decrease over the life cycle of the project as decisions are reached and as deliverables are accepted.

◆ The ability of stakeholders to influence the final characteristics of the project's product, without significantly impacting cost and schedule, is highest at the start of the project and decreases as the project progresses toward completion. Figure 1-3 illustrates the cost of making changes and correcting errors typically increases substantially as the project approaches completion.

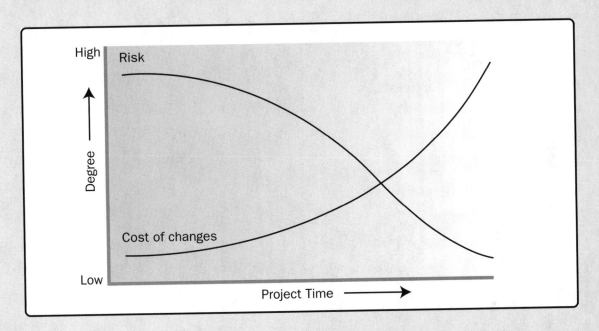

Figure 1-3. Impact of Variables Over Time

# 1.6 PROJECT STAKEHOLDERS

A stakeholder is an individual, group, or organization that may affect, be affected by, or perceive itself to be affected by a decision, activity, or outcome of a project. Project stakeholders may be internal or external to the project, they may be actively involved, passively involved, or unaware of the project. Project stakeholders may have a positive or negative impact on the project, or be positively or negatively impacted by the project. Examples of stakeholders include but are not limited to:

◆ *Internal stakeholders:*

- Sponsor,
- Resource manager,
- Project management office (PMO),
- Portfolio steering committee,
- Program manager,
- Project managers of other projects, and
- Team members.

◆ *External stakeholders:*

- Customers,
- End users,
- Suppliers,
- Shareholders
- Regulatory bodies, and
- Competitors

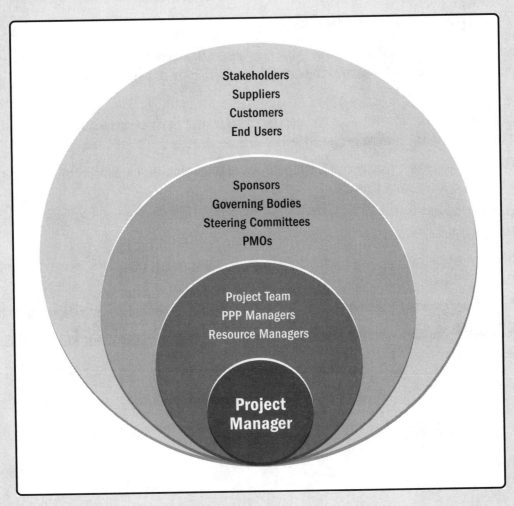

**Figure 1-4. Examples of Project Stakeholders**

Figure 1-4 shows examples of project stakeholders. Stakeholder involvement may range from occasional contributions in surveys and focus groups to full project sponsorship that includes the provision of financial, political, or other types of support. The type and level of project involvement can change over the course of the project's life cycle. Therefore, successfully identifying, analyzing, and engaging stakeholders and effectively managing their project expectations and participation throughout the project life cycle is critical to project success.

# 1.7 ROLE OF THE PROJECT MANAGER

The project manager is the person assigned by the performing organization to lead the team responsible for achieving the project objectives. The project manager's reporting relationships are based on the organizational structure and project governance.

In addition to any specific technical skills and general management proficiencies required for the project, project managers should have at least the following attributes:

◆ Knowledge about project management, the business environment, technical aspects, and other information needed to manage the project effectively;

◆ Skills needed to effectively lead the project team, coordinate the work, collaborate with stakeholders, solve problems, and make decisions;

◆ Abilities to develop and manage scope, schedules, budgets, resources, risks, plans, presentations, and reports; and

◆ Other attributes required to successfully manage the project, such as personality, attitude, ethics, and leadership.

Project managers accomplish work through the project team and other stakeholders. Project managers rely on important interpersonal skills, including, but not limited to:

◆ Leadership,

◆ Team building,

◆ Motivating,

◆ Communicating,

◆ Influencing,

◆ Decision making,

◆ Political and cultural awareness,

◆ Negotiating,

◆ Facilitating,

◆ Managing conflict, and

◆ Coaching.

The project manager is successful when the project objectives have been achieved. Another aspect of success is stakeholder satisfaction. The project manager should address stakeholder needs, concerns and expectations to satisfy relevant stakeholders. To be successful, the project manager should tailor the project approach, life cycle, and project management processes to meet the project and product requirements.

# 1.8 PROJECT MANAGEMENT KNOWLEDGE AREAS

The Project Management Knowledge Areas are fields or areas of specialization that are commonly employed when managing projects. A Knowledge Area is a set of processes associated with a particular topic in project management. These 10 Knowledge Areas are used on most projects most of the time. The needs of a specific project may require additional Knowledge Areas. The 10 Knowledge Areas are:

◆ **Project Integration Management.** Project Integration Management includes the processes and activities to identify, define, combine, unify, and coordinate the various processes and project management activities within the Project Management Process Groups.

◆ **Project Scope Management.** Project Scope Management includes the processes required to ensure that the project includes all the work required, and only the work required, to complete the project successfully.

◆ **Project Schedule Management.** Project Schedule Management includes the processes required to manage the timely completion of the project.

◆ **Project Cost Management.** Project Cost Management includes the processes involved in planning, estimating, budgeting, financing, funding, managing, and controlling costs so the project can be completed within the approved budget.

◆ **Project Quality Management.** Project Quality Management includes the processes for incorporating the organization's quality policy regarding planning, managing, and controlling project and product quality requirements, in order to meet stakeholders' expectations.

◆ **Project Resource Management.** Project Resource Management includes the processes to identify, acquire, and manage the resources needed for the successful completion of the project.

◆ **Project Communications Management.** Project Communications Management includes the processes required to ensure timely and appropriate planning, collection, creation, distribution, storage, retrieval, management, control, monitoring, and ultimate disposition of project information.

◆ **Project Risk Management.** Project Risk Management includes the processes of conducting risk management planning, identification, analysis, response planning, response implementation, and monitoring risk on a project.

◆ **Project Procurement Management.** Project Procurement Management includes the processes necessary to purchase or acquire products, services, or results needed from outside the project team.

◆ **Project Stakeholder Management.** Project Stakeholder Management includes the processes required to identify the people, groups, or organizations that could impact or be impacted by the project, to analyze stakeholder expectations and their impact on the project, and to develop appropriate management strategies for effectively engaging stakeholders in project decisions and execution.

# 1.9 PROJECT MANAGEMENT PROCESS GROUPS

This standard describes the project management processes employed to meet project objectives. Project management processes are grouped in five Project Management Process Groups:

◆ **Initiating Process Group.** The process(es) performed to define a new project or a new phase of an existing project by obtaining authorization to start the project or phase. Initiating processes are described in Section 2.

◆ **Planning Process Group.** The process(es) required to establish the scope of the project, refine the objectives, and define the course of action required to attain the objectives that the project was undertaken to achieve. Planning processes are described in Section 3.

◆ **Executing Process Group.** The process(es) performed to complete the work defined in the project management plan to satisfy the project requirements. Executing processes are described in Section 4.

◆ **Monitoring and Controlling Process Group.** The process(es) required to track, review, and regulate the progress and performance of the project; identify any areas in which changes to the plan are required; and initiate the corresponding changes. Monitoring and Controlling processes are described in Section 5.

◆ **Closing Process Group.** The process(es) performed to formally complete or close a project, phase, or contract. Closing processes are described in Section 6.

These five Process Groups are independent of the application areas, (such as marketing, information services, or accounting) or industry focus (such as construction, aerospace, telecommunications). Individual processes in the Process Groups are often iterated prior to completing a phase or a project. The number of process iterations and interactions between processes varies based on the needs of the project. Processes generally fall into one of three categories:

◆ **Processes used once or at predefined points in the project.** Developing the project charter and closing the project or phase are examples.

◆ **Processes that are performed periodically as needed.** Acquiring resources is performed when resources are needed. Conducting procurements will be performed prior to needing the procured item.

◆ **Processes that are performed continuously throughout the project.** Defining activities may occur throughout the project life cycle, especially when the project uses rolling wave planning or an adaptive development approach. Many of the monitoring and control processes are ongoing from the start of the project, until it is closed out.

The output of one process generally becomes an input to another process or is a deliverable of the project or project phase. For example, the project management plan and project documents (e.g., risk register, responsibility assignment matrix, etc.) produced in the Planning Process Group are provided to the Executing Process Group where updates are made. Figure 1-4 illustrates an example of how Process Groups can overlap during a project or phase.

Process Groups are not project phases. If the project is divided into phases, the processes in the Process Groups interact within each phase. It is possible that all Process Groups could be represented within a phase, as illustrated in Figure 1-5. As projects are separated into distinct phases, such as concept development, feasibility study, design, prototype, build, or test, etc., processes in each of the Process Groups are repeated as necessary in each phase until the completion criteria for that phase have been satisfied.

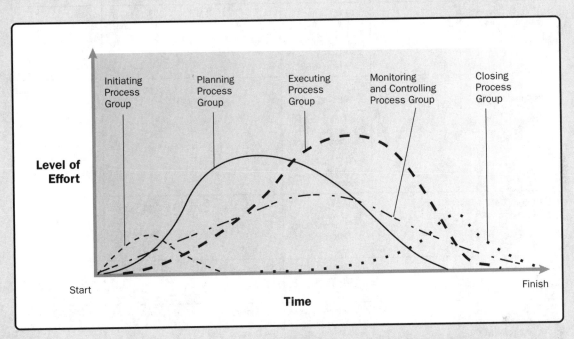

**Figure 1-5. Example of Process Group Interactions Within a Project or Phase**

Table 1-1 shows the 49 processes mapped to the Process Groups and Knowledge Areas.

| Knowledge Areas | Project Management Process Groups | | | | |
|---|---|---|---|---|---|
| | Initiating Process Group | Planning Process Group | Executing Process Group | Monitoring and Controlling Process Group | Closing Process Group |
| **4. Project Integration Management** | 4.1 Develop Project Charter | 4.2 Develop Project Management Plan | 4.3 Direct and Manage Project Work<br>4.4 Manage Project Knowledge | 4.5 Monitor and Control Project Work<br>4.6 Perform Integrated Change Control | 4.7 Close Project or Phase |
| **5. Project Scope Management** | | 5.1 Plan Scope Management<br>5.2 Collect Requirements<br>5.3 Define Scope<br>5.4 Create WBS | | 5.5 Validate Scope<br>5.6 Control Scope | |
| **6. Project Schedule Management** | | 6.1 Plan Schedule Management<br>6.2 Define Activities<br>6.3 Sequence Activities<br>6.4 Estimate Activity Durations<br>6.5 Develop Schedule | | 6.6 Control Schedule | |
| **7. Project Cost Management** | | 7.1 Plan Cost Management<br>7.2 Estimate Costs<br>7.3 Determine Budget | | 7.4 Control Costs | |
| **8. Project Quality Management** | | 8.1 Plan Quality Management | 8.2 Manage Quality | 8.3 Control Quality | |
| **9. Project Resource Management** | | 9.1 Plan Resource Management<br>9.2 Estimate Activity Resources | 9.3 Acquire Resources<br>9.4 Develop Team<br>9.5 Manage Team | 9.6 Control Resources | |
| **10. Project Communications Management** | | 10.1 Plan Communications Management | 10.2 Manage Communications | 10.3 Monitor Communications | |
| **11. Project Risk Management** | | 11.1 Plan Risk Management<br>11.2 Identify Risks<br>11.3 Perform Qualitative Risk Analysis<br>11.4 Perform Quantitative Risk Analysis<br>11.5 Plan Risk Responses | 11.6 Implement Risk Responses | 11.7 Monitor Risks | |
| **12. Project Procurement Management** | | 12.1 Plan Procurement Management | 12.2 Conduct Procurements | 12.3 Control Procurements | |
| **13. Project Stakeholder Management** | 13.1 Identify Stakeholders | 13.2 Plan Stakeholder Engagement | 13.3 Manage Stakeholder Engagement | 13.4 Monitor Stakeholder Engagement | |

# 1.10 ENTERPRISE ENVIRONMENTAL FACTORS AND ORGANIZATIONAL PROCESS ASSETS

Projects exist and operate in environments that may have an influence on them. These influences can have a favorable or unfavorable impact on the project. Two major categories of influences are enterprise environmental factors (EEFs) and organizational process assets (OPAs).

EEFs originate from the environment outside of the project and often outside of the enterprise. These factors refer to conditions, which are not under the control of the project team, that influence, constrain, or direct the project. EEFs may have an impact at the enterprise, portfolio, program, or project level. (Refer to Section 2.2 in the *PMBOK® Guide* for additional information on EEFs.) One set of such factors are the internal organizational culture, structure and governance. Examples in this area include but are not limited to: vision, mission, values, beliefs, cultural norms, hierarchy, and authority relationships.

OPAs are internal to the enterprise. These may arise from the enterprise itself, a portfolio, a program, another project, or a combination of these. OPAs are the plans, processes, policies, procedures, and knowledge bases specific to and used by the performing organization. These assets influence the management of the project. Examples include but are not limited to: change control procedures, templates, information from previous projects, and lessons learned repositories. (Refer to Section 2.3 in the *PMBOK® Guide* for additional information on OPAs).

# 1.11 TAILORING THE PROJECT ARTIFACTS

The term artifact in this context includes project management processes, inputs, tools, techniques, outputs, EEFs, and OPAs. The project manager and the project management team select and adapt the appropriate artifacts for use on their specific project. This selection and adaptation activity is known as tailoring. Tailoring is necessary because each project is unique; therefore, not every process, input, tool, technique, or output is required on every project.

The project management plan is the most prevalent artifact. It has many components, such as the subsidiary management plans, baselines, and a description of the project life cycle. Subsidiary management plans are plans associated with a specific aspect or Knowledge Area of the project, for example, a schedule management plan, risk management plan and change management plan. Part of tailoring is identifying the project management plan components needed for a particular project. The project management plan is an input and project management plan updates are an output of many processes in this standard. Rather than listing the individual project management plan components in the input/output tables, examples of the components that *may* be inputs or *may* be updated as outputs are listed beneath the input/output tables for each process. The possible components are listed as examples only. These inputs and outputs are not required and are not the only inputs or updates to the project management plan that a project manager may use in that particular process.

The project management plan is one of the primary project artifacts, but there are other documents that are not part of the project management plan that are used to manage the project. These other documents are called project documents. Similar to project management plan components, project documents needed for a process will depend on the individual project. The project manager is accountable for identifying the project documents needed for a process and the project documents that will be updated as an output of a process. The project documents listed beneath the input/output tables throughout this standard are possible examples of project documents, not a comprehensive list.

Table 1-2 is a representative list of project management plan components and project documents. It is not complete list, but it does provide a representation of the types of documents that are often used to help manage a project.

**Table 1-2. Project Management Plan and Project Documents**

| Project Management Plan | Project Documents | |
|---|---|---|
| 1. Scope management plan | 1. Activity attributes | 20. Quality metrics |
| 2. Requirements management plan | 2. Activity list | 21. Quality report |
| 3. Schedule management plan | 3. Assumption log | 22. Requirements documentation |
| 4. Cost management plan | 4. Basis of estimates | 23. Requirements traceability matrix |
| 5. Quality management plan | 5. Change log | 24. Resource breakdown structure |
| 6. Resource management plan | 6. Cost estimates | 25. Resource calendars |
| 7. Communications management plan | 7. Cost forecasts | 26. Resource requirements |
| 8. Risk management plan | 8. Duration estimates | 27. Risk register |
| 9. Procurement management plan | 9. Issue log | 28. Risk report |
| 10. Stakeholder engagement plan | 10. Lessons learned register | 29. Schedule data |
| 11. Change management plan | 11. Milestone list | 30. Schedule forecasts |
| 12. Configuration management plan | 12. Physical resource assignments | 31. Stakeholder register |
| 13. Scope baseline | 13. Project calendars | 32. Team charter |
| 14. Schedule baseline | 14. Project communications | 33. Test and evaluation documents |
| 15. Cost baseline | 15. Project schedule | |
| 16. Performance measurement baseline | 16. Project schedule network diagram | |
| 17. Project life cycle description | 17. Project scope statement | |
| 18. Development approach | 18. Project team assignments | |
| 19. Management reviews | 19. Quality control measurements | |

Business documents are documents that are generally originated outside of the project, and are used as inputs to the project. Examples of business documents include the business case and benefits management plan. The use of the business documents will depend on the company culture and project initiation process.

The enterprise environmental factors that influence the project and the organizational process assets available to the project will depend on the project and project environment and are not listed in this standard.

# 2

## INITIATING PROCESS GROUP

The Initiating Process Group consists of those processes performed to define a new project or a new phase of an existing project by obtaining authorization to start the project or phase. The purpose of the Initiating Process Group is to align the stakeholders' expectations and the project purpose, inform stakeholders of the scope and objectives, and discuss how their participation in the project and its associated phases can help to ensure their expectations are met. Within the Initiating processes, the initial scope is defined and initial financial resources are committed. Stakeholders who will interact and influence the overall outcome of the project are identified. If not already assigned, the project manager is appointed. This information is captured in the project charter and stakeholder register. When the project charter is approved, the project is officially authorized, and the project manager is authorized to apply organizational resources to project activities.

The key benefits of this Process Group are that only projects that are aligned with the organization's strategic objectives are authorized and that the business case, benefits, and stakeholders are considered from the start of the project. In some organizations, the project manager is involved in developing the business case and defining the benefits. In those organizations, the project manager generally helps write the project charter; in other organizations, the pre-project work is done by the project sponsor, project management office (PMO), portfolio steering committee, or other stakeholder group. This standard assumes the project has been approved by the sponsor or other governing body and they have reviewed the business documents prior to authorizing the project.

Business documents are documents that are generally originated outside of the project, but are used as input to the project. Examples of business documents include the business case, and benefits management plan. Figure 2-1 shows the sponsor and the business documents in relation to the Initiating Processes.

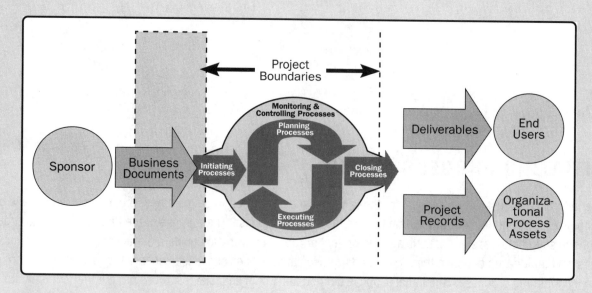

Figure 2-1. Project Boundaries

As described in Section 1.5, projects are often divided into phases. When this is done, information from processes in the Initiating Process Group is reexamined to determine if the information is still valid. Revisiting the Initiating processes at the start of each phase helps keep the project focused on the business need that the project was undertaken to address. The project charter, business documents, and success criteria are verified. The influence, drivers, expectations, and objectives of the project stakeholders are reviewed.

Involving the sponsors, customers, and other stakeholders during initiation creates a shared understanding of success criteria. It also increases the likelihood of deliverable acceptance when the project is complete, and stakeholder satisfaction throughout the project.

The Initiating Process Group includes the project management processes identified in Sections 2.1 through 2.2.

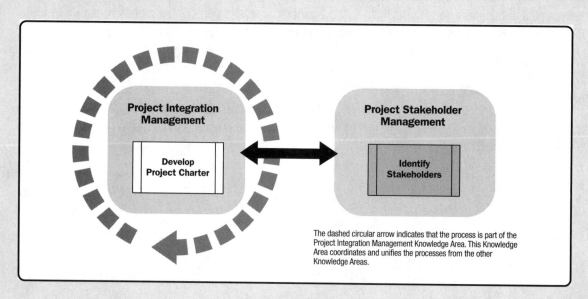

Figure 2-2. Initiating Process Group

## 2.1 DEVELOP PROJECT CHARTER

Develop Project Charter is the process of developing a document that formally authorizes the existence of a project and provides the project manager with the authority to apply organizational resources to project activities. The key benefits of this process are that it provides a direct link between the project and the strategic objectives of the organization, creates a formal record of the project, and shows the organizational commitment to the project. This process is performed once, or at predefined points in the project. The inputs and outputs of this process are shown in Figure 2-3.

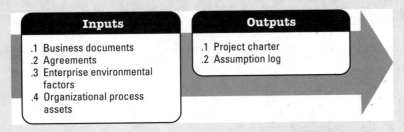

**Figure 2-3. Develop Project Charter: Inputs and Outputs**

## 2.2 IDENTIFY STAKEHOLDERS

Identify Stakeholders is the process of identifying project stakeholders regularly and analyzing and documenting relevant information regarding their interests, involvement, interdependencies, influence, and potential impact on project success. The key benefit of this process is that it enables the project team to identify the appropriate focus for engagement of each stakeholder or group of stakeholders. This process is performed periodically throughout the project as needed. The inputs and outputs of this process are depicted in Figure 2-4.

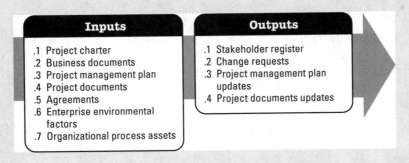

**Figure 2-4. Identify Stakeholders: Inputs and Outputs**

The needs of the project determine which components of the project management plan and which project documents are necessary.

## 2.2.1 PROJECT MANAGEMENT PLAN COMPONENTS

Examples of project management plan components that may be inputs for this process include but are not limited to:

◆ Communications management plan, and

◆ Stakeholder engagement plan.

## 2.2.2 PROJECT DOCUMENTS EXAMPLES

Examples of project documents that may be inputs for this process include but are not limited to:

◆ Change log,

◆ Issue log, and

◆ Requirements documentation.

## 2.2.3 PROJECT MANAGEMENT PLAN UPDATES

Examples of project management plan components that may be updated as a result of this process include but are not limited to:

◆ Requirements management plan,

◆ Communications management plan,

◆ Risk management plan, and

◆ Stakeholder engagement plan.

## 2.2.4 PROJECT DOCUMENTS UPDATES

Examples of project documents that may be updated as a result of this process include but are not limited to:

◆ Assumption log,

◆ Issue log, and

◆ Risk register.

# 3

## PLANNING PROCESS GROUP

The Planning Process Group consists of those processes that establish the total scope of the effort, define and refine the objectives, and develop the course of action required to attain those objectives. The processes in the Planning Process Group develop the components of the project management plan and the project documents used to carry out the project. The nature of a project may require the use of repeated feedback loops for additional analysis. As more project information or characteristics are gathered and understood, additional planning will likely be required. Significant changes that occur throughout the project life cycle may initiate a need to revisit one or more of the planning processes and, possibly, one or both of the Initiating processes. This ongoing refinement of the project management plan is called progressive elaboration, indicating that planning and documentation are iterative or ongoing activities. The key benefit of this Process Group is to define the course of action to successfully complete the project or phase.

The project management team seeks input and encourages involvement from relevant stakeholders while planning the project and developing the project management plan and project documents. When the initial planning effort is completed, the approved version of the project management plan is considered a baseline. Throughout the project, the Monitoring and Controlling processes compare the project performance to the baselines.

The Planning Process Group (Figure 3-1) includes the project management processes identified in Sections 3.1 to 3.24.

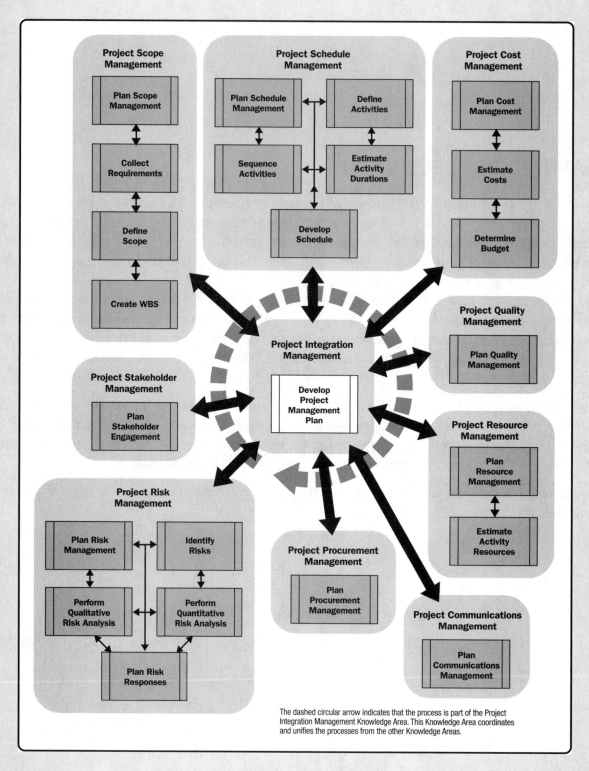

The dashed circular arrow indicates that the process is part of the Project Integration Management Knowledge Area. This Knowledge Area coordinates and unifies the processes from the other Knowledge Areas.

Figure 3-1. Planning Process Group

## 3.1 DEVELOP PROJECT MANAGEMENT PLAN

Develop Project Management Plan is the process of defining, preparing, and coordinating all plan components and consolidating them into an integrated project management plan. The key benefit of this process is the production of a comprehensive document that defines the basis of all project work and how the work will be performed. This process is performed once or at predefined points in the project. The inputs and outputs of this process are depicted in Figure 3-2.

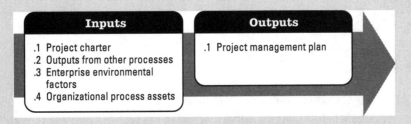

**Figure 3-2. Develop Project Management Plan: Inputs and Outputs**

The needs of the project determine which components of the project management plan and which project documents are necessary.

## 3.2 PLAN SCOPE MANAGEMENT

Plan Scope Management is the process of creating a scope management plan that documents how the project and product scope will be defined, validated, and controlled. The key benefit of this process is that it provides guidance and direction on how scope will be managed throughout the project. This process is performed once or at predefined points in the project. The inputs and outputs of this process are depicted in Figure 3-3.

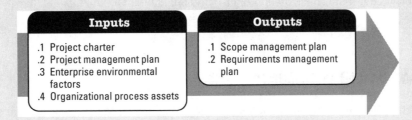

**Figure 3-3. Plan Scope Management: Inputs and Outputs**

The needs of the project determine which components of the project management plan are necessary.

### 3.2.1 PROJECT MANAGEMENT PLAN COMPONENTS

Examples of project management plan components that may be inputs for this process include but are not limited to:

◆ Quality management plan,

◆ Project life cycle description, and

◆ Development approach.

## 3.3 COLLECT REQUIREMENTS

Collect Requirements is the process of determining, documenting, and managing stakeholder needs and requirements to meet objectives. The key benefit of this process is that it provides the basis for defining the product scope and project scope. This process is performed once or at predefined points in the project. The inputs and outputs of this process are depicted in Figure 3-4.

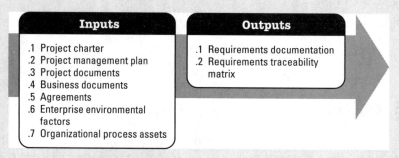

**Inputs**

.1 Project charter
.2 Project management plan
.3 Project documents
.4 Business documents
.5 Agreements
.6 Enterprise environmental factors
.7 Organizational process assets

**Outputs**

.1 Requirements documentation
.2 Requirements traceability matrix

Figure 3-4. Collect Requirements: Inputs and Outputs

The needs of the project determine which components of the project management plan and which project documents are necessary.

### 3.3.1 PROJECT MANAGEMENT PLAN COMPONENTS

Examples of project management plan components that may be inputs for this process include but are not limited to:

◆ Scope management plan,

◆ Requirements management plan, and

◆ Stakeholder engagement plan.

## 3.3.2 PROJECT DOCUMENTS EXAMPLES

Examples of project documents that may be inputs for this process include but are not limited to:

◆ Assumption log,

◆ Lessons learned register, and

◆ Stakeholder register.

# 3.4 DEFINE SCOPE

Define Scope is the process of developing a detailed description of the project and product. The key benefit of this process is that it describes the product, service, or result boundaries and acceptance criteria. This process is performed once or at predefined points in the project. The inputs and outputs of this process are depicted in Figure 3-5.

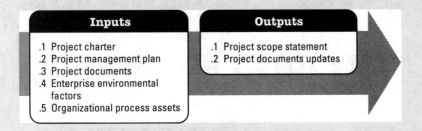

**Figure 3-5. Define Scope: Inputs and Outputs**

The needs of the project determine which components of the project management plan and which project documents are necessary.

## 3.4.1 PROJECT MANAGEMENT PLAN COMPONENTS

An example of a project management plan component that may be an input for this process includes but is not limited to the scope management plan.

## 3.4.2 PROJECT DOCUMENTS EXAMPLES

Examples of project documents that may be inputs for this process include but are not limited to:

◆ Assumption log,

◆ Requirements documentation, and

◆ Risk register.

### 3.4.3 PROJECT DOCUMENTS UPDATES

Project documents that may be updated as a result of this process include but are not limited to:

◆ Assumption log,

◆ Requirements documentation,

◆ Requirements traceability matrix, and

◆ Stakeholder register.

## 3.5 CREATE WBS

Create Work Breakdown Structure (WBS) is the process of subdividing project deliverables and project work into smaller, more manageable components. The key benefit of this process is that it provides a framework of what has to be delivered. This process is performed once or at predefined points in the project. The inputs and outputs of this process are depicted in Figure 3-6.

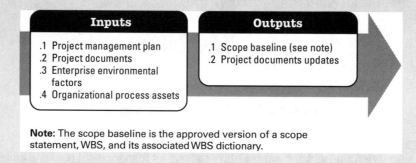

**Figure 3-6. Create WBS: Inputs and Outputs**

The needs of the project determine which components of the project management plan and which project documents are necessary.

### 3.5.1 PROJECT MANAGEMENT PLAN COMPONENTS

An example of a project management plan component that may be an input for this process includes but is not limited to the scope management plan.

## 3.5.2 PROJECT DOCUMENTS EXAMPLES

Examples of project documents that may be inputs for this process include but are not limited to:

◆ Project scope statement, and

◆ Requirements documentation.

## 3.5.3 PROJECT DOCUMENTS UPDATES

Project document that may be updated as a result of this process include but is not limited to:

◆ Assumption log, and

◆ Requirements documentation.

# 3.6 PLAN SCHEDULE MANAGEMENT

Plan Schedule Management is the process of establishing the policies, procedures, and documentation for planning, developing, managing, executing, and controlling the project schedule. The key benefit of this process is that it provides guidance and direction on how the project schedule will be managed throughout the project. This process is performed once or at predefined points in the project. The inputs and outputs of this process are depicted in Figure 3-7.

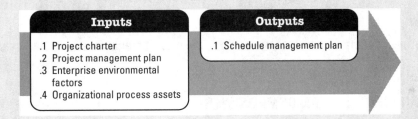

Figure 3-7. Plan Schedule Management: Inputs and Outputs

The needs of the project determine which components of the project management plan are necessary.

### 3.6.1 PROJECT MANAGEMENT PLAN COMPONENTS

Examples of project management plan components that may be inputs for this process include but are not limited to:

◆ Scope management plan, and

◆ Development approach.

## 3.7 DEFINE ACTIVITIES

Define Activities is the process of identifying and documenting the specific actions to be performed to produce the project deliverables. The key benefit of this process is that it decomposes work packages into schedule activities that provide a basis for estimating, scheduling, executing, monitoring, and controlling the project work. This process is performed throughout the project. The inputs and outputs of this process are depicted in Figure 3-8.

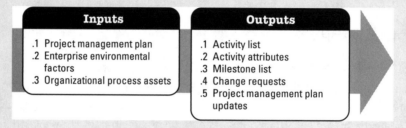

| Inputs | Outputs |
|---|---|
| .1 Project management plan<br>.2 Enterprise environmental factors<br>.3 Organizational process assets | .1 Activity list<br>.2 Activity attributes<br>.3 Milestone list<br>.4 Change requests<br>.5 Project management plan updates |

Figure 3-8. Define Activities: Inputs and Outputs

The needs of the project determine which components of the project management plan are necessary.

### 3.7.1 PROJECT MANAGEMENT PLAN COMPONENTS

Examples of project management plan components that may be inputs for this process include but are not limited to:

◆ Schedule management plan, and

◆ Scope baseline.

### 3.7.2 PROJECT MANAGEMENT PLAN UPDATES

Components of the project management plan that may be updated as a result of this process include but are not limited to:

◆ Schedule baseline, and

◆ Cost baseline.

## 3.8 SEQUENCE ACTIVITIES

Sequence Activities is the process of identifying and documenting relationships among the project activities. The key benefit of this process is that it defines the logical sequence of work to obtain the greatest efficiency given all project constraints. This process is performed throughout the project. The inputs and outputs of this process are depicted in Figure 3-9.

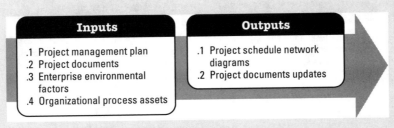

**Figure 3-9. Sequence Activities: Inputs and Outputs**

The needs of the project determine which components of the project management plan and which project documents are necessary.

### 3.8.1 PROJECT MANAGEMENT PLAN COMPONENTS

Examples of project management plan components that may be inputs for this process include but are not limited to:

◆ Schedule management plan, and

◆ Scope baseline.

### 3.8.2 PROJECT DOCUMENTS EXAMPLES

Examples of project documents that may be inputs for this process include but are not limited to:

◆ Activity attributes,

◆ Activity list,

◆ Assumption log, and

◆ Milestone list.

### 3.8.3 PROJECT DOCUMENTS UPDATES

Project documents that may be updated as a result of this process include but are not limited to:

◆ Activity attributes,

◆ Activity list,

◆ Assumption log, and

◆ Milestone list.

# 3.9 ESTIMATE ACTIVITY DURATIONS

Estimate Activity Durations is the process of estimating the number of work periods needed to complete individual activities with estimated resources. The key benefit of this process is that it provides the amount of time each activity will take to complete. This process is performed throughout the project. The inputs and outputs of this process are depicted in Figure 3-10.

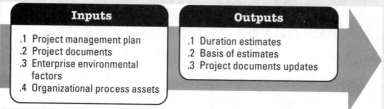

**Inputs**

.1 Project management plan
.2 Project documents
.3 Enterprise environmental factors
.4 Organizational process assets

**Outputs**

.1 Duration estimates
.2 Basis of estimates
.3 Project documents updates

Figure 3-10. Estimate Activity Durations: Inputs and Outputs

The needs of the project determine which components of the project management plan and which project documents are necessary.

## 3.9.1 PROJECT MANAGEMENT PLAN COMPONENTS

Examples of project management plan components that may be inputs for this process include but are not limited to:

◆ Schedule management plan, and

◆ Scope baseline.

## 3.9.2 PROJECT DOCUMENTS EXAMPLES

Examples of project documents that may be inputs for this process include but are not limited to:

◆ Activity attributes,

◆ Activity list,

◆ Assumption log,

◆ Lessons learned register,

◆ Milestone list,

◆ Project team assignments,

◆ Resource breakdown structure,

◆ Resource calendars,

◆ Resource requirements, and

◆ Risk register.

### 3.9.3 PROJECT DOCUMENTS UPDATES

Project documents that may be updated as a result of this process include but are not limited to:

◆ Activity attributes,

◆ Assumption log,

◆ Lessons learned register.

## 3.10 DEVELOP SCHEDULE

Develop Schedule is the process of analyzing activity sequences, durations, resource requirements, and schedule constraints to create a schedule model for project execution and monitoring and controlling. The key benefit of this process is that it generates a schedule model with planned dates for completing project activities. This process is performed throughout the project. The inputs and outputs of this process are depicted in Figure 3-11.

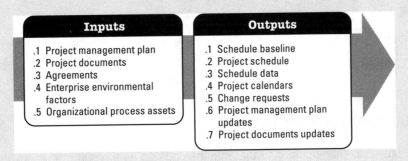

**Figure 3-11. Develop Schedule: Inputs and Outputs**

The needs of the project determine which components of the project management plan and which project documents are necessary.

### 3.10.1 PROJECT MANAGEMENT PLAN COMPONENTS

Examples of project management plan components that may be inputs for this process include but are not limited to:

◆ Schedule management plan, and

◆ Scope baseline.

## 3.10.2 PROJECT DOCUMENTS EXAMPLES

Examples of project documents that may be inputs for this process include but are not limited to:

◆ Activity attributes,

◆ Activity list,

◆ Assumption log,

◆ Basis of estimates,

◆ Duration estimates,

◆ Lessons learned register,

◆ Milestone list,

◆ Project schedule network diagram,

◆ Project team assignments,

◆ Resource calendars,

◆ Resource requirements, and

◆ Risk register.


## 3.10.3 PROJECT MANAGEMENT PLAN UPDATES

Components of the project management plan that may be updated as a result of this process include but are not limited to:

◆ Schedule management plan, and

◆ Cost baseline.


## 3.10.4 PROJECT DOCUMENTS UPDATES

Project documents that may be updated as a result of this process include but are not limited to:

◆ Activity attributes,

◆ Assumption log,

◆ Duration estimates,

◆ Lessons learned register,

◆ Resource requirements, and

◆ Risk register.

# 3.11 PLAN COST MANAGEMENT

Plan Cost Management is the process of defining how the project costs will be estimated, budgeted, managed, monitored, and controlled. The key benefit of this process is that it provides guidance and direction on how the project costs will be managed throughout the project. This process is performed once, or at predefined points in the project. The inputs and outputs of this process are depicted in Figure 3-12.

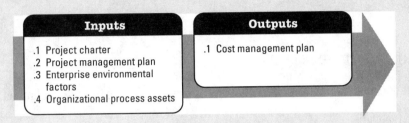

**Figure 3-12. Plan Cost Management: Inputs and Outputs**

The needs of the project determine which components of the project management plan are necessary.

## 3.11.1 PROJECT MANAGEMENT PLAN COMPONENTS

Examples of project management plan components that may be inputs for this process include but are not limited to:

◆ Schedule management plan, and

◆ Risk management plan.

# 3.12 ESTIMATE COSTS

Estimate Costs is the process of developing an approximation of the monetary resources needed to complete project work. The key benefit of this process is that it determines the monetary resources required for the project. This process is performed periodically throughout the project as needed. The inputs and outputs of this process are depicted in Figure 3-13.

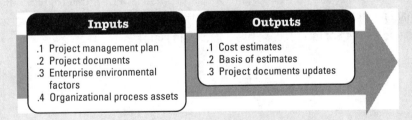

**Figure 3-13. Estimate Costs: Inputs and Outputs**

The needs of the project determine which components of the project management plan and which project documents are necessary.

### 3.12.1 PROJECT MANAGEMENT PLAN COMPONENTS

Examples of project management plan components that may be inputs for this process include but are not limited to:

◆ Cost management plan,

◆ Quality management plan, and

◆ Scope baseline.


### 3.12.2 PROJECT DOCUMENTS EXAMPLES

Examples of project documents that may be inputs for this process include but are not limited to:

◆ Lessons learned register,

◆ Project schedule,

◆ Resource requirements, and

◆ Risk register.


### 3.12.3 PROJECT DOCUMENTS UPDATES

Project documents that may be updated as a result of this process include but are not limited to:

◆ Assumption log,

◆ Lessons learned register, and

◆ Risk register.


## 3.13 DETERMINE BUDGET

Determine Budget is the process of aggregating the estimated costs of individual activities or work packages to establish an authorized cost baseline. The key benefit of this process is that it determines the cost baseline against which project performance can be monitored and controlled. This process is performed once or at predefined points in the project. The inputs and outputs of this process are depicted in Figure 3-14.

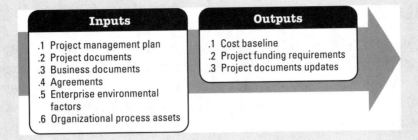

| Inputs | Outputs |
|---|---|
| .1 Project management plan | .1 Cost baseline |
| .2 Project documents | .2 Project funding requirements |
| .3 Business documents | .3 Project documents updates |
| .4 Agreements | |
| .5 Enterprise environmental factors | |
| .6 Organizational process assets | |

**Figure 3-14. Determine Budget: Inputs and Outputs**

The needs of the project determine which components of the project management plan and which project documents are necessary.

### 3.13.1 PROJECT MANAGEMENT PLAN COMPONENTS

Examples of project management plan components that may be inputs for this process include but are not limited to:

◆ Cost management plan,

◆ Resource management plan, and

◆ Scope baseline.

### 3.13.2 PROJECT DOCUMENTS EXAMPLES

Examples of project documents that may be inputs for this process include but are not limited to:

◆ Basis of estimates,

◆ Cost estimates,

◆ Project schedule, and

◆ Risk register.

### 3.13.3 PROJECT DOCUMENTS UPDATES

Project documents that may be updated as a result of this process include but are not limited to:

◆ Cost estimates,

◆ Project schedule, and

◆ Risk register.

# 3.14 PLAN QUALITY MANAGEMENT

Plan Quality Management is the process of identifying quality requirements and/or standards for the project and its deliverables, and documenting how the project will demonstrate compliance with quality requirements and/or standards. The key benefit of this process is that it provides guidance and direction on how quality will be managed and verified throughout the project. This process is performed once or at predefined points in the project. The inputs and outputs of this process are shown in Figure 3-15.

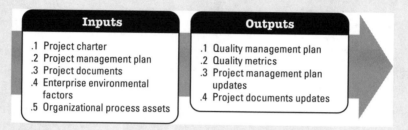

**Figure 3-15. Plan Quality Management: Inputs and Outputs**

The needs of the project determine which components of the project management plan and which project documents are necessary.

## 3.14.1 PROJECT MANAGEMENT PLAN COMPONENTS

Examples of project management plan components that may be inputs for this process include but are not limited to:

◆ Requirements management plan,

◆ Risk management plan,

◆ Stakeholder engagement plan, and

◆ Scope baseline.

## 3.14.2 PROJECT DOCUMENTS EXAMPLES

Examples of project documents that may be inputs for this process include but are not limited to:

◆ Assumption log,

◆ Requirements documentation,

◆ Requirements traceability matrix,

◆ Risk register, and

◆ Stakeholder register.

### 3.14.3 PROJECT MANAGEMENT PLAN UPDATES

Examples of project management plan components that may be updated as a result of this process include but are not limited to:

◆ Risk management plan, and

◆ Scope baseline.

### 3.14.4 PROJECT DOCUMENTS UPDATES

Project documents that may be updated as a result of this process include but are not limited to:

◆ Lessons learned register,

◆ Requirements traceability matrix,

◆ Risk register, and

◆ Stakeholder register.

## 3.15 PLAN RESOURCE MANAGEMENT

Plan Resource Management is the process of defining how to estimate, acquire, manage, and utilize physical and team resources. The key benefit of this process is that it establishes the approach and level of management effort needed for managing project resources based on the type and complexity of the project. This process is performed once or at predefined points in the project. The inputs and outputs of this process are shown in Figure 3-16.

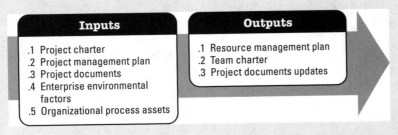

**Figure 3-16. Plan Resource Management: Inputs and Outputs**

The needs of the project determine which components of the project management plan and which project documents are necessary.

### 3.15.1 PROJECT MANAGEMENT PLAN COMPONENTS

Examples of project management plan components that may be inputs for this process include but are not limited to:

◆ Quality management plan, and

◆ Scope baseline.

### 3.15.2 PROJECT DOCUMENTS EXAMPLES

Examples of project documents that may be inputs for this process include but are not limited to:

◆ Project schedule,

◆ Requirements documentation,

◆ Risk register, and

◆ Stakeholder register.

### 3.15.3 PROJECT DOCUMENTS UPDATES

Project documents that may be updated as a result of this process include but are not limited to:

◆ Assumption log, and

◆ Risk register.

## 3.16 ESTIMATE ACTIVITY RESOURCES

Estimate Activity Resources is the process of estimating team resources and the type and quantities of materials, equipment, and supplies necessary to perform project work. The key benefit of this process is that it identifies the type, quantity, and characteristics of resources required to complete the project. This process is performed periodically throughout the project as needed. The inputs and outputs of this process are depicted in Figure 3-17.

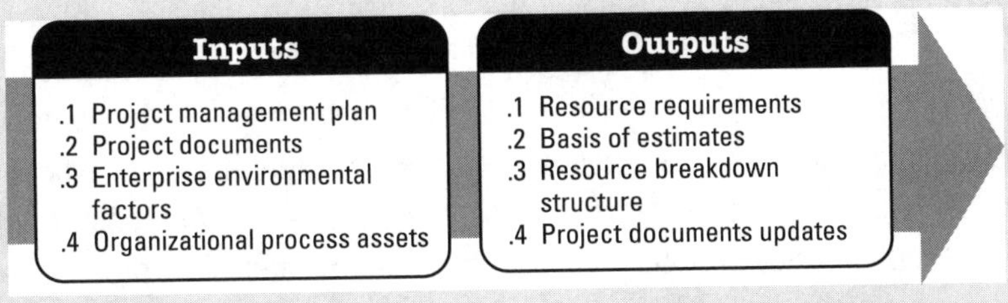

| Inputs | Outputs |
| --- | --- |
| .1 Project management plan<br>.2 Project documents<br>.3 Enterprise environmental factors<br>.4 Organizational process assets | .1 Resource requirements<br>.2 Basis of estimates<br>.3 Resource breakdown structure<br>.4 Project documents updates |

**Figure 3-17. Estimate Activity Resources: Inputs and Outputs**

The needs of the project determine which components of the project management plan and which project documents are necessary.

### 3.16.1 PROJECT MANAGEMENT PLAN COMPONENTS

Examples of project management plan components that may be inputs for this process include but are not limited to:

◆ Resource management plan, and

◆ Scope baseline.

### 3.16.2 PROJECT DOCUMENTS EXAMPLES

Examples of project documents that may be inputs for this process include but are not limited to:

◆ Activity attributes,

◆ Activity list,

◆ Assumption log,

◆ Cost estimates,

◆ Resource calendars, and

◆ Risk register.

### 3.16.3 PROJECT DOCUMENTS UPDATES

Project documents that may be updated as a result of this process include but are not limited to:

◆ Activity attributes,

◆ Assumption log,

◆ Lessons learned register.

# 3.17 PLAN COMMUNICATIONS MANAGEMENT

Plan Communications Management is the process of developing an appropriate approach and plan for project communication activities based on the information needs of each stakeholder or group, available organizational assets, and the needs of the project. The key benefit of this process is a documented approach to effectively and efficiently engage stakeholders by presenting relevant information in a timely manner. This process is performed periodically throughout the project as needed. The inputs and outputs of this process are depicted in Figure 3-18.

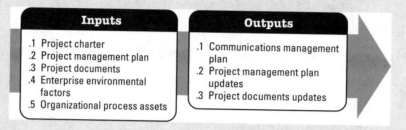

| Inputs | Outputs |
|---|---|
| .1 Project charter<br>.2 Project management plan<br>.3 Project documents<br>.4 Enterprise environmental factors<br>.5 Organizational process assets | .1 Communications management plan<br>.2 Project management plan updates<br>.3 Project documents updates |

Figure 3-18. Plan Communications Management: Inputs and Outputs

The needs of the project determine which components of the project management plan and which project documents are necessary.

## 3.17.1 PROJECT MANAGEMENT PLAN COMPONENTS

Examples of project management plan components that may be inputs for this process include but are not limited to:

◆ Resource management plan, and

◆ Stakeholder engagement plan.

## 3.17.2 PROJECT DOCUMENTS EXAMPLES

Examples of project documents that may be inputs for this process include but are not limited to:

◆ Requirements documentation, and

◆ Stakeholder register.

## 3.17.3 PROJECT MANAGEMENT PLAN UPDATES

Components of the project management plan that may be updated as a result of this process include but are not limited to the stakeholder engagement plan.

### 3.17.4 PROJECT DOCUMENTS UPDATES

Project documents that may be updated as a result of this process include but are not limited to:

◆ Project schedule, and

◆ Stakeholder register.

## 3.18 PLAN RISK MANAGEMENT

Plan Risk Management is the process of defining how to conduct risk management activities for a project. The key benefit of this process is that it ensures that the degree, type, and visibility of risk management are proportionate to both the risks and the importance of the project to the organization and other stakeholders. This process is performed once or at predefined points in the project. The inputs and output of this process are depicted in Figure 3-19.

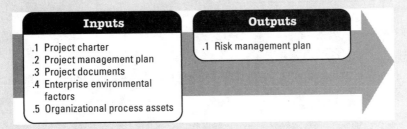

**Figure 3-19. Plan Risk Management: Inputs and Outputs**

The needs of the project determine which components of the project management plan and which project documents are necessary.

### 3.18.1 PROJECT MANAGEMENT PLAN COMPONENTS

In planning Project Risk Management, all available components of the project management plan should be taken into consideration in order to ensure risk management is consistent with the needs of the project.

### 3.18.2 PROJECT DOCUMENTS EXAMPLES

An example of a project document that may be an input for this process includes but is not limited to the stakeholder register.

# 3.19 IDENTIFY RISKS

Identify Risks is the process of identifying individual project risks as well as sources of overall project risk, and documenting their characteristics. The key benefit of this process is the documentation of the existing individual project risks and the sources of overall project risk. It also brings together information so the project team can respond appropriately to the identified risks. This process is performed throughout the project. The inputs and outputs of this process are depicted in Figure 3-20.

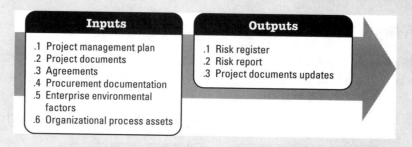

**Figure 3-20. Identify Risks: Inputs and Outputs**

The needs of the project determine which components of the project management plan and which project documents are necessary.

## 3.19.1 PROJECT MANAGEMENT PLAN COMPONENTS

Examples of project management plan components that may be inputs for this process include but are not limited to:

◆ Requirements management plan,

◆ Schedule management plan,

◆ Cost management plan,

◆ Quality management plan,

◆ Resource management plan,

◆ Risk management plan,

◆ Scope baseline,

◆ Schedule baseline, and

◆ Cost baseline.

## 3.19.2 PROJECT DOCUMENTS EXAMPLES

Examples of project documents that may be inputs for this process include but are not limited to:

◆ Assumption log,

◆ Cost estimates,

◆ Duration estimates,

◆ Issue log,

◆ Lessons learned register,

◆ Requirements documentation,

◆ Resource requirements, and

◆ Stakeholder register.

## 3.19.3 PROJECT DOCUMENTS UPDATES

Project documents that may be updated as a result of this process include but are not limited to:

◆ Assumption log,

◆ Issue log, and

◆ Lessons learned register.

## 3.20 PERFORM QUALITATIVE RISK ANALYSIS

Perform Qualitative Risk Analysis is the process of prioritizing individual project risks for further analysis or action by assessing their probability of occurrence and impact as well as other characteristics. The key benefit of this process is that it focuses efforts on high-priority risks. This process is performed throughout the project. The inputs and outputs of this process are depicted in Figure 3-21.

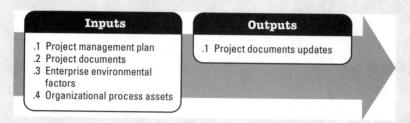

**Figure 3-21. Perform Qualitative Risk Analysis: Inputs and Outputs**

The needs of the project determine which components of the project management plan and which project documents are necessary.

### 3.20.1 PROJECT MANAGEMENT PLAN COMPONENTS

An example of a project management plan component that may be an input for this process includes but is not limited to the risk management plan.

### 3.20.2 PROJECT DOCUMENTS EXAMPLES

Examples of project documents that may be inputs for this process include but are not limited to:

◆ Assumption log,

◆ Risk register, and

◆ Stakeholder register.

### 3.20.3 PROJECT DOCUMENTS UPDATES

Project documents that may be updated as a result of this process include but are not limited to:

◆ Assumption log,

◆ Issue log,

◆ Risk register, and

◆ Risk report.

## 3.21 PERFORM QUANTITATIVE RISK ANALYSIS

Perform Quantitative Risk Analysis is the process of numerically analyzing the combined effect of identified individual project risks and other sources of uncertainty on overall project objectives. The key benefit of this process is that it quantifies overall project risk exposure and can also provide additional quantitative risk information to support risk response planning. This process is performed throughout the project. The inputs and outputs of this process are depicted in Figure 3-22.

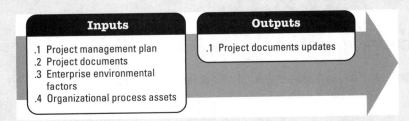

**Figure 3-22. Perform Quantitative Risk Analysis: Inputs and Outputs**

The needs of the project determine which components of the project management plan and which project documents are necessary.

### 3.21.1 PROJECT MANAGEMENT PLAN COMPONENTS

Examples of project management plan components that may be inputs for this process include but are not limited to:

◆ Risk management plan,

◆ Scope baseline,

◆ Schedule baseline, and

◆ Cost baseline.

## 3.21.2 PROJECT DOCUMENTS EXAMPLES

Examples of project documents that may be inputs for this process include but are not limited to:

◆ Assumption log,

◆ Basis of estimates,

◆ Cost estimates,

◆ Cost forecasts,

◆ Duration estimates,

◆ Milestone list,

◆ Resource requirements,

◆ Risk register,

◆ Risk report, and

◆ Schedule forecasts.

## 3.21.3 PROJECT DOCUMENTS UPDATES

Project documents that may be updated as a result of this process include but are not limited to the risk report.

## 3.22 PLAN RISK RESPONSES

Plan Risk Responses is the process of developing options, selecting strategies, and agreeing on actions to address overall project risk exposure as well as to treat individual project risks. The key benefit of this process is that it identifies appropriate ways to address overall project risk and individual project risks. This process also allocates resources and inserts activities into project documents and the project management plan as needed. This process is performed throughout the project. The inputs and outputs of this process are depicted in Figure 3-23.

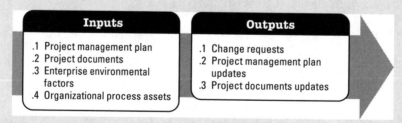

**Figure 3-23. Plan Risk Responses: Inputs and Outputs**

The needs of the project determine which components of the project management plan and which project documents are necessary.

### 3.22.1 PROJECT MANAGEMENT PLAN COMPONENTS

Examples of project management plan components that may be inputs for this process include but are not limited to:

◆ Resource management plan,

◆ Risk management plan, and

◆ Cost baseline.

### 3.22.2 PROJECT DOCUMENTS EXAMPLES

Examples of project documents that may be inputs for this process include but are not limited to:

◆ Lessons learned register,

◆ Project schedule,

◆ Project team assignments,

◆ Resource calendars,

◆ Risk register,

◆ Risk report, and

◆ Stakeholder register.

### 3.22.3 PROJECT MANAGEMENT PLAN UPDATES

Components of the project management plan that may be updated as a result of this process include but are not limited to:

◆ Schedule management plan,

◆ Cost management plan,

◆ Quality management plan,

◆ Resource management plan,

◆ Procurement management plan,

◆ Scope baseline,

◆ Schedule baseline, and

◆ Cost baseline.

### 3.22.4 PROJECT DOCUMENTS UPDATES

Project documents that may be updated as a result of this process include but are not limited to:

◆ Assumption log,

◆ Cost forecasts,

◆ Lessons learned register,

◆ Project schedule,

◆ Project team assignments,

◆ Risk register, and

◆ Risk report.

## 3.23 PLAN PROCUREMENT MANAGEMENT

Plan Procurement Management is the process of documenting project procurement decisions, specifying the approach, and identifying potential sellers. The key benefit of this process is that it determines whether to acquire goods and services from outside the project and, if so, what to acquire as well as how and when to acquire it. Goods and services may be procured from other parts of the performing organization or from external sources. This process is performed once or at predefined points in the project. The inputs and outputs of this process are depicted in Figure 3-24.

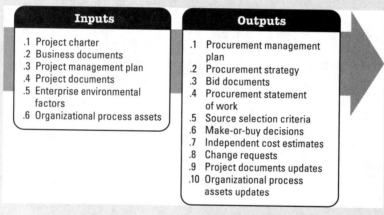

**Inputs**

.1 Project charter
.2 Business documents
.3 Project management plan
.4 Project documents
.5 Enterprise environmental factors
.6 Organizational process assets

**Outputs**

.1 Procurement management plan
.2 Procurement strategy
.3 Bid documents
.4 Procurement statement of work
.5 Source selection criteria
.6 Make-or-buy decisions
.7 Independent cost estimates
.8 Change requests
.9 Project documents updates
.10 Organizational process assets updates

Figure 3-24. Plan Procurement Management: Inputs and Outputs

The needs of the project determine which components of the project management plan and which project documents are necessary.

### 3.23.1 PROJECT MANAGEMENT PLAN COMPONENTS

Examples of project management plan components that may be inputs for this process include but are not limited to:

◆ Scope management plan,

◆ Quality management plan,

◆ Resource management plan, and

◆ Scope baseline.

### 3.23.2 PROJECT DOCUMENTS EXAMPLES

Examples of project documents that may be inputs for this process include but are not limited to:

◆ Milestone list,

◆ Project team assignments,

◆ Requirements documentation,

◆ Requirements traceability matrix,

◆ Resource requirements,

◆ Risk register, and

◆ Stakeholder register.

### 3.23.3 PROJECT DOCUMENTS UPDATES

Project documents that may be updated as a result of this process include but are not limited to:

◆ Lessons learned register,

◆ Milestone list,

◆ Requirements documentation,

◆ Requirements traceability matrix,

◆ Risk register, and

◆ Stakeholder register.

# 3.24 PLAN STAKEHOLDER ENGAGEMENT

Plan Stakeholder Engagement is the process of developing approaches to involve project stakeholders based on their needs, expectations, interests, and potential impact on the project. The key benefit is that it provides an actionable plan to interact with stakeholders effectively. This process is performed periodically throughout the project as needed. The inputs and outputs of this process are depicted in Figure 3-25.

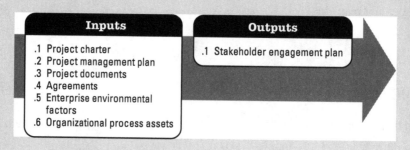

**Figure 3-25. Plan Stakeholder Engagement: Inputs and Outputs**

The needs of the project determine which components of the project management plan and which project documents are necessary.

## 3.24.1 PROJECT MANAGEMENT PLAN COMPONENTS

Examples of project management plan components that may be inputs for this process include but are not limited to:

◆ Resource management plan,

◆ Communications management plan, and

◆ Risk management plan.

## 3.24.2 PROJECT DOCUMENTS EXAMPLES

Examples of project documents that may be inputs for this process include but are not limited to:

◆ Assumption log,

◆ Change log,

◆ Issue log,

◆ Project schedule,

◆ Risk register, and

◆ Stakeholder register.

# 4

## EXECUTING PROCESS GROUP

The Executing Process Group consists of those processes performed to complete the work defined in the project management plan to satisfy the project requirements. This Process Group involves coordinating resources, managing stakeholder engagement, and integrating and performing the activities of the project in accordance with the project management plan. The key benefit of this Process Group is that the work needed to meet the project requirements and objectives is performed according to plan. A large portion of the project budget, resources, and time is expended in performing the Executing Process Group processes. The processes in the Executing Process Group may generate change requests. If approved, the change requests may trigger one or more planning processes that result in a modified management plan, project documents, and possibly new baselines. The Executing Process Group (Figure 4-1) includes the project management processes identified in Sections 4.1 through 4.10.

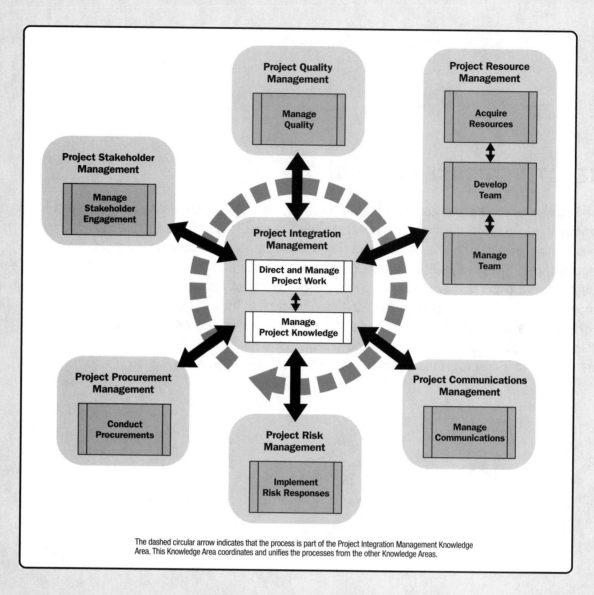

The dashed circular arrow indicates that the process is part of the Project Integration Management Knowledge Area. This Knowledge Area coordinates and unifies the processes from the other Knowledge Areas.

**Figure 4-1. Executing Process Group**

# 4.1 DIRECT AND MANAGE PROJECT WORK

Direct and Manage Project Work is the process of leading and performing the work defined in the project management plan and implementing approved changes to achieve the project's objectives. The key benefit of this process is that it provides overall management of the project work and deliverables, thus improving the probability of project success. This process is performed throughout the project. The inputs and outputs of this process are depicted in Figure 4-2.

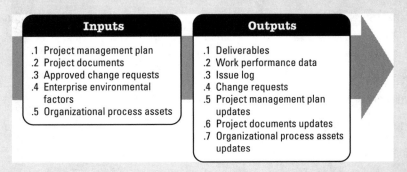

| Inputs | Outputs |
|---|---|
| .1 Project management plan | .1 Deliverables |
| .2 Project documents | .2 Work performance data |
| .3 Approved change requests | .3 Issue log |
| .4 Enterprise environmental factors | .4 Change requests |
| .5 Organizational process assets | .5 Project management plan updates |
| | .6 Project documents updates |
| | .7 Organizational process assets updates |

Figure 4-2. Direct and Manage Project Work: Inputs and Outputs

The needs of the project determine which components of the project management plan and which project documents are necessary.

## 4.1.1 PROJECT MANAGEMENT PLAN COMPONENTS

Any component of the project management plan may be an input for this process.

## 4.1.2 PROJECT DOCUMENTS EXAMPLES

Examples of project documents that may be inputs for this process include but are not limited to:

◆ Change log,

◆ Lessons learned register,

◆ Milestone list,

◆ Project communications,

◆ Project schedule,

◆ Requirements traceability matrix,

◆ Risk register, and

◆ Risk report.

### 4.1.3 PROJECT MANAGEMENT PLAN UPDATES

Any component of the project management plan may be updated as a result of this process.

### 4.1.4 PROJECT DOCUMENTS UPDATES

Project documents that may be updated as a result of this process include but are not limited to:

◆ Activity list,

◆ Assumption log,

◆ Lessons learned register,

◆ Requirements documentation,

◆ Risk register, and

◆ Stakeholder register.

## 4.2 MANAGE PROJECT KNOWLEDGE

Manage Project Knowledge is the process of using existing knowledge and creating new knowledge to achieve the project's objectives and contribute to organizational learning. The key benefits of this process are that prior organizational knowledge is leveraged to produce or improve the project outcomes and that knowledge created by the project is available to support organizational operations and future projects or phases. This process is performed throughout the project. The inputs and outputs of this process are depicted in Figure 4-3.

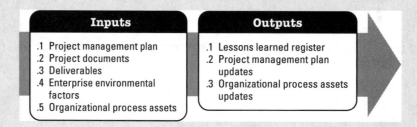

**Figure 4-3. Manage Project Knowledge: Inputs and Outputs**

The needs of the project determine which components of the project management plan and which project documents are necessary.

### 4.2.1 PROJECT MANAGEMENT PLAN COMPONENTS

All components of the project management plan may be inputs for this process.

### 4.2.2 PROJECT DOCUMENTS EXAMPLES

Examples of project documents that may be inputs for this process include but are not limited to:

◆ Lessons learned register,

◆ Project team assignments,

◆ Resource breakdown structure,

◆ Source selection criteria, and

◆ Stakeholder register.

### 4.2.3 PROJECT MANAGEMENT PLAN UPDATES

Any component of the project management plan may be updated as a result of this process.

## 4.3 MANAGE QUALITY

Manage Quality is the process of translating the quality management plan into executable quality activities that incorporate the organization's quality policies into the project. The key benefit of this process is that it increases the probability of meeting the quality objectives, as well as identifying ineffective processes and causes of poor quality. This process is performed throughout the project. The inputs and outputs of this process are shown in Figure 4-4.

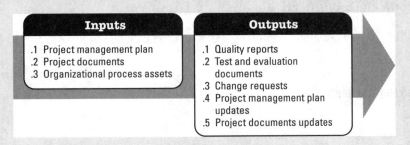

**Figure 4-4. Manage Quality: Inputs and Outputs**

The needs of the project determine which components of the project management plan and which project documents are necessary.

### 4.3.1 PROJECT MANAGEMENT PLAN COMPONENTS

An example of a project management plan component that may be an input for this process includes but is not limited to the quality management plan.

### 4.3.2 PROJECT DOCUMENTS EXAMPLES

Examples of project documents that may be inputs for this process include but are not limited to:

◆ Lessons learned register,

◆ Quality control measurements,

◆ Quality metrics, and

◆ Risk report.

### 4.3.3 PROJECT MANAGEMENT PLAN UPDATES

Components of the project management plan that may be updated as a result of this process include but are not limited to:

◆ Quality management plan,

◆ Scope baseline,

◆ Schedule baseline,

◆ Cost baseline.

### 4.3.4 PROJECT DOCUMENTS UPDATES

Project documents that may be updated as a result of this process include but are not limited to:

◆ Issue log,

◆ Lessons learned register, and

◆ Risk register.

## 4.4 ACQUIRE RESOURCES

Acquire Resources is the process of obtaining team members, facilities, equipment, materials, supplies, and other resources necessary to complete project work. The key benefit of this process is that it outlines and guides the selection of resources and assigns them to their respective activities. This process is performed periodically throughout the project as needed. The inputs and outputs of this process are shown in Figure 4-5.

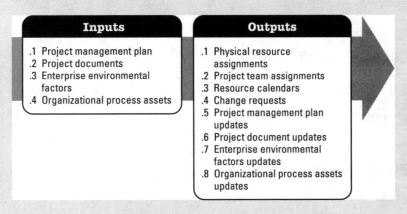

**Figure 4-5. Acquire Resources: Inputs and Outputs**

The needs of the project determine which components of the project management plan and which project documents are necessary.

### 4.4.1 PROJECT MANAGEMENT PLAN COMPONENTS

Examples of project management plan components that may be inputs for this process include but are not limited to:

◆ Resource management plan,

◆ Procurement management plan, and

◆ Cost baseline.

### 4.4.2 PROJECT DOCUMENTS EXAMPLES

Examples of project documents that may be inputs for this process include but are not limited to:

◆ Project schedule

◆ Resource calendars,

◆ Resource requirements, and

◆ Stakeholder register.

### 4.4.3 PROJECT MANAGEMENT PLAN UPDATES

Components of the project management plan that may be updated as a result of this process include but are not limited to:

◆ Resource management plan, and

◆ Cost baseline.

### 4.4.4 PROJECT DOCUMENTS UPDATES

Project documents that may be updated as a result of this process include but are not limited to:

◆ Lessons learned register,

◆ Project schedule,

◆ Resource breakdown structure,

◆ Resource calendars,

◆ Resource requirements,

◆ Risk register, and

◆ Stakeholder register.

## 4.5 DEVELOP TEAM

Develop Team is the process of improving competencies, team member interaction, and overall team environment to enhance project performance. The key benefit of this process is that it results in improved teamwork, enhanced interpersonal skills and competencies, motivated employees, reduced attrition, and improved overall project performance. This process is performed throughout the project. The inputs and outputs of this process are shown in Figure 4-6.

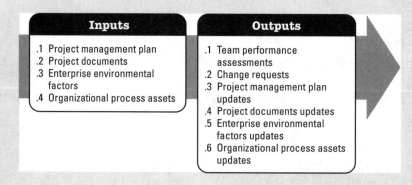

| Inputs | Outputs |
|---|---|
| .1 Project management plan<br>.2 Project documents<br>.3 Enterprise environmental factors<br>.4 Organizational process assets | .1 Team performance assessments<br>.2 Change requests<br>.3 Project management plan updates<br>.4 Project documents updates<br>.5 Enterprise environmental factors updates<br>.6 Organizational process assets updates |

**Figure 4-6. Develop Team: Inputs and Outputs**

The needs of the project determine which components of the project management plan and which project documents are necessary.

### 4.5.1 PROJECT MANAGEMENT PLAN COMPONENTS

An example of a project management plan component that may be an input for this process includes but is not limited to the resource management plan.

### 4.5.2 PROJECT DOCUMENTS EXAMPLES

Examples of project documents that may be inputs for this process include but are not limited to:

◆ Lessons learned register,

◆ Project schedule,

◆ Project team assignments,

◆ Resource calendars, and

◆ Team charter.

### 4.5.3 PROJECT MANAGEMENT PLAN UPDATES

A component of the project management plan that may be updated as a result of this process includes but is not limited to the resource management plan.

### 4.5.4 PROJECT DOCUMENTS UPDATES

A project document that may be updated as a result of this process includes but is not limited to:

◆ Lessons learned register,

◆ Project schedule,

◆ Project team assignments,

◆ Resource calendars, and

◆ Team charter.

## 4.6 MANAGE TEAM

Manage Team is the process of tracking team member performance, providing feedback, resolving issues, and managing team changes to optimize project performance. The key benefit of this process is that it influences team behavior, manages conflict, and resolves issues. This process is performed throughout the project. The inputs and outputs of this process are shown in Figure 4-7.

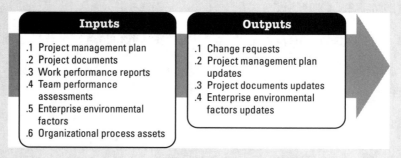

| Inputs | Outputs |
|---|---|
| .1 Project management plan<br>.2 Project documents<br>.3 Work performance reports<br>.4 Team performance assessments<br>.5 Enterprise environmental factors<br>.6 Organizational process assets | .1 Change requests<br>.2 Project management plan updates<br>.3 Project documents updates<br>.4 Enterprise environmental factors updates |

Figure 4-7. Manage Team: Inputs and Outputs

The needs of the project determine which components of the project management plan and which project documents are necessary.

### 4.6.1 PROJECT MANAGEMENT PLAN COMPONENTS

An example of a project management plan component that may be an input for this process includes but is not limited to the resource management plan.

### 4.6.2 PROJECT DOCUMENTS EXAMPLES

Examples of project documents that may be inputs for this process include but are not limited to:

◆ Issue log,

◆ Lessons learned register,

◆ Project team assignments, and

◆ Team charter.

### 4.6.3 PROJECT MANAGEMENT PLAN UPDATES

Components of the project management plan that may be updated as a result of this process include but are not limited to:

◆ Resource management plan,

◆ Schedule baseline, and

◆ Cost baseline.

### 4.6.4 PROJECT DOCUMENTS UPDATES

Project documents that may be updated as a result of this process include but are not limited to:

◆ Issue log,

◆ Lessons learned register, and

◆ Project team assignments.

## 4.7 MANAGE COMMUNICATIONS

Manage Communications is the process of ensuring timely and appropriate collection, creation, distribution, storage, retrieval, management, monitoring, and the ultimate disposition of project information. The key benefit of this process is that it enables an efficient and effective information flow between the project team and the stakeholders. This process is performed throughout the project. The inputs and outputs of this process are depicted in Figure 4-8.

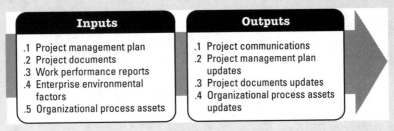

**Figure 4-8. Manage Communications: Inputs and Outputs**

The needs of the project determine which components of the project management plan and which project documents are necessary.

### 4.7.1 PROJECT MANAGEMENT PLAN COMPONENTS

Examples of project management plan components that may be inputs for this process include but are not limited to:

◆ Resource management plan,

◆ Communications management plan, and

◆ Stakeholder engagement plan.


### 4.7.2 PROJECT DOCUMENTS EXAMPLE

Examples of project documents that may be inputs for this process include but are not limited to:

◆ Change log,

◆ Issue log,

◆ Lessons learned register,

◆ Quality report,

◆ Risk report, and

◆ Stakeholder register.


### 4.7.3 PROJECT MANAGEMENT PLAN UPDATES

Examples of the project management plan components that may be updated as a result of this process include but are not limited to:

◆ Communications management plan, and

◆ Stakeholder engagement plan.


### 4.7.4 PROJECT DOCUMENTS UPDATES

Project documents that may be updated as a result of this process include but are not limited to:

◆ Issue log,

◆ Lessons learned register,

◆ Project schedule,

◆ Risk register, and

◆ Stakeholder register.

# 4.8 IMPLEMENT RISK RESPONSES

Implement Risk Responses is the process of implementing agreed-upon risk response plans. The key benefit of this process is that it ensures that agreed-upon risk responses are executed as planned in order to address overall project risk exposure, as well as to minimize individual project threats and maximize individual project opportunities. This process is performed throughout the project. The inputs and outputs of this process are depicted in Figure 4-9.

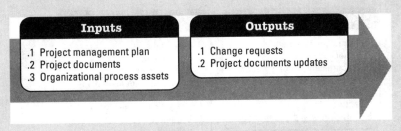

**Figure 4-9. Implement Risk Responses: Inputs and Outputs**

The needs of the project determine which components of the project management plan and which project documents are necessary.

## 4.8.1 PROJECT MANAGEMENT PLAN COMPONENTS

An example of a project management plan component that may be an input for this process includes but is not limited to the risk management plan.

## 4.8.2 PROJECT DOCUMENTS EXAMPLES

Examples of project documents that may be inputs for this process include but are not limited to:

◆ Lessons learned register,

◆ Risk register, and

◆ Risk report.

## 4.8.3 PROJECT DOCUMENTS UPDATES

Project documents that may be updated as a result of this process include but are not limited to:

◆ Issue log,

◆ Lessons learned register,

◆ Project team assignments,

◆ Risk register, and

◆ Risk report.

# 4.9 CONDUCT PROCUREMENTS

Conduct Procurements is the process of obtaining seller responses, selecting a seller, and awarding a contract. The key benefit of this process is that it selects a qualified seller and implements the legal agreement for delivery. This process is performed periodically throughout the project as needed. The inputs and outputs of this process are depicted in Figure 4-10.

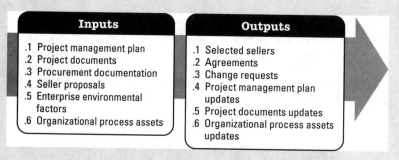

| Inputs | Outputs |
|---|---|
| .1 Project management plan | .1 Selected sellers |
| .2 Project documents | .2 Agreements |
| .3 Procurement documentation | .3 Change requests |
| .4 Seller proposals | .4 Project management plan updates |
| .5 Enterprise environmental factors | .5 Project documents updates |
| .6 Organizational process assets | .6 Organizational process assets updates |

Figure 4-10. Conduct Procurements: Inputs and Outputs

The needs of the project determine which components of the project management plan and which project documents are necessary.

## 4.9.1 PROJECT MANAGEMENT PLAN COMPONENTS

Examples of project management plan components that may be inputs for this process include but are not limited to:

◆ Scope management plan,

◆ Requirements management plan,

◆ Communications management plan,

◆ Risk management plan,

◆ Procurement management plan,

◆ Configuration management plan, and

◆ Cost baseline.

## 4.9.2 PROJECT DOCUMENTS EXAMPLES

Examples of project documents that may be inputs for this process include but are not limited to:

◆ Lessons learned register,

◆ Project schedule,

◆ Requirements documentation,

◆ Risk register, and

◆ Stakeholder register.


## 4.9.3 PROJECT MANAGEMENT PLAN UPDATES

Components of the project management plan that may be updated as a result of this process include but are not limited to:

◆ Requirements management plan,

◆ Quality management plan,

◆ Communications management plan,

◆ Risk management plan,

◆ Procurement management plan,

◆ Scope baseline,

◆ Schedule baseline, and

◆ Cost baseline.


## 4.9.4 PROJECT DOCUMENTS UPDATES

Project documents that may be updated as a result of this process include but are not limited to:

◆ Lessons learned register,

◆ Requirements documentation,

◆ Requirements traceability matrix,

◆ Resource calendars,

◆ Risk register, and

◆ Stakeholder register.

# 4.10 MANAGE STAKEHOLDER ENGAGEMENT

Manage Stakeholder Engagement is the process of communicating and working with stakeholders to meet their needs and expectations, address issues, and foster appropriate stakeholder involvement. The key benefit of this process is that it allows the project manager to increase support and minimize resistance from stakeholders. This process is performed throughout the project. The inputs and outputs of this process are depicted in Figure 4-11.

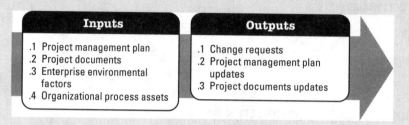

**Figure 4-11. Manage Stakeholder Engagement: Inputs and Outputs**

The needs of the project determine which components of the project management plan and which project documents are necessary.

## 4.10.1 PROJECT MANAGEMENT PLAN COMPONENTS

Examples of project management plan components that may be inputs for this process include but are not limited to:

◆ Communications management plan,

◆ Risk management plan,

◆ Stakeholder engagement plan, and

◆ Change management plan.

## 4.10.2 PROJECT DOCUMENTS EXAMPLES

Examples of project documents that may be inputs for this process include but are not limited to:

◆ Change log,

◆ Issue log,

◆ Lessons learned register, and

◆ Stakeholder register.

## 4.10.3 PROJECT MANAGEMENT PLAN UPDATES

Components of the project management plan that may be updated as a result of this process include but are not limited to:

◆ Communications management plan, and

◆ Stakeholder engagement plan.


## 4.10.4 PROJECT DOCUMENTS UPDATES

Project documents that may be updated as a result of this process include but are not limited to:

◆ Change log,

◆ Issue log,

◆ Lessons learned register, and

◆ Stakeholder register.

# 5

## MONITORING AND CONTROLLING PROCESS GROUP

The Monitoring and Controlling Process Group consists of those processes required to track, review, and regulate the progress and performance of the project; identify any areas in which changes to the plan are required; and initiate the corresponding changes. Monitoring is collecting project performance data, producing performance measures, and reporting and disseminating performance information. Controlling is comparing actual performance with planned performance, analyzing variances, assessing trends to effect process improvements, evaluating possible alternatives, and recommending appropriate corrective action as needed. The key benefit of this Process Group is that project performance is measured and analyzed at regular intervals, appropriate events, or when exception conditions occur in order to identify and correct variances from the project management plan. The Monitoring and Controlling Process Group also involves:

◆ Evaluating change requests and deciding on the appropriate response;

◆ Recommending corrective or preventive action in anticipation of possible problems;

◆ Monitoring the ongoing project activities against the project management plan and project baselines; and

◆ Influencing the factors that could circumvent the change control process so only approved changes are implemented.

Continuous monitoring provides the project team and other stakeholders with insight into the status of the project and identifies any areas that require additional attention. The Monitoring and Controlling Process Group monitors and controls the work being done within each Knowledge Area, each Process Group, each life cycle phase, and the project as a whole. The Monitoring and Controlling Process Group (Figure 5-1) includes the project management processes identified in Sections 5.1 through 5.12.

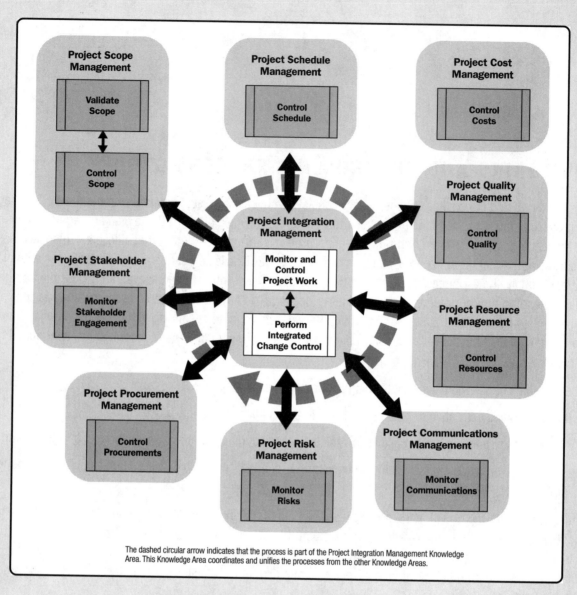

The dashed circular arrow indicates that the process is part of the Project Integration Management Knowledge Area. This Knowledge Area coordinates and unifies the processes from the other Knowledge Areas.

Figure 5-1. Monitoring and Controlling Process Group

# 5.1 MONITOR AND CONTROL PROJECT WORK

Monitor and Control Project Work is the process of tracking, reviewing, and reporting the overall progress to meet the performance objectives defined in the project management plan. The key benefit of this process is that it allows stakeholders to understand the current state of the project, to recognize the actions taken to address any performance issues, and to have visibility into the future project status with cost and schedule forecasts. This process is performed throughout the project. The inputs and outputs for this process are depicted in Figure 5-2.

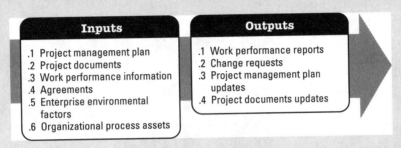

**Figure 5-2. Monitor and Control Project Work: Inputs and Outputs**

The needs of the project determine which components of the project management plan and which project documents are necessary.

## 5.1.1 PROJECT MANAGEMENT PLAN COMPONENTS

Any component of the project management plan may be an input for this process.

## 5.1.2 PROJECT DOCUMENTS EXAMPLES

Examples of project documents that may be inputs for this process include but are not limited to:

◆ Assumption log,

◆ Basis of estimates,

◆ Cost forecasts,

◆ Issue log,

◆ Lessons learned register,

◆ Milestone list,

◆ Quality reports,

◆ Risk register,

◆ Risk report, and

◆ Schedule forecasts.

### 5.1.3 PROJECT MANAGEMENT PLAN UPDATES

Any component of the project management plan may be updated as a result of this process.

### 5.1.4 PROJECT DOCUMENTS UPDATES

Project documents that may be updated as a result of this process include but are not limited to:

◆ Cost forecasts,

◆ Issue log,

◆ Lessons learned register,

◆ Risk register, and

◆ Schedule forecasts.

## 5.2 PERFORM INTEGRATED CHANGE CONTROL

Perform Integrated Change Control is the process of reviewing all change requests; approving changes and managing changes to deliverables, organizational process assets, project documents, and the project management plan; and communicating the decisions. This process reviews all requests for changes to project documents, deliverables, or the project management plan, and determines the resolution of the change requests. The key benefit of this process is that it allows for documented changes within the project to be considered in an integrated manner while addressing overall project risk, which often arises from changes made without consideration of the overall project objectives or plans. This process is performed throughout the project. The inputs and outputs of this process are depicted in Figure 5-3.

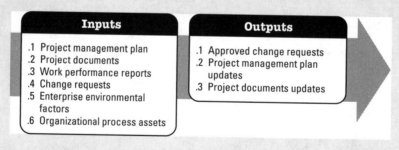

**Figure 5-3. Perform Integrated Change Control: Inputs and Outputs**

The needs of the project determine which components of the project management plan and which project documents are necessary.

### 5.2.1 PROJECT MANAGEMENT PLAN COMPONENTS

Examples of project management plan components that may be inputs for this process include but are not limited to:

◆ Change management plan,

◆ Configuration management plan,

◆ Scope baseline,

◆ Schedule baseline, and

◆ Cost baseline.

### 5.2.2 PROJECT DOCUMENTS EXAMPLES

Examples of project documents that may be inputs for this process include but are not limited to:

◆ Basis of estimates,

◆ Requirements traceability matrix,

◆ Risk report, and

◆ Change log.

### 5.2.3 PROJECT MANAGEMENT PLAN UPDATES

Any component of the project management plan may be updated as a result of this process.

### 5.2.4 PROJECT DOCUMENTS UPDATES

Any formally controlled project document may be changed as a result of this process. A project document that is normally updated as a result of this process is the change log. The change log is used to document changes that occur during a project.

# 5.3 VALIDATE SCOPE

Validate Scope is the process of formalizing acceptance of the completed project deliverables. The key benefit of this process is that it brings objectivity to the acceptance process and increases the probability of final product, service, or result acceptance by validating each deliverable. This process is performed periodically throughout the project as needed. The inputs and outputs of this process are depicted in Figure 5-4.

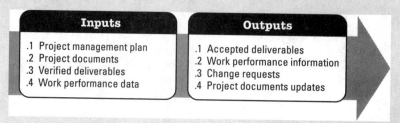

**Figure 5-4. Validate Scope: Inputs and Outputs**

The needs of the project determine which components of the project management plan and which project documents are necessary.

## 5.3.1 PROJECT MANAGEMENT PLAN COMPONENTS

Examples of project management plan components that may be inputs for this process include but are not limited to:

◆ Scope management plan,

◆ Requirements management plan, and

◆ Scope baseline.

## 5.3.2 PROJECT DOCUMENTS EXAMPLES

Examples of project documents that may be inputs for this process include but are not limited to:

◆ Lessons learned register,

◆ Quality reports,

◆ Requirements documentation, and

◆ Requirements traceability matrix.

### 5.3.3 PROJECT DOCUMENTS UPDATES

Examples of project documents that may be updated as a result of this process include but are not limited to:

◆ Lessons learned register,

◆ Requirements documentation, and

◆ Requirements traceability matrix.

## 5.4 CONTROL SCOPE

Control Scope is the process of monitoring the status of the project and product scope and managing changes to the scope baseline. The key benefit of this process is that the scope baseline is maintained throughout the project. This process is performed throughout the project. The inputs and outputs of this process are depicted in Figure 5-5.

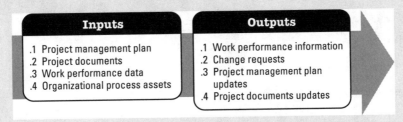

| Inputs | Outputs |
| --- | --- |
| .1 Project management plan<br>.2 Project documents<br>.3 Work performance data<br>.4 Organizational process assets | .1 Work performance information<br>.2 Change requests<br>.3 Project management plan updates<br>.4 Project documents updates |

**Figure 5-5. Control Scope: Inputs and Outputs**

The needs of the project determine which components of the project management plan and which project documents are necessary.

### 5.4.1 PROJECT MANAGEMENT PLAN COMPONENTS

Examples of project management plan components that may be inputs for this process include but are not limited to:

◆ Scope management plan,

◆ Requirements management plan,

◆ Change management plan,

◆ Configuration management plan,

◆ Scope baseline, and

◆ Performance measurement baseline.

## 5.4.2 PROJECT DOCUMENTS EXAMPLES

Examples of project documents that may be inputs for this process include but are not limited to:

◆ Lessons learned register,

◆ Requirements documentation, and

◆ Requirements traceability matrix.

## 5.4.3 PROJECT MANAGEMENT PLAN UPDATES

Components of the project management plan that may be updated as a result of this process include but are not limited to:

◆ Scope management plan,

◆ Scope baseline,

◆ Schedule baseline,

◆ Cost baseline and

◆ Performance measurement baseline.

## 5.4.4 PROJECT DOCUMENTS UPDATES

Project documents that may be updated as a result of this process include but are not limited to:

◆ Lessons learned register,

◆ Requirements documentation, and

◆ Requirements traceability matrix.

## 5.5 CONTROL SCHEDULE

Control Schedule is the process of monitoring the status of the project to update the project schedule and manage changes to the schedule baseline. The key benefit of this process is that the schedule baseline is maintained throughout the project. This process is performed throughout the project. The inputs and outputs of this process are depicted in Figure 5-6.

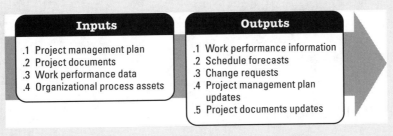

**Figure 5-6. Control Schedule: Inputs and Outputs**

The needs of the project determine which components of the project management plan and which project documents are necessary.

### 5.5.1 PROJECT MANAGEMENT PLAN COMPONENTS

Examples of project management plan components that may be inputs for this process include but are not limited to:

◆ Schedule management plan,

◆ Schedule baseline,

◆ Scope baseline, and

◆ Performance measurement baseline.

### 5.5.2 PROJECT DOCUMENTS EXAMPLES

Examples of project documents that may be inputs for this process include but are not limited to:

◆ Lessons learned register,

◆ Project calendars,

◆ Project schedule,

◆ Resource calendars, and

◆ Schedule data.

### 5.5.3 PROJECT MANAGEMENT PLAN UPDATES

Components of the project management plan that may be updated as a result of this process include but are not limited to:

◆ Schedule management plan,

◆ Schedule baseline, and

◆ Cost baseline and

◆ Performance measurement baseline.

### 5.5.4 PROJECT DOCUMENTS UPDATES

Project documents that may be updated as a result of this process include but are not limited to:

◆ Assumption log,

◆ Basis of estimates,

◆ Lessons learned register,

◆ Project schedule,

◆ Resource calendars,

◆ Risk register, and

◆ Schedule data.

## 5.6 CONTROL COSTS

Control Costs is the process of monitoring the status of the project to update the project costs and managing changes to the cost baseline. The key benefit of this process is that the cost baseline is maintained throughout the project. This process is performed throughout the project. The inputs and outputs of this process are depicted in Figure 5-7.

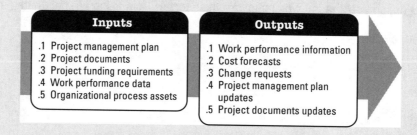

**Figure 5-7. Control Costs: Inputs and Outputs**

The needs of the project determine which components of the project management plan are necessary.

### 5.6.1 PROJECT MANAGEMENT PLAN COMPONENTS

Examples of project management plan components that may be inputs for this process include but are not limited to:

◆ Cost management plan,

◆ Cost baseline, and

◆ Performance measurement baseline.

### 5.6.2 PROJECT DOCUMENTS EXAMPLES

An example of a project document that may an input for this process includes but is not limited to the lessons learned register.

### 5.6.3 PROJECT MANAGEMENT PLAN UPDATES

Components of the project management plan that may be updated as a result of this process include but are not limited to:

◆ Cost management plan,

◆ Cost baseline, and

◆ Performance measurement baseline.

### 5.6.4 PROJECT DOCUMENTS UPDATES

Project documents that may be updated as a result of this process include but are not limited to:

◆ Assumption log,

◆ Basis of estimates,

◆ Cost estimates,

◆ Lessons learned register, and

◆ Risk register.

## 5.7 CONTROL QUALITY

Control Quality is the process of monitoring and recording results of executing the quality management activities to assess performance and ensure the project outputs are complete, correct, and meet customer expectations. The key benefit of this process is verifying that project deliverables and work meet the requirements specified by key stakeholders for final acceptance. This process is performed throughout the project. The inputs and outputs of this process are shown in Figure 5-8.

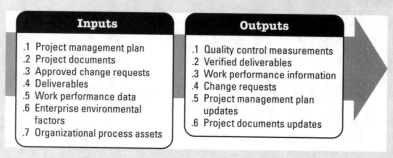

**Figure 5-8. Control Quality: Inputs and Outputs**

The needs of the project determine which components of the project management plan and which project documents are necessary.

### 5.7.1 PROJECT MANAGEMENT PLAN COMPONENTS

An example of a project management plan component that may be an input for this process includes but is not limited to the quality management plan.

### 5.7.2 PROJECT DOCUMENTS EXAMPLES

Examples of project documents that may be inputs for this process include but are not limited to:

◆ Lessons learned register,

◆ Quality metrics, and

◆ Test and evaluation documents.

### 5.7.3 PROJECT MANAGEMENT PLAN UPDATES

A component of the project management plan that may be updated as a result of this process includes but is not limited to the quality management plan.

### 5.7.4 PROJECT DOCUMENTS UPDATES

Project documents that may be updated as a result of this process include but are not limited to:

◆ Issue log,

◆ Lessons learned register,

◆ Risk register, and

◆ Test and evaluation documents.

## 5.8 CONTROL RESOURCES

Control Resources is the process of ensuring that the physical resources assigned and allocated to the project are available as planned, as well as monitoring the planned versus actual utilization of resources and taking corrective action as necessary. The key benefit of this process is ensuring that the assigned resources are available to the project at the right time and in the right place and are released when no longer needed. This process is performed throughout the project. The inputs and outputs of this process are shown in Figure 5-9.

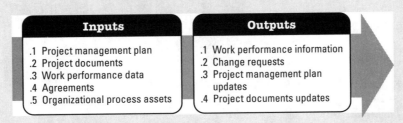

| Inputs | Outputs |
|---|---|
| .1 Project management plan<br>.2 Project documents<br>.3 Work performance data<br>.4 Agreements<br>.5 Organizational process assets | .1 Work performance information<br>.2 Change requests<br>.3 Project management plan updates<br>.4 Project documents updates |

Figure 5-9. Control Resources: Inputs and Outputs

The needs of the project determine which components of the project management plan and which project documents are necessary.

### 5.8.1 PROJECT MANAGEMENT PLAN COMPONENTS

An example of a project management plan component that may be an input for this process includes but is not limited to the resource management plan.

### 5.8.2 PROJECT DOCUMENTS EXAMPLES

Examples of project documents that may be inputs for this process include but are not limited to:

◆ Issue log,

◆ Lessons learned register,

◆ Physical resource assignments,

◆ Project schedule

◆ Resource breakdown structure,

◆ Resource requirements, and

◆ Risk register.

### 5.8.3 PROJECT MANAGEMENT PLAN UPDATES

A component of the project management plan that may be updated as a result of this process includes but is not limited to:

◆ Resource management plan,

◆ Schedule baseline, and

◆ Cost baseline.

### 5.8.4 PROJECT DOCUMENTS UPDATES

Project documents that may be updated as a result of this process include but are not limited to:

◆ Assumption log,

◆ Issue log,

◆ Lessons learned register,

◆ Physical resource assignments,

◆ Resource breakdown structure, and

◆ Risk register.

## 5.9 MONITOR COMMUNICATIONS

Monitor Communications is the process of ensuring the information needs of the project and its stakeholders are met. The key benefit of this process is the optimal information flow as defined in the communications management plan and stakeholder engagement plan. This process is performed throughout the project. The inputs and outputs of this process are depicted in Figure 5-10.

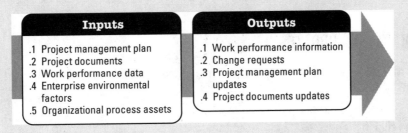

**Inputs**
.1 Project management plan
.2 Project documents
.3 Work performance data
.4 Enterprise environmental factors
.5 Organizational process assets

**Outputs**
.1 Work performance information
.2 Change requests
.3 Project management plan updates
.4 Project documents updates

Figure 5-10. Monitor Communications: Inputs and Outputs

The needs of the project determine which components of the project management plan and which project documents are necessary.

### 5.9.1 PROJECT MANAGEMENT PLAN COMPONENTS

Examples of project management plan components that may be inputs for this process include but are not limited to:

◆ Resource management plan,

◆ Communications management plan, and

◆ Stakeholder engagement plan.

### 5.9.2 PROJECT DOCUMENTS EXAMPLES

Examples of project documents that may be inputs for this process include but are not limited to:

◆ Issue log,

◆ Lessons learned register, and

◆ Project communications.

### 5.9.3 PROJECT MANAGEMENT PLAN UPDATES

Components of the project management plan that may be updated as a result of this process include but are not limited to:

◆ Communications management plan, and

◆ Stakeholder engagement plan.

### 5.9.4 PROJECT DOCUMENTS UPDATES

Project documents that may be updated as a result of this process include but are not limited to:

◆ Issue log,

◆ Lessons learned register, and

◆ Stakeholder register.

## 5.10 MONITOR RISKS

Monitor Risks is the process of monitoring the implementation of agreed-upon risk response plans, tracking identified risks, identifying and analyzing new risks, and evaluating risk process effectiveness throughout the project. The key benefit of this process is that it enables project decisions to be based on current information about overall project risk exposure and individual project risks. This process is performed throughout the project. The inputs and outputs of this process are depicted in Figure 5-11.

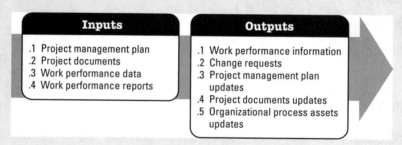

**Figure 5-11. Monitor Risks: Inputs and Outputs**

The needs of the project determine which components of the project management plan and which project documents are necessary.

### 5.10.1 PROJECT MANAGEMENT PLAN COMPONENTS

An example of a project management plan component that may be an input for this process includes but is not limited to the risk management plan.

### 5.10.2 PROJECT DOCUMENTS EXAMPLES

Examples of project documents that may be inputs for this process include but are not limited to:

◆ Issue log,

◆ Lessons learned register,

◆ Risk register, and

◆ Risk report.

### 5.10.3 PROJECT MANAGEMENT PLAN UPDATES

Any component of the project management plan may be updated as a result of this process.

### 5.10.4 PROJECT DOCUMENTS UPDATES

Project documents that may be updated as a result of this process include but are not limited to:

◆ Assumption log,

◆ Issue log,

◆ Lessons learned register,

◆ Risk register, and

◆ Risk report.

## 5.11 CONTROL PROCUREMENTS

Control Procurements is the process of managing procurement relationships, monitoring contract performance and making changes and corrections as appropriate, and closing out contracts. The key benefit of this process is that it ensures that both the seller's and buyer's performance meets the project's requirements according to the terms of the legal agreements. This process is performed throughout the project, when procurements are active. The inputs and outputs of this process are depicted in Figure 5-12.

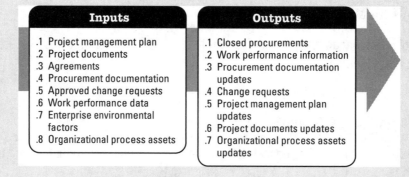

| Inputs | Outputs |
|---|---|
| .1 Project management plan | .1 Closed procurements |
| .2 Project documents | .2 Work performance information |
| .3 Agreements | .3 Procurement documentation updates |
| .4 Procurement documentation | .4 Change requests |
| .5 Approved change requests | .5 Project management plan updates |
| .6 Work performance data | .6 Project documents updates |
| .7 Enterprise environmental factors | .7 Organizational process assets updates |
| .8 Organizational process assets | |

Figure 5-12. Control Procurements: Inputs and Outputs

The needs of the project determine which components of the project management plan and which project documents are necessary.

## 5.11.1 PROJECT MANAGEMENT PLAN COMPONENTS

Examples of project management plan components that may be inputs for this process include but are not limited to:

◆ Requirements management plan,

◆ Risk management plan,

◆ Procurement management plan,

◆ Change management plan, and

◆ Schedule baseline.

## 5.11.2 PROJECT DOCUMENTS EXAMPLES

Examples of project documents that may be inputs for this process include but are not limited to:

◆ Assumption log,

◆ Lessons learned register,

◆ Milestone list,

◆ Quality reports,

◆ Requirements documentation,

◆ Requirements traceability matrix,

◆ Risk register, and

◆ Stakeholder register.

### 5.11.3 PROJECT MANAGEMENT PLAN UPDATES

Components of the project management plan that may be updated as a result of this process include but are not limited to:

◆ Risk management plan,

◆ Procurement management plan,

◆ Schedule baseline, and

◆ Cost baseline.

### 5.11.4 PROJECT DOCUMENTS UPDATES

Project documents that may be updated as a result of this process include but are not limited to:

◆ Lessons learned register,

◆ Resource requirements,

◆ Requirements traceability matrix,

◆ Risk register, and

◆ Stakeholder register.

## 5.12 MONITOR STAKEHOLDER ENGAGEMENT

Monitor Stakeholder Engagement is the process of monitoring project stakeholder relationships, and tailoring strategies for engaging stakeholders through modification of engagement strategies and plans. The key benefit of this process is that it maintains or increases the efficiency and effectiveness of stakeholder engagement activities as the project evolves and its environment changes. This process is performed throughout the project. The inputs and outputs of this process are depicted in Figure 5-13.

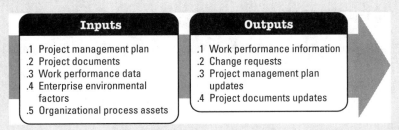

**Figure 5-13. Monitor Stakeholder Engagement: Inputs and Outputs**

The needs of the project determine which components of the project management plan and which project documents are necessary.

### 5.12.1 PROJECT MANAGEMENT PLAN COMPONENTS

Examples of project management plan components that may be inputs for this process include but are not limited to:

◆ Resource management plan,

◆ Communications management plan, and

◆ Stakeholder engagement plan.


### 5.12.2 PROJECT DOCUMENTS EXAMPLES

Examples of project documents that may be inputs for this process include but are not limited to:

◆ Issue log,

◆ Lessons learned register,

◆ Project communications,

◆ Risk register, and

◆ Stakeholder register.


### 5.12.3 PROJECT MANAGEMENT PLAN UPDATES

Components of the project management plan that may be updated as a result of this process include but are not limited to:

◆ Resource management plan,

◆ Communications management plan, and

◆ Stakeholder engagement plan.


### 5.12.4 PROJECT DOCUMENTS UPDATES

Project documents that may be updated as a result of this process include but are not limited to:

◆ Issue log,

◆ Lessons learned register,

◆ Risk register, and

◆ Stakeholder register.

# 6

# CLOSING PROCESS GROUP

The Closing Process Group consists of the process(es) performed to formally complete or close a project, phase, or contract. This Process Group verifies that the defined processes are completed within all of the Process Groups to close the project or phase, as appropriate, and formally establishes that the project or project phase is complete. The key benefit of this Process Group is that phases, projects, and contracts are closed out appropriately. While there is only one process in this Process Group, organizations may have their own processes associated with project, phase, or contract closure. Therefore, the term Process Group is maintained.

This Process Group may also address the early closure of the project, for example, aborted projects or cancelled projects.

The Closing Process Group (Figure 6-1) includes the project management process identified in Section 6.1.

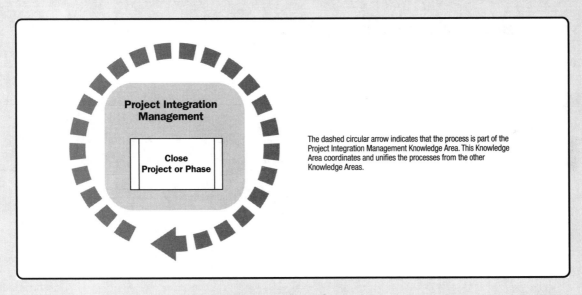

Figure 6-1. Closing Process Group

# 6.1 CLOSE PROJECT OR PHASE

Close Project or Phase is the process of finalizing all activities for the project, phase, or contract. The key benefits of this process are the project or phase information is archived, the planned work is completed, and organizational resources are released to pursue new endeavors. This process is performed once or at predefined points in the project. The inputs and outputs of this process are depicted in Figure 6-2.

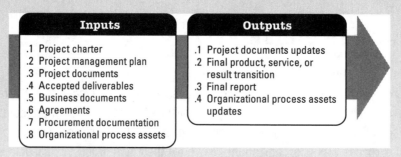

**Figure 6-2. Close Project or Phase: Inputs and Outputs**

The needs of the project determine which components of the project management plan and which project documents are necessary.

## 6.1.1 PROJECT MANAGEMENT PLAN COMPONENTS

All components of the project management plan may be inputs to this process.

## 6.1.2 PROJECT DOCUMENTS EXAMPLES

Examples of project documents that may be inputs for this process include but are not limited to:

- ◆ Assumption log,
- ◆ Basis of estimates,
- ◆ Change log,
- ◆ Issue log,
- ◆ Lessons learned register,
- ◆ Milestone list,
- ◆ Project communications,
- ◆ Quality control measurements,
- ◆ Quality reports,
- ◆ Requirements documentation,
- ◆ Risk register, and
- ◆ Risk report.

## 6.1.3 PROJECT DOCUMENTS UPDATES

Any project documents that may be updated as a result of this process include but are not limited to the lessons learned register.

# Part 3

# Appendices, Glossary, and Index

# APPENDIX X1
# SIXTH EDITION CHANGES

The purpose of this appendix is to provide an overview of the changes made to *A Guide to the Project Management Body of Knowledge (PMBOK® Guide)*—Fifth Edition to create the *PMBOK® Guide*—Sixth Edition.

## X1.1 SCOPE OF UPDATE

The approved scope for the *PMBOK® Guide*—Sixth Edition includes:

◆ Review the following and determine whether the material will be included or excluded in the new editions, and track the disposition:

■ All material relevant to Sections 1 through 13, Annex A1, and the Glossary that was deferred during the development of *A Guide to the Project Management Body of Knowledge (PMBOK® Guide)*—Fifth Edition

■ All comments and feedback relevant to Sections 1 through 13, Annex A1, and the Glossary of *A Guide to the Project Management Body of Knowledge (PMBOK® Guide)*—Fifth Edition that have been received by PMI since the initial development and publication.

◆ Review, interpret, and ensure appropriate alignment with ISO 21500 in the development of the standard.

◆ Ensure harmonization with any other relevant PMI foundational standards.

◆ Consider the project manager role delineation study results and other PMI research studies for incorporation as appropriate.

◆ Review, conduct, and analyze research for significant additions, deletions, and changes to the Sixth Edition and possibly for strategic input to future editions.

With that directive in mind, the update team focused on bringing greater consistency and clarity by refining and standardizing the processes, inputs, tools and techniques, and outputs.

## X1.2 RULES FOR HARMONIZATION BETWEEN GLOSSARY TERMS AND THE *PMI LEXICON OF PROJECT MANAGEMENT TERMS*

To ensure that terms used in the *PMBOK® Guide* align with the *PMI Lexicon of Project Management Terms*[1] and harmonize with other relevant PMI standards, the Sixth Edition followed these business rules:

◆ For terms found in both the *PMBOK® Guide* and the *PMI Lexicon, the definition* from the *PMI Lexicon* is used.

◆ Where terms used in the *PMBOK® Guide* are not found in the *PMI Lexicon* but are found in other relevant PMI standards, the definitions of the terms should be identical. If the definitions do not align with the respective standards, the term is elevated to the PMI Lexicon team for assistance in creating an acceptable common definition.


## X1.3 RULES FOR HANDLING INPUTS AND OUTPUTS

The following business rules were used to provide consistency in the order and information within the inputs and outputs for each project management process:

◆ *Fundamental Rules:*

  ■ Inputs are any documents that are key to the process.

  ■ Outputs should become an input to another project management process unless the output is a terminal output or embedded within another input such as project documents.

  ■ Inputs should come from an output from another project management process unless the input comes from outside the project.

◆ *Project Documents Rules:*

  ■ When specific project documents are identified the first time, they are listed as a specific output. Subsequently, they are listed as "project documents updates" in the output list, and described in the section narrative.

  ■ When any project document is an input, the term "project documents" is listed and the specific project documents are described in the section narrative.

◆ *Project Management Plan Rules:*

  ■ For those planning processes that create a subsidiary plan, the project charter is the first input and the project management plan is the second input.

  ■ The process that creates a component of the project management plan lists the component specifically. Subsequently, components are listed as "project management plan updates" in the output list, and described in the section narrative.

  ■ When the project management plan serves as a process input, specific components of the project management plan that may be considered are described in the section narrative.


[1] Project Management Institute. 2016. *The PMI Lexicon of Project Management Terms.* Available from http://www.pmi.org/Lexiconterms

◆ *Sequencing Rules:*

■ If the project charter is an input, it is the first input.

■ When the project management plan is an input or output, the subsidiary management plans are listed in the order of the sections in the *PMBOK® Guide* where they are produced as an output, followed by baselines and then any other plans.

■ Project documents are listed in alphabetical order.

■ Enterprise environmental factors and organizational process assets are listed last in that order.

■ When updates are an output they are listed in the following sequence:

  ○ Project management plan updates,

  ○ Project documents updates, and

  ○ Organizational process assets updates.

## X1.4 RULES FOR HANDLING TOOLS AND TECHNIQUES

The Sixth Edition endeavored to reduce the number of tools and techniques by focusing on those that are currently used on most projects most of the time. Based on academic and market research a number of tools and techniques were eliminated. In order to reduce repetition a tool or technique is described the first time it is listed and subsequent processes using that tool or technique refer back to the earlier description.

The Sixth Edition grouped some of the commonly used tools and techniques by their intent. Not all tools and techniques fall within a group, but for those tools or techniques that are part of a group, the group is listed and then examples of tools and techniques in that group are described in the narrative. The tools and techniques groups are:

◆ Data gathering,

◆ Data analysis,

◆ Data representation,

◆ Decision-making,

◆ Communication skills, and

◆ Interpersonal and team skills.

Appendix X6 identifies all the tools and techniques in the *PMBOK® Guide* by group, where appropriate, and lists the processes where they are used.

## X1.5 PROJECT MANAGEMENT PLAN

Not every component of the project management plan is created in a separate process. Such components are considered to be created in the Develop Project Management Plan process. They include the change management plan, configuration management plan, performance measurement baseline, project life cycle, development approach, and management reviews.

## X1.6 SECTION 1—INTRODUCTION

The Introduction section was significantly rewritten. Introductory information about projects, programs, and portfolios that aligns with other PMI foundational standards remains. However, there is new information on project and development life cycles, project phases, and phase gates. This information provides a high-level overview on selecting development approaches from predictive, iterative, incremental and adaptive, based on the nature of the project. New information on business documents includes the business case and the benefits management plan.

## X1.7 SECTION 2—THE ENVIRONMENT IN WHICH PROJECTS OPERATE

The content of Section 2 was significantly rewritten. Information on organizational process assets and enterprise environmental factors remains. However, there is new content on governance, management elements, and organizational structure types.

## X1.8 SECTION 3—THE ROLE OF THE PROJECT MANAGER

This is a new section that outlines the project manager's role on the team. It includes information on the project manager's sphere of influence and competencies. PMI's Talent Triangle® is discussed with its emphasis on strategic and business management skills, technical project management skills, and leadership skills. Leadership styles and personality are also discussed as part of this section. The final part of this section focuses on the project manager as an integrator.

## X1.9 AGILE

Since the Fifth Edition of the *PMBOK® Guide* there has been more adoption of agile and adaptive methodologies in the management of projects. The Sixth Edition has included a subsection called Considerations for Adaptive Environments at the beginning of Sections 4 through 13. Some agile-specific tools and techniques have been introduced into the *PMBOK® Guide*, such as sprint and iteration planning. Appendix X3 describes the use of agile, adaptive, iterative, and hybrid approaches from the perspective of the Project Management Process Groups.

## X1.10 KNOWLEDGE AREA FRONT MATERIAL

Each of the Knowledge Area sections includes standardized material prior to introducing the first process. The material is presented in the following subsections:

◆ **Key Concepts.** Collects key concepts associated with the specific knowledge area. This information was presented in earlier editions; in this edition it is consolidated and presented for consistency between knowledge areas. These key concepts are compiled in Appendix X4.

◆ **Trends and Emerging Practices**. The profession of project management continues to evolve. However, the purpose of the *PMBOK® Guide* is not to lead the industry; it is to describe what is considered good practice on most projects most of the time. This subsection identifies some of the trends or emerging practices that are occurring, but that may not be practiced on most projects.

◆ **Tailoring Considerations**. The Sixth Edition emphasizes the importance of tailoring all aspects of the project to meet the needs of the organization, environment, stakeholders and other variables. This subsection identifies areas the project manager can consider when tailoring their project. These tailoring considerations are compiled in Appendix X5.

◆ **Considerations for Agile/Adaptive Environments**. This subsection identifies some of the areas where adaptive approaches may differ from predictive approaches in the particular Knowledge Area.

## X1.11 KNOWLEDGE AREA AND PROCESS CHANGES

Two Knowledge Areas names were changed to more closely reflect the work that is done.

◆ Project Time Management was changed to Project Schedule Management to reflect that the project schedule is defined and managed during the project, whereas time is not managed.

◆ Both team resources and physical resources are addressed in the Sixth Edition. Thus, the Knowledge Area Project Human Resource Management was changed to Project Resource Management.

One process was removed and three new processes were added, to reflect changes in the way projects are managed in practice. One process was moved between Knowledge Areas. These changes are summarized below, and discussed in the relevant Knowledge Area section:

◆ Manage Project Knowledge (Section 4.4)—Added.

◆ Estimate Activity Resources (Section 6.4)—Moved to Project Resource Management.

◆ Control Resources (Section 9.6)—Added.

◆ Implement Risk Responses (Section 11.6)—Added.

◆ Close Procurements (Section 12.4)—Eliminated.

Several process names were changed to improve consistency across the processes and to improve clarity. Research indicates that project managers tend to monitor, facilitate, and manage rather than control, particularly in processes that involve interactions with people. Therefore, process names for Control Communications, Control Risks, and Control Stakeholder Engagement were changed to Monitor Communications, Monitor Risks, and Monitor Stakeholder Engagement. The list below summarizes all the process name changes:

◆ Perform Quality Assurance (Section 8.2)—Changed to Manage Quality.

◆ Plan Human Resource Management (Section 9.1)—Changed to Plan Resource Management.

◆ Acquire Project Team (Section 9.2)—Changed to Acquire Resources.

◆ Develop Project Team (Section 9.3)—Changed to Develop Team.

◆ Manage Project Team (Section 9.4)—Changed to Manage Team.

◆ Control Communications (Section 10.3)—Changed to Monitor Communications

◆ Control Risks (Section 11.6)—Changed to Monitor Risks.

◆ Plan Stakeholder Management (Section 13.2)—Changed to Plan Stakeholder Engagement.

◆ Control Stakeholder Engagement (Section 13.4)—Changed to Monitor Stakeholder Engagement.

## X1.12 SECTION 4—PROJECT INTEGRATION MANAGEMENT CHANGES

A new process, Manage Project Knowledge, was added. This is a result of many deferred comments from the Fifth Edition indicating the need to address knowledge management in projects. A key output of this process is the lessons learned register. This register is used throughout many of the processes in the Sixth Edition. This emphasizes the need to learn continually throughout the project rather than waiting until the end to reflect.

Business documents are inputs to the Develop Project Charter and Close Project or Phase processes. The introduction of business documents underscores the importance of staying attuned to the business case and benefits management throughout the project. Administrative closure activities for procurements have been absorbed into the Close Project or Phase process.

Changes consistent with information described in Sections X1.1 through X1.11 were implemented. Table X1-1 summarizes the Section 4 processes:

**Table X1-1. Section 4 Changes**

| Fifth Edition Processes | Sixth Edition Processes |
|---|---|
| 4.1 Develop Project Charter | 4.1 Develop Project Charter |
| 4.2 Develop Project Management Plan | 4.2 Develop Project Management Plan |
| 4.3 Direct and Manage Project Work | 4.3 Direct and Manage Project Work |
| 4.4 Monitor and Control Project Work | 4.4 Manage Project Knowledge |
| 4.5 Perform Integrated Change Control | 4.5 Monitor and Control Project Work |
| 4.6 Close Project or Phase | 4.6 Perform Integrated Change Control |
| | 4.7 Close Project or Phase |

## X1.13 SECTION 5—PROJECT SCOPE MANAGEMENT CHANGES

The Sixth Edition team collaborated with The Standard for Business Analysis to ensure that both foundational standards were aligned, though not duplicative. No changes to process names were necessary.

Changes consistent with information described in Sections X1.1 through X1.11 were implemented.

## X1.14 SECTION 6—PROJECT SCHEDULE MANAGEMENT CHANGES

Section 6 was renamed from Project Time Management to Project Schedule Management. Research indicated support for the name change as project managers do not manage time, they define and manage the project schedule. Due to the shift in focus and renaming of Project Human Resource Management to Project Resource Management, the process Estimate Activity Resources was moved from this Knowledge Area to Project Resource Management. Some agile concepts were incorporated into the Develop Schedule process. Figures and associated text were updated to clarify scheduling concepts addressed in the section.

Changes consistent with information described in Sections X1.1 through X1.11 were implemented. Table X1-2 summarizes the Section 6 processes:

Table X1-2. Section 6 Changes

| Fifth Edition Processes | Sixth Edition Processes |
|---|---|
| 6.1 Plan Schedule Management | 6.1 Plan Schedule Management |
| 6.2 Define Activities | 6.2 Define Activities |
| 6.3 Sequence Activities | 6.3 Sequence Activities |
| 6.4 Estimate Activity Resources | 6.4 Estimate Activity Durations |
| 6.5 Estimate Activity Durations | 6.5 Develop Schedule |
| 6.6 Develop Schedule | 6.6 Control Schedule |
| 6.7 Control Schedule | |

## X1.15 SECTION 7—PROJECT COST MANAGEMENT CHANGES

Changes consistent with information described in Sections X1.1 through X1.11 were implemented.

## X1.16 SECTION 8—PROJECT QUALITY MANAGEMENT CHANGES

Academic and market research was conducted regarding the Perform Quality Assurance process. Research indicated that many of the quality tools and techniques that were identified previously are not widely used in today's projects. The profession focuses more on managing quality through the quality management plan. Thus, the Perform Quality Assurance process shifted focus and the name was changed to Manage Quality.

Changes consistent with information described in Sections X1.1 through X1.11 were implemented. Table X1-3 summarizes the Section 8 processes:

Table X1-3. Section 8 Changes

| Fifth Edition Processes | Sixth Edition Processes |
|---|---|
| 8.1 Plan Quality Management | 8.1 Plan Quality Management |
| 8.2 Perform Quality Assurance | 8.2 Manage Quality |
| 8.3 Control Quality | 8.3 Control Quality |

# X1.17 SECTION 9—PROJECT RESOURCE MANAGEMENT CHANGES

The Sixth Edition expanded the scope of this section from its previous focus on human resources to include all resources. To distinguish between human resources and other resources, the term team resources is used to refer to human resources and the term physical resources is used to refer to other resources. The Estimate Activity Resources process was transferred into this Knowledge Area from Project Schedule Management, and a new process Control Resources was added. The word "project" was eliminated from Develop Team and Manage Team as it is inferred that the only team the project manager is concerned about developing and managing is the project team.

Changes consistent with information described in Sections X1.1 through X1.11 were implemented. Table X1-4 summarizes the Section 9 processes:

**Table X1-4. Section 9 Changes**

| Fifth Edition Processes | Sixth Edition Processes |
|---|---|
| 9.1 Plan Human Resource Management | 9.1 Plan Resource Management |
| 9.2 Acquire Project Team | 9.2 Estimate Activity Resources |
| 9.3 Develop Project Team | 9.3 Acquire Resources |
| 9.4 Manage Project Team | 9.4 Develop Team |
|  | 9.5 Manage Team |
|  | 9.6 Control Resources |

# X1.18 SECTION 10—PROJECT COMMUNICATIONS MANAGEMENT CHANGES

A subtle but important distinction was made in this section about project communication. The term "communication" indicates the act of communicating, such as facilitating a meeting, giving information and active listening. The term "communications" indicates the artifacts of communication, such as memos, presentations, and emails. Because it is not possible to control how and when people communicate, the name of the Control Communications process has been changed to Monitor Communications.

Changes consistent with information described in Sections X1.1 through X1.11 were implemented. Table X1-5 summarizes the Section 10 processes:

**Table X1-5. Section 10 Changes**

| Fifth Edition Processes | Sixth Edition Processes |
|---|---|
| 10.1 Plan Communications Management | 10.1 Plan Communications Management |
| 10.2 Manage Communications | 10.2 Manage Communications |
| 10.3 Control Communications | 10.3 Monitor Communications |

## X1.19 SECTION 11—PROJECT RISK MANAGEMENT CHANGES

An increased emphasis on overall project risk was integrated throughout the risk management processes. A new process, Implement Risk Responses, was added. This process is part of the Executing Process Group. The new process emphasizes the importance of not just planning risk responses, but implementing them as well. A new risk response "escalate" was introduced to indicate that if risks are identified that are outside the scope of the project objectives, they should be passed to the relevant person or part of the organization. Because risks are uncertain future events or conditions, they cannot be controlled; however, they can be monitored. Thus, the process Control Risks was renamed to Monitor Risks.

Changes consistent with information described in Sections X1.1 through X1.11 were implemented. Table X1-6 summarizes the Section 11 processes:

**Table X1-6. Section 11 Changes**

| Fifth Edition Processes | Sixth Edition Processes |
|---|---|
| 11.1 Plan Risk Management | 11.1 Plan Risk Management |
| 11.2 Identify Risks | 11.2 Identify Risks |
| 11.3 Perform Qualitative Risk Analysis | 11.3 Perform Qualitative Risk Analysis |
| 11.4 Perform Quantitative Risk Analysis | 11.4 Perform Quantitative Risk Analysis |
| 11.5 Plan Risk Responses | 11.5 Plan Risk Responses |
| 11.6 Control Risks | 11.6 Implement Risk Responses |
|  | 11.7 Monitor Risks |

# X1.20 SECTION 12—PROJECT PROCUREMENT MANAGEMENT CHANGES

Much of the information in this Knowledge Area was updated to reflect a more global perspective. Many projects are conducted with stakeholders in various countries, or by organizations with offices in multiple countries.

Market research shows that very few project managers actually close out procurements. Someone in contracts, procurement or legal departments usually has that authority. Therefore, information from Close Procurements about evaluating all completed deliverables and comparing them to the contract was absorbed into Control Procurements. Information about administrative, communications, and records was moved to Close Project or Phase.

Changes consistent with information described in Sections X1.1 through X1.11 were implemented. Table X1-7 summarizes the Section 12 processes:

Table X1-7. Section 12 Changes

| Fifth Edition Processes | Sixth Edition Processes |
| --- | --- |
| 12.1 Plan Procurement Management | 12.1 Plan Procurement Management |
| 12.2 Conduct Procurements | 12.2 Conduct Procurements |
| 12.3 Administer Procurements | 12.3 Control Procurements |
| 12.4 Close Procurements | |

# X1.21 SECTION 13—PROJECT STAKEHOLDER MANAGEMENT CHANGES

In keeping with current research and practice, a shift was made to focus on stakeholder engagement rather than stakeholder management. Because project managers rarely, if ever, have the ability to control stakeholders, Control Stakeholder Engagement was renamed to Monitor Stakeholder Engagement.

Changes consistent with information described in Sections X1.1 through X1.11 were implemented. Table X1-8 summarizes the Section 13 processes:

Table X1-8. Section 13 Changes

| Fifth Edition Processes | Sixth Edition Processes |
|---|---|
| 13.1 Identify Stakeholders | 13.1 Identify Stakeholders |
| 13.2 Plan Stakeholder Management | 13.2 Plan Stakeholder Engagement |
| 13.3 Manage Stakeholder Engagement | 13.3 Manage Stakeholder Engagement |
| 13.4 Control Stakeholder Engagement | 13.4 Monitor Stakeholder Engagement |

# X1.22 GLOSSARY

The glossary of the *PMBOK® Guide*—Sixth Edition was updated to clarify meaning and improve the quality and accuracy of any translations. Terms that are not used in the Sixth Edition, or are not used differently from everyday usage, were eliminated.

# APPENDIX X2
# CONTRIBUTORS AND REVIEWERS OF
# THE *PMBOK® GUIDE*—SIXTH EDITION

PMI volunteers first attempted to codify the Project Management Body of Knowledge in the *Special Report on Ethics, Standards, and Accreditation,* published in 1983. Since that time, other volunteers have come forward to update and improve that original document and contribute to this globally recognized standard for project management, PMI's *A Guide to the Project Management Body of Knowledge (PMBOK® Guide).* This appendix lists, those individuals who have contributed to the development and production of the *PMBOK® Guide* – Sixth Edition. No list can adequately portray all the contributions of those who have volunteered to develop the *PMBOK® Guide* – Sixth Edition.

The Project Management Institute is grateful to all of these individuals for their support and acknowledges their contributions to the project management profession.

## X2.1 *PMBOK® GUIDE*—SIXTH EDITION CORE COMMITTEE

The following individuals served as members, were contributors of text or concepts, and served as leaders within the Project Core Committee:

Cyndi Snyder Dionisio, MBA, PMP, Chair
David A. Hillson, PhD, PMI Fellow, HonFAPM, Vice Chair (Volunteer Engagement Lead & Section 11 Lead)
Lynda Bourne, DPM, FACS (Sections 10 & 13 Lead)
Larkland A. Brown, PMP, PMI-ACP (Section 6 Lead)
Pan C.P. Kao, PhD, PMP, (Sections 7 & 12 Lead)
Mercedes Martinez Sanz, PMP (Section 4 Lead)
Alejandro Romero-Torres, PhD, PMP, (Document Quality & Management Lead & Section 5 Lead)
Guy Schleffer, PfMP, PMP, (Sections 8 & 9 Lead)
Michael J. Stratton, PhD, PMP (Section 1, 2, & 3 Lead)†
Kristin L. Vitello, Standards Project Specialist
Gwen Whitman, EMBA, PfMP (Project Communications Lead)

---

†Deceased. The core committee and PMI acknowledge Michael J. Stratton for his work on the *PMBOK Guide -* Sixth Edition. Mike was dedicated to the profession and this work is a testament of his contributions to the field of project management.

---

## X2.2 SIGNIFICANT CONTRIBUTORS

In addition to the members of the Project Core Committee, the following individuals provided significant input or concepts:

Ernest Baker, PMP, PRINCE2® Practitioner
Cheryl Burcham, PMP
Guido Caciagli, B., PMP
Jimmy I. Char, PMP, SDI
Cătălin-Teodor Dogaru, PhD, MBA
Andrés Falcón, PMP
Anna Maria Felici, PMP
Jesse Fewell, CST, PMI-ACP
Eren Gokce, MBA, PMP
Pamela S. Goodhue, MBA, PMP
Franco R. Graziano, MPA, PMP
Mike Griffiths, PMP, PMI-ACP
Joy Gumz, CPA, PMP
Salah M. Haswah, PMP, PgMP
Puja Kasariya, PMP
Srikanth Krishnamoorthy, PMP, PGDSA
Tom Magee, MBA, PMP
David A. Maynard, MBA, PMP
Bob Mahler, PMP, PMI-RMP
Frank R. Parth, MBA, PMP
Dattatraya Y. Pathak, PMP, PfMP
Judy Payne, PhD, MBA
Nagy Attalla Saad, PMP, ITIL
Davidov Shai
Kavita Sharma, PMP, RMP
Jurgen T. Sturany, PMP
Dirk Withake, PgMP, PMP

## X2.3 *PMBOK® GUIDE*—SIXTH EDITION CONTENT COMMITTEE

The following individuals were contributors of text or concepts and provided recommendations on drafts of the *PMBOK® Guide*—Sixth Edition:

Vahid Azadmanesh, MBA, PMP

Brad Bigelow, PMP, MSP

Wayne R. Brantley, MSEd, PMP

Marcelo A. Briola PhD, PMP

Michael C. Broadway, PMP

Mariana Nella Caffarena Bolivar

Steven Flannes

Sandra Fonseca, PhD, CISA, CRISC

Theofanis C. Giotis, PMP, PMI-ACP

Piyush Govil, BE, PMP

Rex M. Holmlin, PE, PMP

Éamonn V. Kelly, DBA, PMP

Srikanth Krishnamoorthy

Fabiano de Alcântara de Lima, PhD, PMP

Shashank Neppalli

Andrea Pantano

Kristine Persun, PMP

Piyush Prakash PMP, Prince 2

Raju N. Rao, PMP, SCPM

Krupakar Reddy, PMP, PRINCE2 Practitioner

Emadeldin Seddik, PhD, PMP

Tejas V. Sura, PMP, PfMP

Nicholas Tovar

Fede Varchavsky, MBA, PMP

Angelo Valle, PhD, CRK

Ronald H. Verheijden, PMP

# X2.4 REVIEWERS

## X2.4.1 SME REVIEW

In addition to the members of the Committee, the following individuals provided their review and recommendations on drafts of the standard:

David P. Bieg, PMI-PBA
James F. Carilli, PMP, PgMP
Shika Carter, PMP, PgMP
Dan Deakin, PMP, CISSP
Theofanis C. Giotis, PMP, PMI-ACP
Dave Gunner, MSc, PMP
George Jucan, PMP
Ginger Levin, PhD, PMP, PgMP
Vanina Mangano, PMP, PMI-RMP
Juan Carlos Moreno, MBA, PMP
Marvin R. Nelson, MBA, SCPM
Klaus Nielsen, MBA, PMP
Chris Richards, PMP
Ivan Rincon, MBA, PMP
Shaligram Pokharel, REng (Nepal), PhD
Paul E. Shaltry, MA, PMP
Carolina Gabriela Spindola, PMP, SSBB
Langeswaran Supramaniam, C Build E FCABE, PMP
Michael A Yinger

## X2.4.2 FINAL EXPOSURE DRAFT REVIEW (STANDARD PORTION)

In addition to the members of the Committee, the following individuals provided recommendations for improving the Exposure Draft of the *PMBOK® Guide*—Sixth Edition (standard portion):

Ahmed A. Raouf Hamdy, PhD, PMP

Farhad Abdollahyan, PMP, OPM3 CP

Adil Abdulghani

Tetsuhide Abe, PMP

Klaus Abert

Ayodeji R. Abitogun, MBA, PMP

Taiwo Abraham

Mohammad I. Abu Irshaid, PMP, PfMP

Manuel Acosta A.

Phill C. Akinwale, MSc, PMP

Mazen Al Bazreh

Jose Rafael Alcala Gomez, PMP

Ameer Ali

Hammam Zayed Alkouz, PMP, PMI-RMP

Bill Allbee, PMP

Charmaine Y. Allen, PMP, PBA

Kristin L. Allen, PE, PMP

Abdulaziz Almalki

Ayman Alminawi, MBA, PMP

Ahmad Moh. Al-Musallami, MSc, PMP

Imad Alsadeq, P3M3, MB

Mohammed Ahmad S. Al-Shamsi, PhD, PEng

Essam Alsultan, MBA, PMP

Haluk Altunel, PhD, PMP

Priscilla S. R. Alves, PMP

Angelo Amaral

Barnabas Seth Amarteifio, PMP, ITIL (Expert)

Wilson Anandaraj, MBA, PMP

Guillermo Anton

John Aogon, PMP

Hamid Aougab, PMP, PMI-ACP

Charalampos Apostolopoulos, PhD, PMP

Rodolfo Arguello

Abd Razak B Ariffin, PMP

Deepak Arora, MBA, PMP

C. H. ArunPrabu, PMP

Zaher Asfari, MBA, PMI-ACP

Ayman Atallah, BE, PMP

Reza Atashfaraz, MSc, PMP

Sharaf A. Attas, PMP, PMI-RMP

Abdurazaq Attuwaijri

Ashraf M Awwad, MSc, PMP

Vikram Kumar B. T.

Nabeel Eltyeb Babiker, PMP, P3O

Mohamed A Badie, PMP, Prince2 Practitioner

Smitha Balakrishnan

Saket Bansal, PMP, PMI-ACP

Manuel F. Baquero V., MSc, PMP

Haytham Baraka, PMP, CCP

Robert Barclay

Karuna Basu

Joy Beatty, PMI-PBA, CBAP

Frances Bellows, PMP, ACP

Peter G. Bembir, MPhil, PMP

Anis Ben Hassen, Msc Project/ Programme/Portfolio Management, PMP

Racquel Benedict

German Bernate, MPM

Bryan D. Berthot, MBA, PMP

Karl F. Best, PMP, CStd

Shantanu Bhamare, PMP, LIMC

Jasbir Singh Bhogal, PMP, ITIL-V3

Michael M. Bissonette, MBA, PfMP

Molly Blake-Michaels, MS, PMP

Nigel Blampied, PE, PMP

Wolfgang Blickle, PMP, PMI-ACP

Jaqueline Boeck

Dennis L. Bolles, PMP

Kiron D. Bondale, PMP, PMI-RMP

Raúl Borges, PMP

Farid F. Bouges, PhD, PMP, PfMP

Joao Boyadjian

Damiano Bragantini, PMP

Ralf Braune

Kevin Brennan

Naga Pradeep Buddhavarapu, PMP

David E. Buehler, PMP

Susan M. Burk

Andrea Caccamese, PMP, Prince2 Practitioner

Roberto A. Cadena Legaspi, PMP, MCI

Shawna D. Camp, MBA, PMP

Iker Castillo, PMP

Igor Castro

Helena Cedersjö, MSc, PMP

Balasubramanian Chandrasekaran, BE, PMP

Joo-Kwan Chang

Panos Chatzipanos, PhD, Dr Eur Ing

Pengzhi Chen, PMP, MSC

Wilson Lee Chung, PMP

Xavier Clerfeuille, MSc, SSL Black Belt

Martin A. Collado, PMP, ITIL

Sergio Luis Conte, PhD, PMP

Lawrence (Larry) Cooper, PMP, PMI-ACP

Hélio R. Costa, DSc

Scott Cunningham

Adriano Jose da Silva Neves, PhD, PMP

Hernán D'Adamo, MPM, PMP

Michelle Daigle, PMP

Larry C Dalton, PfMP, PgMP

Farshid Damirchilo, MSc

Tran Dang

Teodor Darabaneanu, PMP, MEng

Russell W. Darnall, DM, PMP

Edson G. Freitas, PMP

Jean-Michel de Jaeger, EMBA, PMP

Maria Angela de Souza Fernandes

Allan E. Dean PMP, PgMP

G. Murat Dengiz, PMP

Valerie P. Denney, DBA, PMP

Jacqueline E. Dennis, PMP, PgMP

Konika Dey, MCA, PMP

Cyndi Snyder Dionisio, MBA, PMP

Ajay Kumar Dixit, MBA, B Tech

Roland Doerr, MSc, PMP

Rex Wotan Dominguez Chang

Jorge Duenas-Lozano

Stephen M. Duffield, MPM, CPPD

Josée Dufour, PMP

Darya Duma, PEng, PMP

Keiran J. Dunne, PhD

Awab Elameer, PMP, PMI-SP

Khaled EL-Nakib, MSc, PMP

Yasir Elsadig, PMP, PfMP

Majdi N. Elyyan, PMP, PMI-RMP

Pedro Engrácia

Mark W. Erwin, PMP, PMI-ACP

Behnam Faizabadi, PhD, PMP

Marco Falcao, PMP, PMI-RMP

Puian Masudi Far, PhDc, PMP

Jamil Faraj

Saurater Faraday, PMI-RMP

Fereydoun Fardad, PMP, PRINCE2

Sergio Ferreto Gutiérrez, MPM, MBA

David Foley, MBA

Les Foley, MPM, PMP

Gloria Folle Estrada, PMP

Frank P. Forte, PMP

Laura Franch, PMP

Nestor C. Gabarda Jr., ECE, PMP

Jaime Garcia Castro, PMP

Sam Ghavanloo, PMP

Ing Gustavo Giannattasio MBA, PMP

Sheila Gibbs

Carl M. Gilbert, PMP PfMP

Theofanis Giotis, PhDc, PMP

José Abranches Gonçalves, MSc, PMP

Juan Carlos González, PMP, PMI-ACP

Jean Gouix, PMP, PgMP

Therese Graff

Scott M. Graffius, PMP, CSM

Brian Grafsgaard, PMP, PgMP

Sara Grilli Colombo

Anita Griner

Maxim Grishin, PhD, PMP

Robert C Grove, MBA, PMP

David Guan, PMP

Juan E. Guarache, V, BEng, PMP

Pier Luigi Guida

Vijay Guliani, PMP, PMI-PBA

Tomasz Gutmanski

Omar Haddad, CAPM, PMP

Mustafa Hafizoglu, PMP

Yoshifumi Hamamichi

Simon Harris, PMP, CGEIT

Patti M. Harter, PMP

Sean Shraden Hasley, MSIT-PM

Ahmed Hassan

Akram Hassan, PhD, PMP

Susumu Hayakawa, PMP

Bruce A. Hayes, PMP

Guangcheng He, PMP

David G. Hendrickson, PMP

Barbara Henrich

Baruch Herrera

Sergio Herrera-Apestigue, PMP, P3O

Robert Hierholtz, PhD, MBA, PMP

Robert N. Higgins V, PMP, ITIL Expert

David A. Hillson, PhD, PMI Fellow, HonFAPM

Shirley Hinton, PMP

Kenji Hiraishi, MsE, PMP

Lenora Holmsten, PMP, MPM

Jenny Anne Horst-Martz, JD, PMP

Alfred J. Howard, PMP, ITIL Expert

Cynthia L. Hoxey, PMP

Gheorghe Hriscu, PMP, CGEIT

Ananth HV PMP, CSM

Guillermo A. Ibañez, PMP, ITIL

Victor Manuel Ibanez Salazar, PMP, MA

Waleed Idris

Shuichi Ikeda, PMP

Andrea Innocenti PMP, CGEIT

Can Izgi, PMP

Pablo Jaramillo

Tariq Javed, MS, PMP

Cari Jewell, PMP, MISST

Gabriela Jimenez P.

Icvillajoe Joe

Tony Johnson, PMP, PfMP

Michele J. Jones, PMP

Yves Jordan, PMP

Alisher Kabildjanov, PMP

SS Kanagaraj, PMP, ITIL

Naoki Kasahara, PMP

Arcady Katnikov

Suhail Khaled

Basher Khalil

Aaron Ho Khong, PMP, ITIL Expert

M. Raashid Kiani, PMP, CSM

Taeyoung Kim, PMP

Ariel S. Kirshbom, PMP, ACP

Konstantinos Kirytopoulos,
PhD, PMP

Ian Koenig PMP

Athens Kolias, MPM, PMP

Henry Kondo, PMP, PfMP

Maciej Koszykowski,
PMP, PMI-RMP

Rouzbeh Kotobzadeh,
PMP, PMI-ACP

Srikanth Krishnamoorthy,
PMP, PGDSA

Amit Kumar

Devesh Kumar

Pramit Kumar, PMP

Rakesh Kumar, MBA, PMP

Santosh Kumar

S. Y. Satish Kumar

Abhilash Kuzhikat, PMP, CISA

Thierry Labriet

G.Lakshmi Sekhar, PMP, PMI-SP

Boon Soon Lam

Vincent Hiu Sing Lam, PMP

Ruchie Lamba

Deborah Langlois MBA, PMP

Alvaro Latorre,MsC, PMP

Olivier Lazar

Chang-Hee Lee, PMP, CISA

Cheryl G. Lee, PMP, PMI-PBA

Oliver F. Lehmann, MSc, PMP

Michael J Leisegang, PMP

Craig Letavec, PgMP, PfMP

Jean-Pierre Lhomme, PMP

Junquan Liu

Shihan Liu

Tong Liu (James Liu), PhD, PMP

Anand Loganathan, MS

Anand Lokhande, PMP

Nancy Lopez

Samuel López González de Murillo,
MPM, PMP

Carlos López Javier, MBA, PMP

Zheng Lou, MBA, PMP

Sérgio Lourenço, PMP, PMI-RMP

Catia Lourenço

Hugo Kleber Magalhães Lourenço,
PMP, ACP

Amy S. Lugibihl, PMP

Sergio O. Lugo, MBA, PMP

Vijaya Prasanth M. L., PMP, MCTS

José Carlos Machicao, MSc, PMP

Frederick G. Mackaden,
CRISC, PMP

Jas Madhur

Krishan Gopal Maheshwari,
PMP, ITILv3 Expert

Konstantinos Maliakas,
MSc (PM), PMP

Rich Maltzman, PMP

Vaios Maniotis

Antonio Marino, PMP, PMI-ACP

Gaitan Marius Titi, Eng, PMP

Photoula Markou-Voskou

Lou Marks, PMP

Cristian Martín Corrales, MPM, PMP

Mike McElroy, MHA, PMP

Jon McGlothian, MBA, PMP

William T. McNamara, PMP

Rob D. Meadows, MBA, PMP

Alain Patrick Medenou,
PMP, PRINCE2 Practitioner

Lourdes Medina, PMP, PfMP

Peter Berndt de Souza Mello,
PMI-SP, PMP

Yan Bello Mendez

Ernst Menet, PMP

Sunil Meshram, PMP

Mohammed M'Hamdi, PMP

Lubomira Mihailova, MBA, PMP

Gloria J. Miller, PMP

Romeo Mitchell, MSc, BSc

Mannan Mohammed, Peng, PMP

Venkatram Vasi Mohanvasi

Ricardo Monteiro

Paula Morais

Maciej Mordaka, PMP

Rachel A. Morris, PMP

Doris Moss

Henrique Moura, PMP, PMI-RMP

Timur Mukharyamov, PhD, PMP

Antonio Muntaner, PMP

Muktesh Murthy, MBA (IS), PMP

Lemya Musa M. Idris,
PMP, PMI-PBA

Khalid M. Musleh, PMP, PMI-RMP

Syed Ahsan Mustaqeem, PE, PMP

Todd Nielsen Myers, MBA, PMP

Narayanaswamy Nagarajan, PMP

Kiran Nalam

Faig Nasibov, PMP

Asad Naveed, PMP, RMP

Serge Patrick N'Guessan,
MSIS, PMP

Praveen K. Nidumolu,
PMP, PMI-ACP

Eric Nielsen, PMP

Jeffrey S. Nielsen, PMP, PgMP

Víctor Nieva Martín-Portugués, PMP

Michael C. Nollet, PMP, PMI-ACP

Takamasa Nomura

Ernesto Antonio Noya Carbajal

Mufaro M. Nyachoto,
PMI-PBA, CAPM

Conor O'Brien,
MBA (Tech Open), PMP

Peter O'Driscoll

Michael O. Ogberuhor, PMP, EVP

Bayonle Oladoja, PMP, PRINCE2

Antonio Oliva González, PMP, EMPM

Habeeb Omar, PgMP, PfMP

Stefan Ondek, PMP

Marian Oprea, PMP, ITIL

Henrique Ortega-Tenorio, PMP

Venkateswar Oruganti, FIETE, PMP

Musab Abdalmageed Osman
Abubakar

Jaime Andres Alvarez Ospina,
PMP, PMI-RMP

Tabitha A. Palmer, PMP

Neeraj Pandit, PMP

Luke Panezich, PMP, PMI-ACP

Hariyo Pangarso

Laura Paton, PMP, PMI-PBA

Seenivasan Pavanasam,
PMP, PgMP

Anil Peer, PEng, PMP

Mauricio Perez Calvo,
PMP, PMI-RMP

Dana Persada Mulyoto, MBA, PMP

LEE Nan Phin, PMP, CSM

Luca Pietrandrea

Crispin ("Kik") Piney, BSc, PgMP

Jose Angelo Pinto, PMP, OPM3 CP

Narendra Pondugula, PMP, PMI-ACP

Hin-Fei Poon

Svetlana Prahova, PMP

B. K. Subramanya Prasad, PMP, CSM

T.V. Prasanna Raaj, PMP

Suhail Qadir, PMP, BTech

Collin Quiring, PMP, OPM3

Nader K. Rad, PMP

Noalur Rahim, PMP

Prashanth Bagepalli Rajarao,
BE, PMP

S. Ramani, PgMP, PfMP

Gurdev S. Randhawa, PMP

Alakananda Rao, PMP

Vicky Restrepo, PMP

Raman Rezaei

Tashfeen Riaz, PMP, MPM

Juan Carlos Rincón Acuña,
PhD, PMP

Juan Sebastian Rivera Ortiz

Dan Roman, PMP, PMI-ACP

Rafael Fernando Ronces Rosas,
PMP, ITIL

David W. Ross, PMP, PgMP

Kaydashov Ruslan, PMP

Philip Leslie Russell, PMP

Mohamed Salah Eldien Saad, PMP

Eyad Saadeh, PfMP, PgMP

Imad Sabonji, PMP

Kumar Sadasivan, PMP

Mihail Sadeanu, PhD, PMP

Gopal Sahai, PMP, PMI-PBA

Joudi Ahmad Said, PMP, MSc

Ibrahim Saig, PhD, PMP, MRCPI

Brian Salk, PhD, PMP

Omar A. Samaniego, PMP, PMI-RMP

Abubaker Sami, PfMP, PgMP

Carlos Sánchez Golding, PMP

Yiannis Sandis, MSc, PMP

Iván S. Tejera Santana,
PMP, PMI-ACP

Murali Santhanam, PMP, BCom

Subhendu Sarangi

Saikat Sarkar, PMP

Shreesh Sarvagya

Supriya Saxena

Nicole Schelter, PMP

Kathy Schwalbe, PhD, PMP

Dion Serben

Marcus Gregorio Serrano,
MBA, PMP

Isaac Sethian, MBA, PMP

Bruce G. Shapiro, PMP

Ian Sharpe, 4-DM CPPD

Cindy C Shelton, PMP, PMI-ACP

Nitin Shende, PMP, PRINCE2

Gregory P. Shetler, PhD, PgMP

Patricia C. C. Sibinelli, MEng, PMP

Alexsandro Silva

Christopher M. Simonek, PMP

Rohit Singh

Sathya Sivagurunathan

Venkatramanan S., PMP

Michelle A. Sobers, MS

Pamela L. Soderholm, PMP

Khaled Soliman

Mauro Sotille, PMP, PMI-RMP

Sriram Srinivasan, PMP, CGEIT

Pranay Srivastava, PMP, CSM

Alexander Stamenov

Jamie Stasch

John Stenbeck, PMP, PMI-ACP

Michael J. Stratton, PhD, PMP

S. Sudha, PMP

John L. Sullivan, MEd, PMP

Karen Z. Sullivan, PMP, PSM

Surichaqui

Yasuji Suzuki, PMP

Mark A. Swiderski, PMP, MBA

Titus K. Syengo, PMP

Paul S. Szwed, DSc, PMP

Hadi Tahmasbi Ashtiani

Shoji Tajima, PMP, ITC

Peter Tashkoff, PMP

Ahmet Taspinar

Gokrem Tekir

Sunil Telkar PMP, PGDBL

Sal J. Thompson, MBA, PMP

Mark S. Tolbert, PMP, PMI-ACP

Mukund Toro, PMP

Stephen Tower, PMP, MBCI

John Tracy, PMP, MBA

Biagio Tramontana, Eng, PMP

Micol Trezza, MBA, PMP

Konstantin Trunin, PMP

Ahmet Tümay, PhD, PMPM.

Jeffery Tyler, PMP

Hafiz Umar, MBA, PMP

Krishnakant T. Upadhyaya, PMP

Atta Ur Rahman, MBA, PMP

Ebenezer Uy

Madhavan V.

Ali Vahedi Diz, PgMP, PfMP

Tom Van Medegael, PMP

Stephen VanArsdale

Enid T. Vargas Maldonado,
    PMP, PMI-PBA

Paola D. Vargas

Allam V. V. S. Venu, PMP, PgMP

Roberto Villa, PMP

Tiziano Villa, PMP, PMI-ACP

Benjamin Villar Lurquin, Bs

Dave Violette, MPM, PMP

Vijay Srinivas Vittalam PMP, RMP

Julian Vivas

Sameh Wahba, PMP, CPMC

Prakash Waknis, PMP

Xiaojin Wang, PhD, PMP

Tsunefumi Watanabe, PMP

Barbara A. Waters, MBA, PMP

Shayla P. Watson, MA

Patrick Weaver, PMP, PMI-SP

Kevin R. Wegryn, PMP, Security+

Lars Wendestam, MSc, PMP

Jan Werewka, PMP

Carol E. P. Whitaker, MBA, PMP

Sean Whitaker, MBA, PMP

Angela Wick, PMP, PBA

Michal P. Wieteska

J. Craig Williams

Malgorzata Wolny

Sek-Kay Steve Wong, MBA, PMP

Louise M. Worsley

Yan Wu, APME, PMP

Clement C. L. Yeung, PMP

Cynthia J. Young,
    PhD, PMP, LSSMBB

Gordon Young

Alan E. Yue, PMP, PMI-ACP

Hany I. Zahran

Saeed Zamani

Alessandri Zapata Rosas, PMP

Azam M. Zaqzouq, MCT, PMP

Salim Zid, MSc, PMP

Eire Emilio Zimmermann

Marcin Zmigrodzki, PhD, PgMP

## X2.4.3 FINAL EXPOSURE DRAFT REVIEW (GUIDE PORTION)

In addition to the members of the Committee, the following individuals provided recommendations for improving the Exposure Draft of the *PMBOK® Guide*—Sixth Edition (guide portion):

Farhad Abdollahyan, PMP, OPM3CP

Tetsuhide Abe, PMP

Ali Abedi, PhD, PMP

Amir Mansour Abdollahi, MSc, PE

Eric Aboagye

Umesh AC

Jer Adamsson

Carles Adell, MPM, PMP

Mounir A. Ajam, RMP, GPM-bTM

Uğur Aksoylu, PMP

Tarik Al Hraki, PMP, PMI-RMP

Melad Al Aqra, PMP, MIET

Amer Albuttma, BSc, PMP

Jose Rafael Alcala Gomez, PMP

Filippo Alessandro, PMP

Hammam Zayed Alkouz,
PMP, PMI-RMP

Eric Allen

Wasel A. Al-Muhammad, MBA, PMP

Turki Mohammed Alqawsi, MITM

Imad Alsadeq, MB, P3M3

Haluk Altunel, PhD, PMP

Barnabas Seth Amarteifio,
PMP, ITIL (Expert)

Serge Amon, MBA, PMP

Abd Razak B Ariffin, PMP

Sridhar Arjula

Kalpesh Ashar, PMP, PMI-ACP

Vijaya C. Avula, PMP, ACP

Andy Bacon, PMP, CSP

Andrey Badin

Sherif I. Bakr, PMP, MBA

Karuna Basu

Chandra Beaveridge, BEng, PMP

Jane Alam Belgaum, PMP

Stefan Bertschi, PhD

Harwinder Singh Bhatia,
PMP, PMI-ACP

Jasbir Singh Bhogal, PMP, ITIL-V3

Jayaram Bhogi PMP, CSM

Michael M. Bissonette, MBA, MS

Greta Blash, PMP, PMI-ACP

Steve Blash, PMP, PMI-ACP

Dennis L. Bolles, PMP

Rodolphe Boudet, PMP

Farid F. Bouges, PhD, PfMP, PMP

Damiano Bragantini, PMP

Ralf Braune, PhD, PMP

Maria del Carmen Brown, PMP

James N. Bullock,
PMP, ASQ CMQ/OE

Andy Burns PMP, PMI-ACP

Nicola Bussoni, PMP

Roberto A. Cadena Legaspi,
PMP, MCI

Carla M. Campion,
BEng (Hons), PMP

Shika Carter, PMP, PgMP

Luis Casacó, MA, PMP

Guillermo A. Cepeda L.,
PMP, PMI-RMP

Kristine Chapman

Panos Chatzipanos,
PhD, Dr Eur Eng.

Satish Chhiba

Aditya Chinni

Virgiliu Cimpoeru, PhDc, PMP

Jorge Omar Clemente, PMP, CPA

Martin A. Collado, PMP, ITIL

Sergio Luis Conte, PhD, PMP

Franco Cosenza, PGDipBA, PMP

Veronica Cruz

Ron Cwik MBA, PMP

Yudha P. Damiat, PMP, PMI-SP

Farshid Damirchilo, MSc

William H. Dannenmaier, PMP, MBA

Sankalpa Dash

Gina Davidovic PMP, PgMP

Beatriz Benezra Dehtear, MBA

G. Murat Dengiz, PMP

Stephen A. Devaux, PMP, MSPM

Shanmugasundaram Dhandapani

Sachin S. Dhaygude, PMP, PMI-ACP

Ivana Dilparic

Marcelo Sans Dodson, DBA,PMP

Nedal A. Dudin, PMP, PBA

Jorge A. Dueñas, PMP, AVS

Eunice Duran Tapia, PMP, PfMP

Wael K. Elmetwaly, PMP, PMI-ACP

Talha M. El-Gazzar, PMP

Carol Elliott, MBA, PMP

Larry Elwood, PMP, CISSP

Angela England

Marco Falcao, PMP, PMI-RMP

Puian Masudi Far, PhDc, PMP

Jared Farnum

Jose L. Fernandez-Sanchez, PhD

Eduardo S. Fiol, PMP

Regis Fitzgibbon

Garry Flemings

Carlos Augusto Freitas, CAPM, PMP

Scott J. Friedman, PMP, ACG

MAG Sanaa Fuchs

Nestor C. Gabarda Jr., ECE, PMP

Robert M. Galbraith, PMP

Carl M. Gilbert, PMP, PfMP

Theofanis Giotis, PhDc, PMP

Dhananjay Gokhale

José Abranches Gonçalves, MSc, PMP

Herbert G. Gonder, PMP

Edward Gorni, PMP, MSc

Julie Grabb PMP, B Math

Stuart Gray

Christiane Gresse von Wangenheim, Dr. rer. nat., PMP

Grzegorz Grzesiak

Ahmed Guessous, PMP

Neeraj Gupta, PMP, CSM

Sunita Gupta

Raj Guttha PhD, PMP

Mustafa Hafizoglu, PMP

Kazuro Haga, PMP, PMI-RMP

Yoshifumi Hamamichi

Simon Harris, PMP, CGEIT

Gabrielle B. Haskins, PMP

Hossam Hassan

Madhavi Hawa, MBA

Randell R. Hayes II, PMP, MBA

Guangcheng He, PMP

Kym Henderson, RFD, MSc (Comp)

Sergio Herrera-Apestigue, PMP, P3O

Robert Hierholtz, PhD, MBA, PMP

Bob Hillier, PMP

Aaron Ho Khong, PMP, ITIL Expert

Scott C. Holbrook, PMP, CISSP

Regina Holzinger, PhD, PMP

Christina M. House, MBA, PMP

Gheorghe Hriscu, PMP, CGEIT

Terri Anne Iacobucci, SPHR, PMP

Guillermo A. Ibañez, PMP, ITIL

Can Izgi, PMP

Anand Jayaraman PMP, MCA

Anil K. Jayavarapu, PMP

Cari Jewell, PMP, MISST

Martina Jirickova

Alan John

Tony Johnson, PMP, PfMP

Michele J. Jones, PMP

Rajesh G. Kadwe, PMP

Orhan Kalayci, PMP, CBAP

Samer Faker Kamal, PMP, LEED AP BD+C

Surendran Kamalanathan

Vaijayantee Kamat, PMP

Nils Kandelin

Carl Karshagen, PMP

Anton Kartamyshev

Scott Kashkin, MS, PMP

Katsuichi Kawamitsu, PMP, ITC

Rachel V. Keen, PMP

Suhail Khaled

Jamal Khalid

Eng. Ahmed Samir Khalil, PMP, OPM3-CP

Basher Khalil

Ranga Raju Kidambi

Mostafa K. Kilani, BEng, PMP

Diwakar Killamsetty

Taeyoung Kim, PMP

Konstantinos Kirytopoulos, PhD, PMP

Kashinath Kodliwadmanth

Maarten Koens, PMP

Dwaraka Ramana Kompally, MBA, PMP

Henry Kondo, PMP, PfMP

Maciej Koszykowski, PMP, PMI-RMP

Ahmed A F Krimly

Srikanth Krishnamoorthy, PMP, PGDSA

Bret Kuhne

Avinash Kumar, PMP

Pramit Kumar, PMP

Thomas M. Kurihara

Andrew Lakritz

Boon Soon Lam

Luc R. Lang PMP

Jon Lazarus

Chang-Hee Lee PMP, CISA

Ivan Lee PMP, PMI-ACP

Oliver F. Lehmann, MSc, PMP

Katherine A. Leigh

Donald LePage

Peter Liakos, PMP, Cert APM

Tong Liu, PhD, PMP

Chandra Sekhar Lolla Venkata Satya

Stefania Lombardi, PhDc, PMP

Daniel D. Lopez, CSP, PMP

Zheng Lou, MBA, PMP

Sérgio Lourenço, PMP, PMI-RMP

Hugo Kleber Magalhães Lourenço, PMP, ACP

Xiang Luo, PMP, PMI-PBA

José Carlos Machicao, PMP, MSc

Sowjanya Machiraju, MS, PMP

Robert Mahler

Mostafa M. Abbas, PMP, OCE

Konstantinos Maliakas, MSc (PM), PMP

Rich Maltzman, PMP

Ammar Mango

Antonio Marino, PMP, PMI-ACP

Gaitan Marius Titi, Eng, PMP

Lou Marks, PMP

Rodrigo Marques da Rocha

Ronnie Maschk, PMP

Maria T Mata-Sivera, PMP

Kurisinkal Mathew

Stephen J. Matney, CEM, PMP

David A. Maynard, MBA, PMP

Pierre Mbeniyaba Mboundou

Thomas McCabe

Jon McGlothian, MBA, PMP

Alan McLoughlin, PMP, PMI-ACP

Ernst Menet, PMP

Mohammed M'Hamdi, PMP

Roberta Miglioranza, PMP, Prince2

Gloria J. Miller, PMP

Daniel Minahan, MSPM, PMP

Javier A Miranda, PMP, PMI-ACP

Saddam Mohammed Babikr
  Mohammed

Venkatramvasi Mohanvasi, PMP

Maciej Mordaka, PMP

Paola Morgese, PMP

Moises Moshinsky, MSc, PMP

Henrique Moura, PMP, PMI-RMP

Nathan Mourfield

Alison K. Munro, MSc, PMP

Khalid M. Musleh, PMP, PMI-RMP

Vasudev Narayanan

Faig Nasibov, PMP

Daud Nasir, PMP, LSSBB

Nasrullah

Nghi M. Nguyen, PhD, PMP

Eric Nielsen, PMP

Yamanta Raj Niroula, PMP

Emily Nyindodo

Peter O'Driscoll

Kiyohisa Okada

Bayonle Oladoja, PMP, PRINCE2

Sofia Olguin

Edward C. Olszanowski III,
  PMP, EMBA

Austen B. Omonyo, PhD, PMP

Stefan Ondek, PMP

Tom Oommen

H. Metin Ornek, PMP, MBA

Juan Carlos Pacheco

Durgadevi S. Padmanaban,
  MBA, PMP

Ravindranath Palahalli

Boopathy Pallavapuram, PMP

Rajeev R. Pandey

Luke Panezich, PMP, PMI-ACP

Sungjoon Park, PMP

Gino Parravidino Jacobo, PMP, ITIL

Richard L. Pascoe, PMP

George Pasieka, PMP

Sneha Patel, PMP

Satyabrata Pati, PMP

Seenivasan Pavanasam PMP, PgMP

R. Anthoney Pavelich, PMP

P. B. Ramesh, PMP, ACP

Brent C. Peters, BA

Yvan Petit, PhD, PMP

Crispin ("Kik") Piney, BSc, PgMP

Jose Angelo Pinto, PMP, OPM3 CP

Napoleón Posada, MBA, PMP

B K Subramanya Prasad, PMP, CSM

Carl W. Pro, PMP, PMI-RMP

Srikanth PV

Nader K. Rad, PMP

Karen Rainford, EdD, PMP

S. Ramani, PfMP, PgMP

Niranjana Koodavalli Ramaswamy,
  BE Mech, PGDM

Jesus Esteban Ramirez, BEng, eCS

Michele Ranaldo, PMP

Gurdev S. Randhawa, PMP

Sreekiran K. Ranganna, PMP, MBA

Alakananda Rao

Muhammad Sauood ur Rauf, PMP

P. Ravikumar, PMP, PMI-ACP

Michael Reed, PMP, PfMP

Messias Reis, PMP

Alexander V. Revin, PMP

Mohammadreza Rezaei

Gustavo Ribas

David B. Rich, PMP

Gregg D. Richie, PMP, MCTS

Edgar Robleto Cuadra

Bernard Roduit

David Roe, PMP

Rafael Fernando Ronces Rosas,
  PMP, ITIL

Prakash Roshan

William S. Ruggles, PMP, CSSMBB

Nagy Attalla Saad, PMP, ITIL

Natesa Sabapathy, PhD, PMP

Kumar Sadasivan, PMP

Dzhamshid Safin, PhD, PMP

Edgardo S. Safranchik, PMP

Ibrahim Mohammed Ali Saig

Naoto Sakaue

Xavier Salas Ceciliano, MSc, PMP

Anderson Sales

Floriano Salvaterra, PMP, IPMA-C

Omar A. Samaniego, PMP, PMI-RMP

Abubaker Sami, PfMP, PgMP

Angela Sammon

P. Sampathkumar, MBA, PMP

Iván S. Tejera Santana,
  PMP, PMI-ACP

Luciana de Jesus Santos, PMP

Aminu Sarafa, PMP, CCP

Darpan Saravia, PMP, CSM

Tamara Scatcherd

Stephen M. Schneider, PhD, PMP

Ludwig Schreier, Eur Ing, PMP

Birgitte Sharif, PMP

Sanjeev Sharma

Alexander Shavrin, PhD, PMP

Nitin Shende, PMP, PRINCE2

Luqman Shantal, PMP, TOGAF

N. K. Shrivastava, PMP, SPC4

Mohamad Sibai

Gustavo Silva

Sumit Kumar Sinha, PMP

Ronald Zack Sionakides, MBA, PMP

Klas Skogmar, EMBA, PMP

J. Greg Smith, EVP

Kenneth F. Smith, PhD, PMP

Pamela L. Soderholm, PMP

John Paul Soltesz
Sheilina Somani, RPP, PMP
Mauro Sotille, PMP, PMI-RMP
Setty Sreelatha, PMP, PMI-ACP
Shishir Srivastav, PMP, CSM
Pranay Srivastava, PMP, CSM
John Stenbeck, PMP, PMI-ACP
Jim Stewart
Yasuji Suzuki, PMP
Mark A. Swiderski, PMP, MBA
Ahmed Taha, PMP, PMI-RMP
Francis Taiwo, PMP, PMI-ACP
Yahya Tatar, PMP, MBA
Gerhard J. Tekes, PMP, PMI-RMP
Gokrem Tekir
João Paulo Tinoco
Claudia A. Tocantins, MSc, PMP
Mukund Toro, PMP
Juan Torres Vela
Stephen Tower, PMP, MBCI
Brenda Tracy
John Tracy, MBA, PMP

Konstantin Trunin, PMP
Tassos Tsochataridis, MSc, PMP
Krishnakant T. Upadhyaya, PMP
Ali Vahedi Diz, PgMP, PfMP
Jorge Valdés Garciatorres,
  PMP, SMC
Jose Felix Valdez-Torero, PMP
Tom Van Medegael, PMP
Raymond Z van Tonder,
  PMP, ND Elec Eng
Ravi Vanukuru, BE, PMP
Ricardo Viana Vargas, MSc, PMP
Neelanshu Varma, PMP
Debbie Varn, PMP, SHRM-SCP
Vijay Vemana, PgMP, PMP
Nagesh V., PMP
Aloysio Vianna Jr., DEng, PMP
Roberto Villa, PMP
Jorge Villanueva, MSc (PM), PMP
Dave Violette, MPM, PMP
Yiannis Vithynos PMP, PMI-ACP
Steve Waddell, MBA, PMP

Xiaojin Wang, PhD, PMP
J. LeRoy Ward, PMP, PgMP
Toshiyuki Henry Watanabe, PE, PMP
Ashleigh Waters, PMP
Ganesh Watve, MBA, PMP
Patrick Weaver, PMP, PMI-SP
Michal P. Wieteska
Roger Wild, PMP
Rebecca A. Winston, JD
Lisa Wolf
Carlos Magno Xavier, PhD, PMP
Wenyi Xiao, PMP
Haotian Xu, CAPM
Clement C. L. Yeung, PMP
Saeed Zamani
Azam M. Zaqzouq, MCT, PMP
Omran M. Zbeida, PMP, BSP
Marcin Zmigrodzki, PMP, PgMP
Rolf Dieter Zschau, PMP
Alan Zucker, PMP, CSM

## X2.5 PMI STANDARDS PROGRAM MEMBER ADVISORY GROUP (MAG)

The following individuals served as members of the PMI Standards Program Member Advisory Group during development of the *PMBOK® Guide*—Sixth Edition:

Maria Cristina Barbero, PMP, PMI-ACP
Brian Grafsgaard, PMP, PgMP
Hagit Landman, PMP, PMI-SP
Yvan Petit, PhD, PMP
Chris Stevens, PhD
Dave Violette, MPM, PMP
John Zlockie, MBA, PMP, PMI Standards Manager

## X2.6 CONSENSUS BODY REVIEW

The following individuals served as members of the PMI Standards Program Consensus Body:

Nigel Blampied, PE, PMP
Dennis L. Bolles, PMP
Chris Cartwright, MPM, PMP
Sergio Coronado, PhD
Andrea Demaria, PMP
John L. Dettbarn, Jr., DSc, PE
Charles T. Follin, PMP
Laurence Goldsmith, MBA, PMP
Dana J Goulston, PMP
Brian Grafsgaard, PMP, PgMP
David Gunner, PMP
Dorothy L. Kangas, PMP
Thomas Kurihara
Hagit Landman, PMP, PMI-SP
Timothy MacFadyen
Harold "Mike" Mosley, Jr., PE, PMP
Eric S Norman, PMP, PgMP
Nanette Patton, MSBA, PMP
Yvan Petit, PhD, PMP
Crispin ("Kik") Piney, BSc, PgMP
Michael Reed, PMP, PfMP
David W. Ross, PMP, PgMP
Paul E. Shaltry, PMP
Chris Stevens, PhD
Adam D. Sykes, MS, PMP
Matthew D. Tomlinson, PMP, PgMP
Dave Violette, MPM, PMP

## X2.7 PRODUCTION STAFF

Special mention is due to the following employees of PMI:

Donn Greenberg, Manager, Publications
Roberta Storer, Product Editor
Stephen A. Townsend, Director of Network Programs
Barbara Walsh, Publications Production Supervisor

# APPENDIX X3
# AGILE, ITERATIVE, ADAPTIVE, AND
# HYBRID PROJECT ENVIRONMENTS

This appendix explores the nuances of how the Project Management Process Groups described in *The Standard for Project Management* are performed with respect to the project environment and life cycle.

Section 1.2.4.1 of the *PMBOK® Guide* states that the "project life cycle needs to be flexible enough to deal with the variety of factors included in the project." It is the nature of projects to evolve as more detailed and specific information becomes available. This ability to evolve and adapt is more relevant in environments with a high degree of change and uncertainty or with a wide variation of stakeholder interpretation and expectations.

## X3.1 THE CONTINUUM OF PROJECT LIFE CYCLES

To understand the application of the process in adaptive projects, the continuum of project life cycles should be defined. The *PMBOK® Guide* Glossary describes the project life cycle as "the series of phases that a project passes through from its start to its completion." Within a project life cycle, there are generally one or more phases that are associated with the development of the product, service, or result. These are called a development life cycle. Development life cycles can be predictive (plan-driven), adaptive (agile), iterative, incremental, or a hybrid.

Figure X3-1 shows the various ways in which requirements and plans are handled, how risk and cost are managed, schedule considerations, and how the involvement of key stakeholders is handled depending on the type of life cycle being employed.

| Predictive | Iterative | Incremental | Agile |
|---|---|---|---|
| Requirements are defined up-front before development begins | Requirements can be elaborated at periodic intervals during delivery | | Requirements are elaborated frequently during delivery |
| Deliver plans for the eventual deliverable. Then deliver only a single final product at end of project timeline | Delivery can be divided into subsets of the overall product | | Delivery occurs frequently with customer-valued subsets of the overall product |
| Change is constrained as much as possible | Change is incorporated at periodic intervals | | Change is incorporated in real-time during delivery |
| Key stakeholders are involved at specific milestones | Key stakeholders are regularly involved | | Key stakeholders are continuously involved |
| Risk and cost are controlled by detailed planning of mostly knowable considerations | Risk and cost are controlled by progressively elaborating the plans with new information | | Risk and cost are controlled as requirements and constraints emerge |

**Figure X3-1. The Continuum of Project Life Cycles**

Predictive project life cycles are characterized by an emphasis on specification of requirements and detailed planning during the beginning phases of a project. Detailed plans based on known requirements and constraints may reduce risk and cost. Milestones for key stakeholder involvement are also planned. As execution of the detailed plan progresses, the monitoring and controlling processes focus on constraining changes that might impact the scope, schedule, or budget.

Highly adaptive or agile life cycles for projects are characterized by progressive elaboration of requirements based on short iterative planning and executing cycles. Risk and cost are reduced by progressive evolution of initial plans. Key stakeholders are continuously involved and provide frequent feedback which enables responding to changes more quickly and also leads to better quality.

The following considerations apply to the center of the life cycle continuum: (a) risk and cost are reduced by iterative evolution of initial plans; and (b) key stakeholders have more opportunities to be involved in incremental, iterative, and agile cycles than stakeholders at the project milestones of highly predictive life cycles.

Project life cycles in the center of the life cycle continuum tend to align more closely with the predictive side or the agile side of the continuum depending on the way requirements are specified, how risk and cost are handled, and the nature of key stakeholder involvement. Projects in this part of the continuum may utilize hybrid project methods.

It should be emphasized that development life cycles are complex and multidimensional. Often, the different phases in a given project employ different life cycles, just as distinct projects within a given program may each be executed differently.

## X3.2 PROJECT PHASES

Section 1.2.4.2 of the *PMBOK® Guide* defines phases as "a collection of logically related project activities that culminates in the completion of one or more deliverables." Processes in each of the Process Groups are repeated as necessary in each phase until the completion criteria for that phase have been satisfied.

Projects on the more adaptive side of the continuum make use of two recurring patterns of project phase relationships as described in Sections X3.2.1 and X3.2.2.

### X3.2.1 SEQUENTIAL ITERATION-BASED PHASES

Adaptive projects are often decomposed into a sequence of phases called Iterations. Each iteration utilizes the relevant project management processes. These iterations create a cadence of predictable, timeboxed pre-agreed, consistent duration that aids with scheduling.

Performing the process groups repeatedly incurs overhead. The overhead is considered necessary to effectively manage projects with high degrees of complexity, uncertainty, and change. The effort level for iteration-based phases is illustrated in Figure X3-2.

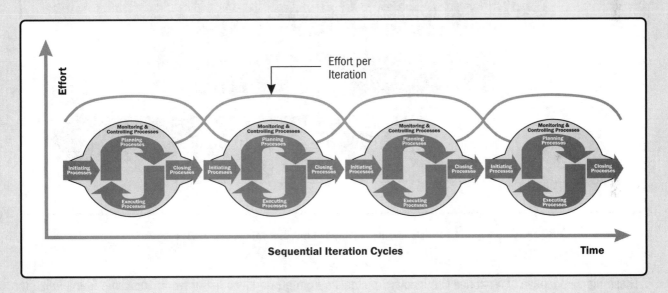

Figure X3-2. Level of Effort for Process Groups across Iteration Cycles

## X3.2.2 CONTINUOUS OVERLAPPING PHASES

Projects that are highly adaptive will often perform all of the project management process groups continuously throughout the project life cycle. Inspired by techniques from lean thinking, the approach is often referred to as "continuous and adaptive planning," which acknowledges that once work starts, the plan will change, and the plan needs to reflect this new knowledge. The intent is to aggressively refine and improve all elements of the project management plan, beyond the prescheduled checkpoints associated with Iterations. The interaction of the Process Groups in this approach is illustrated in Figure X3-3.

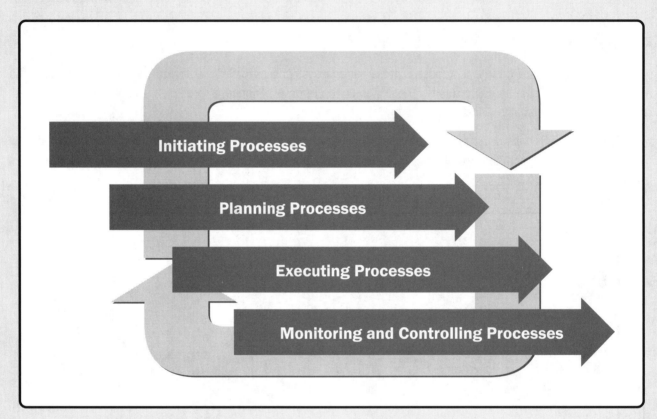

**Figure X3-3. Relationship of Process Groups in Continuous Phases**

These highly adaptive approaches continuously pull tasks from a prioritized list of work. This aims to minimize the overhead of managing Process Groups repeatedly, by removing the start and end of iteration activities. Continuous pull systems can be viewed as microiterations with an emphasis on maximizing the time available on execution rather than management. They do however need their own planning, tracking, and adjustment mechanisms to keep them on track and adapt to changes.

# X3.3 PROCESS GROUPS IN ADAPTIVE ENVIRONMENTS

As shown in the previous section, each of the Project Management Process Groups occurs in projects across the project life cycle continuum. There are some variations in how the Process Groups interact within adaptive and highly adaptive life cycles.

## X3.3.1 INITIATING PROCESS GROUP

Initiating processes are those processes performed to define a new project or a new phase of an existing project by obtaining authorization to start the project or phase. Adaptive projects revisit and revalidate the project charter on a frequent basis. As the project progresses, competing priorities and changing dynamics may cause the project constraints and success criteria to become obsolete. For this reason, the Initiating processes are performed regularly on adaptive projects in order to ensure the project is moving within constraints and toward goals that reflect the latest information.

Adaptive projects rely heavily on a knowledgeable customer or designated customer representative who can state needs and desires, and provide feedback on the emerging deliverable on a continuous, ongoing basis. Identifying this stakeholder or other stakeholders at the start of the project permits frequent interactions when performing Execution and Monitoring and Controlling processes. The associated feedback ensures that the correct project outputs are delivered. As indicated previously, an Initiating process is typically conducted on each iterative cycle of an adaptive life cycle project.

## X3.3.2 PLANNING PROCESS GROUP

Planning processes are those processes required to establish the scope of the project, refine the objectives, and define the course of action required to attain the objectives that the project was undertaken to achieve.

Highly predictive project life cycles are generally characterized by few changes to project scope and high stakeholder alignment. These projects benefit from detailed up-front planning. Adaptive life cycles, on the other hand, develop a set of high-level plans for the initial requirements and progressively elaborate requirements to an appropriate level of detail for the planning cycle. Therefore, predictive and adaptive life cycles differ as to how much planning is done and when it is done.

Additionally, projects navigating high degrees of complexity and uncertainty should involve as many team members and stakeholders as possible in the planning processes. The intent is to overcome uncertainty by incorporating a wide band of input into planning.

## X3.3.3 EXECUTING PROCESS GROUP

Executing processes are those processes performed to complete the work defined in the project management plan to satisfy the project requirements.

Work in agile, iterative, and adaptive project life cycles is directed and managed through iterations. Each iteration is a short, fixed time period to undertake work followed by a demonstration of functionality or design. Based on the demonstration, relevant stakeholders and the team conduct a retrospective review. The demonstration and review helps check progress against the plan and determines if any changes to the project scope, schedule, or execution processes are necessary. These sessions also help manage stakeholder engagement by showing increments of work done and discussing future work. The retrospective allows issues with the execution approach to be identified and discussed in a timely fashion along with ideas for improvements. Retrospectives are a primary tool to manage project knowledge and develop the team through discussions of what is working well and team-based problem solving.

While work is undertaken via short iterations, it is also tracked and managed against longer-term project delivery timeframes. Trends of development speed, spend, defect rates, and team capacity that are tracked at an iteration level are summed and extrapolated at a project level to track completion performance. Highly adaptive approaches aim to utilize specialized team knowledge for task completion. Rather than a project manager selecting and sequencing work, higher-level objectives are explained and the team members are empowered to self-organize specific tasks as a group to best meet those objectives. This leads to the creation of practical plans with high levels of buy-in from the team members.

Junior teams working on highly adaptive projects typically need coaching and work assignments before reaching this empowered team state. However, with progressive trials within the confines of a short iteration, teams are reviewed as part of the retrospective to determine if they acquired the required skills to perform without coaching.

### X3.3.4 MONITORING AND CONTROLLING PROCESS GROUP

Monitoring and Controlling processes are those processes required to track, review, and regulate the progress and performance of the project; identify any areas in which changes to the plan are required; and initiate the corresponding changes.

Iterative, agile, and adaptive approaches track, review, and regulate progress and performance by maintaining a backlog. The backlog is prioritized by a business representative with help from the project team who estimates and provides information about technical dependencies. Work is pulled from the top of the backlog for the next iteration based on business priority and team capacity. Requests for change and defect reports are evaluated by the business representative in consultation with the team for technical input and are prioritized accordingly in the backlog of work.

This single-list-of-work-and-changes approach originated in project environ-ments with very high rates of change that tended to overwhelm any attempts to separate change requests from originally planned work. Combining these work streams into a single backlog that can be easily resequenced provides a single place for stakeholders to manage and control project work, perform change control, and validate scope.

As prioritized tasks and changes are pulled from the backlog and completed via iterations, trends, and metrics on work performed, change effort and defect rates are calculated. By sampling progress frequently via short iterations, measures of team capacity and progress against the original scope are made by measuring the number of change impacts and defect remediation efforts. This allows estimates of cost, schedule, and scope to be made based on real progress rates and change impacts.

These metrics and projections are shared with project stakeholders via trend graphs (information radiators) to communicate progress, share issues, drive continuous improvement activities, and manage stakeholder expectations.

### X3.3.5 CLOSING PROCESS GROUP

The Closing processes are the processes performed to formally complete or close a project, phase, or contract. Work on iterative, adaptive, and agile projects is prioritized to undertake the highest business value items first. So, if the Closing Process Group prematurely closes a project or phase, there is a high chance that some useful business value will already have been generated. This allows premature closure to be less of a failure due to sunk costs and more of an early benefits realization, quick win, or proof of concept for the business.

# APPENDIX X4
# SUMMARY OF KEY CONCEPTS FOR KNOWLEDGE AREAS

The purpose of this appendix is to provide a summary of the sections on Key Concepts for each of the Knowledge Areas in Sections 4-13. It can be used as an aid for project practitioners, a checklist of learning objectives for providers of project management training, or as a study aid by those preparing for certification.

## X4.1 KEY CONCEPTS FOR PROJECT INTEGRATION MANAGEMENT

Key concepts for Project Integration Management include:

◆ Project Integration Management is the specific responsibility of the project manager and it cannot be delegated or transferred. The project manager is the one that combines the results from all the other Knowledge Areas to provide an overall view of the project. The project manager is ultimately responsible for the project as a whole.

◆ Projects and project management are integrative by nature, with most tasks involving more than one Knowledge Area.

◆ The relationships of processes within the Project Management Process Groups and between the Project Management Process

◆ Project Integration Management is about:

  ■ Ensuring that the due dates of project deliverables, the project life cycle, and the benefits realization plan are aligned;

  ■ Providing a project management plan to achieve the project objectives;

  ■ Ensuring the creation and the use of appropriate knowledge to and from the project;

  ■ Managing project performance and changes to the project activities;

  ■ Making integrated decisions regarding key changes impacting the project;

  ■ Measuring and monitoring progress and taking appropriate action;

  ■ Collecting, analyzing and communicating project information to relevant stakeholders;

  ■ Completing all the work of the project and formally closing each phase, contract, and the project as a whole; and

  ■ Managing phase transitions when necessary.

## X4.2 KEY CONCEPTS FOR PROJECT SCOPE MANAGEMENT

Key concepts for Project Scope Management include:

◆ Scope can refer to product scope (the features and functions that characterize a product, service, or result), or to project scope (the work performed to deliver a product, service, or result with the specified features and functions).

◆ Project life cycles range along a continuum from predictive to adaptive or agile. In a life cycle that uses a predictive approach, the project deliverables are defined at the beginning of the project and any changes to the scope are progressively managed. In an adaptive or agile approach, the deliverables are developed over multiple iterations where a detailed scope is defined and approved for each iteration when it begins.

◆ Completion of the project scope is measured against the project management plan. Completion of the product scope is measured against the product requirements.

## X4.3 KEY CONCEPTS FOR PROJECT SCHEDULE MANAGEMENT

Key concepts for Project Schedule Management include:

◆ Project scheduling provides a detailed plan that represents how and when the project will deliver the products, services, and results defined in the project scope.

◆ The project schedule is used as a tool for communication, managing stakeholder expectations, and a basis for performance reporting.

◆ When possible, the detailed project schedule should remain flexible throughout the project to adjust for knowledge gained, increased understanding of the risk, and value-added activities.

## X4.4 KEY CONCEPTS FOR PROJECT COST MANAGEMENT

Key concepts for Project Cost Management include:

◆ Project Cost Management is primarily concerned with the cost of the resources needed to complete project activities, but it should also consider the effect of project decisions on the subsequent recurring cost of using, maintaining, and supporting project deliverables.

◆ Different stakeholders will measure project costs in different ways and at different times. Stakeholder requirements for managing costs should be considered explicitly.

◆ Predicting and analyzing the prospective financial performance of the project's product may be performed outside the project, or it may be part of Project Cost Management.

# X4.5 KEY CONCEPTS FOR PROJECT QUALITY MANAGEMENT

Key concepts for Project Quality Management include:

◆ Project Quality Management addresses the management of the project and the deliverables of the project. It applies to all projects, regardless of the nature of their deliverables. Quality measures and techniques are specific to the type of deliverables being produced by the project.

◆ Quality and grade are different concepts. Quality is "the degree to which a set of inherent characteristics fulfills requirements" (ISO 9000).[1] Grade is a category assigned to deliverables having the same functional use but different technical characteristics. The project manager and team are responsible for managing trade-offs associated with delivering the required levels of both quality and grade.

◆ Prevention is preferred over inspection. It is better to design quality into deliverables, rather than to find quality issues during inspection. The cost of preventing mistakes is generally much less than the cost of correcting mistakes when they are found by inspection or during usage.

◆ Project managers may need to be familiar with sampling. Attribute sampling (the result either conforms or does not conform) and variable sampling (the result is rated on a continuous scale that measures the degree of conformity).

◆ Many projects establish tolerances and control limits for project and product measurements. Tolerances (the specified range of acceptable results) and control limits (the boundaries of common variation in a statistically stable process or process performance).

◆ The cost of quality (COQ) includes all costs incurred over the life of the product by investment in preventing nonconformance to requirements, appraising the product or service for conformance to requirements, and failing to meet requirements (rework). Cost of quality is often the concern of program management, portfolio management, the PMO, or operations.

◆ The most effective quality management is achieved when quality is incorporated into the planning and designing of the project and product, and when organizational culture is aware and committed to quality.

---

[1] International Standards Organization. 2015. Quality Management Systems—Fundamentals and Vocabulary. Geneva: Author.

## X4.6 KEY CONCEPTS FOR PROJECT RESOURCE MANAGEMENT

Key concepts for Project Resource Management include:

◆ Project resources include both physical resources (equipment, materials, facilities, and infrastructure) and team resources (individuals with assigned project roles and responsibilities).

◆ Different skills and competences are needed to manage team resources versus physical resources.

◆ The project manager should be both the leader and the manager of the project team, and should invest suitable effort in acquiring, managing, motivating, and empowering team members.

◆ The project manager should be aware of team influences such as the team environment, geographical location of team members, communication among stakeholders, organizational change management, internal and external politics, cultural issues, and organizational uniqueness.

◆ The project manager is responsible for proactively developing team skills and competences while retaining and improving team satisfaction and motivation.

◆ Physical resource management is concentrated on allocating and utilizing the physical resources needed for successful completion of the project in an efficient and effective way. Failure to manage and control resources efficiently may reduce the chance of completing the project successfully.

## X4.7 KEY CONCEPTS FOR PROJECT COMMUNICATIONS MANAGEMENT

Key concepts for Project Communications Management include:

◆ *Communication* is the process of exchanging information, intended or involuntary, between individuals and/ or groups. *Communications* describes the means by which information can be sent or received, either through activities, such as meetings and presentations, or artifacts, such as emails, social media, project reports, or project documentation. Project Communications Management addresses both the process of communication, as well as management of communications activities and artifacts.

◆ Effective communication creates a bridge between diverse stakeholders whose differences will generally have an impact or influence upon the project execution or outcome, so it is vital that all communication is clear and concise.

◆ Communication activities include internal and external, formal and informal, written and oral.

◆ Communication can be directed upwards to senior management stakeholders, downwards to team members, or horizontally to peers. This will affect the format and content of the message.

- Communication takes place consciously or unconsciously through words, facial expressions, gestures and other actions. It includes developing strategies and plans for suitable communications artifacts, and the application of skills to enhance effectiveness.

- Effort is required to prevent misunderstandings and miscommunication, and the methods, messengers, and messages should be carefully selected.

- Effective communication depends on defining the purpose of communication, understanding the receiver of the communications, and monitoring effectiveness.

## X4.8 KEY CONCEPTS FOR PROJECT RISK MANAGEMENT

Key concepts for Project Risk Management include:

- All projects are risky. Organizations choose to take project risk in order to create value, while balancing risk and reward.

- Project Risk Management aims to identify and manage risks that are not covered by other project management processes.

- Risk exists at two levels within every project: *Individual project risk* is an uncertain event or condition that, if it occurs, has a positive or negative effect on one or more project objectives. *Overall project risk* is the effect of uncertainty on the project as a whole, arising from all sources of uncertainty including individual risks, representing the exposure of stakeholders to the implications of variations in project outcome, both positive and negative. Project Risk Management processes address both levels of risk in projects.

- Individual project risks can have a positive or negative effect on project objectives if they occur. Overall project risk can also be positive or negative.

- Risks will continue to emerge during the lifetime of the project, so Project Risk Management processes should be conducted iteratively.

- In order to manage risk effectively on a particular project, the project team needs to know what level of risk exposure is acceptable in pursuit of project objectives. This is defined by measurable risk thresholds that reflect the risk appetite of the organization and project stakeholders.

# X4.9 KEY CONCEPTS FOR PROJECT PROCUREMENT MANAGEMENT

Key concepts for project procurement management include:

◆ The project manager should be familiar enough with the procurement process to make intelligent decisions regarding contracts and contractual relationships.

◆ Procurement involves agreements that describe the relationship between a buyer and a seller. Agreements can be simple or complex, and the procurement approach should reflect the degree of complexity. An agreement can be a contract, a service-level agreement, an understanding, a memorandum of agreement, or a purchase order.

◆ Agreements must comply with local, national, and international laws regarding contracts.

◆ The project manager should ensure that all procurements meet the specific needs of the project, while working with procurement specialists to ensure organizational policies are followed.

◆ The legally binding nature of an agreement means it will be subjected to a more extensive approval process, often involving the legal department, to ensure that it adequately describes the products, services, or results that the seller is agreeing to provide, while being in compliance with the laws and regulations regarding procurements.

◆ A complex project may involve multiple contracts simultaneously or in sequence. The buyer-seller relationship may exist at many levels on any one project, and between organizations internal to and external to the acquiring organization.

# X4.10 KEY CONCEPTS FOR PROJECT STAKEHOLDER MANAGEMENT

Key concepts for project stakeholder management include:

◆ Every project has stakeholders who are impacted by or can impact the project in a positive or negative way. Some stakeholders will have a limited ability to influence the project's work or outcomes; others will have significant influence on the project and its expected outcomes.

◆ The ability of the project manager and team to correctly identify and engage all of the stakeholders in an appropriate way can mean the difference between project success and failure.

◆ To increase the chances of success, the process of stakeholder identification and engagement should commence as soon as possible after the project charter has been approved, the project manager has been assigned, and the team begins to form.

◆ The key to effective stakeholder engagement is a focus on continuous communication with all stakeholders. Stakeholder satisfaction should be identified and managed as a key project objective.

◆ The process of identifying and engaging stakeholders for the benefit of the project is iterative, and should be reviewed and updated routinely, particularly when the project moves into a new phase, or if there are significant changes in the organization or the wider stakeholder community.

# APPENDIX X5
# SUMMARY OF TAILORING CONSIDERATIONS
# FOR KNOWLEDGE AREAS

The purpose of this appendix is to provide a summary of the Tailoring Concepts sections for each of the Knowledge Areas in Sections 4 through 13. Because each project is unique, this information can be used to aid practitioners in determining how to tailor processes, inputs, tools and techniques, and outputs for a project. This information can also help determine the degree of rigor that should be applied to the various processes in a Knowledge Area.

## X5.1 PROJECT INTEGRATION MANAGEMENT

Considerations for tailoring project integration management include but are not limited to:

◆ **Project life cycle.** What is an appropriate project life cycle? What phases should comprise the project life cycle?

◆ **Development life cycle**. What development life cycle and approach is appropriate for the product, service or result? Is a predictive or adaptive approach appropriate? If adaptive, should the product be developed incrementally or iteratively? Is a hybrid approach best?

◆ **Management approaches**. What management processes are most effective based on the organizational culture and the complexity of the project?

◆ **Knowledge management.** How will knowledge be managed in the project to foster a collaborative working environment?

◆ **Change**. How will change be managed in the project?

◆ **Governance**. What control boards, committees, and other stakeholders are part of the project? What are the project status reporting requirements?

◆ **Lessons learned**. What information should be collected throughout and at the end of the project? How will historical information and lessons learned be made available to future projects?

◆ **Benefits**. When and how should benefits be reported: at the end of the project or at the end of each iteration or phase?

## X5.2 PROJECT SCOPE MANAGEMENT

Considerations for tailoring project scope management include but are not limited to:

◆ **Knowledge and requirements management**. Does the organization have formal or informal knowledge and requirements management systems? What guidelines should the project manager establish for requirements to be reused in the future?

◆ **Validation and control**. Does the organization have existing formal or informal validation and control-related policies, procedures, and guidelines?

◆ **Use of agile approach**. Does the organization use agile approaches in managing projects? Is the development approach iterative or incremental? Is a predictive approach used? Will a hybrid approach be productive?

◆ **Governance**. Does the organization have formal or informal audit and governance policies, procedures, and guidelines?

## X5.3 PROJECT SCHEDULE MANAGEMENT

Considerations for tailoring project schedule management include but are not limited to:

◆ **Life cycle approach.** What is the most appropriate life cycle approach that allows for a detailed schedule?

◆ **Duration and resource.** What are the factors influencing durations, such as the correlation between resource availability and productivity?

◆ **Project dimensions.** How will the presence of project complexity, technological uncertainty, product novelty, pace or progress tracking, (such as earned value management, percentage complete, red-yellow-green (stop light) indicators) impact the desired level of control?

◆ **Technology support.** Is technology used to develop, record, transmit, receive, and store project schedule model information and is it readily accessible?

## X5.4 PROJECT COST MANAGEMENT

Considerations for tailoring project cost management include but are not limited to:

◆ **Knowledge management**. Does the organization have a formal knowledge management and financial databases repository that a project manager is required to use and is readily accessible?

◆ **Estimating and budgeting**. Does the organization have existing formal or informal cost estimating and budgeting-related policies, procedures, and guidelines?

◆ **Earned value management**. Does the organization use earned value management in managing projects?

◆ **Use of agile approach**. Does the organization use agile methodologies in managing projects? How does this impact cost estimating?

◆ **Governance**. Does the organization have formal or informal audit and governance policies, procedures, and guidelines?

## X5.5 PROJECT QUALITY MANAGEMENT

Considerations for tailoring project quality management include but are not limited to:

◆ **Policy compliance and auditing**. What quality policies and procedures exist in the organization? What quality tools, techniques, and templates are used in the organization?

◆ **Standards and regulatory compliance**. Are there any specific quality standards in the industry that need to be applied? Are there any specific governmental, legal, or regulatory constraints that need to be taken into consideration?

◆ **Continuous improvement**. How will quality improvement be managed in the project? Is it managed at the organizational level or at the level of each project?

◆ **Stakeholder engagement**. Is there a collaborative environment with stakeholders and suppliers?

## X5.6 PROJECT RESOURCE MANAGEMENT

Considerations for tailoring project resource management include but are not limited to:

◆ **Diversity**. What is the diversity background of the team?

◆ **Physical location**. What is the physical location of team members and physical resources?

◆ **Industry-specific resources**. What special resources are needed in in the industry?

◆ **Acquisition of team members**. How will team members be acquired for the project? Are team resources full-time or part-time on the project?

◆ **Development and management of team**. How is team development managed for the project? Are there organizational tools to manage team development or will new ones need to be established? Will the team need special training to manage diversity?

◆ **Life cycle approaches**. What life cycle approach will be used on the project?

## X5.7 PROJECT COMMUNICATIONS MANAGEMENT

Considerations for tailoring project communications management include but are not limited to:

◆ **Stakeholders**. Are the stakeholders internal or external to the organization, or both?

◆ **Physical location**. What is the physical location of team members? Is the team colocated? Is the team in the same geographical area? Is the team distributed across multiple time zones?

◆ **Communications technology**. What technology is available to develop, record, transmit, retrieve, track, and store communication artifacts? What technologies are most appropriate and cost effective for communicating to stakeholders?

◆ **Language**. Language is a main factor to consider in communication activities. Is one language used? Or are many languages used? Have allowances been made to adjust to the complexity of team members from diverse language groups?

◆ **Knowledge management**. Does the organization have a formal knowledge management repository? Is the repository used?

## X5.8 PROJECT RISK MANAGEMENT

Considerations for tailoring project risk management include but are not limited to:

◆ **Project size**. Does the project's size in terms of budget, duration, scope, or team size require a more detailed approach to risk management? Or is it small enough to justify a simplified risk process?

◆ **Project complexity**. Is a robust risk approach demanded by high levels of innovation, new technology, commercial arrangements, interfaces, or external dependencies that increase project complexity? Or is the project simple enough that a reduced risk process will suffice?

◆ **Project importance**. How strategically important is the project? Is the level of risk increased for this project because it aims to produce breakthrough opportunities, addresses significant blocks to organizational performance, or involves major product innovation?

◆ **Development approach**. Is this a waterfall project where risk processes can be followed sequentially and iteratively, or does the project follow an agile approach where risk is addressed at the start of each iteration as well as during execution?

## X5.9 PROJECT PROCUREMENT MANAGEMENT

Considerations for tailoring project procurement management include but are not limited to:

◆ **Complexity of procurement**. Is there one main procurement or are there multiple procurements at different times with different sellers that add to the complexity of the procurements?

◆ **Physical location**. Are the buyers and sellers in the same location or reasonably close or in different time zones, countries, or continents?

◆ **Governance and regulatory environment**. Are local laws and regulations regarding procurement activities integrated with the organization's procurement policies? How does this affect contract auditing requirements?

◆ **Availability of contractors**. Are there available contractors who are capable of performing the work?

# X5.10 PROJECT STAKEHOLDER MANAGEMENT

Considerations for tailoring project stakeholder management include but are not limited to:

◆ **Stakeholder diversity**. How many stakeholders are there? How diverse is the culture within the stakeholder community?

◆ **Complexity of stakeholder relationships**. How complex are the relationships within the stakeholder community? The more networks a stakeholder or stakeholder group participates in, the more complex the networks of information and misinformation the stakeholder may receive.

◆ **Communication technology**. What communication technology is available? What support mechanisms are in place to ensure that best value is achieved from the technology?

# APPENDIX X6
# TOOLS AND TECHNIQUES

## X6.1 INTRODUCTION

The *PMBOK® Guide* - Sixth Edition presents tools and techniques differently from previous editions. Where appropriate, this edition groups tools and techniques by their purpose. The group name describes the intent of what needs to be done and the tools and techniques in the group represent different methods to accomplish the intent. For example, data gathering is a group with the intent of gathering data and information. Brainstorming, interviews, and market research are among the techniques that can be used to gather data and information.

This approach reflects the emphasis in the Sixth Edition on the importance of tailoring the information presented in the *PMBOK® Guide* to the needs of the environment, situation, organization, or project.

There are 132 individual tools and techniques in the *PMBOK® Guide* – Sixth Edition. These are not the only tools and techniques that can be used to manage a project. They represent those tools and techniques that are considered to be good practice on most projects most of the time. Some are mentioned once and some appear many times in the *PMBOK® Guide*.

To assist practitioners in identifying where specific tools and techniques are used, this appendix identifies each tool and technique, the group to which it belongs (if appropriate), and the process(es) where it is listed in the *PMBOK® Guide*. The process in which a tool or technique is described in the guide is in boldface type. In other processes where the tool or technique is listed, it will reference the process in which it is described. Processes may provide additional verbiage on how a tool or technique is used in a particular process.

## X6.2 TOOLS AND TECHNIQUES GROUPS

The following tools and techniques groups are used throughout the *PMBOK® Guide*:

◆ **Data gathering techniques.** Used to collect data and information from a variety of sources. There are nine data gathering tools and techniques.

◆ **Data analysis techniques.** Used to organize, assess, and evaluate data and information. There are 27 data analysis tools and techniques.

◆ **Data representation techniques.** Used to show graphic representations or other methods used to convey data and information. There are 16 data representation tools and techniques.

◆ **Decision-making techniques.** Used to select a course of action from different alternatives. There are three decision-making tools and techniques.

◆ **Communication skills.** Used to transfer information between stakeholders. There are four communication skills tools and techniques.

◆ **Interpersonal and team skills.** Used to effectively lead and interact with team members and other stakeholders. There are 17 interpersonal and team skills tools and techniques.

There are 59 ungrouped tools and techniques.

Table X6-1. Categorization and Index of Tools and Techniques

| Tool and Technique | Knowledge Area[A] | | | | | | | | | |
|---|---|---|---|---|---|---|---|---|---|---|
| | Integration | Scope | Schedule | Cost | Quality | Resources | Communication | Risk | Procurement | Stakeholder |
| **Data Gathering Tools and Techniques** | | | | | | | | | | |
| Benchmarking | | 5.2 | | | **8.1** | | | | | 13.2 |
| Brainstorming | **4.1**, 4.2 | 5.2 | | | 8.1 | | | 11.2 | | 13.1 |
| Check sheets | | | | | **8.3** | | | | | |
| Checklists | 4.2 | | | | 8.2, 8.3 | | | **11.2** | | |
| Focus groups | 4.1, 4.2 | **5.2** | | | | | | | | |
| Interviews | 4.1, 4.2 | **5.2** | | | 8.1 | | | 11.2, 11.3, 11.4, 11.5 | | |
| Market research | | | | | | | | | **12.1** | |
| Questionnaires and surveys | | **5.2** | | | 8.3 | | | | | 13.1 |
| Statistical sampling | | | | | **8.3** | | | | | |

| Tool and Technique | Knowledge Area[A] | | | | | | | | | |
|---|---|---|---|---|---|---|---|---|---|---|
| | Integration | Scope | Schedule | Cost | Quality | Resources | Communication | Risk | Procurement | Stakeholder |
| **Data Analysis Tools and Techniques** | | | | | | | | | | |
| Alternatives analysis | 4.5, 4.6 | 5.1, 5.3 | 6.1, 6.4 | 7.1, 7.2 | 8.2 | **9.2**, 9.6 | | 11.5 | | 13.4 |
| Assessment of other risk parameters | | | | | | | | **11.3** | | |
| Assumption and constraint analysis | | | | | | | | **11.2** | | 13.2 |
| Cost of quality | | | | 7.2 | **8.1** | | | | | |
| Cost-benefit analysis | 4.5, 4.6 | | | | **8.1** | 9.6 | | 11.5 | | |
| Decision tree analysis | | | | | | | | **11.4** | | |
| Document analysis | 4.7 | **5.2** | | | 8.2 | | | 11.2 | | 13.1 |
| Earned value analysis | 4.5 | | 6.6 | **7.4** | | | | | 12.3 | |
| Influence diagrams | | | | | | | | **11.4** | | |
| Iteration burndown chart | | | **6.6** | | | | | | | |
| Make-or-buy analysis | | | | | | | | | **12.1** | |
| Performance reviews | | | **6.6** | | 8.3 | 9.6 | | | 12.3 | |
| Process analysis | | | | | **8.2** | | | | | |
| Proposal evaluation | | | | | | | | | **12.2** | |

| Tool and Technique | Knowledge Area[A] | | | | | | | | | |
|---|---|---|---|---|---|---|---|---|---|---|
| | Integration | Scope | Schedule | Cost | Quality | Resources | Communication | Risk | Procurement | Stakeholder |
| **Data Analysis Tools and Techniques** *(cont.)* | | | | | | | | | | |
| Regression analysis | **4.7** | | | | | | | | | |
| Reserve analysis | | | 6.4 | **7.2**, 7.3, 7.4 | | | | 11.7 | | |
| Risk data quality assessment | | | | | | | | **11.3** | | |
| Risk probability and impact assessment | | | | | | | | **11.3** | | |
| Root cause analysis | 4.5 | | | | 8.2, 8.3 | | | 11.2 | | 13.2, 13.4 |
| Sensitivity analysis | | | | | | | | **11.4** | | |
| Simulation | | | 6.5 | | | | | **11.4** | | |
| Stakeholder analysis | | | | | | | | 11.1 | | **13.1**, 13.4 |
| SWOT analysis | | | | | | | | **11.2** | | |
| Technical performance analysis | | | | | | | | **11.7** | | |
| Trend analysis | **4.5**, 4.7 | 5.6 | 6.6 | 7.4 | | 9.6 | | | 12.3 | |
| Variance analysis | **4.5**, 4.7 | 5.6 | 6.6 | 7.4 | | | | | | |
| What-if scenario analysis | | | **6.5**, 6.6 | | | | | | | |

| Tool and Technique | Knowledge Area[A] | | | | | | | | | |
|---|---|---|---|---|---|---|---|---|---|---|
| | Integration | Scope | Schedule | Cost | Quality | Resources | Communication | Risk | Procurement | Stakeholder |
| **Data Representation Tools and Techniques** | | | | | | | | | | |
| Affinity diagrams | | **5.2** | | | 8.2 | | | | | |
| Cause-and-effect diagrams | | | | | **8.2**, 8.3 | | | | | |
| Control charts | | | | | **8.3** | | | | | |
| Flowcharts | | | | | **8.1**, 8.2 | | | | | |
| Hierarchical charts | | | | | | 9.1 | | 11.3 | | |
| Histograms | | | | | **8.2**, 8.3 | | | | | |
| Logical data model | | | | | **8.1** | | | | | |
| Matrix diagrams | | | | | **8.1**, 8.2 | | | | | |
| Mind mapping | | **5.2** | | | 8.1 | | | | | 13.2 |
| Prioritization/ ranking | | | | | | | | | | **13.2** |
| Probability and impact matrix | | | | | | | | **11.3** | | |
| Responsibility assignment matrix | | | | | | 9.1 | | | | |
| Scatter diagrams | | | | | **8.2**, 8.3 | | | | | |
| Stakeholder engagement assessment matrix | | | | | | | 10.1, 10.3 | | | **13.2**, 13.4 |
| Stakeholder mapping/ representation | | | | | | | | | | **13.1** |
| Text-oriented formats | | | | | | 9.1 | | | | |
| **Decision-Making Tools and Techniques** | | | | | | | | | | |
| Multicriteria decision analysis | 4.6 | 5.2, 5.3 | | | **8.1**, 8.2 | 9.3 | | 11.5 | | 13.4 |
| Voting | 4.5, 4.6 | **5.2**, 5.5 | 6.4 | 7.2 | | | | | | 13.4 |
| Autocratic decision making | 4.6 | 5.2 | | | | | | | | |
| **Communication Skills Tools and Techniques** | | | | | | | | | | |
| Communication competence | | | | | | | **10.2** | | | |
| Feedback | | | | | | | **10.2** | | | 13.4 |
| Nonverbal | | | | | | | **10.2** | | | |
| Presentations | | | | | | | **10.2** | | | 13.4 |

Table X6-1. Categorization and Index of Tools and Techniques *(cont.)*

| Tool and Technique | Knowledge Area^A | | | | | | | | | |
|---|---|---|---|---|---|---|---|---|---|---|
| | Integration | Scope | Schedule | Cost | Quality | Resources | Communication | Risk | Procurement | Stakeholder |
| **Interpersonal and Team Skills Tools and Techniques** | | | | | | | | | | |
| Active listening | 4.4 | | | | | | **10.2** | | | 13.4 |
| Communication styles assessment | | | | | | | **10.1** | | | |
| Conflict management | 4.1, 4.2 | | | | | 9.4, **9.5** | 10.2 | | | 13.3 |
| Cultural awareness | | | | | | | **10.1**, 10.2 | | | 13.3, 13.4 |
| Decision making | | | | | | **9.5** | | | | |
| Emotional intelligence | | | | | | **9.5** | | | | |
| Facilitation | **4.1**, 4.2, 4.4 | 5.2, 5.3 | | | | | | 11.2, 11.3, 11.4, 11.5 | | |
| Influencing | | | | | | 9.4, **9.5**, 9.6 | | 11.6 | | |
| Leadership | 4.4 | | | | | **9.5** | | | | 13.4 |
| Meeting management | 4.1, 4.2 | | | | | | **10.2** | | | |
| Motivation | | | | | | **9.4** | | | | |
| Negotiation | | | | | | 9.3, 9.4, 9.6 | | | **12.2** | 13.3 |
| Networking | 4.4 | | | | | | **10.2** | | | 13.4 |
| Nominal group technique | | **5.2** | | | | | | | | |
| Observation/ conversation | | **5.2** | | | | | 10.3 | | | 13.3 |
| Political awareness | 4.4 | | | | | | **10.1**, 10.2 | | | 13.3, 13.4 |
| Team building | | | | | | **9.4** | | | | |

## Table X6-1. Categorization and Index of Tools and Techniques *(cont.)*

| Tool and Technique | Knowledge Area[A] | | | | | | | | | |
|---|---|---|---|---|---|---|---|---|---|---|
| | Integration | Scope | Schedule | Cost | Quality | Resources | Communication | Risk | Procurement | Stakeholder |
| **Ungrouped Tools and Techniques** | | | | | | | | | | |
| Advertising | | | | | | | | | **12.2** | |
| Agile release planning | | | **6.5** | | | | | | | |
| Analogous estimating | | | **6.4** | 7.2 | | 9.2 | | | | |
| Audits | | | | | **8.2** | | | 11.7 | 12.3 | |
| Bidder conferences | | | | | | | | | **12.2** | |
| Bottom-up estimating | | | **6.4** | 7.2 | | 9.2 | | | | |
| Change control tools | **4.6** | | | | | | | | | |
| Claims administration | | | | | | | | | **12.3** | |
| Colocation | | | | | | **9.4** | | | | |
| Communication methods | | | | | | | **10.1**, 10.2 | | | |
| Communication models | | | | | | | **10.1** | | | |
| Communication requirements analysis | | | | | | | **10.1** | | | |
| Communication technology | | | | | | 9.4 | **10.1**, 10.2 | | | |
| Context diagram | | **5.2** | | | | | | | | |
| Contingent response strategies | | | | | | | | **11.5** | | |
| Cost aggregation | | | | **7.3** | | | | | | |
| Critical path method | | | **6.5**, 6.6 | | | | | | | |

691

| Tool and Technique | Knowledge Area[A] | | | | | | | | | |
|---|---|---|---|---|---|---|---|---|---|---|
| | Integration | Scope | Schedule | Cost | Quality | Resources | Communication | Risk | Procurement | Stakeholder |
| **Ungrouped Tools and Techniques *(cont.)*** | | | | | | | | | | |
| Decomposition | | **5.4** | 6.2 | | | | | | | |
| Dependency determination and integration | | | **6.3** | | | | | | | |
| Design for X | | | | | 8.2 | | | | | |
| Expert judgment | **4.1**, 4.2, 4.3, 4.4, 4.5, 4.6, 4.7 | 5.1, 5.2, 5.3, 5.4 | 6.1, 6.2, 6.4 | 7.1, 7.2, 7.3, 7.4 | 8.1 | 9.1, 9.2 | 10.1, 10.3 | 11.1, 11.2, 11.3, 11.4, 11.5, 11.6 | 12.1, 12.2, 12.3 | 13.1, 13.2, 13.3 |
| Financing | | | | **7.3** | | | | | | |
| Funding limit reconciliation | | | | **7.3** | | | | | | |
| Ground rules | | | | | | | | | | **13.3** |
| Historical information review | | | | **7.3** | | | | | | |
| Individual and team assessments | | | | | | 9.4 | | | | |
| Information management | **4.4** | | | | | | | | | |
| Inspection | | 5.5 | | | 8.3 | | | | 12.3 | |
| Knowledge management | **4.4** | | | | | | | | | |
| Leads and lags | | | **6.3**, 6.5, 6.6 | | | | | | | |
| Meetings | 4.1, 4.2, 4.3, 4.5, 4.6, 4.7 | 5.1 | 6.1, 6.2, 6.4 | 7.1 | 8.1, 8.3 | 9.1, 9.2, 9.4 | **10.1**, 10,2, 10.3 | 11.1, 11.2, 11.3, 11.7 | 12.1 | 13.1, 13.2, 13.3, 13.4 |

## Table X6-1. Categorization and Index of Tools and Techniques *(cont.)*

| Tool and Technique | Knowledge Area[A] | | | | | | | | | |
|---|---|---|---|---|---|---|---|---|---|---|
| | Integration | Scope | Schedule | Cost | Quality | Resources | Communication | Risk | Procurement | Stakeholder |
| **Ungrouped Tools and Techniques** *(cont.)* | | | | | | | | | | |
| Organizational theory | | | | | | **9.1** | | | | |
| Parametric estimating | | | **6.4** | 7.2 | | 9.2 | | | | |
| Pre-assignment | | | | | | **9.3** | | | | |
| Precedence diagramming method | | | **6.3** | | | | | | | |
| Problem solving | | | | | **8.2** | 9.6 | | | | |
| Product analysis | | **5.3** | | | | | | | | |
| Project management information system | **4.3** | | 6.3, 6.5, 6.6 | 7.2, 7.4 | | 9.2, 9.5, 9.6 | 10.2, 10.3 | 11.6 | | |
| Project reporting | | | | | **8.2** | | | | | |
| Prompt lists | | | | | | | | **11.2** | | |
| Prototypes | | **5.2** | | | | | | | | |
| Quality improvement methods | | | | | **8.2** | | | | | |
| Recognition and rewards | | | | | | **9.4** | | | | |
| Representations of uncertainty | | | | | | | | **11.4** | | |
| Resource optimization | | | **6.5**, 6.6 | | | | | | | |
| Risk categorization | | | | | | | | **11.3** | | |
| Rolling wave planning | | | **6.2** | | | | | | | |

| Tool and Technique | Knowledge Area[A] | | | | | | | | | |
|---|---|---|---|---|---|---|---|---|---|---|
| | Integration | Scope | Schedule | Cost | Quality | Resources | Communication | Risk | Procurement | Stakeholder |
| **Ungrouped Tools and Techniques** *(cont.)* | | | | | | | | | | |
| Schedule compression | | | **6.5**, 6.6 | | | | | | | |
| Schedule network analysis | | | **6.5** | | | | | | | |
| Source selection analysis | | | | | | | | | 12.1 | |
| Strategies for opportunities | | | | | | | | 11.5 | | |
| Strategies for overall project risk | | | | | | | | 11.5 | | |
| Strategies for threats | | | | | | | | 11.5 | | |
| Test and inspection planning | | | | | 8.1 | | | | | |
| Testing/product evaluations | | | | | 8.3 | | | | | |
| Three-point estimating | | | 6.4 | 7.2 | | | | | | |
| To-complete performance index | | | | 7.4 | | | | | | |
| Training | | | | | | 9.4 | | | | |
| Virtual teams | | | | | | **9.3**, 9.4 | | | | |

[A] The boldface entries indicate the section numbers of the processes where a tool or technique is described.

# GLOSSARY

## 1. INCLUSIONS AND EXCLUSIONS

This glossary includes terms that are:

◆ Unique or nearly unique to project management (e.g., project scope statement, work package, work breakdown structure, critical path method).

◆ Not unique to project management, but used differently or with a narrower meaning in project management than in general everyday usage (e.g., early start date).

This glossary generally does not include:

◆ Application area-specific terms.

◆ Terms used in project management that do not differ in any material way from everyday use (e.g., calendar day, delay).

◆ Compound terms whose meaning is clear from the meanings of the component parts.

◆ Variants when the meaning of the variant is clear from the base term.

◆ Terms that are used only once and are not critical to understanding the point of the sentence. This can include a list of examples that would not have each term defined in the Glossary.

# 2. COMMON ACRONYMS

| | |
|---|---|
| AC | actual cost |
| BAC | budget at completion |
| CCB | change control board |
| COQ | cost of quality |
| CPAF | cost plus award fee |
| CPFF | cost plus fixed fee |
| CPI | cost performance index |
| CPIF | cost plus incentive fee |
| CPM | critical path method |
| CV | cost variance |
| EAC | estimate at completion |
| EF | early finish date |
| ES | early start date |
| ETC | estimate to complete |
| EV | earned value |
| EVM | earned value management |
| FF | finish-to-finish |
| FFP | firm fixed price |
| FPEPA | fixed price with economic price adjustment |
| FPIF | fixed price incentive fee |
| FS | finish to start |
| IFB | invitation for bid |

| | |
|---|---|
| LF | late finish date |
| LOE | level of effort |
| LS | late start date |
| OBS | organizational breakdown structure |
| PDM | precedence diagramming method |
| PMBOK | Project Management Body of Knowledge |
| PV | planned value |
| QFD | quality function deployment |
| RACI | responsible, accountable, consult, and inform |
| RAM | responsibility assignment matrix |
| RBS | risk breakdown structure |
| RFI | request for information |
| RFP | request for proposal |
| RFQ | request for quotation |
| SF | start-to-finish |
| SOW | statement of work |
| SPI | schedule performance index |
| SS | start-to-start |
| SV | schedule variance |
| SWOT | strengths, weaknesses, opportunities, and threats |
| T&M | time and material contract |
| VAC | variance at completion |
| WBS | work breakdown structure |

# 3. DEFINITIONS

Many of the words defined here have broader, and in some cases different, dictionary definitions. In some cases, a single glossary term consists of multiple words (e.g., root cause analysis).

**Acceptance Criteria.** A set of conditions that is required to be met before deliverables are accepted.

**Accepted Deliverables.** Products, results, or capabilities produced by a project and validated by the project customer or sponsors as meeting their specified acceptance criteria.

**Accuracy.** Within the quality management system, accuracy is an assessment of correctness.

**Acquire Resources.** The process of obtaining team members, facilities, equipment, materials, supplies, and other resources necessary to complete project work.

**Acquisition.** Obtaining human and material resources necessary to perform project activities. Acquisition implies a cost of resources, and is not necessarily financial.

**Activity.** A distinct, scheduled portion of work performed during the course of a project.

**Activity Attributes.** Multiple attributes associated with each schedule activity that can be included within the activity list. Activity attributes include activity codes, predecessor activities, successor activities, logical relationships, leads and lags, resource requirements, imposed dates, constraints, and assumptions.

**Activity Duration.** The time in calendar units between the start and finish of a schedule activity. See also duration.

**Activity Duration Estimates.** The quantitative assessments of the likely number of time periods that are required to complete an activity.

**Activity List.** A documented tabulation of schedule activities that shows the activity description, activity identifier, and a sufficiently detailed scope of work description so project team members understand what work is to be performed.

**Activity-on-Node (AON).** See precedence diagramming method (PDM).

**Actual Cost (AC).** The realized cost incurred for the work performed on an activity during a specific time period.

**Actual Duration.** The time in calendar units between the actual start date of the schedule activity and either the data date of the project schedule if the schedule activity is in progress or the actual finish date if the schedule activity is complete.

**Adaptive Life Cycle.** A project life cycle that is iterative or incremental.

**Affinity Diagrams.** A technique that allows large numbers of ideas to be classified into groups for review and analysis.

**Agreements.** Any document or communication that defines the initial intentions of a project. This can take the form of a contract, memorandum of understanding (MOU), letters of agreement, verbal agreements, email, etc.

**Alternative Analysis.** A technique used to evaluate identified options in order to select the options or approaches to use to execute and perform the work of the project.

**Analogous Estimating.** A technique for estimating the duration or cost of an activity or a project using historical data from a similar activity or project.

**Analytical Techniques.** Various techniques used to evaluate, analyze, or forecast potential outcomes based on possible variations of project or environmental variables and their relationships with other variables.

**Assumption.** A factor in the planning process that is considered to be true, real, or certain, without proof or demonstration.

**Assumption Log.** A project document used to record all assumptions and constraints throughout the project life cycle.

**Attribute Sampling.** Method of measuring quality that consists of noting the presence (or absence) of some characteristic (attribute) in each of the units under consideration.

**Authority.** The right to apply project resources, expend funds, make decisions, or give approvals.

**Backward Pass.** A critical path method technique for calculating the late start and late finish dates by working backward through the schedule model from the project end date.

**Bar Chart.** A graphic display of schedule-related information. In the typical bar chart, schedule activities or work breakdown structure components are listed down the left side of the chart, dates are shown across the top, and activity durations are shown as date-placed horizontal bars. See also Gantt chart.

**Baseline.** The approved version of a work product that can be changed only through formal change control procedures and is used as a basis for comparison to actual results.

**Basis of Estimates.** Supporting documentation outlining the details used in establishing project estimates such as assumptions, constraints, level of detail, ranges, and confidence levels.

**Benchmarking.** The comparison of actual or planned products, processes, and practices to those of comparable organizations to identify best practices, generate ideas for improvement, and provide a basis for measuring performance.

**Benefits Management Plan.** The documented explanation defining the processes for creating, maximizing, and sustaining the benefits provided by a project or program.

**Bid Documents.** All documents used to solicit information, quotations, or proposals from prospective sellers.

**Bidder Conference.** The meetings with prospective sellers prior to the preparation of a bid or proposal to ensure all prospective vendors have a clear and common understanding of the procurement. Also known as contractor conferences, vendor conferences, or pre-bid conferences.

**Bottom-Up Estimating.** A method of estimating project duration or cost by aggregating the estimates of the lower-level components of the work breakdown structure (WBS).

**Budget.** The approved estimate for the project or any work breakdown structure component or any schedule activity.

**Budget at Completion (BAC).** The sum of all budgets established for the work to be performed.

**Buffer.** *See reserve.*

**Business Case.** A documented economic feasibility study used to establish validity of the benefits of a selected component lacking sufficient definition and that is used as a basis for the authorization of further project management activities.

**Business Value.** The net quantifiable benefit derived from a business endeavor. The benefit may be tangible, intangible, or both.

**Cause and Effect Diagram.** A decomposition technique that helps trace an undesirable effect back to its root cause.

**Change.** A modification to any formally controlled deliverable, project management plan component, or project document.

**Change Control.** A process whereby modifications to documents, deliverables, or baselines associated with the project are identified, documented, approved, or rejected.

**Change Control Board (CCB).** A formally chartered group responsible for reviewing, evaluating, approving, delaying, or rejecting changes to the project, and for recording and communicating such decisions.

**Change Control System.** A set of procedures that describes how modifications to the project deliverables and documentation are managed and controlled.

**Change Control Tools.** Manual or automated tools to assist with change and/or configuration management. At a minimum, the tools should support the activities of the CCB.

**Change Log.** A comprehensive list of changes submitted during the project and their current status.

**Change Management Plan.** A component of the project management plan that establishes the change control board, documents the extent of its authority, and describes how the change control system will be implemented.

**Change Request.** A formal proposal to modify a document, deliverable, or baseline.

**Charter.** *See project charter.*

**Checklist Analysis.** A technique for systematically reviewing materials using a list for accuracy and completeness.

**Check Sheet.** A tally sheet that can be used as a checklist when gathering data.

**Claim.** A request, demand, or assertion of rights by a seller against a buyer, or vice versa, for consideration, compensation, or payment under the terms of a legally binding contract, such as for a disputed change.

**Claims Administration.** The process of processing, adjudicating, and communicating contract claims.

**Close Project or Phase.** The process of finalizing all activities for the project, phase, or contract.

**Closing Process Group.** The process(es) performed to formally complete or close a project, phase, or contract.

**Code of Accounts.** A numbering system used to uniquely identify each component of the work breakdown structure (WBS).

**Collect Requirements.** The process of determining, documenting, and managing stakeholder needs and requirements to meet project objectives.

**Colocation.** An organizational placement strategy where the project team members are physically located close to one another in order to improve communication, working relationships, and productivity.

**Communication Methods.** A systematic procedure, technique, or process used to transfer information among project stakeholders.

**Communication Models.** A description, analogy, or schematic used to represent how the communication process will be performed for the project.

**Communication Requirements Analysis.** An analytical technique to determine the information needs of the project stakeholders through interviews, workshops, study of lessons learned from previous projects, etc.

**Communications Management Plan.** A component of the project, program, or portfolio management plan that describes how, when, and by whom information about the project will be administered and disseminated.

**Communication Styles Assessment.** A technique to identify the preferred communication method, format, and content for stakeholders for planned communication activities.

**Communication Technology.** Specific tools, systems, computer programs, etc., used to transfer information among project stakeholders.

**Conduct Procurements.** The process of obtaining seller responses, selecting a seller, and awarding a contract.

**Configuration Management Plan.** A component of the project management plan that describes how to identify and account for project artifacts under configuration control, and how to record and report changes to them.

**Configuration Management System.** A collection of procedures used to track project artifacts and monitor and control changes to these artifacts.

**Conformance.** Within the quality management system, conformance is a general concept of delivering results that fall within the limits that define acceptable variation for a quality requirement.

**Constraint.** A limiting factor that affects the execution of a project, program, portfolio, or process.

**Context Diagrams.** A visual depiction of the product scope showing a business system (process, equipment, computer system, etc.), and how people and other systems (actors) interact with it.

**Contingency.** An event or occurrence that could affect the execution of the project that may be accounted for with a reserve.

**Contingency Reserve.** Time or money allocated in the schedule or cost baseline for known risks with active response strategies.

**Contingent Response Strategies.** Responses provided which may be used in the event that a specific trigger occurs.

**Contract.** A contract is a mutually binding agreement that obligates the seller to provide the specified product or service or result and obligates the buyer to pay for it.

**Contract Change Control System.** The system used to collect, track, adjudicate, and communicate changes to a contract.

**Control.** Comparing actual performance with planned performance, analyzing variances, assessing trends to effect process improvements, evaluating possible alternatives, and recommending appropriate corrective action as needed.

**Control Account.** A management control point where scope, budget, actual cost, and schedule are integrated and compared to earned value for performance measurement.

**Control Chart.** A graphic display of process data over time and against established control limits, which has a centerline that assists in detecting a trend of plotted values toward either control limit.

**Control Costs.** The process of monitoring the status of the project to update the project costs and manage changes to the cost baseline.

**Control Limits.** The area composed of three standard deviations on either side of the centerline or mean of a normal distribution of data plotted on a control chart, which reflects the expected variation in the data. See also specification limits.

**Control Procurements.** The process of managing procurement relationships, monitoring contract performance, making changes and corrections as appropriate, and closing out contracts.

**Control Quality.** The process of monitoring and recording results of executing the quality management activities to assess performance and ensure the project outputs are complete, correct, and meet customer expectations.

**Control Resources.** The process of ensuring that the physical resources assigned and allocated to the project are available as planned, as well as monitoring the planned versus actual utilization of resources and performing corrective action as necessary.

**Control Schedule.** The process of monitoring the status of the project to update the project schedule and manage changes to the schedule baseline.

**Control Scope.** The process of monitoring the status of the project and product scope and managing changes to the scope baaseline.

**Corrective Action.** An intentional activity that realigns the performance of the project work with the project management plan.

**Cost Aggregation.** Summing the lower-level cost estimates associated with the various work packages for a given level within the project's WBS or for a given cost control account.

**Cost Baseline.** The approved version of the time-phased project budget, excluding any management reserves, which can be changed only through formal change control procedures and is used as a basis for comparison to actual results.

**Cost-Benefit Analysis.** A financial analysis tool used to determine the benefits provided by a project against its costs.

**Cost Management Plan.** A component of a project or program management plan that describes how costs will be planned, structured, and controlled.

**Cost of Quality (CoQ).** All costs incurred over the life of the product by investment in preventing nonconformance to requirements, appraisal of the product or service for conformance to requirements, and failure to meet requirements.

**Cost Performance Index (CPI).** A measure of the cost efficiency of budgeted resources expressed as the ratio of earned value to actual cost.

**Cost Plus Award Fee Contract (CPAF).** A category of contract that involves payments to the seller for all legitimate actual costs incurred for completed work, plus an award fee representing seller profit.

**Cost Plus Fixed Fee Contract (CPFF).** A type of cost-reimbursable contract where the buyer reimburses the seller for the seller's allowable costs (allowable costs are defined by the contract) plus a fixed amount of profit (fee).

**Cost Plus Incentive Fee Contract (CPIF).** A type of cost-reimbursable contract where the buyer reimburses the seller for the seller's allowable costs (allowable costs are defined by the contract), and the seller earns its profit if it meets defined performance criteria.

**Cost-Reimbursable Contract.** A type of contract involving payment to the seller for the seller's actual costs, plus a fee typically representing the seller's profit.

**Cost Variance (CV).** The amount of budget deficit or surplus at a given point in time, expressed as the difference between the earned value and the actual cost.

**Crashing.** A technique used to shorten the schedule duration for the least incremental cost by adding resources.

**Create WBS.** The process of subdividing project deliverables and project work into smaller, more manageable components.

**Criteria.** Standards, rules, or tests on which a judgment or decision can be based or by which a product, service, result, or process can be evaluated.

**Critical Path.** The sequence of activities that represents the longest path through a project, which determines the shortest possible duration.

**Critical Path Activity.** Any activity on the critical path in a project schedule.

**Critical Path Method (CPM).** A method used to estimate the minimum project duration and determine the amount of schedule flexibility on the logical network paths within the schedule model.

**Data.** Discrete, unorganized, unprocessed measurements or raw observations.

**Data Analysis Techniques.** Techniques used to organize, assess, and evaluate data and information.

**Data Date.** A point in time when the status of the project is recorded.

**Data Gathering Techniques.** Techniques used to collect data and information from a variety of sources.

**Data Representation Techniques.** Graphic representations or other methods used to convey data and information.

**Decision-Making Techniques.** Techniques used to select a course of action from different alternatives.

**Decision Tree Analysis.** A diagramming and calculation technique for evaluating the implications of a chain of multiple options in the presence of uncertainty.

**Decomposition.** A technique used for dividing and subdividing the project scope and project deliverables into smaller, more manageable parts.

**Defect.** An imperfection or deficiency in a project component where that component does not meet its requirements or specifications and needs to be either repaired or replaced.

**Defect Repair.** An intentional activity to modify a nonconforming product or product component.

**Define Activities.** The process of identifying and documenting the specific actions to be performed to produce the project deliverables.

**Define Scope.** The process of developing a detailed description of the project and product.

**Deliverable.** Any unique and verifiable product, result, or capability to perform a service that is required to be produced to complete a process, phase, or project.

**Dependency.** *See logical relationship.*

**Determine Budget.** The process of aggregating the estimated costs of individual activities or work packages to establish an authorized cost baseline.

**Development Approach.** The method used to create and evolve the product, service, or result during the project life cycle, such as predictive, iterative, incremental, agile, or a hybrid method.

**Develop Project Charter.** The process of developing a document that formally authorizes the existence of a project and provides the project manager with the authority to apply organizational resources to project activities.

**Develop Project Management Plan.** The process of defining, preparing, and coordinating all plan components and consolidating them into an integrated project management plan.

**Develop Schedule.** The process of analyzing activity sequences, durations, resource requirements, and schedule constraints to create the project schedule model for project execution and monitoring and controlling.

**Develop Team.** The process of improving competences, team member interaction, and overall team environment to enhance project performance.

**Diagramming Techniques.** Approaches to presenting information with logical linkages that aid in understanding.

**Direct and Manage Project Work.** The process of leading and performing the work defined in the project management plan and implementing approved changes to achieve the project's objectives.

**Discrete Effort.** An activity that can be planned and measured and that yields a specific output. [Note: Discrete effort is one of three earned value management (EVM) types of activities used to measure work performance.]

**Discretionary Dependency.** A relationship that is established based on knowledge of best practices within a particular application area or an aspect of the project where a specific sequence is desired.

**Documentation Reviews.** The process of gathering a corpus of information and reviewing it to determine accuracy and completeness.

**Duration.** The total number of work periods required to complete an activity or work breakdown structure component, expressed in hours, days, or weeks. Contrast with effort.

**Early Finish Date (EF).** In the critical path method, the earliest possible point in time when the uncompleted portions of a schedule activity can finish based on the schedule network logic, the data date, and any schedule constraints.

**Early Start Date (ES).** In the critical path method, the earliest possible point in time when the uncompleted portions of a schedule activity can start based on the schedule network logic, the data date, and any schedule constraints.

**Earned Value (EV).** The measure of work performed expressed in terms of the budget authorized for that work.

**Earned Value Management.** A methodology that combines scope, schedule, and resource measurements to assess project performance and progress.

**Effort.** The number of labor units required to complete a schedule activity or work breakdown structure component, often expressed in hours, days, or weeks. *Contrast with duration.*

**Emotional Intelligence.** The ability to identify, assess, and manage the personal emotions of oneself and other people, as well as the collective emotions of groups of people.

**Enterprise Environmental Factors.** Conditions, not under the immediate control of the team, that influence, constrain, or direct the project, program, or portfolio.

**Estimate.** A quantitative assessment of the likely amount or outcome of a variable, such as project costs, resources, effort, or durations.

**Estimate Activity Durations.** The process of estimating the number of work periods needed to complete individual activities with the estimated resources.

**Estimate Activity Resources.** The process of estimating team resources and the type and quantities of material, equipment, and supplies necessary to perform project work.

**Estimate at Completion (EAC).** The expected total cost of completing all work expressed as the sum of the actual cost to date and the estimate to complete.

**Estimate Costs.** The process of developing an approximation of the monetary resources needed to complete project work.

**Estimate to Complete (ETC).** The expected cost to finish all the remaining project work.

**Execute.** Directing, managing, performing, and accomplishing the project work; providing the deliverables; and providing work performance information.

**Executing Process Group.** Those processes performed to complete the work defined in the project management plan to satisfy the project requirements.

**Expert Judgment.** Judgment provided based upon expertise in an application area, knowledge area, discipline, industry, etc., as appropriate for the activity being performed. Such expertise may be provided by any group or person with specialized education, knowledge, skill, experience, or training.

**Explicit Knowledge.** Knowledge that can be codified using symbols such as words, numbers, and pictures.

**External Dependency.** A relationship between project activities and non-project activities.

**Fallback Plan.** An alternative set of actions and tasks available in the event that the primary plan needs to be abandoned because of issues, risks, or other causes.

**Fast Tracking.** A schedule compression technique in which activities or phases normally done in sequence are performed in parallel for at least a portion of their duration.

**Fee.** Represents profit as a component of compensation to a seller.

**Finish Date.** A point in time associated with a schedule activity's completion. Usually qualified by one of the following: actual, planned, estimated, scheduled, early, late, baseline, target, or current.

**Finish-to-Finish (FF).** A logical relationship in which a successor activity cannot finish until a predecessor activity has finished.

**Finish-to-Start (FS).** A logical relationship in which a successor activity cannot start until a predecessor activity has finished.

**Firm Fixed Price Contract (FFP).** A type of fixed price contract where the buyer pays the seller a set amount (as defined by the contract), regardless of the seller's costs.

**Fishbone diagram.** *See Cause and Effect Diagram.*

**Fixed-Price Contract.** An agreement that sets the fee that will be paid for a defined scope of work regardless of the cost or effort to deliver it.

**Fixed Price Incentive Fee Contract (FPIF).** A type of contract where the buyer pays the seller a set amount (as defined by the contract), and the seller can earn an additional amount if the seller meets defined performance criteria.

**Fixed Price with Economic Price Adjustment Contract (FPEPA).** A fixed-price contract, but with a special provision allowing for predefined final adjustments to the contract price due to changed conditions, such as inflation changes, or cost increases (or decreases) for specific commodities.

**Float.** Also called slack. *See total float and free float.*

**Flowchart.** The depiction in a diagram format of the inputs, process actions, and outputs of one or more processes within a system.

**Focus Groups.** An elicitation technique that brings together prequalified stakeholders and subject matter experts to learn about their expectations and attitudes about a proposed product, service, or result.

**Forecast.** An estimate or prediction of conditions and events in the project's future based on information and knowledge available at the time of the forecast.

**Forward Pass.** A critical path method technique for calculating the early start and early finish dates by working forward through the schedule model from the project start date or a given point in time.

**Free Float.** The amount of time that a schedule activity can be delayed without delaying the early start date of any successor or violating a schedule constraint.

**Functional Organization.** An organizational structure in which staff is grouped by areas of specialization and the project manager has limited authority to assign work and apply resources.

**Funding Limit Reconciliation**. The process of comparing the planned expenditure of project funds against any limits on the commitment of funds for the project to identify any variances between the funding limits and the planned expenditures.

**Gantt Chart.** A bar chart of schedule information where activities are listed on the vertical axis, dates are shown on the horizontal axis, and activity durations are shown as horizontal bars placed according to start and finish dates.

**Grade.** A category or rank used to distinguish items that have the same functional use but do not share the same requirements for quality.

**Ground Rules.** Expectations regarding acceptable behavior by project team members.

**Histogram.** A bar chart that shows the graphical representation of numerical data.

**Historical Information.** Documents and data on prior projects including project files, records, correspondence, closed contracts, and closed projects.

**Identify Risks.** The process of identifying individual risks as well as sources of overall risk and documenting their characteristics.

**Identify Stakeholders.** The process of identifying project stakeholders regularly and analyzing and documenting relevant information regarding their interests, involvement, interdependencies, influence, and potential impact on project success.

**Implement Risk Responses.** The process of implementing agreed-upon risk response plans.

**Imposed Date.** A fixed date imposed on a schedule activity or schedule milestone, usually in the form of a "start no earlier than" and "finish no later than" date.

**Incentive Fee.** A set of financial incentives related to cost, schedule, or technical performance of the seller.

**Incremental Life Cycle.** An adaptive project life cycle in which the deliverable is produced through a series of iterations that successively add functionality within a predetermined time frame. The deliverable contains the necessary and sufficient capability to be considered complete only after the final iteration.

**Independent Estimates.** A process of using a third party to obtain and analyze information to support prediction of cost, schedule, or other items.

**Influence Diagram.** A graphical representation of situations showing causal influences, time ordering of events, and other relationships among variables and outcomes.

**Information.** Organized or structured data, processed for a specific purpose to make it meaningful, valuable, and useful in specific contexts.

**Information Management Systems.** Facilities, processes, and procedures used to collect, store, and distribute information between producers and consumers of information in physical or electronic format.

**Initiating Process Group.** Those processes performed to define a new project or a new phase of an existing project by obtaining authorization to start the project or phase.

**Input.** Any item, whether internal or external to the project, which is required by a process before that process proceeds. May be an output from a predecessor process.

**Inspection.** Examination of a work product to determine whether it conforms to documented standards.

**Interpersonal and Team Skills.** Skills used to effectively lead and interact with team members and other stakeholders.

**Interpersonal Skills.** Skills used to establish and maintain relationships with other people.

**Interviews.** A formal or informal approach to elicit information from stakeholders by talking to them directly.

**Invitation for Bid (IFB).** Generally, this term is equivalent to request for proposal. However, in some application areas, it may have a narrower or more specific meaning.

**Issue.** A current condition or situation that may have an impact on the project objectives.

**Issue Log.** A project document where information about issues is recorded and monitored.

**Iterative Life Cycle.** A project life cycle where the project scope is generally determined early in the project life cycle, but time and cost estimates are routinely modified as the project team's understanding of the product increases. Iterations develop the product through a series of repeated cycles, while increments successively add to the functionality of the product.

**Knowledge.** A mixture of experience, values and beliefs, contextual information, intuition, and insight that people use to make sense of new experiences and information.

**Lag.** The amount of time whereby a successor activity will be delayed with respect to a predecessor activity.

**Late Finish Date (LF).** In the critical path method, the latest possible point in time when the uncompleted portions of a schedule activity can finish based on the schedule network, the project completion date, and any schedule constraints.

**Late Start Date (LS).** In the critical path method, the latest possible point in time when the uncompleted portions of a schedule activity can start based on the schedule network logic, the project completion date, and any schedule constraints.

**Lead.** The amount of time whereby a successor activity can be advanced with respect to a predecessor activity.

**Lessons Learned.** The knowledge gained during a project which shows how project events were addressed or should be addressed in the future for the purpose of improving future performance.

**Lessons Learned Register.** A project document used to record knowledge gained during a project so that it can be used in the current project and entered into the lessons learned repository.

**Lessons Learned Repository.** A store of historical information about lessons learned in projects.

**Level of Effort (LOE).** An activity that does not produce definitive end products and is measured by the passage of time.

**Life Cycle.** *See project life cycle.*

**Log.** A document used to record and describe or denote selected items identified during execution of a process or activity. Usually used with a modifier, such as issue, change, or assumption.

**Logical Relationship.** A dependency between two activities, or between an activity and a milestone.

**Make-or-Buy Analysis.** The process of gathering and organizing data about product requirements and analyzing them against available alternatives including the purchase or internal manufacture of the product.

**Make-or-Buy Decisions.** Decisions made regarding the external purchase or internal manufacture of a product.

**Manage Communications.** Manage Communications is the process of ensuring timely and appropriate collection, creation, distribution, storage, retrieval, management, monitoring, and the ultimate disposition of project information.

**Management Reserve.** An amount of the project budget or project schedule held outside of the performance measurement baseline (PMB) for management control purposes, that is reserved for unforeseen work that is within scope of the project.

**Management Skills.** The ability to plan, organize, direct, and control individuals or groups of people to achieve specific goals.

**Manage Project Knowledge.** The process of using existing knowledge and creating new knowledge to achieve the project's objectives and contribute to organizational learning.

**Manage Quality.** The process of translating the quality management plan into executable quality activities that incorporate the organization's quality policies into the project.

**Manage Stakeholder Engagement.** The process of communicating and working with stakeholders to meet their needs and expectations, address issues, and foster appropriate stakeholder involvement.

**Manage Team.** The process of tracking team member performance, providing feedback, resolving issues, and managing team changes to optimize project performance.

**Mandatory Dependency.** A relationship that is contractually required or inherent in the nature of the work.

**Master Schedule.** A summary-level project schedule that identifies the major deliverables and work breakdown structure components and key schedule milestones. *See also milestone schedule.*

**Matrix Diagrams.** A quality management and control tool used to perform data analysis within the organizational structure created in the matrix. The matrix diagram seeks to show the strength of relationships between factors, causes, and objectives that exist between the rows and columns that form the matrix.

**Matrix Organization.** Any organizational structure in which the project manager shares responsibility with the functional managers for assigning priorities and for directing the work of persons assigned to the project.

**Methodology.** A system of practices, techniques, procedures, and rules used by those who work in a discipline.

**Milestone.** A significant point or event in a project, program, or portfolio.

**Milestone Schedule.** A type of schedule that presents milestones with planned dates. See also master schedule.

**Mind-Mapping.** A technique used to consolidate ideas created through individual brainstorming sessions into a single map to reflect commonality and differences in understanding and to generate new ideas.

**Monitor.** Collect project performance data, produce performance measures, and report and disseminate performance information.

**Monitor and Control Project Work.** The process of tracking, reviewing, and reporting overall progress to meet the performance objectives defined in the project management plan.

**Monitor Communications.** The process of ensuring that the information needs of the project and its stakeholders are met.

**Monitoring and Controlling Process Group.** Those processes required to track, review, and regulate the progress and performance of the project; identify any areas in which changes to the plan are required; and initiate the corresponding changes.

**Monitor Risks.** The process of monitoring the implementation of agreed-upon risk response plans, tracking identified risks, identifying and analyzing new risks, and evaluating risk process effectiveness throughout the project.

**Monitor Stakeholder Engagement.** The process of monitoring project stakeholder relationships, and tailoring strategies for engaging stakeholders through the modification of engagement strategies and plans.

**Monte Carlo Simulation.** An analysis technique where a computer model is iterated many times, with the input values chosen at random for each iteration driven by the input data, including probability distributions and probabilistic branches. Outputs are generated to represent the range of possible outcomes for the project.

**Multicriteria Decision Analysis.** This technique utilizes a decision matrix to provide a systematic analytical approach for establishing criteria, such as risk levels, uncertainty, and valuation, to evaluate and rank many ideas.

**Network.** *See project schedule network diagram.*

**Network Logic.** All activity dependencies in a project schedule network diagram.

**Network Path.** A sequence of activities connected by logical relationships in a project schedule network diagram.

**Networking.** Establishing connections and relationships with other people from the same or other organizations.

**Node.** A point at which dependency lines connect on a schedule network diagram.

**Nominal Group Technique.** A technique that enhances brainstorming with a voting process used to rank the most useful ideas for further brainstorming or for prioritization.

**Objective.** Something toward which work is to be directed, a strategic position to be attained, a purpose to be achieved, a result to be obtained, a product to be produced, or a service to be performed.

**Opportunity.** A risk that would have a positive effect on one or more project objectives.

**Organizational Breakdown Structure (OBS).** A hierarchical representation of the project organization, which illustrates the relationship between project activities and the organizational units that will perform those activities.

**Organizational Learning.** A discipline concerned with the way individuals, groups, and organizations develop knowledge.

**Organizational Process Assets.** Plans, processes, policies, procedures, and knowledge bases that are specific to and used by the performing organization.

**Output.** A product, result, or service generated by a process. May be an input to a successor process.

**Overall Project Risk.** The effect of uncertainty on the project as a whole, arising from all sources of uncertainty including individual risks, representing the exposure of stakeholders to the implications of variations in project outcome, both positive and negative.

**Parametric Estimating.** An estimating technique in which an algorithm is used to calculate cost or duration based on historical data and project parameters.

**Path Convergence.** A relationship in which a schedule activity has more than one predecessor.

**Path Divergence.** A relationship in which a schedule activity has more than one successor.

**Percent Complete.** An estimate expressed as a percent of the amount of work that has been completed on an activity or a work breakdown structure component.

**Performance Measurement Baseline (PMB).** Integrated scope, schedule, and cost baselines used for comparison to manage, measure, and control project execution.

**Performance Reviews.** A technique that is used to measure, compare, and analyze actual performance of work in progress on the project against the baseline.

**Perform Integrated Change Control.** The process of reviewing all change requests; approving changes and managing changes to deliverables, organizational process assets, project documents, and the project management plan; and communicating the decisions.

**Perform Qualitative Risk Analysis.** The process of prioritizing individual project risks for further analysis or action by assessing their probability of occurrence and impact as well as other characteristics.

**Perform Quantitative Risk Analysis.** The process of numerically analyzing the combined effect of identified individual project risks and other sources of uncertainty on overall project objectives.

**Phase.** *See project phase.*

**Phase Gate.** A review at the end of a phase in which a decision is made to continue to the next phase, to continue with modification, or to end a project or program.

**Plan Communications Management.** The process of developing an appropriate approach and plan for project communication activities based on the information needs of each stakeholder or group, available organizational assets, and the needs of the project.

**Plan Cost Management.** The process of defining how the project costs will be estimated, budgeted, managed, monitored, and controlled.

**Planned Value (PV).** The authorized budget assigned to scheduled work.

**Planning Package.** A work breakdown structure component below the control account with known work content but without detailed schedule activities. See also control account.

**Planning Process Group.** Those processes required to establish the scope of the project, refine the objectives, and define the course of action required to attain the objectives that the project was undertaken to achieve.

**Plan Procurement Management.** The process of documenting project procurement decisions, specifying the approach, and identifying potential sellers.

**Plan Quality Management.** The process of identifying quality requirements and/or standards for the project and its deliverables, and documenting how the project will demonstrate compliance with quality requirements and/or standards.

**Plan Resource Management.** The process of defining how to estimate, acquire, manage, and utilize physical and team resources.

**Plan Risk Management.** The process of defining how to conduct risk management activities for a project.

**Plan Risk Responses.** The process of developing options, selecting strategies, and agreeing on actions to address overall project risk exposure, as well as to treat individual project risks.

**Plan Schedule Management.** The process of establishing the policies, procedures, and documentation for planning, developing, managing, executing, and controlling the project schedule.

**Plan Scope Management.** The process of creating a scope management plan that documents how the project and product scope will be defined, validated, and controlled.

**Plan Stakeholder Engagement.** The process of developing approaches to involve project stakeholders, based on their needs, expectations, interests, and potential impact on the project.

**Plurality.** Decisions made by the largest block in a group, even if a majority is not achieved.

**Policy.** A structured pattern of actions adopted by an organization such that the organization's policy can be explained as a set of basic principles that govern the organization's conduct.

**Portfolio.** Projects, programs, subsidiary portfolios, and operations managed as a group to achieve strategic objectives.

**Portfolio Management.** The centralized management of one or more portfolios to achieve strategic objectives.

**Practice.** A specific type of professional or management activity that contributes to the execution of a process and that may employ one or more techniques and tools.

**Precedence Diagramming Method (PDM).** A technique used for constructing a schedule model in which activities are represented by nodes and are graphically linked by one or more logical relationships to show the sequence in which the activities are to be performed.

**Precedence Relationship.** A logical dependency used in the precedence diagramming method.

**Predecessor Activity.** An activity that logically comes before a dependent activity in a schedule.

**Predictive Life Cycle.** A form of project life cycle in which the project scope, time, and cost are determined in the early phases of the life cycle.

**Preventive Action.** An intentional activity that ensures the future performance of the project work is aligned with the project management plan.

**Probability and Impact Matrix.** A grid for mapping the probability of occurrence of each risk and its impact on project objectives if that risk occurs.

**Procedure.** An established method of accomplishing a consistent performance or result, a procedure typically can be described as the sequence of steps that will be used to execute a process.

**Process.** A systematic series of activities directed towards causing an end result such that one or more inputs will be acted upon to create one or more outputs.

**Procurement Audits.** The review of contracts and contracting processes for completeness, accuracy, and effectiveness.

**Procurement Documentation.** All documents used in signing, executing, and closing an agreement. Procurement documentation may include documents predating the project.

**Procurement Management Plan.** A component of the project or program management plan that describes how a project team will acquire goods and services from outside of the performing organization.

**Procurement Statement of Work.** Describes the procurement item in sufficient detail to allow prospective sellers to determine if they are capable of providing the products, services, or results.

**Procurement Strategy.** The approach by the buyer to determine the project delivery method and the type of legally binding agreement(s) that should be used to deliver the desired results.

**Product.** An artifact that is produced, is quantifiable, and can be either an end item in itself or a component item. Additional words for products are material and goods. See also deliverable.

**Product Analysis.** For projects that have a product as a deliverable, it is a tool to define scope that generally means asking questions about a product and forming answers to describe the use, characteristics, and other relevant aspects of what is going to be manufactured.

**Product Life Cycle.** The series of phases that represent the evolution of a product, from concept through delivery, growth, maturity, and to retirement.

**Product Scope.** The features and functions that characterize a product, service, or result.

**Product Scope Description.** The documented narrative description of the product scope.

**Program**. Related projects, subsidiary programs, and program activities that are managed in a coordinated manner to obtain benefits not available from managing them individually.

**Program Management.** The application of knowledge, skills, and principles to a program to achieve the program objectives and obtain benefits and control not available by managing program components individually.

**Progressive Elaboration.** The iterative process of increasing the level of detail in a project management plan as greater amounts of information and more accurate estimates become available.

**Project.** A temporary endeavor undertaken to create a unique product, service, or result.

**Project Calendar.** A calendar that identifies working days and shifts that are available for scheduled activities.

**Project Charter.** A document issued by the project initiator or sponsor that formally authorizes the existence of a project and provides the project manager with the authority to apply organizational resources to project activities.

**Project Communications Management.** Project Communications Management includes the processes required to ensure timely and appropriate planning, collection, creation, distribution, storage, retrieval, management, control, monitoring, and ultimate disposition of project information.

**Project Cost Management.** Project Cost Management includes the processes involved in planning, estimating, budgeting, financing, funding, managing, and controlling costs so the project can be completed within the approved budget.

**Project Funding Requirements.** Forecast project costs to be paid that are derived from the cost baseline for total or periodic requirements, including projected expenditures plus anticipated liabilities.

**Project Governance.** The framework, functions, and processes that guide project management activities in order to create a unique product, service, or result to meet organizational, strategic, and operational goals.

**Project Initiation.** Launching a process that can result in the authorization of a new project.

**Project Integration Management.** Project Integration Management includes the processes and activities to identify, define, combine, unify, and coordinate the various processes and project management activities within the Project Management Process Groups.

**Project Life Cycle.** The series of phases that a project passes through from its start to its completion.

**Project Management.** The application of knowledge, skills, tools, and techniques to project activities to meet the project requirements.

**Project Management Body of Knowledge.** A term that describes the knowledge within the profession of project management. The project management body of knowledge includes proven traditional practices that are widely applied as well as innovative practices that are emerging in the profession.

**Project Management Information System.** An information system consisting of the tools and techniques used to gather, integrate, and disseminate the outputs of project management processes.

**Project Management Knowledge Area.** An identified area of project management defined by its knowledge requirements and described in terms of its component processes, practices, inputs, outputs, tools, and techniques.

**Project Management Office (PMO).** A management structure that standardizes the project-related governance processes and facilitates the sharing of resources, methodologies, tools, and techniques.

**Project Management Plan.** The document that describes how the project will be executed, monitored and controlled, and closed.

**Project Management Process Group.** A logical grouping of project management inputs, tools and techniques, and outputs. The Project Management Process Groups include initiating processes, planning processes, executing processes, monitoring and controlling processes, and closing processes. Project Management Process Groups are not project phases.

**Project Management System.** The aggregation of the processes, tools, techniques, methodologies, resources, and procedures to manage a project.

**Project Management Team.** The members of the project team who are directly involved in project management activities. *See also Project Team.*

**Project Manager (PM).** The person assigned by the performing organization to lead the team that is responsible for achieving the project objectives.

**Project Organization Chart.** A document that graphically depicts the project team members and their interrelationships for a specific project.

**Project Phase.** A collection of logically related project activities that culminates in the completion of one or more deliverables.

**Project Procurement Management.** Project Procurement Management includes the processes necessary to purchase or acquire products, services, or results needed from outside the project team.

**Project Quality Management.** Project Quality Management includes the processes for incorporating the organization's quality policy regarding planning, managing, and controlling project and product quality requirements, in order to meet stakeholders' expectations.

**Project Resource Management.** Project Resource Management includes the processes to identify, acquire, and manage the resources needed for the successful completion of the project.

**Project Risk Management.** Project Risk Management includes the processes of conducting risk management planning, identification, analysis, response planning, response implementation, and monitoring risk on a project.

**Project Schedule.** An output of a schedule model that presents linked activities with planned dates, durations, milestones, and resources.

**Project Schedule Management.** Project Schedule Management includes the processes required to manage the timely completion of the project.

**Project Schedule Network Diagram.** A graphical representation of the logical relationships among the project schedule activities.

**Project Scope.** The work performed to deliver a product, service, or result with the specified features and functions.

**Project Scope Management.** Project Scope Management includes the processes required to ensure that the project includes all the work required, and only the work required, to complete the project successfully.

**Project Scope Statement.** The description of the project scope, major deliverables, and exclusions.

**Project Stakeholder Management.** Project Stakeholder Management includes the processes required to identify the people, groups, or organizations that could impact or be impacted by the project, to analyze stakeholder expectations and their impact on the project, and to develop appropriate management strategies for effectively engaging stakeholders in project decisions and execution.

**Project Team.** A set of individuals who support the project manager in performing the work of the project to achieve its objectives. See also Project Management Team.

**Project Team Directory.** A documented list of project team members, their project roles, and communication information.

**Proposal Evaluation Techniques.** The process of reviewing proposals provided by suppliers to support contract award decisions.

**Prototypes.** A method of obtaining early feedback on requirements by providing a working model of the expected product before actually building it.

**Quality.** The degree to which a set of inherent characteristics fulfills requirements.

**Quality Audits.** A quality audit is a structured, independent process to determine if project activities comply with organizational and project policies, processes, and procedures.

**Quality Checklists.** A structured tool used to verify that a set of required steps has been performed.

**Quality Control Measurements.** The documented results of control quality activities.

**Quality Management Plan.** A component of the project or program management plan that describes how applicable policies, procedures, and guidelines will be implemented to achieve the quality objectives.

**Quality Management System.** The organizational framework whose structure provides the policies, processes, procedures, and resources required to implement the quality management plan. The typical project quality management plan should be compatible to the organization's quality management system.

**Quality Metrics.** A description of a project or product attribute and how to measure it.

**Quality Policy.** A policy specific to the Project Quality Management Knowledge Area, it establishes the basic principles that should govern the organization's actions as it implements its system for quality management.

**Quality Report.** A project document that includes quality management issues, recommendations for corrective actions, and a summary of findings from quality control activities and may include recommendations for process, project, and product improvements.

**Quality Requirement.** A condition or capability that will be used to assess conformance by validating the acceptability of an attribute for the quality of a result.

**Questionnaires.** Written sets of questions designed to quickly accumulate information from a large number of respondents.

**RACI Chart.** A common type of responsibility assignment matrix that uses responsible, accountable, consult, and inform statuses to define the involvement of stakeholders in project activities.

**Regression Analysis.** An analytical technique where a series of input variables are examined in relation to their corresponding output results in order to develop a mathematical or statistical relationship.

**Regulations.** Requirements imposed by a governmental body. These requirements can establish product, process, or service characteristics, including applicable administrative provisions that have government-mandated compliance.

**Request for Information (RFI).** A type of procurement document whereby the buyer requests a potential seller to provide various pieces of information related to a product or service or seller capability.

**Request for Proposal (RFP).** A type of procurement document used to request proposals from prospective sellers of products or services. In some application areas, it may have a narrower or more specific meaning.

**Request for Quotation (RFQ).** A type of procurement document used to request price quotations from prospective sellers of common or standard products or services. Sometimes used in place of request for proposal and, in some application areas, it may have a narrower or more specific meaning.

**Requirement.** A condition or capability that is necessary to be present in a product, service, or result to satisfy a business need.

**Requirements Documentation.** A description of how individual requirements meet the business need for the project.

**Requirements Management Plan.** A component of the project or program management plan that describes how requirements will be analyzed, documented, and managed.

**Requirements Traceability Matrix.** A grid that links product requirements from their origin to the deliverables that satisfy them.

**Reserve.** A provision in the project management plan to mitigate cost and/or schedule risk. Often used with a modifier (e.g., management reserve, contingency reserve) to provide further detail on what types of risk are meant to be mitigated.

**Reserve Analysis.** An analytical technique to determine the essential features and relationships of components in the project management plan to establish a reserve for the schedule duration, budget, estimated cost, or funds for a project.

**Residual Risk.** The risk that remains after risk responses have been implemented.

**Resource.** A team member or any physical item needed to complete the project.

**Resource Breakdown Structure.** A hierarchical representation of resources by category and type.

**Resource Calendar.** A calendar that identifies the working days and shifts upon which each specific resource is available.

**Resource Histogram.** A bar chart showing the amount of time that a resource is scheduled to work over a series of time periods.

**Resource Leveling.** A resource optimization technique in which adjustments are made to the project schedule to optimize the allocation of resources and which may affect critical path. *See also resource optimization technique and resource smoothing.*

**Resource Management Plan.** A component of the project management plan that describes how project resources are acquired, allocated, monitored, and controlled.

**Resource Manager.** An individual with management authority over one or more resources.

**Resource Optimization Technique.** A technique in which activity start and finish dates are adjusted to balance demand for resources with the available supply. *See also resource leveling and resource smoothing.*

**Resource Requirements.** The types and quantities of resources required for each activity in a work package.

**Resource Smoothing.** A resource optimization technique in which free and total float are used without affecting the critical path. See also resource leveling and resource optimization technique.

**Responsibility.** An assignment that can be delegated within a project management plan such that the assigned resource incurs a duty to perform the requirements of the assignment.

**Responsibility Assignment Matrix (RAM).** A grid that shows the project resources assigned to each work package.

**Result.** An output from performing project management processes and activities. Results include outcomes (e.g., integrated systems, revised process, restructured organization, tests, trained personnel, etc.) and documents (e.g., policies, plans, studies, procedures, specifications, reports, etc.). See also deliverable.

**Rework.** Action taken to bring a defective or nonconforming component into compliance with requirements or specifications.

**Risk.** An uncertain event or condition that, if it occurs, has a positive or negative effect on one or more project objectives.

**Risk Acceptance.** A risk response strategy whereby the project team decides to acknowledge the risk and not take any action unless the risk occurs.

**Risk Appetite.** The degree of uncertainty an organization or individual is willing to accept in anticipation of a reward.

**Risk Audit.** A type of audit used to consider the effectiveness of the risk management process.

**Risk Avoidance.** A risk response strategy whereby the project team acts to eliminate the threat or protect the project from its impact.

**Risk Breakdown Structure (RBS).** A hierarchical representation of potential sources of risks.

**Risk Categorization.** Organization by sources of risk (e.g., using the RBS), the area of the project affected (e.g., using the WBS), or other useful category (e.g., project phase) to determine the areas of the project most exposed to the effects of uncertainty.

**Risk Category.** A group of potential causes of risk.

**Risk Data Quality Assessment.** Technique to evaluate the degree to which the data about risks is useful for risk management.

**Risk Enhancement.** A risk response strategy whereby the project team acts to increase the probability of occurrence or impact of an opportunity.

**Risk Escalation.** A risk response strategy whereby the team acknowledges that a risk is outside of its sphere of influence and shifts the ownership of the risk to a higher level of the organization where it is more effectively managed.

**Risk Exploiting.** A risk response strategy whereby the project team acts to ensure that an opportunity occurs.

**Risk Exposure.** An aggregate measure of the potential impact of all risks at any given point in time in a project, program, or portfolio.

**Risk Management Plan.** A component of the project, program, or portfolio management plan that describes how risk management activities will be structured and performed.

**Risk Mitigation.** A risk response strategy whereby the project team acts to decrease the probability of occurrence or impact of a threat.

**Risk Owner.** The person responsible for monitoring the risks and for selecting and implementing an appropriate risk response strategy.

**Risk Register.** A repository in which outputs of risk management processes are recorded.

**Risk Report.** A project document developed progressively throughout the Project Risk Management processes, which summarizes information on individual project risks and the level of overall project risk.

**Risk Review.** A meeting to examine and document the effectiveness of risk responses in dealing with overall project risk and with identified individual project risks.

**Risk Sharing.** A risk response strategy whereby the project team allocates ownership of an opportunity to a third party who is best able to capture the benefit of that opportunity.

**Risk Threshold.** The measure of acceptable variation around an objective that reflects the risk appetite of the organization and stakeholders. *See also risk appetite.*

**Risk Transference.** A risk response strategy whereby the project team shifts the impact of a threat to a third party, together with ownership of the response.

**Role.** A defined function to be performed by a project team member, such as testing, filing, inspecting, or coding.

**Rolling Wave Planning.** An iterative planning technique in which the work to be accomplished in the near term is planned in detail, while the work in the future is planned at a higher level.

**Root Cause Analysis.** An analytical technique used to determine the basic underlying reason that causes a variance or a defect or a risk. A root cause may underlie more than one variance or defect or risk.

**Schedule.** *See project schedule and schedule model.*

**Schedule Baseline.** The approved version of a schedule model that can be changed using formal change control procedures and is used as the basis for comparison to actual results.

**Schedule Compression.** A technique used to shorten the schedule duration without reducing the project scope.

**Schedule Data.** The collection of information for describing and controlling the schedule.

**Schedule Forecasts.** Estimates or predictions of conditions and events in the project's future based on information and knowledge available at the time the schedule is calculated.

**Schedule Management Plan.** A component of the project or program management plan that establishes the criteria and the activities for developing, monitoring, and controlling the schedule.

**Schedule Model.** A representation of the plan for executing the project's activities including durations, dependencies, and other planning information, used to produce a project schedule along with other scheduling artifacts.

**Schedule Network Analysis.** A technique to identify early and late start dates, as well as early and late finish dates, for the uncompleted portions of project activities.

**Schedule Performance Index (SPI).** A measure of schedule efficiency expressed as the ratio of earned value to planned value.

**Schedule Variance (SV).** A measure of schedule performance expressed as the difference between the earned value and the planned value.

**Scheduling Tool.** A tool that provides schedule component names, definitions, structural relationships, and formats that support the application of a scheduling method.

**Scope.** The sum of the products, services, and results to be provided as a project. See also project scope and product scope.

**Scope Baseline.** The approved version of a scope statement, work breakdown structure (WBS), and its associated WBS dictionary, that can be changed using formal change control procedures and is used as a basis for comparison to actual results.

**Scope Creep.** The uncontrolled expansion to product or project scope without adjustments to time, cost, and resources.

**Scope Management Plan.** A component of the project or program management plan that describes how the scope will be defined, developed, monitored, controlled, and validated.

**Secondary Risk.** A risk that arises as a direct result of implementing a risk response.

**Self-Organizing Teams.** A team formation where the team functions with an absence of centralized control.

**Seller.** A provider or supplier of products, services, or results to an organization.

**Seller Proposals.** Formal responses from sellers to a request for proposal or other procurement document specifying the price, commercial terms of sale, and technical specifications or capabilities the seller will do for the requesting organization that, if accepted, would bind the seller to perform the resulting agreement.

**Sensitivity Analysis.** An analysis technique to determine which individual project risks or other sources of uncertainty have the most potential impact on project outcomes, by correlating variations in project outcomes with variations in elements of a quantitative risk analysis model.

**Sequence Activities.** The process of identifying and documenting relationships among the project activities.

**Service Level Agreement (SLA).** A contract between a service provider (either internal or external) and the end user that defines the level of service expected from the service provider.

**Simulation.** An analytical technique that models the combined effect of uncertainties to evaluate their potential impact on objectives.

**Source Selection Criteria.** A set of attributes desired by the buyer which a seller is required to meet or exceed to be selected for a contract.

**Specification.** A precise statement of the needs to be satisfied and the essential characteristics that are required.

**Specification Limits.** The area, on either side of the centerline, or mean, of data plotted on a control chart that meets the customer's requirements for a product or service. This area may be greater than or less than the area defined by the control limits. See also control limits.

**Sponsor.** A person or group who provides resources and support for the project, program, or portfolio and is accountable for enabling success.

**Sponsoring Organization.** The entity responsible for providing the project's sponsor and a conduit for project funding or other project resources.

**Stakeholder.** An individual, group, or organization that may affect, be affected by, or perceive itself to be affected by a decision, activity, or outcome of a project, program, or portfolio.

**Stakeholder Analysis.** A technique of systematically gathering and analyzing quantitative and qualitative information to determine whose interests should be taken into account throughout the project.

**Stakeholder Engagement Assessment Matrix.** A matrix that compares current and desired stakeholder engagement levels.

**Stakeholder Engagement Plan.** A component of the project management plan that identifies the strategies and actions required to promote productive involvement of stakeholders in project or program decision making and execution.

**Stakeholder Register.** A project document including the identification, assessment, and classification of project stakeholders.

**Standard.** A document established by an authority, custom, or general consent as a model or example.

**Start Date.** A point in time associated with a schedule activity's start, usually qualified by one of the following: actual, planned, estimated, scheduled, early, late, target, baseline, or current.

**Start-to-Finish (SF).** A logical relationship in which a predecessor activity cannot finish until a successor activity has started.

**Start-to-Start (SS).** A logical relationship in which a successor activity cannot start until a predecessor activity has started.

**Statement of Work (SOW).** A narrative description of products, services, or results to be delivered by the project.

**Statistical Sampling.** Choosing part of a population of interest for inspection.

**Successor Activity.** A dependent activity that logically comes after another activity in a schedule.

**Summary Activity.** A group of related schedule activities aggregated and displayed as a single activity.

**SWOT Analysis.** Analysis of strengths, weaknesses, opportunities, and threats of an organization, project, or option.

**Tacit Knowledge.** Personal knowledge that can be difficult to articulate and share such as beliefs, experience, and insights.

**Tailoring.** Determining the appropriate combination of processes, inputs, tools, techniques, outputs, and life cycle phases to manage a project.

**Team Charter.** A document that records the team values, agreements, and operating guidelines, as well as establishing clear expectations regarding acceptable behavior by project team members.

**Team Management Plan.** A component of the resource management plan that describes when and how team members will be acquired and how long they will be needed.

**Technique.** A defined systematic procedure employed by a human resource to perform an activity to produce a product or result or deliver a service, and that may employ one or more tools.

**Templates.** A partially complete document in a predefined format that provides a defined structure for collecting, organizing, and presenting information and data.

**Test and Evaluation Documents.** Project documents that describe the activities used to determine if the product meets the quality objectives stated in the quality management plan.

**Threat.** A risk that would have a negative effect on one or more project objectives.

**Three-Point Estimating.** A technique used to estimate cost or duration by applying an average or weighted average of optimistic, pessimistic, and most likely estimates when there is uncertainty with the individual activity estimates.

**Threshold.** A predetermined value of a measurable project variable that represents a limit that requires action to be taken if it is reached.

**Time and Material Contract (T&M).** A type of contract that is a hybrid contractual arrangement containing aspects of both cost-reimbursable and fixed-price contracts.

**To-Complete Performance Index (TCPI).** A measure of the cost performance that is required to be achieved with the remaining resources in order to meet a specified management goal, expressed as the ratio of the cost to finish the outstanding work to the remaining budget.

**Tolerance.** The quantified description of acceptable variation for a quality requirement.

**Tool.** Something tangible, such as a template or software program, used in performing an activity to produce a product or result.

**Tornado Diagram.** A special type of bar chart used in sensitivity analysis for comparing the relative importance of the variables.

**Total Float.** The amount of time that a schedule activity can be delayed or extended from its early start date without delaying the project finish date or violating a schedule constraint.

**Trend Analysis.** An analytical technique that uses mathematical models to forecast future outcomes based on historical results.

**Trigger Condition.** An event or situation that indicates that a risk is about to occur.

**Unanimity.** Agreement by everyone in the group on a single course of action.

**Update.** A modification to any deliverable, project management plan component, or project document that is not under formal change control.

**Validate Scope.** The process of formalizing acceptance of the completed project deliverables.

**Validation.** The assurance that a product, service, or result meets the needs of the customer and other identified stakeholders. Contrast with *verification*.

**Variance.** A quantifiable deviation, departure, or divergence away from a known baseline or expected value.

**Variance Analysis.** A technique for determining the cause and degree of difference between the baseline and actual performance.

**Variance At Completion (VAC).** A projection of the amount of budget deficit or surplus, expressed as the difference between the budget at completion and the estimate at completion.

**Variation.** An actual condition that is different from the expected condition that is contained in the baseline plan.

**Verification.** The evaluation of whether or not a product, service, or result complies with a regulation, requirement, specification, or imposed condition. Contrast with *validation*.

**Verified Deliverables.** Completed project deliverables that have been checked and confirmed for correctness through the Control Quality process.

**Virtual Teams.** Groups of people with a shared goal who fulfill their roles with little or no time spent meeting face to face.

**Voice of the Customer.** A planning technique used to provide products, services, and results that truly reflect customer requirements by translating those customer requirements into the appropriate technical requirements for each phase of project product development.

**WBS Dictionary.** A document that provides detailed deliverable, activity, and scheduling information about each component in the work breakdown structure.

**What-If Scenario Analysis.** The process of evaluating scenarios in order to predict their effect on project objectives.

**Work Breakdown Structure (WBS).** A hierarchical decomposition of the total scope of work to be carried out by the project team to accomplish the project objectives and create the required deliverables.

**Work Breakdown Structure Component.** An entry in the work breakdown structure that can be at any level.

**Work Package.** The work defined at the lowest level of the work breakdown structure for which cost and duration are estimated and managed.

**Work Performance Data.** The raw observations and measurements identified during activities being performed to carry out the project work.

**Work Performance Information.** The performance data collected from controlling processes, analyzed in comparison with project management plan components, project documents, and other work performance information.

**Work Performance Reports.** The physical or electronic representation of work performance information compiled in project documents, intended to generate decisions, actions, or awareness.

# INDEX

## A

Agile release planning, 216

Agreements, 460, 698. *See also* Contract(s); Service level agreements
    as input, 78, 109, 125, 141, 208, 251, 355, 413, 496, 510, 519
    master services, 465
    as output, 489

Alternative dispute resolution (ADR), 498

Alternatives analysis, 111, 119, 202, 245, 292, 325, 356, 446, 533
    definition, 699

Ambiguity risk, 398, 399

Analogous estimating, 200, 244, 324, 699

Analytical techniques, 699

AON. *See* Activity-on-node

Approved change request, 115
    as input, 93, 300, 301, 495, 496
    as output, 120
    quality audits and, 295
    schedule baseline and, 229

Artifacts
    communication, 375
    project, 558–559

Assessments, individual and team, 342

Assets. *See* Organizational process assets (OPAs)

Assignment matrix (RAM), 317

Assumption(s), 33, 699

Assumption and constraint analysis, 415, 521

Assumption log
    definition, 699
    as input, 108, 124, 141, 152, 188, 198, 207, 280, 323, 412, 421, 430, 495, 519
    as output, 81, 97, 155, 194, 204, 221, 230, 247, 270, 320, 327, 358, 418, 427, 448, 458, 515

Attribute(s), 149

Attribute sampling, 274, 699

Audio conferencing, 340

Audits, 118, 276, 498
    configuration item verification and, 118
    procurement, 494, 714
    quality, 290, 294–295, 296, 718
    risk, 456, 458, 720

Authority, 699. *See also* Governance frameworks

Autocratic decision making, 119, 144

Automated tools, 73, 118

Avoidance, overall project risk and, 445

# B

BAC. *See* Budget at completion

Backward pass, 210, 699

Bar chart, 217, 699

Baseline(s), 87, 699. *See also* Cost baseline; Scope baseline

Baseline schedule. *See* Schedule baseline

Basis of estimates, 108, 204, 699
    as input, 116, 124, 208, 250, 430
    as output, 229, 230, 247, 270, 326

Benchmarking, 143, 281, 699

Benefits management, project success and, 546–547

Benefits management plan, 33, 251, 469, 509, 699

Best practices
    benchmarking and, 143, 281, 399
    discretionary dependencies and, 191

Beta distribution, 245

Bid(s), 477. *See also* Proposals
    winning bidder and, 462

Bidder. *See* Seller(s)

Bidder conferences, 487, 699

Bid documents, 477, 485, 699

BIM. *See* Building information model

Body of knowledge (BOK), 1, 2, 69

BOK. *See* Body of knowledge

Bottom-up estimating, 324
    definition, 700
    description of, 202, 244

Brainstorming, 78, 80, 85, 142, 144, 281, 414, 416, 511

Brain writing, 511

Bubble chart, 425–426

Budget(s)
    definition, 700
    time-phased project, 87, 248, 254

Budget at completion (BAC), 261, 262, 264, 430, 700

Buffer. *See* Reserve

Building information model (BIM), 463

Burndown chart, 226

*Business Analysis for Practitioners: A Practice Guide,* 7, 33, 140

Business case
    business documents and, 77–78
    definition, 700
    as input, 125, 251, 469, 509
    project, 30–32
Business documents, 29–30
    business case and, 77–78
    definition, 559
    as input, 125, 141, 251, 469, 509
    project life cycle and, 30
    project management, 29–30
Business environment, 10
Business management plan, 125
Business management skills, 58–60
    PMI Talent Triangle® and, 56, 57
Business requirements, 148
Business value, 8, 10, 148
    definition, 7, 700
    state transition and, 6
Buyer
    procurement process and, 461
    seller and, 460–461
    trial engagements and, 464
    winning bidder, 462
Buyer-seller relationship, 461

# C

CA. *See* Control account
Calendar. *See* Project calendar; Resource calendars
Cause-and-effect diagrams, 293, 294, 304, 700
CCB. *See* Change control board
Change(s)
    contested, 498
    definition, 700
    projects and, 6
Change control. *See also* Perform Integrated Change Control process
    meetings, 120
    procedures, 40
    tools, 118–119, 700

Change control board (CCB), 115, 120, 700
Change control system, 700. *See also* Contract change control system
Change log
    definition, 700
    as input, 92, 124, 382, 510, 519, 525
    as output, 529
Change management plan, 88, 116, 169, 495, 525, 700
Change request(s). *See also* Approved change request; Change management plan; Perform Integrated Change Control process; Requested change
    approved change requests review, 305
    components requiring, 171, 186, 221, 229, 287, 297, 351, 358, 387, 393, 490, 500, 515, 529
    definition, 700
    as input, 117, 301
    as output, 96, 112, 166, 170, 186, 220, 228, 269, 296, 306, 334, 343, 350, 357, 393, 447, 451, 457, 479, 489, 499, 514, 528, 535
    project baselines and, 115
    status tracking, 124
    tools and, 119
    types of, 96, 112
Charter. *See* Develop Project Charter process; Project charter; Team charter
Checklist(s), 85, 302, 414. *See also* Quality checklists
Checklist analysis, 700
Check sheet, 302, 700
Claim, 700
Claims administration, 498, 701
Closed procurements, 499
Close Project or Phase process, 121–128, 634–635
    definition, 701
    inputs, 124–126
    outputs, 127–128
    overview, 121–123
    tools and techniques, 126–127
Closing Process Group, 23, 633–635
    definition, 701
    inputs and outputs, 634
    overview of, 633
Code of accounts, 701
*Code of Ethics and Professional Conduct,* 3

Intellectual property rights, 470, 480, 483, 485, 491, 495

Interactive communication, 374

Interdependencies, 14, 16, 102–103

Internal dependencies, 192

Internal rate of return (IRR), 34, 473

Internal stakeholders, 550

Interpersonal and team skills, 709

Interpersonal communication, 374

Interpersonal skills, 144–145, 153
    definition, 709
    "soft" skills, 53
    team skills and, 332–333, 341, 348–350, 357, 375–376, 386, 392, 416, 424, 432, 442, 451, 488, 527, 534
    types of, 80, 104, 534, 552

Interviews, 80, 85, 142, 282, 414, 432, 709

Invitation for bid (IFB), 709

IRR. *See* Internal rate of return

Ishikawa diagrams, 293

Issue, 709

Issue log
    definition, 709
    as input, 124, 347, 354, 382, 390, 412, 455, 510, 519, 525, 532
    as output, 96, 113, 297, 306, 351, 358, 387, 393, 418, 427, 452, 458, 515, 529, 536

Iteration backlog, 203, 226

Iteration burndown chart, 226

Iteration length, 182

Iteration planning, 215

Iterative activity, 33

Iterative life cycle, 19, 151, 709

Iterative planning technique, 185, 721

Iterative process, 205, 209, 411

# J

JAD. *See* Joint application design/development (JAD) sessions

"Job shadowing," 145

Joint application design/development (JAD) sessions, 145

Joint venture, 444, 445, 476

Judgment. *See* Expert judgment

# K

Kaizen, 310

Kanban system, 177

Key concepts
    Project Communications Management and, 360–363
    Project Cost Management and, 233
    Project Integration Management and, 72
    Project Procurement Management and, 460–462
    Project Quality Management and, 273–275
    Project Resource Management and, 309–310
    Project Risk Management and, 397–398
    Project Schedule Management and, 175
    Project Scope Management and, 131
    Project Stakeholder Engagement and, 504–505

Key performance indicators (KPIs), 95, 389

Key stakeholder list, 81, 314, 368, 509

Knowledge, 709. *See also* Manage Project Knowledge process
    body of, 1
    explicit, 100, 706
    product, management of, 73
    project management and, 16
    project manager and, 52
    repositories for, 41
    tacit, 100, 724

Knowledge Areas, 23–25, 553
    mapping of, 24–25, 556
    overview, 23–25
    *PMBOK® Guide* key components and, 18
    Process Groups and, 24–25, 556

Knowledge management, 133, 365
    misconceptions, 100
    product, 73
    project, 73
    tools and techniques, 103

Known risks, 31, 399

"Known-unknowns," 202, 245

KPIs. *See* Key performance indicators

# L

Lag(s)
adjusting, 228
definition, 193, 709
example of, 192
leads and, 192–193, 214
Language, 365
Late finish date (LF), 210, 709
Late start date (LS), 210, 709
Law of diminishing returns, 197
Lead(s)
adjusting, 228
definition, 192, 709
example of, 192
lags and, 192–193, 214
Leader(s), qualities and skills of, 61–62
Leadership, 534
management compared to, 64–66
styles, 65
Leadership skills, 60–63, 350
getting things done, 62–63
people, dealing with, 60
PMI Talent Triangle® and, 56, 57
politics, power and, 62–63
qualities and, 61–62
Lean Six Sigma, 275
Least cost method, 473
Legal requirements, 78, 369, 370
Legal rights, 512
Lessons learned, 208. *See also* Retrospectives
definition, 709
meetings, 305
tailoring considerations, 74
Lessons learned register
definition, 709
description of, 104
as input, 92, 101, 108, 124, 141, 165, 169, 198, 208, 225, 242, 291, 300, 339, 347, 354, 382, 390, 412, 440, 450, 455, 484, 495, 525, 532
as output, 97, 104, 113, 167, 171, 204, 221, 230, 247, 270, 287, 297, 306, 327, 335, 344, 351, 358, 387, 393, 418, 448, 452, 458, 480, 491, 500, 529, 536

Lessons learned repository
definition, 709
as output, 128, 501
Leveling. *See* Resource leveling
Level of accuracy, 182, 238
Level of effort (LoE), 300, 325, 450, 709
Level of precision, 238
Lexicon. *See PMI Lexicon of Project Management Terms*
LF. *See* Late finish date
Life cycle. *See also* Iterative life cycle; Predictive life cycle; Product life cycle; Project life cycle
attributes and, 20
definition, 710
development, 19, 74
incremental, 19, 708
iterative, 19, 151, 709
predictive, 19, 714
Life cycle approach, 178, 311
Listening techniques, 386, 534. *See also* Active listening
LoE. *See* Level of effort
Log, 710. *See also* Issue log
Logical data model, 284
Logical relationship, 710. *See also* Precedence Diagramming Method (PDM); Precedence relationship
Logic bar chart, 218
Logistics, 464
Long-lead items, 464
LS. *See* Late start date

# M

Majority, 144
Make-or-buy analysis, 473, 476, 710
Make-or-buy decisions, 473, 479, 710
Make versus buy decision, 241
Manageability, risk and, 424
Manage Communications process, 379–388, 605–606
definition, 710
inputs, 381–383
outputs, 387–388
overview, 379–381
tools and techniques, 383–386

# Q

QFD. *See* Quality Function Deployment

Qualifications only selection method, 473

Qualitative risk analysis. *See* Perform Qualitative Risk Analysis process

Quality. *See also* Plan Quality Management process; Project Quality Management
  definition, 718
  grade and, 274

Quality assurance, 289. *See also* Manage Quality process

Quality audits, 290, 294–296, 718

Quality checklists, 292, 718

Quality control measurements
  definition, 718
  as input, 124, 291
  as output, 305

Quality function deployment, 145

Quality improvement
  initiatives, 275
  methods, 296

Quality management. *See* Project Quality Management

Quality management plan, 87, 320. *See also* Manage Quality process; Plan Quality Management process; Project Quality Management
  definition, 718
  as input, 135, 241, 314, 411, 469
  as output, 286, 297, 447, 490

Quality management system, 718

Quality metrics
  definition, 718
  as input, 291, 300
  as output, 287

Quality policy, 718

Quality report, 108, 124, 165, 296, 382, 495, 718

Quality requirements, 148, 718

Quality standards. *See* Standard

Quantitative risk analysis. *See* Perform Quantitative Risk Analysis process

Questionnaires, 143, 303, 511, 718

Quotation, 477

# R

RACI. *See* Responsible, accountable, consult and inform (RACI) chart

RACI chart, 317, 718

RAM. *See* Assignment matrix; Responsibility assignment matrix

RBS. *See* Resource breakdown structure; Risk breakdown structure

RCA. *See* Root cause analysis

Recognition, 319, 341–342

Regression analysis, 126, 718

Regulations, 718

Regulatory bodies, 550

Report(s). *See also* Quality report; Risk report
  final, 127–128
  project, 123, 361, 362, 388
  work performance, 26

Reporting formats, 182, 239, 408, 455, 525

Requested change. *See also* Change requests

Request for information (RFI), 477, 718

Request for proposal (RFP), 477, 718

Request for quotation (RFQ), 477, 719

Requirement(s). *See also* High-level requirements; Product requirements
  business, 148
  classifications, 148
  cross-functional, 145
  definition, 719
  functional, 118, 148
  legal, 78, 369, 370
  nonfunctional, 148
  organizational communication, 369, 383, 391, 520, 525, 533
  project, 148
  quality, 148, 718
  solution, 148
  stakeholder, 148
  transition and readiness, 148

Requirements documentation, 147–148. *See also* Collect Requirements process; Contract(s)
  definition, 719
  as input, 124, 152, 157, 165, 169, 280, 314, 368, 412, 470, 485, 495, 510
  as output, 97, 147–148, 155, 162, 167, 171, 480, 491

*Requirements Management: A Practice Guide,* 132

---

Virtual teams, 311, 333, 340, 725
Visual management tools, 73
VOC. *See* Voice of the Customer
Voice of the Customer (VOC), 145, 726
Voting, 111, 119, 144, 534

# W

Walkthroughs, 166, 224, 303, 498
Watch list, risks and, 423, 427, 440, 455
Waterfall development approach, 135, 185
Waterfall life cycles, 19
Waterfall model-based projects, 299, 400
WBS. *See* Work breakdown structure
WBS dictionary, 162, 726
WBS ID, 186
What-if scenario analysis, 213, 227, 726
Work breakdown structure (WBS). *See also* Create WBS process
    approaches to, 159
    as output, 161
    cost management plan and, 239
    data representation and, 316
    definition, 726
    planned value and, 261
    planning package and, 161
    samples, 159–160
    scope baseline and, 242
Work breakdown structure component, 726
*Work Breakdown Structures, Practice Standard for – Second Edition*, 161
Work packages, 157
    decomposition and, 158, 183, 185
    definition, 726
    description of, 161
    level of detail and, 158
    progressive elaboration and, 186
Work performance data, 26
    definition, 726
    as input, 165, 169, 225, 260, 301, 355, 390, 456, 496, 532
    as output, 95

Work performance information, 26, 357
    definition, 726
    as input, 109, 535
    as output, 166, 170, 228, 305, 392, 457, 499
Work performance reports, 26
    definition, 726
    as input, 116, 347, 382, 456
    as output, 106, 615
Workshops, 145. *See also* Facilitated workshops
Written communication, 360, 361. *See also* E-mail 5 Cs of, 361, 362–363

# X

X, Design for X (DfX), 295